Creating Teacher Immediacy in Online Learning Environments

Steven D'Agustino
Fordham University, USA

A volume in the Advances in Educational Technologies and Instructional Design (AETID) Book Series

Information Science REFERENCE
An Imprint of IGI Global

Published in the United States of America by
Information Science Reference (an imprint of IGI Global)
701 E. Chocolate Avenue
Hershey PA, USA 17033
Tel: 717-533-8845
Fax: 717-533-8661
E-mail: cust@igi-global.com
Web site: http://www.igi-global.com

Library of Congress Cataloging-in-Publication Data

Names: D'Agustino, Steven, 1965- editor.
Title: Teacher immediacy in online learning environments / Steven D'Agustino, editor.
Description: Hershey, PA : Information Science Reference, [2016] | Includes bibliographical references and index.
Identifiers: LCCN 2016002935| ISBN 9781466699953 (hardcover) | ISBN 9781466699960 (ebook)
Subjects: LCSH: Web-based instruction. | Individualized instruction. | Teacher-student relationships. | Communication in education.
Classification: LCC LB1044.87 .T42 2016 | DDC 371.33/44678--dc23 LC record available at http://lccn.loc.gov/2016002935

This book is published in the IGI Global book series Advances in Educational Technologies and Instructional Design (AETID) (ISSN: 2326-8905; eISSN: 2326-8913)

British Cataloguing in Publication Data
A Cataloguing in Publication record for this book is available from the British Library.

For electronic access to this publication, please contact: eresources@igi-global.com.

Advances in Educational Technologies and Instructional Design (AETID) Book Series

Lawrence A. Tomei
Robert Morris University, USA

ISSN: 2326-8905
EISSN: 2326-8913

Mission

Education has undergone, and continues to undergo, immense changes in the way it is enacted and distributed to both child and adult learners. From distance education, Massive-Open-Online-Courses (MOOCs), and electronic tablets in the classroom, technology is now an integral part of the educational experience and is also affecting the way educators communicate information to students.

The **Advances in Educational Technologies & Instructional Design (AETID) Book Series** is a resource where researchers, students, administrators, and educators alike can find the most updated research and theories regarding technology's integration within education and its effect on teaching as a practice.

Coverage

- Bring-Your-Own-Device
- Collaboration Tools
- Social Media Effects on Education
- Digital Divide in Education
- Instructional Design
- Higher Education Technologies
- Adaptive Learning
- Online Media in Classrooms
- Classroom Response Systems
- Curriculum Development

IGI Global is currently accepting manuscripts for publication within this series. To submit a proposal for a volume in this series, please contact our Acquisition Editors at Acquisitions@igi-global.com or visit: http://www.igi-global.com/publish/.

The Advances in Educational Technologies and Instructional Design (AETID) Book Series (ISSN 2326-8905) is published by IGI Global, 701 E. Chocolate Avenue, Hershey, PA 17033-1240, USA, www.igi-global.com. This series is composed of titles available for purchase individually; each title is edited to be contextually exclusive from any other title within the series. For pricing and ordering information please visit http://www.igi-global.com/book-series/advances-educational-technologies-instructional-design/73678. Postmaster: Send all address changes to above address.

This book is dedicated to Daniel and Thomas D'Agustino

Editorial Advisory Board

Table of Contents

Detailed Table of Contents

The role of the instructor in any learning environment is a good motivator for students. It is important to understand how the instructor's position can be viewed in the online learning environment. The principal role of the instructor in any learning environment is to assist students in making connections and identifying significance through an educational process. This chapter, examined from an instructional designer and instructor's point of view, sets out to explore the effectiveness of the online teaching presence as an adequate investment of time for the student's benefit.

The author examines instructor presence by considering its historical role, the many important tasks that instruction presence accomplishes, and many ways instructional presence can be shown in online learning. Instructor presence has historically fulfilled four key functions: guidance, socialization, motivation, and coordination. Tasks that instructor presence can help with include welcoming and orienting learners, providing grades and explanations for grades, communicating course and instructor expectations and feedback on learner work, offering follow-up questions and comments, and moderating discussions. Seven techniques suggested to provide a sense of instructor presence include scheduling predetermined, regular appearances online, providing quick responses to comments and assignments, making occasional instructor posts throughout course discussions, offering periodic, brief, personal comments, providing special periods of instructor access, simulating presence by means of prerecorded audio or video clips and using instructor representatives.

Attention to the quality issues of distance education in higher education has focused primarily on courses. Entire academic programs are now delivered online, and faculty members must spend a significant amount of resources in addressing curricular-issues of online programs, as opposed to pedagogical issues for the courses they teach. Priorities for instructor interactivity and immediacy can become explicit goals for all learning experiences in academic programs. This chapter is organized in three parts: (1) the value of using interactivity/immediacy in the design of extended learning academic programs, (2) instructional design best practices for developing interactivity and immediacy in online academic programs, and (3) recommendations for different level of academic programs, including undergraduate, master's, doctoral, and specialized programs, including teacher education, certificates, and professional development.

online environment. Specifically, the issue of effective interaction is investigated, including: (1) the application of formative feedback practices; (2) the application of student self-assessment to encourage deeper learning; and (3) the integration of rubric use in assessment activities. The chapter concludes, recommending that practical application of teaching strategies such as: (1) using rubrics; and (2) encouraging student self-assessment, has the effect of enhancing teacher interaction and improving both the student experience and the student learning outcomes in an online environment. The chapter aims to contribute to the literature associated with online university education by validating best practices which assists in developing more effective online courses.

Due to a growing number of online courses and programs, educators' interest in using audio and video feedback in asynchronous online environment has increased. Studies have found evidence that the use of audio and video feedback in asynchronous online courses can increase instructor presence and enhance online community interactions. The purpose of this chapter is to share research findings on audio and video feedback and to overview qualities of effective feedback. The chapter also presents potential benefits and limitations of audio and video feedback in online environments. Researchers and practitioners interested in implementing both types of feedback in online courses will find solutions, recommendations and possible future research directions.

Dissemination of teaching-learning information through online and distance-learning methods can only be effective if the materials are interactively presented among all the stakeholders, that is, the teacher, the learner, and the content itself. The content being used need to dynamically respond according to the prevailing learning circumstances that may demand the interactivity involving text, video, audio, graphics, and animation in a real-time environment. Based on this premise, Macromedia Director-MX Lessons Development system, abbreviated in this work as MAD-LED Model, was envisaged. The MAD-LED Model utilises the combination of nonverbal immediacy and multimedia Macromedia Director-MX technologies. The situational variable of teacher nonverbal immediacy is associated with student's motivation to study and is thus essential for effective classroom instruction. The multimedia Macromedia Director-MX tools such as cast, stage, score, and control panel are used to design and develop animation utilising the text, video, audio, and graphics.

Foreword

Online education is of interest to those of us who are involved in creating alternative learning spaces inside and outside institutional settings because it holds the potential to open new avenues of knowledge and opportunity not currently available or within reach of certain populations, especially in poorer areas in the United States or across the globe. *Creating Teacher Immediacy in Online Learning Environments* is especially relevant for educators, researchers, instructional designers and learners who are interested in the development of effective, interactive and interpersonal asynchronous online learning environments. The chapters within provide research on new models of student engagement and insights on how to harness the full potential of social media and interactive tools to enable a richer, more personally satisfying experience for students and better learning outcomes.

Typically in distance learning environments interactions are often limited to text-based asynchronous discussion boards. Asynchronous discussions provide opportunities for instructors to survey student understanding and identify areas that require additional attention. A type of formative assessment, instructors can use student comments to gauge student learning as it is occurring. A consideration of questioning techniques is essential as online instructors set the direction of the discussion through anticipatory questions or prompts. Questions enables instructors to assess (1) student engagement – how involved students are with the learning activities and content, (2) student motivation – the level of student self-inducement to achieve their goals, (3) student preparation – the degree to which students are remaining current with the progression through the course content, (4) student thinking – an identification of the cognitive strategies students are employing, (5) student understanding – the degree to which students are acquiring knowledge of the content and meeting learning objectives and (6) student creativity – the degree to which students are integrating new learning into pre-existing knowledge to generate new ideas. While discussion boards have advantages – allowing student reflection before posting ideas, empowering students who have a more text-based approach to learning and communicating – asynchronous discussion have a number of failings. Unless designed and moderated effectively, they can be static and unfocussed. Often instructors use discussion boards as a kind of homework assignment, and prompts can take the form of direct information-based questioning. Discussion, in this scenario, becomes questioning and rather than collaboratively making meaning, students simply post their best guess at the "right answer." Created in this form as a kind of assessment strategy, student participation becomes motivated primarily by externally imposed criteria in the form of grading by the instructor and can devolve into a way of checking if students have done the reading. Instructor presence in online discussions can also be problematic as students inevitably defer to their comments and instructor assent and validation can become the prime mover. These failures can obviously plague video and/or based discussion tools as well which, while more effective at mimicking synchronous interactions, can also fail to empower students to dig more deeply into difficult questions that move beyond providing answers to content-based questions. The point here is that instructor immediacy is not tool-dependent. Rather, immediacy requires a purposeful design process that focuses on how students can collaboratively create shared meanings in intellectually and academically rigorous ways.

Thousands of free courses are offered online by universities, including MIT, Harvard, Stanford and Columbia University. Over 10 million users a month access Kahn Academy's content, whose mantra is clearly stated on the home page of the Web site, "You can learn anything. For free. For everyone. Forever." New technologies, such as whiteboard screencasting and hand drawing software, allow people to create and share information in ways never before possible; however, today modern e-learning pedagogy is not dissimilar to that experienced by University of Illinois students in the 1960s when classroom computer terminals were linked to resources supporting piped-in lectures by their professors or to the 1950s and 1960s skill and drill system of the Programmed Logic for Automatic Teaching Operations (PLATO). When one considers that e-learning evolved from the earliest communications technologies, radio in the 1920s, then television in the 1930s and by government institutions that are often slow to change, it is not so surprising that many of the popular platforms' features, functionality and delivery mechanisms are stalled in 1.0.

Khan Academy has been criticized for its "sit and get" instructional strategy, for its focus on decontextualized procedural knowledge and its emphasis on foundational rather than conceptual learning (Kerr, 2015). Others warn that there are close connections between behaviorism and adaptive learning systems, such as Knewton, and the teaching machines of B.F. Skinner (Watters, 2015). While these solutions may provide students with baseline knowledge that can serve to inform or remediate, as with all prototypes that have gone through the testing phase with bugs identified, perhaps it's time for a radical shift beyond online education broadcast networks and from response and awards-based learning mechanisms to action-centric spaces for collaboration, creation and innovation. In the Vygotskian view, social interaction plays a fundamental role in the cognitive development of learning. The Internet, not Facebook, is the social network. The amount of casually generated information online is staggering and growing. Every minute of the day, YouTube users upload more than 72 hours of new video, Facebook users share 2,460,000 pieces of data and Pintrest users pin 3,472 images. The tracks of social interaction and learning have been laid and oncoming are the tools that have the potential to close the gap between classes of people who have had varying classroom experiences from K-12 to community college to university and beyond.

What could these new action-centric spaces for collaboration, creation and innovation look like? In the Bronx, NY students in public schools learned how to use CAD software through two different collaborative experiences. In the first, teenagers addressed how they could motivate their peers to exercise more through the invention of a foot-peddled scooter that charges handheld devices. They researched ideas for their invention online, accessed tutorials to learn how to use CAD software to design and prototype the invention and worked on the tutorials individually and collaboratively, asking each other questions when they hit snags. Their tutorials were supplemented with twice-weekly direct online interaction with an expert instructor who answered their specific questions about the functionality of the software and the application of it to their design. While observing the teens use the software to build models of their invention in real time, the instructor was also able to suggest useful modifications as well as contributed to the overall design of the mechanism. Over three months, the teenagers became expert users of the software and also produced two prototypes of their invention that were featured on YouTube and other online publications that were seen by their teachers and peers. The recognition that the teenagers received elevated not only their self-perceptions of worthiness through their contributions to society, but also that of their schools administrators and staff who felt connected to the teens' success. In a second collaboration, teenagers who already had familiarity with CAD, 3D animation and coding were given the task to design a game that would teach other teens how to use CAD software. The teens had a deadline of four weeks to design and deliver a demonstration game that included a compelling story line with motivation to learn CAD and the task to learn how to build mechanisms using CAD software. The teens formed a team that they named JAVAK, a letter for each first letter of their names. Each day the team worked together onsite or in a combination of onsite and virtually to design, develop the assets and program the game. They also blogged a record of their development progress, which provides highly informative insights into how the incentive of designing their own product for their peers drove them to learn more and more skills across new software tools that would help them to complete the final deliverable. The final product is not only a testament to what young people can learn with available tools of technology, but also to the form they envision that learning can take online.

As you read the chapters of this book, ask yourself, how can you use the information within to build your own action-centric spaces. Also, ask yourself about the spaces and eLearning experiences that the authors describe. Are they are designed to be highly interactive, collaborative and adaptive to students' needs through the real-time engagement of the instructor? Do they blend both offline and online experiences and content that supports the use of tools of creation? What benefits are the students receiving? Are they learning new knowledge and being encouraged to synthesize what they learn? Do students have choice through an environment that offers online tutorials, collaborative on and offline experiences with their instructor and peers, opportunities to virtually construct mechanisms, then print out files and reconstruct them offline? Today's technology offers amazing opportunities to leapfrog existing classroom practices and create exciting spaces for all young people to thrive and create their own futures today. Where will you take it?

Creating Teacher Immediacy in Online Learning Environments offers insights into instructor presence through a number of lenses. Some authors focus on effective tools to create, develop and sustain immediacy, others examine and recommend effective practices. Several authors offer global perspectives, broadening the conversation in interesting and innovative ways. Essentially, the collections reminds us that the human component of teaching and learning remains paramount regardless of the instructional setting.

Karen P. Kaun
Makeosity, Inc., USA

Karen P. Kaun *is an e-learning innovator, entrepreneur and leading figure in the maker movement whose work in the public and private sector and schools domestically and internationally has been featured in the media for its innovation including the book Design, Make, Play, Growing the Next Generation of STEM Innovators (2013). Dr. Kaun's programs support k-8 educators to integrate new technologies (e.g. 3D design, robotics) with their classroom curriculum and teaching practices. Her newest initiative is the launch of Makeosity, an on and offline community that immerses students in science, technology, engineering, art and math (STEAM) through making and invention. Makeosity (www.makeosity.com) is a space for youth to incubate and create new ideas such as its patent pending "Energy Scooter" designed by middle school girls with Autodesk Fusion 360 software and partially 3D printed. The scooter has been showcased across the globe including in Seoul, Korea where Dr. Kaun was a keynote speaker at Autodesk University Korea on the future of manufacturing.*

REFERENCES

Kerr. (2015). *Behaviourism and adaptive learning.* Retrieved from https://adaptivelearninginelt.wordpress.com/tag/knewton/

Waters. (2015). *Education technology and skinners box.* Retrieved from https://educationfuturism.com/education-technology-and-skinners-box-76a669c48461#.63cts8qee

Preface

With the continuing growth of asynchronous online learning environments in higher education, instructors, instructional designers, program developers and students have created a set of structures and practices for these new virtual spaces. Currently, online learning has greater legitimacy than during the period following its broad adoption. As a result, the conversation among researchers, practitioners and designers has moved from a defensive posture, to a tool-based conversation (LMS selection for example) to identifying promising instructional practices. Attention has evolved from issues around content curation and creation to issues around immediacy. One might call this the *interactive turn*. The interactive turn is characterized by a focus on the human components of teaching and learning in asynchronous spaces populated by simulacra – video and audio recordings, icons and avatars.

In many ways, interaction in online learning environments mirrors the structures of interaction in traditional classrooms: teacher-centered, information based and assessment driven. Certainly these are all reasonable methods of interaction but they discount a number of inevitable and often inadvertent characteristics of in-person communication. These include the emergent quality of discussions that often lead to a meaning-making in an inquiry-based community. In other words, instructors and students, when in each other's presence, can collaboratively determine why they think they know what they think they know. It is possible to recreate this emergent quality in online learning environments, but ironically, the more highly planned, developed and content-laden an online course is, the less space remains for students to exert their influence on the direction learning will take. An *un-designed remainder,* some space that allows for students to have agency, must somehow be designed.

Students often learn from the physical presence of their instructor – her comportment, facial expressions and movement through physical space. This important aspect, the *modelling function*, provides students with a real-time embodiment of how an academic thinks, what she thinks about and, perhaps most importantly, what this thinking looks like in action. Often in online environments, modelling takes place through recordings and comments in discussions forums. In fact, it can be argued that the mediated quality of asynchronous learning provides instructors and learners with more time to reflect upon their self-presentation and thus, to be more deliberate.

The following collection, *Creating Teacher Immediacy in Online Learning Environments,* is especially relevant as the environment of teaching and learning is rapidly evolving. With the ubiquity of communication technology and its attendant ease of use, face-to-face interactions in the traditional classroom are becoming augmented, and in some cases supplanted, by asynchronous interaction. These changes can be alarming in the sense that they are driven by technological and cultural evolution (and in some cases cost), rather than emerging from instructional best practices identified by educators. This is not to suggest that a retrenchment is in order and that they only truly valuable interactions (for instructional purposes) take place face-to-face in real time. But, best practices for providing students with the sense that their teacher is a "real person" who is invested in the development remains an essential feature. The challenge for educators is to identify best practices to accomplish this.

The target audiences for this book are educators, researchers, instructional designers and learners who are interested in the development of effective, interactive and interpersonal asynchronous online learning environments. Specifically, the audience includes: course designers for online programs in higher education, faculty who teach online, higher education administrators for online programs (deans and directors), educational and instructional technologists, educational media specialists, educational software designers, higher-education researchers, undergraduate and graduate schools of education, teacher preparation programs and clinical field supervisors of teachers. The following brief descriptions of each chapter provide a preview of the text.

Building Teaching Presence in Online Classes
Oliver Dreon

Teaching online presents a challenge to instructors who have never learned online. This chapter digs deeply into how instructors new to the online environment can employ recommended strategies to enhance their presence. The author also examines a variety of technologies to support his effort and concludes with a valuable discussion of design principles that support teacher presence.

Instructor Immediacy and Authenticity
Caroline M. Crawford

Instructor beliefs and behaviors as a method of examining how to support student success through immediacy is an innovative and exciting way to examine immediacy. Cognitive vulnerability is a novel and essential feature of this chapter which, rather than focusing on technology, investigates the human components of teaching and learning.

Emphasizing Instructor Presence in Digital Learning Environments
Rachael O. Afolabi

This chapter explores online teacher presence from the perspective of both instructional designer and instructor. Instructor presence requires a commitment of time and resources of both designers – how can presence be built into the course, what tools can facilitate it? – and instructors – what is an appropriate amount of interaction? These are central questions in online learning environments that this chapter explores with an eye on student learning outcomes.

"I'm Here for You": Instructor Presence Online
Kelly R. Elander

Zeroing in on one instructor's practices, this chapter examines the variety of ways instructor presence is accomplished as well as the many opportunities for creating immediacy are available through standard instructional tasks that are regularly performed. The author suggest seven techniques to enhance instructor presence which range from scheduling regular online appearances to providing special periods of instructor access. Strategies to simulate presence through pre-recorded audio and video content are also described.

Interactivity and Immediacy in Online Academic Programs
Neal Shambaugh

While interactivity and immediacy are increasingly perceived as integral components of online learning, they are often added on while the class is in progress and mediated through standard communication tools. This chapter describes how interactivity should be the focus of the design phase of instruction and includes best practices for building in immediacy. The chapter concludes with recommendations for a variety of online academic programs.

The Human Element
Melanie Hibbert, Kristine Rodriguez Kerr, Adrienne A. Garber, Matthea Marquart

Instructional videos are emerging as common components of online courses. This chapter examines the effectiveness of instructional videos as opportunities for immediacy using a specific set of evaluative criteria. The authors unpack the concept of immediacy and make essential recommendations for instructors.

Leveraging Teaching Presence in Online Courses
Kun Huang, Sang Joon Lee, Ashley Dugan

The authors employ the community of inquiry framework as a way to understand the social, cognitive and teaching presences of instructors in online environments. The chapter focuses on instructional design and organization and directed facilitation. The chapter also provides essential and specific strategies and examples for leveraging teacher presence in online courses. The chapter concludes with the student perspective of the recommended strategies.

Synchronous and Asynchronous Tools Optimizing Online Learning in the English-Speaking Caribbean
Paulette Stewart

The analysis of the effectiveness of asynchronous and synchronous tools used in the online education program at The University of the West Indies Open Campus that forms the center of this study provides a needed focus on the learning styles and needs of adult learners, who are self-directed, self-motivated and goal-oriented. Also, so-called non-traditional students are an increasing majority in higher education and in online learning environments. The study traces the movement from asynchronous communication and collaboration tools to synchronous tools and documents the effects of this evolution on instructional practices, student engagement and student learning outcomes.

Facebook Mediated Learning Environments in Pakistan
Tazeen Hussain

Exploring teacher immediacy in online learning environments by focusing on the use of social media is an interesting way to examine how interaction can be managed absent a learning management system. The study is based on teaching practice in Indus Valley School of Art and Architecture and Department of Visual Studies, University of Karachi. The author focuses on how immediacy can be harnessed to improve learning outcomes. The chapter highlights how technological innovation and changes in social interaction can be integrated into teaching and learning with positive results.

Instructional Strategies for Synchronous Components of Online Courses
Matthea Marquart, Michael Fleming, Sam A. Rosenthal, Melanie Hibbert

The authors provide a practical toolkit of strategies and best practices for increasing immediacy and interactivity through the use of synchronous online webinars. The chapter is both a valuable examination and description of the broader implementation model and technology support system that makes these webinars effective.

Understanding Strategies of Teacher-Student Interaction
Tarryn L. Kille

A descriptive case study, this chapter explores strategies intended to reduce psychological distance in the online environment. Employing a theoretical approach, the author investigates formative feedback practices, student self-assessment tools and the use of rubrics. The chapter identifies best practices for enhancing interaction, improving the student experience and positively affecting student learning.

Using Audio and Video Feedback to Increase Instructor Presence in Asynchronous Online Courses
Larisa Olesova, Jered Borup

As audio and video have emerged as common tools in the development of instructor presence online, this chapter provides a needed examination of effective uses of this strategy. The authors share both benefits and limitations of audio and video and provide valuable source of solutions, recommendations and effective practices for increasing instructor presence.

Macromedia Director-MX Lessons Development (MAD-LED) Model:
The Immediacy of Online-Distance Teaching-Learning in Multimedia and Real-Time Environments
Jameson Mbale, Manish Wadhwa

This chapter focuses on a specific instructional design tool that focuses on enhancing online learning through the use of video, audio, graphics and animation in a synchronous environment. The chapter examines how student motivation is heightened through the use of these interactive elements and how learning outcomes are improved as a result.

Students' Perceptions of the Online Instructors' Roles in a Massive Open Online Course
Hengtao Tang, Shuyan Wang, Yingxiao Qian, Kyle Peck

The rise and subsequent sinking back to earth of Massive Open Online Courses (MOOCs) has resulted in a reassessment of the effectiveness of this instructional modality. While the access promise of MOOC's is still being realized, the instructional effectiveness and acquired student competencies are still in question – resulting in a clear need to identify effective instructional practices in this environment. This chapter provides a needed, practical and insightful look at students' perceptions of the instructor role and how the humanization of that role impacts the student learning experience.

An Entertaining Game-Like Learning Environment in a Virtual World for Education
Hsiao-Cheng (Sandrine) Han, Junsong Zhang, Nasim Peikazadi, Ge Shi, Annie Hung, Colette P. L. Doan, Sandra Filippelli

This chapter explores the possibilities, benefits, and difficulties of developing game-like virtual environments for education as a way to describe instructor presence form a different perspective. The chapter concludes with examples of such environments and suggestions for how to create game-like experiences for students.

Creating Teacher Immediacy in Online Learning Environments is a valuable toolkit for instructional designers, media specialists and subject matter experts to create and sustain effective online learning environments, essentially rescuing this area from early for-profit endeavors which have done some harm to the perceived legitimacy of online education at the University level. The collection identifies strategies for greater personalization of online learning environments with an eye on greater student success and supports the developers of online programs in the creation of context and culture specific online offerings so that online offerings do not become generic and technology-driven but retain their specific culture and character (so that courses offered online and University A differ from courses offered online at University B).

This volume is essential reading because online learning still has a perceived lack of legitimacy, is imperiled by the movement towards looking at education as simply another form of "content," a perspective that which swallowed journalism, book publishing and music. This authors locate online learning in pedagogy rather than in technology. Technology is certainly a central feature but technologies evolve rapidly – foundational principles (best practices) for teaching and learning in online environments with a specific focus on instructor immediacy and presence – are essential.

Chapter 1
Building Teaching Presence in Online Classes

Oliver Dreon
Millersville University, USA

ABSTRACT

In their framework outlining educational experiences for online students, Garrison, Anderson, and Archer (2000) identify and explain the critical elements of a Community of Inquiry that support instruction and learning. The elements include: cognitive presence, social presence, and teaching presence. While an online educational experience is impacted by the interplay of all three presences, new online teachers may struggle with developing a teaching presence since their own educational experiences as students may be very different from the ones they encounter as online instructors (Lortie, 1975). In this book chapter, the importance of teaching presence will be discussed. Strategies for developing online teacher presence will be examined and technologies for fostering teacher presence will be outlined. The chapter concludes with broad design principles that apply to the construction of online learning environments that foster a strong teacher presence.

INTRODUCTION

Distance learning is exploding in higher education. In their report tracking online education in the United States, Allen and Seaman (2014) found that of the more than 21 million students enrolled in degree granting institutions of higher education, one third had taken at least one online class during their collegiate experience. Examining online enrollments since 2002, the researchers found that the online student population has grown at "a compound annual growth rate of 16.1 percent" despite collegiate populations only increasing at an annual rate of 2.5 percent over that time period (Allen & Seaman, 2014, p. 15). But why are more students enrolling in online classes? In a 2011 survey of university leaders, respondents felt that most students enrolled in online classes because the courses offered greater flexibility in scheduling than face-to-face classes would (Allen & Seaman, 2011). Despite the flexibility, many students struggle in online classes. Xu and Jaggars (2013) examined 500,000 courses taken by over 40,000 community and technical college students in Washington State. The researchers studied

DOI: 10.4018/978-1-4666-9995-3.ch001

students' success in online courses relative to their ability to do so in face-to-face courses. Looking at different sub-groups of students based on academic preparedness, age, gender, race and socioeconomic status, the study found that every sub-group performed significantly better in their face-to-face courses than their online ones. While a number of factors may contribute to a student's success in an online class, instructors have little control over the vast majority of them. For instance, Wojciechowski and Palmer (2005) found that a student's GPA, reading ability and previous online course experience were strong predictors of success in online classes. Although these student characteristics may play a role in students' success in online classes, various studies have shown that instructor involvement can positively impact online students' satisfaction and perceived learning (Fredricksen, et al, 2000; Shea, et al, 2002).

In this chapter, the role of teaching presence in online classes will be examined. The construct of "teaching presence" was first introduced as part of Garrison, Anderson and Archer's Community of Inquiry framework (2000). The chapter begins with an overview of the Community of Inquiry framework before focusing specifically on teaching presence and how it can be fostered in online classes. The chapter will also discuss some of the challenges that online instructors face when teaching online classes and discuss how face-to-face instruction can provide some guidance for developing teaching presence online. Drawing on Chickering and Gamson's seven principles of quality undergraduate education (1987), the chapter will outline how these principles which were originally developed for face-to-face instruction can be fostered in online learning environments. Strategies for developing online teacher presence will be examined and different technologies for fostering teacher presence will be outlined. The chapter concludes with recommendations that support the facilitation of online learning environments that foster a strong teacher presence.

BACKGROUND

In their examination of computer-based conferencing in higher education, Garrison, Archer and Anderson (2000) introduced the Community of Inquiry framework as way to describe a "worthwhile educational experience" for students. The framework involves three overlapping "presences" which help to describe the overall learning activities with which students and instructors must engage. The framework includes: social presence, cognitive presence and teaching presence. Social presence in an online class helps to develop the affective dimensions of learning and foster interpersonal relationships between a student and their peers. Developing social presence helps a student feel more connected in online classes and more open to express their ideas and collaborate with their peers. Social presence helps to form a risk-free classroom where students can share their knowledge, experience and emotions and work together to build a cohesive learning community (Dikkers, Whiteside & Lewis, 2013). In their research examining social presence in online classes, Richardson and Swan (2003) found that students who felt more socially connected in their online classes had higher rates of satisfaction and perceived learning than students who did not.

Cognitive presence involves students engaging in critical discourse of course content and analyzing assigned material to construct understanding and meaning. While social presence relates to affective dimensions and the overall cohesion of the classroom community, cognitive presence focuses on the critical thinking processes with which students must engage to learn in an online community. Garrison and Archer (2010) introduced the construct of "practical inquiry" where students cycle through phases of initiation, exploration, integration and resolution to assimilate the "public and private worlds of the learner." Cognitive presence has been associated with student satisfaction and learning outcomes in online courses (Aykol & Garrison, 2011).

MAIN FOCUS OF THE CHAPTER

Teaching Presence

Taken on their own, the social and cognitive presences capture much of the interactions with which students engage in online classes. These interactions do not happen, however, without the involvement and expertise of an instructor (Dikkers, Whiteside & Lewis, 2013; Shea et al, 2010; Bengert, 2008). The last element of the Community of Inquiry framework examines the instructor's critical role in online classes. Anderson, Rourke, Garrison and Archer (2001) define teaching presence as:

the design, facilitation, and direction of cognitive and social processes for the purpose of realizing personally meaningful and educationally worthwhile outcomes. (p. 5)

This definition demonstrates this critical interplay between an instructor and the social and cognitive presences developed in an online class. In their examination of the different components of the Community of Inquiry framework, Shea and colleagues (2010) found that social presence indicators were directly impacted by teaching presence. They write "as instructor teaching presence rises or falls, there is a correlating rise or fall in student social presence" (Shea et al, 2010, p. 13) This echoes research by Bangert (2008) that found correlation between an instructor's involvement and the social and cognitive presences apparent in online classes. Clearly, instructors play a critical role in the development of a Community of Inquiry.

In Garrison's 2011 book *E-Learning in the 21st Century*, he expands the "teaching presence" construct further and discusses the different roles that instructors must play online. To develop a strong teaching presence, instructors must provide *design and organization* in online classes so students can capably access course material and requirements. Through the design and organization of online classes, instructors communicate curricular standards to students, identify resources that students will use and explain the learning outcomes that students must meet. Instructors also outline instructional and behavioral expectations in the class and define the processes with which student learning will assessed.

Beyond designing and organizing online classes, instructors must also *direct instruction* to help students learn content. In this role, instructors collect instructional materials from diverse sources and guide students as they navigate their online educational journey. They assess student learning and provide purposeful feedback that can help students develop. In the direct instruction role, instructors also assist students with technical challenges they might experience and work to make the overall online experience seamless and educationally worthwhile.

Lastly online instructors must *facilitate discourse*. While this instructor-facilitated discourse helps students learn content through participation and interaction, it also helps to create the climate for learning by encouraging and reinforcing positive student behavior. In discussion forums, instructors foster teacher presence by being an active participant but not a central figure in discussions. Instead, instructors work to draw students into the conversation and ask probing questions that help to extend the discussion in new directions. The instructor can also help to refocus conversations that drift away from the intended purpose of the discussion. Through their involvement, instructors help students move intentionally through the phases of practical inquiry.

Examining these roles further it becomes clear that a teacher's presence begins before a single student enters an online class and increases as students start to navigate course content and participate in discussion. From designing and developing classes in learning management system to fostering discourse in discussion forums to assessing student learning, the instructor plays a central role in the overall learning experience for online students. Considering the skillset needed for success, the roles extend far beyond an instructor's content knowledge and involve leveraging managerial, pedagogical, technical, social and intellectual domains (Garrison, 2011).

CHALLENGES

While instructors' content knowledge is often revered, it is becoming increasingly clear that their impact extends beyond this knowledge base. For instance, Ray and Kafka (2014) examined the well-being of 30,000 college graduates and found that respondents who had engaged positively with a faculty member on campus were more likely to report being engaged in their future workplace. This echoes work from Chambliss and Takacs (2014). In their book, *How College Works*, the authors found that undergraduates were more likely to major in a field if they had an inspiring and caring faculty member in an introductory course. Students were also equally likely to write off an entire field if they had a single negative experience with a professor. Student/teacher interaction, whether occurring in an online or face-to-face class, impacts how students react to course content and how much they learn.

Educause Center for Analysis and Research (2014) examined instructors' perceptions of the efficacy of online instruction. Almost half of instructors with online teaching experience felt that students could learn more effectively in online learning environments. For instructors with no online experience, the rate fell to only 29 percent. Clearly, teaching online can help instructors better visualize opportunities to impact student learning. But what if the instructor has no previous experience in online classes, either as a student or as a teacher? In his book *Schoolteacher: A Sociological Study*, Lortie (1975) introduces the concept of apprenticeship of observation. As they navigate their education as students, Lortie argues, budding instructors are actually being apprenticed into the practice of teaching. They observe how classrooms are used and how content is taught. When these students eventually enter classrooms as teachers, this apprenticeship informs how they use the learning spaces they encounter and how they engage students in the learning process. They map their experiences as students in classroom spaces onto the classroom spaces they encounter as teachers. These learning histories present a challenge when an instructor begins to teach in online learning environments of which they have no prior experience. Instructors who may be quite adept at fostering discourse in a face-to-face setting may struggle seeing how this can be accomplished in online environments.

Several organizations have developed materials to assist instructors when teaching online. For instance, Blackboard, Quality Matters and others have developed rubrics and course review processes to help instructors with designing online courses that reflect best practices in online education (e.g. Sener, 2006). While these approaches assist instructors with the development of online classes, they tend to focus mostly on the design and organization element of teaching presence. For instance, the rubrics assess the inclusion of items that outline expectations to students and detail institutional policies. The rubrics also evaluate whether clear learning objectives are included and assessment procedures are outlined. As the rubrics and review processes provide guidance with the roles of organization and design that are critical in developing teaching presence, they tend to focus less on the other roles (facilitate discourse and direct instruction) that also play a large factor in fostering a strong teacher presence. Clearly, a more comprehensive approach is needed to capture holistically all of the roles inherent in the element of teaching presence.

PRINCIPLES OF GOOD INSTRUCTION

Expanding the lens beyond online instruction may provide some guidance for new online instructors hoping to create an effective teaching presence. Chickering & Gamson (1987) outlined seven principles for good instructional practices in undergraduate education. Although the principles were originally intended for face-to-face instruction, they can serve as a framework fostering online teacher presence as well. Beyond the design and organizational role that is captured in the rubrics provided by Quality Matters and others, these principles highlight the roles of facilitating discourse and providing direct instruction. These principles include:

1. Encourage Contact between Students and Faculty

Chickering and Gamson (1987) write "frequent student-faculty contact in and out of classes is the most important factor in student involvement and motivation" (p. 3). In online classes, this may be difficult to imagine since there is no physical learning environment. Regardless of the type of learning environment, however, students need to know that instructors are present and available if they need assistance. To meet this principle, online instructors can provide different means of communication (email, phone, etc.) that students can use if they are struggling. Instructors can also leverage both asynchronous and synchronous means of communication to encourage contact. For instance, instructors can provide online office hours using Skype or chat rooms where students can visit when they are having difficulty. These synchronous discussions can help to foster more social connections in online classes (Hrastinksi, 2008). Additionally, instructors should monitor students' progress in course materials and contact students who may be falling behind. Motivation is at the heart of this principle. Students are more invested and motivated when they know an instructor is present to assist with their learning.

2. Develop Reciprocity and Cooperation Among Students

This principle bridges all three presences in the Community of Inquiry framework. As Chickering and Gamson write, "good learning, like good work, is collaborative and social, not competitive and isolated. Working with others increases involvement in learning" (1987, p. 3). The instructor plays a critical role in how students interact with the class. This principle can be achieved by designing activities and assessments that require more than individualized participation on the part of students. Online classes should be more than independent studies of content where individual students navigate readings and construct meaning on their own. Through effective design and thoughtful facilitation, online instructors can support the development of social and cognitive presence by structuring asynchronous communication avenues that require students to discuss content with one another and work together to solve problems and complete assignments.

3. Encourage Active Learning

"Learning is not a spectator sport," Chickering and Gamson write. To learn, students "must talk about what they are learning, write about it, relate it to past experiences, apply it to their daily lives. They must make what they learn part of themselves" (1987, p. 4). Many collegiate instructors struggle when incorporating active learning strategies in face-to-face environments (Michael, 2007). When the classroom moves to an online setting, the challenges can multiply. Despite the incorporation of discussion forums and online videos, students can still be passive learners in online classes. The hallmark of active learning is that students are doing meaningful activities that require them to think about what they are learning (Bonwell & Eison, 1991). Active learning in an online class requires that do students do more than just complete a series of isolated activities. Students must be provided the opportunity to reflect, evaluate, analyze, synthesize and communicate their work to the instructor and to the peers (Fink, 2003). Focusing on active learning provides some guidance for instructors who are designing and facilitating online classes. In synchronous environments, for instance, instructors can utilize peer instruction strategies where students discuss concepts in small groups and support small-group problem solving (Crouch & Mazur, 2001). In asynchronous environments, instructors can utilize case studies to foster more authentic, problem-based discussions where students apply content (Dixson, 2010)

4. Give Prompt Feedback

"Students need help in assessing existing knowledge and competence… and frequent opportunities to perform and receive suggestions for improvement" (Chickering & Gamson, 1987, p. 4). Learning management systems offer numerous assessment opportunities for online instructors. From quizzes to paper submission systems to rubrics, instructors have a multitude of tools to assess student learning. The power of assessment is the opportunity for students to grow and develop based on assessment data. Utilizing a series of targeted formative and summative assessment strategies can enhance student learning and provide a wealth of information to guide instruction. These assessments, however, are only powerful when effective feedback is given to students in a timely manner. Wiggins (2012) provides "seven keys to effective feedback" which include goal-referenced, tangible and transparent, user-friendly, timely, ongoing, consistent, and progress toward a goal. Incorporating these strategies in an online class can help create a culture where student development is fostered. As Jan Chappuis writes in her book on the *Seven Strategies of Assessment for Learning* (2104), "effective feedback occurs during learning." She writes:

How do we show students that it's not only okay to make mistakes but that when they occur, they are to be welcomed as information about next steps in learning? We cultivate this mindset when we offer feedback with opportunities to improve during the learning. Feedback is most effective in improving achievement if it is delivered while there is still time to act on it. (p. 68)

Besides helping students develop and improve, providing ongoing, timely feedback demonstrates that the instructor is available to direct instruction and facilitate student learning, one of the roles outlined in Garrison's teacher presence construct.

5. Emphasize Time on Task

"Students need help in learning effective time management." Chickering and Gamson (1987) write. "Allocating realistic amounts of time means effective learning for students and effective teaching for faculty" (p. 4). In online classes, time management can be challenging for students. Most students take online classes because of the flexibility that the classes provide. This flexibility, however, can undermine effective time management. To emphasize time on task, instructors can utilize some simple strategies that help students manage their time more effectively. Communicating realistic due dates early in the course can help students plan their work better. Including estimated times for completing readings, watching videos and other assigned tasks can support students in navigating the various expectations outlined in an online module. Returning to Xu and Jaggers' 2013 study of online classes in Washington, the researchers found that older, non-traditional students were more adaptable to the constraints and expectations of online classes. As they juggled work and family commitments in addition to educational ones, older students may possess better time management skills than younger students. While instructors cannot control the age or time management abilities of their students, they can better emphasize time on task by communicating clear expectations and time frames for students.

6. Communicate High Expectations

Some students may take online classes because they think it provides an easier academic route than a face-to-face class would. Online classes, however, must hold students to similar expectations that their face-to-face counterparts would. "High expectations are import for everyone – for the poorly prepared, for those unwilling to exert themselves and for the bright and well motivated. Expecting students to perform well becomes a self-fulfilling prophecy when teachers and institutions hold high expectations of themselves and make extra efforts" (Chickering & Gamson, 1987, p. 5). In online classes, instructors can communicate high expectations by providing examples for students that showcase the level of participation in discussion forums or the quality of work for assignments. Instructors can also use of rubrics to communicate their expectations to students.

7. Respect Diverse Talents and Ways of Learning

"There are many roads to learning," Chickering and Gamson (1987) write. "Students need the opportunity to show their talents and learn in ways that work for them" (p. 5). In online classes, it can be difficult to recognize students' talents and ways of learning since all communication and interaction is mediated via technology. Designing for these differences, however, can make a class more engaging and more student-centered. The principles of Universal Design for Learning (UDL) offer some powerful avenues for instructors teaching through digital means (Rose & Meyer, 2002). For instance, when instructors provide instructional content in multiple ways, students can engage with text-based readings, videos and audio files. Providing content through multiple means supports students that may have a variety of learning differences. Other UDL principle encourages instructors to offer multiple means of engagement and expression. Online instructors can incorporate these principles by offering students choice in how they want to demonstrate their learning. For instance, rather than assigning a paper for all students, an online instructor could offer a variety of assessment options from which students could choose. Some students could use moviemaking software to create a digital story analyzing the content in depth. Other students may choose to conduct an online presentation sharing their research. Providing choice helps to motivate students and provides opportunities to "show their talents" in the online space.

While Chickering and Gamson's work emerged long before the explosion of online education, the principles can provide a support structure for new or developing online instructors. By bridging between face-to-face and online instruction, the seven principles can serve as a way for online teachers to foster a teaching presence mindful of the design, instruction and discourse the leads to quality undergraduate education.

SUPPORTING ONLINE CLASSES

Returning specifically to the pedagogy of online learning, it can be challenging for a new online teacher to manage all of the roles outlined in Garrison's teaching presence framework. Savery (2005) examined the types of instructor interactions that engaged students and promoted their learning. To contribute to a successful learning environment for students and instructors, Savery argues that instructors need to be "VOCAL" – Visible, Organized, Compassionate, Analytical and a Leader-by-example. While the acronym itself might be easy to follow, some explanation may be needed to connect the descriptors to online instruction. While Savery offers these strategies as a descriptive analysis of quality online instruction, they can also serve as important considerations for instructors who are facilitating online classes and wanting to foster a strong teaching presence.

1. **Be visible.** Students need to interact with their instructors, especially in online learning environments. While it can be difficult to have a "teaching presence" in a digitally mediated space, it's not impossible. Instructors can start by participating in online discussions and by providing opportunities for students to engage in synchronous chats. In their study of factors that impact classroom community in online classes, Young and Bruce (2011) found that students saw "being present" and "active online" as critical instructor behaviors that influenced student engagement. Dixson (2010) found that offering multiple communication avenues for students also fostered more active participation in online classes and more student-instructor interaction. After examining interactivity in online classes, Martin, Parker and Deale (2012) found that an instructor's presence was instrumental in engaging students and suggested using synchronous tools to foster more student engagement and provide more immediate feedback. One way to be more visible in online classes is for instructors to use synchronous tools (chat, virtual classrooms, etc.) to hold scheduled office hours online. This strategy can provide additional opportunities for instructors to interact with their students, which can have powerful impacts on their learning. For instance, Lavooy and Newlin (2008) found that the frequency of students' attendance in online office hours correlated with their final grades in the class. These synchronous opportunities can demonstrate to students that an online instructor is present, active online and available to support their learning.
2. **Be organized.** Learning management systems (LMS) offer opportunities for organizing content and communication easily. While an instructor doesn't necessarily have to use all of the organiza-

tion structures available in an LMS, it's critical that they communicate the organization clearly to students. Making the organizational structures transparent for students will help them find materials and will promote more participation in class. In their study of students' views of instructor presence in online courses, Hodges and Cowan (2012) found that organizational issues were identified as the most important behaviors for online teachers. Items such as "makes course requirements clear," "creates a course that is easy to navigate," and "provides clear instruction on how to participate in course learning activities" were identified as the most critical behaviors for online instructors by students. One way to respond to these factors is for instructors to create an online orientation video that outlines the organizational system they are using and where students can access the critical components of the class. In their book, *The Virtual Student*, Palloff and Pratt (2003) recommend incorporating an online orientation as one of the first activities in any online class. They write:

Regardless of how it is delivered, an orientation is critical for virtual students if they are to have any likelihood of success in in online courses. Instructors and program administrators cannot assume that students will intuitively know how to access a course or navigate it. (Palloff & Pratt, 2003, p. 73)

By offering orientations to their online classes through recorded screencasts, online instructors can guide students through the organizations systems being employed to better support their navigation of course content. While Palloff and Pratt suggest that any method of online orientation would be beneficial, more recent research outlines the power of video-based tutorials. For instance, after examining the learning resources offered in an online instructional technology class, Li, Fu, Zhao and Leh (2010) found that students, especially those with lower technical proficiency, preferred video-based learning resources over text-based ones.

3. **Be compassionate.** In Savery's work, being compassionate means providing opportunities for student-instructor and student-student interaction. A compassionate instructor recognizes that all classes, even online ones, have a social component that needs to be fostered. While many instructors may see this as running counter to Chickering and Gamson's principle of communicating high expectations, being compassionate does not mean lowering goals for students engaged in online classes. Returning to Garrison's teacher presence framework, directing instruction involves more than organizing content, conducting assessment and providing feedback. For instance, in Baran, Correia and Thompson's ethnographic study of exemplary online teachers (2013), participants cited "knowing their students" and "enhancing teacher-student relationships" as critical components to successful online learning classes. As one online teacher in the study discussed when considering her interaction with her students:

I need to talk to you. I need to know how you are thinking and how much you understand...Because I always feel like, I am trying to help you become a better you. So I have to know you. (Baran, Correia & Thompson, 2013)

Being compassionate also means that instructors must recognize the technological challenges that can emerge in online classes and help student navigate these challenges compassionately and supportively.

In their study, Song, Singleton, Hill and Koh (2004) found that students' feeling comfortable with online technologies was an influencing factor for the perceived success of an online class. To navigate these hurdles, instructors could include short tutorials that demonstrate how certain technologies can be used. Instructors can also include a "Help" discussion forum where students can ask for technical assistance when it's needed (Wang & Chen, 2010). By including these elements, instructors communicate their desire to support students in times of need and demonstrate their compassion for struggling students.

4. **Be analytical.** Analytical instructors provide clear expectations and guidelines for planned assessments and offer timely feedback on student work. Returning to Hodges and Cowan's study of successful online instructors, several factors were identified that relate directly to assessment and feedback in online classes. For instance, participating students identified "provides timely feedback on assignments and projects" and "lets me know how I am doing in the course" as critical behaviors employed by successful online instructors. In her meta-analysis of research on student persistence in online programs, Hart (2012) found that quality and promptness of instructor feedback on student work was found to have an influence on student ability to successfully complete online classes.

Analytical online instructors also examine statistics to identify different degrees of participation and work to motivate underperforming students. For instance, Wilson, Pollock and Hamman (2007) found that students' performance in online classes was strongly related to the number of posts they read and the number of "in-depth" posts they contributed. Recognizing this impact on student learning, analytical instructors can work to foster more interaction and engagement from underperforming students by examining participation statistics and reaching out to those students who are not as involved. Analytical online instructors utilize data from assessments and from the learning management system to promote more student engagement and support student learning.

5. **Be a leader-by-example.** Online instructors model good behavior and participate fully in the online class. While there is some overlap with being visible, being a leader-by-example extends the instructor's role a little further. Instructors need to model the behaviors and cognitive expectations that they desire from students. If students are asked to introduce themselves at the start of the class, instructor should do the same to model the expectations for students. If specific discussion board guidelines are provided to scaffold student participation, instructors must adhere to these guidelines as well. In their survey of online instructors nationally, Heuer and King (2004) outlined five main roles that educators take on when teaching an online class: planner, model, coach, facilitator and communicator. While the roles ebb and flow during the management of an online class, instructors must "be a leader in modeling online behavior" for students (Heuer & King, 2004, p. 6). For instance, in a cross class study conducted by Choi, Land and Turgeon (2008), researchers found that instructors' continuous modeling of questioning techniques used in online discussion forums influenced students' use of the strategies. By modeling expected behaviors, instructors can provide what Brown Collins and Duguid call a "cognitive apprenticeship" (1989). By being a leader-by-example, an online instructor can help to acculturate students into the practices of a class by modeling the expected activity and discourse of the space. Being a leader-by-example means that instructors both "walk the walk" and "talk the talk" in their online classes.

FUTURE RESEARCH DIRECTIONS

While research on communities of inquiry and the interdependent elements of social, cognitive and teaching presence continues, research examining factors that influence the preparation and training of online instructors to effectively support online learners is slow to develop. The importance of strong teaching presence in online classes is well documented. Little research, however, has examined how online instructors gain proficiency with the tools and strategies to foster teaching presence. One possible research avenue is an investigation of online teacher's self-efficacy beliefs. Bandura (1997) defines self-efficacy as ''one's beliefs in one's capacity to organize and execute the courses of action required to produce given attainments'' (p. 3). Connected to online teaching, self-efficacy would refer to an online instructor's belief in their ability to organize and execute actions to promote student learning. While teacher efficacy is well researched in face-to-face learning environments, the construct has not been fully examined in online settings. In face-to-face learning environments, teachers' efficacy beliefs have been related to student achievement (Ross, 1992), increased job satisfaction (Caprara, Barbarnelli, Borgogni & Steca, 2003), greater commitment to the teaching profession (Coladarci, 1992) and greater levels of organization and planning (Allinder, 1994). Research exploring the connection between teacher efficacy and the development of teaching presence could inform how we support new online instructors as they design courses and facilitate learning online.

CONCLUSION

Garrison and Archer's Community of Inquiry framework captures the complex nature of online learning by introducing the constructs of teaching, social and cognitive presences. While each of these presences represent different aspects of online classes, teaching presence is critical since it can foster student engagement and participation that leads to student learning. To foster positive teaching presence, an instructor must manage roles that include design and organization, direct instruction and facilitating discourse. While many instructors may struggle with visualizing these roles when they teach online for the first time, bridging between quality face-to-face instruction and online opportunities can provide guidance. Although they were originally designed for face-to-face learning environments, Chickering and Gamson's seven principles for quality undergraduate instruction marries well to the activities and roles that instructors must play to foster teaching presence in online classes.

REFERENCES

Akyol, Z., & Garrison, D. R. (2011). Understanding cognitive presence in an online and blended community of inquiry: Assessing outcomes and processes for deep approaches to learning. *British Journal of Educational Technology*, *42*(2), 233–250. doi:10.1111/j.1467-8535.2009.01029.x

Allen, I. E., & Seaman, J. (2011). Going the distance: Online education in the United States. Sloan Consortium.

Allen, I. E., & Seaman, J. (2014). *Grade change: Tracking online education in the United States, 2013.* Babson Survey Research Group and Quahog Research Group, LLC.

Allinder, R. M. (1994). The relationship between efficacy and the instructional practices of special education teachers and consultants. *Teacher Education and Special Education*, *17*(2), 86–95. doi:10.1177/088840649401700203

Anderson, T., Rourke, L., Archer, W., & Garrison, R. (2001). Assessing teaching presence in computer conferencing transcripts. *Journal of Asynchronous Learning Networks*, *5*(2).

Bandura, A. (1997). *Self-efficacy: The exercise of control.* New York: W.H. Freeman.

Bangert, A. (2008). The influence of social presence and teaching presence on the quality of online critical inquiry. *Journal of Computing in Higher Education*, *20*(1), 34–61. doi:10.1007/BF03033431

Baran, E., Correia, A. P., & Thompson, A. (2013). Tracing successful online teaching in higher education: Voices of exemplary online teachers. *Teachers College Record*, *115*(3), 1–41.

Bonwell, C. C., & Eison, J. A. (1991). Active Learning: Creating Excitement in the Classroom. 1991 ASHE-ERIC Higher Education Reports. ERIC Clearinghouse on Higher Education, The George Washington University.

Brown, J. S., Collins, A., & Duguid, P. (1989). Situated cognition and the culture of learning. *Educational Researcher*, *18*(1), 32–42. doi:10.3102/0013189X018001032

Caprara, G. V., Barbaranelli, C., Borgogni, L., & Steca, P. (2003). Efficacy beliefs as determinants of teachers' job satisfaction. *Journal of Educational Psychology*, *95*(4), 821–832. doi:10.1037/0022-0663.95.4.821

Chambliss, D., & Takacs, C. (2014). *How College Works*. Boston: Harvard University Press. doi:10.4159/harvard.9780674726093

Chappuis, J. (2014). *Seven Strategies of Assessment for Learning*. New York: Pearson.

Chickering, A. W., & Gamson, Z. F. (1987). Seven principles for good practice in undergraduate education. *AAHE Bulletin*, *3*, 7.

Choi, I., Land, S. M., & Turgeon, A. (2008). Instructor modeling and online question prompts for supporting peer-questioning during online discussion. *Journal of Educational Technology Systems*, *36*(3), 255–275. doi:10.2190/ET.36.3.c

Coladarci, T. (1992). Teachers' sense of efficacy and commitment to teaching. *Journal of Experimental Education*, *60*(4), 323–337. doi:10.1080/00220973.1992.9943869

Crouch, C. H., & Mazur, E. (2001). Peer instruction: Ten years of experience and results. *American Journal of Physics*, *69*(9), 970–977. doi:10.1119/1.1374249

Dahlstrom, E., & Brooks, D. C. (2014). ECAR Study of Faculty and Information Technology, 2014. Louisville, CO: ECAR.

Dikkers, A. G., Whiteside, A. L., & Lewis, S. (2013). Virtual high school teacher and student reactions to the social presence model. *Journal of Interactive Online Learning*, *12*(3), 156–170.

Dixson, M. D. (2012). Creating effective student engagement in online courses: What do students find engaging? *Journal of the Scholarship of Teaching and Learning*, *10*(2), 1–13.

Fink, L. D. (2003). *Creating Significant Learning Experiences: An Integrated Approach to Designing College Courses*. San Francisco, CA: Jossey-Bass.

Fredericksen, E., Pickett, A., Shea, P., Pelz, W., & Swan, K. (2000). Student satisfaction and perceived learning with on-line courses: Principles and examples from the SUNY learning network. *Journal of Asynchronous Learning Networks*, *4*(2), 7–41.

Garrison, D. R. (2011). *E-learning in the 21st century: A framework for research and practice*. Taylor & Francis.

Garrison, D. R., Anderson, T., & Archer, W. (2000). Critical inquiry in a text-based environment: Computer conferencing in higher education. *The Internet and Higher Education*, *2*(2–3), 87–105.

Hart, C. (2012). Factors associated with student persistence in an online program of study: A review of the literature. *Journal of Interactive Online Learning*, *11*(1), 19–42.

Heuer, B. P., & King, K. P. (2004). Leading the band: The role of the instructor in online learning for educators. *Journal of Interactive Online Learning*, *3*(1), 1–11.

Hodges, C. B., & Forrest Cowan, S. (2012). Preservice teachers' views of instructor presence in online courses. *Journal of Digital Learning in Teacher Education*, *28*(4), 139–145. doi:10.1080/21532974.2012.10784694

Hrastinski, S. (2008). Asynchronous and synchronous e-learning. *EDUCAUSE Quarterly*, *31*(4), 51–55.

Lavooy, M., & Newlin, M. (2008). Online chats and cyber-office hours: Everything but the office. *International Journal on E-Learning*, *7*(1), 107–116.

Lortie, D. C. (1975). *School teacher: A sociological inquiry*. Chicago: University of Chicago Press.

Martin, F., Parker, M. A., & Deale, D. F. (2012). Examining interactivity in synchronous virtual classrooms. *The International Review of Research in Open and Distributed Learning*, *13*(3), 228–261.

Michael, J. (2007). Faculty perceptions about barriers to active learning. *College Teaching*, *55*(2), 42–47. doi:10.3200/CTCH.55.2.42-47

Palloff, R. M., & Pratt, K. (2003). *The virtual student: A profile and guide to working with online learners*. John Wiley & Sons.

Ray, J., & Kafka, S. (2014). Life in college matters for life after college. *Gallup Latest News, Economy.* Retrieved from http://www. gallup.com/poll/168848/life-college-matters-life-college.aspx

Richardson, J. C., & Swan, K. (2003). Examing social presence in online courses in relation to students' perceived learning and satisfaction. *Journal of Asynchronous Learning Networks*, *7*(1), 69–83.

Rose, D. H., & Meyer, A. (2002). *Teaching every student in the digital age: Universal design for learning*. Alexandria, VA: Association for Supervision and Curriculum Development.

Ross, J. A. (1992). Teacher efficacy and the effects of coaching on student achievement. *Canadian Journal of Education*, *17*(1), 51–65. doi:10.2307/1495395

Savery, J. (2005). BE VOCAL: Characteristics of successful online instructors. *Journal of Interactive Online Learning*, *4*(2), 141–153.

Sener, J. (2006). Quality Matters: Inter-institutional quality improvement for online courses. *Journal of Asynchronous Learning Networks*, *10*(1), 69–80.

Shea, P., Hayes, S., Vickers, J., Gozza-Cohen, M., Uzuner, S., Mehta, R., & Rangan, P. et al. (2010). A re-examination of the community of inquiry framework: Social network and content analysis. *The Internet and Higher Education*, *13*(1), 10–21. doi:10.1016/j.iheduc.2009.11.002

Shea, P., Swan, K., Fredericksen, E., & Pickett, A. (2002). Student satisfaction and reported learning in the SUNY learning network. *Elements of Quality Online Education*, *3*, 145-156.

Shea, P. J., Fredericksen, E. E., Pickett, A. M., & Pelz, W. E. (2003). A preliminary investigation of "teaching presence" in the SUNY learning network. *Elements of Quality Online Education: Practice and Direction, 4*, 279-312.

Wang, Y. M., & Chen, D. V. (2011). Instructors as Architects—Designing Learning Spaces for Discussion-Based Online Courses. *Journal of Educational Technology Systems*, *39*(3), 281–294. doi:10.2190/ET.39.3.e

Wiggins, G. (2012). Seven keys to effective feedback. *Educational Leadership*, *70*(1), 10–18.

Wilson, B. M., Pollock, P. H., & Hamann, K. (2007). Does active learning enhance learner outcomes? Evidence from discussion participation in online classes. *Journal of Political Science Education*, *3*(2), 131–142. doi:10.1080/15512160701338304

Wojciechowski, A., & Palmer, L. B. (2005). Individual student characteristics: Can any be predictors of success in online classes? *Online Journal of Distance Learning Administration*, *8*(2).

Xu, D., & Jaggars, S. S. (2013). *Adaptability to Online Learning: Differences across Types of Students and Academic Subject Areas*. CCRC Working Paper No. 54. Community College Research Center, Columbia University.

Young, S., & Bruce, M. A. (2011). Classroom community and student engagement in online courses. *MERLOT Journal of Online Learning and Teaching*, *7*(2), 219–230.

Chapter 2
Instructor Immediacy and Authenticity:
Engaging in Cognitive Vulnerability within the Online Instructional Environment

Caroline M. Crawford
University of Houston – Clear Lake, USA

ABSTRACT

Online instructors necessitate the implementation of immediacy and authenticity on a continuous basis within an instructional endeavor. Towards more fully understanding the immediacy and authenticity of an instructor's efforts, aspects related to interactive activities, instructor's philosophical beliefs systems, and understanding cognitive vulnerability within an online instructional environment are vitally important to learner success. Further, while developing a community of practice supports the instructor's efforts to engage learners more fully within the instructional success capable within an online instructional environment, while also focusing upon enhancing the talent pool within the course environment. A talent-propelled instructional environment supports the learners while also enhancing the instructor's viability and strength of positive instructional experience.

INTRODUCTION

As with each new innovation that is integrated into the instructional environment, the cries that teachers will no longer be needed and that teachers will become extinct arise. From the time that radio was introduced, to film and even television, each societal shift was introduced into the instructional environment and the inherent fear mongering that teachers will be retired due to inherent extinction of viable need has been realized as ridiculous. With the latest introduction of the Digital Age's Internet access and Information Age's conceptual freedom of information on a global scale, again cries arose that quality instructors will become an unnecessary job that would be fondly remembered by the older generations (Arnett, 2013; Galant, 2013; Kessler, 2013; Kopp, 2013; Ravitch, 2013; Trucano, 2015). Again, after a longer

DOI: 10.4018/978-1-4666-9995-3.ch002

period than one might have imagined, society again come to the realization that the instructor is inherently necessary and ultimately a vital component throughout the shifting influences of the Digital Age.

Information Age's Impact upon Teaching and Learning

Of interest is the discussions revolving around labels, as pertains to the name Information Age, Digital Age, or perhaps even Computer Age. What is most important within these labels that define the shift from traditional engagement with knowledge and attainment of information through a process defined by time and effort, within the Information Age the digitally-based availability of information is merely a few mouse clicks or a few finger movements away. Meaning, the concept of "knowledge is power" has shifted within the Information Age; previously controlling the knowledge was how power was defined, but within the Information Age all knowledge is available quickly so the power is held by those persons who have cognitive skills and who can work with the information in creatively new and different ways of understanding. Knowledge is no longer the power broker within society; instead, the ability to produce new information that is not only personalized but also creatively meets a societal need reflects a Knowledge Economy thought process. Technological progress has merely made knowledge available more swiftly and more easily than ever before; within the Information Age the knowledge overload is a concern, wherein the ability to use information in new and different ways is not only shifting the educational arena but also the world of business and industry. The impact of the Information Age upon the educational system is obvious, as knowledge acquisition must be framed beyond the traditional face-to-face instructional environment and towards an anywhere-anytime cognitive availability.

Instructor Immediacy and the Instructional Experience

The instructor is vitally important within this Information Age shift must be recognized, as the instructor's immediacy and instructional presence within an instructional environment inherently reflects the necessary conditions and support structures inherent within any cognitive endeavor. Yet, what is instructor immediacy? One may suggest that instructor immediacy is the ability of an instructor to communicate and engage learners with the subject matter and with course colleagues, across distances of time, space and knowledge base. As described by Cheese, Thomas and Craig (2008), although associated with the realm of business and industry, the conception of talent-propelled organizations recognize the following realization that educational institutions are only now beginning to comprehend:

... the conditions faced by every organization in the search for talent are changing with astonishing rapidity in every part of the world. Familiar talent pools are shrinking, new ones are emerging; new technologies are transforming the nature of work, the skills demanded at work and the ways in which people can work; new elements are arriving in the global talent mix with new attitudes and ambitions. All these trends are making talent an ever more critical and complex issue for every organization. (p. 2)

As the business and industry realm recognizes the importance associated with not only talented people inherent throughout organizational personnel, but also the shifting types of talent that are emerging more swiftly than one might imagine. This suggests the need for even more high quality instructors, who bring forward a sense of immediacy and authenticity that supports the learners even more fully than previously realized. As Naisbitt emphasized within one of his best-selling books entitled *High Tech*

/ *High Touch* (1999), the continued emphasis upon the technological realm will naturally drive people towards a deep-seated need for communal connections. Not only is this currently viewed through the innumerable social media realms and "oversharing" that may be a reflection of the need to somehow connect with other humans on a deeper level than previously imagined, but the strides associated with online and distributed learning over the previous decade has shifted to further emphasis upon a more humanistic, holistic approach towards understanding the connective needs of learners within a sanitary, descriptively cold learning environment that is beautifully instructionally designed and the usability of learners may be assured, but the motivational and connective needs of humans are recognized as inherently viable and indispensably necessary to continuously engage the learners and enhance the cognitive efforts towards understanding subject matter information.

Learner's Motivation and Self-Regulation Efforts

The instructor not only imparts knowledge and cognitively supports the learner's understanding of information through Bloom's Taxonomy of the Cognitive Domain (Bloom, 1956; Bloom, Englhart, Furst, Hill & Krathwohl, 1956) and Anderson and Krathwohl's Revised Taxonomy of the Cognitive Domain for the Digital Age (Anderson & Krathwohl, 2001), but the instructor offers a motivational and self-regulatory immediacy and authenticity to an instructional environment that a talented instructional designer, learning management system or simulated gaming environment may support but currently cannot attain to the same level as an instructor who has the ability to engage, motivate and cognitively connect the learner with the information as well as within the larger community of understanding.

In a strangely satisfying manner, the self-study and reflective teaching efforts that continue to engage academics and scholars in strongly opinionated discussions, on both ends of the opinion spectrum, has brought forward significant recognition of the importance and inherent impact of the instructor upon the learner. From this author's own ethnographic efforts and understandings that also encompassed significant ongoing yet cursory self-study reflective engagement, components revolving around instructor immediacy and authenticity brought forward extended understandings of interactive activities, the impact of the instructor's philosophical beliefs systems upon the instructional environment and the learner's potential towards enhanced understanding of the subject matter, as well as the true impact of an instructor upon the learner's implicit cognitive vulnerability. Each of these intriguing areas of instructor impact are addressed, within this chapter, as each of these understandings arose through working within online learning environments.

The objective of this chapter is to frame an understanding of instructor immediacy and authenticity within different types of instructional environments. There is special attention focused upon online and other forms of distributed instructional environments, through real world and learned experiences over an almost thirty year professional educator experience. This extended professional experience evolved in understanding from a secondary classroom teacher experience to realizing the potential cognitive impact and instructional recognition of technological tools, towards a continuously developing and expanding recognition of the strengths inherent within Digital Age instructional possibilities. Also framed within this discussion is the effort towards more fully recognizing and appreciating the true impact of an instructor not merely upon the learner's instructional experience but more deeply, upon the learner's ability to engage with the knowledge more fully and supportively modeling a safe environment in which the learners can "think outside the box" in new and creative ways.

BACKGROUND

Since Dewey (1910/1991, 1938) first began to wonder about educational experiences to Gardner, 1995), Koestler (1969) and Kolb (1984) focusing upon the intriguing aspects of the learning process, instructors and learners have been a central focus of interest and attention. Teacher immediacy and quality instructional efforts have further enhanced the scholarly discussions and enhanced an interest in understanding, since the Industrial Age classroom environment was created (Anderson, 1979; Brookfield, 1995; Grossera & Lombard, 2008; Lave & Wenger, 1991) brings forward discussions revolving around teacher immediacy, teacher effectiveness, and teacher impact within different instructional environments (Backs, 2012; Brown, Collins & Duguid, 1989; Hadjioannou, 2007, Kreijins, Kirschener, & Jochems, 2003; Laurillard, 1993, 2002a, 2002b; Mullen & Tallent-Runnels, 2006; Park, 2013; Park & Bonk, 2007; Reilly, 2014; Sobel, Sands & Dunlap, 2009; Swan, 2002; Woods & Baker, 2004). Yet shifting understandings of the Information Age have brought forward differentiated understandings of human talent, as suggested by Cheese, Thomas and Craig (2008):

First, the key factor in determining the success of any organization is its ability to use human talent - to discover it, develop it, deploy it, motivate and energize it. Human talent - the combined capacity and will of people to achieve an organization's goals - is a productive resource like no other, with a unique capacity to add value to an organization. (p. 1)

Distance education is an intriguingly innovative and difficult effort, not only from an instructional design aspect but also considerations towards successful knowledge acquisition, evaluative assessment, learner engagement and instructional prowess understandings. Much as within any instructional environment, the traditional aspects apply. Yet within today's fast-changing world, what we call *distance education* is quickly shifting and in the throes of being inherently redefined and expanded. Expanding the thought process from an understanding of distance education towards a more holistic thought process revolving around the concept of distributed learning environments may support the impact and importance of instructor immediacy.

Distributed learning environments are an intriguing instructional effort, no matter if persons are focused upon totally online learning environments, blended or hybrid learning environments, mobile learning, massive open online courses (MOOCs) or the newer views of MOOCs towards small private online courses (SPOCs) or even newly termed corporate open online courses (COOCs), with an interesting new focus upon connectivist MOOCs (cMOOCs) and extended MOOCs (xMOOCs).Yes, the primary focus of any instructional environment is upon successful knowledge attainment by the learners. This is the same ultimate focus as within face-to-face traditional instructional environments. Yet within a time allocation and distance understanding, the potential impact of the instructor's importance towards learner support and engagement has continued as a realized area of impact.

Instructor Immediacy and Online Learning

Chickering and Gamson (1987, 1999) as well as Chickering and Ehrmann (1996) have focused upon good practice as revolves around the concept of instructor immediacy, specifically revolving around undergraduate education. These aspects include the following:

- Encourages student-faculty contact
- Encourages cooperation among students
- Encourages active learning
- Gives prompt feedback
- Emphasizes time on task
- Communicates high expectations
- Respects diverse talents and ways of learning (Chickering & Gamson, 1987, p. 1-2 ; 1999, p. 76)

Also of interest is the discussion that the presence of these aspects multiply as introduced within the instructional environment, wherein "together, they employ six powerful forces in education: activity; diversity; interaction; cooperation; expectations; responsibility" (Chickering & Gamson, 1987, p. 3). These elements of good practice occur not merely within the face-to-face environment, but are equally important and engaging aspects of instructor immediacy and engagement within online learning environments. These seven principles were even introduced as a model towards evaluating online teaching and instructor immediacy (Bangert, 2004), engaging in a constructivist understanding of the good practices that were broken into a Likert-style quantitative questionnaire, focusing upon a master's-level online statistics course, that implemented the grouping of 35 prompts into topic areas designated as: student faculty contact; cooperation among students; active learning; prompt feedback; time on task; high expectations; diverse talents and ways of learning; and the "overall" (pp. 229-230) course questions delineated as:

- This course was valuable.
- This course improved my understanding of educational statistics.
- Taking this course increased my interest in educational statistics. (Bangert, 2004, p. 230)

Ultimately, instructor immediacy is reflected through good practice within any style of instructional environment, whether it be a traditional face-to-face instructional environment, a blended learning approach, or a distributed learning environment also known as online learning.

The instructional immediacy and authenticity brought forward through not only the instructor's facilitative and moderating efforts, but also the inherent impact of the instructor's understanding of the differentiated flow of learning, understanding and enhancement associated with cognitive efforts in new and different ways, continue to ultimately remain within the domain of the instructor. Through the instructor's understanding of perceived and real immediacy by the learners, and the inherent authenticity of reactive and proactive approaches towards the learner's recognized yet momentarily and continuously shifting needs, the instructor does bring quite a lot to the instructional environment.

INSTRUCTOR IMMEDIACY AND AUTHENTICITY: THE MEAT OF THE DISCUSSION

An interesting discussion as concerns instructor immediacy and authenticity emphasizes an understanding revolving around interactive communications as an undergirding of any instructional experience. An initial reaction is a two-way style of interactive communications, between the learner and the instructor. Garrison (1989) and Garrison and Shale (1990) focused upon the transactional approaches associated with the instructor-learner communicative efforts as functional approaches towards understanding the information, with a focused effort to, "avoid the restrictive trap of describing distance education based upon its existing forms and structures" (p. 25), although the functional understanding of the learning process was reframed with an attempt towards considering the teaching and learning functional process as the central focus of any type of distance education endeavor. Yet this is a simplistic understanding of the depth and breadth of influence upon the learner within an instructional environment. Towards recognizing the inherent social and communicative nature of the instructional process, an understanding focused upon interactive activities is offered.

A next area of interest is focused upon the conception of a philosophical beliefs system. Although the primary focus is upon the instructor's philosophical beliefs systems that are in place and, consequently, directly impact the course design, course modeling and mentoring efforts, collegial environment, impact upon the community of learning or perhaps community of practice (Lave & Wenger, 1991; Wenger, 1998, 2009, 2010; Wenger, McDermott & Snyder, 2002) efforts, facilitative efforts and mentoring learners, as well as recognition that the instructor has a direct impact upon supporting the learner's cognitive vulnerability and strengths associated with learning and more fully engaging with the course subject matter.

This concept of cognitive vulnerability may be viewed as an instructor's ability to engage with each learner on an intellectual as well as empathic level of understanding, towards meeting the intellectual and cognitive needs of the learner, beyond acting as a support effort and more so towards engaging with the learners and the subject matter in new and different ways, towards attempting to ensure that the learners develop a basic understanding of the knowledge base while continuing to cajole and enhance the learner towards working with the information in new and different ways, towards higher order thinking skills, and towards a potential recognition of current subject matter knowledge gaps that the learners may be able to address in new and innovative manners.

Each of these three aspects of the instructor's immediacy and authenticity may be described as a scientific recognition of procedural efforts, while an empathic view of an instructor's efforts may also reflect an acknowledgement of the artistic nature of an instructor's engagement with the subject matter, within the instructional design and learner needs associated with instructional enhancements, as well as knowing and understanding what the learner may need even though the learner may be unable to verbalize their needs to the instructor. The immediacy of the instructor's understanding and facilitative role, while also representing an authenticity with the learners so as to reflect an approachability and collegial mentorship effort that more fully engages the learners with the subject matter, within the instructional environment, as well as a collegial approach with learner colleagues that also integrates a motivational component and sense of engagement and recognition within the learning environment. Although each of these three aspects may seem separated by thought process and emphasis within the instructional environment, the instructor's sense of immediacy and authenticity more fully embraces the all-encompassing nature of each topic as stand-alone areas of vital importance but also the overlay and ability of each topic to seep into and impact each of the other areas of emphasis.

Interactive Activities

Defining terms of use within this discussion is of vital importance, as the terms *interactions* and *interactivities* within the instructional environment are treated quite differently by scholars, wherein some scholars interchange the terms, while other scholars state that these terms are quite separate in definition as well as in implementation. Roblyer and Ekhaml (2000) offer a beautifully articulated reflection of the differentiation in terminology designation, as follows:

Gilbert and Moore (1998) note that an accepted definition of interactivity in the literature on computer-mediated instruction is a reciprocal exchange between the technology and the learner, a process which he says is referred to as "feedback." Gilbert and Moore use the terms "interaction" and interactivity" interchangeably. However, Wagner (1994, 1997) draws a sharp distinction between them. Like Gilbert and Moore, she says that "interaction" is an interplay and exchange in which individuals and groups influence each other. Thus, interaction is when there are "reciprocal events requiring two objects and two actions (p. 20). On the other hand, she says "interactivity" seems to have emerged from "descriptions of technological capability for establishing connections from point-to-point ... in realtime" (p. 20). Thus, interaction focuses on people's behaviors, while interactivity focuses on characteristics of the technology systems.

Even if one accepts this distinction, it is evident that these qualities are linked and that both are necessary to achieve the qualities students find so desirable. Also, it is clear that there is a relationship between these two qualities in distance courses. Technologies that allow high interactivity seem necessary to allow high person-to-person, person-to-group, and person-to-system interaction. (para. 4-5)

These definitions are inherent to this discussion, as *interactions* and *interactivities* are separately articulated from the term implemented in this discussion, being *interactive activities* wherein there is indeed a technological interface and impact upon the initial frame of the discussion; however, *interactivity* is not an appropriate label for this discussion due to the inherent social allocation and necessary emphasis upon not only the instructor's immediacy and perceived authenticity throughout the instructional process and while working with the learners, but also due to the pronounced emphasis upon the reflective focus upon one's own learning within the "self" designation, as well as within the community consideration that emphasizes not merely the in-course learning community of colleagues, but also the professional community, personal community and larger social community as additional frames of understanding the developing knowledge base, thinking about the information in new and different ways, as well as creatively focusing upon higher order thinking skills progression (Bloom, 1956; Bloom, Englhart, Furst, Hill & Krathwohl, 1956; Anderson & Krathwohl, 2001).

As interactive activities focus upon interactions based upon several different aspects and considerations a background in critical interactions within any instructional environment, with special consideration towards distance learning environments, resulted in several different interactive activity considerations arising over the previous decade or two:

- Learner-content (Moore, 1989)
- Learner-interface (Hillman, Willis & Gunawardena, 1994)
- Learner-instructor (Moore, 1989)
- Learner-learner (Moore, 1989)
- Learner-self (Crawford, 2001)
- Learner-community (Burnham & Walden, 1997)
- Instructor-community (Crawford, 2001)
- Instructor-content (Crawford, 2001)
- Instructor-interface (Crawford, 2001)
- Instructor-self (Crawford, 2001;2003)

An interesting shift in thought is Crawford's (2001, 2003) focus upon the instructor's engagement within and impact upon the instructional environment, which is rarely included in the discussions revolving around distance education environments and interactive activities.

The primary focus within the list of interactive activities revolves around the learner and the instructor as separate yet clearly articulated persons who are actively engaged within the instructional environment. The person or persons holding the label of instructor or facilitative moderator interact with the same level of information, interface and social aspects as does the learner. Actually, the instructor must more fully engage in interactive activities within the instructional environment due to the lively engagement motivational efforts as well as consistent integration of new, timely and socially or culturally relevant information that may support the learner's ability to make connections with the course subject matter. At the same time, the instructor is working "behind the scenes" towards ensuring that the course environment is working properly and assignment efforts are fully evaluated with detailed, thoughtful and supportive feedback emphasized towards each learner's progressive course efforts. These evaluative efforts are not only private endeavors, but the public engagement within asynchronous environments such as discussion boards as well as synchronous environments such as video conference calls, telephone conversations, chat sessions, and other immediacy-focused efforts emphasize the nuanced yet complex nature of the instructor's role within an online or distributed instructional environment.

A question with which the author has struggled, is how the instructor successfully engages in all forms of interactive activities within innumerable course environments, while still ensuring that the instructor immediacy and engaging authenticity are inherently valid for the learners. Within the author's own level of comfort, including careful and continuous efforts towards analysis and re-analysis of the subject matter and the learners, while also considering the viability of different technological components that must be continuously considered as viable instructional support but may not yet be ready to begin integrating into the instructional environment, are all elements that have been addressed over the years. The author was overjoyed when Internet speeds and accessibility finally developed to the point that the learners could easily access streaming video vignettes from home, from work and even from their smart phones. This currently inconsequential consideration was hugely significant in the author's efforts towards instructor immediacy and authenticity, as the author's efforts towards worthwhile instructor-specific video products could be readily accessed and finally had the opportunity to impact the learners more directly. Lesson overviews, lesson explanations, sample assignment products, and even offering a personalized approach towards instructional assessment all became readily available and more easily implemented. As well as the learner accessibility recognition, an additional consideration is the intriguing emphasis upon the personalized video vignettes as perceived instructor immediacy and authenticity. Meaning, the unit introduction video vignettes offered the perception of personalization that the learners desired, not only the ability to perceive a sense of in-class lecture-style or conversational-style understandings, but also the personalization perceived through the vocal intonation, headshots and additional aspects that helped the learners perceive a stronger connection and understanding with the instructor.

The embracing of a more fully developed understanding of interactive activities throughout the instructional experience, and particularly impactful within an online or distributed instructional environment, may support the instructor's understanding of internal-to-course as well as external influences upon the learner's conceptualization and understanding of the subject matter. Within this thought process and instructional venue, the needs of the learners and understandings associated with the learner's interactive activity needs and expectations can support the instructor's efforts towards not only self-sufficiency, enhancement and course engagement, but more fully towards understanding aspects of the learner that support the ability to engage in more authentic ways within the instructional environment while also ensuring the sense of immediacy that is integrally important when learners are at a distance. As such, the impact of the instructor upon the perceived successes of the distance education environment are inherent within any discussion revolving around online instructional environments and learner success.

Instructor's Philosophical Beliefs Systems

A journey towards understanding an instructor's philosophical beliefs systems can be a difficult undertaking, with significant reflection and a need for not only an open mind but also a desire to research beyond what one perceives as "true". After all, there is an overabundance of research suggesting that so many instructors teach the way that they were taught (Austin, 2002; Bell, 1997; Bransford, Brown & Cocking, 1999; Caffarella & Zinn, 1999; Fenwick, 2000; Gibbs & Coffey, 2004; Hativa & Goodyear, 2001; Kember, 1997; Kolb, 1984; Lortie, 1975; Menges, 2000; Nespor, 1987; Nisbett & Ross, 1980; Oleson & Hora, 2012; Pajares, 1992; Putnam & Borko, 2000; Saroyan & Amundsen, 2004; Shavelson & Stern, 1981; Shulman, 1987; Smylie, 1989; Trigwell, Prosser & Waterhouse, 1999; Umbach, 2007). Yet the ability to reflect upon one's own instructional understandings can support instructor immediacy and authenticity by understanding one's own belief systems and efforts. Associated with online learning environments and associated distributed learning efforts, a worthwhile endeavor. As suggested by Siemens (2002):

The growth and success of elearning is closely linked to the design of quality learning, enabled through the use of technology. Instructional designers play the pivotal role of bringing together these disparate fields - for the benefit of students, instructors, and organizations. Many of the concerns of online learning drop out rates, learner resistance, and poor learner performance can be addressed through a structured design process. The resulting benefits - reduced design costs, consistent look and feel, transparency, quality control, standardization - make organizational investment in ID a simple decision. (Siemens, 2002, para. 11)

Based upon the importance and impact of the instructor within the distance learning environment, an understanding of the instructor's philosophical beliefs systems must be addressed. Yet, what does this even mean? The instructor impacts almost every aspect of the distance education endeavor, with an initial focus upon framing the course through the instructor's philosophical beliefs about learning and teaching, including:

- Learning Theories and The Impact Upon Instructional Success
- How the Instructor Believes that She Learns
- How the Instructor Designs Online Courses
- How the Instructor Instructs
- How the Instructor Believes that Other People Learn
- How the Instructor Believes the Subject is "Best" Taught

Learning theories undergird each aspect of an instructor's implementation of a distance education environment, including not only instructional interactions but especially instructional expectations. Yet, what is a learning theory? Driscoll (2004) defines a learning theory as the following:

A learning theory, therefore, comprises a set of constructs linking observed changes in performance with what is thought to bring about those changes. Constructs refer to the concepts theorists invent to identify psychological variables. Memory, for example, is a construct implicated in cognitive perspectives on learning. In other words, we look at the fact that people can demonstrate the same performance time after time and reason that they do so because they have remembered it. We have invented the concept of memory to explain this result. (p. 9)

An understanding of learning theories as a conceptual understanding helps supports the thought process associated with thinking through one's own philosophical beliefs systems, wherein one questions their own beliefs about not only their own areas of comfort and personal understandings, but also their own beliefs about the ways that other people view the world and learn information. Everyone is different, with distinctly different "flavors" and mixes of learning theories implemented so as to reflect responses to each of the above questions. For example, how might an instructor believe that she learns information most easily and fully? What are the processes that are not only comfortable to her, but also that supports her efforts towards remembering and understanding new information? Now, does she implement the same instructional processes to learn the subject matter that she teaches? This is an important question, as an additional important question is how the instructor believes that others learn the information. There are those persons who cannot perceive that one can learn any new information outside of a behavioral realm wherein the instructor is the font of knowledge and the learner is a blank slate into which the instructor pours new information.

Yet on the other side of the metaphorical pendulum swing, there are instructors who strongly hold the opinion that a radical constructivist instructional approach, such as discovery learning without any instructional knowledge base building nor necessary guidance, is the most appropriate way through which people learn. Recognizing these differences as an instructor, as well as recognizing the differences in the learner's viewpoints associated with learning, can more readily engage the instructor towards understanding the needs of the learners, the instructional immediacy and level of continuous engagement that will be necessary and appropriate within an online instructional environment when implementing different ways of presenting information within an online or distributed instructional environment. As well, the instructor must always consider the authenticity of the instructional environment. Embracing the appropriateness of the subject matter is vital, especially when considering one's own philosophical beliefs and ways that the online course is instructionally designed. Will the knowledge base be carefully framed and presented to the learners, or will the learners work out the information in different ways? Will there be a desire for team-based collegial projects, or will the course be solely individual in nature? Yes, of course the subject matter, level of learner understanding associated with the subject matter, and quality of learner experiences are necessary to recognize, but after a full analysis of the course needs and associated learner needs, the course must be designed towards meeting specific instructional objectives that are directly aligned with the learner assessments.

Whether the instructor designs a distance education course environment does impact a course structure and frames the initial conceptual impact upon the subject matter and the student learner, yet the instructor further impacts the online course environment based upon the instructor's beliefs about herself, the subject matter, appropriate instructional persona, type of online community that is necessary and appropriate to model, as well as the instructor's belief about the learners and the way or ways that the learner may most appropriately and most fully engage with the subject matter towards knowledge acquisition.

Cognitive Vulnerability Theory

At this point, Crawford's developing Cognitive Vulnerability theory (Crawford, 2015; Crawford & Smith, 2015) begins to explain the nuanced importance of the instructor's immediacy and authenticity within an online instructional environment. Recognition of the learner's vulnerable nature within an instructional environment may be regulated and understood by an instructor's efforts towards interacting with the learners more fully within an instructional environment, while modeling appropriate and collegial interactive efforts within this same environment enhances the learner's understandings as regards expectations and community involvement within the online learning environment; however, moving beyond a more simplistic view of the instructor's impact upon the learners is necessary and appropriate. An important question to ask is, what is *vulnerability*? Bennett (2007) reflects upon this question and offers:

Vulnerability is not good or bad, it is simply real. Some kinds of vulnerability feel awesome and some feel terrifying. All vulnerability is profoundly experiential and memorable. The more we learn how to nurture our vulnerability, the more intimacy we can experience and the safer and happier we are likely to be in the world.

But live in a culture where vulnerability is ridiculed, abused, medicated and repressed. Because of this, many reading this article do not even know about their vulnerability – consciously. Some literally have been abused out of a connection to their vulnerability. In these people, vulnerability seems bad and the need to "escape it" drives much of what they do. (para. 7-8)

Once one considered the sense of vulnerability within another person, especially when recognizing the experience-based and memory-focused impact upon one's cognitive abilities, as well as the societal views that vulnerability is somehow shameful and must be hidden away, a recognition may begin to arise that reflects upon the most vulnerable nature of the learning process. After all, endeavoring to learn new information and use this information in new and different ways is very much a vulnerable endeavor. As such, it is the task of the instructor to ensure that each learner's level of comfortableness, acceptance and freedom towards engaging with the information in new and different ways is ensured as occurring within a safe and supportive, collegial environment. The instructor's immediacy and authenticity throughout the course will not only model the level of vulnerability that is deemed acceptable within the online instructional environment, but the facilitative role of the instructor has the opportunity to enhance the learner's comfortableness and sense of vulnerability, to more fully work with the course subject matter, ask questions, think "outside the box" and a most frightening endeavor for most learners is to "get it wrong" and expect the potential public humiliation that may ensue. Instead of developing a course culture of perfectionism, one may suggest that modeling and engaging in a vulnerable course culture wherein creativity, innovation and recognizing that all learning efforts will include rethinking of understandings and reframing conceptual frameworks of understanding (Vygotsky, 1933/1966, 1934, 1934/1987, 1935, 1962, 1978a, 1978b, 1981). The role of the instructor is to define the course culture and appropriate behaviors, not only through modeling and facilitating throughout the course experience, but also towards ensuring the instructor's immediacy and authenticity engage in understandings revolving around cognitive vulnerability as an instructional experience.

The instructor's cognitive impact upon the learning as an individual, as well as the learners within the larger community of learning environment, more directly frames the instructor's importance as a cognitive model who reflects a cognitive strength and belief in the ability of each learner yet who also has an opportunity to engage the learning community, in reality to engage each learner within the learning community, towards thinking about the subject matter in new and different ways that are beyond the initial bounds of the instructional objectives as stated within the online instructional environment. Not only may the subject matter focus necessarily impart an understanding of the knowledge base upon the learner, nor perhaps even implement an understanding and test-check of the subject matter within a real world environment so as to engage within higher order thinking skills (Bloom, 1956; Bloom, Englhart, Furst, Hill & Krathwohl, 1956; Anderson & Krathwohl, 2001), but the impact of the instructor upon the learner's engagement with the subject matter in new and innovative ways towards more fully thinking *outside the box* embraces the cognitive efforts and cognitive vulnerability of each learner within a safe and trusted community environment, towards framing the subject matter in new and innovative ways so as to more fully engage with the subject matter knowledge base and not only shift from short term memory towards long-term implicit memory understandings of the information, but also offers the potential towards engaging the learners in a more innovative and creative understanding of the subject matter that moves beyond knowledge acquisition and higher order thinking skills, and towards a cognitively vulnerable and positively supportive instructional environment that the instructor carefully designs, develops, implements and supportively engages through different forms of modeling and positive reinforcement of cognitively vulnerable efforts, so as to fully engage the learners in a cognitively vulnerable instructional environment that moves beyond an instructional environment and more so towards a more fully articulated and framed academic and scholarly engagement with the information as not only learners but also as collegial co-contributors.

SOLUTIONS AND RECOMMENDATIONS

The issues revolving around the concept of the online or distributed learning environment instructor must be fully emphasized, so as to more fully articulate the significant impact that the instructor has upon the course culture through the modeling endeavors and facilitative understandings in each instance viewed by the learners. The instructor sets the tone for the course, and the learners clearly understand not only the instructor's role in the course but also the learner's own role and level of collegial importance based upon the instructor's efforts. How does the instructor set the tone for the course? This is an interesting question, as this is dependent upon the learners within the course experience and the subject matter focus of the instructional experience. However, after stating as much, there are basic aspects worthy of implementation.

Engaging in the Instructional Environment

First is the expectation that the instructor reaches out to engage the learners early and through an extended period at the beginning of the learning experience. Emails of introduction, professional information shared through textual display, as well as sharing of external resources are vital. Also important is the recognition of each learner's posted professional introduction of themselves; it is vitally important for the instructional facilitator, the course lead, to professionally respond to each learner's posted information within an online environment as early as possible within the course experience, not only towards ensuring a feeling of engagement between the learners and the course experience but also towards representing a community of engagement feeling within the course. After all, learners are curious by nature and will review not only colleague communications but especially the instructor's responses to learner colleagues; the initial instructor communications with all learners within the learning environment will be reviewed by all learner colleagues, and set the initial tone and level of expectation and experience throughout the rest of the learning experience. An instructor's sense of immediacy and sense of authenticity throughout the digital realm wherein instruction occurs impacts the success of the course experience, but more so the quality of instructional experience by each of the learners.

Humanness: Humanizing the Instructional Environment

Of course the instructor traditionally holds the position of power and control within an instructional environment. Yet instead of focusing upon wielding the power and control, one could more comfortably expand one's sense of "humanness", the social construction of connectedness in essential engagement and understanding within our own socialization and species, and understanding towards focusing more fully upon "the power of vulnerability" (Brown, 2010, 2011). Professionally commiserating within a collegial instructional environment, understanding each other's strengths and sharing knowledge understanding and additional supportive resources within an open instructional environment may offer a more fully articulated and enhanced opportunity towards framing the full strength of an instructional endeavor. The openness displayed by the instructor, the sharing of professional experiences and understandings by the instructor, reflects a mentoring effort that many learners will follow; this type of guidance by the instructor sets the level of professional expectation and engagement throughout the instructional experience, that has the opportunity to more fully engage learners with not only the information but also with other learner colleague connections. These types of efforts by the instructor offer an immediacy of engagement and comfortableness by learners within the course experience, resulting in a level of motivation and self-efficacy that develop into an inherent engagement for a significant percentage of learners.

Instructor as a Reflective Practitioner and Facilitator

The instructor may expand their own knowledge and understanding through a sense of self-study and reflective analysis upon one's own instructional experiences, while also more fully critically analyzing one's quality and reputation as an instructor. Although the author find that most learners do willingly defer to the instructor within an instructional environment, the author also find that learners easily engage in a community of practice environment (Lave & Wenger, 1991; Wenger, 1998, 2009, 2010; Wenger, McDermott & Snyder, 2002) wherein the instructor defines herself as a collegial member of the learning community and as a mentor-type scholar with the sole purpose being an enhancement of the instructional experience and not only the attainment of the knowledge base but a focus upon higher order thinking skills during which the instructor emphasizes the desire to highlight the strengths of the learners within the community, and continuously supports the learner needs more quietly and respectfully. With an instructor engaging in a reflective analysis and self-study throughout an instructional experience delves into a professional self-understanding that further defines the instructor's professionalism, while also reflecting a level of vulnerability and engagement within the course experience that supports the community-building of the learning experience and subsequent engagement of the learners through the stated or unstated recognition that the instructor is just as engaged in the course as are the learners.

This authenticity within the instructional realm directly impacts the authenticity, vulnerability and engagement of the learners in a positive manner; when the instructor is allowing herself to be vulnerable and self-reflectivity is "on display" for the learners, this style of instructional engagement and learner mentorship supports the learners on innumerable levels of collegiality, subject matter engagement, and ability towards a comfortableness with questioning and analyzing the subject matter under study in a professional, positive manner.

With approximately thirty years of instructional experience, and recognizing that the author is always working on strengthening her own instructional immediacy and authenticity, the efforts associated with working towards enhanced interactive activities, more fully understanding one's own and continuously developing sense of philosophical beliefs systems, as well as focusing upon authenticity through cognitive vulnerability within the author's own professional and personal realm, it is comforting to openly state that the author is never going to finish her journey forward. As a recommendation, the author urges that instructors strive to be more kind to themselves, while also working towards being the strongest possible instructor for the learners. Everything is a progressive journey, and every journey is recursive in nature. Enjoy the journey, and especially enjoy your learners' experiences as your own.

FUTURE RESEARCH DIRECTIONS

The book's focus upon the instructor within different types of online learning environments is not only timely, but appears to be a significantly growing area of interest within the academic, business and industry and training worlds (Bawane & Spector, 2009; Mehra, 2002). At first, the emphasis within online instructional environments was the instructional design focus wherein "if we build it, they will come" which this author found to be quite ridiculous. Yes, the instructional design efforts were respectable and quite important, but a holistic approach towards the instructional process is normally a more prudent approach. Additionally, this author watched as pretty and fun graphics and multimedia vignettes were integrated throughout the vast majority of online courses, as learning management systems grew in attraction and the higher education organizations desperately attempted to pull together online courses and then online degree programs, sometimes without enhanced consideration towards quality of the learner experience. This author was deemed as a bit annoying, mandating that access time for the learners was more important than silly and annoying "fun" animated GIFs, while the graphics and interactive interfaces that were integrated into the online courses were instructionally relevant and supported the learner's understanding of the subject matter. A third consideration that the author finds curious, and one may suggest is still in its infancy, is the administrative perception of online courses mandate that instructors be involved in the online courses seven days a week, seemingly twenty-four hours a day (Brauckman & Schwarz, 2015; Wilson, 1998; Root, Molgaard & Malone, 2015; St. Phard, 2015). Much as this author heard during her years as a classroom teacher in middle school and high school, today this author hears "shaming" conversations revolving around "if you cared about the students, then you'd give more of your time" somehow suggesting that an instructor's endeavors are not inherently intrusive into other job responsibilities or that the instructor doesn't care about the students or associated job responsibilities. Considering that the conception of instructor immediacy has the potential to be wielded as a negative administrative tool, future research directions would do well to focus upon the dichotomy between time, quality and monetary allocation. The instructor within an online instructional environment endeavors to fulfill the instructional obligations of a strong instructional experience for the learners, but the question must always be asked, "how much is too much?" when it comes to instructor immediacy as framed through the lens of accountability.

CONCLUSION

Instructor immediacy and authenticity within an online instructional environment are inherently vital aspects towards supporting a learner's successful journey through a potentially rough terrain. Yet after stating as much, the instructor has innumerable talents and skill sets to bring forward within an online instructional environment. The ability to successfully engage the learners within an online environment, to not only survive but to more so thrive and enhance the initial experience into a truly enviable course experience is supported through the recognition and integration of the course culture, modeling by the course instructor, and facilitative efforts that support the cognitive vulnerability of not only the instructor's modeling but more importantly the comfortableness of the learners to reach beyond the role of the learner and endeavor towards a collegial community of practice wherein it is a safe environment to test, fail, and then succeed to greater lengths than any learner had originally imagined as possible.

REFERENCES

Anderson, J. F. (1979). Teacher immediacy as a predictor of teaching effectiveness. In D. Nimmo (Ed.), *Communication Yearbook III* (pp. 543–559). New Brunswick, NJ: Transaction Books.

Anderson, L.W., & Krathwohl. (Eds.). (2001). *A taxonomy for learning, teaching, and assessing: A revision of Bloom's Taxonomy of Educational Objectives*. New York: Longman.

Arnett, T. (2013, August 26). Will computers replace teachers? *Clayton Christensen Institute for Disruptive Innovation*. Retrieved from http://www.christenseninstitute.org/will-computers-replace-teachers/

Austin, A. E. (2002). Preparing the next generation of faculty: Graduate school as socialization to the academic career. *The Journal of Higher Education*, *73*(1), 94–122. doi:10.1353/jhe.2002.0001

Backs, A. (2012). *Dragging the Y Generation into E-Learning: A study of engaging averse online learners. In 2012 Annual Proceedings* (Vol. 1, pp. 38–40). Bloomington, IN: Association for Educational Communications and Technology.

Bangert, A. W. (2004). The seven principles of good practice: A framework for evaluating on-line teaching. *The Internet and Higher Education*, *7*(3), 217–232. doi:10.1016/j.iheduc.2004.06.003

Bawane, J., & Spector, J. M. (2009, November). Prioritization of online instructor roles: Implications for competency-based teacher education programs. *Distance Education*, *30*(3), 383–397. doi:10.1080/01587910903236536

Bell, M. (1997). The development of expertise. *Journal of Professional Development*, *68*(2), 34–38.

Bennett, J. (2007). Great actors access vulnerability. *The Jason Bennett Actor's Workshop*. Retrieved from http://www.jbactors.com/actingreading/actorsaccessvulnerability.html

Bloom, B. S. (1984). *Taxomony of educational objectives*. Boston, MA: Allyn and Bacon.

Bloom, B. S., Englhart, M. D., Furst, E. J., Hill, W. H., & Krathwohl, D. R. (Eds.). (1956). *Taxonomy of educational objectives, the classification of educational goals, Handbook I: cognitive domain*. New York: Longmans.

Bransford, J. D., Brown, A. L., & Cocking, R. D. (Eds.). (1999). *How people learn: Brain, mind, experience, and school*. Washington, DC: National Academy Press.

Brauckmann, S., & Schwarz, A. (2015). No time to manage? The trade-off between relevant tasks and actual priorities of school leaders in Germany. *International Journal of Educational Management*, *29*(6), 749–765. doi:10.1108/IJEM-10-2014-0138

Brookfield, S. D. (1995). *Becoming a critically reflective teacher*. San Francisco: Jossey-Bass.

Brown, B. (2010, December). The power of vulnerability. *TEDxHouston*. TED Conferences, LCC. Retrieved from http://www.ted.com/talks/brene_brown_on_vulnerability.html

Brown, B. (2011, January). *Brene Brown: The power of vulnerability*. Retrieved from: http://www.youtube.com/watch?v=iCvmsMzlF7o

Brown, J. S., Collins, A., & Duguid, P. (1989). Situated cognition and the culture of learning. *Educational Researcher*, *18*(1), 32–42. doi:10.3102/0013189X018001032

Burnham, B., & Walden, B. (1997). Interactions in distance education: A report from the other side. In *Proceedings of the Adult Education Research Conference*. Oklahoma State University. Available: http://www.edst.educ.ubc.ca/aerc/1997/97burnham.html

Caffarella, R. S., & Zinn, L. F. (1999). Professional development for faculty: A conceptual framework of barriers and supports. *Innovative Higher Education*, *23*(4), 241–254. doi:10.1023/A:1022978806131

Cheese, P., Thomas, R. J., & Craig, E. (2008). *The talent powered organization: Strategies for globalization, talent management and high performance*. London, UK: Kogan Page Publishers.

Chickering, A. W., & Ehrmann, S. C. (1996, October). Implementing the seven principles: Technology as lever. *AAHE Bulletin*, *49*(2), 3–6.

Chickering, A. W., & Gamson, Z. F. (1987, March). Seven principles of good practice in undergraduate education. *AAHE Bulletin*, *39*(7), 3–7. Retrieved from https://scholar.vt.edu/access/content/user/adevans/Public/DVDPortfolio/Samples/samples/training/track_d/Introduction/Best%20Practices/Article%20-%207%20Principles%20of%20Good%20Practice%20in%20Undergrad%20Ed.pdf

Chickering, A. W., & Gamson, Z. F. (1999, Winter). Development and adaptations of the seven principles for good practice in undergraduate education. *New Directions for Teaching and Learning*, *80*(80), 75–81. doi:10.1002/tl.8006

Crawford, C. (2015). Vulnerability in learning. In J. Spector (Ed.), *The SAGE Encyclopedia of Educational Technology* (pp. 832–835). Thousand Oaks, CA: SAGE Publications, Inc.; doi:10.4135/9781483346397.n338

Crawford, C. M. (2001). Developing webs of significance through communications: Appropriate interactive activities for distributed learning environments. *Campus-Wide Information Systems Journal, 18*(2), 68–72. doi:10.1108/10650740110386675

Crawford, C. M. (2003). Emerging learning environments: Enhancing the online community. *Academic Exchange Quarterly, 7*(4), 131–135.

Crawford, C. M., & Smith, M. S. (2015). Rethinking Bloom's Taxonomy: Implicit Cognitive Vulnerability as an impetus towards higher order thinking skills. In Z. Jin (Ed.), *Exploring Implicit Cognition: Learning, Memory, and Social Cognitive Processes* (pp. 86–103). Hershey, PA: Information Science Reference.

Dewey, J. (1938). *Experience and education*. New York: The Macmillan Company.

Dewey, J. (1991). *How we think*. New York: Prometheus. (Original work published 1910)

Driscoll, M. P. (2004). *Psychology of Learning for Instruction* (3rd ed.). New York: Pearson Education.

Fenwick, T. J. (2000). Expanding conceptions of experiential learning: A review of the five contemporary perspectives on cognition. *Adult Education Quarterly, 50*(4), 243–272. doi:10.1177/07417130022087035

Galant, R. (2013, March 26). What if students learn faster without teachers? *Cable News Network (CNN)*. Retrieved from http://www.cnn.com/2013/02/27/opinion/ted-prize-students-teach-themselves/index.html

Gardner, S. (1995). Inquiry is no mere conversation (or discussion or dialogue): Facilitation is hard work! *Critical and Creative Thinking: The Australasian Journal of Philosophy for Children, 3*(2), 38–49.

Garrison, D. R. (1989). *Understanding distance education: A framework for the future*. London: Routledge.

Garrison, D. R., & Shale, D. (1990). *Education at a distance: From issues to practice*. Melbourne, FL: Krieger.

Gibbs, G., & Coffey, M. (2004). The impact of training of university teachers on their teaching skills, their approach to teaching, and the approach to learning of their students. *Active Learning in Higher Education, 5*(1), 87–100. doi:10.1177/1469787404040463

Gilbert, L., & Moore, D. R. (1998). Building interactivity into web courses: Tools for social and instructional interaction. *Educational Technology, 38*(3), 29–35.

Grossera, M. M., & Lombard, B. J. J. (2008). The relationship between culture and the development of critical thinking abilities of prospective teachers. *Teaching and Teacher Education, 24*(5), 1364–1375. doi:10.1016/j.tate.2007.10.001

Hadjioannou, X. (2007, June). Bringing the background to the foreground: What do classroom environments that support authentic discussions look like? *American Educational Research Journal, 44*(2), 370–399. doi:10.3102/0002831207302173

Hativa, N., & Goodyear, P. (Eds.). (2001). *Teacher thinking, beliefs, and knowledge in higher education*. Norwell, MA: Kluwer Academic Publishers.

Hillman, D., Willis, D. J., & Gunawardena, C. (1994). Learner-interface interaction in distance education: An extension of contemporary models and strategies for practitioners. *American Journal of Distance Education*, *8*(2), 30–42. doi:10.1080/08923649409526853

Kember, D. (1997). A reconceptualisation of the research into university academics' conceptions of teaching. *Learning and Instruction*, *7*(3), 255–27. doi:10.1016/S0959-4752(96)00028-X

Kessler, A. (2013, June 2). Professors are about to get an online education: Georgia Tech's new Internet master's degree in computer science is the future. *The Wall Street Journal*. Retrieved from http://www.wsj.com/articles/SB10001424127887324659404578504761168566272

Koestler, A. (1969). *The act of creation* (Danube edition). London: Pan.

Kolb, D. A. (1984). *Experiential learning: Experience as a source of learning and development*. Englewood Cliffs, NJ: Prentice-Hall.

Kopp, W. (2013, April 8). Computers can't replace real teachers. *Cable News Network (CNN)*. Retrieved from http://www.cnn.com/2013/04/08/opinion/kopp-kids-real-teachers/index.html

Kreijns, K., Kirschener, P. A., & Jochems, W. (2003). Identifying the pitfalls for social interaction in computer-supported collaborative learning environments: A review of the research. *Computers in Human Behavior*, *19*(3), 335–353. doi:10.1016/S0747-5632(02)00057-2

Laurillard, D. (1993). *Rethinking university teaching: A framework for the effective use of educational technology*. London: Routledge.

Laurillard, D. (2002a, January/February). Rethinking teaching for the knowledge society. *Educause Review*. Retrieved from http://net.educause.edu/ir/library/pdf/erm0201.pdf

Laurillard, D. (2002b). *Rethinking university teaching: A framework for the effective use of educational technology* (2nd ed.). London: RoutledgeFalmer. doi:10.4324/9780203304846

Lave, J., & Wenger, E. (1991). *Situated learning: Legitimate peripheral participation*. Cambridge, UK: Cambridge University Press. doi:10.1017/CBO9780511815355

Lortie, D. C. (1975). *Schoolteacher: A sociological study*. Chicago, IL: University of Chicago Press.

Mehra, B. (2002, March). Bias in qualitative research: Voices from an online classroom. *Qualitative Report*, *7*(1), 1–19. Retrieved from http://nsuworks.nova.edu/cgi/viewcontent.cgi?article=1986&context=tqr

Menges, R. (2000). Shortcomings of research on evaluating and improving teaching in higher education. *New Directions for Teaching and Learning*, *83*(83), 5–11. doi:10.1002/tl.8301

Moore, M. (1989). Three types of interaction. *American Journal of Distance Education*, *3*(2), 1–7. doi:10.1080/08923648909526659

Mullen, G. E., & Tallent-Runnels, M. K. (2006). Student outcomes and perceptions of instructors' demands and support in online and traditional classrooms. *The Internet and Higher Education*, *9*(4), 257–266. doi:10.1016/j.iheduc.2006.08.005

Naisbitt, J. (1999). *High tech/ high touch: Technology and our search for meaning*. New York: Broadway Books.

Nespor, J. (1987). The role of beliefs in the practice of teaching. *Journal of Curriculum Studies*, *19*(4), 317–328. doi:10.1080/0022027870190403

Nisbett, R., & Ross, L. (1980). *Human inference: Strategies and shortcomings of social judgment*. Englewood Cliffs, NJ: Prentice-Hall, Inc.

Oleson, A., & Hora, M. T. (2012, September). *Teaching the way they were taught? Revisiting the sources of teaching knowledge and the role of prior experience in shaping faculty teaching practices.* Wisconsin Center for Education Research, School of Education, University of Wisconsin-Madison. Retrieved from http://www.wcer.wisc.edu/publications/workingpapers/Working_Paper_No_2012_09.pdf

Pajares, M. F. (1992). Teachers' beliefs and educational research: Cleaning up a messy construct. *Review of Educational Research*, *62*(3), 307–332. doi:10.3102/00346543062003307

Park, J. Y. (2013). Student interactivity and teacher participation: An application of legitimate peripheral participation in higher education online learning environments. *Technology, Pedagogy and Education*, *24*(3), 389–406. doi:10.1080/1475939X.2014.935743

Park, Y. J., & Bonk, C. J. (2007, September). Is online life a breeze? A case study for promoting synchronous learning in a blended graduate course. *MERLOT Journal of Online Learning and Teaching*, *3*(3), 307-323. Retrieved from http://www.anitacrawley.net/Articles/Park2007%20pedagogical%20strategies%20for%20integ%20of%20syn.pdf

Putnam, R. T., & Borko, H. (2000). What do new views of knowledge and thinking have to say about research on teacher learning? *Educational Researcher*, *29*(1), 4–15. doi:10.3102/0013189X029001004

Ravitch, D. (2013, July 17). Diane Ravitch: 3 dubious uses of technology in schools: Technology can inspire creativity or dehumanize learning. *Scientific American*, *309*(2). Retrieved from http://www.scientificamerican.com/article/diane-ravitch-3-dubious-uses-technology-in-schools/

Reilly, C. (2014). Online teaching as the art of hosting: Designing social interactions to promote engagement. In *Proceedings of World Conference on E-Learning in Corporate, Government, Healthcare, and Higher Education 2014* (pp. 1635-1641). Chesapeake, VA: Association for the Advancement of Computing in Education (AACE).

Roblyer, M. D., & Ekhaml, L. (2000, Spring). How interactive are YOUR distance courses? A rubric for assessing interaction in distance learning. *Online Journal of Distance Learning Administration*, *3*(2). Retrieved from http://www.westga.edu/~distance/roblyer32.html

Root, M. V., Molgaard, L. K., & Malone, E. (2015). Creation of a metric for faculty effort in teaching in the veterinary curriculum. *Journal of Veterinary Medical Education, 42*(3), 66-68. 10.3138/jvme.0414-046R

Saroyan, A., & Amundsen, C. (2004). *Rethinking teaching in higher education: From a course design workshop to a faculty development framework.* Sterling, VA: Stylus Publishing.

Shavelson, R. J., & Stern, P. (1981). Research on teachers' pedagogical thoughts, judgments, decisions, and behavior. *Review of Educational Research*, *51*(4), 455–498. doi:10.3102/00346543051004455

Shulman, L. (1987). Knowledge and teaching: Foundations of the new reform. *Harvard Educational Review*, *57*(1), 1–21. doi:10.17763/haer.57.1.j463w79r56455411

Siemens, G. (2002, September 30). *Instructional design in elearning*. Retrieved from http://www.elearnspace.org/Articles/InstructionalDesign.htm

Smylie, M. A. (1989). Teachers' views of the effectiveness of sources of learning to teach. *The Elementary School Journal*, *89*(5), 543–558. doi:10.1086/461591

Sobel, D. M., Sands, D. I., & Dunlap, J. C. (2009). Teaching intricate content online: It can be done and done well. *Action in Teacher Education*, *30*(4), 28–44. doi:10.1080/01626620.2009.10734450

St. Phard, J., Jr. (2015). Distance education through the lens of USDLA members: A white paper. *Distance Learning 12*(2), 15-21. Retrieved from http://search.proquest.com/openview/fdbfe622e1eb011eafa1cafe097c3c6e/1?pq-origsite=gscholar

Swan, K. (2002). Building learning communities in online courses: The importance of interaction. *Education Communication and Information*, *2*(1), 23–49. doi:10.1080/1463631022000005016

Trigwell, K., Prosser, M., & Waterhouse, F. (1999). Relations between teachers' approaches to teaching and students' approaches to learning. *Higher Education*, *37*(1), 57–70. doi:10.1023/A:1003548313194

Trucano, M. (2015, February 24). Will technology replace teachers? No, but … *EduTech*. Retrieved from http://blogs.worldbank.org/edutech/tech-and-teachers

Umbach, P. (2007). Faculty cultures and college teaching. In R. P. Perry & J. C. Smart (Eds.), *The Scholarship of Teaching and Learning in Higher Education: An Evidence-Based Perspective* (pp. 263–317). Netherlands: Springer. doi:10.1007/1-4020-5742-3_8

Vygotsky, L. (1934). Thinking and speaking. Cambridge, MA: The MIT Press.

Vygotsky, L. S. (1933/1966). Play and its role in the mental development of the child. *Social Psychology*, *12*(6), 62–76.

Vygotsky, L. S. (1935). *Mental development of children during education*. Moscow: Uchpedzig.

Vygotsky, L. S. (1962). *Thought and Language*. Cambridge, MA: MIT Press. doi:10.1037/11193-000

Vygotsky, L. S. (1978a). *Mind in society*. Cambridge, MA: Harvard University Press.

Vygotsky, L. S. (1978b). *Mind in society: The development of higher psychological processes* (M. Cole, V. John-Steiner, S. Scribner, & E. Souberman, Trans. & Eds.). Cambridge, MA: Harvard University.

Vygotsky, L. S. (1981). The genesis of higher mental functions. In J. V. Wertsch (Ed.), *The Concept of Activity in Soviet Psychology*. Armonk, NY: Sharpe.

Vygotsky, L. S. (1987). *The collected works of L. S. Vygotsky* (R. W. Rieber & A. Carton, Eds.). New York: Plenum Press. (Original work published 1934)

Wagner, E. D. (1994). In support of a functional definition of interaction. *American Journal of Distance Education*, *8*(2), 6–26. doi:10.1080/08923649409526852

Wagner, E. D. (1997). In support of a functional definition of interaction. *New Directions for Teaching and Learning*, *71*, 19–26. doi:10.1002/tl.7103

Wenger, E. (1998). *Communities of practice: Learning, meaning, and identity*. Cambridge: Cambridge University Press. doi:10.1017/CBO9780511803932

Wenger, E. (2009). *Digital habitats*. Portland: CPsquare.

Wenger, E. (2010). Communities of practice and social learning systems: the career of a concept. In C. Blackmore (Ed.), *Social Learning Systems and Communities of Practice*. Springer Verlag and the Open University. doi:10.1007/978-1-84996-133-2_11

Wenger, E., McDermott, R., & Snyder, W. M. (2002). *Cultivating communities of practice*. Harvard Business Press.

Wilson, C. (1998, Fall). Concerns of instructors delivering distance learning via the WWW. *Online Journal of Distance Learning Administration*, *1*(3). Retrieved from http://www.westga.edu/~distance/ojdla/fall13/wilson13.html

Woods, R. H., & Baker, J. D. (2004, August). Interaction and immediacy in online learning. *The International Review of Research in Open and Distributed Learning*, *5*(2). Retrieved from http://www.irrodl.org/index.php/irrodl/article/view/186/268

KEY TERMS AND DEFINITIONS

Cognition: Within an instructional environment, this is the mental efforts associated with learning new information.

Cognitive Vulnerability: The humanness and comfortableness felt within instructionally relevant situations that enhance one's ability to engage with the subject matter and share new, creative, innovative ideas with co-learners without fear of reprisal or reprimand.

Collegiality: The ability to offer a professionally appropriate and working relationship-oriented representation to one's co-learners.

Distributed Learning Environments: A term that includes all types of instructionally-focused environments that bring together persons from different times, locations and technological product interfaces, towards focused learning efforts.

Humanness: The ability to think, feel and share kindness with others. The social construction of connectedness in essential engagement and understanding within our own socialization and species.

Instructor Authenticity: The effort of an instructor to fully represent their personality, professionalism, interest and engagement within an instructional environment.

Instructor Immediacy: The ability of an instructor to communicate and engage learners with the subject matter and with course colleagues, across distances of time, space and knowledge base.

Instructor's Philosophical Beliefs Systems: This is an instructor's understanding of not only who the instructor is as a professional, but more so the instructor's understandings associated with the instructional environment milieu.

Interactive Activity: These are different ways to implement instructional environmental tools towards working within and learning information in new and different ways.

Online Instruction: This is a term that is slowly being replaced by distributed learning environments, due to the shifts in technological ability that are currently allowing for a portability of communicative environment that was not previously a viable consideration.

Chapter 3
Emphasizing Instructor Presence in Digital Learning Environments

Rachael Olubukola Afolabi
Carlow University, USA

ABSTRACT

The role of the instructor in any learning environment is a good motivator for students. It is important to understand how the instructor's position can be viewed in the online learning environment. The principal role of the instructor in any learning environment is to assist students in making connections and identifying significance through an educational process. This chapter, examined from an instructional designer and instructor's point of view, sets out to explore the effectiveness of the online teaching presence as an adequate investment of time for the student's benefit.

INTRODUCTION

Teaching online has evolved through a myriad of structures without following a particular set of standards in course structure or development. The expectations of traditional teaching is defined and understood when a student comes into a pre-set venue at a pre-set time to listen and learn from an instructor who gives a lecture on a particular topic in a field of study usually in a degree track. With online teaching, several institutions have adopted the "self-paced" and/or an asynchronous, student-centered education model. While the asynchronous method has proven successful in many online learning environments, there is a gap in the instructor and or student relationship and mentorship that learning should provide.

Until recently there have not been a set standards set up for the purposes of teaching online. The International Association for K-12 Online Learning (iNACOL) formerly known as the North American Council for Online Learning, have established themselves as essential resources for educators by compiling research, advocating for positive policy changes and helping to create effective standards. iNACOL designed a National Standards for Quality Online Teaching to provide states, districts, online

DOI: 10.4018/978-1-4666-9995-3.ch003

programs, and other organizations with a set of quality guidelines for online teaching and instructional design (Kennedy & Archambault, 2012). The initiative began with a thorough literature review of existing online teaching quality standards, a cross-reference of standards, followed by a survey of iNACOL members and experts to ensure the efficiency of the standards adopted.

Part of the results that yielded from this survey revealed that online technologies for learning can provide active learning for students; however, using the technology alone is not enough to foster learning. It is important that online instructors redefine the methods utilized in the traditional classroom by enhancing existing pedagogical practices within a technology based environment.

One of the "seven principles" for good practice in undergraduate education which was first established in 1987 by the American Association for Higher Education identifies one of its components as "encourage student-faculty contact" (Hudgins, Orellana & Simonson, 2009). While these principles were designed and formed as a foundation for the traditional classroom, they are an important consideration of instructor practice in the online classroom.

The role of the instructor in any learning environment is a good place to start and align how those positions can translate into the online learning environment. The principal role of the instructor in any learning environment is to assist students in making connections and identifying the significance through an educational process. According to Anderson, Rourke, Garrison, and Archer in Preisman (2014), teaching presence consists of three critical roles for the instructor which are as follows:

1. The first responsibility is the designing and organization of the learning experience, which takes place prior to and during the run of the course.
2. Secondly, instructors are responsible for the creating, implementing, and the monitoring of activities that encourage communication and interaction between the students, teachers, and content resources.
3. Finally, instructors must contribute academic knowledge and relevant experiences through forms of direct instruction.

The above roles of the online instructor align back to these three positions. This chapter, examined from an instructional designer and instructor's point of view, sets out to explore the effectiveness of the online teaching presence as an adequate investment of time for the student's benefit. The motivation behind this chapter arises from observations from an instructional designer while working with faculty to create online courses. The perspective and perceived notion of several instructors is that online learning is more demanding and time consuming than face-to-face instruction (Bollinger & Waslik, 2009; Harber & Mills; 2008, Worley & Tesdell, 2009). This usually poses a challenge for instructional designers to decide on the best use of educational technology and instructional choices not only to meet the student learning outcomes, but also to be a smart investment of the instructor's time.

'Technology-mediated learning' is essential for online instruction; however, the challenges associated with the organizing and developing of online courses is forming the sensation of a "real-life" experience in the digital classroom. Hansen & Bryant (2005), argue that humanizing the online learning environment will increase the student's comfort level, and most significantly put a form of reduction within the psychological path or distance between the instructors and students. In essence, creating an environment that has an almost immediate response that can facilitate students' investment within the learning process.

Instructor presence in the online classroom is a theory of affective learning based on the concept of instructor verbal and nonverbal behaviors that are related to student attitudes and instructional outcomes'' (Rodriguez, Plax, & Kearney, 1996). Immediacy also relates to course design, same as defining it on how an instructor or teacher deliberately arranges a set of external events to support the learner's internal learning process. According to Swan (2001), it was reported, from statistics and opinion shared by students, that they had increased interaction with the subject matter (course), when they had direct contact with the instructor. Online instructors need to acknowledge this fact by creating a sense of presence with intent in their courses so that students know that somebody is leading their educational experience. Ragan, Bigatel, Kennan, & Dillon (2012), expands on this by highlighting how instructor online presence consists of three dimensions:

- **Persona:** This is the instructor's personality, teaching style, and interests. These are all the characteristics that go into the students' impression of the instructor.
- **Social:** This denotes the relationship or connections that is set up between the instructors and the students and that among students to build a learning community.
- **Instructional:** This refers to the role, and the process the instructor plays is to assist the students through the learning process.

Why is the Instructor Presence Needed?

The traditional face-to-face classrooms have an instructor present coordinating the class session; this is unlike the online space where there is no physicality. The online environment is a virtual space where the peers or the instructors are not physically seen, differences in time zones might be different in several cases, but class activities are designed to be mostly asynchronous, so students have the ability to participate at their convenience. Ragan, Bigatel, Kennan, & Dillon (2012), poses the question "how do I convey to the students that there is somebody who is participating, who is the leader in this educational experience?" Because of the nature of online learning which involves the lack of a physical presence in online classes, building a learning community is important to enhance participation and a drive to learn (Ladyshewsky, 2013). When instructors don't seem present, this has a significant effect on student learning.

Lack of Instructor Presence can have Negative Consequences for the Learner

Students that are engaged in online programs especially need more of an instructor presence compared to on-campus students who see their instructors face-to-face. For students in an online academic environment, the instructor becomes the connection to the learning institution (Ragan, Bigatel, Kennan, & Dillon, 2012). This presence is the glue that holds the system together, and it is important for the learner to get to know the instructor on an almost personal level. Ragan, Bigatel, Kennan, & Dillon (2012) further discusses that the traditional student may not be interested in this idea of a learning community because of their social circles. This crowd does not typically see the need for the instructional experience also to contain the dimension of the online instructor presence. However, the online learner values the importance of the online instructor presence and may feel isolated from the experience, from the physical dimension of the learning institution when the instructor does not constantly make their presence known in the online classroom.

Course Development Design Considerations for Instructor Presence

Instructional designers create courses through a combination of instructional design and delivery with the perception of the instructor as the leader and facilitator (deNoyelles, Cobb & Lowe, 2012). Several modes of course developing media can aid the creation of the instructor presence in the mode of online course delivery; a few include examples include the use of videos, photos, and narratives, depending on the instructor's comfort level with the platform. The proper use of these teaching resources need to be timed and fitted accurately in the course design phase which should go along with proper time appropriation, and the consideration of the student's time on task for each activity.

It is important that in the process of online course design and planning, instructional designers do not get carried away by using "too much technology". Despite the fact that teaching in a technology based environment invites the temptation to use all the available pieces available, it is sometimes helpful to keep things simple. Instructional designers should never advocate using all the technologies available within a course (Kelly, 2014). The idea is to identify the gaps in a course where it may see that the student is seemingly "alone" and incorporate the strategy of the instructor presence in that section. This draws the student back and invites a whole new level of inquiry. The use of technology in learning should be an accepted pedagogical need in inquiry and not a random selection of technology based on availability. With the guidance of an instructional designer, instructors can make the decisions on what type of technology should be used for creating an instructor's presence in the online classroom, and how this ultimately contributes to the learner's experience.

Indication of Engagement in the Online Classroom

An online instructor could define their presence in the online classroom by using several fora such as announcements, discussion board posts, and the uploading of photos and videos by the instructor, which will require the student's view during course session. It is not enough to log in and monitor a course; instructors need to show that they are active in the course (Ragan, Bigatel, Kennan, & Dillon, 2012).

Several institutions use learning management systems that have the ability to monitor the presence of students and their daily/weekly participation in the online classroom (Seaman & Tinti-Kane, 2013). In the same manner, it is important that instructors be guided in making the same effort in participating or "showing up" in the online classroom for interaction with their students, rather than just coming in to grade assignments. A learning management system dashboard with the capability that provides instructors and departmental chairs and deans with data on how much presence an instructor has "logged" in the online classroom may be helpful for the instructor to manage his or her presence (Ragan, Bigatel, Kennan, & Dillon, 2012). Instructor presence is considered the most important aspect of an online course (Boettcher & Conrad, 2010). This is largely due to the fact that instructors are the leaders in this learning process. A student will always be on the lookout for guidance from their instructors.

Research has shown that a significant component in students' performance and satisfaction with their online course is the active participation of the instructor within their course (Picciano, 2002; Rovai, 2002; Swan & Shih, 2005). Typically, every student wants to relate to their instructors throughout their online learning experience. There is a general criticism that constantly arises in literature which involves online instructors who do not give time or respond to students in a timely manner or sometimes provide little or no response. Several institutions do not give instructors a guideline or mandate on how much they need to "be in" the classroom. And so many online instructors consider themselves as "facilitators" rather than experts in the field where their students look up to them and crave their attention throughout the learning process. This is a need that should be addressed in many learning institutions and to be adequately taken into consideration the active participation of the instructor, alongside their interactions with students, which helps them to be "present" in an online course. The Instructor presence is important because it contributes in bridging the distance, and address feelings of isolation students may feel when learning online.

According to Mandemach, Gonzales, & Garrett (2006), instructor presence includes three elements: teaching presence, instructor immediacy, and social presence.

- *Teaching presence* is a perception described in Garrison, Anderson, and Archer's (2000) Community of Inquiry framework. This perception argues that the instructors are "the binding element" in the learning experience. Instructors not only create but also help to sustain the learning community. Teaching presence can be established in three ways; course design, facilitation and direct instruction.
  - *Course design* involves activities such as instructional design and curriculum development, the creation and integration of a variety of learning activities into the course, and assessment of participant learning outcomes.
  - *Facilitation and direct instruction* is a major consideration in the course which consists of setting the course environment, encouraging learner participation in course activities, and acknowledging participant responses (Traver, Volchok, Bidjerano & Shea, 2014). Direct instruction encompasses tasks such as, regulating the amount of material covered, posing questions that guide participants' learning, summarizing discussions, and confirming understanding through assessment and feedback. Each of these interrelated processes helps shape the student learning experience (Mandemach, Gonzales, & Garrett, 2006).
- Instructor immediacy involves communication behaviors that reduce "social and psychological distance between people" (Arbaugh, 2001). It includes using humor (somctimes) and participant names, encouraging participation during discussion, and sharing personal stories.
- Social presence is the ability of an individual to project themselves as a "real person" in the online learning environment (Garrison et al., 2000). Self-disclosure can be a simple way in which the idea of social presence manifests itself in an online class, an example is a way one goes about sharing work and professional interests, and modeling open, respectful communication. For instance, one of the ways an instructor demonstrates this principle is through his or her online biographies in which he or she shares information about his or her hobbies and research interests.

The following examples are listed techniques to establish instructor presence:

- A form of 'pre-notification'; this can be done by sending welcoming messages and necessary preliminary information about the course before it begins.
- Creating a 'meet the instructor' and 'course navigation' videos to initiate students to social presence and help establish expectations.
- Sharing information related to personal and professional interests.
- A good platform or site to help students relate and associate with instructors.
- Using the announcement forum to communicate important information about the course.

- Setting expectations at the beginning of the course for how often messages will be checked and how frequently.
- Creating a variety of formats to help eliminate untimeliness to students' responses such as email, phone calls and several other means available.
- Sharing the instructor's expertise with students.
- Using names when asking students to explain rationale or posing questions to them.
- Monitoring student progress.
- Finding a platform to participate with students to solve their problems.

As defined by Anderson, Rourke, Garrison and Archer (2000), teaching presence is "the design, facilitation and direction of cognitive and social processes for the purpose of realizing personally meaningful and educationally worthwhile learning outcomes". The instructor usually begins to establish a personal teaching presence in the first class meeting. From this, students create their opinions and make assumptions about the instructor and the organization of the course, from the first meeting.

These are the major roles which will come into action before and during the establishment and operation of the learning community. The design process provides instructors opportunities to instill their own teaching presence by establishing a personalized tone within the course content. This is done through organizing the course components, through the use of visual and audio instructional components, and by allowing students, through the planned instructional components and organization of the course, to see the personal enthusiasm and interests that inspire the teacher's attraction to the subject. Another role of the instructor is to develop and implement activities to encourage effective communication between students, likewise dialog between the teacher and the student, and active interaction of the students with the content. The third role comes to play when the instructor includes subject matter expertise through a variety of forms of direct instruction. In these three roles, the instructor will set the foundations of the personal teaching presence in the first class meeting.

The instructor usually strives to establish these three roles involved in creating teaching presence throughout the course; however the standard of community of inquiry that integrates cognitive, social, and teaching elements that go beyond social exchanges begins in the first class meeting. Garrison, Anderson, and Archer (2000) have developed a conceptual model of online learning that is referred to as the "community of inquiry" model.

The above model postulates that deep and meaningful learning results when there are sufficient levels of three component "presences." First on the list is an adequate degree of *cognitive presence*, in such a way that serious learning can take place in an environment that supports the development and growth of critical thinking skills. Cognitive presence is grounded in and defined by the study of a particular content; thus, it works within the epistemological, cultural, and social expression of the content in an approach that supports the development of critical thinking skills. The second, *social presence* relates to the establishment of a supportive environment such that students feel the necessary degree of comfort and safety to express their ideas in a collaborative context. The absence of social presence leads to an inability to express disagreements, share viewpoints, explore differences, and accept support and confirmation from peers and teacher. Finally, informal education, as opposed to informal learning opportunities, *teaching presence* is critical for a variety of reasons.

The importance of the instructor's presence in the online learning environment is summed up effectively when Oztok and Brett (2011), stated that "studying online communities through the concept of social presence could provide a fundamental understanding of how individuals connect, communicate, interact, and form relationships as they work collaboratively in an online environment." Overall, the instructor's presence in the online classroom is the core for the learner because the teacher acts as a supporter and facilitator inside the classroom. This role helps instructors shape the culture of their online classes and improve student learning.

For years, educators have collected and evaluated students' stories about what is considered "best" teaching and learning experiences. The results of analyzing these stories has been consistent in terms of what students see as important characteristics of engaging, memorable, and impactful learning experiences (Dunlap & Lowenthal, 2010a, in Dunlap, J., & Lowenthal, P. 2014). Online students often feel the absence of their instructor and do complain about missing the presence of their instructor or professor from the course (Smith & Taveras, 2005). Educators continue to discuss the importance and the challenges of establishing and maintaining a presence in service to students learning in online courses. The absence of social presence abraded the overall aesthetic learning experience and undermined student learning.

Instructor feedback in an online course raises a number of challenges which are distinct from teaching in traditional classroom face-to-face environments. In the case of classroom feedback, this can be provided in different ways using informal discussions before or after class, when an assignment is being explained, through nonverbal communication, and in real time (Getzlaf, Perry, Toffner, Lamarche, & Edwards, 2009, in Dunlap & Lowenthal, 2014). At the onset of online learning, several educators found this to be more challenging in an online course, but can still be replicated. The personal contact between students and the instructor are key factors influencing a student's perceived satisfaction with his or her learning (Ladyshewsky, R. K. (2013).The 'instructor to student' interaction is found to be one of the most significant variable influencing student satisfaction in a survey of online students (Marks, Sibley, & Arbaugh, 2005 in, in Dunlap, J., & Lowenthal, P). (2014). Teacher immediacy in providing feedback is also an important factor in student satisfaction.

Perspectives of Online Instructor Presence

This section focuses on the significance of the instructor's online presence and the analysis of the teaching presence from the viewpoint of the instructional designer and instructor. In the online classroom, does it matter if the teacher is there? What is a teacher's contribution to emerging patterns of interactions in online classroom discussions? These questions will be addressed with these perspectives and channels used in online classrooms:

1. Synchronous and Asynchronous Communications.
2. Social Networking in the Online Learning Environment.
3. Online Office Hours.
4. Course Midpoint Check.
5. Welcome/Introductory Video.
6. Instructor and Student Identification.

SYNCHRONOUS AND ASYNCHRONOUS COMMUNICATIONS

Synchronous tools enable communication and collaboration in a "real-time" mode. These tools allow individuals to connect at a single point in time, at the same time. This method has the advantage of being able to engage people instantly and at the same point in time. On the other hand, Asynchronous tools enable communication and collaboration over a period through a "different time-different place" mode. These methods allow people to connect at each person's convenience and own schedule. Asynchronous tools are valuable for supporting dialog and collaboration over a period and providing people with resources and information that are instantly accessible, anytime.

In online learning, synchronous e-learning is commonly supported by media such as videoconferencing and chat, and has the potential to support e-learners in the development of learning communities (Hrastinski, 2008). Learners and teachers experience synchronous e-learning as more social and avoid frustration by asking and answering questions in real time. Synchronous sessions help e-learners feel like participants rather than isolates. This method of teaching and communicating in the online learning environment works well for many learners with no issues of getting on the internet. However, synchronous e-learning is a challenge for several learners who have no access to the internet or to the applications that make synchronous e-learning a possibility. Hrastinski (2008) further argues that this context of Isolation in the classroom can be overcome by more continued contact by becoming aware of themselves as members of a community rather than as isolated individuals communicating with the computer.

This is an advantage of asynchronous e-learning where most of the time, the learning is done on a self-paced basis by the learner. One of the unique features of online learning is the ability to support different learners' at various times of the day (Harasim, 1996), thus enabling students the flexibility to "attend" classes at their own convenience.

These two methods of instructor interaction provide options for both the instructor and the learners. Instructors could select synchronous or asynchronous methods of instruction for various sections of their courses, as they see fit. Regardless of what method an instructor goes with, here are some classroom practices that online instructors should keep in mind that works for keeping the instructor presence online.

Incorporate Interactive Reflective eLearning Activities

Dewey once said that 'Reflective learning is a 'meaning-making' process that moves a learner from one experience to the next with deeper understanding of its relationships with and connections to other experiences and ideas.' Interactive activities in the service of teaching and learning should be viewed in context and in relationship with teaching methods and delivery systems available to the instructor (Berge, Z. L. (2002). In relating the two ideas together according to Dewey again, reflections need to happen in a community; interacting with others.

It is important for the online instructor to maintain an active participation presence in any interactive activity that is incorporated into an online class. Simply allowing the eLearning activity to run as a "robot" course, without providing input or feedback, giving the student an impression of a lost feeling where they are unsure of whether they are in the right or wrong place, or how to connect the activity with real life experiences without the guidance of the instructor.

Virtual Helping Hand

Like in a traditional classroom, it should not be assumed that all learners in an online classroom are aware of what they are doing. Though many online learners work autonomously, they may need support from time to time. Russo, T., & Benson, S. (2005), discusses that when students find online classes impersonal or isolating, they may disengage completely simply by dropping out of the course or failing to finish the course. Whatever the form of support needed by the student, there should be a reliable communication process that the learner can easily access. This may be technical or subject related. A reliable form of communication for the instructor should be available with a turnaround time provided since they will not be able to get help from a face-to-face instructor. This form of assistance that addresses their concerns and answers immediate pressing questions makes students feel a sense of community in their online classroom.

Align the Course Objectives to Real World Concepts

Synchronous or asynchronous learners need motivation in their online classes and want the course content to reflect some relationship with their learning goals. Whether a course is run synchronously or asynchronously, it is helpful for the instructor to understand each learner and their expectations of how the class is expected to relate to their goals. This can be done with icebreaker activities that help in understanding each individual student and their background. Just like in a face-to-face context, this opportunity helps learners to connect and engage in small group discussions (Garrison, D. R. (2006). These activities can be crafted in methods that ask the student how they intend to apply the knowledge at the end of the course to their professional goals. This is where an instructor can stress the real world benefits of completing the course by defining and recommending how they can use the subject in their real lives.

Effective Assessments

Every learning experience should be finalized with an effective assessment strategy. Intentionally linking the assessment of student learning outcomes of service-learning with reflection, allows each to inform and reinforce the other (Ash, S. L., Clayton, P. H., & Atkinson, M. P. (2005). There is no learning experience that is completed without an effective assessment strategy, and this is doubly important for online learners. Integrating quizzes and exams with full feedback to test learners' knowledge and check their progress is important for the learner to see that their progress is being tracked and monitored by the instructor. This also gives the instructor a chance to gauge his or her own progress as the course progresses, so that he or she can fix incorrect learning behaviors and improve on his or her flaws.

SOCIAL NETWORKING IN THE ONLINE LEARNING ENVIRONMENT

The advent of technology brought about the use of social networking. This has enabled the construction of knowledge and experiences as essential to online communication tools that are significant pieces for fostering online socialization and networking (Bruyn, 2004; Zapalska, Brozik, 2006). This defines how collaborative learning provides a ground for having a learning community where a group of learners comes together for exchanging, sharing their ideas and experiences (Bruyn, 2004; Neo, 2005).

Social networking has the potential to facilitate interaction, communication and collaboration and, as a result, have been prominently featured in discussions centering on the use of technology to support and amplify educational endeavors (Greenhow, Robelia, & Hughes, 2009; Veletsianos, in Veletsianos,

G., & Navarrete, C. (2012). Empirical research on their role in online education is limited, even though researchers have identified an accelerating use of social software informal learning contexts (Schroeder, Minocha, & Schneider, 2010). Veletsianos, G., & Navarrete, C. (2012).

In several learning institutions, social media is largely blocked in schools due to privacy, security, and copyright concerns (Greenhow, C. (2011). In the United States, the National Educational Technology Plan published in November 2010, and recent educational standards, both assume 24/7 access and use of newer web technologies for learning and advocating appropriation of technologies students already use, and prefer to use, for educational purposes.

In addressing this from an instructor's context, it is important to understand and identify the meaning of social media. Social media is a 21st century term used to broadly define a variety of networked tools or technologies that emphasize the social aspects of the Internet as a channel for communication, collaboration, and creative expression, and is often interchangeable with the terms Web 2.0 and social software (Dabbagh & Reo, 2011a). Sites such as Facebook, Twitter, YouTube, Foursquare, and various wiki-style sites which are already firmly integrated into the personal lives of several students, allows faculty the opportunity to customize course material to facilitate and accomplish learning expectations and goals (McLoughlin & Lee, 2008, in Churcher, K. M., Downs, E., & Tewksbury, D. (2014). When an online instructor makes use of social networking tools in the online classroom, it is with the goal that students can learn further through dialogue and interaction with others which is central to knowledge generation (Churcher, K. M., Downs, E., & Tewksbury, D. (2014). The benefit of using social media such as Facebook or wikis is that these technologies connect with students where they spend much of their time, thus creating virtual communities of practice and a virtual public sphere for discussion (Lave & Wenger, 1991; Wenger, White, & Smith, 2009, in Churcher, K. M., Downs, E., & Tewksbury, D. (2014). When using social media in the online classroom, the role and the presence of the instructor is not solely to disseminate information, but rather to moderate the trajectory of user-generated content and community knowledge-sharing (Wenger, White, & Smith, 2009). Applying Dewey's theory of past knowledge and experience to shape meaning and construct new knowledge (Lambert et al, 2001), sites such as Facebook, Twitter, Bloggers etc. are already familiar to learners who use these technologies in their day-to-day lives. The instructor's presence in the online classroom using social media requires skills moderation in ensuring effective learning while keeping to how learners collaborate in creating knowledge (Lazonder, Wilhelm, & Ootes, 2003). With the instructor as a mediator to keep discussions and activities on track, the community of practice takes a sense of ownership over its own knowledge, while at the same time working within the framework of the instructor's course objectives and goals. The instructor's use of skill media in an online course also presents the instructor as a "real" person. With online teaching, several studies have shown that students feel isolated without the constant communication and feedback from an instructor (Erichsen & Bolliger, 2011; Reilly, Gallagher-Lepak & Killion, 2012). Social media can present itself as almost real time communication because it is an ongoing discussion of ideas from students who come from different backgrounds.

ONLINE OFFICE HOURS

Office hours are essential for student learning and as this is done in the traditional classroom successfully; it is equally important in the online classroom. Traditionally, office hours have taken place face-to-face and can be limited by conflicting instructor-student schedules and student participation. Lih-Ching, &

Beasley (2006), discuss how the importance of office hours makes for a successful faculty member. Furthermore, Lih-Ching, & Beasley (2006), describe that faculty office hours working with students in a college general chemistry class, were one of several factors which resulted in higher student retention and better performance on standard (Dougherty, Bowen, Berger, Rees,Mellon, & Pulliam, 1995, in Lih-Ching, & Beasley (2006).

Electronic office hours is not a new concept; however with new advances in technology, there are more creative ways of making practical use of this concept (Wallace and Wallace, 2001). Examples of the technologies used for electronic office hours include: chat rooms (synchronous), E-mail (asynchronous), cell phones (synchronous), voicemail (asynchronous), etc. While several of these technologies can be used synchronously and asynchronously, it is important that online instructors set up standard times for their students to connect with them online (Cifuentes & Lents, 2011). Online instructors typically use this standard template to describe what their office hours are in the syllabus for an online class.

Office Hours: Since this is an online course, there are no office hours. However, you may email me at any time to discuss anything that you like. I check my email daily, so I should respond to your email within 24-48 hours.

The above example does not give the learners any confidence that when they run into difficulty in their class or have a pressing question for the instructor, they will be available to help out the student. Instructors' office hours have been traditionally used in higher education to enhance student advising and learning (Wallace & Wallace, 2001). In several institutions, office hours usually occur during daytime hours in accordance with a faculty's conventional working schedule. With online learning growing more in several institutions, and many students commuting back and forth, in addition to work, the traditional office hours makes it difficult for them to use such conventionally scheduled appointments. Consequently, both faculty and students are left seeking a better solution which could enhance student advising and learning without the schedule and travel limitations

imposed by face-to-face office hours. Despite the positive benefits of student–faculty contact outside of the classroom, most studies have found that actual communication between faculty and their students is infrequent, and largely limited to formal and structured situations such as classroom lectures (Pascarella 1980; Jasma and Kopper, 1999; Nadler and Nadler 2000). The traditional practice of holding office hours has long been a required part of a professor's teaching responsibilities, which is designed to provide students the opportunity for informal communication beyond the classroom to seek additional help and ask questions. This practice also fosters the instructor's presence in the online classroom. When students are aware that there is an option to connect with their instructor in the online classroom, there is a better chance of retention. In their study of e-learning environments, Jafari, McGee and Carmean (2006) also found that students preferred free and popular communication technologies such as IMs and video chat, and wanted these technologies to be used in the online classroom for easier access to connecting with their instructor.

COURSE MIDPOINT CHECK

This section builds up on the previous section on the instructor's presence at different points in time of the online course. The course midpoint check gives both instructor and student a chance to get back with each other to access the progress of the course. The concept of the course midpoint check has proved particularly effective in an entirely online course when a telephone conversation was made by the instructor to the student. The instructor followed up with the student to see how their class was progressing and if he or she had any concerns as he or she moved along (Sorensen & Baylen, 2009). Course evaluations indicated that the students appreciated this contact by the instructor. This is especially useful and helpful for students that are struggling, and this may give them an opportunity to catch up in their courses. An instructor's perspective on using midpoint, formative course evaluations, helps to make adjustments to the students' needs for the second part of the course (Rallis, 1994).

WELCOME/INTRODUCTORY VIDEO

There is a significant importance in creating a welcome message to students before the course begins and during the time the course is running. This is a significant step in establishing your online identity to the learners. The goal of creating a welcome or introductory is not to discuss the entire syllabus in a video message; the idea is to welcome students and develop a comfortable class environment; introduce the class syllabus, schedule, protocols, and to/or build a weekly routine.

Since e-learning has become a reality for many students in higher education, the sense of isolation in online courses has also become a reality of which Moore (1980) has warned that students' sense of distance can threaten their ability to learn. (Garrison, Anderson, & Archer, 2000) discussed how the community of inquiry framework has provided insight into ways that online interactions can improve students' and instructors' social presence and learning. New video technologies have been able to improve these interactions and thus more easily support the development of communities of inquiry. According to Borup, Graham & Velasquez, 2011), a significant amount of students indicated feeling that the video-based communication made their instructors seem more real, present, and familiar, and that these relationships were similar to face-to-face instruction. Video communication impacted students' social presence in similar ways, although to a lesser degree than they believed it impacted instructor social presence.

The homework (readings, videos) must be structured for the students to prepare them for in-class activities. For most teachers (and students), videos are preferably used for delivering the out-of-class segment of the instruction. Instructors have used videos produced by third-party sources such as the Kahn Academy (http://www.khanacademy.org/) and BozemanScience (http://www.bozemanscience.com/science-videos/) or are creating their own using education technology applications like *Camtasia, PaperShow, and ShowMe* or by way of iPad apps such as *Educreations* and *Explain Everything*. These videos are subsequently posted on-line by way of iTunes U, Podcasts, and YouTube or on course management systems like Blackboard or Moodle.

A study conducted by Jones, Naugle & Kolloff (2008), reviewed the use of introductory videos and the supporting script that provided opportunities for establishing teaching presence in the following three ways. First, you begin to establish teaching presence by providing organizational services to help prepare students for the current online course. This includes the design and structure of the course (the instructional design and planning phase of the course), and at the same time the efforts to communicate the organization and expectations to the students. The introductory video can aid in communicating the organization and expectations to the students. At the same time, this step is critical in modeling appropriate etiquette and demonstrating efficient use of the technology. The second aspect of creating teaching presence is facilitating discourse. The instructor facilitates discourse after the students have viewed the video and/or read the scripts. They have a good direction of where to begin the course, and where to go online to communicate with the other students in the class as well as where to go to seek answers to questions. Finally, teachers provide intellectual leadership and share their knowledge of the subject matter with their students. The instructors must be able to communicate the intellectual climate of the course and serve as a model for their students.

From this study, the authors found that students participating in a Web-supported course do indeed value the instructor and student relationship (Jones, Naugle, & Kolloff, 2008). Therefore, students appreciate having the opportunity to meet the instructor "virtually" using introductory videos before the course begins, regardless of whether the course is offered fully online, or if only a portion of the class meetings will be "online." Participants in these studies reported that they valued having the opportunity to meet the instructor of the course through the introductory video. The students stated their preference was to have a sense of learning from a real person (when receiving instruction via the course site) and not just from text-based instruction. Students also stated that they value the opportunity to "get to know the instructor" before the beginning of class. Students see the relationship that is forming from the beginning of the course, and from the students' perspectives, it had a direct impact on their progress in the class.

There were some key differences found in this study. When students were asked if the introductory video helped them to prepare for the course, 65% of the students from the hybrid course said "Yes," while in the fully online course, 81% of the participants responded "Yes." One possible explanation for this difference is that the online students were more dependent on the online instructional products. Students from the hybrid course had the opportunity to meet with the instructor face-to-face multiple times throughout the term. Therefore, the students' need for "start-up" information or introductory instructions was not solely dependent on watching the video.

There is extensive literature on the effect of instructional video podcasts, which can have a positive impact on student attitudes (Bolliger, Supanakorn, & Boggs, 2010; Fernandez, Simo, & Sallan, 2009; Hill & Nelson, 2011; Holbrook & Dupont, 2010; Lonn & Teasley, 2009); student behavior (Chester, Buntine, Hammond, & Atkinson, 2011; Foertsch, Moses, Strikwerda, & Litzkow, 2002; McCombs & Liu, 2007); and student performance (Alpay & Gulati, 2010; Crippen & Earl, 2004; Traphagan, Kusera, & Kishi, 2010; Vajoczki, Watt, Marquis, & Holshausen, 2010). All of this bodes well for their use in the online or hybrid classroom (Herreid, C. F., & Schiller, N. A. (2013). Recent changes in higher education have impacted teachers' abilities to provide students with personalized feedback. Evans (2013) stated that ''feedback to students needs to be considered against the backdrop of the 'massification' and 'consumerization' of higher education''. Higgins et al. (2002) suggested that providing personalized feedback has become more difficult as class sizes increase and instructor-student personal contact opportunities decrease. This is especially true in learning environments where teachers and students are separated in space and time for all or most of the course. Despite these changes, students still desire verbal feedback from their instructors (National Union of Students, 2008). Graham (2006) explained, ''Many learners want the convenience offered by a distributed environment yet do not want to sacrifice the social interactions and human touch they are used to in a face-to-face classroom''. Although feedback in distributed environments has traditionally been asynchronous text (Parsad and Lewis 2009), new innovations in technology have the potential to improve instructor feedback and provide students with the human touch that they desire (Oncu and Cakir 2011).

INSTRUCTOR AND STUDENT IDENTIFICATION

A picture speaks a thousand words. Because of the issue of isolation in the online classroom, instructors and students are encouraged to put a face to the name of their colleagues. According to the research on social presence and technology, increasing or bolstering levels of social presence often leads to more effective communication (Frisby, Limperos, Record, Downs, & Kercsmar, 2013). A social presence can manifest in many ways depending on the format of technology and the context of interaction. Although face-to-face settings are considered to have the most social presence, new technologies allow for social presence to exist in computer-mediated interactions as well. Of particular interest to the online instructional context, instructors can now interact with students via synchronous chat with web calling and video from web cameras. These channels allow for social cues to be captured and evaluated by students and instructors, which should enhance perceptions of social presence (So & Brush, 2008). Theoretically, there are many benefits associated with increased social presence in online instructional settings, but empirical validation of these effects is varied. As mentioned, some of the earliest social presence studies (e.g., Short et al., 1976) compared text-based mediums with those of audio and video modalities. These modalities differ in that diverse factors identified by Allmendinger (2010) are introduced which may contribute to perceptions of presence.

Specifically, text contributes visual factors; audio contributes vocalic, and video contributes visual factors and nonverbal factors. In online learning environments, researchers have manipulated technological features and formats associated with online courses to understand social presence and its subsequent effects. Extensive research has linked social presence in online learning environments to increased perceptions of learning (Arbaugh, 2005; Richardson & Swan, 2003), satisfaction with the course (Richardson & Swan, 2003; Swan & Shih, 2005), and learning satisfaction (Arbaugh & Benbunan-Finch, 2006). While this body of research seems to show that social presence in online environments has relatively positive effects, there is still a need for researchers to more systematically investigate exactly which type of online formats and modes of instruction are most effective in bolstering instructor–student relationships and actual (rather than perceived) learning. Even though it is well documented that social presence can increase instructor immediacy (Cui et al., 2012; Schutt, Allen, & Laumakis, 2009), it remains unclear how the differences in online instructional formats impact particular aspects of the instructor–student relationship. More specifically, social presence likely influences both the rhetorical and relational goals of instructors and students in online instructional settings. Previous research has examined how the use of technology may affect perceptions of an instructor's credibility, or students' perceptions of an instructor's caring, trustworthiness, and competence.

Undoubtedly, it is challenging to institute a teaching presence in an online course, especially when using heavily text-based resources. Producing teaching resources like the introductory video does more than allow the students to see or hear the instructor. From the student's viewpoint, the significance is to have an "experience" with the instructor. Several human factors like hearing instructor's tone, voice and understanding their personality, making eye contact, allows students to have an idea about the instructor to make the information more real, and adds value for the students (Jones, Naugle, & Kolloff, 2008). Regardless of the time and effort it takes for a course design team (the instructor, the instructional designer, and media specialist) to develop and produce resources that reinforce their presence in the classroom, these are highly valued by students.

SUMMARY

Research has shown that several online course assessment and evaluation surveys show that most students appreciate the opportunity to know their instructor and have a personal connection with them. Students become more fully engaged when presented with the opportunity to learn more about their instructor, through several means. Weaver and Qi (2005) recommend that online instructors should take the time to understand factors that influence students' participation in class within "the framework of the classroom as a social organization". The models described in this chapter show that elements of the online classroom's formal and informal structures and of students' attributes are directly related to presence and interaction. A key point suggests that student interaction is largely influenced by the organization of the online classroom and the presence of the instructor. Instructor interaction in the classroom is equally critical in promoting student engagement. When interaction is done effectively, students can reflect on the class experience, tying it back to the instructor that made their presence known in the classroom and linking those experiences together.

REFERENCES

Anderson, T., Rourke, L., Garrison, D. R., & Archer, W. (2001). Assessing teaching presence in a computer conferencing context. *Journal of Asynchronous Learning Networks*, *5*(2), 1–17.

Arbaugh, J. B., & Hwang, A. (2006). Does "teaching presence" exist in online MBA courses? *The Internet and Higher Education*, *9*(1), 9–21. doi:10.1016/j.iheduc.2005.12.001

Ash, S. L., Clayton, P. H., & Atkinson, M. P. (2005). Integrating reflection and assessment to capture and improve student learning. *Michigan Journal of Community Service Learning*, *11*(2).

Berge, Z. L. (2002). Active, interactive, and reflective elearning. *Quarterly Review of Distance Education*, *3*(2), 181–190.

Bolliger, D., & Waslik, O. (2009). Factors influencing faculty satisfaction with online teaching and learning in higher education. *Distance Education*, *30*(1), 103–116. doi:10.1080/01587910902845949

Borup, J., Graham, C. R., & Velasquez, A. (2011). The use of asynchronous video communication to improve instructor immediacy and social presence in a blended learning environment. In *Blended learning across disciplines: Models for implementation*, (pp. 38-57). Academic Press.

Bruyn, L. L. (2004). Monitoring Online Communication: Can the development of convergence and social presence indicate an interactive learning environment? *Distance Education*, *25*(1), 67–81. doi:10.1080/0158791042000212468

Chen, B., Raible, J., Bauer, & Thompson. (2015). Welcome Message. In K. Thompson & B. Chen (Eds.), *Teaching Online Pedagogical Repository*. Orlando, FL: University of Central Florida Center for Distributed Learning. Retrieved February 27, 2015 from https://topr.online.ucf.edu/index.php?title=Welcome_Message&oldid=3906

Chickering, A. W., & Gamson, Z. F. (1987). Seven principles for good practice in undergraduate education. *AAHE Bulletin*, *3*, 7.

Churcher, K. M., Downs, E., & Tewksbury, D. (2014). "Friending" Vygotsky: A Social Constructivist Pedagogy of Knowledge Building Through Classroom Social Media Use. *The Journal of Effective Teaching, 33*.

Cifuentes, O. E., & Lents, N. H. (2011). Increasing student-teacher interactions at an urban commuter campus through instant messaging and online office hours. *Electronic Journal of Science Education, 14*(1).

Dabbagh, N., & Kitsantas, A. (2012). Personal Learning Environments, social media, and self- regulated learning: A natural formula for connecting formal and informal learning. *The Internet and Higher Education, 15*(1), 3–8. doi:10.1016/j.iheduc.2011.06.002

Dabbagh, N., & Reo, R. (2011a). Back to the future: Tracing the roots and learning affordances of social software. In M. J. W. Lee & C. McLoughlin (Eds.), *Web 2.0-based e-learning: Applying social informatics for tertiary teaching* (pp. 1–20). Hershey, PA: IGI Global. doi:10.4018/978-1-60566-294-7.ch001

deNoyelles, A., Cobb, C., & Lowe, D. (2012). Influence of Reduced Seat Time on Satisfaction and Perception of Course Development Goals: A Case Study in Faculty Development. *Journal of Asynchronous Learning Networks, 16*(2), 85–98.

Dunlap, J., & Lowenthal, P. (2014). *The power of presence: Our quest for the right mix of social presence in online courses. Real Life Distance Education: Case Studies in Practice*. Charlotte, NC: Information Age Publishing.

Dupin-Bryant, P. A., & DuCharme-Hansen, B. A. (2005). Assessing student needs in web-based distance education. *International Journal of Instructional Technology and Distance Learning, 2*(1), 39-47.

Erichsen, E. A., & Bolliger, D. U. (2011). Towards understanding international graduate student isolation in traditional and online environments. *Educational Technology Research and Development, 59*(3), 309–326. doi:10.1007/s11423-010-9161-6

Garrison, D. R. (2006). Online collaboration principles. *Journal of Asynchronous Learning Networks, 10*(1), 25–34.

Gazi, Z. A., Aksal, F. A., & Öztuğ, O. (2012). *Online Social Networking: A Synergy for Learning*. Retrieved from http://www.iojes.net/userfiles/Article/IOJES_967.pdf_br

Greenhow, C. (2011). Online social networks and learning. *On the Horizon, 19*(1), 4–12. doi:10.1108/10748121111107663

Harasim, L. (1996). *Online education. Computer networking and scholarly communication in the twenty-first-century university*. Academic Press.

Herreid, C. F., & Schiller, N. A. (2013). Case studies and the flipped classroom. *Journal of College Science Teaching, 42*(5), 62–66.

Hrastinski, S. (2008). Asynchronous and synchronous e-learning. *EDUCAUSE Quarterly, 31*(4), 51–55.

Hudgins T.L., Orellana, A. & Simonson, M. (2009). *The perfect online course: best practices for designing and teaching*. Academic Press.

Jafari, A., McGee, P., & Carmean, C. (2006). Managing Courses, Defining Learning: What Faculty, Students, and Administrators Want. *EDUCAUSE Review*, *41*(4), 50–71. Retrieved from http://www.educause.edu/EDUCAUSE+Review/EDUCAUSEReviewMagazineVolume41/ManagingCoursesDefiningLearnin/158070

Jones, P., Naugle, K., & Kolloff, M. (2008). *Teacher presence: Using introductory videos in online and hybrid courses*. Learning Solutions Magazine.

Kelly, R. (2014). *Creating a Sense of Instructor Presense in the Online Classroom*. Retrieved August 4, 2015 from http://www.facultyfocus.com/articles/online-education/creating-a-sense-of-instructor-presence-in-the-online-classroom/

Kennedy, K., & Archambault, L. (2012). Offering Preservice Teachers Field Experiences in K-12 Online Learning A National Survey of Teacher Education Programs. *Journal of Teacher Education*, *63*(3), 185–200. doi:10.1177/0022487111433651

Ladyshewsky, R. K. (2013). Instructor presence in online courses and student satisfaction. *International Journal for the Scholarship of Teaching and Learning*, *7*(1), 13. doi:10.20429/ijsotl.2013.070113

Lazonder, A. W., Wilhelm, P., & Ootes, S. A. W. (2003). Using sentence openers to foster student interaction in computer-mediated learning environments. *Computers & Education*, *41*(3), 291–308. doi:10.1016/S0360-1315(03)00050-2

Lih-Ching, C. W., & Beasley, W. (2006). Integrating Instant Messenger into Online Office Hours to Enhance Synchronous Online Interaction in Teacher Education. *International Journal of Instructional Media*, *33*(3), 277–287.

National Standards for Quality Online Courses. (n.d.). Retrieved from http://www.inacol.org/cms/wp-content/uploads/2013/02/iNACOL_CourseStandards_2011.pdf_br

Oztok, M., & Brett, C. (2011). Social presence and online learning: A review of the research. *Journal of Distance Education*, *25*(3), 1–10.

Pappas, C. (2015). *Ten Invaluable tips to develop asynchronous learning*. Retrieved July 2, 2015 from https://www.docebo.com/2015/06/22/10-invaluable-tips-to-develop-asynchronous-learning/

Preisman, K. A. (2014). Teaching Presence in Online Education: From the Instructor's Point of View. *Online Learning*, *10*(3), 1–16.

Ragan, L. C., Bigatel, P. M., Kennan, S. S., & Dillon, J. M. (2012). From Research to Practice: Towards the Development of an Integrated and Comprehensive Faculty Development Program. *Journal of Asynchronous Learning Networks*, *16*(5), 71–86.

Rallis, H. (1994). *Creating teaching and learning partnerships with students: Helping faculty listen to student voices*. Academic Press.

Reilly, J. R., Gallagher-Lepak, S., & Killion, C. (2012). "Me and My Computer": Emotional Factors in Online Learning. *Nursing Education Perspectives*, *33*(2), 100–105. doi:10.5480/1536-5026-33.2.100 PMID:22616408

Russo, T., & Benson, S. (2005). Learning with invisible others: Perceptions of online presence and their relationship to cognitive and affective learning. *Journal of Educational Technology & Society*, *8*(1), 54–62.

Seaman, J., & Tinti-Kane, H. (2013). *Social media for teaching and learning*. Pearson Learning Systems.

So, H. J., & Brush, T. A. (2008). Student perceptions of collaborative learning, social presence and satisfaction in a blended learning environment: Relationships and critical factors. *Computers & Education*, *51*(1), 318–336. doi:10.1016/j.compedu.2007.05.009

Sorensen, C. K., & Baylen, D. M. (2009). *Learning online. The perfect online course: Best practices for designing and teaching*. Academic Press.

Swan, K., & Shih, L. F. (2005). On the nature and development of social presence in online course discussions. *Journal of Asynchronous Learning Networks*, *9*(3), 115–136.

The Online Learning Definitions Project. (n.d.). Retrieved from http://www.inacol.org/cms/wp- content/uploads/2013/04/iNACOL_DefinitionsProject.pdf_br

Traver, A. E., Volchok, E., Bidjerano, T., & Shea, P. (2014). Correlating community college students' perceptions of community of inquiry presences with their completion of blended courses. *The Internet and Higher Education*, *20*, 1–9. doi:10.1016/j.iheduc.2013.09.001

Veletsianos, G., & Navarrete, C. (2012). Online social networks as formal learning environments: Learner experiences and activities. *The International Review of Research in Open and Distributed Learning*, *13*(1), 144–166.

Vesely, P., Bloom, L., & Sherlock, J. (2007). Key elements of building online community: Comparing faculty and student perceptions. *MERLOT Journal of Online Learning and Teaching*, *3*(3), 234–246.

Wenger, E., White, N., & Smith, J. (2009). *Digital habitats: Stewarding technology for communities*. CP Square Press.

Chapter 4
"I'm Here for You": Instructor Presence Online

Kelly R. Elander
Harding University, USA

ABSTRACT

The author examines instructor presence by considering its historical role, the many important tasks that instruction presence accomplishes, and many ways instructional presence can be shown in online learning. Instructor presence has historically fulfilled four key functions: guidance, socialization, motivation, and coordination. Tasks that instructor presence can help with include welcoming and orienting learners, providing grades and explanations for grades, communicating course and instructor expectations and feedback on learner work, offering follow-up questions and comments, and moderating discussions. Seven techniques suggested to provide a sense of instructor presence include scheduling predetermined, regular appearances online, providing quick responses to comments and assignments, making occasional instructor posts throughout course discussions, offering periodic, brief, personal comments, providing special periods of instructor access, simulating presence by means of prerecorded audio or video clips and using instructor representatives.

INTRODUCTION

Everyone who has attended K-12, higher education, or training classes has probably been in a situation in which the class is about to begin, everyone is seated…and then the unexpected happens: the instructor never arrives. Initially, most people will wait politely, assuming the instructor was delayed, or is sick and sending a replacement, or that someone will come tell them what is going on. However, once it becomes apparent that the instructor isn't coming, confusion and indecision can set in. The students begin to wonder what they should do. Leave? Wait longer? Call someone? Look in other classrooms to see if the class is meeting somewhere else? Sit and read the next assignment in the textbook? Everyone in class has a different idea of what to do.

What began as a well-planned and carefully orchestrated meeting that brings together dozens of people with a common purpose quickly degenerates into various factions, each ready to choose a different course

DOI: 10.4018/978-1-4666-9995-3.ch004

of action. This perhaps familiar illustration explains what can happen in an online class if there is a perception that the instructor is absent. How does an online instructor help learners dispersed across great distances and varied settings feel like the instructor is right there with them as they learn and interact?

This chapter will examine the background and influence of instructor presence on online learning. The concept of instructor presence in e-learning actually encompasses a number of concepts, with each having an impact upon learners, influencing their satisfaction with and academic success in the online courses. This chapter will also consider why instructor presence is important to e-learning and what forms it ought to take. It will explain that research and experience have revealed the following:

- Instructor presence has always been important to e-learning.
- Instructor presence fulfills important tasks in e-learning.
- Instructor presence can be used in different ways to help e-learning.

INSTRUCTOR PRESENCE HAS ALWAYS BEEN IMPORTANT TO E-LEARNING

After the Internet became widely used by more segments of society in the 1990's, all kinds of communication, transactions, and business processes migrated to this new platform. Those in the fields of education and training looked for ways to capitalize on this new, worldwide network. Many people designing early online learning projects envisioned that once instructional materials, tutorials, and Web-based training courses and tools were online, learners would just access the information and teach themselves (Beer, 2000; Rosenberg, 2001). This thinking arose from the assumption that most online learners would be adults learning job skills on their own time. Since adult learning theory said adults want autonomy in their learning (Rovai, Ponton, & Baker, 2008), and Deci & Ryan's (2000) Self Determination Theory of learning motivation also advocated learner autonomy, the move toward self-study seemed logical.

However, early Internet learning pioneers discovered that learners using computer-mediated communication have very different needs from learners in a face-to-face classroom (Allen, 2003; Beer, 2000; Chute, Thompson, & Hancock, 1999). Online learners were not content with self-directed learning. Instead, online learners needed and expected to be guided through the strange new world of e-learning (Dirkx & Smith, 2004; Sorensen, 2004). This unexpected need for help—combined with other obstacles such as technical malfunctions led to high drop-out rates in e-learning courses (Barrett, 2009; Neuhauser, Bender, & Stromberg, 2000; Seaton & Schwier, 2014). Research revealed that many e-learners felt isolated, disconnected, and not part of an organized class (Borup, West & Graham, 2011; Russo & Benson, 2005; Seaton & Schwier, 2014). In online classes with an instructor learners associated their satisfaction with their interactions with the instructor (Borup, West, & Graham, 2011).

Since removing the instructor altogether online didn't seem to work, e-learning researchers and course designers began exploring what role the instructor would take in online learning (Dubuclet, 2008). Studies (Bonk, Wisher, & Lee, 2004; Lehman & Conceição, 2010; Seaton & Schwier, 2014) eventually revealed that online learners look to instructors to provide four key functions:

- Guidance
- Socialization
- Motivation
- Coordination

Guidance

The first thing online learners expect from the instructor is guidance. Online instructors need to be more than facilitators, they must direct learners by explaining information and activities, including being available to answer questions (Alutu, 2006; Bonk, Wisher, & Lee, 2004; Dirkx & Smith, 2004; Seaton & Schwier, 2014). Just as computer technology provided simple feedback to users in the form of sounds, pop-ups, symbols, and labels to help users operate their computers and software, e-learning course developers came to learn that online learners also needed feedback, especially human interaction to use online courses.

E-learning researchers explored all the ways interaction can affect the e-learning environment, which eventually led to Moore's Transactional Distance Theory. Moore's theory helps explain why interaction between the learner and the instructor helps make the distance and separation between two parties seem less and describes the four basic kinds of interaction (instructor-learner, learner-learner, learner- interface, and learner-online materials) that can be provided in an online course to reduce the sense of distance between instructors and learners. (Baker, 2010; Woods & Baker, 2004).

Moore and others identified a few different kinds of interaction influencing online learners (Baker, 2010). These interactions included learner-to instructor interactions, learner-to-learner interactions, interaction between the learner and the learning interface, and interaction between the learner and online materials or programs created used to present information (such as a multimedia presentation). Still the most impactful interaction was that between learner and instructor (Jones, Naugle, & Kolloff, 2008; Ladyshewsky, 2013; Reio & Crim, 2006). Alutu (2006) has suggested that even online self-directed or self-guided activities should be preceded by instructor guidance in order to be effective. Some early online learners rated their entire online learning experience based on how visible and helpful the instructor was (Bischoff, 2000).

Figure 1. Moore's Transactional Distance Theory

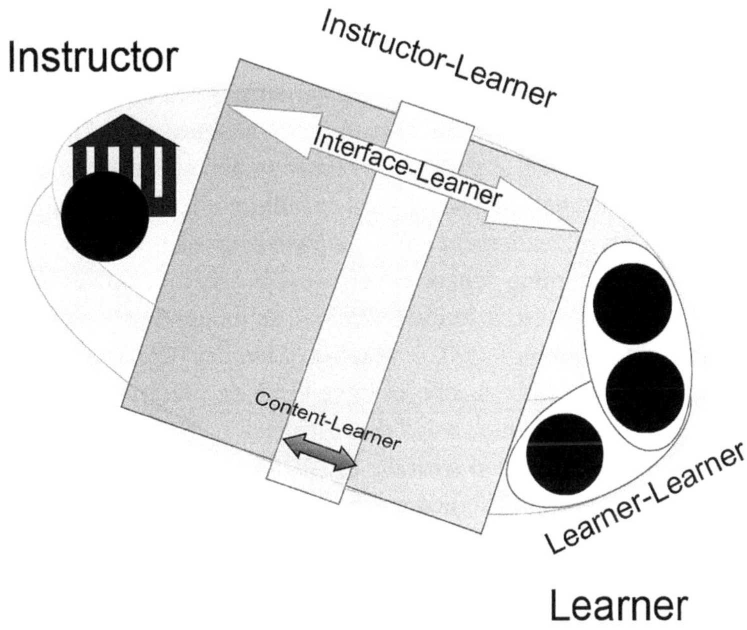

It became apparent that online learners wanted to know their instructor and feel that he or she was present ready to come to their aid anywhere in the course (Alutu, 2006; Dirkx & Smith, 2004; Seaton & Schwier, 2014; Stewart, August 21, 2014). This is why introducing the instructor at the start of a course has became a standard, necessary ritual in e-learning courses. For example, a decade or so ago at the training center at one large consulting company, the course designers began showing a photo of the instructor at the start of each course because they found it improved the learner's connection to the instructor, making him or her more "real."

It was also found that learners—especially learners new to e-learning—would not intuitively know what to do or where to go in an online class without some guidance (Simonson, Smaldino, Albright, & Zvacek, 2003). When instructors seemed absent learners were confused and frustrated, distracting them from learning. Thus it was found that instructor guidance could help new learners avoid this confusion or frustration as they began their online courses (White, 2000). Instructor guidance has remained a key feature in online learning, even when course designers have sought to try newer learner-centered constructivist learning approaches. All instructional approaches recognize the importance of instructor guidance at the start of a course

Instructor guidance can take many forms: leading by example, starting conversations in discussion areas, providing informative feedback, asking reflective questions, and showing how to express ideas in a productive and professional way. Online universities such as the University of Phoenix and Capella University have built their success on the principle of instructor guidance (Palloff & Pratt, 2003; White & Weight, 2000). Some online instructors, feared their comments online would dominate and suppress learner comments and withheld their own posts, only to wind up receiving very negative feedback from their learners (Morgan, 2011). When an online instructor does not post and communicate with the learners, the learners get the impression the instructor doesn't exist (Dennen, 2010; Stone & Chapman, 2006).

Socialization

In addition to providing guidance, e-learning instructors have always needed to create a social connection to their learners and between learners. Online classes, like any other human interaction, needs to include social rituals, such as meeting and greeting, building rapport, developing respect and trust, and creating relationships. Without such social protocols, it is much harder to work with learners because all others would be perceived as strangers. This principle is seen in the business world in the important ceremonial event in large work projects known as the kick-off meeting in which everyone who will be involved with the project gets to meet one another. The success or failure of teamwork and communication on a project can be traced to whether all team members were present at the kick-off meeting (Wright, 2009).

Researchers studying online learning dynamics began calling this socialization role of the instructor "*social presence*" (Garrison, Anderson, & Archer, 2003). The model that has been widely accepted as best describing online instructor presence, the Community of Inquiry (COI) model (Garrison, Anderson, & Archer, 2003) defines social presence as one of three kinds of presence instructors must create for a successful online class. It describes three ways the instructor embodies presence in an online class. *Social presence* refers to human interaction with the instructor and others. *Teaching presence* refers to the sense that the course has been well-designed and orchestrated. *Cognitive presence* refers to the way learners are able to mentally engage, reflect, and internalize their understanding of the topic. Certain settings or materials may result in overlapping kinds of presence.

Figure 2. Traditional Community of Inquiry Model

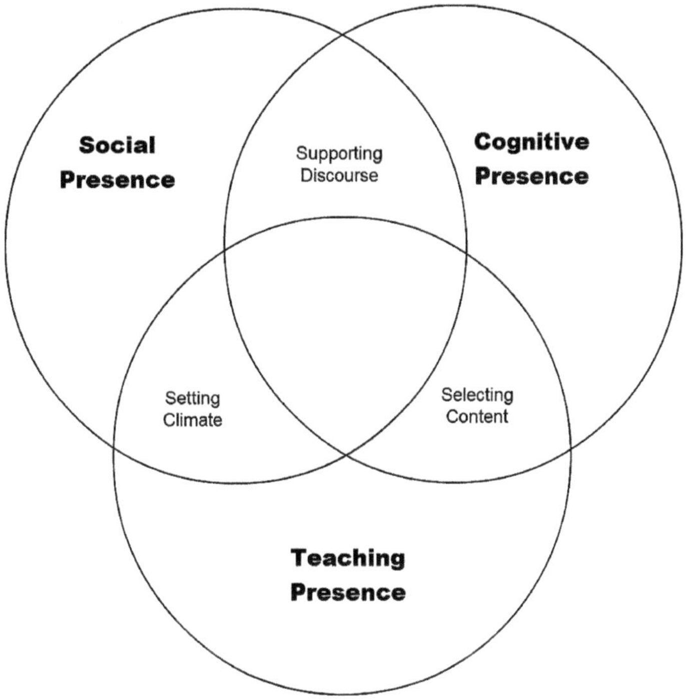

Social presence refers to the closeness created as people meet and relate to each other and find commonalities (Annand, 2011). Instructors who make no effort at social interaction or bonding with learners are not perceived by learners as a real, significant person (Lehman & Conceição, 2010). Therefore, when there is no social presence, learners will be less understanding, patient, or forgiving of any errors the learner perceives the instructor makes in the class.

Recently, some scholars have sought to add an additional dimension to the COI model to identify the dimension of emotions, feelings, attitudes, and states of mind that have also influenced online relationships (Anderson, 2014; Cleveland-Innes & Campbell, 2012; Rienties & Rivers, 2014; and Sorensen, 2004). Still others have sought to expand the COI model to show that the manner of communication for each presence sphere is also a variable (Kreijns, Van Acker, Vermeulen, & Van Buuren, 2014). For example, a video recording of an orientation session or an instruction session might be used in place of a live instructor session. The newest components recommended to be added to the COI model are another form of presence, encompassing emotions, and the identification of communication mediums as another variable for implementing the four spheres of presence.

Despite these additions to the COI model, the focus of this chapter is confined to the three original spheres of presence. Thus, research has found that social presence in online courses is crucial, starting with welcoming emails and the instructor introducing himself or herself (including sharing things about family members, hobbies, interests, and other such characteristics) (Fullmer-Umari, 2000). The social presence dimension might also include private, friendly, occasional one-on-one conversations with individual learners by chat, phone, or some other program (Arbaugh, 2010). Today, online instructors

Figure 3. The most complete and expanded version of the Community of Inquiry Model (2.0)

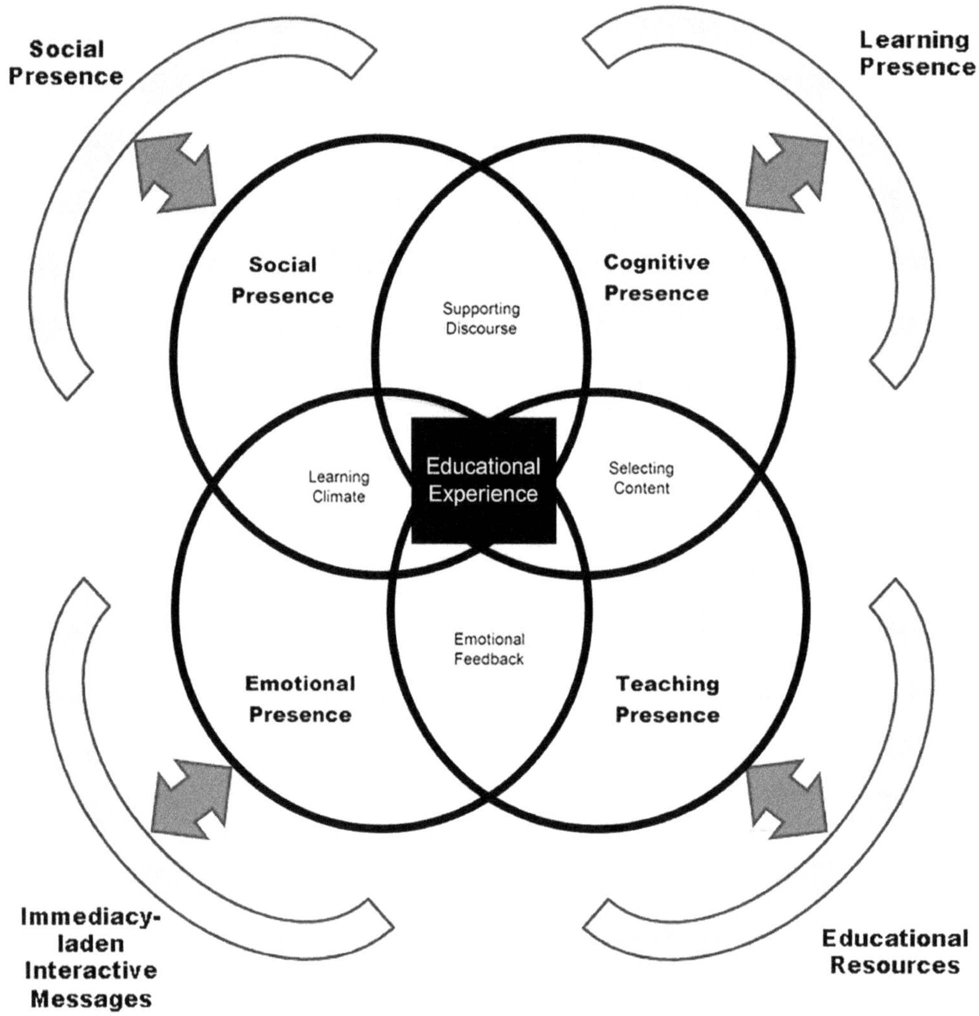

typically provide photos of themselves to create social presence and may also use introductory audio files and videos (Jones, Naugle, & Kolloff, 2008). There is, however, still some debate in the literature about whether prerecorded video or audio self-introductions can provide the same level of social connection that live communication can (Sheridan & Kelly, 2010).

Experienced online instructors enhance their social presence by noting and mentioning details about the learners in conversations, referring to learners by name, providing encouraging remarks, and including friendly banter in discussion posts to make interactions warmer. Some course designers even provide a discussion space in online courses for learners to talk socially with their peers on topics unrelated to the class and assignments. These virtual *lounges* or *café's* enable learners to share their personal struggles and concerns and receive social support.

Constructivist, collaborative online learning approaches often stressed the need to make classes into communities of learning, where all participants felt connected to each other and the industry or profession connected to the class. This emphasis also enhances the perception of the instructor's social presence (Wolfe, 2000). Some instructors even reported being able to build stronger relationships with online students than they did with students in traditional classrooms (Arbaugh, 2010).

Motivation

Merely knowing that an instructor was present and monitoring on- and off-line interactions between learners often kept class members engaged (Houtman, Maros, & Meacock, 2014). Additional incentives might come by having the instructor clearly spell out his or her expectations through grading rubrics and activity instructions. However, learning theorists have concluded that external motivation (using rewards and punishments) is not sufficient to build deep, meaningful knowledge (Furlich, 2013). Instead, the hope is that once the online learners become interested and involved in the topic he or she will become more intrinsically compelled (that is, self-motivated) to seek out the answers and solutions to activities and exercises. In fact some motivational theories acknowledge that self motivated learners are goal-oriented and will perform granted they understand clearly expectations and feel they can be successful (Schank, 1997). So, online instructors will often initially use expectations and grades to provide a starting framework for learners to motivate themselves throughout the course.

An instructor will use his or her presence to become more directly involved with the learners as they engaged in course activities (Houtman, Maros, & Meacock, 2014; Jones, 2011). Merely asking and/or encouraging a learner to engage in an online discussion or team project can influence a learner's motivation (Jones, 2011).The online instructor's presence as he or she virtually checks in with teams working on a project can provide the opportunity to motivate by simple corrective comments or encourage the group to value the input of quieter group members during the collaborative processes. By being present, the online instructor help motivate teams to stay on topic. And just as the instructor can monitor learner engagement and team dynamics, he or she can also examine interactions within the class and seek to make them more effective. By being present in the e-learning trenches with the learners, the instructor can keep learners engaged and motivated.

Coordination

Instructor presence also serves a coordinating function in online classes, especially during discussion and team interactions. Researchers have stressed the need for instructors to moderate learner interactions with all parties involved (Hanover Research Council, 2009) in online learning. According to Moore's Theory of Transactional distance, the smoother the interactions are in an online course, the closer the participants feel to each other and the instructor, allowing learners to forget, in a sense, the physical distances between them, and allowing them to focus entirely on the subject at hand.

In addition to peer-to-peer interactions, learners must also learn to work with online content tools, resources, and the course interface itself. Tutorials or support desks can help with these needs, but the instructors can use these needs to establish a stronger sense of presence and help coordinate learner success. For instance, the instructor might hold an introductory class session or workshop on how to interact with the course content and the course interface. While experience has shown learners don't typically denigrate instructors who lack of technical knowledge of e-learning systems (Priest, 2000), there is still the opportunity to use such situations to cultivate trust and appreciation from learners. Instructors who are well acquainted with the course Learning Management System (LMS) to share their knowledge of the system with learners, showing them quicker, easier ways to do tasks within the interface. Instructors can also help coordinate learners' efforts to find information, and recommended tools to help learners produce their best work.

The literature is clear there is no "perfect formula" for instructor presence, but it is also clear that instructor presence is vital for guidance, socialization, motivation, and coordination.

Instructor Presence Fulfills Important Tasks in E-learning

Though there are many different kinds of online courses and structures used today, research and experience continue to show that instructor presence provides vital functions in all e-learning courses (Hodges & Cowan, 2012; Richardson, Koehler, Besser, Caskurlu, Lim, & Mueller, 2015). Much of current research on instructor presence seeks to improve upon methods that have been identified and find new and better ways to manifest the sense of presence learners need (Hodges & Cowan, 2012; Richardson, Koehler, Besser, Caskurlu, Lim, & Mueller, 2015). However, some of the standard practices that have developed, thus far, for online instructor presence include the following:

- Welcoming and orienting learners.
- Providing grades and explanations for grades.
- Communicating course and instructor expectations, and providing analysis, suggestions, and feedback on learner work.
- Offering follow-up questions and clarifying responses to learner comments.
- Moderating discussions, including pointing out relationships and connections between learner posts.

Welcoming and Orienting Learners

The first instructor presence task in any course is establishing a social connection between the instructor and learners, associated with social presence, in the traditional COI model. Maintaining a high profile and frequent involvement is especially important at the beginning of a course (Arbaugh, 2010). Instructors need to make sure learners are welcomed, made to feel important (Carwile, 2007), and are provided the instructions needed to get started. Typically, this starts with self introductions by the instructor and learners.

In a physical classroom, social rapport is accomplished through the use of what Mehrabian describes as immediacy behaviors (1969). These verbal messages and non-verbal gestures, shown in *Table 1*, personalize the instructor, and help him or her to acknowledge and value the learners.

It might help to think of immediacy behaviors as the things people use when trying to make friends and build relationships. One of the challenges of online learning is that many of the immediacy communicated non-verbally in a classroom cannot be conveyed online except with the most elaborate person-to-person video systems. Even then, it's nearly impossible to do with a full class of learners. Online written communication is notoriously inadequate for communicating the tone and attitude behind the text. Recent studies of teacher immediacy behaviors have sought to find a way to reintroduce the tone and attitude into online courses to help create a stronger sense of social presence (Richardson, Koehler, Besser, Caskurlu, Lim, & Mueller, 2015).

Table 1. Typical Immediacy Behaviors

Non-Verbal	Verbal
Smiling	Humor
Eye contact	Use of student names
Vocal expressiveness	Sharing of personal examples and stories
Gestures	Praising good learner work
Leaning forward	Engaging in conversations with learners
Body movements.	Emoticons
Touching others	Encouragement learners to join discussions
Facing one another	Allowing learners to address the instructor by his or her first name
Head nods	Expressing emotions and opinions
	Following-up on student comments
	Encouraging future contact with the students
	Responding promptly to learner comments, assignments, and questions
	Using inclusive pronouns like "we" and "our"
	Continuing a discussion thread
	Asking questions
	Reflection on the course itself
	Agreeing with others
	Offering specific advice
	Instructors disclose details about themselves
	Greetings

Note: This table contains the generally espoused immediacy behaviors (Baker, 2010a; Furlich, 2013; Kucuk, 2009; Lehman & Conceição, 2010; Lowenthal & Parscal, 2008; Walkem, 2013).

Besides welcoming the class and creating a positive impression, the instructor orients the learner through guidance, suggestions, and recommendations about available tools and resources. He or she also offers to help or answer questions whenever needed.

Providing Grades and Explanations for Grades

In e-learning, just as in traditional classroom learning, the instructor needs to make clear what the assignments are and what the expectations are to receive a good grade, thus helping learners achieve the grade they desire. As stated earlier, the original COI model is a useful tool illustrating the three dimensions of instructor's presence in an online class. The first dimension, already mentioned, is *social presence*. The second dimension in the traditional COI model is *teaching presence*. Unlike social presence, teaching presence has to do with the construction and design of the course, activities, time frames, and grades. Ladyshewsky (2013, p. 3) among others (Arbaugh, 2010; Kupczynski, Ice, Wiesenmayer, & McClusky, 2010) categorize teaching presence into three functions:

- The design and organization of the course.
- How the course is facilitated (discussions, team projects, and so on).
- How much direct instruction takes place.

Thus, part of teaching presence is organizing the assessment or grading component of the course, including rubrics, examples, modeling good practices (Hanover report, 2009) and ensuring that grading is clear and fair in all situations. Prior to the giving of assignments and grading, teaching presence would have meant the instructor created a course structure that is logical, useful, and well-formatted. Teaching presence means designing and developing the learning modules and lessons, readings, materials and activities that will enable learners construct their knowledge effectively. Strategies and tasks may vary but necessary knowledge should be obtainable.

As the concierge of good learning, the instructor steps in when online conversations are getting off course, becoming counterproductive, or need to be pushed in the right direction. As a teaching professional, the instructor should protect the learners' psychological safety and freedom to function in the learning process. The physical classroom creates an atmosphere of accountability, which is reinforced by the immediacy behaviors or the instructor and non-verbal communications from classmates. Online these restraints are not present and thus inappropriate communication becomes more possible. The third dimension in the traditional COI model is *cognitive presence*. Cognitive presence has to do with interactions and situations that enable the learner to grapple with information or concepts, and reflect upon and analyze material so he or she can create a deeper, more meaningful understanding of the subject. Instead of promoting *verbal* engagement, cognitive presence creates *mental* engagement.

There are many ways to get people thinking and processing on a deeper level, but one of the most common is to lead them into a discussion in which they have to articulate their understanding, listen to other positions, reevaluate their position, and then revise their understanding, if appropriate. Research indicates that written, asynchronous communication online (discussion groups or forums) are beneficial in stimulating deeper cognitive learning by causing the learner to think carefully about how to respond to other comments, spend time reflecting on his or her message while composing it, and editing that message after further thought and analysis (Sorensen, 2004).

COMMUNICATING COURSE AND INSTRUCTOR EXPECTATIONS, AND PROVIDING ANALYSIS, SUGGESTIONS, AND FEEDBACK ON LEARNER WORK

Many have seen the instructor's role in online courses as a coach and role-model demonstrating the expected scholarship and behavior in the online course (Bischoff, 2000; Chung, 2005; Panko, 2005). The learners may be unsure about what is considered an appropriate, scholarly discussion post and may be unsure how to comment upon or disagree with the posts of others in a professional, academically appropriate way. The instructor can demonstrate the kinds of comments, questions, and analyses the learners should make (Seaton & Schwier, 2014). Further, Preisman (2014) and Dubuclet (2008) discovered the quantity of comments the instructor makes is not as important as the usefulness and instructional quality of his or her comments.

Offering Follow-Up Questions and Clarifying Responses to Learner Comments

The instructor must also ensure that the points of instruction are clearly understood by the learners (Arbaugh, 2010). Learners look to the instructor to answer questions, clarify muddled points, fill in any missing details, and defuse misunderstandings. The instructor often does this by offering follow-up questions and clarifying responses to learner comments

Much has been said about self-confidence and self-efficacy as motivational components in learning. When a learner posts a fledgling idea, trying to express a concept that might be just a little fuzzy or misstated, the instructor can affirm the effort, gently reassuring and bolstering the learner's confidence while clarifying the point. If a more corrective comment is needed, the online instructor should comment privately rather than in front of the group. The Hanover Research Council report (2009) recommends that instructors contact learners privately by phone to give corrective feedback. Other private and personal platforms for feedback include email, video clips (like that provided by VoiceThreads), or one-to-one Skype calls. Tools such as VoiceThread™ enable instructors to create recorded video feedback for learners, thus providing critique and advice for learners. This potentially provides more personal communication by providing visuals that communicate non-verbal immediacy behaviors. Such communication provides guidance, instructor presence, and concern.

Explaining Relationships or Connections between the Different Learner Posts

Individual learners posting to a discussion board will often be highly focused on getting the content and wording of their own post correct. The instructor should serve in a moderating role by pointing out

Figure 4. Tools such as VoiceThread™ enable instructors to create recorded video feedback for learners, thus providing critique and advice for learners. This potentially provides more personal communication by providing visuals that communicate non-verbal immediacy behaviors.

connections between the words and ideas from various learner posts (Hanover Research Council, 2009). Instructors and course developers generally hope that by doing so, the learners will eventually be looking for such connections themselves. In addition to spotting connections, the instructor can recognize and highlight key points that are made so the group will stay focused on the vital topics and concepts.

Instructor Presence Can Be Used in Different Ways to Help E-learning

The next question, then, is this: How can the online instructor best communicate the presence that is needed in online learning? This section will provide suggestions based on the discussions in the research literature. It is unrealistic and impractical for instructors to be present twenty-four hours a day on the chance that a learner might suddenly have question. Thus, the challenge of instructor presence is in how to effectively manage learner perceptions so that it *seems* the instructor is continually present.

To understand the dynamics at work, consider the illustration of a shepherd protecting of his flock. The shepherd can't watch every sheep every moment. Instead, he merely creates the perception that the shepherd is nearby and ready so the sheep will not dare stray and predators will not attack based on the belief that the shepherd is watching and ready to react. In order to communicate the sense of oversight or readiness, the shepherd employs various techniques. Online instructors should take a similar approach to maintain a sense of presence while not actually monitoring the course every minute.

There are seven techniques suggested to provide the sense of ongoing instructor presence:

- Schedule predetermined, regular appearances online.
- Provide quick responses to comments and assignments.
- Have occasional instructor postings peppered throughout course discussions.
- Providing periodic, brief, personal comments.
- Provide special periods of instructor access, such as a Q&A session and online office hours.
- Simulate presence in the form of prerecorded audio or video clips.
- Use instructor representatives.

Schedule Predetermined, Regular Appearances Online

One way instructor presence is communicated is through scheduled appearances. This may include a welcoming meeting, course schedules, events, and timelines, weekly virtual office hours, and prescheduled periodic meetings, such as at the beginning or end of a unit. How might these work? First, a welcoming email, photos or a video of the instructor, or a live, synchronous event can all be ways the instructor introduces himself or herself to the learners and begins creating social presence. Next, the course structure and timeline can be presented. The more the learners perceive the online course as well-constructed, logical, well-timed, and smooth-running, the more they perceive that the instructor is present (Preisman, 2014). Before or during the class, learners should be notified of weekly, virtual office hours. This approach will be discussed more in an upcoming section. Finally, the instructor should schedule one or more events during the course in which learners will meet together with the instructor in a live conference call or teleconference. Live events can be difficult to schedule when learners come from varied time zones, however, so the instructor may need to do some juggling or schedule two live events with some of the class attending one and the rest attending the other.

Going back to the shepherd analogy, if the shepherd leads the flock out to the fields in the morning and back to the barn in the evening, the sheep imagine that the shepherd has been present all day. Having regularly scheduled events throughout the course helps learners to feel the instructor is always present.

Provide Quick Responses to Comments and Assignments

One of the times learners specifically look for instructor presence (and will miss its absence!) is after an assignment has been turned it. Learners may have uncertainties about whether they did the assignment correctly, turned it in properly, and got a good grade. Some online instructors manage learner expectations about grading turn-around time by stating a response time in the syllabus of twenty-four or forty-eight hours for feedback and grades. Timely feedback is strongly recommended for promoting instructor presence (Hanover Research Council, 2009; Hodges & Cowan, 2012, Plante & Asselin, 2014).

Feedback that learners will associate with instructor presence should be personal, individualized, and employ various verbal immediacy behaviors. There has been some debate in the literature whether rich media feedback (for example, video) provides any greater sense of presence than written feedback (Giesbers, Rienties, Tempelaar, & Gijselaers, 2014).

Have Occasional Instructor Postings Peppered throughout Course Discussions

For the instructor to seem present between scheduled appearances, he or she should participate in learner discussions. The instructor must be perceived as both present and immediate before learners can associate the instructor with social or cognitive presence (Arbaugh, 2010). The instructor does not need to respond to every student post, but can sometimes address multiple student posts with a post or two. The posts also do need not to be at any regular interval or any set number of times. In fact, the number of postings does not necessarily correlate with a higher sense of presence (Dubuclet, 2008). However, if the instructor posts very rarely or not at all, it will be perceived as instructor absence or indifference.

Assigned discussion posts in online courses typically have a scheduled window of access when the majority of learners will post. To spread out the sense of presence, the instructor should not always post within this window. The instructor should respond sometimes to early posts, encouraging others to join the discussion, and sometimes join in the discussion later, after a more people have posted. Part of this process is steering the class to a deeper level of discussion; however, the instructor should come across as a co-participant who is exploring the topic along with the learners (Dubuclet, 2008; Dennen, 2011).

Provide Periodic, Brief, Personal Comments

To create a sense of presence, instructors also need to send informal welcoming messages at the beginning of the course, socialize in informal forums (such as virtual lounges or cafés) to get to know the learners, and send reassuring comments to encourage and support learners who may need a boost (Hanover Research Council, 2009). Instructor comments should not be all course-oriented. Studies suggests that to promote the immediacy behavior discussed earlier, some posts need to include personal stories or examples, humor, and acknowledgement of the learners individuals. Posts can also be brief, simply asking a question or making an observation.

Provide Special Periods of Instructor Access, such as a Q&A Session and Online Office Hours

One practice mentioned earlier for enhancing instructor presence is the use of virtual office hours, or prescheduled Q&A sessions (Hanover Research Council, 2009; Lehman & Conceição, 2010). These sessions provide learners a time when they can be certain the instructor will be present to immediately address their questions or concerns, whether in chat, audio, or video form. Attendance at scheduled office hours should be optional for learners (Lehman & Conceição, 2010). Even those who have chosen not to attend still have the perception of instructor presence because they know the instructor is available.

Simulate Presence in the Form of Prerecorded Audio or Video Clips

Recent research has explored the use of audio and video that was prerecorded by the instructor as a tool to communicate richer, more personal presence than written replies (Borup, West, & Graham, 2011; Bozkaya, 2008; Priesman, 2014). One area in which this has been tried the most is during the course welcome process in an effort to humanize the instructor and make a personal connection to the learner.

There have also been efforts to use prerecorded lectures in video or audio form in an effort to humanize the lecture (Borup, West, & Graham, 2011). Although this kind of media content has been recommended in some settings, research has not proven rich media content (that is, video, web conferencing, and podcasting) is more effective than written forms of communication (Bozkaya, 2008; Giesbers, Rienties, Tempelaar, & Gijselaers, 2014; Preisman, 2014; Sheridan & Kelly, 2010). Recently simple video recording tools such as VoiceThread® have been suggested as a way to create asynchronous video discussions in discussion post areas.

Additionally, simple video recording tools have been used by some online instructors to provide personalized grading feedback or critiques without the logistical difficulties of scheduling phone calls (Henderson & Phillips, 2015). The recent interest in using video may, in part, be that video provides the chance to show non-verbal teacher immediacy behaviors in an online class.

Use Instructor Representatives

Much of this chapter has focused on what the instructor can do to expand the learners' sense of instructor presence online. Since instructor presence is clearly important, some literature has discussed using impression management techniques to enhance perceptions of presence online (Houtman, Makos, & Meacock, 2014). Impression management techniques are methods of generating a perception of something that may or may not be true. There are also more physical or simulated ways to make the instructor seem present in many places at once. The six instructor representative approaches currently in use or suggested are

- Automated System Responses
- Automated Intelligent Learning Agents or Guides
- Teams or Two or More Instructors
- Teaching Assistants
- Virtual Student Helpers
- Telepresence Robots

Automated System Responses

First, though certainly not the best, is simply the use of automatic replies. Learners who are technologically savvy will likely recognized system generated communication as just that. However, going back to Moore's Transactional Distance Theory, learners' interaction with the interface and online materials is supposed to help shrink the distance between learners and the instructor. If the learner sends his or her assignment (Gunderson, Theiss, Wood, Conti-OHare, 2014), the learning management system (LMS) can send an automated notification to the learner that the assignment was received. The LMS (such as Canvas™ or Blackboard™) can also send reminders about upcoming office hours, notify learners when an assignment is due, signal when someone has commented on their comment, or alert learners that a grade has been posted. In a sense, the LMS engages in some teaching presence activities.

Automated Intelligent Learning Agents or Guides

The second instructor representative approach is learning agents. These are automated guides that could handle certain course functions based on some action or input by the learner. Research in the area of artificial intelligence (AI) has been moving toward machines that can learn and make some decisions

Figure 5.

based on experience or circumstances. In the future, instructors could be partnered with an AI *bot* to help extend the reach of their online presence (Bonk, Wisher, & Lee, 2004).

Teams of Two or More Instructors

The third instructor representative approach is the more conventional approach of having two or more instructors assigned to the class. This would allow the instructors to split up their time so that one instructor or the other is present nearly all the time. This could be done by pairing instructors from opposite sides of the world (that is, opposite time zones) so that each instructor is present during his or her daytime.

Teaching Assistants

Another instructor representative approach, which historically has been used in higher learning classrooms, is the use of teaching assistants (TAs), who can, on the behalf of the instructor, perform certain functions, such as grade assignments against a rubric. As Anderson (2004) described it, the instructor's influence and presence might be spread out by using assignment graders, discussion post moderators, or even students to help to provide some feedback on the behalf of the instructor.

Virtual Student Helpers

The fifth instructor representative approach is having virtual student helpers. This unusual approach is the use of a "virtual student" within the class acting as an informal coach to steer the other students to the right behaviors, action, and work (Nagel, Blignaut, & Cronjé, 2007). The virtual student is not an actual student but an "avatar" or persona of a student, with a back story and personality. In reality, the virtual student is a helping instructor or TA. This approach raises some ethical eyebrows, but perhaps if learners are told of the possibility of this method being used in a pre-course disclaimer, the practice might be better accepted.

Telepresence Robots

The last instructor representative approach is telepresence robots. In hybrid classes that use physical locations in conjunction with online courses, a few educational programs (such as Michigan State and the University of North Carolina pharmacy school) have employed telepresence robots as virtual representatives (Meyer, February 2015; Roscorta, May 2015). A telepresence robot (from vendors such as,, and mantarobot.com) is a machine on wheels nearly the height of a person that is remotely controlled so it can move around within classrooms. The robots have a display screen where a person's head would be so learners can see the instructor's face at the normal height of a person. Telepresence robots use a display, such as a tablet, mounted on a remote-controlled cart. The instructor uses live, streaming video on the tablet to show real-time instructor presence. The instructor can remotely move the cart around the room to simulate movement and physical presence. This approach conveys instructor presence through live video and audio with an object that provides a physical presence. The telepresence robot would not work well in a course that is exclusively online, but since many courses use both virtual and physical settings, such a robot might prove very useful.

Figure 6. Telepresence Robots

CONCLUSION

History and practical experience support the idea that instructor presence is crucial to any online learning. While the role and manner of instructional presence may have changed over time, the fact remains that online learners need to be able to feel connected with someone, primarily the instructor. As more and more higher learning and professional training courses move online and class sizes increase, one's strategic approach to providing instructor presence may spell the difference between a learner's e-learning success or failure.

Any online instructor would do well to become familiar with the Community of Inquiry (COI) model and its social, teaching, and cognitive presence, as well as emotional presence described in the expanded model. Additionally, instructors should become well versed in verbal and non-verbal immediacy behaviors so the course platform and materials can be used to create a connection to one's learners.

REFERENCES

Allen, M. W. (2003). *Michael Allen's guide to e-learning: Building interactive, fun, and effective learning programs for any company*. Hoboken, NJ: Wiley.

Alutu, A. N. G. (2006). The guidance role of the instructor in the teaching and learning process. *Journal of Instructional Psychology*, *33*(1), 44–49.

Anderson, T. (2004). Teaching in an online learning context. In T. Anderson & F. Elloumi (Eds.), *Theory and Practice of Online Learning*. Athabasca University.

Anderson, T. (2014, December 16). *New report on emotional presence in online education.* [Web log post]. Retrieved from http://terrya.edublogs.org/2014/12/16/new-report-on-emotional-presence-in-online-education/

Arbaugh, J. B. (2010). Sage, guide, both, or even more? An examination of instructor activity in online MBA courses. *Computers & Education*, *55*(3), 1234–1244. doi:10.1016/j.compedu.2010.05.020

Baker, C. (2010). The impact of instructor immediacy and presence for online student affective learning, cognition, and motivation. *The Journal of Educators Online*, *7*(1).

Baker, J. D. (2010). Perceptions of immediacy, cohesiveness, and learning in online courses. *Christian Perspectives in Education*, *4*(1), 1–14.

Beer, V. (2000). *The web learning fieldbook: Using the world wide web to build workplace learning environments.* San Francisco: Jossey-Bass.

Bischoff, A. (2000). The elements of effective online teaching. In K. W. White & B. H. Weight (Eds.), The Online Teaching Guide: A Handbook of Attitudes, Strategies, and Techniques for the Virtual Classroom, (pp. 57-72). Academic Press.

Bonk, C. J., Wisher, R. A., & Lee, J. Y. (2004). Moderating learner-centered e-learning: Problems and solutions, benefits and implications. In T. S. Roberts (Ed.), Online Collaborative Learning: Theory and Practice, (pp. 54-85). Academic Press.

Borup, J., West, R. E., & Graham, C. R. (2011). Improving online social presence through asynchronous video. *The Internet and Higher Education*, *15*(3), 195–203. doi:10.1016/j.iheduc.2011.11.001

Carwile, J. (2007). A constructivist approach to online teaching and learning. *Inquiry*, *12*(1), 68–73.

Chute, A., Thompson, M., & Hancock, B. (1999). *The McGraw-Hill handbook of distance learning: An implementation guide for trainers & human resource professionals.* New York: McGraw Hill.

Cleveland-Innes, M., & Campbell, P. (2012). Emotional presence, learning, and the online learning environment. *International Review of Research in Open and Distance Learning*, *13*(4), 269–292.

Dennen, V. P. (2011). Facilitator presence and identity in online discourse: Use of positioning theory as an analytic framework. *Instructional Science*, *39*(4), 527–541. doi:10.1007/s11251-010-9139-0

Dirkx, J., & Smith, R. O. (2004). Thinking out of a bowl of spaghetti: Learning to learn in online collaborative groups. In T. S. Roberts (Ed.), Online Collaborative Learning: Theory and Practice, (pp. 132-159). Academic Press.

Dobo, N. (2014). *What it's like to have a robot for a teacher.* [Web blog post]. Retrieved from http://www.slate.com/ articles/technology/future_tense/2014

Dubuclet, K. S. (2008). *Teaching presence: A focus on the instructor's role in online collaborative learning*. (Unpublished doctoral dissertation). University of Southern Mississippi.

Fullmer-Umari, M. (2000). Getting ready: The Syllabus and other online indispensables. In K. W. White & B. H. Weight (Eds.), The Online Teaching Guide, (pp. 95-111). Boston: Allyn and Bacon.

Furlich, S. (2013). Enhancing on-line teaching with verbal immediacy through self-theory. In T. Bastiaens & G. Marks (Eds.), *Proceedings of E-Learn: World Conference on E-Learning in Corporate, Government, Healthcare, and Higher Education 2013* (pp. 694-703). Chesapeake, VA: Association for the Advancement of Computing in Education (AACE).

Garrison, D. (2011). *E-Learning in the 21st century: A framework for research and practice* (2nd ed.). London: Routledge/Taylor and Francis.

Garrison, D., Anderson, T., & Archer, W. (2000). Critical inquiry in a text-based environment; computer conferencing in higher education. *The Internet and Higher Education*, *2*(2-3), 87–105. doi:10.1016/S1096-7516(00)00016-6

Garrison, D., Anderson, T., & Archer, W. (2003). A theory of critical inquiry in online distance education. In M. G. Moore & W. G. Anderson (Eds.), Handbook of Distance Education, (pp. 113-127). Mahwah, NJ: Erlbaum.

Giesbers, B., Rienties, B., Tempelaar, D. T., & Gijselaers, W. (2014). Why Increased Social Presence through Web Videoconferencing Does Not Automatically Lead to Improved Learning. *E-Learning and Digital Media*, *11*(1), 31–45. doi:10.2304/elea.2014.11.1.31

Gunderson, B. J., Theiss, M. A., Wood, L. K., & Conti-OHare, M. (2014). Using a telephone call to increase social presence in online classes. *Nursing Education Perspectives*, *35*(5), 338–339. doi:10.5480/11-569 PMID:25291933

Hanover Research Council. (2009). *Best practices in online teaching strategies*. Retrieved from http://www.uwec.edu/AcadAff/resources/edtech/upload/Best-Practices-in-Online-Teaching-Strategies-Membership.pdf

Henderson, M., & Phillips, M. (2015). Video-based feedback on student assessment: Scarily personal. *Australasian Journal of Educational Technology*, *61*(1), 51–66.

Hodges, C. B., & Cowan, S. F. (2012). Preservice teachers' view of instructor presence in online courses. *Journal of Digital Learning in Teacher Education*, *28*(4), 139–145. doi:10.1080/21532974.2012.10784694

Hosler, K. A., & Arend, B. D. (2012). The importance of course design, feedback, and facilitation: Student perceptions of the relationship between teaching presence and cognitive presence. *Educational Media International*, *49*(3), 217–229. doi:10.1080/09523987.2012.738014

Jaggars, S. S., Edgecombe, N., & Stacey, G. W. (2014). *Creating an effective online instructor presence*. Community College Research Center, Teachers College, Columbia University.

Jones, I. M. (2011). Can you see me now? Defining teaching presence in the online classroom through building a learning community. *Journal of Legal Studies Education*, *28*(1), 67–116. doi:10.1111/j.1744-1722.2010.01085.x

Kreijns, K., Van Acker, F., Vermeulen, M., & Van Buuren, H. (2014). Community of inquiry: Social presence revisited. *E-Learning and Digital Media*, *11*(1), 5–18. doi:10.2304/elea.2014.11.1.5

Kupczynski, L., Ice, P., Wiesenmayer, R., & McCluskey, F. (2010). Student perceptions of the relationship between indicators of teaching presence and success in online courses. *Journal of Interactive Online Learning*, *9*(1), 23–43.

Lehman, R. M., & Conceição, S. C. (2010). *Creating a Sense of Presence in Online Teaching: How to 'Be There' for Distance Learners*. San Francisco: Jossey-Bass.

Lowenthal, P. R., & Parscal, T. (2008). Teaching presence. *The Learning Curve, 3*(4), 1-2, 4.

Mehradbian, A. (1969). Methods and designs: Some referents and measures of non-verbal behavior. *Behavior Research Methods and Instrumentation*, *1*(6), 203–207. doi:10.3758/BF03208096

Metro-Roland, D. & Farber, P. (2010). Lost causes: Online instruction and the integrity of presence. *Philosophy of Education*.

Meyer, L. (2015). Michigan State telepresence robots for online students. *Campus Technology*.

Mollen, A., & Wilson, H. (2009). Engagement, telepresence, and interactivity in online consumer experience: Reconciling scholastic and managerial perspectives. *Journal of Business Research*, *63*(9-10), 919–925. doi:10.1016/j.jbusres.2009.05.014

Morgan, T. (2011). Online classroom or community-in-the-making? Instructor conceptualizations and teaching presence in international online contexts. *Journal of Distance Education*, *25*(1).

Nagel, L., Blignaut, S., & Cronjé, J. (2007). Methical Jane: Perspectives on an Undisclosed Virtual Student. *Journal of Computer-Mediated Communication*, *12*(4), 1346–1368. doi:10.1111/j.1083-6101.2007.00376.x

Neuhauser, P., Bender, R., & Stromberg, K. (2000). *Culture.com*. Toronto: John Wiley & Sons.

Panko, M. (2005). Teaching beliefs and the practice of e-moderators: Presage, process, and product. *Education in a Changing World*.

Plante, K., & Asselin, M. E. (2014). Best practices for creating social presence and caring behaviors online. *Nursing Education Perspectives*, *35*(4), 219–223. doi:10.5480/13-1094.1 PMID:25158415

Preisman, K. A. (2014). Teaching Presence in Online Education: From the Instructor's Point of View. *Online Learning, 18*(3). Retrieved from http://files.eric.ed.gov/fulltext/ EJ1043166.pdf

Richardson, J. C., Koehler, A. A., Besser, E. D., Caskurlu, S., Lim, J. E., & Mueller, C. M. (2015). Conceptualizing and investigating instructor presence in online learning environments. *International Review of Research in Open and Distributed Learning*, *16*(3), 256–297.

Rienties, B., & Alden Rivers, B. (2014). *Measuring and Understanding Learner Emotions: Evidence and Prospects*. Learning Analytics Review 1, Learning Analytics Community Exchange (LACE). Retrieved from http://www.laceproject.eu/learning-analyticsreview/meas

Rodriguez, A. L., & Fahara, M. F. (2010). Online teaching styles: A study in distance education. *International Journal of University Teaching and Faculty*, *1*(2), 1–14.

Roscoria, T. (2015, May). *Telepresence helps universities connect virtual students with campus life.* [Web Blog Post]. Retrieved fromhttp://www.govtech.com/education/Telepresence-Helps-Universities-Connect-Virtual-Students-With-Campus-Life.html

Rosenberg, M. J. (2001). *Building successful online learning in your organization: E-learning strategies for delivering knowledge in the digital age.* New York: McGraw Hill.

Rovai, A. P., Ponton, M. K., & Baker, J. D. (2008). *Distance learning in higher education: Programmatic approach to planning, design, instruction, evaluation, and accreditation.* New York: Teachers College Press.

Russo, T., & Benson, S. (2005). Learning with invisible others: Perceptions of online presence and their relationship to cognitive and affective learning. *Journal of Educational Technology & Society, 8*(1), 54–62.

Ryan, R. M., & Deci, E. I. (2000). Intrinsic and extrinsic motivation: Classic definitions and new directions. *Contemporary Educational Psychology, 25*(1), 54–67. doi:10.1006/ceps.1999.1020 PMID:10620381

Schank, R. (1997). *Virtual learning, A revolutionary approach to building a highly skilled workforce.* New York: McGraw-Hill.

Seaton, J. X., & Schwier, R. (2014). An exploratory case study of online instructors: Factors associated with instructor engagement. *International Journal of E-learning &. Distance Education, 29*(1), 1–16.

Sheridan, K., & Kelly, M. A. (2010). The indicators of instructor presence that are important to students in online courses. *Journal of Online Learning and Teaching, 6*(4).

Simonson, M., Smaldino, S., Albright, M., & Zvacek, S. (2003). *Teaching and learning at a distance: Foundations of distance education* (2nd ed.). Upper Saddle River, NJ: Merrill.

Sorensen, E. K. (2004). Reflection and intellectual amplification in online communities of collaborative learning. In T. S. Roberts (Ed.), Online Collaborative Learning: Theory and Practice, (pp. 242-261). doi:10.4018/978-1-59140-174-2.ch011

Stenbom, S., Cleveland-Innes, M., & Hrastinski, S. (2014). Online Coaching as a Relationship of Inquiry: Mathematics, online help, and emotional presence. In *Eden 2014.* Oxford, UK: Eden.

Stewart, M. (2014, August 21,) *Designing for emergence: The role of the instructor in student- centered learning.* [Web Blog Post]. Retrieved from http://www.hybridpedagogy.com/ Journal/designing-emergence-role-instructor-student-centered-learning

Walkem, K. (2014). Instructional immediacy in elearning. *Collegian (Royal College of Nursing, Australia), 21*(3), 179–184. doi:10.1016/j.colegn.2013.02.004 PMID:25632711

Wolfe, C. (2000). Learning and teaching on the World Wide Web. In C. R. Wolfe (Ed.), *Learning and teaching on the World Wide Web* (pp. 1–22). San Diego, CA: Academic Press.

Wright, R. (2009). Effective kickoff meetings. *Internal Aditor.*

Chapter 5
Interactivity and Immediacy in Online Academic Programs

Neal Shambaugh
West Virginia University, USA

ABSTRACT

Attention to the quality issues of distance education in higher education has focused primarily on courses. Entire academic programs are now delivered online, and faculty members must spend a significant amount of resources in addressing curricular-issues of online programs, as opposed to pedagogical issues for the courses they teach. Priorities for instructor interactivity and immediacy can become explicit goals for all learning experiences in academic programs. This chapter is organized in three parts: (1) the value of using interactivity/immediacy in the design of extended learning academic programs, (2) instructional design best practices for developing interactivity and immediacy in online academic programs, and (3) recommendations for different level of academic programs, including undergraduate, master's, doctoral, and specialized programs, including teacher education, certificates, and professional development.

VALUE OF DESIGNING INTERACTIVITY IN ONLINE ACADEMIC PROGRAMS

The call for increased and improved interactivity between instructor and student in distance education courses also applies to online academic programs. Interactivity and immediacy in courses have been a principal concern of faculty with teaching responsibilities. However, the advising of students that faculty may never meet in person with online programs becomes an important teaching activity. Potential and active students need contact with instructors and staff for information, advising, and human support to begin, move through, and complete an online program. The development of student support systems with new interactive features may increasingly be needed to guide student matriculation in a way that is seamless, automated where possible, and with human contacts as needed.

Student needs are partly informational but also social and emotional, and students view interaction with faculty and staff as the benchmark for quality advising and instruction. Moving academic programs online requires faculty attention to maintain, re-examine, and specify the quality of interaction in courses and advising as an explicit program feature. Thus, one quality measure of online programs becomes

DOI: 10.4018/978-1-4666-9995-3.ch005

interactivity, the degree to which participants in an academic program develop contact and interaction with the world (Miller, 1973), or as Garrison and Shale (1990) have defined all forms of education (including that delivered at a distance) as essentially interactions between content, students, and teachers.

The characteristics of present and future students suggest that interactivity and immediacy be given high priority as design features to be implemented and evaluated across all features of an online academic program. The oldest of the so-called Millennials (also known as Generation Y) are now in their thirties. Millennials see additional education as programs in which they can apply what they learn and still maintain a social life. Behind this group are Generation Z students, born in the mid-1990s, who want to "grow up" now. Rather than feeling entitled as the previous group is sometimes characterized as, Generation Z students are ready to apply their independence, curiosity, and maturity to real-world activities (Levit, 2015). These future college students may prefer educational programs that interact with the real world and provide the "immediacy" to apply what they are learning. Interactivity and immediacy become marketing key words for future college students now in middle and high school.

The first section of this chapter includes the following subsections: role of interactivity in student success in online programs, features of interactivity to attract students, and the value of interactivity as an accountability measure for program monitoring.

Defining Student Success with Interactivity

How do students view success? Students typically regard success in most academic programs as completing a program and using that program for career purposes (Bauerlein, 2009). Outside any debates about the purpose for college, students in graduate distance education programs in particular see the credentials, whether a certificate or a master's degree, as leading to advancement or new careers. Students in these post-undergraduate programs still value the quality of the program in terms of courses, faculty, and responsiveness to student concerns as they inquire, apply to, move through, and complete a program. Interactivity may form the central criterion for attracting and keeping students.

Given the quality assurance pressure that has been brought to bear on online courses, online academic programs can include courses and other experiences that are more tightly designed with program outcomes in mind. Thus, the learning outcomes and subsequent learning products from those courses can be examined for their potential in helping students and instructors achieve those program outcomes. In terms of interactivity, the online academic program can be evaluated in terms of the (a) "interaction of the behaviors of students and instructors and (b) interactivity or the characteristics of the technology systems" (Roblyer & Ekhaml, 2000, pp. 1-2). While interaction and interactivity are frequently used interchangeably, considering the differences as defined above can help educators keep the student-instructor, as well as the student-instructor-system, in the foreground of planning, implementation, and ongoing evaluation.

Matching program goals with interactions. Given the vocational focus of potential students, online academic programs could consider the skills valued in real-world organizations and organize their programs along those skills. Wasko, Teigland, Leidner and Jarvenpaa (2011) identify the following organizational skills: (1) leading a large virtual team of people with diverse demographic backgrounds from across the world without any formal authority over these individuals, (2) successfully developing and implementing strategies under pressure, (3) networking to acquire necessary information and resources, and (4) building trust and managing cross-cultural conflict without face-to-face communication (p. 650).

These organizational skills can be reduced to the following key terms and collectively considered as a skill-learning goal for online academic programs: virtual peer leadership, strategy implementation, information and resource networking, and conflict management.

Thus, if the purpose for the academic program, particularly master's level programs, is vocational, then a direct connection can be made between organizational needs and program outcomes. Although this connection is usually identified in new program proposals, the connection between needs and outcomes needs to show up in the design and evaluation across all courses. What other student experiences, outside of courses, build on these student outcomes? The program skill outcomes of peer leadership, strategy implementation, information and resource networking, as well as conflict management, could be regarded as categories of periodic program evaluation.

Program design activity by the instructional designer and faculty/staff can be framed into a general design question, which is stated as follows: *What x-interactivity and interactions assist y-students and teachers to achieve z-outcomes?* A question cognitively triggers humans to respond. Here Y-participants, students and teachers, can be regarded as co-learners although with different roles (Shambaugh & Magliaro, 2005). The Z-outcomes in our example include peer leadership, strategy implementation, information and resource networking, and conflict management. This question can also be framed as a design research question, so that the program can be systematically studied. Ongoing program study includes "data sources" that are then routinely collected by all those involved in the program so that program evaluation can expand beyond "we have to do it" to actual program improvement.

Attracting and Retaining Students

Interactivity features in online academic programs can be used to attract new students and constitute unique program identities and competitive features. Potential students are drawn to online programs, because they can obtain further education without pausing their careers and life responsibilities (Ruffalo Noel Levitz, 2015). However, one downside to some online programs is the psychological distance that some students experience as compared to their experiences with face-to-face instruction, which include both verbal and non-verbal behaviors. Research has documented the connection between teacher immediacy behaviors and student learning, most recently acknowledging the impact of these behaviors on student motivation, which in turn influence cognitive learning (Swan & Shea, 2005). Faculty members that continually work to understand their students are in a more informed position to make interactivity and immediacy decisions in courses and other learning activities. Decisions on systematic use of interactivity across a program provide unique attributes with which to market these programs for potential students. A unique program identity could develop over time and itself become a branding feature.

The communications literature has identified five forms of social support that students need: informational, emotional, esteem, tangible aid, and social networks (Walther & Boyd, 2002). Social support categories such as these can become criteria for design, implementation, and evaluation of courses and programs. If a program attracts students tapping its interactive and immediacy features and particularly those that address social support needs, then student retention, the other side of the student enrollment numbers challenge, requires that these features be truly offered before, during, and after enrollment. Enrolled students would value any interactivity in online academic programs in which advising and matriculation guides them to timely program completion.

Monitoring and Growing Programs

Ongoing program evaluation is key to monitoring attracting and retaining students, which are key priorities for academic institutions (Selinger, 2015). Because interactivity and immediacy are designed to reduce psychological distance between people, interactivity and immediacy provide accountability measures for program monitoring and program improvement. One benefit from online academic programs is that the criteria for program success and overall program value for students and institution has been established through institutional requirements for new programs and the increased accountability of online programs (Cafferella, 2002).

The functions of interactivity in online academic programs, as suggested by Sims (1999), Wenger (1998), and Wenger et al (2002), can serve as overall program goals and include the following:

1. Enabling learner control.
2. Facilitating student input to program changes.
3. Allowing for communication and participation.
4. Acting as an aid to meaningful learning (Sims, 1999)
5. Creating learning communities (Wenger, 1998; Wenger et al, 2002).

In program discussions one can translate the above interactivity functions into questions, such as "How does our program enable learner control?" How does our program enable student feedback to contribute to program improvement?" "In what ways do courses and other experiences specify varied means of communication and participation that help students?" The meaningful learning function of interactivity can be specified in learning outcomes. As an example, the organizational skills identified earlier of virtual peer leadership, strategy implementation, information and resource networking, and conflict management could be used to design courses and other learning experiences with online academic programs. Thus, the question becomes of "How does our program use interactivity to support program goals as well as individual course goals?"

The fifth program goal, creating learning communities, was added to the Sims (1999) list in order to address the social nature of humans who share common work practices. The Community of Practice (CoP) construct, which was initially grounded in the work of Lave and Wenger (1991), provides physical and virtual structures of activity in which people can learn from one another.

INSTRUCTIONAL DESIGN BEST PRACTICES FOR INTERACTIVITY IN HIGH EDUCATION ACADEMIC PROGRAMS

The second section of this chapter includes the following subsections: first, a systematic analysis and decision-making process is described, a process to determine how interactivity supports learner outcomes and examines the contextual issues of any new innovation. The second subsection section provides recommendations for quality feedback, and the third section provides recommendations on the use of video and program level immediacy and interactivity decisions.

Systematic Analysis and Decision-Making

One way to ensure interactivity in online academic programs is through a systematic analysis and decision process. While instructional design can involve significant time and resources, four important questions regarding learners, content, context, and instruction (Shambaugh & Magliaro, 2005) can provide assistance to developers and instructors. The first three questions provide analysis. What are the student learning characteristics? What is the nature of the content to be learned? What are the major constraints? The answers to these questions provide input to answering the fourth question, which includes design decisions, "What are the specific interactive features to help these students learn the "content"?

Question 1 – Who are the learners? The characteristics of the young people who will enroll in academic programs will require authentic activities, ones that serve to simulate or even become real activities with real consequences. The design of interactivity into learning environments and academic programs can tap a knowledge base consisting of learning principles regarding self-regulation, multimedia learning (Mayer, 2001), motivation, and collaborative and cooperative learning (Abrami, Bernard, Bures, Borokhovski & Tamim, 2012). The more one knows about one's learners the more responsive design and teaching decisions can be made for a course or program. While there are many approaches to profiling the learner, the most overarching approach is through the use of learner characteristics, the various categories that differentiate one person from another.

Question 2 – What is the content? Determining the "full range of the content to be taught," the second instructional design question, prompts designers and instructors to think through the nature of the content to be learned by humans. By understanding what is being asked of the learner to know, to do, or to value, a complete set of learning outcomes can be specified up front. If learning outcomes require problem solving, critical thinking, designing, or other intellectual performance, a social learning and affective issues component needs to be addressed. Thus, the full range of learning outcomes may involve team skills or social interaction in which problems are addressed and options proposed, meaning that these sensibilities, attitudes, and skills need to be and can be assessed (Wiggins & McTighe, 2006). The implications for any course or any academic program where intellectual activity is pursued means that course and program assessments must take into account the full range of human performance that may be required. Acknowledging the demands made upon the learner, the designer/instructor can more appropriately specify interactive learning opportunities where the teaching and assessment are typically intertwined. Frequently, course syllabi do not specify the social nature or affective issues in course learning outcomes.

Question 3 – What are the constraints? While there are many constraints in any instructional problem, most notably time, institutional factors play a large role in the context of any instructional problem in higher education. Success in increasing enrollment produces needs to staff courses and providing student advising. A best practice is to involve faculty, students, and staffs in an ongoing program review, which identifies potential students, examines potential student needs, and existing gaps or adjustments to curriculum. Meanwhile, a limited pool of quality instructors forces academic units to secure adjuncts. A best practice here requires initial attention to vetting, orienting, and evaluating adjunct instructors, after which professional development of adjuncts is recommended, although this stage will add more pressures on support staff. As student numbers increase, the function of advising suggests creating and staffing an advising center for both undergraduate and graduate students. A centralized center provides consistent advising, tracks student performance within a program, and relieves faculty of some of the advising demands. In addition, a centralized center can be responsible for program data collection and review practicum settings for some programs where they are required by accreditation bodies.

Budget pressures further limit the addition of tenure-line faculty who would advise higher numbers of graduate students. In institutions where the reward system prioritizes peer-reviewed research publications over teaching, existing faculty face pressures from increased teaching and advising. A best practice recommendation is to re-examine policies of departments for workload categories of teaching and advising, and any program content area coordination responsibilities. Existing staff descriptions and training may need to evolve to provide critical support to students and faculty. Workload and other resource issues must be taken into account when considering additions, changes, or deletions of programs.

Another set of constraints is instructional development time, supporting staff for training and ongoing assistance, and changing technologies. A major technological constraint/resource for online programs is the Learning Management System (LMS). Two types of affordances include the capability of the LMS for interactivity (Arbaugh & Benbunan-Fich, 2007) and its ease of use by students (Kirschner et al., 2004). Rubin, Fernandes and Avgerinou (2013) determined that "the affordances of the LMS affect instructors, the teaching, social, and cognitive presence within the courses, as well as student satisfaction" (p. 55). Their study determined that this impact on the three types of presence is based partly on course design and instructor actions (Akyol & Garrison, 2010, 2011), but also student perceptions of the LMS for communication and ease of use.

As the LMS provides the delivery technology, budget and staff support from university, college, and departments becomes a primary consideration. One best practice recommendation includes funding of a college-supported center where technology and training support are centralized. Staff members become familiar with academic programs and faculty needs. Such a center becomes, as with a centralized advising center, a visible priority for fund-raising and development activities, and subsequently supports recruitment activities. Some institutions have implemented online quality review programs, such as Quality Matters or the best practices model for online course design of Vai and Sosulski (2011), to provide some consistency in online program features. These quality approaches recommend specific requirements for engaging students and activities that directly support clear and measurable learning outcomes. Careful consideration needs to be made to the demand in resources, such as staff support and faculty time, that will be needed by the institution and individual units to implement such an institutional review process, as well as faculty resistance to any mandated program.

Question 4 – What program features support engagement? Knowing the learners, learning outcomes, and the major constraints provides "front-end" awareness to make decisions for online courses and programs. Such decisions take into account, as Roblyer and Ekhaml (2000) have differentiated, not only the technical issues of interactivity, but the social configuration of interaction between students and instructor. To help us make design decisions, we can return to the design research question to ask and answer the following question: *What x-interactions assist y-students and teachers to achieve z-outcomes?* Again, this design question is based on the idea of Garrison and Shale (1990) that education involves interactions between content, students, and teachers. The response to this question includes decisions on teaching and assessment and how both are related (Herrington, Reeves & Oliver, 2010). One way that the design of interactive learning activities involving teaching/assessment issues can be configured is to tap the research base behind models of teaching, those approaches (e.g., cooperative learning, discussion, direct instruction, advance organizers), which are based on years of research (Joyce, Weil, & Calhoun, 2014).

In summary, systematically thinking through four instructional design questions provides a means to re-examine who the learners are, what is to be learned, what are the limitations, and how designed instruction can incorporate this knowledge into interactive features in both course and program design.

Recommendations for Quality Feedback in Online Courses

Students value quality feedback in any course setting. Three factors that constitute quality feedback in courses and programs include timeliness, consistency, and responsiveness. Timeliness or the speed with which feedback is provided may be the number one attribute that students cite in instructor evaluations. Timeliness in program queries and matriculation issues between a student, advisor, and/or staff person can be just as valuable. Programs can specify for staff and faculty a rough metric for timely feedback of 24 hours for student queries or within a week for student work. Consistency in feedback can sometimes vary over a semester and requires vigilance and practice from the instructor.

Consistent feedback in courses requires that what an instructor says about course policies and procedures is the same across all students. Another aspect of consistency involves feedback on tasks, and while feedback, verbal or written, may vary based on student performance on tasks, an overall consistency is applied. A common complaint from students is hearing that "the instructor changed his mind over the semester so that we weren't ever sure as to what was expected." Timely and consistent information and advice in courses and at the program level are crucial for the program's reputation and student success.

The most difficult feature to achieve for quality feedback is responsiveness or appropriate feedback given the course, the learner, and the context of the course. Being timely and consistent are not enough. Responsive feedback adjusts to unique student needs and past performance. Responsiveness is context-dependent and is qualitative in nature, as opposed to time and consistency-matching features. Responsiveness, while addressing task performance also involves being psychologically supportive or encouraging and an awareness of a person's bio-psycho-social traits. Anderson et al (2001) provides a valuable way of looking at responsive feedback in online settings in terms of verbal immediacy. One type of verbal immediacy includes affective responses between participants, or personal expressions of emotion and feelings, as well as beliefs and values. Cohesive responses, meanwhile, are those online behaviors that build and sustain a sense of group commitment. A third type of verbal immediacy includes interactive responses or behaviors that provide some evidence that another person is engaged to the activity.

Recommendations for Interactivity and Immediacy

Video use. A key skill set for online college instructors to master is video. There are different ways to produce moving images with sounds, including screencasting, video movies, and animation, in a rough order of the skills needed to produce them. Screencasting tools, which record what occurs on the computer screen, have been used to record lectures, presentations, and webinars as well as how-to-use videos for online tools. These tools record screen movement (e.g., cursor movement, drawing, web page access, media) as well as the instructor's voice. Screencasting tools may also be able to insert into the video still images and other video files, and use post-production features to process audio and provide a range of audio and video effects. The resulting file can be exported to an external source and linked in the online LMS. In contrast, traditional movies require attention to audio and lighting and can require significant time and expense to produce. Simulations provide students with near-authentic experiences and have proven very useful in medical schools and professional education (Tekian et al, 1999). While the benefits are high, the work to produce them and keep their content current, however, can be significant.

Video is a typical feature of flipped classrooms where F2F instruction is delivered online with video clips. The classroom setting provides student assistance to work through problems and questions, which may have been raised from the instructional video or subsequent student practice. The amount of time to produce the video clips can be substantial, although economies are realized in future deliveries, even with periodic revision. The key to flipped classrooms is more about what happens in the classroom to support student needs, as well as a competent and responsive instructor (Ogden, Pyzdrowski & Shambaugh, 2014).

The overall value of video as a technology in online academic programs is to increase the type, scope, and depth of interactivity and interaction for the individual student, in particular providing feedback on student performance. Recommendations for video include the following:

- Provide professional development to faculty on the use of video to support learning outcomes.
- Introduce faculty to habits of documenting their courses in terms of activity and student learning products. Screen captures, still images, and summary videos can be used to document teaching activity and showcase for others, faculty and students alike, the nature of what it means to increase interactivity and immediacy.
- Tap the systematic features of instructional design to keep learning in the forefront of teaching decisions.
- Consider the use of screencasting products as an appropriate tool to manage faculty needs to record, edit, and provide an adequate level of post-production.

Undergraduate programs. Undergraduate programs remain predominantly F2F deliveries with online courses used to meet requirements for any common core, academic minor or electives. Online delivery is increasingly being offered in the summer to meet student demand to complete course requirements and minors. Interactive features chosen for undergraduate courses and programs need to be made based on what we are coming to know as today's or tomorrow's undergraduate. This group has been assumed to be characterized by stable features, but uncertain occupational prospects and the social impact from technology and media are influencing new and rapidly changing attributes of young people (Levine & Dean, 2012). Online programs stand to benefit from offering this age group different means of interacting that resonate with social media-based features of their adolescent development. Internal challenges to any re-examination of curriculum will have to address long-standing views by faculty and administrators on what constitutes a "course" and a "program," as well as who the students are. To attract these students, programs need to be designed as interactive programs, rather than add-on features to courses. Responsive academic programs will need to be based on an ongoing review of students, learning outcomes (i.e., "What do you want the graduates to be able to know, do, and value?). The students now in middle and secondary schools will be attracted to programs which market themselves as relevant to their working futures, provide ongoing support that adjusts to their needs, and programs in which they can apply their independence, curiosity, and maturity to real-world activities (Levit, 2015).

Another group of potential undergraduates for online programs is an increasing number of adult students who are place-bound members of families or who military veterans (Ruffalo Noel Levitz, 2015). Traditional institutions will need to examine these audiences for how programs serve their needs, a process that can occur if an institution implements ongoing program review to identify gaps and re-examine the profile of the undergraduate student.

In light of these changes, the following recommendations to address interactivity and immediacy in undergraduate programs are suggested:

- Interactive features will require the ability of the student to communicate with program staff, academic advisors, and course instructors.
- Communications, in terms of text, audio, and video, need to be as seamless as possible and function not only within courses but across programs.
- Personalized learning systems research builds on the features of personalized learning (Wolf, 2010), including flexibility, expanded/redefined teacher role, project-based and authentic learning, student-driven learning paths, and a mastery/competence plan.
- Advising becomes a more dynamic ongoing function, partly automated but keyed to student needs and the time constraints of staff and faculty.
- Public schools have already begun to use dashboards to organize and present information. The value of this visual information for higher education enables institutions to visually represent data from a number of systems. Dashboards enable instructors to monitor student use of online systems (pulling data from an LMS, for example) and program performance. Data is collected, stored, and visually made accessible in the background, while staff and faculty can intervene when necessary. Technology support will need to obtain training on third party vendor products, which enable the trainer to build dashboards on the institutions server and work with spreadsheet data.

Master's programs. Master's programs are designed to enhance one's current skills, perhaps building on a certificate program or providing a new career path. A master's program may consist of professional tracks that enable programs to market their master's programs to specific audiences. The culminating event of many master's programs may provide a capstone course, project, or thesis. The development of skills and competencies drives the design of the program and forms the basis for program goals and course assessment. In turn, engagement features are specified which primarily contribute to knowledge and skill competencies for those tracks, although increasing variety and appeal are not trivial purposes for engaging activities and media materials. Suggestions for program interaction and immediacy in master's programs include the following:

- Adding interactivity features in student support features creates a unique competitive marketing feature for programs. Including testimonials and student case studies demonstrate what they get to do in the program and what they do in their future job.
- Master's level students who encounter online courses and online programs for the first time need a clear orientation to help them be successful. Video orientation using video or screencasting tools provides a personal approach.
- More student-support interactivity is needed to help students while they are in a master's program. These café-like environments should be designed to attract students and provide human-connections with video chat capabilities, features that support not only Communities of Practice but purposeful conversations (Brown, 2005).

- Developing an online community for master's students needs (a) an LMS system, which provides consistent features across courses in a program and an (b) online student support function, which may or may not exist in an LMS.
- The basis for interactive features within courses should be based on program goals. In this way interactivity in individual course instructors supports course learning outcomes as well as interactive consistency across the program.
- Team-building activities can use video and group-chat features to work together on assigned projects, a feature typical in LMS systems. Interactive feedback through audio, video and/or text annotations can be accomplished by screencasting or other software products.
- Student work organized by competencies can be archived online on portfolio sites or portfolio links to a campus LMS. With adequate permission policies in place, portfolios of past work can provide valuable examples of work to students and evidence for program and institutional accreditation.
- The capability of students to complete coursework on mobile devices adds to the responsibilities of technology support groups as well as individual faculty.
- Online course development may need professional development to help faculty address any quality assurance rubric items.
- Each student could also have their own online site connected to the LMS where they can post their portfolio of course-produced artifacts, as well as showcasing other attributes of their personal and work history.
- Video conferencing remains an interactive option in courses, but not often used in the support of program goals. Developing a learning community can be supported using video conferencing tools for advising, information, in-house and external webinars, and other educational uses.

Doctoral programs. Many of the recommendations for master's programs can be adopted in doctoral programs, particularly those which are delivered as hybrid or completely online programs. Some master's programs, while principally vocational in focus, may feed students into doctoral programs. Two major questions face prospective students in doctoral programs, questions that have implications for the design of those programs and interactive program features. First, what will they use a doctoral degree for and will the program prepare them for that use? Second, are they sufficiently motivated to complete a program? Prospective students may seek initials behind their name and continue in their present position or may desire teaching or research tracks in higher education. Research positions carry teaching responsibilities, while some students seek the doctoral degree to primarily teach in higher education institutions. Whatever their focus might be, most doctoral programs feature foundational cores in content areas and research skills plus specialization courses, in addition to conducting original research and reporting the results in a dissertation. In almost all cases, continued motivation to develop research skills, select a research topic, and complete original research becomes a major issue to completing a doctoral program. A curricular question for faculty in doctoral programs becomes "How can we better support students across their program and what role do interactive features play?"

Interactivity within doctoral programs becomes a key strategy to achieving Communities of Practice (CoP) as people move through a doctoral program collectively. Wenger's et al (2002) seven principles for cultivating communities of practice (CoP) include (1) designing for evolution, (2) opening a dialogue between inside and outside perspectives, (3) inviting different levels of participation, (4) developing public and private community spaces, (5) focusing on value, (6) combining familiarity and excitement, and (7) creating a rhythm for the community. To address these principles, the following recommendations are suggested:

- Tap existing personal networks from formal doctoral program cohort groups or informal networks of people developed from individual courses.
- Discover common member interests for research topics, collective activity for other program experiences, or projects outside the doctoral group.
- Part of the key to designing CoP is not to restrict its activities to only tasks required in the program. Request within the LMS and/or other systems features that support conversation, dialogue, and activity both within the program and outside, and to disseminate conversation and ideas within and outside the systems.
- Assign a community facilitator, such as a rotating faculty member, program coordinator, or even a senior graduate student, to monitor conversation and encourages dialogue within and outside the community itself (Brown, 2005). Students gain experience at different levels of the community, whether active or peripheral, or core group or coordinator (Wenger et al, 2002). One or more senior facilitators could easily be identified from more experienced graduate students to lead the doctoral community and receive practicum credit hours. A program requirement could be x-credit hours of community facilitation giving the students documented experience at team-building particularly online experience with teams at a distance.
- Add group facilitation skills as a program outcome and give students practice at working and leading groups.

One of Wenger's (2002) principles, "focusing on value," applies to all academic programs and how these principles can be addressed through interactive course and program features. People participate in a community because there are clear reasons for doing so. As new students move through an academic program, the human productivity of the CoP is contributed, such as papers, projects, and dissertations, and service contributions. A CoP taps the current expertise and emotional support of current group members. Ideas and problems can be forwarded to the group as well as hearing about the experiences of current members. This repository of student and faculty work, which we could regard as intellectual community capital, also serves to disseminate its expertise and value to the outside world and will naturally attract future students to join the program and make their own contributions.

FUTURE RESEARCH DIRECTIONS

- *Development of best practices for creating and sustaining interactivity and immediacy.* How do these practices support course and program outcomes, and the role of instructional design to guide this development?
- *Ongoing study of specific interactivity and immediacy features.* Rubin et al. (2013) has studied the effect of the LMS on online learning outcomes (McGill & Klobas, 2009) and determined that the "affordances of the learning interface affect the Community of Inquiry, and that satisfaction with the LMS hosting a course has a significant independent effect on course satisfaction" (p. 57).

- *New generations of learning management systems.* How does a LMS with increased participant interactions and increased transparency in the use media resources improve the learner experience?
- *Design, development, and evaluation of student support systems.* How can a systematic design, development, and evaluation process inform teaching and program changes?
- *Customized learning support.* How can personalized learning systems, which adapt to student needs, be used for student learning, program completion, and provide data for ongoing program improvement.

CONCLUSION

Interactivity and immediacy can become academic program goals. Such decisions can be made and evaluated across a program and not show up as "hit or miss" features in courses. Interactivity can also become a key marketing strategy. If prospective students value interactivity, they will be attracted to programs, which systematically provide this activity. Interactivity decisions can be systematically made through instructional design. Asking questions about students, content, and constraints lead to informed decisions about interactive features that support learner outcomes. Interactive features must serve a purpose and instructional design can help developers and instructors to examine assumptions behind decisions. An important issue for any academic program is monitoring its performance. Given the increased resources applied to accountability, the "success" of programs must be defined in annual program reviews and how interactivity contributes to student learning and program "success," whatever success is defined to consist of. Finally, all faculty need to be a part of curriculum decisions. Faculty will increasingly need to assume a responsibility to think as much about "programs" as they think about the courses they teach. Such a move will spark resistance by the status quo.

REFERENCES

Abrami, P. C., Bernard, R. M., Bures, E. M., Borokhovski, E., & Tamim, R. M. (2012). Interaction in distance education and online learning: Using evidence and theory to improve practice. In L. Moller & J. B. Huett (Eds.), *The next generation of distance education: Unconstrained learning*. New York: Springer. doi:10.1007/978-1-4614-1785-9_4

Akyol, Z., & Garrison, D. R. (2010). The development of a Community of Inquiry over time in an online course: Understanding the progression and integration of social, cognitive and teaching presence. *Journal of Asynchronous Learning Networks*, *12*(3–4), 4–22.

Akyol, Z., & Garrison, D. R. (2011). Understanding cognitive presence in an online and blended community of inquiry: Assessing outcomes and processes for deep approaches to learning. *British Journal of Educational Technology*, *42*(2), 233–250. doi:10.1111/j.1467-8535.2009.01029.x

Anderson, T., Rourke, L., Garrison, D. R., & Archer, W. (2001). Assessing teaching presence in a computer conferencing context. *Journal of Asynchronous Learning Networks*, *5*(2), 1–17. Also available at http://www.aln.org/alnweb/journal/jaln-vol5issue2v2.htm

Arbaugh, J. B., & Benbunan-Fich, R. (2007). The importance of participant interaction in online environments. *Decision Support Systems*, *43*(3), 853–865. doi:10.1016/j.dss.2006.12.013

Bauerlein, M. (2009). *The dumbest generation: How the digital age stupefies young Americans and jeopardizes our future (or, don't trust anyway under 30)*. London: Jeremy Tarcher/Penguin.

Brown, J. (2005). *The world café: Shaping our futures through conversations that matter*. San Francisco, CA: Berrett-Koehler Publishers.

Cafferella, R. (2002). *Planning programs for adult learners*. San Francisco, CA: Jossey-Bass.

Garrison, D. R., & Shale, D. (Eds.). (1990). *Education at a distance: From issues to practice*. Melbourne, Florida: Krieger.

Herrington, J., Reeves, T. C., & Oliver, R. (2010). *A guide to authentic e-learning*. New York: Routledge.

Joyce, B. R., Weil, M., & Calhoun, E. (2014). *Models of teaching* (9th ed.). Boston, MA: Pearson.

Kirschner, P., Strijbos, J. W., Kreijns, K., & Beers, P. J. (2004). Designing electronic collaborative environments. *Educational Technology Research and Development*, *52*(3), 47–66. doi:10.1007/BF02504675

Lave, J., & Senger, E. (1991). *Situated learning: Legitimate peripheral participation*. Cambridge: Cambridge University Press. doi:10.1017/CBO9780511815355

Levine, A., & Dean, D. (2012). Today's students: Same as always, but more so. *Chronicle of Higher Education*. Retrieved from http://chronicle.com/article/Todays-Students-Same-as/134234/ on June 28, 2015.

Levit, A. (2015). Make way for Generation Z. *New York Times*. Accessed April 21, 2015 at http://www.nytimes.com/2015/03/29/jobs/make-way-for-generation-z.html?_r=0

Mayer, R. E. (2009). *Multimedia learning* (2nd ed.). New York: Cambridge University Press. doi:10.1017/CBO9780511811678

McGill, J., & Klobas, J. E. (2009). A task-technology fit view of learning management system impact. *Computers & Education*, *52*(2), 496508. doi:10.1016/j.compedu.2008.10.002

Miller, D. (1973). *George Herbert Mead: Self, language, and the world*. Austin, Texas: University of Texas Press.

Ogden, L., Pyzdrowski, L., & Shambaugh, N. (2014). A teaching model for the college algebra flipped classroom. In J. Keengwe, G. Onchwari, & J. Oigara (Eds.), *Promoting active learning through the flipped classroom model* (pp. 47–70). Hershey, PA: IGI Global. doi:10.4018/978-1-4666-4987-3.ch003

Roblyer, M., & Ekhaml, L. (2000). How interactive are YOUR distance courses? A rubric for assessing interaction in distance learning. *Online Journal of Distance Learning Administration.* Retrieved on November 8, 2015 from http://www.westga.edu/distance/roblyer32.html

Rubin, B., Fernandes, R., & Avgerinous, M. D. (2013). The effects of technology on the Community of Inquiry and satisfaction with online courses. *The Internet and Higher Education*, *17*, 48–57. doi:10.1016/j.iheduc.2012.09.006

Ruffalo Noel Levitz. (2015). 2015 *Adult learner marketing and recruitment practices benchmark report*. Retrieved November 8, 2015 from www.noellevitz.com/BenchmarkReports

Selinger, J. (2015). The view from the top: What presidents think about financial sustainability, student outcomes, and the future of higher education. *The Chronicle of Higher Education*.

Shambaugh, R. N., & Magliaro, S. G. (2005). *Instructional design: A systematic approach to reflective practice*. Boston, MA: Allyn & Bacon.

Sims, R. (1999). Interactivity on stage: Strategies for learner-designer communication. *Australasian Journal of Educational Technology*, *15*(3), 257–272. Retrieved from http://www.ascilite.org.au/ajet/ajet15/sims.html

Swan, K., & Shea, P. (2005). The development of virtual learning communities. In S. R. Hiltz & R. Goldman (Eds.), *Learning together online: Research on asynchronous learning networks* (pp. 239–260). Mahwah, NJ: Erlbaum.

Tekian, A., McGuire, C. H., McGaghie, W. C., & Associates. C (1999). Innovative simulations for assessing professional competence. Chicago, IL: Department of Medical Education, University of Illinois, Chicago.

Vai, M., & Sosulski, K. (2011). *Essentials of online course design: A standards-based guide*. New York: Routledge.

Walther, J. B., & Boyd, S. (2002). Attraction to computer-mediated social support. In C. A. Lin & D. Atkin (Eds.), *Communications technology and society: Audience adoption and uses of the new media* (pp. 153–188). Cresskill, NJ: Hampton Press.

Wasko, M., Teigland, R., Leidner, D., & Jarvenpaa, S. (2011). Stepping into the Internet: New ventures in virtual worlds. *MIS Quarterly: Management Information Systems*, *35*(3), 645–652.

Wenger, E. (1998). *Communities of practice: Learning, meaning, and identity*. Cambridge, MA: Cambridge University Press. doi:10.1017/CBO9780511803932

Wenger, E., McDermott, R., & Snyder, W. M. (2002). *Cultivating communities of practice*. Cambridge, MA: Harvard Business Press.

Wiggins, G., & McTighe, J. (2006). Understanding by design (2nd ed.). Upper Saddle River, NJ: Merrill/Prentice-Hall.

Wolf, M. A. (2010). Innovate to educate: System [Re]design for personalized learning: A report from the 2010 symposium. Washington, DC: Software & Information Industry Association (SIAA).

ADDITIONAL READING

Anderson, T. (2008). *Theory and practice of online learning* (2nd ed.). Edmonton, AB: AU Press.

Clark, R. E. (1994). Media will never influence learning. *Educational Technology Research and Development*, *42*(1), 21–29. doi:10.1007/BF02299088

Kozma, R. B. (1994). Will media influence learning: Reframing the debate. *Educational Technology Research and Development*, *42*(2), 7–19. doi:10.1007/BF02299087

Swan, K. (2005). *Interface matters: What research says about the mediating effects of course interfaces.* Paper presented at the 20th Annual Conference on Distance Teaching and Learning, Madison, Wisconsin. Retrieved from http://www.uwex.edu/disted/conference/Resource_library/proceedings/04_1076.pdf

Winn, W. (2002). Current trends in educational technology research: The study of learning environments. *Educational Technology Review*, *14*(3), 331–351.

Wolf, M. A. (2010). *Innovate to educate: System [Re]design for personalized learning: A report from the*

Chapter 6
The Human Element:
Fostering Instructor Presence through Online Instructional Videos

Melanie Hibbert
Columbia University, USA

Adrienne A. Garber
Columbia University, USA

Kristine Rodriguez Kerr
Columbia University, USA

Matthea Marquart
Columbia University, USA

ABSTRACT

One of the affordances of instructional videos in online courses is that they provide the opportunity for faculty to increase their instructor presence in asynchronous learning environments. This chapter draws upon qualitative interview data collected from student perspectives about their experiences with online course media, and discusses emergent themes from student interviews related to increased instructor presence such as trustworthiness (social context, branding, production values, nonverbal communication), personalization (humor, colloquial language), and feedback. That is, videos that encompassed these qualities were evaluated and discussed in ways that reflected more social presence (Dunlap & Lowenthal, 2014) and instructor immediacy (Baker, 2010), and less social distance (Magee & Smith, 2013). Our findings suggest that online instructional videos can be an effective tool to reduce social distance between instructors and students. This chapter concludes with suggestions for online education practitioners on how to produce and use instructional videos to increase instructor presence and immediacy.

INTRODUCTION

The videos are definitely better than just reading the material because it has more of that human element. (Student interview, 2014)

The importance of the above student quote is made more significant when one considers the well-documented experiences of isolation that are commonly reported by students of online courses. In addition to feeling isolated from each other, Smith and Taveras (2005) point out that online students often

DOI: 10.4018/978-1-4666-9995-3.ch006

complain about feeling as though their professors were absent from their online courses. However, we believe the above quote, taken from one of several in-depth qualitative interviews with online students at Columbia University School of Professional Studies, alludes to the felt sense of connection that can be communicated via asynchronous instructional video.

As a team comprised of instructional designers, media specialists, and online support strategists, we became interested in unpacking the notion of "human element" as something to actively strive to develop within our online learning courses. Achieved in a variety of ways, this chapter focuses specifically on instructional videos within online courses and our belief that these videos can be developed for, by, and with instructors as strategic tools to increase social presence (Dunlap & Lowenthal, 2014) and instructor immediacy (Baker, 2010), and lessen social distance (Magee & Smith, 2013). Drawing from qualitative interviews with students across numerous online courses, we offer suggestions at the conclusion of this chapter to that end. That is, we suggest a variety of ways for online education practitioners to produce asynchronous instructional video as a means of positively impacting students' felt sense of instructor presence and immediacy by carefully considering both the verbal and nonverbal elements of instructional video. These findings have design implications for instructors, instructional designers, media specialists and subject matter experts. In offering these research-based suggestions, we would like to stress the importance of striving to understand context in any educational design process. That is, these suggestions are not meant as generic, tech-driven concepts, but rather as possible tools to be thoughtfully adapted across a variety of online contexts.

It hopefully is then fitting that we begin the following background section with information on our context, before discussing the history of educational videos as well as theories of social distance and immediacy that serve as our conceptual frame.

BACKGROUND

Context

The School of Professional Studies at Columbia University (SPS) is part of the Graduate School of Arts and Sciences. SPS offers a variety of master's degrees and certificate programs built around emerging and interdisciplinary professions. Of these degrees and programs, approximately half offer courses that are delivered as online or hybrid, meaning that a significant amount of course activities occur both synchronously and asynchronously in online learning environments (although there are a handful of face-to-face residency sessions per semester). Courses in the online programs are hosted on the learning management system (LMS) Canvas, where the majority of the course materials are posted and social exchanges occur: syllabi, case studies, readings, quizzes, resources, discussion forums, assignments, etc. Most of the courses also have weekly "live sessions" integrated directly into the LMS and hosted on the webinar platform Adobe Connect, where students and faculty members meet for approximately 60-90 minutes in virtual real-time events that encompass lectures, class discussion, group work, student presentations, and other forms of classroom interactions.

An internal development team at this graduate school (including instructional designers, course developers, educational technologists, online instructional support, and media producers) collaborate with faculty to produce and execute these online courses. The production cycle for these courses typically occur the semester prior to when the course runs. By the start of the production cycle, the academic program directors have approved the course syllabi, so there is an already-established scope and sequence to the course with course learning objectives aligned with the larger program objectives. Together with the instructional designer, the faculty member further plans their courses by distilling course-level learning objectives into individual class session learning objectives that are aligned with assessments and instructional strategies in a course design document. The faculty member works closely with the instructional designer and other team members to articulate media opportunities, technology needs, webinar format, and other course elements that realize his or her course design plan.

Due to the fact that SPS historically has not offered tenure in its organizational structure, the faculty at SPS are adjuncts or lecturers, unless they have a dual appointment as a tenured faculty member through another school at the university. Most are professionals in the field, often working as consultants or full-time employees at organizations and agencies, such as advertising firms, accounting firms, consulting firms, or technology companies. As the programs in this school are designed for professionals in emerging fields, it is an intention of the school to hire faculty who are highly active in and responsive to the practicalities of their professions and industries. Thus, like most institutions of higher education in the U.S., SPS relies heavily on adjunct and contingent instructors. According to the American Association of University Professors' tabulation of data from the U.S. Department of Education Integrated Postsecondary Education Data System (IPEDS), part-time faculty at all postsecondary institutions that participate in federal student aid programs made up 51.4% of instructional staff in 2011, up from 31.4% in 1976 (Curtis, 2014).

The student profiles for this graduate school vary by degree and program; for instance, the average age of a student entering a program in actuarial science is 23, whereas the average age of a student entering the landscape architecture program is 40. The median age of the student population is 27 years old; 25% are international citizens. Seventeen percent of all students held advanced degrees upon admission, and 25% of mid-career students (defined as those with over 10 years of experience) held advanced degrees upon admission. This graduate student population is comprised of adult learners whom (to generalize) embody adult learner characteristics such as self-direction, internal motivation, and goal orientation (Fidishun, 2000).

Educational Video

Video has been a tool supporting education for many years (Sheppard, 2003). In WWII, filmstrips were studied as a resource for training soldiers (Hovland, Lumsdaine, & Sheffield, 1949). Instructional television developed in the 1950s and 1960s, and Public Broadcasting Service (PBS) began in 1970, which created a wide range of educational television content such as Sesame Street. Video is a medium that has the ability to involve both auditory and visual symbol systems, creating a multisensory environment. There are many educational possibilities offered via video, such as simulations, dynamic modeling, conceptual visualizations, narrative content, etc. (Baggett, 1984).

In online education and distance learning, video regularly has an integral role in course delivery. Since students are not present in a physical classroom, videos are often used to convey information that would typically be delivered during classroom time, such as instructional lectures. In the context of SPS, the videos our team produces have a wide range in both purpose and production value; some of the types of media we have created include animated pieces, documentaries, guest speaker interviews, content lectures, simulations, scripted scenarios with actors, and other types of videos. Based on this work, we have found that video pieces produced for our online courses have allowed instructors to expand opportunities for students to individualize their learning experience by giving them the opportunity to consume said videos while learning at their own pace and according to their interest, prior knowledge, and learning objectives. Further, as suggested by Anderson's Online Learning theory, our research shows that learning effectiveness in using instructional videos is influenced by the interactions and communication fostered by and among the instructor and his or her students (Anderson, 2004). The level of interaction depends on instructor immediacy and instructor presence established in the online learning environment.

Social Distance

In describing the theoretical logic connecting power to social distance, Magee and Smith (2013) define social distance as an experience, or subjective perception, of distance from one person to another. In their review of research on social distance, Magee and Smith emphasize the "degree of felt closeness to another person" as an important aspect of social distance (2013, p. 159). Similar to their borrowing of research on social closeness (Kelly et al 1983), which depends critically on the interdependence of two actors, we seek to make a further link to the theorizing of social presence in the field on online learning. That is, this study is based on the recognition that online learning is most effective when it is conceived as an inherently social endeavor and designed with social interactions between instructors and learners in mind. Social distance, in particular the social distance between instructors and learners, can be lessened by design efforts that seek to increased instructor social presence.

Increasingly used as a theoretical framing in the field of computer mediated online learning, numerous authors have recognized social presence as one of the most important aspects of online learning (Sung & Mayer, 2012). Social presence in this context was initially defined as the degree to which a person is perceived as "real" in mediated communications (Gunawardena & Zittle, 1997; Tu, 2002; Yen & Tu, 2011). Tu and McIssac (2002) worked to further defined social presence for online learning environments as the degree of feeling, perception, and reaction of being connected via CMC to another intellectual entity. In their review of this literature, Sung and Mayer (2013) note numerous studies that highlight social presence as positively impacting online learners' interaction and learning, learners' achievement, learners' satisfaction, and the development of a sense of community. Not surprisingly, numerous studies have noted that a lack of social presence occurs in courses that also have reported higher levels of student frustration, negative attitudes toward the teacher's effectiveness, and lower level of reported affective learning (Sung & Mayer, 2012). In research that has been conducted about cognitive, social and teaching presence, the consensus is that "teaching presence is a significant determinate of student satisfaction, perceived learning and sense of community" (Garrison, 2007, p.67).

Although the importance of cultivating strong social presence for online courses is clear, as Dunlap & Lowenthal (2015) note, it often remains challenging to establish a consistent and adequate level of social presence in the development of online courses. This may be due, in part, to what Sung and Mayer (2013) list as part of the fundamental nature of social presence—that social presence may relate to feeling rather than reason. Despite this difficulty, we agree with Kim, Kwon, & Cho's statement that "social presence, among other factors, is an important concept to be facilitated, developed, and sustained in distance higher education" (2011, p. 1512). In conducting this research study, we first seek to understand learners' sense of instructor social presence in online environments by working to "identify the facets (or factors) of online learners' affective feelings of social presence" (Sung & Mayer, 2013, p. 1739). We aim to then use these findings to make suggestions for instructional designers, media specialists, and subject matter experts to create and sustain teaching and social presence by "setting the climate" (Garrison, 2007), specifically through online video.

It is important to note, that we see this work as answering Remesal & Colomina (2013) call for research that "should consider the instructor as a highly responsible agent of SP [social presence] in any e-learning experience" (p. 366). With this in mind, the following section explores theories of communication immediacy as a way to impact instructor social and teaching presence in online courses.

Immediacy

For decades, educational communication scholars have studied immediacy behaviors (and their relationship to student attitudes and learning) in face-to-face classrooms and traditional spaces of learning. Originally conceptualized by Mehrabian (1967, 1969, 1981), immediacy refers to the use of communication behaviors that reduce social and psychological distance between two individuals. Immediacy behaviors include both verbal and nonverbal forms of expression, which can be purposefully incorporated by instructors within a learning environment. As Wood and Backer (2004) explain, an example of verbal immediacy would be an instructor use of the word "we" to foster an increased felt sense of closeness among learners. Wood and Baker's examples of nonverbal immediacy, which can also increase a felt sense of closeness among learners, include facial expressions, eye contact, posture, proximity, and touch. Particularly because of the verbal and nonverbal distinction, we found this conceptual framing useful in our analysis of instructors' use of video in the online context. That is, we see conceptual overlap in the discussion of "multi-dimensionality of immediacy behaviors" with the multimodal affordances of instructional video. This overlap, we argue, becomes particularly important when considered in the context of online learning environments. "The online learning environment allows instructors to incorporate verbally immediate behaviors easily with careful design of the course content and written interactions with students" (Baker, 2010, p. 5). Video is a medium that allows for instructors to communicate with their students through verbal and nonverbal means.

Although immediacy was originally developed in the interpersonal communication context, decades of research has sought to better understand instructor immediacy in online learning environments (Arbaguh, 2001). Focusing on instructor immediacy in online learning environments, Baker's 2010 study documents a statistically significant positive relationship between instructor immediacy and instructor presence. Not surprisingly given the review of research on social presence above, Baker's study also notes the linear combination of instructor immediacy and presence was also a statistically significant predictor of student affective learning, cognition, and motivation. It is important to note that "weak manipulations of teacher immediacy" in online environments did not show this correlation (Campbell, 2014). Wood and Baker (2002) point out that interaction alone, does not create a positive social dynamic in the online classroom. Rather they found that an instructor's understanding of immediacy dynamics was essential for impacting the quality of communication. In our research we view asynchronous instructional video as a site to thoughtfully design instructor verbal and non-verbal immediacy behaviors within online courses.

METHODS

Thirteen graduate students enrolled in part-time master's degree programs were interviewed for this study. These interviews entailed in-depth semi-structured conversations, conducted in order to gain an understanding of the "lived experience" of students as viewers, including therefore and how they perceived their course videos (Seidman, 2012). Semi-structured interviews have an exploratory nature, allowing participants to provide detailed descriptions of the subject and to reconstruct and integrate the meaning of their experiences (Kvale, 1996; Seidman, 2012). Although the interviews were guided by an Interview Protocol, they were conversational, and allowed for the interviewer to ask participants to repeat, elaborate upon, or clarify topics they discussed.

In addition to verbal interviews, user experience "talk-throughs" were conducted in the interview sessions, in which participants watched online instructional videos that were both part of and outside of their program content. In these talk-throughs, participants watched videos in real time, and discussed what they noticed, made meaning from, what stood out to them, and in general articulated their viewing experiences and reactions aloud. The talk-throughs and verbal interviews were recorded via screen-capture software and audio recording devices. The interviews lasted between 30-60 minutes, and were conducted over phone, Skype, and in-person at times convenient to participants. Once the interviews were completed, they were transcribed and uploaded to the cloud-based data management system. The interviews were subsequently analyzed for emerging themes using the data analysis method of grounded theory (Glaser & Strauss, 1967). These findings are guided through frameworks of instructor social distance and immediacy, as outlined above.

FINDINGS

The analysis of the qualitative data suggest that videos offer a way to reduce social distance in online educational spaces, as well as communicate instructor presence to students enrolled in online master's programs at SPS. These findings echo the work of Borup, West, and Graham (2011) who found "a large majority of students indicated feeling that the video-based communication made their instructors seem more real, present, and familiar" (p. 195). The findings are organized around three themes: trustworthiness, personalization, and feedback, and direct quotes from interview transcripts are excerpted and analyzed to support these themes.

Trustworthiness

[Guest speaker] seems like a trusted resource. He speaks with authority and confidence. Also I know [the professor] is from that world and has a broad professional network, and she will curate people top in their field. —Student interview, 2014

Establishing trustworthiness is one way to reduce social distance (Buchan et al, 2002). Particularly salient in educational contexts, trust and low social distance create environments conducive for learning. As Sung and Mayer (2013) found in their literature review, social presence and low social distance positively impacts online learners' satisfaction and achievement. The following section discusses qualitative data excerpts from student interviews, in which participants explained their experiences with online instructional videos in relation to trustworthiness. These findings have design implications for producing online instructional videos, as certain trustworthiness factors can be intentionally implemented in order to reduce the social distance between instructors and learners. This section is organized around three subcategories related to trustworthiness.

Social Context and Nonverbal Communication

Throughout several of the interview talk-throughs, as participants verbalized what they were watching and their sense-making, many discussed how a speaker seemed like an "authority" from their impressions. As one participant articulated, *"the speaker seems like an authority"*; another explained regarding another video, "[the speaker] *seemed like a trusted resource"*; still another said, "[the speaker] *definitely seems like an expert."* When prompted to further explain why they believed the speaker was an expert, participants responded by addressing one (or both) dimensions: a). the social context with which the speaker was associated; and b). the nonverbal communication (such as body language).

When discussing the trustworthiness of speakers in relation to their social contexts, students generally spoke of two reasons why they trusted a speaker: because of the presenter's association with other people they trusted, or because of the organization or institution with which the speaker was connected. In the example that begins this section, the interviewed student explained the credibility she assigned the instructor, and that she knows the instructor is involved in *"that world"* (in this instance, the New York City advertising field). To offer some background, the participant was discussing a course in a communications program. The instructor she refers to (*"from that world"*) has over 15 years of experience in the marketing and advertising business; previously, this instructor ran a major marketing campaigns in Asia, and also worked for many years at well-known advertising agencies in New York City.

In the interview excerpt highlighted at the beginning of the section, the participant makes the assumption that the instructor arranged for this guest speaker to be in one of the course videos (which in this specific example, that was the case; in other courses, the media team or the program director arrange for industry speakers to appear on camera). The student assumed the instructor invited the speaker to explain his professional experiences to the class, and knowing the instructor is "*from that world*" (implying the instructor has industry knowledge and expertise), by association, the student trusted the speaker to also have expertise and industry knowledge. In other examples, participants conferred social capital and trustworthiness to speakers who were associated with other guest speakers (not just the faculty member). As one student mentioned, *"I know he's impressive because I met one of his colleagues before at a* [face to face] *residency who was also really good."* In this case, the student associated one of the speaker's professional colleagues with him, and because he found the colleague to be *"really good,"* he described the speaker as *"impressive,"* strictly through social context and association.

Participants also conferred trustworthiness to speakers based on the institution to which they were connected. For example, in one interview a student explained, *"I think he's an authority because he's the Chief Strategy Officer at Deutsch. I mean, Deutsche is a big-deal global agency."* The trustworthiness assigned to this speaker was not through proximity to the instructor, nor through his peers and colleagues, but rather through the respect and trust this student held with the speaker's place of employment (see Figure 1). The student was familiar with this company (Deutsche), and described it as a "*big-deal*" and "*global*" agency. Because of the speaker's high-ranking position at this respected agency, the student described him as an "*authority.*"

Participants evaluated speakers as trustworthy through their social contexts, but they also conferred authoritative status upon speakers through non-verbal elements found in the speakers' on-camera delivery. In one observational interview, a student evaluated the presenter in a video as "*trusted*," and when prompted to elaborate, she explained, "*he speaks with authority and confidence*." This echoed other interviews; rather than assigning trustworthiness related to the content delivered, participants spoke more about the *manner* in which the content was delivered—the posture, the body language, the tone of voice. As one student explained, *"[the speaker] seems confident, conversational, and comfortable."* In another interview, a participant said, "*he speaks in a way that he knows what he's talking about*." In these conversations, students' sense-making focused on the non-verbal aspects communicated through the videos. It should be stated that, of course, students had the contextual knowledge that these speakers are featured in videos, embedded within an institutional course setting, and so it is likely this context influenced their association with the personal qualities of "authority." It should also be noted that many of the videos featured speakers who were white and male, identities associated with power and authority (McIntosh, 2003). However, it is noteworthy that when asked to describe *why* a specific person seemed authoritative (outside of the social and contextual factors), students did not refer to the actual content delivered, (i.e. "the speaker is drawing from sound methodologies in the discipline"). Instead, they discussed the nonverbal communicative resources found in the videos—i.e. the presenter's tone of voice, posture, etc.

Institutional Branding

Throughout talk-throughs conducted with interview participants, in which they watched videos in "real time" and discussed aloud their sense-making of these artifacts, one element that was often considered

Figure 1. A screenshot from a guest speaker video; this speaker was evaluated as trustworthy due to his role and institutional affiliation with an advertising agency

This video is hosted on Kaltura, content copyright by School of Professional Studies, Columbia University, 2015. Screenshot taken by Melanie Hibbert, 2015.

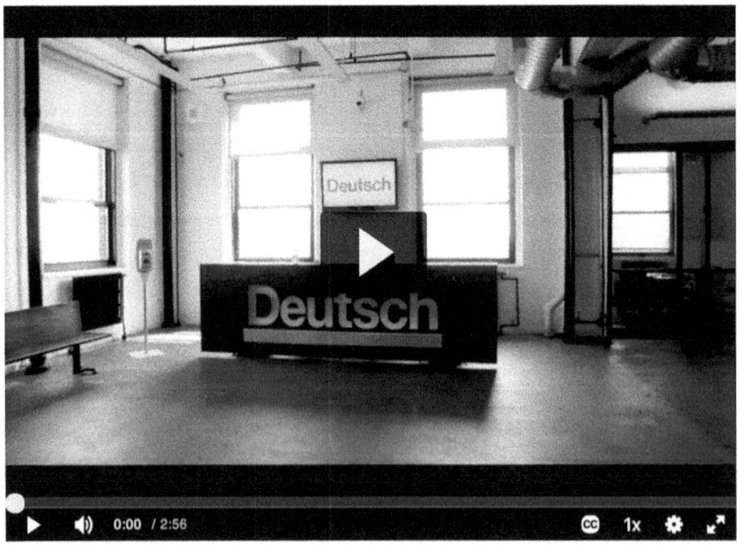

was the institutional branding present in the videos—this includes resources such as the institutional logo, the school's colors, the opening title sequences, etc. These branding elements influenced the ways in which the participants viewed and made-meaning from these videos. In particular, these branding elements were generally talked about in a way that students assigned status to these elements, and evaluated them in such a way that contributed towards their trustworthiness of these artifacts.

All of the videos that interview participants watched and discussed contained institutional branding, such as: a three-second title sequence that includes the institution's colors, logo, as well as text stating the program, School of Professional Studies, and Columbia University (Figure 2). If there was not an opening sequence, the videos had a watermark in the lower right-hand corner; the watermark is a small graphical element of the university's crown logo, containing no text, and is just a symbol. While some of what students discussed in relation to the opening sequence could be considered constructive criticism (such as, *"I would prefer to hear more sound in the opening credits,"* and *"to me, the Columbia blue color seems kind of dark, it almost looks purple"*), participants generally evaluated these branding elements in positive terms. Some interview excerpts include, *"I'm definitely impressed with the Columbia graphics and background*"; "*I like that it's clear it's Columbia's branding*"; "*I really appreciate that there is Columbia branding, I would be disappointed if it wasn't there*"; and "*I like the watermark on the lower right-hand corner*." When asked to further elaborate why they liked it, or why they would be "*disappointed if it wasn't there,*" students responded by explaining the gravitas of the logo, and its explicit connection with the university. For example, one student explained, "*it makes it seem more legit*." Another student said, "*The Columbia logo sets the stage for what you're about to see. It sets the expectation that what you're going to see is high-quality, it's academic.*"

The branded sequences involve a multimodal orchestration of colors, font, movement, and symbols; the reception of these semiotic resources is such that it's associated with the higher education institution.

Figure 2. A screenshot demonstrating institutional branding, from the opening introduction of a course video

This video is hosted on Kaltura, content copyright by School of Professional Studies, Columbia University, 2015. Screenshot taken by Melanie Hibbert, 2015.

The respondents applied a further layer of meaning when this branding is connected with video artifacts; they explained how this semiotic layer confers legitimacy, or "*sets the stage*" that the content will be "*high-quality*." These branded graphic elements contribute to the trustworthiness recipients assign to the online videos, and shape their viewing experiences.

Production Values

If I see that it's not high quality, it makes me more suspicious of it honestly. I feel like it's not going to be as informative and I'd be less likely to watch them. —Excerpt from student interview

Throughout the interviews with participants, production values was a topic explored and investigated, with questions explicitly posed regarding this theme. "Production values" is an all-encompassing term that refers to the look, feel, and general quality of a video. A simplistic definition is that "amateur production values" would be a video created with amateur tools and techniques, such as shaky hand-held camerawork, poor framing of a subject, or distorted audio; "professional production values" might include a studio setting with backdrops and lighting, shot on a tripod, using mixed audio from a microphone. The media created for the online courses by the in-house production team would be considered "professional," (employing professional camerawork, lighting, sound, post-production, etc.); however, there is media in some of the courses that is "amateur," such as screen-captured videos the instructors created themselves. It should be noted that one can produce "professional" seeming production values *without* a media team or expensive studio.

While talking with participants, many spoke of how they viewed something with high production values as more trustworthy; they assigned meaning to the design elements of videos related to the "professionalism," i.e. the camerawork, the lighting, the general look-and-feel. As one student explained, "*If I see that it's not high quality, it makes me more suspicious of it honestly. I feel like it's not going to be as informative and I'd be less likely to watch them.*" This student explains her perspective that "high quality" correlates more with "informative"; and the videos that are not as high of quality, she evaluates as "more suspicious."

Another student discussed his assessment of the videos that he watched in his online courses:

They're definitely well produced. You can tell they're done professionally. The speaker is lit well. The microphone levels are balanced. They're getting video'ed in a nice space. They're definitely professionally done and I can tell. You can tell there are resources, there are university resources spent on ensuring that the videos are of high quality....I'm more likely to tune into something that has like, a title card and then a wipe to the actual lecturer, versus 'here's doctor so- and-so' in a fluorescent room and there's a camera in the back of the classroom and there's a lot of ambient room noise. Whereas you get a more polished video with a little bit of intro and a little bit of intro music and it fades, it just makes it more, it makes it a more enjoyable experience. And it just seems more legitimate. —Student interview, 2014

This participant speaks to the design elements in the videos related to production values—"the speaker is lit well. The microphone levels are balanced. They're getting videoed in a nice space"—and assigns meaning to them, describing the video as, "they're definitely professionally done and I can tell." The student further deduces that because the production values are "professionally done," this implies the university has dedicated resources towards producing these media pieces. The interviewee then contrasts this type of video with a lower-quality video, hypothetically in a *"fluorescent room"* setting, with poor camerawork (*"there's a camera in the back of the classroom"*) and poor audio (*"a lot of ambient room noise"*). The participant considers the distinctions between the two videos—the high quality video and the hypothetical low quality video—and evaluates the differences between the two viewing experiences. He describes the higher quality video as more *"more enjoyable"* and *"more legitimate."* He explains he would confer greater trust in the higher quality video.

These excerpts are pulled from a small sample size, and reflect subjective evaluations related to student experiences with production values related to online instructional videos. However, a consistent theme emerged wherein the students conferred greater trust towards videos they perceived as incorporating higher production values (Figure 3). It should be stated that instructors can establish "professional" seeming production values without large amounts of resources (such as studio space, media production professionals, or high-end equipment and software); rather, simple techniques related to lighting, framing, and audio can be utilized in order to achieve relatively "high" production values. The checklist later in the chapter provides concrete tips for creating quality production values using lo-fi, inexpensive, and simple tools.

Personalization

Mayer (2008) has established the "personalization principle," which asserts that people perform better on individual outcome assessments when words in a multimedia presentation are delivered in a conversational style rather than a formal style. Effective tactics for creating a conversational style include using the first person rather than the third person (such as "you" or "I), as well as directly messaging the learner (Moreno & Mayer, 2004). This also relates to the "voice principle" (Mayer, 2008) which states

Figure 3. A screenshot from a video that could be considered having "high" production values; this was a three-camera shoot, produced in a studio with professional lighting and audio

This video is hosted on Kaltura, content copyright by School of Professional Studies, Columbia University, 2015. Screenshot taken by Melanie Hibbert, 2015.

that people learn more from material delivered by a person, rather than a robotic/artificial voice. While this study did not measure outcome assessments, the qualitative findings from student interviews echo the personalization principle. Students discussed, reflected, and evaluated instructor videos that incorporated humor and informal language in positive terms. These personalized styles and tactics contribute towards the reduction of social distance, and instructor immediacy. As Wood and Backer (2004) explain, using verbal deliveries such as "we" and nonverbal techniques (facial expressions, eye contact, posture, etc) create immediacy, and closer sense of proximity among learners. The following section offers more details related to the subcategory of personalization, focusing on humor and colloquial language.

Humor

The most engaging videos for me is when the professors use wit and humor...I've laughed through some of the videos. There's actually been some slightly witty, funny jokes about what we're learning, and I've actually laughed about them. I'm engaged, I'm reacting to them. Hands down, those are my favorite interviews. Because it keeps you interested. (Student interview, 2014)

This is one example of how a student evaluates the use of humor in a video. The student self-reports that the "most engaging" videos are when the professor uses "wit and humor." This participant explains her response to these videos: "I've actually laughed about them." She then further elaborates that her experiences with videos that incorporate humor are that she is "engaged" and "reacting to them," and it keeps her "interested." To reiterate, videos that the viewer considers humorous are what she also considers "the most engaging" (see Figure 4). The use of humor is one way for instructors to create personalization, and connect with their students. As social presence may relate more to a feeling than reason (Sung & Mayer, 2013), affective qualities have been proposed to further build upon the social

Figure 4. An example of an instructor telling a joke in an online course video, in a lecture related to finance
This video is hosted on Kaltura, content copyright by School of Professional Studies, Columbia University, 2015. Screenshot taken by Melanie Hibbert, 2015.

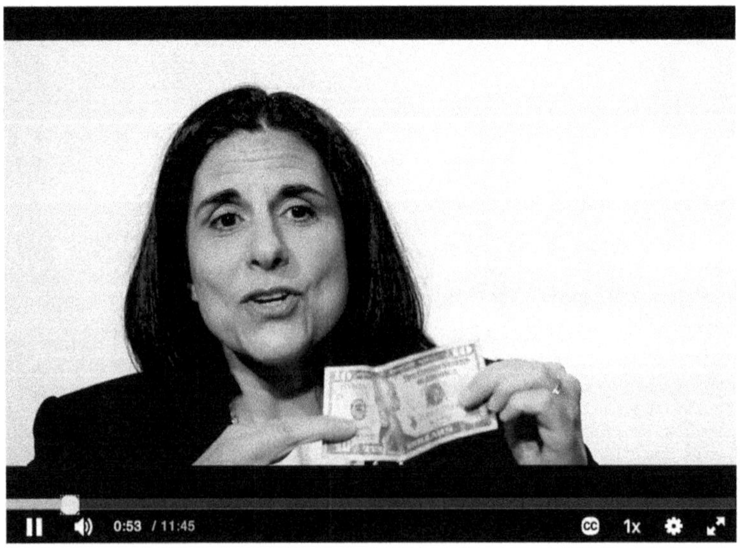

presence framework developed by Garrison, Anderson, and Archer (2000). Use of humor is one quality established by Rourke et al. (2007), and is one way to reduce social distance; it is also considered an important indicator of social presence (King, 2008).

Colloquial Language

The [specific course video] could have been better if the speakers seemed more comfortable. I think because they didn't feel comfortable on camera, the video didn't feel comfortable....it felt very stiff and formal. I think if it had felt more conversational, and they spoke more informally, it would have been better. (Student interview, 2014)

The excerpt from this interview is from a conversation about a video, featuring a faculty member interviewing a guest speaker, which a student evaluated as ineffective. When prompted to explain what could have made the video stronger, the student responded by describing the speakers as uncomfortable, and "stiff and formal." While that might pertain more to the speakers' non-verbal communication and body language, this student also mentioned the speakers' language and manner of speaking. This student describes that if interactions had been more "conversational" and "informal," the video would have been "better."

Informal language and using words such as "we" can reduce social distance and foster instructor immediacy (Wood & Backer, 2004). When producing instructional videos with faculty, we often remind them that videos should not be a replacement for text. Very formal and academic language well suits research articles, papers, and other text-based forms; however, speaking in more informal and conversational tones on video can help connect instructors with their students, and reduce social distance.

Feedback

Feedback is a category that emerged based on interview data when students discussed videos that instructors created themselves through lo-fi tools such as webcams, produced in order to offer individualized feedback or additional instruction for difficult topics. A powerful affordance of online learning management systems is that instructors can use webcams to create personalized videos addressing individual students, such as offering video feedback on a written assignment (as opposed to text-only comments). Video used in this way, as a tool to offer quick feedback produced through lightweight methods, is arguably a way to create instructor immediacy in online environments. Although explored through the one example below, we hope to conduct further research on the use of video as a tool for responsiveness, and a way for instructors to offer feedback and immediacy to their students.

The following demonstrates how an instructor employed lo-fi video tools to connect with students:

And she [the instructor] did all kinds of things, she did the prepared videos that were videoed in your studio, and those were fine, and she did some kind of ad-hoc ones at home, based wherever she was, those were really helpful. And there were the WebEx sessions which she did when we needed it, and she recorded those and posted those as well. (Student interview, 2014)

In this instance, the student explains videos produced by one faculty member in one of his courses. In this case, he was describing an example when the instructional videos were helpful to him in learning the material (specifically, financial math concepts). As he described the videos, his explanation shifted towards the effectiveness of the instructor, and how she filled in gaps for students who were having difficulty understanding the material. First the participant references how the instructor "did the prepared videos that were videoed in your studio"—the student alludes to content-lecture videos created by the online production team. These were unit overview videos, approximately 5-15 minutes long, where the faculty member explained core concepts and illustrated how to work through math formulas. The videos were recorded in a professional studio with professional lighting, audio, and camerawork, although the production values could be considered as relatively basic with "talking head" visuals and solid black or white backdrops.

This participant first describes, "the prepared videos that were videoed in your studio," and then explains, "and she did some kind of ad-hoc ones at home." In that instance, the participant is referring to a series of screen-recorded videos the instructor produced on her own computer, using the screen-capture software Camtasia, accompanied by her presentations on webcam. The instructor created these videos as supplemental resources for her students, and they were generated as a response to needs of students for additional lecture content and exposition. These videos could be described as "lo-fi," with visuals of presentation slides, audio recorded from the built-in microphone of the computer, and run times of approximately 45-60 minutes.

The third element the participant mentions, "there were the WebEx sessions which she did when we needed it, and she recorded those and posted those as well"—in this case, the participant is talking about live webinar sessions, which the instructor held outside of regularly scheduled class times as optional question-and-answer sessions for students looking for additional academic assistance. (These sessions occurred outside of the institutionally supported Adobe Connect webinars, so did not include a technical staff member on hand to assist with facilitation). These webinars were recorded by the faculty member, and then posted as video files on the online course site for students to watch, rewatch, download, etc. An added layer to this discussion is that while the participant is referencing the course "videos," and how they assisted him with learning, a significant dimension to this conversation is that the instructor put in substantial efforts to help students understand the material. The faculty member produced additional screen-recorded lectures, and held optional webinar sessions (which were also recorded as video files)—this was added content created outside of the designated scope of the course, and arose in order to address students' comprehension difficulties.

IMPLICATIONS AND FUTURE RESEARCH

Based on our findings above, factors that we have found that suggest a role in fostering instructor immediacy and presence across asynchronous instructional video include: the instructor's ability to establish trustworthiness through social context and nonverbal communication, institutional branding, and production values; instructors' personalization of videos through humor and colloquial language; and the potential importance of feedback through individualized, quickly produced responses. As noted above, we are hoping in future research to focus specifically on video feedback, and how it relates to social connections. Additional future research considerations include the ways in which interactive tools and videos can increase social presence, and foster instructor immediacy.

To establish increased instructor presence and immediacy in online course through the effective use of instructional videos, online education practitioners can take into account the following suggestions as they design their online learning environments.

RECOMMENDATIONS

Understanding that that a variety of online education practitioners develop content across unique sets of circumstances and resources, we've compiled recommendations that can be thoughtfully adapted across a variety of online contexts. These tips and techniques have been compiled from the above research findings, as well as our team's experience working with online instructors, and address inexpensive and relatively quick ways to increase the production value of instructor-focused video. In addition to being useful for instructional designers and media producers, we developed this table as a tool to help reluctant instructors feel more prepared to both create and be featured in videos to be viewed asynchronously in their online courses. Table 1 provides a checklist summary of these tips and techniques for future reference. Topics covered in Table 1 include: physical set-up, tech set-up, general tips, and editing suggestions.

Table 1. Checklist for instructor-produced videos created with computer webcam

	Physical Set-Up
Lighting	• Set up at least two light sources pointing at your face • If you are recording in a setting with an external light source such as large windows, close the blinds / shades to avoid being back-lit and creating dark shadows across your face • If you wear glasses: turn down your screen's brightness to cut down on the glare on your lenses
Camera angle	• Position the webcam at eye level • Position the webcam at a distance that will show your head and shoulders
Background	• Set up a professional background, such as a wall or bookshelf behind you • Consider branding with school paraphernalia in the background • Consider adding personal touches such as art, specific books, or other
Attire	• Avoid busy patterns, such as stripes or polka dots • Dress professionally
Memory aids	• If you are narrating slides, have your slide notes readily accessible • Tape any talking points near the webcam • Tape any technical reminders near the webcam
	Tech Set-Up
Test recording	Record a short test video to check audio and video quality; make adjustments as needed; determine if you will need an external microphone and/or headset with mouthpiece
	Tips
Professional quality	• Speak naturally; avoid reading word-for-word • Look directly at the camera • Adopt a confident posture • Use the pause button as needed
Personalization	• Be yourself, include your personality via humor, stories, gestures, imperfection • When appropriate, show and discuss course-related physical objects
	Editing (Optional)
Opening	Consider adding a slide with the school name and logo to the start and end of the video for borrowed credibility
Accessibility	Adding closed captioning will make the video more accessible; be cognizant of ADA compliance standards
Interactivity	Use software tools to add in interactive elements

When recording video using webcam, perhaps the most important technique for quality video is sufficient lighting. For a natural look and to ensure that students can see the instructor clearly, instructors should set up a minimum of two light sources directed at the instructor's face. Examples include a desk lamp and daylight from a window, two desk lamps on different sides of the computer, or an overhead light and a standing lamp. Depending on the darkness of the room, more than two light sources may be needed. Lighting not only impacts the ability to see the instructor clearly, but it can also impact the quality of the recording, as computers that must dedicate more resources toward focusing on the instructor's face in the dark may draw resources away from other programs (Figure 5).

For instructors who wear glasses, turning down the screen's brightness will cut down the glare on the lenses, so that the instructor's eyes become visible. Being unable to see the instructor's eyes can create a loss of connection with the instructor.

Another important primary step is setting up the camera angle so that the webcam is approximately at eye level and at a proper distance. Looking significantly down or up at a webcam can seem unprofessional, whereas looking straight into a webcam can make a video seem like the instructor is speaking directly to the students. In addition, the webcam needs to set up at a distance that will show the instructor's head and shoulders. If a webcam is too close, the oddity may distract students from the video content, and if the webcam is too far away, students may not be able to see the instructor clearly. Adjusting distance may involve moving the computer forward or backward on a desk, or moving the instructor's chair (Figure 6).

As mentioned above, setting up the space can also contribute to the sense of "legitimacy" of a video. For a webcam video, this means that the background seen in the video should look professional. This can be accomplished easily at home or in an office by setting up the webcam so that an uncluttered wall or organized bookshelf can be seen in the background. This is also an opportunity for branding a video, for example with a school pennant or framed diploma, or for personalization, for example with personal touches such as art or specific books visible in the background. Branding can add to the trustworthiness of a video, as discussed above (see Figure 7).

The physical set-up can also include setting up any memory aids. Tape any talking points near the webcam, for example on the wall behind the webcam or on the computer monitor next to the webcam. This can help the instructor maintain eye contact with the webcam, rather than looking down to read.

Figure 5. An example of the impact that good quality lighting can make
Screenshot taken by Adrienne Garber, 2016.

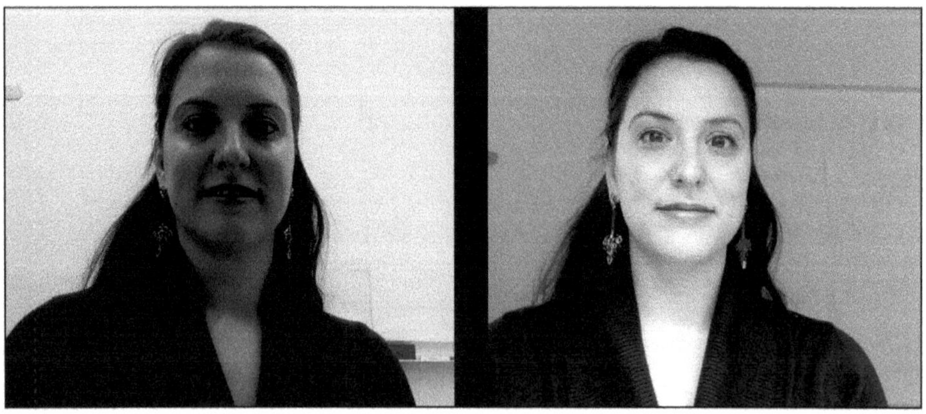

Figure 6. The impact of camera framing and angle
Screenshot taken by Kristine Kerr, 2016.

Figure 7. Examples of different backgrounds
Screenshot taken by Matthea Marquart, 2016.

Preparing bullet points for reference rather than complete sentences to read word-for-word can help the instructor sound more conversational and engaging, which in turn can highlight the instructor's expertise. Any reminders can also be taped near the webcam, for example reminders about posture or to look at the camera so that students feel the instructor is speaking directly to them.

Professionalism and trustworthiness can also be conveyed by attire (Figure 8). Neutral clothing will be less distracting on camera, whereas busy patterns such as stripes or polka dots can distract students and draw attention away from the instructor's points. Depending on the webcam, busy patterns may even appear to move or become three-dimensional.

With the physical set-up complete, including lighting, camera angle, background, attire, and memory aids, instructors should do a quick test of sound and video quality before beginning to record their videos. This test recording can be as short as ten seconds, and will alert the instructor to any adjustments that may need to be made to the physical set-up. For audio, either a headset mic or built-in computer mic should generally work well, but recording this short test video while speaking will alert the instructor to any background noise issues or mic static. Switching from a built-in mic to a headset mic will often

Figure 8. Examples of how presentation and attire influence nonverbal communication
Screenshot taken by Melanie Hibbert, 2016.

resolve issues with background noise, whereas switching from a headset mic to a built-in mic will often resolve issues with mic static or buzzing.

Once the instructor is ready for the actual video recording, a conversational style can help establish a professional level of quality. This includes looking directly at the camera for at least half of the video, speaking naturally rather than reading a script word-for-word, and adopting a confident posture. For longer videos, using the pause button while recording can aid a relaxed style by saving time and avoiding a stressful need to start over, for example when coughing, sneezing, drinking water, or losing a train of thought and needing to refresh one's memory. A conversational style that expresses the instructor's personality through humor, stories, gestures, and references to past experiences can also increase the level of personalization, which can reduce social distance and thereby increase the sense of instructor immediacy. Students can want to get to know their instructors, so demonstrating the instructor's personality in videos can be far superior to robotic script reading. Recording videos also offers the opportunity for personalization via the opportunity to show visuals such as books, art, or other objects related to the course.

If the instructor chooses to edit the video after recording, this introduces an opportunity for additional branding, accessibility, and interactivity. A presentation slide with the school name and logo can easily be added to the start and end of the video for branding that can add to the feeling of legitimacy. Adding closed captioning can make the video more accessible for students with hearing issues or for English language learners. As discussed earlier, many tools offer the ability to add interactive elements to video, such as quiz questions.

CONCLUSION

In conclusion, this study is based on the premise that online learning is most effective when conceived as inherently social and designed with social interactions between instructors and learners in mind. Social presence positively impacts online learners' interaction and learning, learners' achievement, learners' satisfaction, and the development of a sense of community (Sung & Mayer, 2013). Although the importance of creating strong social presence for online courses is clear, it often remains a challenge to establish consistent and adequate levels of social presence in the development of online courses (Dunlap & Lowenthal, 2015). Our findings suggest that online instructional videos can be one way for instructors to create social presence and foster instructor immediacy, as well as reduce social distance in online learning environments.

Employing qualitative research methods including semi-structured interviews and online video "talk throughs," we collected data from 13 students enrolled in master's programs at Columbia University School of Professional Studies. This data was analyzed under the conceptual frameworks of social distance and instructor immediacy, and several themes emerged, including trustworthiness (social context, branding, production values, nonverbal communication), personalization (humor, colloquial language), and feedback. In other words, videos that encompassed these qualities were evaluated and discussed in ways that reflected more social presence and instructor immediacy, and less social distance.

These findings have design implications for practitioners, especially those teaching and/or creating online courses. The design implications and tips for practitioners included above are particularly tailored to those operating with limited resources, who may only have basic tools such as smartphone cameras or built-in webcams. One can still employ these findings (such as adding institutional branding, or using humor) using inexpensive and basic devices. The ecosystem of online education is an ever-growing one, and more research is needed related to the social and affective experiences of students enrolled in online programs.

REFERENCES

Anderson, T. (2004). Towards a theory of online learning. In T. Anderson, & F. Elloumi (Eds.), Theory and practice of online learning (pp. 33-60). Athabasca University Press.

Anderson, T., Rourke, L., Garrison, R., & Archer, W. (2001). Assessing teaching presence in a computer conferencing context. *Journal of Asynchronous Learning Networks*, *5*(2), 1–17.

Arbaugh, J. (2001). How instructors immediacy behaviors affect student satisfaction and learning in web-based courses. *Business Communication Quarterly*, *64*(4), 42–54. doi:10.1177/108056990106400405

Baker, C. (2010). The impact of instructor immediacy and presence for online student affective learning, cognition, and motivation. *The Journal of Educators Online*, *7*(1), 1–30.

Borup, J., West, R., & Graham, C. (2012). Improving online social presence through asynchronous video. *The Internet and Higher Education*, *15*(3), 195–203. doi:10.1016/j.iheduc.2011.11.001

Buchan, N. R., Croson, R. T., & Dawes, R. M. (2002). Swift Neighbors and Persistent Strangers: A Cross-Cultural Investigation of Trust and Reciprocity in Social Exchange1. *American Journal of Sociology*, *108*(1), 168–206. doi:10.1086/344546

Campbell, D. (2014). The influence of teacher immediacy behaviors on Student Performanc in an online course (and the problem of method variance). *Teaching of Psychology*, *41*(2), 163–166. doi:10.1177/0098628314530351

Curtis, J. (2014, April). *The Employment Status of Instructional Staff Members in Higher Education, Fall 2011.* Washington, DC: American Association of University Professors. Retrieved from http://www.aaup.org/sites/default/files/files/AAUP-InstrStaff2011-April2014.pdf

Dewey, J. (1925). Logic: The theory of inquiry (1938). *The Later Works, 1953*, 1-549.

Dunlap, J., & Lowenthal, P. (2014). The power of presence: Our quest for the right mix of social presence in online courses. In A. P. Mizell & A. A. Piña (Eds.), *Real life distance education: Case studies in practice*. Charlotte, NC: Information Age Publishing.

Garrison, D. R. (2007). Online Community of Inquiry Review: Social, Cognitive, and Teaching Presence Issues. *Journal of Asynchronous Learning Networks, 11*(1), 61–72.

Garrison, D. R., & Anderson, T. (1998). *Learning in a networked world. In Distance learners in higher education: Institutional responses for quality outcomes* (pp. 97–112). Madison, WI: Atwood Publishing.

Garrison, D. R., Anderson, T., & Archer, W. (2010). The first decade of the community of inquiry framework: A retrospective. *The Internet and Higher Education, 13*(1), 5–9. doi:10.1016/j.iheduc.2009.10.003

Glaser, B. G., & Strauss, A. L. (1967). *The discovery of grounded theory: Strategies for qualitative research*. Chicago: Aldin.

Gunawardena, C. N., & Zittle, F. J. (1997). Social presence as a predictor of satisfaction within a computer-mediated conferencing environment. *American Journal of Distance Education, 11*(3), 8–26. doi:10.1080/08923649709526970

Jaggars, S. S., Edgecombe, N., & Stacey, G. W. (2013). *Creating an Effective Online Instructor Presence*. Community College Research Center, Columbia University.

Kim, J., Kwon, Y., & Cho, D. (2011). Investigating factors that influence social presense and learning outcomes in distance higher education. *Computers & Education, 57*(2), 1512–1520. doi:10.1016/j.compedu.2011.02.005

King, K. (2008) *Comparison of social presence in voice-based and text-based asynchronous computer conferencing*. (Doctoral dissertation). Retrieved from Proquest.

Kvale, S. (1996). *Interviews*. London: Sage.

Lowenthal, P., & Parscal, T. (2008). Teaching presence online facilitates meaningful learning. *The Learning Curve*, 3(4), 1-2, 4.

Magee, J., & Smith, P. (2013). The social distance theory of power. *Personality and Social Psychology Review, 17*(2), 158–186. doi:10.1177/1088868312472732 PMID:23348983

Mayer, R. E. (2008). Applying the science of learning: Evidence-based principles for the design of multimedia instruction. *The American Psychologist, 63*(8), 762–769. doi:10.1037/0003-066X.63.8.760 PMID:19014238

McIntosh, P. (2003). White privilege and male privilege. *Privilege. Reading (Sunderland)*, 147–160.

Mehrabian, A. (1967). Orientation behaviors and nonverbal attitude communication. *Journal of Communication, 17*(4), 324–332. doi:10.1111/j.1460-2466.1967.tb01190.x PMID:5588696

Mehrabian, A. (1969). Attitudes inferred from non-immediacy of verbal communication. *Journal of Verbal Learning and Verbal Behavior, 6*(2), 294–295. doi:10.1016/S0022-5371(67)80113-0

Mehrabian, A. (1981). *Silent messages: Implicit communication of emotions and attitudes* (2nd ed.). Belmont, CA: Wadsworth.

Moreno, R., & Mayer, R. E. (2004). Personalized messages that promote science learning in virtual environments. *Journal of Educational Psychology, 96*(1), 165–173. doi:10.1037/0022-0663.96.1.165

Myers, S., Zhong, M., & Guan, S. (1998). (1998) Instructor immediacy in the Chinese college classroom. *Communication Studies, 49*(3), 240–254. doi:10.1080/10510979809368534

Remesal, A., & Colomina, R. (2013). Social presence and online collaborative small group work: A socioconstructivist account. *Computers & Education, 60*(1), 357–367. doi:10.1016/j.compedu.2012.07.009

Rourke, L., Anderson, T., Garrison, D. R., & Archer, W. (2007). Assessing social presence in asynchronous text-based computer conferencing. *International Journal of E-Learning & Distance Education, 14*(2), 50–71.

Seidman, I. (2012). *Interviewing as qualitative research: A guide for researchers in education and the social sciences*. New York: Teachers College Press.

Smith, G. G., & Taveras, M. (2005, January). The missing instructor: Does e-learning promote absenteeism? *eLearn Magazine*, 1.

Sung, E., & Mayer, R. (2012). Five Facets of social presence in online distance education. *Computers in Human Behavior, 28*(5), 1738–1747. doi:10.1016/j.chb.2012.04.014

Swan, K. (2003). Developing social presence in online course discussions. In *Learning and teaching with technology: Principles and practices*, (pp. 147-164). Academic Press.

Swan, K., Garrison, D. R., & Richardson, J. (2009). *A constructivist approach to online learning: the Community of Inquiry framework. In Information technology and constructivism in higher education: Progressive learning frameworks*. Hershey, PA: IGI Global.

Swan, K., & Ice, P. (2010). The Community of Inquiry framework ten years later: Introduction to the special issue. *The Internet and Higher Education, 13*(1), 1–4. doi:10.1016/j.iheduc.2009.11.003

Swan, K., & Shih, L. F. (2005). On the nature and development of social presence in online course discussions. *Journal of Asynchronous Learning Networks, 9*(3), 115–136.

Tu, C. (2002). The relationship of social presence in an online learning environment. *The Internet and Higher Education, 5*, 293–318. doi:10.1016/S1096-7516(02)00134-3

Tu, C., & McIsaac, M. (2002). The relationship of social presence and interaction in online classes. *American Journal of Distance Education, 16*(3), 131–150. doi:10.1207/S15389286AJDE1603_2

Woods, R., & Baker, J. (2004). Interaction and Immediacy in Online Learning. *International Review of Research in Open and Distance Learning, 5*(2), 1–13.

KEY TERMS AND DEFINITIONS

Asynchronous Instructional Videos: Pre-recorded videos that contain course content and lecture materials that are not delivered to the students by the instructor in-person or in real-time.

Instructor Immediacy: The use of communication behaviors that reduce social and psychological distance between an instructor and his or her students.

Non-Verbal Immediacy: Behaviors by instructors that have the intended effect of increasing a felt sense of closeness among learners, including but not limited to, facial expressions, eye contact, posture, proximity, and touch.

Online Learning Environment: A structured space created online to facilitate learning and communication by and among students and instructors for the purpose of sharing and creating knowledge.

Production Values: The look, feel, and general quality of a video.

Social Distance: An experience, or subjective perception, of distance from one person to another, often characterized as the degree of felt closeness to another person.

Social Presence: The degree to which a person is perceived as "real" in mediated communications, as well as the degree of feeling, perception, or reaction of being connected to others via mediated communications.

Verbal Immediacy: Behaviors by instructors that have the intended effect of increasing a felt sense of closeness among learners, including but not limited to, the use of inclusive pronouns such as "we" and "our", using personal anecdotes, posing questions to the learners, using humor, initiating discussion, and addressing students by name.

Chapter 7
Leveraging Teaching Presence in Online Courses:
Strategies, Technology, and Student Perspectives

Kun Huang
Mississippi State University, USA

Sang Joon Lee
Mississippi State University, USA

Ashley Dugan
Mississippi State University, USA

ABSTRACT

The Community of Inquiry (CoI) framework has been widely used to guide the research and practice of online courses. In the CoI framework, three essential elements were identified to be critical for a successful online learning experience: social, cognitive, and teaching presences. While the three presences are overlapping and interdependent, teaching presence is known to be key to the creation of a community of inquiry by addressing cognitive and social issues. Starting with an overview of the CoI framework, this chapter mainly focuses on teaching presence and its two dimensions: instructional design and organization and directed facilitation. Specific strategies and examples for each dimension to leveraging teaching presence in a technology-rich online course are presented and described. In addition, a student's learning experience in the course is also shared to provide a student's perspective of the strategies.

INTRODUCTION

This chapter starts with an overview of the Community of Inquiry (CoI) theory, with a particular focus on teaching presence as one of the main elements of CoI. The paper then provides a review of the literature on different aspects of teaching presence, e.g., instructional design and organization, and directed facilitation. For each aspect, guidelines are drawn from the literature review, which are then illustrated and

DOI: 10.4018/978-1-4666-9995-3.ch007

complemented with the authors' own experiences of teaching a technology-rich online course. Specific strategies, examples, and enabling technologies are presented. In addition to illustrating the strategies from the perspective of the instructor who taught the course, the chapter provides a student's account of how she perceived and experienced the strategies. Further, quantitative data regarding students' perceptions of the community of inquiry in the illustrated course are reported to corroborate the description. The chapter ends with the instructor's concluding thoughts and reflections. The goal of this chapter is to present a set of strategies and technologies that can be used to establish and sustain teaching presence in an online course, thereby creating a community of learners.

BACKGROUND

Over the past decade, online education has been growing rapidly. Online courses have become prevalent in higher education. More than 70% of higher education institutions offer online courses, and over 95% of the institutions with 5,000 or more students deliver courses online (Allen & Seaman, 2015). Aslanian and Clinefelter (2012) regard online education as higher education's latest disruptive innovation, which forces colleges and universities to change the way they deliver courses. Pedagogical and technological innovations make it possible to create and deliver online education effectively and efficiently, which leads to the transformation of higher education (Garrison, 2011).

Although the year-to-year growth rate in the number of students taking online courses has been decreasing in the past few years, online education accounts for about 75% of the increase in overall higher education enrollment from 2012 to 2013 in the United States (Allen & Seaman, 2015). According to the 2014 Online Learning Consortium report, *Grade Change: Tracking Online Education in the United States* (Allen & Seaman, 2014), more than seven million students are taking at least one online course.

Colleges and universities see online learning as critical to their institutions' long-term strategy (Allen & Seaman, 2015). Academic leaders believe that the learning outcomes in online education are comparable to those in face-to-face instruction (Allen & Seaman, 2015). Empirical research also shows that distance education is as effective in learning outcomes as face-to-face instruction (Anglin & Morrison, 2000; Cavanaugh, Gillan, Kromrey, Hess, & Blomeyer, 2004; Dean, Stahl, Sylwester, & Peat, 2001).

Students take online courses mainly because online learning allows them to study anywhere at any time while still taking family and work responsibilities (Aslanian & Clinefelt, 2012). With the increasing demand to learn at distance and the fast development of the Internet and other emerging technologies, the growing trend in online learning is expected to continue (Dahlstrom, 2012; Simonson, Smaldino, Albright, & Zvacek, 2012).

While the numbers of online courses and online students have grown, there are a number of concerns and barriers in online education, including the lack of faculty acceptance of online education, lower retention rate, and student readiness for online courses (Allen & Seaman, 2015). A significant number of faculty members in higher education, for example, do not tend to accept the value and legitimacy of online education. More importantly, delivering high quality online courses requires more faculty time and effort, but there are not enough time and resources to design and develop high quality online courses. Due to a lack of training for teaching online, faculty often have limited information and knowledge about what constitutes a successful online course, as well as limited frameworks that guide them to design and deliver an online learning environment.

Community of Inquiry

The CoI framework has been widely used to guide the research and practice of online education (Akyol & Garrison, 2011a). From a collaborative constructivist view of teaching and learning, Garrison, Anderson, and Archer (2000) first introduced the CoI theoretical framework, which focuses on the creation of a community of learners to facilitate reflective discourse and higher-order learning. The collaborative constructivist view recognizes the importance of context and the relationship between personal meaning making and contextual influence. Students construct knowledge by engaging in critical thinking and discourse as a community of learners.

CoI has been used to design, develop, evaluate, understand, explain and prescribe online learning environments where "students can take responsibility and control of their learning through negotiating meaning, diagnosing misconceptions, and challenging accepted beliefs" (Garrison, 2011, p. 22). Such inquiry-based learning approach leads to deep and meaningful learning outcomes. Research has shown the relationship between active engagement in a learning community and deep learning outcomes (Liu, Magjuka, Bonk, & Lee, 2007; Rovai, 2002).

According to Garrison (2011), CoI "represents a process of creating a deep and meaningful (collaborative constructivist) learning experience through the development of three interdependent elements" (p. 22). Social, cognitive, and teaching presences are the three essential elements for a successful online educational experience, and they can be created through interpersonal communications in the community of learners. Social presence is "the ability of participants in a community of inquiry to project themselves socially and emotionally" through the communication channels used in online courses (Garrison et al., 2000, p. 94). Such communication channels may include asynchronous discussion forums, synchronous conferencing tools, or more recent social media channels. According to Garrison et al. (2000), social presence includes "a supportive context for emotional expression, open communication, and group cohesion for building understanding" (p. 101). If online teaching and learning is to be effective and meaningful, appropriate social presence should be established and maintained so that learners can develop personal and affective relationships in the community. Students are then able to share, negotiate, and challenge ideas and meanings, and collaborate with others in the safe and trusted learning environment. When social presence is established, cognitive presence is also enhanced and sustained (Akyol & Garrison, 2011b).

Cognitive presence looks at the cognitive aspects of a learning experience. Cognitive presence indicates the learning and inquiry process through reflection and discourse, and analysis and synthesis (Garrison, Cleveland-Innes, & Fung, 2010). It is closely related to the concept of critical or reflective thinking, which is crucial to inquiry or meaning making. Therefore, it is "at the core of a community of inquiry" (Garrison, 2011, p. 47). Cognitive presence consists of four phases that involve problem recognition, exploration, integration, and resolution. In order to create cognitive presence, support critical inquiry, and achieve higher-order learning outcomes, teachers need to assess critical discourses qualitatively and provide appropriate guidance to support students' knowledge construction through inquiry (Garrison, 2011).

Therefore, teaching presence is key to creating and sustaining a community of inquiry by addressing cognitive and social issues for intended learning outcomes (Garrison et al., 2010). In the following sections, the importance of teaching presence is reviewed, and a case of leveraging teaching presence in an online course is presented.

Importance of Teaching Presence

Anderson, Rourke, Garrison, and Archer (2001) define teaching presence as "the design, facilitation, and direction of cognitive and social processes for the realization of personally meaningful and educationally worthwhile learning outcomes" (p. 5). Since the instructor is the one who establishes and orchestrates both cognitive and social processes of learning, the teaching presence established by the instructor plays a key role in a community of inquiry (Garrison et al., 2010).

Indeed, empirical studies have generated evidence to support the importance of teaching presence in online learning. Teaching presence was found to influence online students' satisfaction (Akyol & Garrison, 2014; Joo, Lim, & Kim, 2011; Swan & Shih, 2005), sense of community (Shea, Li, & Pickett, 2005; 2006), perceived learning (Akyol & Garrison, 2014), and deep approaches to learning (Garrison & Cleveland-Innes, 2005).

Research has further investigated the impact mechanism of teaching presence, which is through its effects on students' perceived social and cognitive presences. Using the CoI Survey (Arbaugh et al., 2008), Garrison et al. (2010) statistically established the causal relationships between teaching presence and the other two CoI elements: social presence and cognitive presence. Teaching presence is necessary to establish a safe and supportive social environment for learning. Swan and Shih (2005) have shown that course design, an aspect of teaching presence, significantly affected students' development of social presence. In addition to helping learners to be socially ready for a community of inquiry, teaching presence is also essential in guiding and promoting learners' cognitive processes. Studies have empirically attested to the significant relationship between learner-perceived teaching presence and cognitive presence (Akyol & Garrison, 2014; Archibald, 2010). Ke (2010) moved a step further to examine the observed, in addition to perceived, social and cognitive presence, and found the same predictive power of course design on the cognitive and social presence observed in online courses. Garrison et al. (2010) posited,

> *... teaching presence is essential in establishing a sense of social presence by engendering an atmosphere of trust, open communication and group cohesion. This sets the stage for purposeful and collaborative learning processes and activities as indicated by the perceived relationship between social and cognitive presence. In this sense, social presence is a mediating factor that provides context for the educational process. The focus then moves to the direct causal relationship between teaching presence and cognitive presence. The assumption is that students are assigned engaging tasks requiring solutions for them to move through the phases of practical inquiry. Once engaged, teaching presence is hypothesized and perceived to have a significant influence in facilitating and directing student learning activities. This perceived relationship has been shown in previous research to be crucial to reach resolution and achieve student perceptions of a successful learning experience (p.35).*

Thus Garrison et al. (2010) provided a more detailed account about how teaching presence interacts with social and cognitive presence at different stages of inquiry. According to Anderson et al. (2001), teaching presence exerts influences on social and cognitive presence in three dimensions: instructional design and organization, facilitating discourse, and direct instruction. Although Garrison, Anderson, and Archer (2010) argued that the three dimensions still hold theoretical and practical merit, recent research appears to suggest two dimensions of teaching presence. While *instructional design and organization* remains a distinct factor, *directed facilitation* has replaced *facilitating discourse* and *direct instruction* (Arbaugh et al., 2008; Shea, 2006).

Plenty of research has examined the positive effects of teaching presence and its relationship with other presences, yet the literature is lacking in providing helpful strategies to establish teaching presence online. Although Garrison and Cleveland-Innes (2005) provided some general guidelines regarding the facilitation of cognitive presence as an instructor, and Garrison (2006) outlined principles for an instructor to support online collaboration, online instructors and instructional designers would benefit from specific strategies and examples to operationalize teaching presence in an online learning environment. Such needs are further intensified by two additional issues. First, the CoI research was initially conducted in the context of computer conferencing. Although later research has evolved to examine asynchronous online discussions, the progress is not in parallel with the fast development of technology that can enable an online instructor to support learning in more diverse ways. New platforms and tools have been updated, many of which have not been accounted for in the research on teaching presence (Garrison, 2007). Shea, Vickers, and Hayes (2010), for example, questioned the narrow focus of the CoI research on online discussions, arguing that such focus may have under-represented the actual teaching presence in online courses.

The second issue is regarding the specific challenges online instructors face in facilitating productive, high-level social and cognitive presence, which can lead to deep learning. Garrison and Cleveland-Innes (2005) have empirically demonstrated that social presence is necessary, but insufficient to create a community of inquiry that results in deep learning. Similarly, Murphy (2004) found that students in an online discussion engaged primarily in social and lower-level cognitive processes, yet did not reach higher levels such as sharing goals and producing shared artifacts. As elaborated by Garrison (2007), online communities of inquiry face the challenge of moving social presence beyond providing socio-emotional support to cultivating purposeful relationships, as well as the challenge of moving students from the exploration phase to the resolution phase of inquiry. It is the instructor's responsibility to address the challenges, yet the current literature has not adequately equipped online instructors to do so.

Therefore, the goal of this chapter is to identify and summarize strategies for each dimension of teaching presence. An online course is used as an example case to illustrate how the strategies were implemented and how technology was used to augment the implementation.

LEVERAGING TEACHING PRESENCE: THE CASE OF AN ONLINE COURSE

The course presented as a case here is a complete online course offered at a large university in the southeastern United States. Each semester, about 25 to 30 students enroll in the course to study topics related to the use of digital tools to support teaching and learning in the 21st century. The students may or may not have prior experience in teaching or training. The overall goals of the course are for students to identify the demands and challenges for education in the 21st century, examine theories related to the integration of digital tools to support different aspects of teaching and learning, demonstrate competency in a few latest digital tools, and apply theories and tools to create web-based learning materials for a target group of learners. The instructor has not previously taught a formal course of the similar nature, although she has taught different components of the course content, mostly in face-to-face settings to a different audience. The course is delivered with the Blackboard Learning Management System (LMS). Although the LMS has its own set of tools, the scope, structure and functionality of these tools can often inhibit just-in-time communications and interactions (Dunlap, 2009). As such, this course has adopted external web-based technology tools to enhance the learning experience.

The remainder of this section describes the strategies the instructor employed in the design and teaching of this online course. Although it is recognized that facilitation of discourse and direct instruction are two unique aspects of teaching, the authors believe that the two practices often occur simultaneously in teaching. As such, the authors adopt Shea's (2006) two dimensions, *instructional design and organization* and *directed facilitation*, as the organizing conceptual framework to present the strategies.

For each dimension, a list of strategies is presented and described. The strategies are illustrated with examples as well as the technology that augmented them. Whenever available, related literature is introduced to support the strategies. To provide a holistic account of the strategies and their implementation, at the end of each dimension, Ashley, a student of this course shares how she and her classmates experienced and perceived the strategies from the receiving end.

Instructional Design and Organization

In the two dimensions of teaching presence, instructional design and organization has more to do with the planning before the delivery of a course. According to Anderson et al. (2001), indicators of instructional design and organization include setting curriculum, designing methods, establishing time parameters, utilizing medium effectively, and establishing netiquette. Recent studies have revealed some additional indicators such as interface design (e.g., Ke, 2010). As such, the strategies outlined here are not limited to the original indicators.

Instructional design is a field in itself. Researchers in this field have already established models and theories (Dick, Carey, & Carey, 2011; Morrison, Ross, Kalman, & Kemp, 2012; Smith & Ragan, 2005). A key principle among instructional design models is the assessment of instructional needs, identification of learning objectives, and the design and development of assessment and learning activities that are aligned with the objectives. Since these models and theories apply to any educational settings, whether online or face-to-face, this chapter does not focus on them. Instead, the strategies introduced here focus on the uniqueness of online teaching and learning. A summary of the strategies and examples can be found in Table 1.

Strategy 1: Take Advantage of the Online Platform to Utilize Learning Materials from Various Sources, in Various Modalities

An advantage of teaching online is the opportunity to utilize various online resources to strengthen the course content. In other words, the instructor can "crowd source" learning materials developed by others, instead of taking the responsibility to create all the course content. Bonk and Zhang (2008) observed that typical online courses rely heavily on text-based assignments and intensive readings. Therefore, in selecting external content, the instructor should keep an open mind to resources beyond the text modality to include materials such as videos, audios, animations, graphs, and web links. Several authors have advocated the concept of learning objects in designing online learning content (e.g., Anderson, 2008; Anderson et al., 2001). Learning objects are essentially small elements of computer-based instruction that can serve as building blocks of learning materials (Wiley, 2002). A learning object can take the form of a video segment, a PowerPoint presentation, an interactive applet, etc. Like Lego pieces, learning objects can be reused and reassembled to achieve different instructional objectives.

Table 1. Teaching presence dimensions, strategies and examples

STRATEGIES	EXAMPLES
Dimension 1: Instructional Design and Organization	
1. Take advantage of the online platform to utilize learning materials from various sources, in various modalities	• Use online resources such as learning object repositories, videos, web links, professional communities, organizations and blogs • Use multiple modalities beyond mere text • Provide access to the latest trends and experts in the field • Identify online materials with interactivity (e.g., self-assessment, practice)
2. Keep online learners in mind when repurposing F2F lecture content	• Enhance F2F PowerPoint with narrations or screencasting (e.g., Camtasia or Jing) • Limit video length • Embed interactivity/assessment within presentation to enhance comprehension (e.g., Articulate Studio)
3. Be mindful of usability to facilitate learning for diverse online learners	• Provide video/audio transcripts to facilitate content review and accommodate disabilities or different devices • Improve LMS navigation by minimizing number of clicks and providing quick access to essential content • Use consistent content layout and organization
4. Design authentic learning activities for students to demonstrate knowledge in multiple ways, with clear guidelines	• Design learning activities that involve real life practice in the discipline (e.g., case studies, project for a target audience) • Allow students to demonstrate knowledge in multiple ways (e.g., blogs for reflection, wikibook to compile and organize important course content, screencast/concept map for visual demonstration) • Incorporate both formal and informal learning activities • Provide clear guidelines
5. Incorporate formal and informal group learning activities	• Combine formal and informal, graded or ungraded group activities • Use group activities to facilitate both learning and social interactions
6. Scaffold students' task management and self-regulation	• Provide weekly agenda with topics, activity checklist, due dates, and upcoming assignments • Establish timeline to maximize quantity and quality of discourse
7. Familiarize learners with course technologies through instructor modeling and practice tasks	• Provides instructor modeling of course technology tools • Provide opportunities for students to practice course technology tools before using them for learning tasks
Dimension 2: Directed Facilitation	
1. Use technology to personalize social activities	• Use online, media-rich personal profile for personal introduction • Use reflective blogging to support social and cognitive interactions • Incorporate icebreaker activities at both class and group levels • Use virtual gift exchange as a group icebreaker activity
2. Scaffold team formation and beginning collaboration	• Use online collaboration canvas for students to share ideas, find common interests, and form teams • Provide sample meeting agenda for the first group meeting
3. Plan for a multi-layered discourse mechanism to move from exploration to resolution phase of inquiry	Prepare students for group work by requiring them to first individually respond to instructor's feedback
4. Provide just-in-time instruction at multiple junctures	• Address learning deficiencies in weekly introduction and grading feedback • Offer "expert perspective" on course projects and case studies
5. Encourage and make use of student-initiated discourse	• Involve students in making course decisions • Incorporate student work in teaching to give recognition and encourage ownership
6. Maintain timely and personalized communications	• Establish and maintain a communication routine • Personalize communication

Online learning repositories such as *Multimedia Educational Resource for Learning and Online Teaching (MERLOT)* provide curated collections of free and open learning objects. An instructor can search such collections by subject, material type, or academic level to locate useful materials. Over time, the instructor can build his or her own collection of learning objects for a given topic or module. Of course, all the learning objects need to be carefully reviewed to ensure the alignment with learning objectives.

In this course, a variety of online resources have been utilized. These resources can contribute to social and cognitive presence in several ways. First, online videos can provide visual explanations to help students understand abstract concepts such as critical thinking. Second, online videos are great in extending class to access experts in the field. For example, students were able to watch talks by Dr. Michael Welsh and Sir Ken Robinson on related course topics. Third, through web links to relevant website, students learned the latest trends in the field. They were able to read *New Media Consortium*'s latest *Horizon Reports* on emerging technology in education, review top 100 tools of the year for learning, and read reviews of books that address hot topics in the field (e.g., *Academically Adrift*). Fourth, students were introduced to online communities of practice through publications by online educational communities such as *Edutopia* and *Educause*. Students also read blogs posted by teachers on website such as *EdTech Teacher*.

While the above resources allowed students to read, listen or watch, the learning activities they afford are still somewhat passive in nature. Additional online resources can engage students more by providing opportunities for them to actively interact or participate. For instance, students could gain first-hand experience about learning styles by assessing their own learning styles through an online survey. Further, an interactive exercise was adopted from *Wisconsin Online*, an online learning object repository, to help students learn and assess their understanding of Bloom's taxonomy, a concept introduced in the course.

Strategy 2: Keep Online Learners in Mind When Repurposing Face-to-Face Lecture Content

When creating content for online courses, instructors often choose to repurpose lecture PowerPoint originally used in face-to-face settings (e.g., Anderson, 2008). Online instructors need to be mindful of the fact that the PowerPoint alone may not be self-explanatory. Therefore, the instructor should carefully review the content from the perspective of an online learner, and add necessary information to help the learner comprehend the materials. Alternatively, the instructor can record narrations to accompany the PowerPoint.

In this course, the instructor recorded narrations for all the PowerPoint presentations using screencasting software *Jing* or *Camtasia*. For videos longer than 10 minutes, they were separated into two or more segments, so that learners will not lose attention after watching a video for a long time. An issue with online presentations, as reported by Ke (2010), is lack of interactivity. A software package the instructor has recently piloted, *Articulate Studio*, can easily convert a narrated PowerPoint into a user-friendly format and present information in a more visual and interactive manner. What's more, such software allows assessment to be embedded within a presentation to test comprehension, thereby enhancing students' cognitive presence.

Strategy 3: Be Mindful of Usability to Facilitate Learning for Diverse Online Learners

Usability characterizes the ease of use and learnability of an interface (Nielsen, 2000). While usability testing is a standard operation in business and industry, it receives much less attention in online learning (Fisher & Wright, 2010). This probably explains why interface design rarely appears in the literature on teaching presence. In studying adult students' experience in online learning, Ke (2010) identified interface design as one of the themes. Online students are diverse. They may have different navigation styles, access a course from different devices, and may have different preferences of the type of media when given a choice. Although most universities adopt an LMS that often has a standard layout, there is usually a certain level of flexibility the instructor can take advantage of to improve students' learning experience.

This course addresses usability in several ways. First, for all the video or audio content created by the instructor, a transcript was provided to the students. In the case of a narrated PowerPoint presentation converted to Flash or web format, students were able to download the PowerPoint file with narration transcripts in its notes (Figure 1). The transcripts not only increase the accessibility for people with disabilities, but also give students options in case they favor one medium over another, or in case their device cannot access one type of media. Further, students could review transcripts multiple times to increase comprehension and retention. The second measure to ensure usability is to minimize the number of clicks students have to go through before accessing an item. For example, for each new module, a quick link was added to the main course navigation menu so that students could directly access instead of having to first visit the modules page before accessing the new module (Figure 2). Further, all the items in a module are usually placed directly within the module's folder without further navigation to sub-folders. Although there may be quite some items within a module, they are organized into several conceptual categories (e.g., agenda, content materials, learning activities), and the organizing scheme is consistent across all the modules. The interface was intended to not only save time for navigation, but also reduce the chance of missing an item due to complexity of navigation.

Strategy 4: Design Authentic Learning Activities for Students to Demonstrate Knowledge in Multiple Ways, with Clear Guidelines

The challenge of designing an online course often lies in the need to identify not only the outcomes of the course, but also the *processes* that lead students to the outcomes. Anderson et al. (2001) has eloquently stated that an online instructor has to "think through the process, structure, evaluation and interaction components of the course" (p.5). Whereas in the classroom setting, the processes can be flexibly implemented and adjusted by the instructor, the online setting requires that the instructor plan them ahead of time. Moreover, the processes have to be translated into specific *learning activities*, that is, what

Figure 1. Narrated presentations are provided in multiple formats

Tools for Reflection

Watch Dr. Huang's short video presentations, OR if you prefer, view PowerPoint and read transcript in the notes section of the PowerPoint files.

- Part 1: Video presentation (4:32) | PowerPoint
- Part 2: Video presentation (3:41) | PowerPoint

Figure 2. Quick link is added for easy navigation to the current module

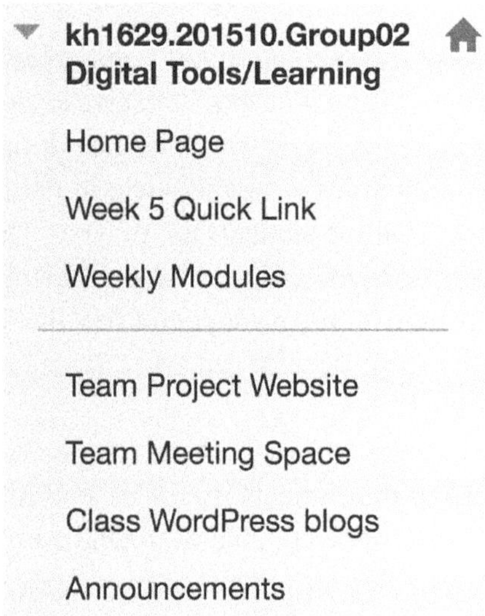

students will *do* in each module of the course. Furthermore, the instructor would not know whether and how students are doing with the learning activities unless certain deliverables are produced. Although the deliverables certainly include those assignments listed in the course syllabus as formal, summative assessments, a face-to-face class usually has additional, informal deliverables, often in the form of class discussions, for the instructor to formatively assess students' thinking and intervene accordingly. Formative assessment is different from summative assessment in that its goal is not only to assess students' learning outcomes at the end of a unit, but more importantly to diagnose students' understanding in the process of learning so that feedback can be provided to shape and improve competence (Sadler, 1989). In the case of an online course, the instructor has to determine what additional, informal deliverables are required to make students' thinking visible (Collins, Brown, & Holum, 1991; Ritchhart, Church, & Morrison, 2011). Such deliverables not only provide the instructor a window to diagnose students' learning progress and interject as necessary, but also challenge students to think deeper and represent their knowledge in a reflective manner (Garrison, 2003).

To promote cognitive presence, it is important for learning activities to expose students to authentic or situated problems and examples – a key strategy found in a recent meta-analysis that significantly impacts critical thinking (Abrami et al., 2015). Considering today's learners and what today's technology has to offer, it is time for online instructors to embrace a variety of learning activities beyond online discussions to engage students in practical applications and authentic problem solving, and to enable them to embody thinking in multiple ways.

In the meantime, it is very important to use clear guidelines and other means of support to communicate expectations of higher order learning. Meyer (2003) urged online instructors to be more directive in course assignments, and argued that the questions an instructor asks determine the level of response.

The learning activities in this course placed a clear focus on the application of knowledge in authentic settings and the production of artifacts with the support of digital tools. As such, in addition to quizzes that assessed students' understanding of content materials, students had to write blog posts to reflect on and make sense of their learning experience, work on a case study to help solve problems encountered by a practitioner in real life, compile as a class a wiki book that introduces to teachers/trainers digital tools to support learning, create a video tutorial to teach a given digital tool, and complete a multi-stage project to design an instructional website utilizing digital tools (Figure 3). In addition to these graded activities, students also worked on informal learning activities. For example, students used a concept-mapping tool, *Bubbl*, to create a concept map that answered the question, "How do people learn in an online class?" and shared their concept map on blogs (Figure 4). Augmented by multiple tools (blogs, wikis, screencasting, concept mapping, and website builder), students had the opportunity to demonstrate their knowledge in different modalities – text, graphics, videos, or a combination of several at the same time.

Clear guidelines were provided for the learning activities. The guidelines for major assignments included the following components: (a) a brief explanation of why and how the activity contributed to course objectives, (b) an overview of the assignment, (c) specific requirements of the assignments, often in the form of question prompts; (d) an explanation of how the assignment would be graded (Figure 5). In addition to the guidelines, examples from past students were also provided to students. The required production of artifacts, detailed guidelines, as well as the examples, challenged students to engage in deep cognitive processing.

Figure 3. Graded course assignments that emphasize application of knowledge

Assignment	Points
Quizzes	50
Case study	100
Reflective blogs	200
Digital tools wikibook	200
Digital tools tutorial	150
Teaching with digital tools (group)	200
Final exam	50
Online activity participation	50
Course paper	100
Total	1100

Figure 4. Concept map created by a student to visually illustrate her idea about online learning

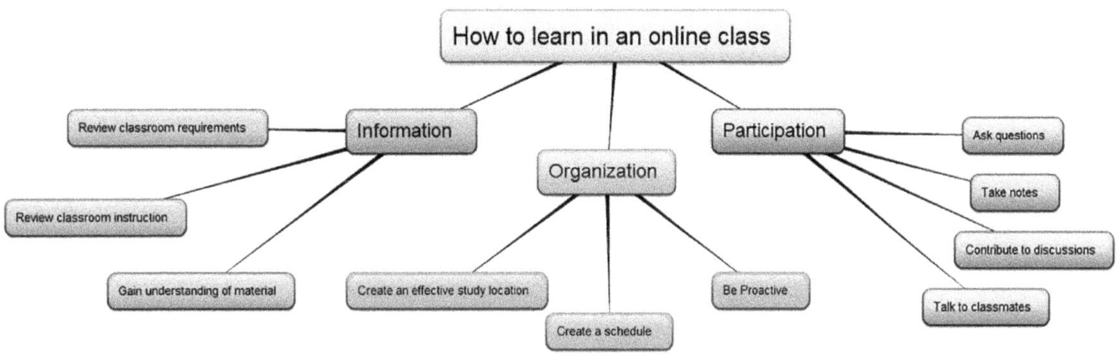

Figure 5. Guidelines for the wikibook assignment

Digital Tools Wikibook #2

The purpose of the Digital Tools Wikibook project is for you to write, as a class, a book that introduces digital tools for each phase of the R2D2 model: Read, Reflect, Display, and Do. The book is written for those teachers or trainers who are looking for good digital tools to aid their teaching or training. The book can also be a great reference when you choose digital tools for your team project. For Wikibook #2 (45 pts), you will write a wiki page about a tool for Reflection.

What should be included in the wiki page?

The following should be on your wiki page:

Title: 4 things you should know about [the tool's name]

Scenario: try to come up with a teaching/learning scenario that uses the tool. It doesn't have to be as long and thorough as the example, but you should use the scenario to demonstrate the use of the tool in an education or training setting (10 pts)

4 things:

1. *What is it?* (10 pts)
Provide a clear explanation of what the tool is and what it does.
2. *How can it benefit Reflection?* (10 pts)
Justify why you think the tool supports the REFLECT phase of R2D2. What are some ways a teacher can use the tool to support reflection? Can it be used by students for active and/or collaborative learning? If so how?
3. *What planning is necessary before using the tool?* (10 pts)
If a teacher is to use the tool in F2F or online teaching, does she/he need to set up anything beforehand? Think thoroughly and explain the technical, logistic, and pedagogical planning involved.
4. *What are some good resources about the tool?* (5 pts)
Provide web links to quality resources if a teacher decides to further explore the tool. The resources can be websites, articles, videos, tutorials, etc.

You are encouraged to add links, insert graphics or embed videos whenever you see necessary. Your wiki page will be evaluated by its clarity, thoroughness, and helpfulness from the perspective of a teacher or trainer.

Strategy 5: Incorporate Formal and Informal Group Learning Activities

While an instructor may be skilled at structuring and facilitating group work in face-to-face settings, they may not feel as comfortable in online settings. Brindley, Walti, and Blaschke (2009) reasoned that an instructor needs be skilled at creating and managing online interactions for successful collaborative learning. With appropriate strategies and tools, online group learning activities not only promote social presence, but also strengthen cognitive presence. Online classes should include a mix of individual and group learning activities (Anderson, 2008). The activities can be formal or informal, graded or ungraded.

In this class, there were two graded group learning activities. The first activity was a group project in which a group of three or four had to work together for a duration of more than 10 weeks to collaboratively design an instructional website. The second activity required that students review and edit classmates' wiki book pages. In addition to the graded group activities, students also participated in other group activities through which they could earn participation points. These activities included reading and commenting on the blog posts and case study responses posted by classmates.

Informal group activities were not for learning purpose per se, but they helped students to know each other. The next section, *directed facilitation*, elaborates more about informal group activities.

Strategy 6: Scaffold Students' Task Management and Self-Regulation

Shea and Bidjerano (2012) found learners' self-regulation to be an important factor that moderates the relationships among teaching, cognitive and social presence. Without face-to-face contact, online learners have to rely on themselves to manage weekly learning tasks through a web interface. The challenge becomes even greater with large-scale projects that require long-term team collaboration at a distance. Online instructors can scaffold learners' self-regulation through effective course design (Dabbagh, 2003).

In this course, an agenda was provided to students each week. The agenda provides the following information: (a) topics covered in the week, (b) a checklist of specific learning tasks stated with action verbs, (c) a checklist of the week's assignments with due dates, and (d) upcoming assignments in the next two weeks (Figure 6). The agenda helped students to preview their tasks and plan their week accordingly. In addition, the current and future assignments provided students with a macro-level view about the course process (Anderson et al., 2001).

Establishing time parameter is an important part of establishing teaching presence (Anderson et al., 2001). To help students manage the big project in the course, the instructor not only gave the students an overview of what the end product should look like, but also divided the project into several progressive milestones with deadlines spaced throughout the semester. For each milestone, specific deliverables were required and detailed guidelines and grading criteria were provided. In negotiating timelines for

Figure 6. An example weekly agenda

Week 3 Agenda

Monday 1/26 – Sunday 2/1

Topics

- Problem solving, critical thinking, creativity … What are they?
- Bloom's taxonomy
- Digital tool: *Lino* online collaboration

Learning activities (all content and instruction can be found in *Week 3* folder)

☐ Review Dr. Huang's introduction to this week's topics
☐ Read/watch all the required content in *Week 3 materials* folder
☐ Post your project idea to *Lino* online collaboration board
☐ Complete Quiz 2
☐ Add your *about.me* profile to your *WordPress* blog
☐ Comment on your classmates' reflective blog #1

Due Assignments

- Sun 2/1: Project idea on *Lino* board – early posting strongly encouraged (participation grade)
- Sun 2/1: Quiz 2 (graded)
- Sun 2/1: *About.me* profile to *WordPress* (participation grade)
- Sun 2/1: Comments on classmate's blog (graded)

Looking ahead: Upcoming Graded Assignments

- Sun 2/8: Reflective blog #2
- Sun 2/15: Group project proposal
- Sun 2/15: Quiz 3

assignments, the instructor had to keep a balance between the ideal and the reality. The reflective blog assignments used to have two deadlines within a week: students had to post their initial reflection by the middle of the week, and respond to others' posts by the end of the week. Students indicated in course evaluations that it was overwhelming for them to work toward two deadlines within a week. As a result, the quality of discourse was compromised. Therefore the instructor adjusted the timeline for the blogging assignments. Students were given two weeks to complete the tasks: they wrote reflections in the first week, and then responded to others' posts in the subsequent week. Reading and responding to others' posts in the second week actually facilitated the transition from previous to the new week, which could help students to be cognitively more prepared.

Strategy 7: Familiarize Learners with Course Technologies through Instructor Modeling and Practice Tasks

When multiple tools are employed in learning activities, one cannot assume that students could use the tools correctly in their first attempt. For instance, it is the instructor's experience that when students used a wiki for the first time, many would opt to use the comment feature instead of directly editing a wiki page. To help students familiarize with the technologies in a course, Anderson et al. (2001) advocated that the instructor model effective use of the tools.

In this course, the instructor modeled the tools in the design and teaching of the course. For example, the lectures were recorded using *Jing* and *Camtasia*, the tools that students would later use to complete their digital tools tutorial project. To model the use of *WordPress* as a blogging tool, the instructor had her own blog and actively used it as a way to communicate with students. Further, the instructor also designed activities for students to practice the tools so that they could be technically ready for completing formal assignments.

Ashley's Experience

In reflecting on her experience with the instructor's design and organization of the course, Ashley wrote the following:

The instructional design strategies implemented in this online course were essential to a fulfilling learning experience. I had taken three online courses prior to this one, and felt definitively that all three were subpar compared to a face-to-face course. This class was different. I felt like I knew some of my classmates and the instructor. The lessons were fascinating and flowed logically with an easily navigable interface. Each week, the topics and technology built new knowledge and skills used in the following weeks. For example, we had a practice assignment using Google Doc to collaboratively write a simple and fun story as a class. This practice prepared us to use Google Doc later for collaborative project work. We never had to simultaneously learn a new technology and provide deep insight using the technology. Also, I appreciated that I could listen to and follow along with the instructor. I know it took more time to provide multiple formats, but it made the absorption of information much simpler.

A strength of the course was that multiple perspectives were provided on each topic. For example, the instructor delivered an overview and insight on a topic via screencast presentation, then an article provided a different perspective, and finally, a YouTube video or TED talk provided an additional analysis.

None took more than 30 minutes, and many took much less. The micro-learning concept meant that I was never bored with the material. I would usually watch the videos before reading the articles. Not only were the video speakers engaging, but they brought an element of humor or human interest that would inspire me to delve deeper into the material.

The variety in the individual and group activities kept the learning interesting. Big picture questions were posed to the students, and practical research, technology, self-reflection, and problem-based learning were emphasized. Many of the assignments required us to take the real-world role of an educator, student, or industry professional. This mindset made the activity more meaningful. Additionally, the milestones for the group project helped me not to feel overwhelmed by a large assignment, and feedback from the instructor ensured that the group could correct any omissions before the final component was due. The integration of manageable activities aided in the processing of information. As a result, my retention of content learned in this course was much higher than in courses that centered on a single textbook.

Directed Facilitation

Once the content materials and activities of an online course are in place through instructional design and organization, the teaching responsibilities step in. Compared with instructional design and organization, the directed facilitation dimension of teaching presence is a more dynamic and interactive process. Conceptually, it involves the facilitation of discourse, as well as direct instruction (Anderson, et al., 2001). In the context of online discussions and computer conferencing, the facilitation of discourse has been further delineated into the following indicators: identifying areas of agreement/disagreement; seeking to reach consensus/understanding; encouraging, acknowledging, or reinforcing student contributions; setting climate for learning; drawing in participants, prompting discussion; and assess and efficacy of the process. The indicators for direct instruction include presenting content/questions; focusing the discussion on specific issues; summarizing the discussion; confirming understanding through assessment and explanatory feedback; diagnosing misconceptions; injecting knowledge from diverse sources; and responding to technical concerns (Anderson et al., 2001).

While the indicators hold true across different settings, they may become more subtle and hard for an instructor to identify and act upon when discourses are distributed across different online learning activities and communication channels outside of online discussion and computer conferencing. Research is still at an early stage to study directed facilitation beyond the context of asynchronous discussions and computer conferencing. In this section, the authors intend to describe a few directed facilitation strategies that were used in the example course to promote social and cognitive presence.

Strategy 1: Use Technology to Personalize Social Activities

To help geographically distant learners to develop trust and feeling of connections in a community of inquiry, online courses usually have some icebreaker activities. A standard practice is to have students post a message to an online discussion forum, sometimes with a picture, to introduce themselves. While this activity serves as a quick way for everyone to introduce themselves, it is also limited by the functionality of discussion forums in most LMS's. Lowenthal and Dunlap (2010) observed shortcomings of text-based introductions, and resorted to digital storytelling to promote social presence. With the prevalence of Web 2.0 tools, it is possible for students to get to know each other by adding more personal touch to such activities.

In this course, students had icebreaker activities both as a large class and within their project team. At the beginning of the class, students were asked to create an online profile on the *about.me* website, where they could provide a brief text introduction, use an image that best represented themselves, and post their own picture. They could also choose to connect their *about.me* profiles to their other social media profiles such as Twitter and Linked-in. Students' profiles were submitted and aggregated using *Google Forms*, which were made available for students to view each other's profiles. Later in class, when students started the reflective blogging activities, they were once again asked to visit and comment on each other's blogs. Such activity was intended for students to both socially interact with each other and cognitively exchange ideas.

After students were placed in project teams, they had an icebreaker activity within teams. They had to utilize any available communication tools (team discussion forum, email, online team meeting, etc.) to find out the three favorite individuals for each team member. Based on what they found, they would post a blog entry on their *WordPress* website in which they would present a virtual gift to each team member. The gift could be an image, video, website, or a quote that was related to the team member's favorite individuals. The virtual gift exchange activity not only helped team members to further acquaint with each other at a more personal level, but also provided them a chance to explore and identify appropriate communication tools for later team collaborations.

Strategy 2: Scaffold Team Formation and Beginning Collaboration

Long-term team project can be intimidating to both the instructor and students in an online class. The instructor has to perform pedagogical, technical, and administrative functions to ensure successful team formation, effective collaboration, and satisfactory project progress and product. Students have to collaborate virtually via different communication and collaboration tools to achieve a common goal and produce shared artifacts. Team formation in an online course is often done by the instructor who assigns students to different teams, often randomly. While this is efficient from the perspective of the instructor, students do not have a chance to identify common interests and goals and form teams accordingly. Once students are placed in teams, one cannot assume that they automatically know how to collaborate, especially at a distance (Nussbaum et al., 2009). Scaffolding team formation and beginning collaboration becomes an essential first step to facilitate teamwork.

In this course, an online tool, *Linoit*, was used to help students identify and form teams with those who shared similar interests. *Linoit* is a web-based collaboration canvas that allows users to post their ideas in the form of sticky notes. Early in the semester, students were asked to individually post to the canvas their ideas about the *Teaching with Digital Tools* project. When they posted theirs, they were also able to see others' ideas, and they were asked to post their sticky notes close to those that were similar to theirs (Figure 7). This activity provided an effective way for students to virtually identify those who shared similar interests, and enabled the instructor to assign teams based on common interests.

As in face-to-face classes, there are always undesirable behaviors in teamwork. To prepare students to be better team players, a wiki activity was set up for students to compile a list of undesirable behaviors from their past teamwork experience. This activity not only served as a reminder for students, but also prepared them for a wiki assignment later in the semester.

Figure 7. Linoit online canvas for students to post and group their project ideas

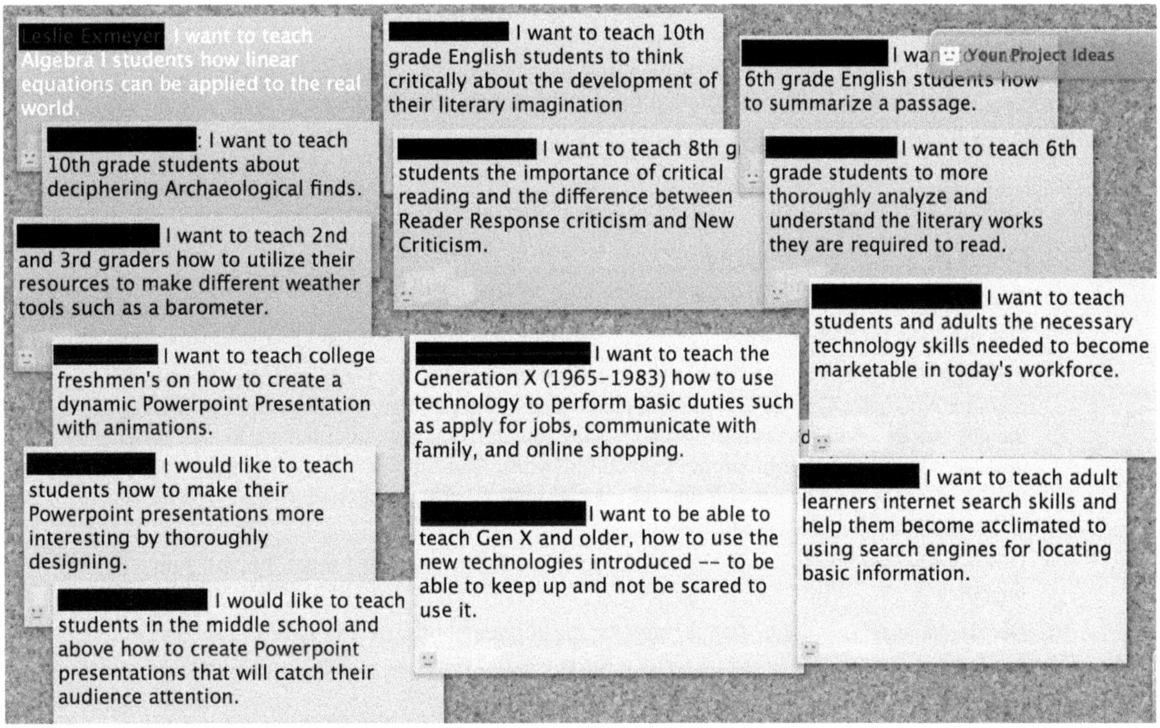

After the teams were formed, members were required to have a synchronous online meeting. A meeting agenda (Figure 8) was provided to guide the teams so they knew what needed to be addressed in order to transition from social encounters to purposeful relationships and cognitive inquiries (Garrison, 2007).

Strategy 3: Plan for a Multi-Layered Discourse Mechanism to Move from Exploration to Resolution Phase of Inquiry

McLoughlin and Luca (2002) stated that in an online environment, an instructor often cannot supervise and support teamwork at the same level as in the face-to-face settings. Teaching presence in teamwork is often limited to the scope of task definition, management and feedback. This may partially explain why cognitive inquiries in online courses often stay at the exploration stage (Garrison, 2007). Researchers have used various strategies and processes to help team collaboration move toward the resolution stage. For example, Nagel and Lotze (2009) employed a double-blind review activity, which brought a deeper dimension of learning to the class and enhanced teaching, cognitive and social presences.

In this course, a multi-layered discourse mechanism was implemented. After teams worked together to submit each milestone of their project, the instructor provided feedback to the team. In the subsequent week, each team member would individually read and respond to the instructor's feedback, so that each member would form his or her own opinion to prepare for team discussions. In the following week, the team would reconvene to review the instructor's feedback, share each other's ideas and work together toward the next milestone of the project. By facilitating discourse between instructor and students, as

Figure 8. A meeting agenda to help students with their first team meeting

How to collaborate as a team

I highly encourage you to use asynchronous online meetings to discuss the project with team members. Here is a sample agenda I drafted for you. As we move on to the next stage, you should manage the project by yourselves.

Discussion agenda:

1. Decide on target learners and topic
2. Decide on how to divide the work
3. Discuss tools for collaboration

   I strongly recommend Google Docs (used for last week's *My Story* assignment). A team member who has a Google account can create a new Google Doc for the team. The sharing of the doc can be set so that everyone who has the link can edit it without having to sign in. The doc can be used in both synchronous meetings (where you can discuss while seeing real time what your team members are typing) and asynchronous settings (each of you is working on a different part of the same document)
4. Discuss who is going to create the new Google Doc for the team and share the link with team members
5. Decide on target finish time (leave room for the alignment of different parts to be coherent)
6. Decide on who is going to finalize the proposal, copy it to Word, and submit to Blackboard for the team
7. Exchange best way of communication for each team member

well as among students, at both individual and team levels, the mechanism was intended to challenge students to negotiate ideas and reach consensus as they worked on the team project.

Strategy 4: Provide Just-in-Time Instruction at Multiple Junctures

Direct instruction in an online course consists not only pre-recorded lectures or other materials prepared beforehand, it is also provided in the form of just-in-time instruction at multiple junctures of an online course. As stated earlier, effective course design can provide opportunities for an instructor to examine students' thinking and work in progress. The instructor needs to remain sensitive to the process of student learning, and diagnose misconceptions and interject when judged necessary (Garrison, 2007).

In this course, the instructor's weekly introductions served as direct instruction. The weekly introductions reviewed and summarized important information from the previous week, and introduced students to the new topics of the week. Moreover, based on students' work in the previous week (e.g., online discussions, personal emails, blog posts, or other submitted assignments), the instructor answered important questions raised by students, and addressed or clarified any misconceptions or confusions. The introduction was intended to help students develop a clear understanding of what they had learned and get ready for what they were about to learn.

Direct instruction was also provided when the instructor offered the "expert perspective." For example, after students spent two weeks working on a case study, the instructor recorded an audio to explain how an expert in the field would approach the issues in the case.

Direct instruction also occurred in the instructor's feedback to student work. When an important issue was detected, the instructor highlighted the issue and provided extensive feedback to help students move toward the right direction. If the issue was found common among several class members, the instructor would escalate the feedback to the entire class.

Strategy 5: Encourage and Make Use of Student-Initiated Discourse

Anderson (2008) found that discourse solely based on teacher-initiated questions and content soon becomes boring to students. A skillful instructor in a face-to-face classroom would encourage students to share their ideas and work, and build teaching on student-initiated discourse. In an online course, encouraging, acknowledging, or reinforcing student contributions can help to establish and maintain productive discourse (Shea et al., 2006). Such practice not only benefits students cognitively, but also helps to establish a sense of trust, openness and safety within a learning community (Anderson, 2008).

In this class, students were given the opportunity to decide for themselves the weight of team members' peer evaluation in their overall project grade. Each student could vote on their preferred percentage, and the majority vote would be used in calculating their project grade. This activity was intended to give students a voice and ownership of their work.

Measures have also been taken to build learning on student-initiated discourse. For example, students were asked to respond to an open-ended question via an online polling system, *PollEverywhere*. In the subsequent week, the instructor used students' responses to generate a word cloud to visually display and discuss the trends in the responses. In her blog, the instructor regularly summarized common threads among students' reflections, identified different perspectives, highlighted "pearls" in students' posts, or featured excellent student works. Links to students' works were embedded in the instructor's posts to help students further explore others' ideas.

Strategy 6: Maintain Timely and Personalized Communications

Instructor immediacy characterizes the extent to which the instructor's communication behaviors reduce the psychological distance between the instructor and students (Moore & Kearsley, 1996). Immediacy behaviors are positively associated with student satisfaction, affect, perceived cognition, motivation, and learning outcomes (Arbaugh, 2001; Baker, 2004). To enhance immediacy, research suggests practices such as addressing students by name, using inclusive personal pronouns such as "we" "us" in communications, responding frequently to students, offering praise, and communicating attentiveness (O'Sullivan, Hunt, & Lippert, 2004).

The instructor maintained timely communications with students throughout the course. During the first couple weeks of a semester, students are often not used to the course schedule and miss participation or assignments. At this early stage, the instructor worked to identify those students and sent individual reminder emails to them. As the semester moved on, the instructor gave students' sense of instructor presence through timely response to emails or questions (usually within 24 hours), and timely feedback to student work. Certainly, this imposed time demands to the instructor. But it is important for the instructor to establish a communication routine and make it known to students. In all her communications with students, the instructor personalized communication by addressing students by name.

Ashley's Experience

Ashley reflected on her experience regarding the directed facilitation aspect of the course:

The Community of Inquiry theory structure of the directed facilitation was impactful to the learning experience. The weekly course content was posted to Blackboard by 9 am on each Monday morning. As I reviewed the email, weekly agenda, and media introduction from the instructor, the goals were clear, and there was always course personalization to keep me motivated. The inclusion of my name or my classmate's names, specific congratulations or questions showed me that the instructor had read our work, and thought of us in the development of the next week's lesson introduction. For example, in one of my blog posts, I included a quote about technology, and the instructor used it in her blog too.

Virtual office hours were available most weeks, but I never called or messaged the instructor during this time. I did not need to, because the instruction was clear. The instructor did request mid-semester course feedback, and then wrote a response on her blog afterwards. This demonstrated a commitment to life-long learning, improvement, and course evolution.

The formation of groups through the Linoit activity gave us insight into our classmate's ideas and beliefs, and established ownership in our team before the project began. The virtual gift exchange activity was also unique and effective. My group worked well together from a distance, and we all attributed that to the gift activity. Plus, it is always nice to receive a gift, and even nicer to receive one that cost the sender nothing except a few minutes in a Google search. Additionally, each student posted the gifts to their blog, and it was fun to look at the gifts everyone in the course received. This encouraged us to look at and comment on our classmate's blogs.

At the beginning of the group project, the instructor inquired via a poll about the percentage of our group project work that should be based on peer assessment. Though my favored percentage was not selected by the majority, I appreciated that I had a vote in the decision. To make our group collaboration smoother, my group selected a standing meeting time every week, to avoid scheduling conflicts. If we needed to meet, the time was reserved for us. If not, we could cancel our meeting via group text (we used the app GroupMe). The requirement of responding to the instructor's feedback individually meant that everyone had to review the comments and prepare for discussion. This eliminated one potential cause of disengagement, and served as a checkpoint to promote an even distribution of work among the group members.

Although the instructor did not teach the Community of Inquiry theory in this particular course, I think it would be valuable to address the theory in online courses of any discipline. When students understand the online learning theory, they recognize the intention of an activity, and can better apply the activity to their individual success in the framework of the theory.

Students' Overall Perceptions of the Community of Inquiry in the Illustrated Course

While Ashley's account of her experience illustrates the perspective from one individual student, it helps to supplement the individual experience with the feedback from the entire class. The CoI survey was administered at the end of the course. Twenty students completed the survey. Students' average ratings of teaching, cognitive, and social presence were 4.62, 4.45, and 4.41 out of 5 respectively. While the data represent only one class without any comparison groups, the ratings are generally at a higher range.

CONCLUSION

In their mixed method study, Kupczynski, Ice, Wiesenmayer, and McCluskey (2010) found that "regardless of learner level, the need for presentation of clear, concise objectives, instructions and general participation guidelines should be a cornerstone of online course development." (p.32). While the general guidelines provide principles for enhance teaching presence, this chapter intends to operationalize the principles by offering specific strategies in the context of an example course.

Although the strategies are anchored in one particular online course, readers will find that most strategies can be applied to any online courses. The authors recognize that for online courses that adopt a Fordism model (Simonson et al., 2012), the instructor is often not responsible for the design of curriculum. Yet the instructor or instructional designer can still benefit from the strategies outlined in this chapter.

Looking ahead, more studies are needed to empirically test the effectiveness of the strategies, especially in settings where new generations of technology are employed to support teaching and learning. Another consideration is the scaling of the strategies. While the constructivist-oriented strategies work well with a relatively small group of learners, it is challenging to maintain high levels of teaching presence for a cohort of more than 30-40 students (Annand, 1999; Anderson & Dron, 2011). With the recent progress in learning analytics, perhaps some of the strategies could be automated in the future to maintain teaching presence in large classes.

REFERENCES

Abrami, P. C., Bernard, R. M., Borokhovski, E., Waddington, D. I., Wade, C. A., & Persson, T. (2015). Strategies for teaching students to think critically: A meta-analysis. *Review of Educational Research*, *85*(2), 275–314.

Akyol, Z., & Garrison, D. R. (2011a). Assessing metacognition in an online community of inquiry. *The Internet and Higher Education*, *14*(3), 183–190. doi:10.1016/j.iheduc.2011.01.005

Akyol, Z., & Garrison, D. R. (2011b). Understanding cognitive presence in an online and blended community of inquiry: Assessing outcomes and processes for deep approaches to learning. *British Journal of Educational Technology*, *42*(2), 233–250. doi:10.1111/j.1467-8535.2009.01029.x

Akyol, Z., & Garrison, D. R. (2014). The development of a community of inquiry over time in an online course: Understanding the progression and integration of social, cognitive and teaching presence. *Journal of Asynchronous Learning Networks*, *12*(3-4), 3–22.

Allen, I. E., & Seaman, J. (2015). *Grade level: Tracking online education in the United States*. Wellesley, MA: Babson Survey Research Group and Quahog Research Group, LLC.

Anderson, T. (2008). *The theory and practice of online learning* (2nd ed.). Edmonton, AB: Athabasca University Press.

Anderson, T., & Dron, J. (2011). Three generations of distance education pedagogy. *The International Review of Research in Open and Distributed Learning*, *12*(3). Retrieved from http://www.irrodl.org/index.php/irrodl/article/view/890/1826

Anderson, T., Rourke, L., Garrison, D. R., & Archer, W. (2001). Assessing teaching presence in a computer conferencing context. *Journal of Asynchronous Learning Networks*, *5*(2). Retrieved from http://cde.athabascau.ca/coi_site/documents/Anderson_Rourke_Garrison_Archer_Teaching_Presence.pdf

Anglin, G. J., & Morrison, G. R. (2000). An analysis of distance education research: Implications for the instructional technologist. *Quarterly Review of Distance Education*, *1*(3), 189–194.

Annand, D. (1999). The problem of computer conferencing for distance-based universities. *Open Learning*, *14*(3), 47–52. doi:10.1080/0268051990140307

Arbaugh, J. B. (2001). How instructor immediacy behaviors affect student satisfaction and learning in web-based courses. *Business Communication Quarterly*, *64*(4), 42–54. doi:10.1177/108056990106400405

Arbaugh, J. B., Cleveland-Innes, M., Diaz, S. R., Garrison, D. R., Ice, P., Richardson, J. C., & Swan, K. P. (2008). Developing a community of inquiry instrument: Testing a measure of the Community of Inquiry framework using a multi-institutional sample. *The Internet and Higher Education*, *11*(3-4), 133–136. doi:10.1016/j.iheduc.2008.06.003

Archibald, D. (2010). Fostering the development of cognitive presence: Initial findings using the community of inquiry survey instrument. *The Internet and Higher Education*, *13*(1-2), 73–74. doi:10.1016/j.iheduc.2009.10.001

Aslanian, C. B., & Clinefelter, D. L. (2012). *Online college students 2012: Comprehensive data on demands and preferences*. Louisville, KY: The Learning House, Inc.

Baker, J. D. (2004). An investigation of relationships among instructor immediacy and affective and cognitive learning in the online classroom. *The Internet and Higher Education*, *7*(1), 1–13. doi:10.1016/j.iheduc.2003.11.006

Bonk, C. J., & Zhang, K. (2008). *Empowering online learning: 100+ activities for reading, reflecting, displaying, and doing*. San Francisco, CA: Jossey-Bass.

Brindley, J. E., Walti, C., & Blaschke, L. M. (2009). Creating effective collaborative learning groups in an online environment. *The International Review of Research in Open and Distributed Learning*, *10*(3).

Cavanaugh, C., Gillan, K. J., Kromrey, J., Hess, M., & Blomeyer, R. (2004). *The effects of distance education on K-12 student outcomes: A meta-analysis*. Naperville, IL: Learning Point Associates.

Collins, A., Brown, J. S., & Holum, A. (2011). Cognitive apprenticeship: Making thinking visible. *American Educator*, *6*(11), 38–46.

Dabbagh, N. (2003). Scaffolding: An important teacher competency in online learning. *TechTrends*, *47*(2), 39–44. doi:10.1007/BF02763424

Dahlstrom, E. (2012). *ECAR study of undergraduate students and information technology*. Louisville, CO: EDUCAUSE Center for Applied Research.

Dean, P. J., Stahl, M. J., Sylwester, D. L., & Peat, J. A. (2001). Effectiveness of combined delivery modalities for distance learning and resident learning. *Quarterly Review of Distance Education*, *2*(3), 247–254.

Dick, W., Carey, L., & Carey, J. (2008). *The systematic design of instruction* (7th ed.). New York: Pearson.

Dunlap, J. C., & Lowenthal, P. R. (2009). Tweeting the night away: Using Twitter to enhance social presence. *Journal of Information Systems Education*, *20*(2). Retrieved from http://www.patricklowenthal.com/publications/Using_Twitter_to_Enhance_Social_Presence.pdf

Fisher, E. A., & Wright, Y. H. (2010). Improving online course design through usability testing. *MERLOT Journal of Online Learning and Teaching*, *6*(1), 228–245.

Garrison, D. R. (2003). Cognitive presence for effective asynchronous online learning: The role of reflective inquiry, self-direction and metacognition. In J. Bourne & J. C. Moore (Eds.), Elements of Quality: Practice and Direction (pp. 47-58). Needham, MA: Sloan-C.

Garrison, D. R. (2006). Online collaboration principles. *Journal of Asynchronous Learning Networks*, *10*(1), 25–34.

Garrison, D. R. (2007). Online community of inquiry review: Social, cognitive, and teaching presence issues. *Journal of Asynchronous Learning Networks*, *11*(1), 61–72.

Garrison, D. R. (2011). *E-Learning in the 21st century: A framework for research and practice* (2nd ed.). New York: Routledge.

Garrison, D. R., Anderson, T., & Archer, W. (2000). Critical inquiry in a text-based environment: Computer conferencing in higher education. *The Internet and Higher Education*, *2*(2-3), 87–105. doi:10.1016/S1096-7516(00)00016-6

Garrison, D. R., & Cleveland-Innes, M. (2005). Facilitating cognitive presence in online learning: Interaction is not enough. *American Journal of Distance Education*, *19*(3), 133–148. doi:10.1207/s15389286ajde1903_2

Garrison, D. R., Cleveland-Innes, M., & Fung, T. S. (2010). Exploring causal relationships among teaching, cognitive and social presence: Student perceptions of the community of inquiry framework. *The Internet and Higher Education*, *13*(1-2), 31–36. doi:10.1016/j.iheduc.2009.10.002

Joo, Y. J., Lim, K. Y., & Kim, E. K. (2011). Online university students' satisfaction and persistence: Examining perceived level of presence, usefulness and ease of use as predictors in a structural model. *Computers & Education*, *57*(2), 1654–1664. doi:10.1016/j.compedu.2011.02.008

Ke, F. (2010). Examining online teaching, cognitive, and social presence for adult students. *Computers & Education*, *55*(2), 808–820. doi:10.1016/j.compedu.2010.03.013

Kupezynski, L., Ice, P., Wiesenmayer, R., & McCluskey, F. (2010). Student perceptions of the relationship between indicators of teaching presence and success in online courses. *Journal of Interactive Online Learning*, *9*(1), 23–43.

Liu, X., Magjuka, R. J., Bonk, C. J., & Lee, S. H. (2007). Does sense of community matter? An examination of participants' perceptions of building learning communities in online courses. *Quarterly Review of Distance Education*, *8*(1), 9–24.

Lowenthal, P. R., & Dunlap, J. C. (2010). From pixel on a screen to real person in your students' lives: Establishing social presence using digital storytelling. *The Internet and Higher Education*, *13*(1-2), 70–72. doi:10.1016/j.iheduc.2009.10.004

McLoughlin, C., & Luca, J. (2002). A learner–centred approach to developing team skills through web–based learning and assessment. *British Journal of Educational Technology*, *33*(5), 571–582. doi:10.1111/1467-8535.00292

Meyer, K. A. (2013). Face-to-face versus threaded discussions: The role of time and higher-order thinking. *Journal of Asynchronous Learning Networks*, *7*(3), 55–65.

Moore, M. G., & Kearsley, G. (1996). *Distance education: A systems view*. Belmont, CA: Wadsworth.

Morrison, G. R., Ross, S. M., Kalman, H. K., & Kemp, J. E. (2012). *Designing effective instruction* (7th ed.). Hoboken, NJ: Wiley.

Murphy, E. (2004). Recognising and promoting collaboration in an online asynchronous discussion. *British Journal of Educational Technology*, *35*(4), 421–431. doi:10.1111/j.0007-1013.2004.00401.x

Nagel, L., & Lotze, T. (2010). Supersizing e-learning: What a CoI survey reveals about teaching presence in a large online class. *The Internet and Higher Education*, *13*(2), 45–51. doi:10.1016/j.iheduc.2009.12.001

Nielsen, J. (2000). *Designing web usability: The practice of simplicity*. Indianapolis, IN: New Riders.

Nussbaum, M., Alvarez, C., McFarlane, A., Gomez, F., Claro, S., & Radovic, D. (2009). Technology as small group face-to-face Collaborative Scaffolding. *Computers & Education*, *52*(1), 147–153. doi:10.1016/j.compedu.2008.07.005

O'Sullivan, P. B., Hunt, S. K., & Lippert, L. R. (2004). Mediated immediacy: A language of affiliation in a technological age. *Journal of Language and Social Psychology*, *23*(4), 464–490. doi:10.1177/0261927X04269588

Ritchhart, R., Church, M., & Morrison, K. (2011). *Making thinking visible: How to promote engagement, understanding, and independence for all learners*. San Francisco, CA: Jossey-Bass.

Rovai, A. P. (2002). Building sense of community at a distance. *International Review of Research in Open and Distance Education*, *5*(2). Retrieved from http://www.irrodl.org/index.php/irrodl/article/view/79/152

Sadler, D. R. (1989). Formative assessment and the design of instructional systems. *Instructional Science*, *18*(2), 119–144. doi:10.1007/BF00117714

Shea, P. (2006). A study of students' sense of learning community in online environments. *Journal of Asynchronous Learning Networks*, *10*(1), 35–44.

Shea, P., & Bidjerano, T. (2012). Learning presence as a moderator in the community of inquiry mode. *Computers & Education*, *59*(2), 316–326. doi:10.1016/j.compedu.2012.01.011

Shea, P., Li, C. S., & Pickett, A. (2006). A study of teaching presence and student sense of learning community in fully online and web-enhanced college courses. *The Internet and Higher Education*, *9*(3), 175–190. doi:10.1016/j.iheduc.2006.06.005

Shea, P., Li, C. S., Swan, K., & Pickett, A. (2005). Developing learning community in online asynchronous college courses: The role of teaching presence. *Journal of Asynchronous Learning Networks*, *9*(4), 59–82.

Shea, P., Vickers, J., & Hayes, S. (2010). Online instructional effort measured through the lens of teaching presence in the community of inquiry framework: A re-examination of measures and approach. *The International Review of Research in Open and Distributed Learning*, *11*(3). Retrieved from http://www.irrodl.org/index.php/irrodl/article/view/915

Simonson, M., Smaldino, S., Albright, M., & Zvacek, S. (2012). *Teaching and learning at a distance: Foundations of distance education* (5th ed.). Boston, MA: Pearson.

Smith, P., & Ragan, T. (2005). *Instructional design* (3rd ed.). Hoboken, NJ: Wiley.

Swan, K., & Shih, L. F. (2005). On the nature and development of social presence in online course discussions. *Journal of Asynchronous Learning Networks*, *9*(3), 115–136.

Wiley, D. A. (2002). *Instructional use of learning objects*. Bloomington, IN: AECT. Retrieved June 26, 2015 from http://www.reusability.org/read/

Chapter 8
Synchronous and Asynchronous Tools Optimizing Online Learning in the English-Speaking Caribbean

Paulette Stewart
The University of the West Indies, Jamaica

ABSTRACT

This chapter examines the effectiveness of asynchronous and synchronous tools used in the online education program at The University of the West Indies Open Campus which is located in the English-speaking Caribbean. The students are adults who are self-directed, goal-oriented and self-motivated learners and are used to the face-to-face mode of delivery. Developers of online programs have applied these learner characteristics to online learning to facilitate students' success. At first, asynchronous tools such as forums were used to deliver online education at The UWI, Open Campus, but in recent time synchronous tools such as Blackboard Collaborate has emerged and has revolutionized online learning in that they provide more scope for e-tutor and student engagement and teacher immediacy. The blend of both synchronous and asynchronous tools has changed e-tutors' pedagogical practices, and enhanced learning.

INTRODUCTION

The request for higher education at a distance has led many universities to implement online education to meet this growing demand and to expand the market share of the education business community. This paradigmatic shift to online learning changes how learning occurs and is communicated through the use of synchronous and asynchronous educational tools. Through these tools, universities that have campuses across a wide geographic region can deliver online education almost equivalent to the conventional instruction. The University of the West Indies is one such university located in the Caribbean with islands scattered over 3 million square kilometres within the Caribbean Sea. The Leeward and Windward

DOI: 10.4018/978-1-4666-9995-3.ch008

Islands are fairly close in proximity to two campuses of the University of the West Indies—St. Augustine in Trinidad and Tobago and the Cave Hill in Barbados. However, these islands are over 1,600 km from Jamaica, where the Mona campus is located (see Figure 1).

Travel from these islands to the Mona campus in Jamaica is usually circuitous, costly, lengthy and difficult. These challenges, together with the demand for online learning and the emergence of information technology that supports interactive communication, have given rise to online learning in the region.

The University of the West Indies (UWI) commenced distance education in 1983 through the UWI Distance Teaching Experiment (UWIDITE). The network linked the three campuses of the UWI in Jamaica, Barbados, and Trinidad and Tobago and the Extra Mural Centres in Antigua, Dominica, and St. Lucia. UWIDITE was the first project in the developing world to use telephone audio conferencing as a principal teaching method. Courses were taught utilizing a combination of print material and teleconferences. There were occasional supplements in the form of video or audio tapes, and some local support by way of tutorials or practicum supervision (Lalor & Stahmer, 1987).

UWIDITE came to an end in 2008 when the fourth campus, The UWI Open Campus, was established to better serve the growing distance education community and to improve the administrative efficiency of distance education offerings. The Open Campus is an amalgamation of the previous Office of the Board for Non-Campus Countries and Distance Education (BNNCDE), the School of Continuing Studies (SCS), the UWI Distance Education Centre (UWIDEC), and the Tertiary Level Institutions Unit (Lalor & Marrett, 1986). To date, this campus has 42 physical sites in 17 English-speaking Caribbean countries (UWI Open Campus, 2015), from which it uses synchronous and asynchronous tools to deliver various programmes.

Figure 1. Map of the Caribbean showing proximity of leeward and windward islands to Jamaica

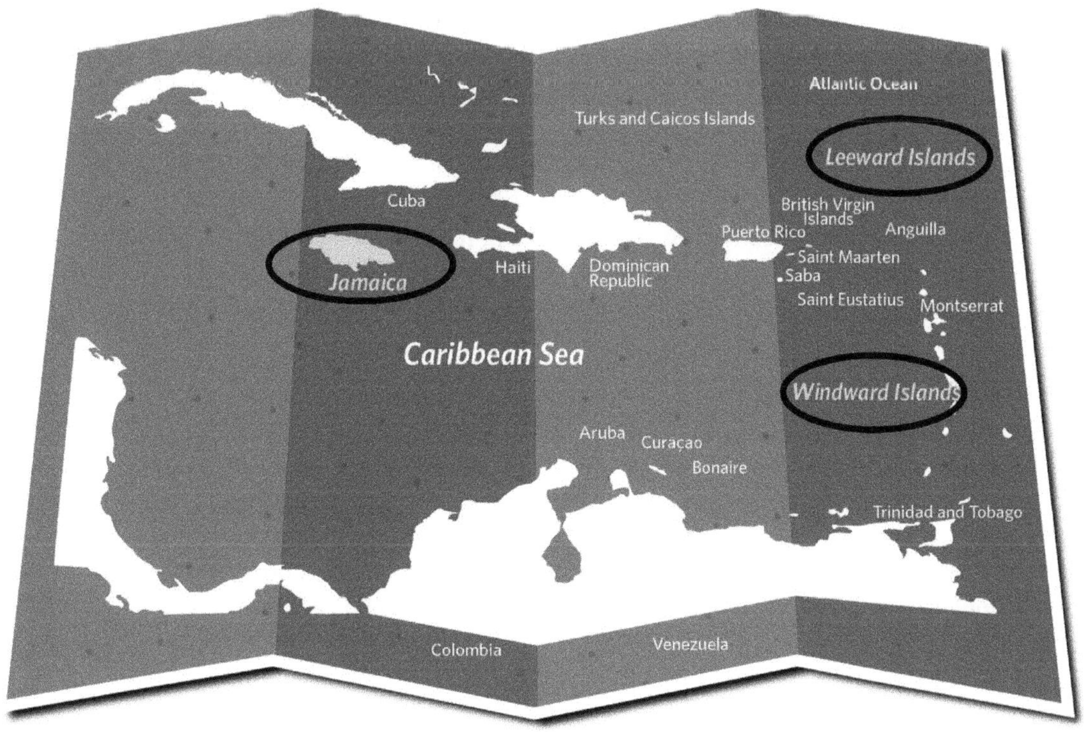

The advancement of media-rich information communication technologies (ICT) has been changing the way online classes are conducted. These technologies are either asynchronous or synchronous. Asynchronous learning takes place virtually but it is delayed because e-tutors and students are not online at the same time. E-tutors or students are engaged in asynchronous activities when they interact in the forum, send e-mails, read threaded discussions, or send text messages. Obasa, Eludire, and Ajao (2013) include e-books in the category of asynchronous tools because they supplement teaching and learning, are static, and do not require interaction. They also include databases because they are repositories of teaching and learning resources. Asynchronous tools are regarded as having a lower level of social presence and therefore require added engagement strategies to create a sense of community and belonging among students.

Synchronous learning takes place virtually in real-time. A number of synchronous tools are being used in online education. These include Blackboard Collaborate and Skype, which allow for video, audio, and web-conferencing. Phone conversations and instant messages may also be included. Synchronous tools create technological immediacy, which promotes teacher presence, cognitive presence, and social presence; moreover, according to Thomson (2014), the right strategies will enable instructors to use these tools to create interesting, informative course work activities and exercises that will fuel students' hunger for learning more. In order to use both asynchronous and synchronous tools effectively in an online educational environment, careful thought has to be given to the pedagogical practices that govern these tools as well as the characteristics of the learners.

The 2013/14 demographic statistics for students of The UWI Open Campus revealed a student population of 6684, with 15.2% being males and 84.8% being females. The majority were in the 24-34 age cohort. Five thousand nine hundred and fourteen (5914) pursued undergraduate degrees and certificate/diploma, while 388 were enrolled in higher degrees and advanced diploma programs. The remaining 391 were specially admitted students (Dass, 2014); that is to say, they were pursuing one or two courses in one of the programs.

The findings of research conducted by Stewart, Bachman, and Johnson (2010) on the demographic characteristics of online learners in the United States revealed similarities to their Caribbean counterparts. These findings suggest that on the one hand, the majority of today's online learners are adults who are usually high school graduates, are employed, and are returning to study after many years away from the formal education system. They are likely to be apprehensive and lacking in confidence about their ability to succeed in online education. On the other hand, research has also shown that today's distance learners are well prepared to engage in online learning activities by virtue of their knowledge of the Internet and web-based technology (Dabbagh, 2007, citing The National Home Study Council, 2000).

Objectives of the Chapter

This chapter discusses the impact that teacher immediacy, which includes teaching presence, cognitive presence, and social presence, has in an online environment. The discussion will include the theoretical framework underpinning teacher immediacy. It also looks at how asynchronous and synchronous tools are used at The UWI Open Campus to enhance teacher immediacy and provide academic and social support to students. It highlights three mini case studies to show real life examples of three categories of teacher immediacy, and finally it looks at some of the implications of teacher immediacy in an online environment.

Background

Teacher Immediacy in an Online Environment

The construct of immediacy is defined as "the extent to which selected communicative behaviors enhance physical or psychological closeness in interpersonal communication (Woods & Baker, 2004, citing Mehrabian, 1967, para. 12). This, they posit, can be understood as "those communication behaviors that reduce perceived distance between people" (Woods & Baker, 2004, citing Thweatt & McCroskey, 1996, para. 12). This is achieved by teacher immediacy which is defined by the Blackwell Reference Online as "communication behaviors that reduce the perceived distance between teacher and students." This conveys a feeling of warmth by e-tutors, positive interpersonal relationship, approachability, and availability for communication (Andersen & Andersen, n.d.). The concept of immediacy is identified as verbal and non-verbal communication and is grounded in the implicit communication theory espoused by Mehrabian in 1969.

Verbal implicit communication refers to stylistic verbal expressions used by teachers to develop within students a degree of like or dislike for their teacher. Gorham's investigation on verbal immediacy establishes that in the learning environment, verbal immediacy can include humor in class, praise of students' work, actions or comments, and willingness of e-tutors to become engaged in conversation with students. This type of communication can be achieved by using the emerging synchronous tools in the online environment. The findings of Gorham's research on verbal immediacy, which was conducted to measure students' perceptions of instructor immediacy on the Verbal Immediacy Scale (VIS), revealed that students' perception ranged from .84 to .90 (Bailie, 2011, citing Baker, 2004). In addition, other research findings have indicated that verbal immediacy shows that there is a relationship between student motivation, perceived cognition and affective learning (Valez & Cano, 2008, citing Christophel, 1990).

Non-verbal immediacy is defined as the implicit use of closeness-inducing behavioral cues (Valez & Cano, 2014, citing Andersen, 1979). In a virtual pedagogical online environment, non-verbal components of immediacy are not as forthright as verbal communication as only a few non-verbal components such as vocal and facial expressiveness can be displayed (Baker, 2010) when there is a synchronous session. These implicit forms of communication deal with transmitting information that is related to feeling, like and dislike, or attitude. The referents of these implicit non-verbal behaviors are emotions, attitudes, or like or dislike. Studies on the effects of nonverbal immediacy conducted by Andersen in 1979 revealed that the more immediate e-tutors are, the more likely they will communicate a close distance, smile, engage in eye contact, use body orientation and gestures, and be vocally expressive (Velez & Cano, 2008, citing Mehrabian, 1981).

The non-verbal immediacy such as vocal and facial expressiveness, bodily positioning, and movement convey affective feelings, warmth, closeness, and belonging (Valez & Cano, 2008, citing Richmond, Gorham, & McCroskey, 1987). These are important in the online learning environment as research has shown that this type of immediacy has "increased students' cognitive learning and information recall, affective learning, and student perception of teacher effectiveness" (Valez & Cano, 2008, citing Powell & Harville, 1990). Sathik and Johnathan (2013) indicated that several studies revealed that the most expressive way humans display emotions is through facial expression, and this is the primary source of information next to words. In addition, they state that a study conducted by Toby et al. in 2008 revealed that facial expression of lecturers kept students motivated and interested during the lecture (Sathik & Johnathan, citing Toby et al., 2008).

This teacher-student relationship that is developed due to teacher immediacy creates in students a positive behavior towards their instructors. This is supported by research that indicates that "teacher immediacy behaviors positively correlate with perceived cognitive, affective, and behavioral learning for students (Mullane, 2014, citing Sanders & Wiseman, 1990). Mullane (2014) also mentions that, "both verbal and nonverbal communication, immediacy behaviors reduce the psychological and/or physical distance between communicators and reducing distance leads to perceived feelings of closeness, directness, and connectedness and generates a direct effect on the relationship between the communicators (Mullane, citing Andersen, Norton, & Nussbaum, 1981; Carrell & Menzel, 2001; King & Witt, 2009; Ozmen, 2011).

The Impact of Teacher Immediacy in Online Environments

Research in the field of online learning indicates that teacher immediacy falls in three categories, which are teaching presence, cognitive presence, and social presence. Garrison, Anderson, and Archer (2000) were the first to differentiate social presence from teaching presence as part of the Communities of Inquiry model. They conceptualized teaching presence as "the design, facilitation, and direction of cognitive and social presence for the purpose of realizing personally meaningful and educationally worthwhile outcomes" (4). Sheridan and Kelly (2010) cited Anderson et al. as referring to these indicators of instructor presence.

Harris cites Garrison et al. (2000) in explaining that teaching presence is established when the course is designed in a manner that involves tasks such as curriculum development, creation, and integration of a variety of learning activities into the course and assessment of participants' outcomes. This includes organizing the course, establishing time parameters, and laying out netiquette criteria (Sheridan & Kelly, 2010, as cited in Anderson et al.). The facilitation includes setting the course climate, encouraging learner participation in course activities, and acknowledging participants' response. This also encompasses encouraging and reinforcing students' contribution, setting the climate for learning, and prompting discussion (Sheridan & Kelly, 2010). Research conducted by Mandernach, Gonzales, and Garrett (2006) shows that facilitation of discourse and instructor visibility is of key importance for establishing teaching presence. It is pointed out by Sheridan and Kelly (2010) that there is a consensus that the e-tutors are accountable to create a space for interaction, engage in discourse with students, provide information and course content, and offer feedback to students in a timely manner. Direct instruction encompasses tasks such as regulating the amount of materials covered, posting questions that guide participants' learning, summarizing discussion and confirming understanding through assessment and feedback. This description makes it evident that teaching presence begins with the preparatory work in designing and developing the course and continues throughout the duration of the course as the e-tutors provide direction and support when necessary (Lowenthal & Parscal, citing Anderson, Rourke, Garrison, & Archer, 2001).

This kind of teacher presence allows for interactive and collaborative learning as mentioned by Wicks (2009, citing Heinecka, Dawson, & Willis, 2001). This is supported by Lev Vygotsky's theory of social constructivism, which is explained as, "all cognitive functions originate in, and must therefore be explained as products of social interactions and that learning was not simply the assimilation and accommodation of new knowledge by learners; it was the process by which learners were integrated into a knowledge community" (GSI Teaching and Resource Center, para. 1). The social constructivism theory is evident in a teacher-present environment because within a social constructivist learning environment students are provided with opportunities to develop meaning by dialoguing, discussing, and debating with other learners. All these activities are done through social interaction. This social interaction creates meaning from current and prior knowledge, thus deepening understanding and extending knowledge for the students. Learners are actively involved in constructing knowledge of a topic using communication and social interactions with peers (Wicks, 2009, as cited in Conole, Dyke, Oliver, & Seale, 2004; Neo, 2008; Siemens, 2004; Snyder, 2009).

The Influence of Cognitive Presence in Online Environments

Teaching presence has shown to have a positive impact on cognitive presence, which is defined by Anderson, Rourke, Garrison, and Archer (2001, as cited by Swan, Garrison, & Richardson, 2009) as "the design, facilitation, and direction of cognitive and social processes for the purpose of realizing personally meaningful and educationally worthwhile learning outcomes" (14). The theory on cognitive presence links back to Dewey's work on reflective thinking and practical inquiry, the literature and research on critical thinking, and the concept development theory work in Vygotsky. This means that achieving cognitive presence in courses requires a focus on higher-order knowledge acquisition and application (Designing for Online Learning, 2012).

The elements for cognitive presence are triggering events, exploration, integration, and reflection (Sheridan & Kelly, 2010). The triggering events element is an important aspect of cognitive learning as it is something that causes students to be excited and motivated to be engaged in the course. This is a likely action that can trigger the other elements and should therefore be acknowledged as very important. The use of a variety of sources provides the means for students to explore the course while using their previous knowledge to make sense of and understand the concepts. This is seen as the element of integration. Finally, upon reflection students should understand the concepts gained from the lesson.

In the article *Designing for Learning 2012*, Garrison and Vaughan (2008) mention that depending on the duration and objectives of the course, course developers can design the course using the elements of cognitive presence in the following manner. Triggering event: use problem-solving strategies as a way of achieving some of their course goals. Exploration: use both individual reflection by the students and the discourse through which the problem formulation occurs. Students should get activities that include exchange of information, brainstorming, and requests for feedback on ideas. Integration: include individual and group reflection which should lead students to reach some convergences by connecting ideas, identifying relationships and patterns, and proposing solutions. Resolution: the group applies and tests solutions in real world scenarios. Learners defend their resolutions and the thinking that supports them.

The Impact of Social Presence in Online Environments

Social presence has been described by Short, Williams, and Christie (1976, as cited in Spear, 2012) as "the degree of salience of another person in an interaction and the consequent salience of an interpersonal relationship" (3). In other words, social presence is the perceived idea by students that there are other students participating in the interaction and the degree to which they believe they know one another (cited in Spear, 2012).

This therefore represents students' feeling of connectedness—social and emotional—with other students. The three elements that surround social presence are: active expression, open communication, and group cohesion. Unlike teacher presence and cognitive presence, social presence is at the level of the students in the online environment.

Active expression involves students' expression of emotion, humor, and self-disclosure, while open communication is their willingness to initiate conversations and respond to one another in an honest and respectful manner. Group cohesion is related to students agreeing with one another and in doing so using terms such as "we" when referring to the group. This also includes using salutation, vocatives, and phatics when addressing classmates. Of importance, at this level, e-tutors have to play a key role by modelling the desired behaviour students are expected to display (Pallof & Pratt, 2003; Pawan et al., 2003, as cited in Sheridan & Kelly, 2010). Short, Williams, and Christie (1976) conducted research and discovered that social presence was very highly correlated with interaction, collaborative learning, and satisfaction. These findings show that social presence is one of the most significant factors to improving instructional effectiveness (Spear, 2012, citing Tu, 2000).

Creating presence in an online learning environment is critical for the students to succeed and for e-tutors to have a positive experience with their class. According to Benshoff and Gibbon (2011), it is critical to create a strong teaching presence when teaching at a distance as it is the binding element in establishing a group of individuals for educational purposes. Along with this, cognitive presence is necessary as it has the potential for advancing meaningful learning in a virtual learning environment and is useful for providing students with opportunities for high levels of in-depth interaction.

METHODOLOGY

A qualitative content analysis was used to identify research and literature regarding teacher immediacy in online learning environments. The inductive approach was used whereby the themes, teacher presence, cognitive presence, and social presence were identified in each research paper and in the literature (Elo & Kynga, 2005). Data were drawn from the findings of these research reports regarding their pedagogical outcomes in online delivery. The results and discussions were used to substantiate the experiences of the researcher's interaction in the online environment. These themes were selected because they are the categories of teacher immediacy (Elo & Kynga, citing Polit & Beck, 2004). A corpus of knowledge from the researcher's environment was used to present three mini case studies on teacher immediacy, providing an engaging description of how teacher immediacy was achieved in the researcher's online environment. The discussions and conclusions were guided by the theoretical frameworks of Mehrabian's implicit communication theory, Vygotsky's social constructivism theory, and Holmberg's theory of guided didactic conversation. These were also used as a means of substantiating the assumptions made by the researcher.

The Synchronous and Asynchronous Tools in the UWI Online Environment

The UWI Open Campus online education initially delivered its online courses asynchronously through the use of a forum. This forum was used for uploading and accessing course content, providing instruction regarding the course, and facilitating interaction between e-tutors and students. The campus-assigned e-mail complemented communication within the learning community. With the introduction of Elluminate Live, a web-conferencing tool, the Open Campus ushered in synchronous delivery alongside its asynchronous tools. However, Elluminate was fraught with challenges such as lengthy delay to gain access and its inability to accommodate a large number of participants during virtual meetings. As a consequence, Blackboard Collaborate, which has a modern and easier-to-use graphical interface and better functionality (Garway, 2011, para. 1) superseded Elluminate Live. Blackboard Collaborate features a new intuitive, modern, and highly accessible web conference client interface as well as more collaboration choices to support both the pedagogical and operational efficiency goals of institutions (Blackboard Help, 2011, p.1). Through its synchronous and asynchronous online technology tool, The UWI Open Campus has been meeting the academic and professional needs of students who are unable to pursue studies on one of its campuses.

The UWI Open Campus uses the Moodle platform, which is a Course Management System (CMS), also known as a Learning Management System or a Virtual Learning Environment (VLE). It is a free web application that educators can use to create effective online learning sites. It allows for the creation of online activities such as storage of course content and management of students' grades. These activities are managed within forums. In this virtual learning environment, the asynchronous tools comprise a forum which includes activities and resources such as assignments, Wiki, quiz, and database. The synchronous tool, called the Blackboard Collaborate platform, features a white board, public and private chat, video, audio and web-conferencing, breakout rooms, PowerPoint import, participant sort, emoticons, and hand raise, among others. In addition to these useful features, there is the capacity for Blackboard Collaborate to accommodate hundreds of users simultaneously without the loss of signal. Blackboard Collaborate is beneficial as it facilitates increased completion rate and retention, eliminates geographical barriers, builds online communities, and accommodates multiple learning styles (Blackboard Help, 2011). The UWI protocol for accessing the synchronous and asynchronous tools is assigned username and password. Figure 2 shows the asynchronous and synchronous tools used in this online environment.

The various synchronous and asynchronous tools facilitate maximum participation by students during course delivery, thereby enhancing learning. This is important since in the online educational setting, "as with any educational technology tool, the purpose for using the tool has to make sense, has to fit in with the curriculum in a pedagogically sound way that supports learning and achievement of the course objectives" (Tag Archives, 2004, par. 5). The Hanover Research Council (2009) also supports this point

Figure 2. Asynchronous and synchronous tools used by UWI open campus

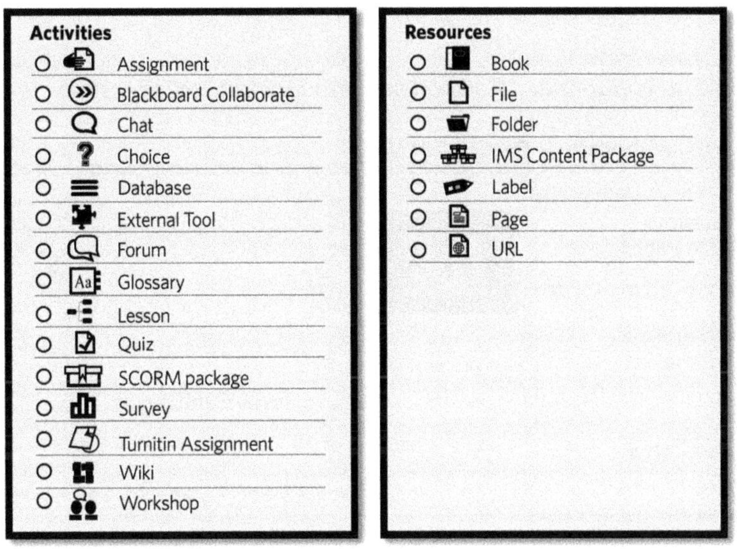

of view by emphasizing that teachers should ensure that pedagogical principles drive the use of technology and not the other way around (p.12). Students access the asynchronous and synchronous tools from the My Courses Page, the first stop in the online environment.

Teacher Immediacy and Synchronous Tools

The first of the three panels is the audio and video panels that facilitate teacher immediacy and encourage real time interaction among instructor and students. This is an example of the implicit communication theorized by Mehrabian, which provides instructors with a framework for fostering psychological closeness through interactions that reduces the physical distance between instructors and students. In the researcher's environment, the course coordinators hold scheduled virtual meetings with students via Blackboard Collaborate to provide an avenue of interaction between e-tutors and students, and students and students similar to what one obtains in a face-to-face environment (see Figure 3).

The audio and video feature facilitates verbal and non-verbal implicit communication. The picture of the e-tutor, the voice that appears in the audio and video panel provides verbal and nonverbal communication throughout the session, which can make a difference in the level of participation from students. Research findings have also indicated that during online sessions, the discussion and the visual cues such as "color, graphics and even the instructor's picture signal expressiveness, accessibility, engagement, and politeness" (Baker, 2010, p. 5, citing O'Sullivan et al., 2004). The discussions are geared towards building cognitive presence as the e-tutor guides, clarifies the concepts, exchanges information, makes suggestions, shares prior experiences, brainstorms new ideas, and suggests alternatives (Redmond, 2014, as cited in Garrison & Anderson, 2003).The e-tutor presence facilitates a meaningful intellectual climate that helps the instructor promptly gauge students' comprehension level and their critical thinking skills. The discussion also facilitates students' cognitive ability as shown by immediacy research that has established that instructor immediacy is positively related to student cognition and affect (Baker, 2010, citing Arbaugh, 2001; Baker, 2004; McAlister, 2001).

Another pedagogical attribute of the audio video component is the use of small-group and whole-class activities to develop the cooperative skills that students will need for the world of work. The small group activities that students are assigned to do when they are placed in separate breakout rooms by e-tutors

Figure 3. The Blackboard collaborate: Components that facilitate teacher immediacy

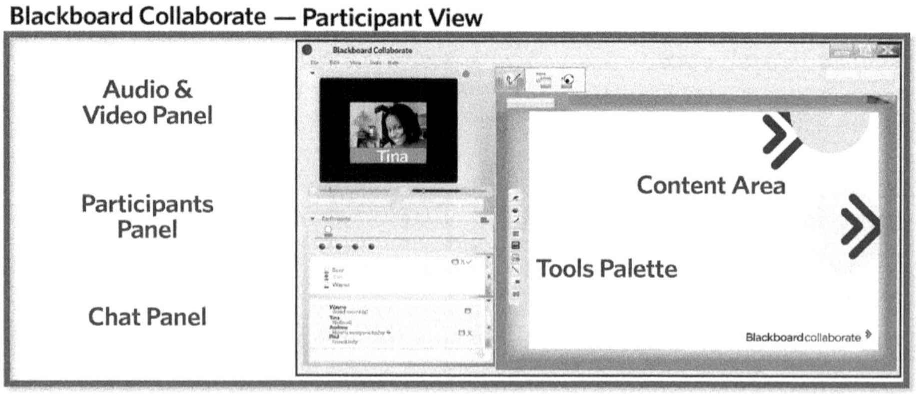

during the synchronous lesson is in support of Vygotsky's social constructivism theory as students are given the opportunity to discuss and debate, which is likely to give them a deeper understanding of the topic. Knabe (2004) cites Koyangi (2003) by stating that in this type of online classroom, students are not perceived as vessels for e-tutors to dump information in their minds, but as students engaged in active learning and discovery.

Knabe (2004) conducted a study on "*Constructivist learning perspectives in the online public relations classroom*" with six participants who had taught in an online environment. He reported that "the most frequent constructivist theme that emerged in the surveys was the value of learning in a social setting. Most of the participants found that learning in a community setting in the online classroom was useful and they indicated success with various teaching methodologies that encouraged peer collaboration in a social context" (4). To support this finding, Knabe cited Roblyer (2003) as describing this constructivist tenet as collaboration between students, with an emphasis on group work as opposed to students demonstrating personal competence on an individual basis.

The Participants Panel that sits beneath the Audio and Video Panel is designed for proactive course management. It gives the e-tutor some level of control over the class during discussion and question and answer sessions as in a face-to-face setting. It displays the names of the students so that the e-tutor can mark the register and address the students by names. In this section, the participants can respond to questions verbally by clicking on the talk icon, or non-verbally by using the option requested by the e-tutor, for example 'yes' and 'no' responses, 'raise hand' or multiple-choice responses (A, B, C, D, E, None) as seen in Figure 4.

There are other tools in this section that encourage students to participate in an orderly manner. For example, the whiteboard has the capacity for e-tutors and students to write on or upload PowerPoints while making a presentation. There are also emoticons that students can click to express their feelings during the session. E-tutors can use this verbal and non-verbal communication toward creating a relationship that will strengthen the academic achievement of students.

Immediately following the Participants Panel is the Chat Panel which allows e-tutors and students to see the comments made by their classmates and to respond to individuals as if they were in a face-to-face classroom setting. E-tutors generally set the requirement for the posting of comments so that such posting does not become chaotic. Students who are able to participate synchronously benefit from the interaction and collaboration identified as major factors in successful learning outcomes because they are able to ask questions for further information or for clarification and get immediate feedback (Higley, 2013, as cited in Bonk & Zhang, 2006; Martinez-Caro, 2011).

This panel facilitates teaching presence, cognitive presence, and social presence by allowing instant didactic communication that Bailie (2011) describes as Holmberg's (1986) theory of guided didactic conversation that focuses on the role of the interaction between the teacher and students in online learn-

Figure 4. Response choices

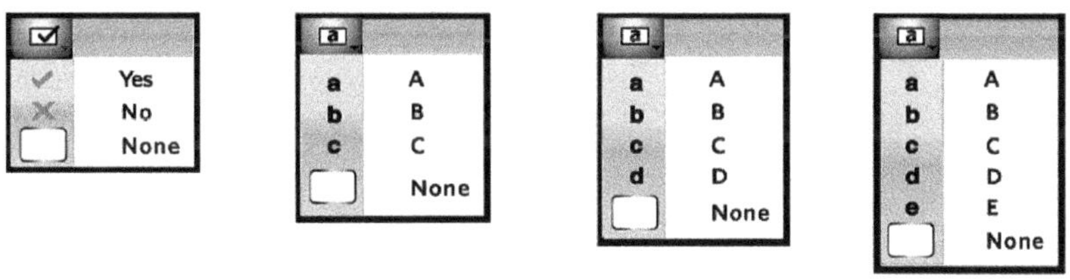

ing. He states that this verbal immediacy will heighten learning outcomes. He also cites the finding of Gorham's investigation on verbal immediacy by stating that this reduces psychological distance because of the recognition of individual students and their ideas and viewpoints. Cognitive presence is achieved by the exchange of information, the connection and application of new ideas. Social presence is gained with the use of the emoticons, the risk free expression, and the encouraged collaboration (McKerlich et al., 2011).

Asynchronous Tools and Teacher Presence

Course developers have to bear in mind the cognition and technology theory in relation to course design, facilitation, and direct instruction to guide them in coordinating the instructional design and learning process with human architecture. The creation of a forum with the use of asynchronous tools where students can respond in written format to graded and learning activities that are inserted in the content of each unit helps students create content that can be shared and discussed among their classmates. It also gives the e-tutors the space to respond with feedback and added information. This has not only fostered cognition but also allows e-tutors to use the six principles of the constructivist-focused online teaching, which are interactive and collaborative learning, facilitating and authentic learning, learner-centered and high quality learning.

The Tutor-Student Exchange which is used by the course coordinator, e-tutors, technical and administrative staff in the researcher online environment is designed to create teacher presence. This exchange is used to address all students in the course simultaneously on matters associated with the course and other issues related to the learning environment. These can include adjustment to course content and schedule, assignments, graded activities, forum posts, and virtual meetings. This forum therefore provides what Ragan describes as proactive course management, one of the 10 best practices of online learning. This satisfies the students' need for the course coordinator and the e-tutor to "serve as the guide, facilitator and "teacher" (Ragan, 2008, p.6).

Students are aware that the e-tutors visit this forum daily in order to give timely responses to their questions and concerns. The administrators ensure that this happens by including it in the job description of course coordinators and e-tutors. Consequently, students use it regularly to communicate with their course coordinator and e-tutor. An important feature of this section is the pop-up box that alerts the course coordinator and the e-tutor that there are messages in this forum from students. The forum is critical since it demonstrates teacher presence, an important objective of the Open Campus. This is referred to as communication immediacy, a concept proposed by Mehrabian in 1971, mentioned earlier in this paper. Students are provided with training so that they will be able to use the tools effectively and efficiently in order to achieve maximum benefit. Figure 5 displays the link to the training session.

Figure 5. Link to the training session

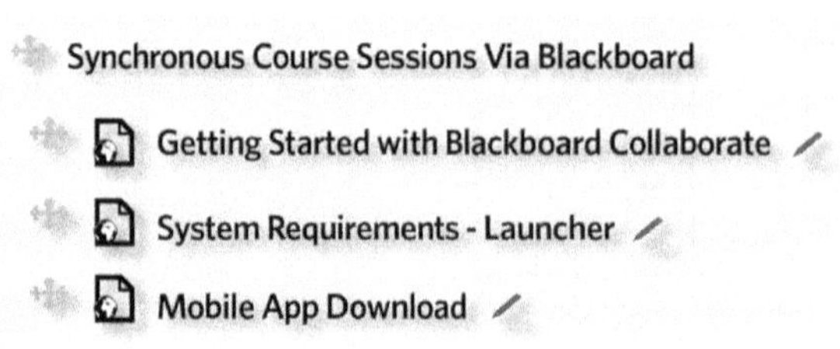

The Learning Forums is another feature designed to create teaching presence as this is divided into manageable units, dated to establish time parameters to guide students on how much to complete over a given period of time. Each unit is placed in a different cell that has, for example, course content, learning and graded activities that provide continuous assessment for students and feedback to e-tutors to ensure that students fully understand the concepts (The Learning Exchange, 2014, para. 6). It allows students to post their answers to the learning activities that are embedded in the units and to respond and make comments to their peers' answers. E-tutors then access the students' posts on assigned learning activities, mark these responses, and give individual feedback as well as overall comments that will correct any misunderstanding of the concepts and extend students' understanding. To support this, Huett (2004) cited Mory as stating that "feedback as an influence on learning is indisputable and undeniable" (para. 4). The author also agrees that e-tutor feedback to students is a critical construct that stimulates active thinking and adds multiple perspectives on a topic since students sometimes give experiences from their various backgrounds.

In addition to allowing feedback from e-tutor and students, the forum permits for extended discussion from students and e-tutor. Boettcher (2011) explains that discussions in an online course are the equivalent of class discussions in a face-to-face class. For this activity, the asynchronous tools are better as students need time for thought and reflection given that the questions usually require critical thinking. This activity is usually done in written form and students usually have an average of two days to respond. This is designed to facilitate the self-paced learning that students need in an online environment. Students also provide peer feedback in this forum, which makes it an excellent pedagogical tool as it has created a platform where students can help one another to understand course concepts and issues, allow the e-tutor to "learn what students are thinking, uncover the connections they are making, and see the accuracy of their thinking processes, not just the end products" (Centre for Teaching Excellence, 2012, para. 6, n.d.). Research conducted by Ertmer et al. (2007, p. 427) establishes that students gain from peer to peer postings in an online environment. These researchers discovered that the quality of students' posting was improved in that "after receiving initial peer feedback, some students realized they had not been as in-depth or constructive as they could have been in providing feedback to others and, as a result, improved the quality of their own feedback." This finding led these researchers to conclude that perhaps the greatest potential benefit of peer feedback lies in the constructive aspect of forming and justifying peer feedback. They explained that this happens when students, through the process of responding to posts, reflect more critically on the discussion postings to which they are providing feedback, as well as their own postings and how they can be improved in a similar manner.

A number of researchers have indicated that teaching presence has an impact on students' success in online learning (Sheridan & Kelly, 2010, citing Bliss & Lawrence, 2009; Garrison & Cleveland-Innes; Fung, 2010, et al.). Shea, Li, and Pickett (2006) conducted research on *"teaching presence and student sense of learning community in fully online and web-enhanced college courses"* with a sample of 1067 online students. Based on the findings, they concluded that there is a clear connection between perceived teaching presence and students' sense of learning community; online students whose instructors exhibited more salient teacher presence behaviors were more likely to experience higher levels of learning and community. Overall, they discovered that "when students reported effective instructional design and organization and 'directed facilitation' of discourse, as defined by the teaching presence section of the instrument, they were more likely to report higher levels of learning community, as measured by Garrison, Anderson & Archer 2000 Classroom Community Index" (184).

Flexible learning is made possible by the use of a blend of asynchronous and synchronous information communication technologies. The online environment allows for teaching and learning to take place at times that are convenient and productive to both the teacher and learners. Carter, 2011 (citing Mueller & Adelman, 2008; Pullam, 2016; Travale, 2007) and others confirm that flexibility of scheduling and the ability to work and study at one's own pace anywhere in the world are reasons that online education is so appealing. She explains that students with families, jobs, and other responsibilities can complete their work at a time in the day that is convenient to them. Also, students who might have jobs that require them to travel are able to take the program with them as they move. The course environment is designed to support the flexibility as the course pages are designed with asynchronous tools that create teacher presence. This makes it easier for students to have access to the support they would need anytime and anywhere.

Real-time presentations are taped so that students can access them at their discretion, watch and re-watch them until they have mastered the concepts presented. The blend therefore facilitates flexibility of time since students can study anywhere and at any time convenient to them. Institutions, such as The UWI Open Campus, which are playing a pivotal role in aiding students to fulfil their educational goals from a distance, will be more attractive to potential post-secondary students locally, regionally, and even beyond the Caribbean region who desire greater flexibility to accommodate their job, personal, or family related circumstances. A spin off for the institution is the increased revenue that will be realized.

Synchronous Tools and Social Presence

An important feature of the synchronous tools in the researcher's environment is that they are suited for the support of social presence. Social presence is the extent to which a student's true self is projected and perceived in an online course (Shea, Li, & Pickett, citing Rourke, Anderson, Garrison, & Archer, 2001). Sheriden and Kelly (2010) mentioned that this represents "students' feeling of the connectedness, both socially and emotionally with others in the online environment" (769). Research including that of Hrastinski (2008) on the potential of asynchronous communication to enhance participation in online discussions has shown that social presence helps to foster knowledge and collaborative learning. A click on the link called Forum on the My Courses page leads to the General and Learning Forums. The asynchronous tools in the General Forum are the Teacher Forum, Tutor Student Exchange, Meet Your Fellow Students, and My Expectation.

The Teacher Forum, the first of the asynchronous tools carries the e-tutor's welcome message, an overview of the course, and the coordinator's expectations for the kinds of interaction that are required of students. This information may also include the technical, social, and academic support that is available to students. Sending preliminary information about the course before it begins is a reflection of teaching presence that is necessary to achieve social presence. Following the Tutor Forum is the Tutor Student Exchange where e-tutors write their personal welcome, the first bit of communication, to the students in their class. It gives the e-tutors the opportunity to connect personally with their students and to begin to build a relationship with them and for students to feel that they are interacting with real people. Winograd (2002) emphasizes that the welcome messages should set the intellectual tone and must be carefully written to give the correct impression.

He continues by stating that this tone should be warm, friendly and personal, letting the readers know that they are important members of the learning community. In the author's experience, a photograph placed on the system by the e-tutor as well as by the students immediately helps everyone put a face to a name and a voice. This not only compensates for the lack of physical presence but also creates camaraderie amongst the e-tutor and students. The UWI Open Campus administrators adopt these best practices as a way of bonding with the students and providing information for their survival in the online environment. An example of a welcome message by an e-tutor is included below (see Figure 6).

Establishing social presence through the welcome message not only provides that personal touch which is critical but also sets the stage for a positive simbiotic relationship between course coordinators and e-tutors with their students as they are about to work together through the Student Tutor Exchange Forum.

Following the Tutor Student Exchange is the Meet Your Fellow Students and E-tutor forum which are designed to humanize the learning environment by making allowance for a social space for students and their e-tutors to introduce themselves. This is very important as it takes account of the necessity for students to become acquainted with one another and for e-tutors to have an inkling of who their students are. In this section, students upload a photograph of themselves which seems to enhance the social presence. This assumption is supported by a study on the *use of personal profiles in a prototype online communication environment* conducted by Kear, Chetwynd, and Jefferis (2014). This study investigated possibilities for using personal profiles to enhance students' sense of social presence. They interviewed online students and 70% of them mentioned that they had uploaded photographs. Two of the themes that emerged from the research were community and putting a face to a name. When these students were asked what prompted them to upload their photograph, they responded that it was done to give a better understanding of who they are. A typical response was, "it makes it more personal when you can see someone's face over the internet, and makes it easier to talk to him/her, instead of him/her being this 'anonymous' stranger behind a computer. I like to be approachable" (n.d.).

E-tutor and students can begin to build a learning community as they become familiar with each other. The inclusion of self-disclosure which includes students' interests and the expectation of the course are ideal ways to create social presence. This can happen because as students read information about their peers they begin to bond together and begin to build a sense of belongingness and group commitment." The following are some samples of how e-tutor and students sometimes introduce themselves. These are edited to remove students' names (see Figure 7).

This initial activity by students does create some excitement among them as they make an effort to get acquainted with one another. This activity sets the foundation for them to build a friendly relationship and to make them feel more comfortable with responding to their peers' learning activities or replying to any requests or comments made by their fellow students such as their expectations of the course. The

Figure 6. Example of welcome message

A warm welcome to my LS32G class. It is good to have you! Extra special welcome to those of you who were with me last semester. I am happy to be working with you again in a new course!

Literature for Children and Young Adults is a very exciting course and the insights you will gain will serve you well in the classroom. Let me encourage you to work smart. This means managing your time properly, being active in the forum and uploading your graded assignments on time. You should also note carefully my comments on your work and endeavour to make the necessary adjustments so that each bit of work is better than the previous one.

You should visit the Tutor/Student forum regularly as this is where I will communicate with you about matters of general interest to the entire class. You may communicate with me as well in the forum and via email if the matter is personal.

Let us all work hard so that we will have a rewarding semester

Your E-tutor

Delete | Reply

Figure 7. Samples of how e-tutor and students sometimes introduce themselves

E-Tutor

Hello Students:

This is my third semester teaching this course LS36B online and I have taught it face to face for four years. I too have been a student in this course. This is a very interesting course, one, I am sure you will find rewarding and enjoyable.

I want to encourage you all to pay attention to the course outline, the course readings, and to participate as best as possible in the discussion forums so as to obtain maximum marks. I will attempt to provide feedback to individual responses - there will be times when the feedback will be general. However, you will receive feedback.

Please feel free to call or text me at any time, if there is anything you think I can help you with.

I wish for you every success!

Regards.

Delete | Reply

Student

Hi Everyone,

I am from Jamaica and I reside in the parish of St. Thomas. This course is important to me because it will enable me to have the necessary skills to select age appropriate literature to improve literacy.

Edit | Delete | Reply

need to use several channels such as announcements on the homepage of the course delivery system, e-mails to students, discussion forums, online lectures, and chats in the researcher's online environment proved ideal. This is confirmed by the literature on social presence.

Research has shown that social presence makes sense in that students need to feel connected to the e-tutor and other students in the course as well as the content of the course (Dixson, 2010, citing Garrison, Anderson, & Archer, 2001; Lewis & Abdul-Hamid, 2006, Rusco & Campbell, 2004, et al.). Several research findings have also shown that, especially on the part of the instructor, social presence is a necessary component to effective online instruction (Dixson, 2010, citing Dennen et al., 2007; Goertz & Kristjansson, 2007, et al.). Social distance can affect students' completion rate as indicated by one study that reported that 43% of the online students complained of inadequate levels of feedback and interaction in their online courses (Virginia Community College System, 2001). A qualitative study of online university students reported that the main negative aspects of the online course were 'feeling lost in cyberspace' because of issues related to delays in getting responses to communication from instructor and other students. In addition, students felt that teachers did not get to know the students personally and that there was no way of reading body language from either fellow students or the instructor (El Mansour & Mupinga, 2007). Similarly, in a qualitative study of online students enrolled in four high-risk community college courses (HRCs), students' primary complaint was a sense of isolation in their online course (Bambara et al., 2009).

The last of the asynchronous tools is the assignment forum. This link takes the e-tutor to the section where the assignments are uploaded. Students use this tool to submit any digital content (files), such as word-processed documents, spreadsheets, images, or audio and video clips as part of their assignment.

The assignments are labeled in-course assignment such as an essay or a project and graded activities and are strategically spaced for self-paced learning and may be submitted individually or as a group. The forum shows the date students can begin to upload the assignment, the due date, the cut-off date, and time. Students are required to post the graded activities within the dates scheduled for the starting and ending of each unit so that when the e-tutor is making a summary of the units, students' responses to the graded activities for each unit can be taken into consideration in the summary. Students are aware that late submission cannot be uploaded because the link automatically closes after the due date and time. This gives the e-tutor control over the collection of the assignments. However, in extenuating circumstances such as ill health or disaster, students are given an extension.

Students work independently when doing these assignments and this promotes self-paced learning because students can balance their work and home activities with the time they are given to upload these assignments. It gives students the opportunity to read the questions as often as they need to understand the task requirements and locate the best resources to accomplish the task so as to produce assignments of high academic standard. The comments offered by e-tutors in the slot provided contribute to cognitive presence as students go through the process of constructing knowledge, inquiring, exploring, and thinking (Online Learning Insights, 2012, para. 2.). According to Annand (2011), this sustained two-way communication from e-tutors and students is essential for distance education because learners negotiate and construct meaningful knowledge while e-tutors provide feedback to students.

The literature on the role of feedback emphasizes that immediate feedback is critical to student learning. Anderson (2008) mentions that detailed timely feedback provided as near in time as possible to the performance of the assessed behavior contributes to motivating and shaping the behavior and mental constructs of students. Students are always eagerly awaiting feedback, sometimes with apprehension, and they are always appreciative of the timely feedback as the examples below indicate (see Figure 8).

The request for feedback on the course is in the last section of the Learning Forums and is labeled "Lessons Learned." This section encourages students to respond to the questions: "What have I learned in this course?" and "How will it impact my future?" They are instructed to post their responses and to look at those of their peers. The summative feedback is designed to provide administration with information

Figure 8. Examples of students' response from e-tutor's feedback

> Good night Dr.
>
> Thanks again for giving me the extra time. Your quick feedback and understanding motivated me to push harder to complete the activity. So I stayed up very late and completed. Thus far, I have posted the essay. If the correct time is 11:55pm I made the deadline.
>
> Again thank you for understanding.
> Respectfully.
>
> Edit | Delete | Reply

> Thank you for your usual quick response I really appreciate this.
> Again thanks a million for the adjustment.
>
> Edit | Delete | Reply

to improve the course in the next offering. This is important as the administrator can use the information to measure the quality and value of the course delivery, which is critical for the continued improvement and success of course design and delivery. The e-tutor can capitalize on the feedback report by using it to inform the update of course content and the teaching strategies for the next delivery session.

This formal student evaluation of the course encapsulates the categories of immediacy. The ratings can be used to improve instruction and personal decisions. Goa (2006) highlighted that in recent times course evaluation includes 'teacher caring.' Teven and McCroskey (1996) studied the relationship of perceived teacher caring with student learning and teacher evaluation and discovered that student perceptions of the caring attitude of their teachers were found to be substantially associated with the students' evaluation of their teachers, their affective learning, and their perceptions of their cognitive learning (cited in Goa, 2006).

CASE STUDY 1: TEACHER IMMEDIACY – ACADEMIC AND SOCIAL SUPPORT

Research has unearthed that e-tutors who exhibit teacher immediacy behaviors experience increased level of students participation and e-tutors enjoy a greater 'breadth' of such participation (Ghamdi, Samarji, & Watt, 2016, cited Friedman, 2013. As the result is reciprocal, it is important that both students and e-tutors feel a sense of togetherness. In the researcher's environment, the welcome message includes a telephone number and a Skype address for the e-tutor that students can use for immediate contact. The promptness of the e-tutor's response in many instances is vital as this can help students who need immediate assistance to complete an assigned task or those who have domestic problems that are preventing them from uploading an assignment on time. Uploading assignments on time is critical because the assignment link closes automatically and students will lose marks because of the lack of submission. Social and academic support are both important for students' survival in the online environment. Students receive social support from their course coordinator and e-tutor through the use of the Teacher Student Exchange Forum, Skype, e-mail, and telephone. Social support is important since social issues can prevent students from completing assignments or sitting examination. The following are examples of the interaction between the course coordinator and students who needed immediate social and academic intervention.

Student 1

This researcher's cellular telephone rang. It was a student from another island. Between her weeping and talking, this author gathered that she was unable to contact her e-tutor to alert him that she was unable to complete and upload her assignment by the scheduled time as a result of marital problems. Her fear of failing was causing her to become distraught. Our lengthy conversation by Skype enabled us to resolve the issue. There was no prior verbal communication with this student. The call was made at 5:30 a.m., which made the researcher realize how desperate the student was. It was therefore critical to transmit verbal and nonverbal immediacy to immediately form a sense of trust and willingness to listen as the situation was considered grave. When this sense of trust was established, connection was made with her on Skype, which contributed to the teacher immediacy as non-verbal communication such as eye contact, the use of direct bodily orientation, use of overall body movement and gestures (Valez & Cano, 2008, citing Richmond et al., 1987) began instantly. The researcher's presence was needed until mid-day when it became evident that the student was out of danger. Based on the author's experience, students sometimes seek academic support when they are faced with challenges, and it is critical that this support be given at all times. A semester later she graduated from the program.

Student 2

This student wanted private immediate feedback to find out why she had received a low mark for her interaction in the course. Had this mark been higher she would have passed the course, hence her urgency to make contact. Sensing the urgency of the matter the course administrator communicated with the researcher and was willing to immediately set up a Blackboard Collaborate meeting for the matter to be discussed. However, in this instance, Skype was the most suitable mode of communication.

Skype, also a synchronous tool, is ideal to provide teacher immediacy for the solution of academic or social problems. However, it is more suited for one-to-one or small group interaction. Though not possessing as many interactive features as Blackboard Collaborate, it allows participants to share screen. Therefore information in different formats can be uploaded for students' viewing during communication. Here is the conversation that the author had with the student who insisted on having detailed information about her low marks for interaction. The conversation continued through word processing because there was difficulty with the sound. The conversation continued as follows (see Figure 9).

Arrangements were made for her to visit the nearest Open Campus site to have one of the technical team members display her data so that she would be convinced that she did not participate as fully as she thought. Ultimately the student was satisfied.

Figure 9. Conversation with students on Skype

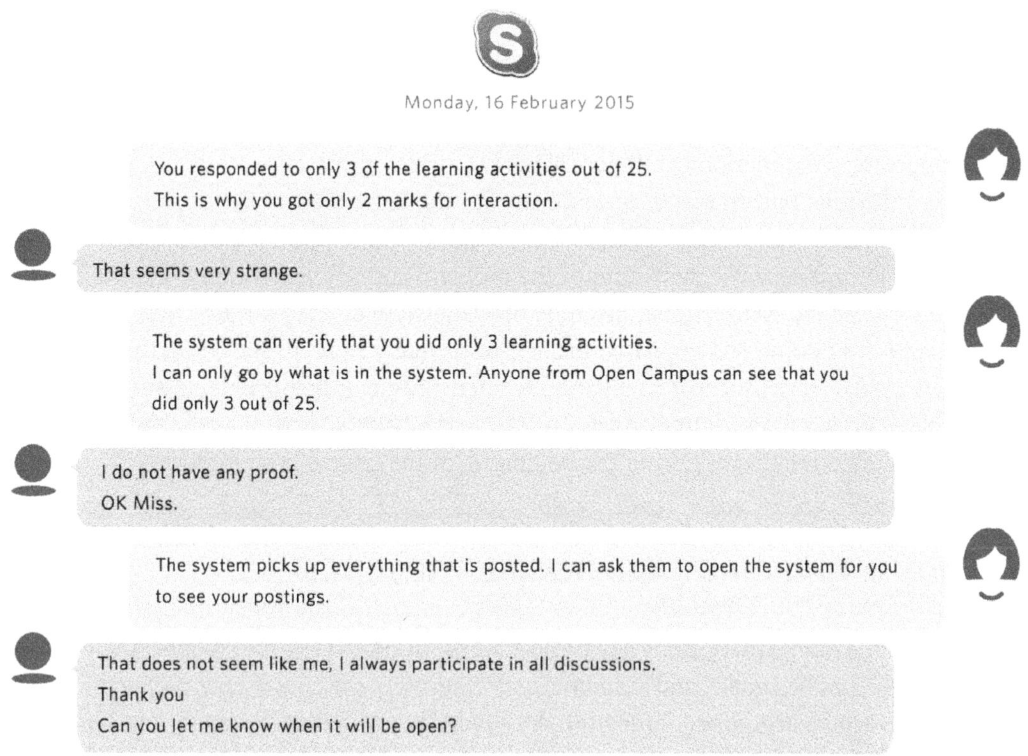

This type of help is not unusual, as Whipp and Lorentz (2008) reported that the findings in their research on social help giving in online education showed that students frequently sought help privately through e-mail, instant messaging, online chats, phone, and face-to-face visits. They added that this study adds support to a growing body of literature that affirms the importance of the instructor in supporting student satisfaction in online courses. The article written by Online Learning Insights states that it is important for students to know that e-tutors are committed to their learning. This commitment can be in the form of timely feedback on assignments which are constructive and personalized. This article emphasises that e-tutors should be supportive even when students' grades are poor.

Student 3

On many occasions e-mails were used to seek social and academic support. Huett (2004) states that email is becoming the communication tool of choice for many because of its ubiquitous nature, relative low cost, global reach, speed, and flexibility. It therefore serves as a bridge between a telephone call and a meeting via Skype or Blackboard Collaborate. E-mails have become an effective communication tool for e-tutors and students especially since cellular phones carry this feature and Wi-Fi is easily available in the English-speaking Caribbean countries. For these reasons, it is used frequently as an asynchronous educational tool within the online environment. Kim (2008) mentions that studies have assessed the use of e-mail in an online environment for academic purposes and discovered that e-mails allow the instructor to maintain relationships with learners and provide on-going support.

In the Open Campus online environment, course coordinators, e-tutors, and students are assigned e-mail addresses for asynchronous communication. On many occasions, they have used this web-based tool instead of the Tutor Student Forum to make contact. One could conjecture that they relish the privacy, the ease and speed of access of the e-mail over that of the Tutor Teacher Forum. Sadat and Rahman (n.d.) commented that e-mail is useful for delivering feedback to learners once a basic understanding of feedback's role in learning has been established. However, course coordinator and e-tutor responses provide timely feedback and ensure that the responses/messages are pedagogically sound (Huett, 2004). The following are two unedited (students' names omitted) forum posts by students seeking academic and social support from the e-tutor (see Figure 10).

As a result of the relationship that was established at the beginning of the course, it is obvious that students feel comfortable explaining their personal and academic problems. Although the nonverbal cues are absent, e-tutors can sense the nature of the problem and act accordingly. The ease of access to e-mails has now closed the transactional distance between students and e-tutors and has improved the response time and in so doing has improved teacher immediacy as well. Based on the author's experience, students do not have any form of trepidation when expressing their problems and seeking support. This is due to the cordial relationship that was built from the beginning of the course. This is one of the reasons building a good relationship from the beginning of the course is so important.

CASE STUDY 2: IMMEDIACY AND SOCIAL PRESENCE

Another feature of the online platform is My Expectations, designed to give students the opportunity to explain their personal, professional, and academic expectations of the course and to state the expectations they have of their e-tutor and course coordinator. A knowledge of students' expectations has pedagogical

Figure 10. Student seeking academic and social support from e-tutor

Student A

I know I have not been participating actively in forums lately but this is because I had a death in my family which has really affected me. I know this is not so important however, I wanted to let you know. On August 4th, my only son, 20 years old died after being sick for a week. The doctors said it was a severe case of pneumonia, and also a cardiac arrest. I am still grappling with shock. I don't know if it will ever get better, and this is really the reason why I am not so active.
I intend to do better in the following units.
Thanks for understanding.

Delete | Reply

E-tutor's Response:

I am very sorry to hear. Please accept my sympathy. I stated in my welcome message that whenever a student is experiencing problems I am to be informed and arrangements will be made to accommodate late assignments.
Hope you will find time to complete the learning activities. I will mark them.
Regards.

Delete | Reply

Student B

I don't fully understand part 2 and part 3 of the project. I would be grateful if you can give me a clearer description as to what I should really do for those parts of the project. I await your response soon.
Thank you very much.
Regards.

Delete | Reply

E-tutor's Response:

Please call me so that we can make arrangements to meet on Skype. Please ensure that you have the Pathfinder assignment so we can discuss the section you are having difficulty understanding.
Regards.

Delete | Reply

implications for the e-tutor in that it informs the learning objectives of the courses which are reflected in the content and assessments). In addition, e-tutors' knowledge of students' expectations can help them to deliberately make arrangements to meet students' expectations. To ensure that this happens, Pappas (2014) posits that the content developer needs to know the students, their skill set, and their level of experience. In addition, it is necessary to know what students want to gain from the course and whether or not they want to master a specific professional skill or expand their knowledge about the subject. This activity sets the foundation for a strong rapport, a sense of belonging and empathy.

In the researcher's environment, as soon as the learning environment is opened for orientation, this page begins to bubble with the postings of students' expectations and their response to the expectations of others. Knowledge of students' expectations is essential as this can initiate a framework for the e-tutor to make the course more specific to students' goals. Some students express this very clearly, as seen in the examples (see Figure 11).

These examples show that students' expectations were reasonable and mostly related to their academic pursuits. Notice should be taken of the emphasis they placed on getting timely feedback from their e-tutor. This was their initial sign of the instructional quality that they expected of e-tutors. Overall instructional quality was also reported as an expectation affecting student retention (Harris, Larrier, & Castano-Bishop, 2011, citing Heyman, 2010). It is likely that if these expectations are met students

Figure 11. Samples of students' expectations of the course

My expectations are as follows:

1. To remain focused and complete my readings and assignments in a timely manner.
2. To attain an exceptional grade overall.
3. To utilize the information gained from the course to aid in my professional development.

I am expecting the e-Tutor and coordinator to be effective facilitators. I expect them to communication information (feedback) in a timely manner and provide the necessary assistance for us to successfully complete the course.

Delete | Reply

My expectations in this course is to use the knowledge and skills that I possess to work hard to achieve the highest grade that is there to attain.
To gain knowledge of the different strategies, and techniques that can help me to enhance my delivery in the teaching and learning process. Share and assist my classmates in every possible way that I can. Make every effort to participate in all discussions and submit my work on time. I am expecting my E-tutor and my course coordinator to be a facilitator and to be very informative. In doing so I know this will help me to achieve my goal and that is to get an 'A' and to be knowledgeable about different aspects in this course. I know that hard work leads to success. I am willing to work hard in order to reach my goal.

Regards.

Delete | Reply

will remain throughout the duration of the courses, as research has indicated that student expectations regarding course demands and course content impacts retention in online courses (Harris, Larrier & Castano-Bishop, 2011, citing Nash, 2005).

Students' Response to Each Other

On a number of occasions students make one-to-one connections with each other by responding to information that is posted in the discussion forum. This is an effective option for facilitation because students can participate in on-going discussion without the e-tutor dominating the discussion. This helps students to establish a social presence which developed into a cohesive group as it can be seen in all three posts that students refer to the group as "we teachers." The following shows students commenting on each others' post. The comments were mixture of approval and correction. Both were always welcome by students (see Figure 12).

It is important that e-tutors make themselves available whether through the asynchronous or synchronous tools as this is a critical component of online teaching. In instances where individualized communication is necessary this should be accommodated.

FUTURE RESEARCH DIRECTIONS

This research discovered that teacher immediacy is critical to students' academic achievement. In order for students to experience this success, this immediacy has to be reciprocal. Therefore, further research needs to be conducted on students' immediacy in the online environment to find out if their level of achievement is comparable to their level of immediacy in their online environment.

Figure 12. Students' comments on each other posts

I think you have addressed questions 1 - 3 very well. I say this because you mentioned information literacy requires one not to only retrieve information, but also to 'recognize when the information is needed, know how to locate it, evaluate it and then use the needed information effectively'. I think this is important due to the fact that we have the Internet, television, radio, and other information resources giving us information which sometimes are untrue. It is therefore important that we as teachers remain up to date with the information available to us and teach our students how to critically evaluate and apply information to solve problems so that they too can become information literate individuals who can one day become an attractive job candidate.

All the best.

Show parent | Edit | Split | Delete | Reply

You post quite informative, I especially appreciate the way you responded to question three. You are absolutely correct in that both information literacy and one's job as teacher is inseparable. We ought to do all that we can to provide and facilitate their learning in the best way possible based on their individual learning style or what appeals to them the most. Since IL is a process, therefore it means that will require time for students to progressively acquire the needed skills to be functional individuals in society.

Show parent | Edit | Split | Delete | Reply

I enjoyed reading your post, it is indeed true information literacy is important for us, as teacher's to know because it is a big part of our day to day activities especially when preparing pedagogical materials for our students. We as teacher need to embrace information literacy as it will enable us to locate, organize and evaluate the information we present to our students based on their needs. Which in turn will create more effective learning and a rich learning environment that will cater to our students learning styles and needs.

Show parent | Edit | Split | Delete | Reply

You seems to have misunderstood the activity that you were required to do. It has to do. It has to do with an academic assignment that you were given, not an assignment that you gave to your gave to your class.

You need to read the assignment more than once to make sure you know what you are asked to do.

Show parent | Edit | Split | Delete | Reply

CONCLUSION

Synchronous and asynchronous communication tools are the centerpiece of online learning as they provide teacher presence, cognitive presence, and social presence, elements that are necessary for efficacious delivery of the content as well as successful learning outcomes. The asynchronous and synchronous tools enable The UWI Open Campus to maintain the interactive component of lesson delivery that achieves social presence among students similar to that of a face-to-face classroom. Verbal implicit communication and verbal immediacy are key factors in online learning; hence, e-tutors should be au fait with the communication styles that the two types of technology offer and be willing to adjust their pedagogical practices to accommodate their use to achieve a higher level of interaction on the part of the students. Course developers need to design courses to allow for teacher presence to ensure that students achieve academically. The evolving nature of asynchronous and synchronous communication tools demands continual training of course coordinators and e-tutors in their use to give them confidence in using the technologies. Addressing the need for training, Burns (2014, para. 3) noted "online instructors are often recruited from face-to-face settings where this intersection of technology, pedagogy, and content is quite different from online settings." This training will guarantee an effective blend of pedagogy and technology to achieve teacher immediacy.

After examining both asynchronous and synchronous tools in the online learning environment of The UWI Open Campus, it is obvious that asynchronous tools should not be regarded as secondary intervention but as complementing the synchronous tools. Therefore, both should be used for realizing course objectives including effective learning. For example, self-paced learning has to be supported by asynchronous tools as it is crucial for time to be given for reflection and for students to function within the ambit of their work and home environment. Synchronous tools are best when there is the need for tutor instruction to increase meaning and understanding of concepts and to provide immediate feedback. It is also best used to eliminate the feeling of isolation and to encourage peer interaction and collaboration. In the same vein, the use of Skype or Blackboard Collaborate to conduct a tutorial session allows students to be involved in virtual discussion. However, the fast pace of the discussion usually does not allow for in-depth thinking about the concepts presented. Nevertheless, after the presentation, e-tutors can post activities in the forum to reinforce the lesson and students can, at their convenience, read, reflect, and research carefully before answering and uploading their responses. Overall, both synchronous and asynchronous tools are able to provide the kind of delivery that is effective and efficient but the effective combination of both will provide a high level to teacher immediacy which is critical in any online learning environment.

REFERENCES

Andersen, J., & Andersen, P. (n.d.). *Teacher immediacy*. Retrieved November 29, 2015 from http://www.blackwellreference.com/public/uid=3/tocnode?id=g9781405131995_chunk_g978140513199525_ss13-1

Anderson, T. (2008). *Teaching in an online learning context*. Retrieved December 2, 2015 from http://davidwees.com/content/role-immediacy-feedback-student-learning/

Annand, D. (2011). Social presence within the community of inquiry framework. *The International Review of Research in Open and Distributed Learning*, *12*(5), 40–56. Retrieved from http://www.irrodl.org/index.php/irrodl/article/view/924/1855

Bailie, J. L. (2011). *The criticality of verbal immediacy in online education: A modified Delpi study*. Retrieved November 25, 2015 from http://www.thejeo.com/Archives/Volume9Number2/BailiePaper.pdf

Baker, C. (2010). *The impact of instructor immediacy and presence for online student*. Retrieved November 16, 2015 from http://www.thejeo.com/Archives/Volume7Number1/BakerPaper.pdf

Bambara, C. S., Habour, C. P., Davies, T. G., & Athey, S. (2009). *Delicate engagement: The lived experience of community college students enrolled in high-risk online courses*. Retrieved on July 2, 2015 from http://crw.sagepub.com/content/36/3/219.short

Blackboard Help. (2011). *Blackboard Collaborate essentials*. Retrieved July 9, 2015, from http://www.open.uwi.edu/sites/default/files/BbC_Essentials_Manual_BbC11_V2_063011.pdf

Blackboard Help. (2015). *Blackboard Collaborate basics for administrators*. Retrieved August 13, 2015, from https://help.blackboard.com/en-us/Learn/Building_Blocks/Blackboard_Collaborate/Administrator/Collaborate_Basics_Administrators

Blackwell Online Dictionary. (n.d.). *Teacher immediacy*. Retrieved November 29, 2015 from http://www.blackwellreference.com/public/uid=3/tocnode?id=g9781405131995_chunk_g978140513199525_ss13-1

Boettcher, J. (2011). *Ten best practices for teaching online: Quick guide for new online faculty*. Retrieved June 25, 2015, from http://www.designingforlearning.info/services/writing/ecoach/tenbest.html

Carter, D. (2011). *Successful online learning: Managing the online learning effectively and efficiently*. Sudbury, MA: Jones and Bartlett Publishers.

Centre for Teaching Excellence. (2012). *Online discussions: Tips for instructors*. Retrieved July 27, 2015, from https://uwaterloo.ca/centre-for-teaching-excellence/teaching-resources/teaching-tips/developing-assignments/blended-learning/online-discussions-tips-instructors

Dabbagh, N. (2007). *The online learner: Characteristics and pedagogical implications*. Retrieved June 30, 2015 from http://www.citejournal.org/vol7/iss3/general/article1.cfm

Dass, A. (2015). *The University of the West Indies statistical review, 2009/10 to 2013/14*. The University of the West Indies. Retrieved July 7, 2015 from http://www.mona.uwi.edu/opair/statistics/2013-2014/Survey%20Reports%20-%20UWI%20STATISTICAL%20REVIEW%202009-10%20TO%202013-14.pdf

Designing for Online Learning. (2012). *E-Coaching tip 36: Cognitive presence in online courses — Are you doing it?* Retrieved November 29, 2015 from http://www.designingforlearning.info/services/writing/ecoach/tips/tip36.html

Dixson, M. (2010). *Creating effective student engagement in online courses: What do students find engaging?* Retrieved November 20, 2015 from file:///C:/Users/10018039/Downloads/1744-6523-1-PB%20 (1).pdf

El Mansour, B., & Mupinga, D. M. (2007). *Students' positive and negative experiences in hybrid and online classes*. Retrieved on August 9, 2015 from http://www.freepatentsonline.com/article/College-Student-Journal/161282247.html

Elo, S., & Kynga, H. (2007). *The qualitative content analysis process*. Retrieved November 29, 2015 from http://academic.csuohio.edu/kneuendorf/c63309/ArticlesFromClassMembers/Amy.pdf

Ertmer, P., Richardson, J., Belland, B., Camin, D., Connolly, P., Coulthard, G., & Mong, C. (2007). Using peer feedback to enhance the quality of student online postings: An exploratory study. *Journal of Computer-Mediated Communication*, *12*(2), 412–433. doi:10.1111/j.1083-6101.2007.00331.x

Fahara, M. F., & Castro, A. L. (2015). *Teaching strategies to promote immediacy in online graduate courses*. Retrieved November 20, 2015 from http://www.openpraxis.org/~openprax/index.php/Open-Praxis/article/viewFile/228/181

Garay, E. (2011). *Elluminate Live! is now Blackboard Collaborate*. Retrieved July 21, 2015, from https://sites.google.com/a/uic.edu/itlnews/announcements/elluminateliveisnowblackboardcollaborate

Garrison, D., & Anderson, T. (2003). *E-learning in the 21st century*. London: Routledge Falmer. doi:10.4324/9780203166093

Garrison, D. R., Anderson, T., & Archer, W. (2000). *Critical inquiry in a text-based environment: Computer conferencing in higher education*. Retrieved November 10, 2015 from http://cde.athabascau.ca/coi_site/documents/Garrison_Anderson_Archer_Critical_Inquiry_model.pdf

Garrison, D. R., & Vaughan, N. D. (2008). *Blended learning in higher education: Framework, principles, and guidelines*. Retrieved November 20, 2015 from http://www.designingforlearning.info/services/writing/ecoach/tips/tip36.html

Ghamdi, A. A., Samarji, A., & Watt, A. (2016). *Essential considerations in distance education in KSA: Teacher immediacy in a virtual teaching and learning environment*. Retrieved on January 2, 2016 from http://www.ijiet.org/show-62-728-1.html

Goa, W. (2006). *Influence of teacher immediacy on student evaluations of teachers in American and Chinese classrooms*. Retrieved December 2, 2015 from http://scholarworks.rit.edu/cgi/viewcontent.cgi?article=8948&context=theses

Graduate Student Instructor Teaching and Resource Center. (n.d.). *Social constructivism*. Retrieved November 8, 2015 from http://gsi.berkeley.edu/gsi-guide-contents/learning-theory-research/social-constructivism/#teaching

Hanover Research Council. (2009). *Best practices in online teaching strategies*. Retrieved June 19, 2015 from http://www.uwec.edu/AcadAff/resources/edtech/upload/Best-Practices-in-Online-Teaching-Strategies-Membership.pdf

Harris, M., Larrier, I., & Castano-Bishop, M. (2011, Winter). Development of the student expectations of online learning survey (SEOLS): A pilot study. *Online Journal of Distance Learning Administration, XIV*, V.

Higley, M. (2013). *Benefits of synchronous and asynchronous e-Learning in an online learning environment*. Retrieved June 18, 2015 from http://elearningindustry.com/benefits-of-synchronous-and-asynchronous-e-learning

Hrastinski, S. (2008). A study of asynchronous and synchronous e-learning methods discovered that each supports different purposes. *EduCause Quarterly,* (1). Retrieved July 5, 2015 from https://net.educause.edu/ir/library/pdf/eqm0848.pdf

Huett, J. (2004). *Email as an educational feedback tool: Relative advantages and implementation guidelines*. Retrieved July 29, 2015 from http://itdl.org/journal/jun_04/article06.htm

IGI Global. (2015). *What is social presence?* Retrieved 2015 from http://www.igi-global.com/dictionary/social-presence/27463

Kear, L., Chetwynd, F., & Jefferis, H. (2014). *Social presence in online learning communities: the role of personal profiles*. Retrieved November 22, 2015 from http://www.researchinlearningtechnology.net/index.php/rlt/article/view/19710

Kim, C. (2008). Using email to enable 3 (effective, efficient, and engaging) learning. *Distance Education, 29*(2), 187–198. doi:10.1080/01587910802154988

Knabe, A. P. (2004). Constructivist learning perspectives in online public relations classrooms. *PRism, 2*. Retrieved November 20, 2015 from http://www.prismjournal.org/fileadmin/Praxis/Files/Journal_Files/Issue2/Knabe.pdf

Lalor, G., & Marrett, C. (1986). *University of the West Indies distance teaching experiment (UWIDITE) report*. Retrieved July 14, 2015 from http://eric.ed.gov/?id=ED290042

Lalor, G., & Stahmer, A. (1987). *The University of the West Indies distance teaching experiment: A case study*. Retrieved August 13, 2015 from http://pdf.usaid.gov/pdf_docs/pnaax696.pdf

Lowenthal, P., & Parscal, T. (2008). *Teaching presence online facilitates meaningful learning*. Retrieved November 22, 2015 from http://www.patricklowenthal.com/publications/TeachingPresenceFacilitates-Learning.pdf

Mandernach, J., Gonzales, R. M., & Garrett, A. L. (2006). *An examination of online instructor presence via threaded discussion participation.* Retrieved November 3, 2015 from http://jolt.merlot.org/vol2no4/mandernach.htm

McKerlich, R. (2011). *Student perceptions of teaching presence, social Presence and cognitive presence in a virtual world.* Retrieved December 1, 2015 from http://jolt.merlot.org/vol7no3/mckerlich_0911.htm

Mona Information Technology Services. (2015). *Programming and administration of the virtual learning environment (2015).* Retrieved August 13, 2015 from http://www.mona.uwi.edu/mits/programming-and-administration-virtual-learning-environment

Morrison, D. (2012). *Critical thinking in the online classroom.* Retrieved on August 7, 2015 from https://onlinelearninginsights.wordpress.com/2012/05/24/critical-thinking-in-the-online-learning-classroom/

Mullane, R. R. (2014). *Students' perception of teacher immediacy behaviors on student success and retention.* Retrieved November 13, 2015 from http://dc.uwm.edu/cgi/viewcontent.cgi?article=1480&context=etd

Obasa, A., Eludire, A., & Ajao, T. (2013). A comparative study of synchronous and asynchronous e-learning resources. *International Journal of Innovative Research in Science, Engineering and Technology, 2*(11). Retrieved from http://www.ijirsct.com/upload/2013/november/3_A-COMPARATIVE.pdf

Pappas, C. (2014). *9 tips to apply adult learning theory to eLearning - eLearning industry.* Retrieved July 20, 2015 from http://elearningindustry.com/9-tips-apply-adult-learning-theory-to-elearning

Ragan, L. (2008). *Best practices in online teaching*. Retrieved July 19, 2015 from http://florida.theorangegrove.org/og/file/489805c0-7346-6cb7-320a-5610cb10f9da/1/onlineedu.pdf

Redmond, P. (2014). Reflection as an indicator of cognitive presence. *E-Learning and Digital Media, 11*(1), 46-46. Retrieved July 19, 2015 from http://ldm.sagepub.com/content/11/1/46.full.pdf html.

Sadat, A., & Rahman, K. (n.d.). *Prospect of email communication as an educational tool for distance education in Bangladesh.* Retrieved August 5, 2015 from http://wikieducator.org/images/7/73/PID_266.pdf

Sathik, M., & Jonathan, S. G. (2013). *Effect of facial expressions on student's comprehension recognition in virtual educational environments.* Retrieved June 28, 2015 from http://www.ncbi.nlm.nih.gov/pmc/articles/PMC3795200/

Shea, P., Li, C. S., & Pickett, A. (2006). *A study of teaching presence and student sense of learning community in fully online and web-enhanced college courses.* Retrieved November 22, 2015 from http://www.sunyresearch.net/hplo/wp-content/uploads/2012/08/Shea-Li-Pickett.pdf

Sheridan, K., & Kelly, M. A. (2010). The indicators of instructor presence that are important to students in online learning. *Journal of Online Learning and Teaching*, *6*(4).

Spear, L. R. (2012). *Social presence, social interaction, collaborative learning, and satisfaction in online and face-to-face courses*. Retrieved November 29, 2015 from http://lib.dr.iastate.edu/cgi/viewcontent.cgi?article=3983&context=etd

Stewart, C., Bachman, C., & Johnson, R. (2010). Students' characteristics and motivation orientations for online and traditional degree programs. *Journal of Online Learning and Teaching*, *6*(2). Retrieved from http://jolt.merlot.org/vol6no2/stewart_0610.htm

Swan, K., Garrison, D. R., & Richardson, J. (2009). *A constructivist approach to online learning: The Community of Inquiry framework*. Retrieved November 15, 2015 from http://www.academia.edu/398997/A_Constructivist_Approach_to_Online_Learning_The_Community_of_Inquiry_Framework

Tag Archives. (2004). *Synchronous tools for online learning the next big thing in online education... learning in real time*. Retrieved June 30, 2015 from https://onlinelearninginsights.wordpress.com/tag/synchronous-tools-for-online-learning/

Thomson, S. (2014). 6 online collaboration tools and strategies for boosting learning - eLearning industry. *E-Learning industry*. Retrieved May 31, 2015 from http://elearningindustry.com/6-online-collaboration-tools-and-strategies-boosting-learning

University of Victoria. (2013). *The continuing studies instructor's welcome message*. Retrieved August 13, 2015 from http://distance.uvic.ca/pdfs/instructors/CS-Instructor-Welcome-Message.pdf

UWI Open Campus. (2014). *The learning exchange*. Retrieved from http://2014.tle.courses.open.uwi.edu/course/view.php?id=272

UWI Open Campus. (2015). *About the open campus, UWI*. Retrieved June 15, 2015 from http://www.open.uwi.edu/about/welcome-uwi-open-campus

Valez, J. L., & Cano, J. (2008). The relationship between teacher immediacy and student motivation. *Journal of Agriculture*, *49*(3).

Whipp, J., & Lorentz, R. A. (2008). *Cognitive and social help Giving in online teaching: An exploratory study*. Retrieved November 30, 2015 from http://epublications.marquette.edu/cgi/viewcontent.cgi?article=1038&context=edu_fac

Wicks, D. J., & Cano, J. (2009). *Educational technology: Emerging theories and online learning environments for adults*. Retrieved November 8, 2015 from https://sites.google.com/a/boisestate.edu/edtechtheories/emerging-theories-and-online-learning-environments-for-adults-1

Winograd, D. (2002). Guidelines for moderating online educational computer conferences. *TechTrends*, *46*(5), 53–57. doi:10.1007/BF02818310

Woods, R. H., & Baker, J. D. (2004). *Interaction and immediacy in online learning*. Retrieved November 29, 2015 from http://www.irrodl.org/index.php/irrodl/article/view/186/268

ADDITIONAL READING

Baker, C. (2010). The impact of instructor immediacy and presence for online student affective learning, cognition, and motivation. Retrieved January 12, 2016 from http://eric.ed.gov/?id=EJ904072

Gunter, G. (2007). The effects of the impact of instructional immediacy on cognition and learning in online classes. Retrieved January 13, 2016 from http://www.waset.org/publications/481

Ni, S. F., & Aust, R. (2008). Examining teacher verbal immediacy and sense of classroom community in online classes. *International Journal on E-Learning*, *7*(3), 477–498.

Swan, K. (2005). On the nature and development of social presence in online course discussions. Paper presented at the annual meeting of the American Educational Research Association.

Chapter 9
Facebook Mediated Learning Environments in Pakistan:
A Study of Teacher Immediacy

Tazeen Hussain
Indus Valley School of Art and Architecture, Pakistan

ABSTRACT

This chapter explores teacher immediacy in online learning environments, focusing on the use of social media - Facebook as a teaching tool in Art and Design education institutions in Pakistan. The study is based on existing teaching practice in Indus Valley School of Art and Architecture and Department of Visual Studies, University of Karachi. Following a mixed method approach including observation and interviews with both teachers and students, the chapter identifies the reasons teachers use Facebook in teaching practice and explores the reasons that limit their use of this potentially immediacy inducing environment. It also includes a study of content including video, links to articles and popular culture manifestations like memes and emoticons, which could be used in teaching via social media and the implications for learning and cognition. The concept of immediacy is explored and the chapter proposes that it be approached more broadly in order to realise the full potential of social media and harness it for better learning and outcomes.

INTRODUCTION

The educational sector all over the world, including Pakistan, is waking up to the possibilities the World Wide Web (www) and Information Communication Technologies (ICTs) can provide for learning as SNS applications become increasingly embedded in our lives, particularly of the tech savvy young people as seen in studies by Ito (2010), Kim and Yun (2007), Livingstone (2002), Selwyn (2009), Siddiqui (2006) and Wang et al (2012). They enable new virtual forums, alongside the traditional classrooms, enabling cognitive and affective learning and overcoming space time barriers by extending the classroom to a

DOI: 10.4018/978-1-4666-9995-3.ch009

virtual space as well as facilitating accessibility from homes, workplaces at any time. These forums are also described as user-centric due to their interlinking capabilities, which enable access and delivery of a variety of content, academic and non-academic, via multiple formats according to the preference and convenience of the learner. In this way these forums can be potentially egalitarian promoting a student-centric environment (Selwyn, 2007; Wood & Baker, 2004). It is also strongly believed that ICTs and the www can play a major role in overcoming global inequalities in education by enabling access to more educational sources and opportunities via online education (Kucuk, 2009; Richards, 2004; Said, 2006,).

As ICT enabled online forums begin to be used widely for the educational purpose world over there is a need to understand the difference between the online learning environment and the real time classroom. Wood & Baker (2004) highlight the salience of teacher immediacy and social presence in educational online environments and demonstrate positive co-relations of teacher immediacy behaviors to cognitive and affective learning.

In Pakistan there is a rising trend amongst teachers and students to use Facebook and other Social network sites (SNS), in an educational context (Hussain, 2015). There are 29, 128,970 Internet users in Pakistan out of which 23,000,000 use Facebook (Internet World Stats, 2015) and most are aged between 18-34 years (PAS, 2014). It is therefore not strange to see teachers of under graduate level institutions reaching out to students via Facebook.

Though existing literature covers various uses of Facebook in educational contexts including student engagement, student motivation, learning management system there is relatively less knowledge about the effects of interactions via Facebook for learning and even less with regards to the developing world. Rambi and N'gambi (2011, 2014) and Ahmed et al (2013) in their studies based in South Africa and Bangladesh point out this asymmetry and both suggest that Facebook's efficacy in educational context might not be universal due to socio-cultural and infrastructural differences in the developing world. Their findings pave the way to the idea that using Facebook to communicate with students might be a means to developing a better understanding of students and overcoming teacher student distance - immediacy.

Facebook being grounded in new media networks allows and eases information sharing due to its interlinking capacity and accessibility via multiple means like PC's, mobile phones and laptops. It is unbiased, that is it allows for information retrieval by individuals irrespective of hierarchy. Facebook sharing being profile-based also allows ownership of information shared. These features have the potential to aid affective and effective learning by allowing autonomy in information access - which is fed by multiple sources instead of only designated academic ones and multiple formats like video, audio, non-academic articles, like newspapers, magazines and blogs.

This exploratory and qualitative study will try to identify and establish immediacy behaviors in online environments by observing existing closed Facebook groups used by teachers in Pakistan as part of pedagogy. This will be followed by discussion with students who are part of the groups. In Karachi, Pakistan using Facebook to communicate with students is an increasingly common practice as the virtual world is as yet rather unregulated and there are no laws against its pedagogical use in educational institutions. Verbal and non-verbal content of Facebook groups will be identified and analyzed for immediacy potential. Results from the observation and discussion will be further explored by undertaking in-depth interviews with teachers to understand their motivations for the usage/non-usage of Facebook as pedagogy and to seek out their views on the merits of online learning environments for teacher immediacy. It is hoped that the study covering two art and design institutions in Karachi, Pakistan will provide an insight into the ground reality of Facebook use against the potential of Facebook aided learning with regards to immediacy in online learning environments, and what can be done to optimize this potential. It also hopes to establish factors that maximize and limit immediacy in online learning.

BACKGROUND

One of the key factors in learning today is teacher immediacy. Research links teachers' immediacy behaviors to effective and affective learning and increased student motivation (Kelley & Gorham 1988; Gorham, 1988; Christophel, 1990) by bridging the gap between teachers and their students.

Immediacy as defined by Mehrabian (1967) is the "extent, to which selected communicative behaviors enhance physical or psychological closeness in interpersonal communication," (Thweatt & McCroskey, 1996, p. 198). It serves to reduce perceived distance between teachers and students (Anderson 1979). Immediacy includes those verbal and non-verbal communication behaviors that produce a sense of closeness including speech and word selection like humor, frequent use of student name, encouraging discussion by following up on student-initiated comments, self disclosure, using 'we' instead of 'I' and body language including facial expression, eye contact, posture and proximity (Kucuk 2009, Wood & Baker 2004). Bell and Daly (1984) extend this understanding to examining the processes individuals use to get others to like them by studying immediacy behaviors that are used to create affinity. In looking at immediacy this way the process of creating affinity becomes an active process in which immediacy is both a result of affinity and vice versa (Wood & Baker 2004).

In the Asian context where cultural codes still play an important role in classrooms and influence attitudes towards new technology and web based forums an understanding of teacher immediacy becomes even more relevant. In many Asian countries the apprentice / teacher model is entrenched in the educational system and change to more autonomous models is an uphill task (Richards, 2004). On the other hand research suggests that due to increase exposure to ICTs, students in Pakistan have developed a preference for more autonomous learning styles (Siddiqui 2006). Teachers are thus faced with the dual challenge of adapting their style of teaching to become responsive to student preferences as well as use mediums and formats which will engage students.

Research shows teachers' adoption of ICTs stem from mainly two reasons: student-centered learning and self and identity (Mumtaz, 2000). Other reasons include student engagement, motivating students to learn and bringing diversity to content. Teacher's previous experience and familiarity with ICTs in non-education context also play an important role (Cox et al., 1999) as well as perception of usefulness of technology and flexibility of educational structures (Buchanan, Sainter & Saunders, 2013).

A factor in ICT mediated learning, which has tremendous potential for aiding immediacy, is that of social presence. Social presence can be described as "degree of salience of the other person in the (mediated) interaction and the consequent salience of the interpersonal relationships" that develops through the interactions facilitated by online learning environments. It measures how real the other person is perceived to be in such environments (cited in Swan & Richardson, 2003, p. 70). Social presence is determined by the inherent qualities of the medium and the perception of the communicator regarding presence in a given medium. In this way social presence differs from immediacy, as it takes into account an additional variable - the medium (Swan & Richardson, 2003)

Short, Williams, and Christie (1976) argue that, social presence between the teacher and student varies with different media. "It affects the nature of the interaction and it interacts with the purpose of the interaction to influence the medium chosen by the individual who wishes to communicate" (cited in Swan & Richardson, 2003). Thus the choice to use Facebook to communicate with students will affect the kind of interactions a teacher or student can have, which might be different from that in actual class environments. However the position assigned by a teacher to Facebook as part of pedagogy, would in turn influence the kind of interactions via Facebook. Gunawardene and Zittle (1997) feel that while mediums and their inherent characteristics are important influences in online behaviors, it is also the perception of the medium used for interaction, in this case Facebook, which effects behavior in online learning environments.

Which ever of the two, Wallace (2003) found social presence to be an important factor in student perception of satisfaction and learning in online learning environments. He found that students felt enabled to create their own social presence with the nature and content of their participation in online environments. Tu and McIsaac, (2002) found perception of social presence was related to two components, intimacy and immediacy, which resulted from the quality of interaction in online environments. Thus social presence could be cultured through adoption of certain behaviors (Swan & Richardson 2003).

Facebook and Educational Environment

Facebook and SNS use in an educational context is characterized by its multiplicity of use. Various studies reveal two main areas of focus, one is the study of Facebook as part of teaching practice, the other is Facebook's use and its sociological implications in educational settings.

Madge et al. (2009) explore reasons of Facebook usage by teachers and reveals student engagement through self-disclosure, motivating students and stimulating teacher student interaction as primary motives. Wang et.al, (2012) explore the potential of Facebook as a learning management tool. Farnham et al, (2012) study of 32 students using So:cl a web application combining browsing, search and social networking finds social media to be an important factor in spurring informal learning. Ahmed et al. (2013) find college students in Bangladesh using Facebook alongside Search Engines for information seeking for both academic as well as non-academic purposes. Their findings suggest that the lack of digitized information and resources in the developing world make SNS driven searches more fruitful than search engines (SE) searches, which are dependent on data digitized by institutions, organizations and governments. These findings are echoed by Hussain (2015) whose study of pedagogical uses of Facebook in Pakistan shows resource sharing to be one of the dominant motives due to lack of education resources in the country. Rambi and Ng'ambi (2011) in their study based on 850 first year university students in Cape Town find that information sharing pedagogy using Facebook helps less confident and academically backward students.

Hewitt & Forte (2006) focus on how students perceive teachers who use Facebook while Mazer, et al, (2007) look at teacher participation on Facebook with regards to its effect on teacher student relations. Harris (2005) explores Facebook with regards to social relations between teachers and students and Rambe & Ng'ambi (2014) explore power relations between students and teachers in Facebook mediated learning environments. Selwyn (2009) after studying the Facebook wall activity of 909 students in a UK university suggests that rather than stimulating student engagement with studies, Facebook has a role to play in student identity politics and can also provide a relatively private space to negotiate role conflict with teachers, administration and work.

LEARNING AND FACEBOOK

New Models of Education

The top-down models of education where information flows downwards from teacher to students and students learn by applying that knowledge to real life situations are based on deductive reasoning processes and are seen as redundant in today's world. There is a growing awareness for a need to replace them with new models based on the bottom-up model where the student sets his own tasks according to a given area of investigation, undertakes research and study and gains the desirable knowledge. This method is based on inductive reasoning and works backwards from inquiry based learning to arrive at established knowledge. The latter approach is thus different from traditional models of education being based on principles of participation and stressing involvement and ownership of learning and activities undertaken by students. Participatory models enable many-to-many communication, interactivity, creativity and autonomy in information seeking and sharing as opposed to the traditional models. In education, this has led to interventions on many fronts including policy, institutional structures, ideology and pedagogy.

Buckingham (1998) highlights the social dimensions of pedagogy by insisting upon a 'focus on the theories of teaching and learning which inform classroom practice-and more specifically on the *social relationships* between teachers and students to which they give rise,' (Buckingham, 1998: p. 3). Differentiating between the two pedagogical approaches 'traditional' which focuses on acquiring information and 'progressive' which emphasizes on conceptual learning through 'readiness' and 'discovery learning' is key to harnessing the participatory and interactive features of the online world and SNS.

Facebook and other social media "employ mobile and web based technologies to create highly interactive platforms via which individuals and communities share, co- create, discuss and modify user generated content." (Keitzman, et al, 2011). Key structural features of these SNS are their interlinking capabilities, many to many communication, ease of accessibility for individual users, interactivity, multiplicity of use, ubiquity and their ability to transcend space and time. Enabled by these features students can become autonomous and take ownership of their learning. In these social forums teachers, books, Internet and other learners are all potential sources of information and support which students access to direct and construct their own learning. SNS enabled forums give these 'Digital Natives' the collaborative interactive and hands on approaches to learning and information and in forms preferred by them. Tapscott (1998) attributes this change in preferred learning styles to the advent of Internet enabled searching and retrieving of information (cited in Bosch, 2013) while Ulmer (1989) points to "the new discursive and conceptual ecology interrelating orality, literacy and videocy", (cited in Green 1998, p. 192).

For teachers too web based learning offers a limitless source of learning and teaching resources and tools, which are in accordance with the preferences of the tech savvy students of today. This marks a departure from the print-based models of learning typical of education (Livingstone, 2002). Along with the teaching and learning styles there is a need to look at evaluation style and methods. Efficacy of learning and teaching via new mediums cannot be judged if evaluations are not responsive to the new forms. Perkel's (2008) study exploring the practice of copy/paste on MySpace as a form of literacy involving social and technical skills gives an insight on the need to change the perception of student learning in accordance with the skills and requirements of the new mediums. Collaboration is another strength of online learning as these forums enable teachers and students to steer and construct learning as a joint process. Indeed Johnson & Johnson (1999) found this collaborative potential to be an important motivating force in learning for students. If SNS are to be harnessed for student motivation and engagement then teaching structures and methods should be crafted to encourage this social dynamic as an intrinsic part of pedagogy.

Facebook: How Is It Relevant

Apart from the potential to reconfigure hierarchies and social relations of classrooms and educational structures SNS also allow identity construction and networking. Facebook and other SNS enable users to create a profile (either public or semi-public), compile and publish a list of other users with whom they share a connection or have 'friended' and have access to people who are their own connections as well as connections of their friends within their confines (Boyd & Ellison, 2008). Thus SNS establish a social context that is absent from other educational tools like LMS. However the social nature of the forum gives rise to concerns about public and private domains with regards to relations between students and teachers.

Studies grounded in Social Presence Theory suggest that communication via ICTs is limited as tool for learning and understanding due to the absence of context (Sproull & Liesler, 1986; Tossell et al., 2012; Walther, 1992, as cited in Richardson & Swan, 2003). SNS being structured around people, (Miller, 2013) reflect unmediated social structures that exist in real life (Wellman, 1988, as cited in Boyd and Ellison, 2008). Facebook allows for visibility of interactions via the wall allowing interactions to be placed in context. Interactions can also be backtracked (Birdsall, 2009; as cited in Rambe & Ng'ambi, 2011). However Boyd & Heer (2006) caution that due to its ability for asynchronous communications and 'digital persistence' the very context can be lost to others accessing an interaction later.

The persistent visibility however can enable both the information seeker and information giver to be transformed through new understanding and command over students, peers, teachers and content. Synchronous and asynchronous interactions in Facebook environments enable meaning making to mirror real-life; a constant construction and deconstruction of meaning enriched by multiple socio-cultural influences and environment allow for better understanding leading to more confidence. Such a process is at work in real time environments as well, but because Facebook provides resources in multiple formats and records interactions, our understanding is built from a richer pool of information. The interactions once recorded on Facebook walls/chats are not lost and can continue to feed our understanding beyond time. In this way online learning environments are different from the traditional learning environments.

There is also evidence to suggest that Facebook is used in representation and identity construction (Selwyn, 2009, Rambi & N'gambi, 2014). Being a virtual forum it can allow students to exert social presence by overcoming issues related to lack of confidence and shyness in a real life class setting. Both suggests that this can build student confidence, allow for further possibilities of engagement and thereby affect learning.

While new opportunities via SNS exist, their potential has yet to be realized. Cuban's (1993) work on technology and pedagogy serves as a good base to view the current trends of technology adoption by teachers. He identifies three categories of teachers, the 'technophiles', the 'preservationists' and the 'cautious optimists'. Hussain (2015) argues that very few teachers integrate technology and curriculum to enable radical changes education practice and structures. Selwyn (2009) cautions that research and accessibility via online sources might lead to dependency on readymade solutions and further detachment with the real world and Livingstone (2002) expresses concern that education should not be made to conform to limitations of technology and virtual environment.

Learning benefits of ICTs are not universally applicable to all learners as Watkins (2009) reports student feeling overwhelmed with the quantity of information available. Ahmed et al, (2013) show even though sources of information gathering available have multiplied, the role of a teacher in an educational experience and its sociological importance in the learning process does not diminish. In fact it is a role that students want and desire (Rambi & N'gambi, 2011, Richard, 2004).-

Immediacy Behaviors in Online Environments

With regards to immediacy producing behaviors such as facial expressions, hand gestures and eye contact, Facebook offers alternatives which merit attention in order to understand its potential. Even though the above stated behaviors are not possible in online environments, these can be overcome by verbal communication behaviors like using first names, sharing personal incidents (self disclosure) and giving a quick response. These behaviors help in creating a participatory learning environment for students and provide the needed social presence thereby encouraging student engagement (Richardson & Swan, 2003).

'Emoticons' and 'memes' are two major visual and graphic elements, which are popular in online environments. Jibril and Abdullah (2013) describe emoticons or "smileys" as socio-emotional suppliers introduced to overcome the lack of non-verbal communication in computer-mediated communication (CMC). They help in understanding the feeling or mood of a message in virtual interactions (Wei, 2012). Emoticons have been credited with lessening the formality of CMC and making it playful (Danet, Reudenberg-Wright, & Rosenbaum-Tamari, 1997; Walther & D'Addario, 2001 as cited in Wie, 2012). They thus function as invaluable emotion enablers in online interactions facilitating understanding by lending expression to the intent or mood behind the written communication. Memes can be described as artifacts of the digital world that have a cognitive and virtual presence. Memes have a social and cultural dimension and are dependent on the purposeful consumption and production by participants of virtual environments. They are an intrinsic part of participatory digital culture (Wiggens & Bowers, 2014)

Ulmer (1994) suggests that the form of content being shared is also an important factor for 'net geners'. Sharing of content in the form of videos and visuals might motivate students to engage with content. The fact that the teacher is aware of student preferences and is sharing content in different formats could also serve to bridge the perceived distance between teacher and student. Thus the form of content shared could also lead to immediacy.

As Wood & Baker (2004) point out, even though interaction is the most important component in online environments it alone cannot "create a positive social dynamic" (p. 2). Wagner's (1994) distinction between interaction and interactivity helps explain this dynamic. She defines interactivity as involving two or more objects or actions and the element of reciprocity. Interaction on the other hand is more then just a reciprocal exchange. It involves mutual influence between two individuals. In context of computer mediated learning, it is this human element that distinguishes interactivity from interaction. Thus "Interactivity may eventually be viewed as a machine attribute, while interaction may be perceived as an outcome of using interactive instructional delivery systems" (Wagner, 1994, p. 26 as cited in Woods & Baker 2004). Research shows students participation being higher in online classes where discussion is valued (Kucek 2009). Teachers are still the key players who shape interactions and set the pattern for how participants of the communication employ any media to build an effective learning community (Rambe & Ng'ambi, 2011).

Research has been concerned with how to promote interpersonal interaction due to the assumption that it will lead to positive communication behaviors such as teacher immediacy, social presence, and sense of community in the online classroom and thus lead to enhanced learning. This however seems like a simplistic approach to a complex matter involving human subjects who are subject to many influences, direct and peripheral. LaRose and Whitten (2000) illustrate that immediacy in web-based forums is a combination of vertical interactions, between teacher and student (teacher immediacy,) and horizontal interactions, between student (student immediacy) and student computer (computer immediacy). According to them learning is thus driven by a combination of immediacy and social presence comprising of incentives through social rewards like approval from teachers and peers and status rewards like an enhanced status of the student. However they tend to overlook the socio-cultural context its implications for students and spaces of interaction. In online forums where identities are not geographically negotiated these influences can pose a challenge to immediacy.

Woods & Baker (2004) include the environment as an important influencing factor and suggest an integration of verbal and non-verbal immediacy to optimize web based learning experience from "mere interaction to authentic intimacy and interpersonal closeness" (Woods & Baker 2004, pp.2). They propose a model of interaction in which the learner who is at the center, interacts with teacher, content, peers and environment. Their model is based on the premise that immediacy is not just a result of who is part of the interaction but also the type or quality of interaction, which in turn is influenced, by all of the above. They also differentiate between the various types of communication: two-way (non - interactive), reactive (quasi interaction) and fully interactive.

There has also not been enough focus on how teachers approach teaching and learning an aspect which has a direct impact on their practice. Elys points out the benefits of ICTs and their potential in pedagogy cannot be examined without a study of how teachers incorporate them in actual practice (cited in Hunter, 1998). Therefore this study focuses on the two as reciprocal and interlinked processes. It examines the structure of the virtual forum, in this case Facebook and the behavioral and psychological implications and effects that communication on such a forum entails. This way a clearer understanding of immediacy behaviors in online environments might be possible and reveal how immediacy affects the processes of learning in online environments.

Method

The study analyzed communication between students and teachers in closed Facebook groups established for study purposes, to identify immediacy behaviors of teachers and students and understand the various factors and reasons affecting them. 3 closed Facebook groups were chosen from undergraduate Art and Design institutions in Karachi, Pakistan, of which two were from Indus Valley School of Art & Architecture and one from Department of Visual Studies, University of Karachi. These groups complemented real-time classrooms.

Facebook communication was observed and analyzed for verbal and nonverbal immediacy behaviors, quality of communication (Wood & Baker, 2004) and nature of content shared. Verbal immediacy behaviors were categorized adapting Verbal Immediacy Indicators from the study of Kucuk (2009). Personalization in messages was interpreted as verbal immediacy and included use of "I" "we", incidences of self-disclosure, approval and encouraging statements. Use of emoticons and exclamation marks was interpreted as Non-verbal immediacy indicators. The purpose was to establish whether students were responsive to verbal or non-verbal immediacy behaviors.

Nature of resources/content shared was categorized into course content and non-course categories and further divided with reference to formats - video, text, memes etc. to establish a preferred format and evaluate if certain formats got a better response.

Quality of communication was categorized in accordance with the categories specified by Wood and Baker (2004). These categories attempted to understand the depth of interactivity. The following categories were used: Interactive (communication between student and teachers with a 'like'), reactive or quasi-interaction (some comment) and full interaction (comments in complete engagement with the post). This was succeeded by interviews with students as to the perceived benefits of study facilitated by Facebook and its ability to overcome teacher student distance by immediacy behaviors. Research by Richardson and Swan (2003) suggests that there is a deeper link between students' perceived benefits of study using CMC and immediacy. Interviews tried to investigate the link. Teachers were interviewed in order to explore their behaviors with reference to immediacy and establish their views about the perceived benefits of employing Facebook for educational purpose.

Results

Observation of three groups over a period of 18 days showed varying activity between the groups- Group 1 being most active and Group 3 least active (see Table 1).

Interviews

Group 1

For students the primary use of Facebook was for convenient communication. They felt that the quality of communication via Facebook depended on the nature of the teacher and the formality of the relationship with students. Respect for teachers was an important aspect in regulating behavior and determining the type of interactions with teachers in the online group. Some students expressed concern over teacher surveillance however they felt that it kept them focused on studies. They felt that fellow students with low proficiency in English were able to participate in discussions taking aid of memes/visuals to express and communicate.

Table 1. Group observations

	Ownership	Description	Purpose
Group 1 - GD	Students set up group and invited teacher to join	Set up by students Not a formal part of course Student led forum Majority student participation Friendly atmosphere	Information sharing Seeking teacher feedback Notice board Discussion Peer motivation
Group 2 - KNYS	Teachers formed the group and told students to join	Formal part of course Teacher led forum Low student participation	Set up by teachers for collaborative design between Karachi and NYC based students Monitoring student interactions Information sharing
Group 3 - AP	Teacher formed the group and told students to join	Formal part of course with participation grade Low participation from teacher and students	Critical thinking Discussion Research and resource sharing

The teacher revealed that he was a moderate user of Facebook and preferred email for communication. Acquisition of a smart phone with a Facebook App resulted in increased interaction via Facebook, as previously he would need to use a desktop or laptop. Real-time interaction of Facebook App was disturbing for him so he did not reply to "useless inbox" and disabled Facebook chat. "Specially when I feel that some one is in urgent need then I don't give them any reply. I will come to class in the morning, I was there today and you remember at one clock at night!" He felt this regulation necessary to discipline students. He was also concerned with the blurring of private and educational spheres on Facebook and felt students tended to overstep boundaries. He preferred face-to-face interaction during class and did not give qualitative feedback on Facebook. "Facebook is just for reminders…deadlines… mostly stern reminders."

He was undecided about Facebook's potential for informal learning and information access. "If I tell them to look it up (resources), they will not bother, so let me share it on the group. In a closed group at least you know they have seen it (shared content) because you get notifications." He recalled that having shared a resource he did not receive any response but received notifications that students had seen it. However the next day some of the students gave a reference to the work shared by him the previous day. "Whether they like or not is besides the point but they have seen it."

Regarding multiple formats, he admitted that he does not share videos due to poor bandwidth, and extremely slow downloading even though students might respond better. Recently bandwidth and video downloading had become better "but I have become set in my habit, it isn't changing, its like I have an allergy to video."

He revealed that he had recently started using emoticons. "I have learnt the smile and wink." He elaborated that until recently he did not understand what the emoticons meant in text-based messages. "Sometimes you get a D, D3….what?"[1] However he was concerned that use of non-verbal communication in virtual environments distanced people from real-time communication. Recalling an incident he explained, "A student posted… I am depressed…oh don't be, here is a hug for you… a virtual hug!" Similarly the number of 'Likes' on the above status outweighed any other types of responses with only one student offering actual support. Facebook also alerted him about students' problems.

With regards to merits of LMS as an alternative to Facebook he felt, Facebook was the better forum to engage students. "Everyone wants to share some thing…show something…. that is why its social media." Facebook also proved useful for student with low class presence and self-esteem as they could experiment with personas. "They are not clear about them selves they are showing a different self at every different platform."

Group 2

Students explained that once the novelty of knowing the NYC students had worn of they lost interest and that led to the low interaction on the group. They felt the group was good for resource sharing and information gathering however lack of understanding of local issues by NYC students limited discussion. Some students suggested Skype sessions during class hours while others felt email contact was better as they were free from monitoring by teachers. Others cited lack of time and interest as factors. Students did not like sharing ideas on open forums and were generally not in favor of collaborative projects.

The teacher felt the group was more beneficial for information sharing than interaction and the Pakistani students were rather passive recipients of information. He felt that the type of resource being shared mattered with more response to a TED lecture than a text based resource. With regards to the discursive potential of Facebook he was skeptical. "It's the way people see Facebook....its social media. So in terms of information exchange its working but in terms of creating a serious discussion around it.... No." Like the previous teacher he also felt that 'Like' option on Facebook restricted discussion and it had to be provoked. "You can have 10 'Likes' and only one comment. I mean nobody knows what you like in it. ....you just like it...that's it."

He felt that Facebook's capacity to make information sharing participatory was its key strength when compared to LMS. However he felt that in order to harness Facebook for co- creation and discussion it needed a formal place in the course with grades for participation. He also felt that students got into the habit of asking others to do their research rather than looking on their own.

Group 3

The group comprised of students from multiple disciplines. Student activity was low and dominated by a few students belonging to Fine Arts. Even though most posts were articles about controversial art there was no evidence of discussion or challenging of ideas. Teacher's activity was limited to notifications about exams and class timings.

Students felt the teacher did not provoke discussion and referred to another teacher's practice of tagging students in relevant articles. Most students were neutral about the group while some felt it was beneficial for resource sharing. One student felt that the resources shared were available via Google too. Some female students expressed reservations about the controversial and explicit nature of the content being shared, they read the articles but did not comment on them. However they found the group useful and did not wish it to be deactivated. Students also reported time constraints and laziness as other reasons for low activity.

The teacher admitted that she had not been active with this particular group, and agreed that her previous practice of provoking discussion had yielded better results. For her multi format resource sharing was the main benefit "because a lot of knowledge that even I come across is online," and she shared it while she read or watched it. "Since I started using Facebook I realized that I am sharing a lot of videos...visuals are so important."

She felt that student participation in a discussion depended on interest level of students in the topic under discussion. She recalled an incidence, in which there was a lot of controversy regarding the design of a local logo. She shared a blog by the designer and an elaborate discussion followed. Controversial issues like gender and those grounded in socio-cultural contexts received more response from students. She felt that more than the form (video or text) response was generated when a resource was shared with a personal comment. She recalled that a student shared two articles with a personal comment and managed to engage his peers. Likewise text accessible through a smart phone or a laptop got a better response than a hard copy of the same text. She felt that participation grades did not ensure interaction: activity on Facebook group was 10%` of her course grade yet participation was low. However her past experience with similar groups was that participation continued beyond the course.

Privacy and self-disclosure was a cause of concern for her. She recalled an incident when Hazara[2] minority was targeted and killed. "In some ways I was coming from this high moral ground...that you should be more considerate of you class fellows (belonging to Hazara minority), you should be more participatory and you are students...what's wrong with you...why aren't you concerned." Students shared the post outside the group. "That's the time when I realized that I should not have shared this kind of information." On the positive side, the post motivated students to collectively take action.

Another benefit was that communication between students and teachers was recorded on walls as opposed to a class where communication was verbal. Apart from this Facebook also provided students with a space to negotiate tensions. She recalled another incident where some students were caught cheating in an exam. The administration decided to cancel the exam for the entire class and organize a retake. Facebook provided students with a forum to express their concern with the decision taken. She pointed out that the communication was never rude but simply an expression of displeasure with the decision taken. The incident had a positive outcome.

She also felt that Facebook groups allowed her an alternate means of assessing student understanding of course content by looking at the content students shared. "I can actually see the growth in terms of knowledge, learning and confidence." However she felt that if institutions could provide an LMS which enable multi-format sharing of resources, and discussion boards she would switch to using LMS, the reason being, "its more professional."

SOLUTIONS AND RECOMMENDATIONS

Reaching out to students via their preferred mediums in this case Facebook can bridge the gap between teachers and students. Being a non-hierarchical social forum it is different to traditional learning environments where teachers and students can build learning together. Simultaneous interaction with teachers, peers, content and socio-cultural environment allows wider exposure and confidence spurring motivation to learn. Due to the easy availability of multiple resources in various formats it allows for a richer educational experience with less effort. Prevalence of the popular culture in online environments allows appropriation of elements like emoticons and memes in learning environments so teachers can speak the language of the students and build immediacy. It supports synchronous and asynchronous communication and allows for greater access as interactions are recorded. Being profile based it also allows more visibility and this enhances teacher's exposure to students and their participation, building better relationships. In this way learning and teaching via Facebook can enable immediacy and social presence. However this is dependent on the way teachers incorporate Facebook in their teaching practice.

Verbal and Non-Verbal Immediacy Behaviors

Prevalence of verbal and non-verbal immediacy behaviors in the observed groups was linked to the nature of the group. Group 1 was not a formal part of the course and was non-academic in nature. Group 2 and 3 were formal components of the course with one having grades for participation. This perhaps contributed to the perception of the group as a more formal space, thus discouraging usage of fun elements (see Figure 1).

With regards to verbal immediacy (the use of "we" "us" etc. and instances of self-disclosure) Group 1 took the lead with Group 3 following. However an important difference was that in Group 1 both teachers and students were engaged but in Group 3 only the teacher, however her interaction was erratic and infrequent. Swan and Richardson (2003) have suggested that immediacy can be cultured. However is culture is fed by socio-cultural norms and imbibed over time. For immediacy in online forums timely response is important, tempered with a more conscious engagement via 'native' communication forms (see Figure 2).

Figure 1. Use of emoticons (non-verbal immediacy) in Facebook groups

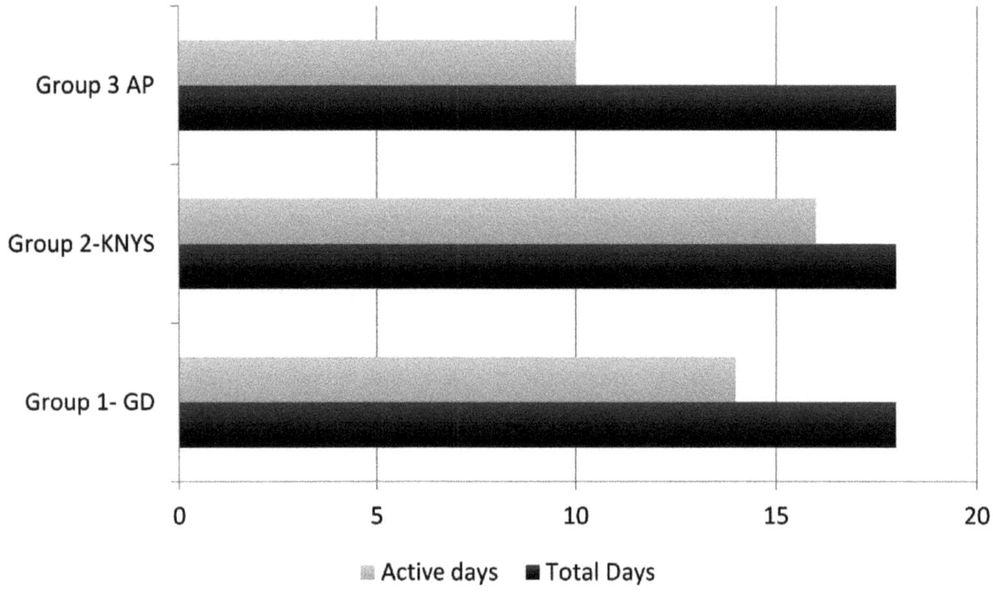

Figure 2. Verbal immediacy use in Facebook groups

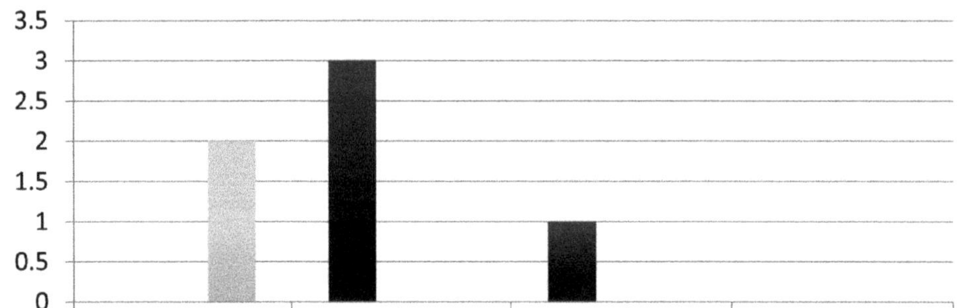

	Teachers	Students	Teachers	Students
	We, us etc.		Self- disclosure	
Group 1- GD	0	3	1	0
Group 2-KNYS	0	0	0	0
Group 3 AP	2	0	0	0

A comparison of immediacy behaviors across the three groups revealed asymmetrical activity: only Group 1 showed significant immediacy. Students led the way in both verbal and non-verbal immediacy behaviors. This could be indicative of a link in student's perception of ownership, Group 1 being student formed, resulting in their setting the tone for interactions with teachers (see Figure 3).

Generation and tech divide also seemed to be a factor. One of the teachers reported unfamiliarity with text-based emoticons as limiting his response to students. However with the acquisition of a smart phone,

Figure 3. Verbal immediacy vs. Non-verbal immediacy in groups

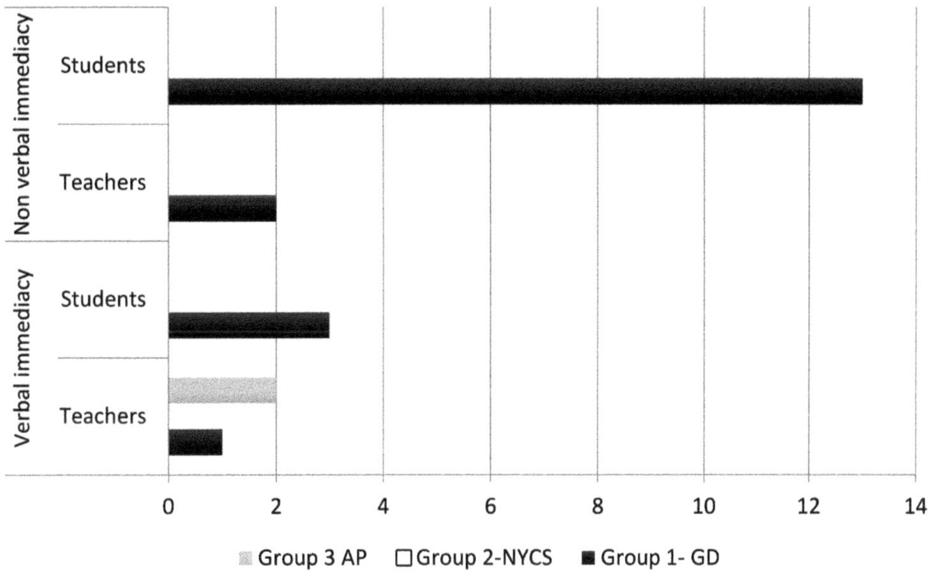

which supported image-based emoticons, he began adopting the practice. Emoticons are embedded in online culture and students might want their online learning experience punctuated by such elements. Ignatius & Kokkonen, (2007) also make a strong case for emoticons being considered as self-disclosure as they represent feelings. Emoticons can alert teachers to student moods where as allowing for tempering of own communication for immediacy.

Online spaces being inhabited by young students can be harnessed for more informal learning where social hierarchies can be reversed and there is room for expression. When choosing online forums teachers might want to keep in mind whether they support emoticons. As image-based emoticons become readily available and new technology enables their use, teachers might consider them for engagement with students.

Immediacy, Interaction and Learning Via Facebook

Potential benefits of immediacy are linked to aiding student learning and better outcomes. By adopting immediacy teachers hope to increase and enhance quality interaction with students (see figure 4).

The quality of interactions amongst the three groups remained unsatisfactory, as the discursive potential of Facebook was not optimally exploited. In Group 1 there was only one incidence of students incorporating relevant resources to shape a discussion. Group 2 due to active teachers fared better, however in both instances of full interaction the teacher instigated discussion. Discrepancy in interactions between Group 3 and the other two groups can be attributed to the lack of teacher involvement. This suggests that teachers are instrumental in shaping the culture of learning online. Furthermore students stated their preference for a more active role from teachers. In Group 1 the teacher limited his interaction citing student discipline as a reason. In online environments where the rate of response matters this might be an important aspect influencing both quantity and quality of interaction. Furthermore Facebook being structured socially might not be suitable for discipline. There might be a need to come up with an alternate strategy for discipline without compromising accessibility.

Figure 4. Quality of interactions in Facebook groups

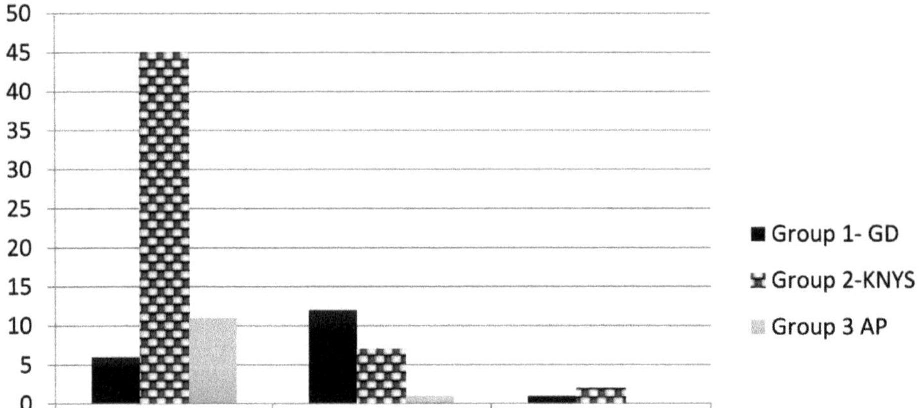

	Interactive	Qausi-interactive	Full
Group 1- GD	6	12	1
Group 2-KNYS	45	7	2
Group 3 AP	11	1	0

It is important to understand the social dynamics of online environments. Even though the teachers in Group 2 exceeded other teachers in terms of activity with a large number of posts being links to course relevant articles, this did not serve to engage students. Students felt resource sharing as the most valuable aspect of the group. On the other hand the teacher felt resource sharing made students complacent and kept them from doing their own research. It might be important for teachers to temper resource sharing with restraint and devise ways to make it more participatory. It might also be a matter of territory. If the online forum is the same as the real-time class in terms of teacher domination, it might be a construed as a negative behavior.

Even though in Group 3 Facebook activity was graded this did not enhance the quality of interaction. The teacher of Group 2 felt controversial topics generated more discussion than purely academic ones. However controversy should not be viewed as immediacy inducing as some students also expressed discomfort with controversial content being shared by their peers. Online boundaries are not geographically defined which means content is not always responsive to socio-cultural norms. This should be kept in mind when sharing resources, as it can have negative effects (see figure 5).

The nature of resource sharing on Facebook remained mostly text based even though teachers admitted that students responded well to video. One of the reasons identified was slow bandwidth connectivity. This perhaps deterred sharing of video by students and teachers. High frequency of articles might be linked to the dearth of digital data and high costs of academic resources in developing countries. Thus newspaper and magazine articles act as alternative information gathering resources. Another limitation, which can be overcome due to availability of content in multiple formats, is language barrier in students with low English proficiency. Livingstone (2002) also highlights problems in understanding due to constraints of academic language. Drawing upon availability of multi-format resources like videos, podcasts these students can construct a better understanding. With improved bandwidth video sharing might be used to improve student understanding.

Figure 5. Comparison of content/resources shared in Facebook groups

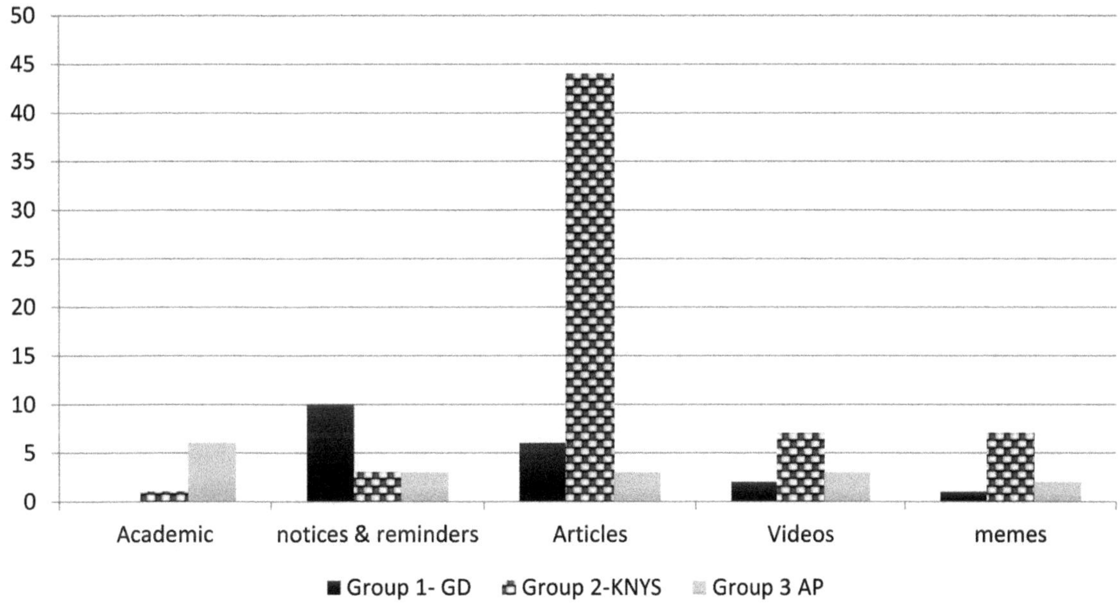

An alternative form that came up was that of a meme. Memes are an intrinsic part of the Internet culture. Students of Group 1 reported that their peers with low proficiency in English were able take part in English based communication taking the aid of memes for expression when language failed them. Memes thus contribute to quality of interactions and can be useful for immediacy. One thing to remember is that memes thrive on socio-cultural relevance and context. Memes can be highly engaging if used by the participants of an interaction sharing a common context. However if the context is missing they will not have the desired results. Online environments and their contents are west centric, which might have contributed to memes having less relevance and therefore not frequently shared in the groups. However increase in locally relevant memes might boost sharing via Facebook and other social media applications.

TOWARDS A SOCIAL THEORY OF LEARNING

Any study of immediacy must take into account the desired end - improving student engagement and learning outcomes. In today's world with education stressing the values of autonomy and critical thinking there might be a need to relook at traditional conceptions of educational practice. Educational instructions will need to be crafted in such a way as to encourage students to construct their own knowledge on their surroundings and take ownership of their educational experience. Teachers will need to realign themselves to this new way of thinking. Social media lends itself well to constructivist learning and a blended approach to learning could be applied by using it alongside formal learning space to see if learning is improved. Studies could also focus on the infrastructural and ideological limitations of teachers regarding educational practice in order to initiate the change to more student centric approaches that promote student autonomy.

It is important to differentiate between types of interaction. For learning interactions to be beneficial teachers will need to play an active role so as to spur discussion beyond the 'like' culture, which is after all a relatively passive behavior in online environments. Cross-cultural studies focusing on the possible uses and connotations of non-verbal behaviors might serve to flesh out the understanding of such behaviors in different cultures. Ahmed et al (2014) suggest an inherent difference in learning styles between West and East. Cross-cultural studies could also help to establish whether students from various parts of the world prefer different formats and content and why.

This study suggests that there is a need to modify behavior and teaching methods in accordance with the social dynamics of online environments, which differ from traditional classrooms. Facebook's potential for social presence is a key determinant to immediacy in the groups. A study, perhaps, with a focus on desirable and undesirable behaviors by teachers keeping this reversal in hierarchy specific to online environments might be useful to establish protocols of online group behaviors. Another dimension is that of extending evaluation to embrace this dynamic. As Perkels (2008) suggests, a move beyond viewing discussion and informed comments as means of assessing student learning might be the way forward. Students can demonstrate learning via linking, sharing of memes, posting videos etc. This could also be an important variable in creating immediacy between teachers and students.

Ownership might be key to Facebook becoming a truly learning and beneficial environment for students. Even though teachers might make the Facebook group a formal component of a course, they will need to think of ways to inculcate ownership. A comparative study focusing on the role Facebook plays in various teachers' pedagogy might reveal what works for promotion of ownership and what does not. This will allow teachers to be able to deliver and design content and instruction in way so as to stimulate ownership.

There might be a strong institutional dynamic at work in the understanding and practice of immediacy behaviors. This study showed a contrast in behaviors between the groups belonging to different institutions, however it did not investigate this aspect. The study was also limited in that it was based upon institutions specializing in art and design, located in a metropolitan. The findings might change in other smaller cities or rural areas and in institutions catering to other disciplines.

CONCLUSION

As Richardson & Swan (2003) explain, in order to understand immediacy in online environments it is important to move beyond counting and categorization of verbal and non-verbal behaviors. As seen in the above study evaluations of immediacy should be approached with a broad understanding of the term immediacy and its implications in the online environment. It is important to note that immediacy has a strong socio-cultural dynamic, what is immediacy producing in one environment might not be viewed so in another.

Facebook as an online learning environment has merits as well as limitations. Even though the use of Facebook to connect with students might itself be viewed as immediate behavior, at the end of the day it's the use of the forum that determines whether it potential is realized. It is essential to recognize the social nature of Facebook in order to harness it for discovery and constructivist learning. Attempts to turn it into a purely academic environment might not be able to produce the desired results. Social presence is an important aspect of learning via Facebook with particular implications for students with low self-esteem. This aspect along with the feature of persistence of asynchronous interactions continues to facilitate teachers' understanding of their students, over time. Fears of surveillance by students and overlapping of public and private spheres by teachers continue to be valid concerns. However there is evidence to support that a sense of ownership of the learning space mitigates these with students and teachers setting and following protocols for online behavior. Facebook also supports Emoticons and memes, which are popular aids for creating immediacy and easing communication. The fact that Facebook is not built for educational purpose allows for a non-hierarchical social environment where teachers learn from students and students learn from teachers. In this way Facebook can be used for a fully interactive learning experience grounded in the principle of mutual influence and mutual benefit. However students still expect teachers to play a leading role.

Broadly, learning via online forums is situated such that it must acknowledge and appropriate the multiple sources available for student learning and evaluation including social media. A blended system synthesizing the two dynamics academic and social might serve to enhance learning and create immediacy. In online environments where socio-cultural contexts are blurred the profile based structure of social media might serve to enhance teachers understanding of student contexts. This can help teachers in creating strategies of learning suitable to individual needs and creating immediacy to optimize learning.

REFERENCES

Ahmed, S., Anik, T. A., Tasnim, M., & Ferdous, H. S. (2013). *Statistical analysis and implications of SNS search in underdeveloped countries.* Paper presented at 25th Australian Computer –Human Interaction Conference: Augmentation, application, Innovation, Collaboration, OZCHI 2013, Adelaide, Australia. Retrieved from https://www.academia.edu/4426905/Statistical_Analysis_and_Implications_of_SNS_Search_in_Under-Developed_Countries

Ajjan, H., & Hartshorne, R. (2008). Investigating faculty decisions to adopt Web 2.0 technologies: Theory and empirical tests. *The Internet and Higher Education*, *11*(2), 71–80. doi:10.1016/j.iheduc.2008.05.002

Andersen, J. F., Andersen, P. A., & Jensen, A. D. (1979). The measurement of immediacy. *Journal of Applied Communication Research*, *7*(2), 153–180. doi:10.1080/00909887909365204

Baringer, D. K., & McCroskey, J. C. (2000). Immediacy in the classroom: Student immediacy. *Communication Education*, *49*(2), 178–186. doi:10.1080/03634520009379204

Bell, R. A., & Daly, J. A. (1984). The affinity-seeking Function of Communication. *Communication Monographs*, *51*(2), 91–115. doi:10.1080/03637758409390188

Bosch, T. E. (2009). Using online social networking for teaching and learning: Facebook use at the University of Cape Town. *Communicatio. South African Journal for Communication Theory and Research*, *35*(2), 185–200.

Boyd, D., & Jeffery, H. (2006). *Profiles as Conversation: Networked Identity Performance on Friendster.* Paper presented at the Hawai'i International Conference on Systems Sciences (HICSS-39) Persistent Conversation Track, Kauai, HI. doi:10.1109/HICSS.2006.394

Boyd, D. M., & Ellison, N. B. (2008). Social Network Sites: Definition, History, and Scholarship. *Journal of Computer-Mediated Communication*, *13*(1), 210–230. doi:10.1111/j.1083-6101.2007.00393.x

Buchanan, T., Sainter, P., & Saunders, G. (2013). Factors affecting faculty use of learning technologies: Implications for models of technology adoption. *Journal of Computing in Higher Education*, *25*(1), 1–11. doi:10.1007/s12528-013-9066-6

Buckingham, D. (1998). *Teaching Popular Culture*. London: UCL Press.

Christophel, D. M. (1990). The relationships among teacher immediacy behaviors, student motivation, and learning. *Communication Education*, *39*(4), 323–340. doi:10.1080/03634529009378813

Cox, M., Preston, C., & Cox, K. (1999). *What Factors Support or Prevent Teachers from Using ICT in their Classrooms?* Paper presented at the British Educational Research Association Annual Conference, Brighton, UK. Retrieved from http://www.leeds.ac.uk/educol/documents/00001304.htm

Cuban, L. (1986). *Teachers and Machines: the classroom use of technology since 1920*. New York: Teachers College Press.

Farnham, S., Lahav, M., Raskino, D., Cheng, L., & Laird-McConnell, T. (2012). So.cl: An interest network for informal learning. In *Proceedings of the International AAAI Conference on Weblogs and Social Media*.

Gorham, J. (1988). The relationship between verbal teacher immediacy behaviors and student learning. *Communication Education*, *37*(1), 40–53. doi:10.1080/03634528809378702

Green, B. (1998). Teaching for difference: Learning Theory and Post-critical pedagogy. In D. Buckingham (Ed.), *Teaching Popular Culture* (pp. 177–197). London: UCL Press.

Gunawardena, C. N., & Zittle, F. J. (1997). Social presence as a predictor of satisfaction within a computer-mediated conferencing environment. *American Journal of Distance Education*, *11*(3), 8–26. doi:10.1080/08923649709526970

Harris, K. (2008, October 16). Using Social Networking Sites as Student Engagement Tools. *Diverse Issues in Higher Education*, *25*(18). Retrieved from http://diverseeducation.com/article/11837/

Hewitt, A., & Forte, A. (2006). *Crossing boundaries: Identity management and student/faculty relationships on the Facebook*. Paper presented at the Computer Supported Cooperative Work Conference, Banff, Canada. Retrieved from: http://andreaforte.net/HewittForteCSCWPoster2006.pdf

Hunter, C. D. (1998). *Technology in the Classroom: Haven't We Heard This Before?* [Class handout]. Retrieved: www2.le.ac.uk/departments/media/dl/documents.../Reading10.pdf

Hussain, T. (2015). Influence of Facebook in Pakistani Pedagogy. *Media Watch*, *6*(3), 326–338. doi:10.15655/mw/2015/v6i3/77895

Ignatius, E., & Kokkonen, M. (2007). Factors contributing to verbal self-disclosure. *Nordic Psychology*, *59*(4), 362–391. doi:10.1027/1901-2276.59.4.362

Ito, M. (2010). Work. In *Hanging out, messing around and Geeking out* (pp. 295–310). MIT Press.

Jibril, T. A., & Abdullah, M. H. (2013). Relevance of Emoticons in Computer-Mediated Communication Contexts: An Overview. *Asian Social Science*, *9*(4). doi:10.5539/ass.v9n4p201

Kelley, D. H., & Gorham, J. (1988). Effects of immediacy on recall of information. *Communication Education*, *37*(3), 198–207. doi:10.1080/03634528809378719

Kietzmann, J. H., Hermkens, K., McCarthy, I. P., & Silvestre, B. S. (2011). Social media? Get serious! Understanding the functional building blocks of social media. *Business Horizons*, *54*(3), 241–251. doi:10.1016/j.bushor.2011.01.005

Kim, K.-H., & Yun, H. (2007). Cying for Me, Cying for Us: Relational Dialectics in a Korean Social Network Site. *Journal of Computer-Mediated Communication*, *13*(1), 298–318. doi:10.1111/j.1083-6101.2007.00397.x

Kucuk, M., (2009). Teacher Immediacy Behaviors And Participation In Computer Mediated Communication. *Turkish Online Journal of Distance Education, 10*(2).

LaRose, R., & Whitten, P. (2000). Re-thinking Instructional Immediacy for Web Courses: A social cognitive exploration. *Communication Education*, *49*(4), 320–338. doi:10.1080/03634520009379221

Lim, D., & Kim, H. (2002). Motivation and learner characteristics affecting online learning and learning applications. *Journal of Educational Technology Systems*, *31*(4), 423–439. doi:10.2190/0LW0-KE8X-MDYH-X27F

Livingstone, S. (2002). Changing Media, changing literacies. In *Young people and New Media* (pp. 211–254). London: Sage.

Livingstone, S. (2010). Interactive, engaging but unequal, critical conclusions from Internet studies. In J. Curran (Ed.), *Media and Society* (pp. 122–142). London: Bloomsbury.

Madge, C., Meek, J., Wellens, J., & Hooley, T. (2009). Facebook, social integration and informal learning at university: 'It is more for socialising and talking to friends about work than for actually doing work'. *Learning, Media and Technology*, *34*(2), 141–155. doi:10.1080/17439880902923606

McQuail, D. (2010). *Mass Communication Theory*. London: Sage.

Mehrabian, A. (1969). Some referents and measures of nonverbal behavior. *Behavior Research Methods and Instrumentation*, *1*(6), 205–207.

Mumtaz, S. (2000). Factors affecting teachers' use of information and communications technology: A review of the literature. *Journal of Information Technology for Teacher Education*, *9*(3), 319–342. doi:10.1080/14759390000200096

Perkel, D. (2006). *Copy and Paste Literacy: Literacy practices in the production of a MySpace profile*. Retrieved April 28, 2014, from http://people.ischool.berkeley.edu/~dperkel/media/dperkel_literacy-myspace.pdf

Richards, C. (2004). From old to new learning: Global imperatives, exemplary Asian dilemmas as a key to cultural change in education. *Globalisation, Societies and Education*, *2*(3), 337–352. doi:10.1080/1476772042000252470

Richardson, J. C., & Swan, K. (2003). Examining social presence in online courses in relation to students' perceived learning and satisfaction. *Journal of Asynchronous Learning Networks*, *7*, 68–82.

Said, A. (2006) Accessing Electronic Information: A study of Pakistan's Digital Library. *INASPR Research and Education Case studies 1*. Oxford, UK: Antony Rowe Ltd. Retrieved from: http://www.hec.gov.pk/PublishingImages/454_diglibpak/454_diglibpak.html

Selwyn, N. (2007). Technology and Education: Learning in the Information Age. In F. Option (Ed.), *Unit 83, MA in Mass Communications (By Distance Learning)*. Department of Media and Communication, University of Leicester.

Selwyn, N. (2009). Faceworking: Exploring students' education-related use of Facebook. *Learning, Media and Technology*, *34*(2), 157–174. doi:10.1080/17439880902923622

Short, J., Williams, E., & Christie, B. (1976). *The social psychology of telecommunications*. London: John Wiley and Sons.

Siddiqui, S. Z. (2006). Study approaches of students in Pakistan: The revised two-factor study process questionnaire experience. *2006 Occasional Report 1*. Retrieved from: http://www.hec.gov.pk/PublishingImages/684_Study-Approaches-of-Students-in-Pakistan/684_Study-Approaches-of-Students-in-Pakistan.html

Thweatt, K. S., & McCroskey, J. C. (1996). Teacher Non-immediacy and Misbehavior: Unintentional negative communication. *Communication Research Reports*, *13*(2), 198–204. doi:10.1080/08824099609362087

Tu, C. H., & McIsaac, M. (2002). The relationship of social presence and interaction in online classes. *American Journal of Distance Education*, *16*(3), 131–150. doi:10.1207/S15389286AJDE1603_2

Wang, Q., Woo, H. L., Quek, L. C., Yang, Y., & Liu, M. (2011). Using the Facebook group as a learning management system: An exploratory study. *British Journal of Educational Technology*, *43*(3), 423–438.

Watkins, C. (2009). What schools are learning about themselves and young technology users. In *The Young and the Digital: What the Migration to Social Network Sites, Games, and Anytime, Anywhere Media Means for Our Future* (pp. 19–46). Beacon Press.

Wei, A. C. Y. (2012). *Emoticons and the non-verbal communication: With reference to Facebook*. (Unpublished master's thesis). Department of Media Studies, Christ University, Bangalore, India.

Wiggins, E. B., & Bowers, G. B. (2014). Memes as genre: A structurational analysis of the memescape. *New Media & Society*, 1–21.

Woods, R. H. Jr, & Baker, J. D. (2004). Interaction and Immediacy in Online Learning. *International Review of Research in Open and Distance Learning*, *5*(2).

KEY TERMS AND DEFINITIONS

Asynchronous: Not occurring at the same time and recorded, persisting in time.

Cognitive Learning: Learning that incorporates and builds upon existing knowledge and information.

Discovery Learning: Also described as inquiry based learning where students are given areas to research and arrive at answers as opposed to looking for answers in prescribed texts.

Emoticons: Graphic representations of facial expressions depicting various human emotions.

Interaction: An exchange between two or more people with varying degrees of engagement.

Internet Meme: A digital artifact that builds upon cognition and is propagated through various digital media. It has a strong socio-cultural component and derives strength from its ubiquity, ability to be shared, appropriated and reproduced in multiple contexts.

Profile: Representation of a user including picture, contacts, personal data, interests and activities.

Social Learning: Similar to cognitive learning but drawing on learning from a pool of peers and social environments.

Social Media: These can be defined as highly interactive virtual social forums connected by mobile or web based technologies where in individuals or groups can share, co-create, discuss and modify content and resources.

Social Presence: The perceived extent of importance of an individual in an interaction in an online environment.

ENDNOTES

1 Text based equivalent of smileys or emoticons.

2 Hazaras are a minority community in Pakistan facing persecution.

Chapter 10
Instructional Strategies for Synchronous Components of Online Courses

Matthea Marquart
Columbia University, USA

Sam A. Rosenthal
Columbia University, USA

Michael Fleming
Columbia University, USA

Melanie Hibbert
Columbia University, USA

ABSTRACT

An effective means of achieving a high degree of interactivity and instructor immediacy in an online course is through the use of synchronous online webinars, herein referred to as live sessions. This chapter outlines the philosophy, techniques, and affordances contained within the School of Professional Studies (SPS) at Columbia University's model for online course support. Of paramount importance to the SPS model is a strong technical support system and a series of replicable class procedures and processes that draw on the strengths of SPS's webinar interfaces and support personnel and on the academic prowess of SPS's instructors. This chapter serves as a practical toolkit of strategies and best practices, with wide potential for implementation, regardless of program size or budget. The authors discuss SPS's model and technologies, some common issues and solutions, and SPS's overarching philosophy. Finally, this chapter offers alternatives for schools with differing needs or constraints, with the core goal of increasing instructor immediacy and fostering student interactivity.

INTRODUCTION

Online course offerings at Columbia University's School of Professional Studies (SPS) have grown substantially in recent years (see Figure 1). SPS is unique in that many of the School's program offerings are directed towards students who already have undergraduate or even, in some cases, graduate level degrees and are furthering their knowledge bases or pursuing new degrees or certificates. The School's instructor base is also unique in that it is largely culled from the professional, not primarily the academic, world, with many faculty pulling double-duty as industry leaders and instructors for SPS

DOI: 10.4018/978-1-4666-9995-3.ch010

online courses. With a student and instructor base that is largely comprised of working professionals, our courses must be highly flexible and adaptable. These background considerations have informed much of the style and mission of the online team at SPS, specifically tasked with building and improving on these online course offerings. For the purposes of our chapter, this team is herein referred to as either the online team, or just SPS.

While keeping the practical needs of instructors and students in mind, the online team has also sought ways to retain the experience and feel of high-quality course offerings that students expect from a highly visible university with a global reputation. It is this tension of considerations that has led the online team to foreground instructor immediacy and student interactivity as the most crucial elements of online courses at SPS.

Therefore, along with providing a multitude of course offerings, central to the School's model is an emphasis on the importance of the instructor to the success of an online course. As some institutions have adopted models which increasingly foreground readings and recorded lectures, SPS has continued to pursue ways to enhance and maintain a strong instructor presence as the core of all online classes.

To this end, SPS has developed a strong synchronous component to online courses, referred to as a *live session*. Live sessions are held weekly, or on another, predetermined schedule, and are conducted in Adobe Connect, a robust web conferencing tool. Within live sessions, students are given the opportunity to interact with their instructors and with each other, through a variety of means, including microphone and video conferencing, instant chat, online polling, and breakout team work. Through a system of training, coaching, and constant feedback, the SPS online team works with instructors to ensure that all of these possibilities for interactivity are utilized during class, providing multiple avenues of interaction for instructors and students.

Figure 1. This chapter is organized like an hourglass, starting with broad ideas about instructor presence in synchronous online class sessions, narrowing to a specific example, and broadening to widely applicable strategies

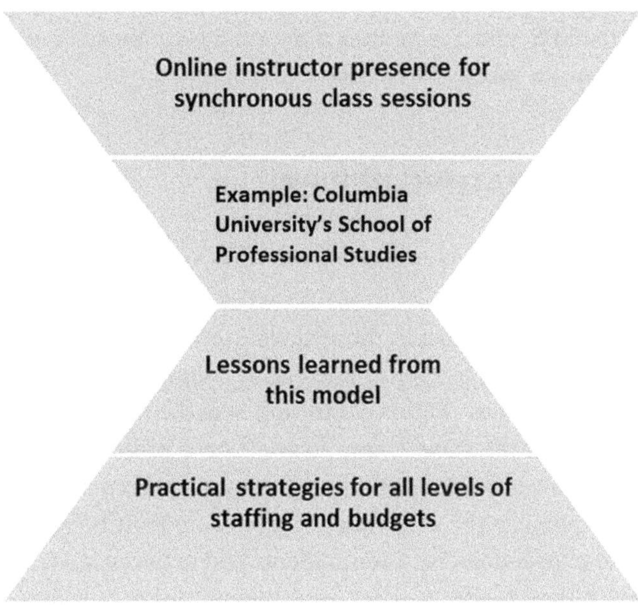

Through extensive work with synchronous class components, the online team has grown to see live class sessions as an essential aspect of enhancing instructor immediacy and fostering class interactivity. The live class session provides an avenue by which the instructor and students can engage in a real-time fashion that generates immediate feedback and reaction, on both sides of the classroom. While we offer some specifics of the School's model here, we also provide alternative solutions and platforms for achieving similar ends. Regardless of program size and affordances, building and executing the right plan for your synchronous class component can be an essential part of a successful and fulfilling online course experience.

In tandem with encouraging instructors to use every available means for interacting with students via Adobe Connect, SPS has provided instructors with a dedicated support person for every live session; the online team believes that this has been critical to the success of synchronous live sessions. Support personnel are responsible for fielding all technical questions that arise during live sessions. This is done in an effort to allow online course instructors to be able to focus entirely on the pedagogical aspects of their course without getting derailed or interrupted by technical issues which students may experience. This is doubly true for the technical assistance which support personnel provide to instructors. Instructors feel secure that they can rely on their dedicated support person to be present for each live session and to be available outside of those sessions for additional troubleshooting and discussion of technical issues. Additionally, live support staff are responsible for submitting once weekly participation reports which contain a mix of qualitative and quantitative feedback designed to relate the key points of the previous live session and highlight issues requiring discussion before the following week's live session.

This mix of technical knowledge and instructor expertise has been an important part of the SPS online course model, but it is by no means the only route to creating a successful instructor presence in an online course. The following is a discussion of the School's attempts to enhance and foreground instructor immediacy in the online environment, towards the end of creating a more engaging, interactive learning system. We will discuss the SPS model, but also recognize the differences and potential constraints working within different environments and institutions, and so will suggest some general best practices, as well as alternative methods for establishing and maintaining a strong instructor presence as the centerpiece of all synchronous online classroom environments. We will also discuss some of the issues which arise within the SPS model, potential workarounds for those issues, and ways of mitigating or heading off some of the issues inherent to online education.

BACKGROUND AND LITERATURE REVIEW

Online Education

The online course space is different from a traditional classroom space. Consider the multiple devices, spaces, and times in which students access online content, as comparatively autonomous students operating on largely uncoordinated schedules. This is contrasted with the physical space of a classroom where a group of students are seated in the same room, focused on a professor. Although online education has in some ways been stigmatized by for-profit companies, and there are inherent limitations, it also invites new ways to reconceptualize the classroom. These include utilizing established and emerging technologies to forge social connections between students and between students and instructors. In this section, we outline some of the broader debates surrounding online education; discuss the literature around webinars, which we generally refer to here as live sessions; and conclude by foregrounding how webinars can facilitate instructor presence in online learning environments.

The term "online course" is defined here as an educational course of study where more than 80% of course activities occur in online or web spaces (Babson Group, 2014). There are many dimensions of the online course which have been cited as beneficial, but some of the most relevant, for the purposes of our discussion, include: the ability to reach different audiences such as nontraditional students, working professionals, and international students; the variability and flexibility of online learning tools; and, finally, the potential reduction of costs, particularly salient due to the increasing tuition of higher education — between 1978 and 2012 the cost of an undergraduate degree increased by 1,120 percent (Jamrisko & Kolet, 2012). The online educational space has many affordances for collapsing distances and creating networks, engendering optimism that it has the potential to create entirely new learning spaces and intellectual and social interactions (Harasim, 1996).

This optimism of online learning — opening access and increasing equity to students; the networking, communication, and adaptive affordances of the online space previously unavailable in the traditional classroom; the more data-driven pedagogy; the more cost-effective credential — is often countered with critiques of online learning. Of the myriad concerns surrounding the advent and increasing popularity of online courses, one of the most oft-discussed counter-arguments is that online courses lack deep engagement and have become automated and factory-like in their degree-awarding models (Feenberg, 2008). In his 1998 essay, "Digital Diploma Mills: The Automation of Higher Education," David Noble argues that emerging online programs of study are impersonal and of low quality, effectively contributing to growing inequities in education. Noble cites a 1959 study of diploma mills, prepared for the American Council on Education, which described the typical diploma mill as having the following traits: "no classrooms," "faculties [who] are often untrained or nonexistent," and "officers [who] are unethical self-seekers whose qualifications are no better than their offerings." Noble argues that these qualifiers are "apt descriptions of the digital diploma mills now in the making."

While it may be true that some platforms of online education are "impersonal" and "of low quality," the School of Professional Studies believes that online courses can be social, personal, and high-quality. At SPS, live sessions are an integral and important aspect of the online course offerings. They provide both a locus of instruction, and a strong sense of instructor presence, effectively operating as a counterpoint to Noble's apprehensions of "no classrooms" and "nonexistent" faculty.

Webinars

Computer-mediated communication (CMC) is integral to online and distance learning. CMC formats are generally divided in two categories: asynchronous (delayed or shifted time) communication and synchronous (real-time) communication (Romiszowski & Mason, 2004; Wang & Hsu, 2008). Asynchronous tools include videos, emails, discussion boards, and other forms of communication that occur in shifted time. These formats support distance learning because of the flexibility offered related to space and time; they allow students more time to read and respond, at their own pace and at times convenient to their schedules (Meyer, 2003). Using a survey methodology, Branon and Essex (2001) found online instructors primarily used asynchronous tools for in-depth and ongoing discussions.

However, asynchronous tools have limitations, especially when considered as a means to replace face-to-face interaction (Wang & Woo, 2007). For instance, asynchronous communication lacks immediate feedback (Gao & Lehman, 2003). In a qualitative study focused on students enrolled in asynchronous online courses, Stodel, Thompson, and MacDonald (2006) found students reported spontaneity, improvisation, and getting to know others as missing from their online courses. Many online courses were previously designed as asynchronous due to technological and/or budget constraints. However, with the increasing prevalence of high-speed Internet, and free or inexpensive real-time communication tools, synchronous tools are increasingly prevalent in online education.

These tools, such as videoconferencing and webinar software, offer different opportunities for instructor-to-student and student-to-student interactions. They allow for multiple participants from multiple sites, and encompass tools such as text chat pods, video conferencing, audio conferencing, slide presentations, and often, other functionality that further enhances the interactive experience. Examples of brand-name webinar software include Adobe Connect, Elluminate, WebEx, and Big Blue Button. Wang and Hsu (2008) list five advantages of synchronous webinars. These are:

1. Affordability;
2. Synchronous communication, such as instant feedback and spontaneity;
3. The ability to facilitate multimedia presentations, especially important while presenting certain types of content;
4. The ability to facilitate multi-level interactions, such as group collaborations; and
5. Recording and archival affordances, so that participants can save and review these sessions.

At SPS, the online team tries to leverage the affordances found within these support platforms, particularly the advantages of synchronous communication, such as discussion and feedback.

Instructor Immediacy

Instructor immediacy requires frequent and purposeful interactions between an instructor and his or her students (Northrup, 2002). In online learning environments, instructor immediacy is tied to discussions, communication, and instructor-student interaction (Blignaut & Trollip, 2003). Being perceived as present or immediate in an online classroom requires "action" and "visibility," in which students are aware that an instructor is attending, participating, listening, and interacting with the class (Picciano, 2002). Instructor immediacy is positioned as a key factor in online course quality and online student experiences; online learners may feel isolated and alienated without instructor-student interactions (Woods & Ebersole, 2003). Jaggars, Edgecome, and Stacey (2013) examined a large data set of online courses at community colleges, and concluded that instructor immediacy and interpersonal interaction were the most important online course quality factors (measured by student performance, retention, and satisfaction). This echoes other research related to how high instructor immediacy leads to increased student satisfaction, motivation, and outcomes (Richardson & Swan, 2003).

Interactive technologies, in particular synchronous webinars, have many affordances for instructor immediacies (such as visual presence, i.e. conveyed via webcams or photos, or synchronous communication, conveyed via interfaces such as chat pods). Live sessions allow for discussion, questions, and spontaneous comments. As Vella (1994) writes, "the dialogue of learning is between two subjects: teacher and student" (p. 13). This dialogue becomes more important in online learning environments. Martin and Parker (2014) found that "Instructors primarily use the virtual classroom to facilitate instructor-student and student-student dialogue." Levin, Whitsett, and Wood (2013) found that many of their online instructors described their relationships with their online students as stronger and "more intimate than those in campus classrooms." Thus, we take the position that instructor presence is a key component of high-quality online courses and that synchronous webinars are a platform that facilitates instructor-student interactions.

Issues, Controversies, Problems

When it comes to online learning, instructor immediacy is paramount to an engaged and fulfilling online learning experience. This is particularly true in the case of synchronous learning. We have come a long way from the early days of distance learning as originally conceived, in which correspondence courses were undertaken via postal service communication, and now live in a reality where video chat and cloud-based web conferencing platforms allow us to connect from myriad devices, from virtually anywhere in the world, with relative ease. With the ubiquity and user-friendliness of video chat platforms such as Google Hangouts and Skype, barriers to delivering a substantive and meaningful online course session are markedly lower. A survey from the Pew Research Center revealed that a majority of respondents believe that by 2020 "there will be mass adoption of teleconferencing and distance learning to leverage expert resources" (Anderson, 2012). Given the proliferation of online course offerings in multitudinous disciplines, there are still surprising ground-floor barriers to synchronous components of online course offerings.

One of the basic impediments to synchronous implementation is that some of the products on the market, in terms of functionality, were not designed with pedagogy in mind. Garcia, Uria, Granda, Suarez, and Gonzales (2007) conducted a review of 20 tools commonly used for synchronous e-learning and found that web conferencing tools such as Acrobat Connect (now called Adobe Connect) and learning tools such as WebEx were designed for different purposes, but were converging in their functionality: "some tools have been specifically designed for synchronous e-learning and others were originally designed for web conferencing, but in their evolution, they have integrated most of the functions included in the tools designed for synchronous e-learning." Web conferencing tools are intended for, and work very well in the case of, video calls and instant meetings with a small group, but the instructional use case for learning tools has entirely different demands. For example, an instructor might meet with a class of students, create a space for collaborative group work, and seamlessly switch between lecture and discussion, to offer just a baseline model of what a synchronous session requires. There are more robust web conference platforms for these activities, however, the cost and complexity often calls for intensive training of the instructor or additional support personnel. Between the user-friendly, but functionally inadequate web conferencing interface, and the comprehensive, but technically involved learning platform, a perfect solution has not yet been developed. To help educational institutions make decisions about which platform to choose, Schullo, Hilbelink, Venable, and Barron (2007) offer their pedagogical evaluation of two web conferencing platforms using the following questions to assess the ability to support instruction:

1. How easy was the system to use? (Usability)
2. How well did the system meet the students' and instructors' needs, technically? (Technical needs for instruction)
3. How did the system help instructors and students meet the educational goals they wanted/needed to accomplish in the live sessions? (Instructional needs)
4. How would the system integrate into an existing infrastructure? (Compatibility)

As the cost for web conferencing solutions comes down and educational technology companies start to provide more directed niche products, specifically tailored to the needs of teaching and learning, the landscape may very well change.

Beyond the issue of choosing the right platform is an even greater concern, that is, one of instructor preparedness. Teaching online is no easy task and teaching in a synchronous modality can often be quite overwhelming to faculty who are new to the environment. Meaningful instructor immediacy rests in the ability of the instructor to convey his or her authenticity and tell his or her story, in spite of technological obstacles. Planning, sound design, training, and support can be powerful remedies to help with the steep learning curve of synchronous teaching and learning.

SOLUTIONS AND RECOMMENDATIONS

The SPS Model

Columbia University's School of Professional Studies has developed a customized model for designing and supporting online and hybrid courses. A majority of courses that take place online undergo a rigorous instructional design process during which faculty work closely with a team of experts to design and build their course in the learning management system (LMS). One member of the Offering Support team — the group who that largely assumes responsibility for the course once it has officially opened to students — is always present during the early stages of the design process to consult on how to most effectively make use of synchronous class time and meet specified learning objectives. The synchronous sessions are only one component of a student's online course experience, but, due to their importance, special consideration is given to their planning and implementation.

After the design phase of a given course has been completed, the course site and attendant materials undergo quality assurance testing to certify that the course is ready for students. At about the same time, the course instructor is trained on the features of the learning management system and the web conferencing platform that they utilize for their respective course. There is additional training for any supplemental educational technologies that are being used for specific assignments or projects in a given course. Prior to the beginning of the term, each course is assigned a dedicated online support specialist who works with their assigned faculty member each week of their course to make sure the live sessions continue to operate at the highest level.

The online team is focused on providing quality technical support in live sessions so that faculty can focus on teaching. While SPS provides training to faculty to ensure that they are comfortable with the technology, it is near impossible to teach a two-hour synchronous session and troubleshoot student issues simultaneously. As a means of offloading technical support work from instructors or facilitating personnel (such as teaching assistants), SPS provides a dedicated online support specialist for every class with synchronous sessions. In this model, instructors benefit from a reduction in disruptions that could potentially derail their lecture while students who are in need of troubleshooting appreciate the direct line of support to help them resolve their issues quickly, so that they can return their attention to class content. It is conceivable that, at some point in the future, educational technologies may be at a place where all users can log in and participate without any technical difficulties; at this moment, we are not there. As McBrien, Jones, and Cheng (2009) write, "we learned from students that technical issues have a strong impact on experiences of 'distance' in online learning....Institutions of higher learning that are implementing cost-reduction measures must not cut resources for web technicians." Levin, Whitsett, and Wood (2013) write that "having a third party mediate [technical] issues proved extremely important to ensuring that student and faculty time would be focused solely on teaching." Therefore, at this juncture, it is critical to have high-quality technical support.

It is important to acknowledge that not all universities or departments have the same staffing, resources, or funding required to sustain this level of support, and so many of the principles we will discuss are flexible enough to apply in different contexts. Even an independent instructor who has a passion for online education can apply these concepts without an Information Technology or administrative team. Next, we will look at how SPS support staff work with instructors on an individual course level.

Planning

Before the course launches, the assigned online support person meets with the instructor and teaching assistants, if applicable, for a virtual kick-off meeting. This meeting takes place in the live session meeting room designated for that respective course and all users log in remotely. At this meeting the instructor shares his or her plans for the synchronous components of the course and asks questions about features that might be useful for completing activities and projects in the synchronous environment. The online support person conducts a diagnostic test with the faculty to make sure that their microphones, webcams, and connectivity are all functioning properly.

Once the course has launched, the online support person schedules a thirty-minute "pre-flight" meeting with the instructor the day before or the day of their first synchronous session to discuss the agenda for the first class. During this meeting, the web conference room is prepared for the live session. This includes building the correct layouts, and assembling the necessary assets and features that are to be used for that week's class. Common live session elements might include a PowerPoint presentation, PDF documents, polling questions, video clips, a chat pod, or breakout rooms to be used for group work. The online support person conducts another technology check with the instructor and troubleshoots any issues that arise then. These pre-flight meetings are held each week a live class session runs to help the instructor prepare and progress (see Figure 2).

Support

Course support takes on many different faces and iterations depending upon a number of factors. These include the teaching style of the instructor, the prior experiences of the online support person, the overall technical knowledge of the students, and the general demands of the course. Cappiccie and Desrosiers (2011), who used Adobe Connect for a social work course, emphasize the necessity of technical support for instructors and students: "It is important to have a contact for technology problems (both during work hours and after work hours)." Ellingson and Notbohm (2012), who used Adobe Connect for a business course, also credit their university's technical support, noting that "as with any technology-dependent venture, technical problems may arrive…[and] troubleshooting can be difficult and time-consuming." There are common recurrent problems, of which anyone running a synchronous session should be aware. These are described below. A summary of recommendations for addressing these issues can be found in Table 1.

Some common issues that might arise for users during a synchronous session include:

Figure 2. SPS's support model for live sessions
Source: Marquart & Fleming, 2014. Used with permission.

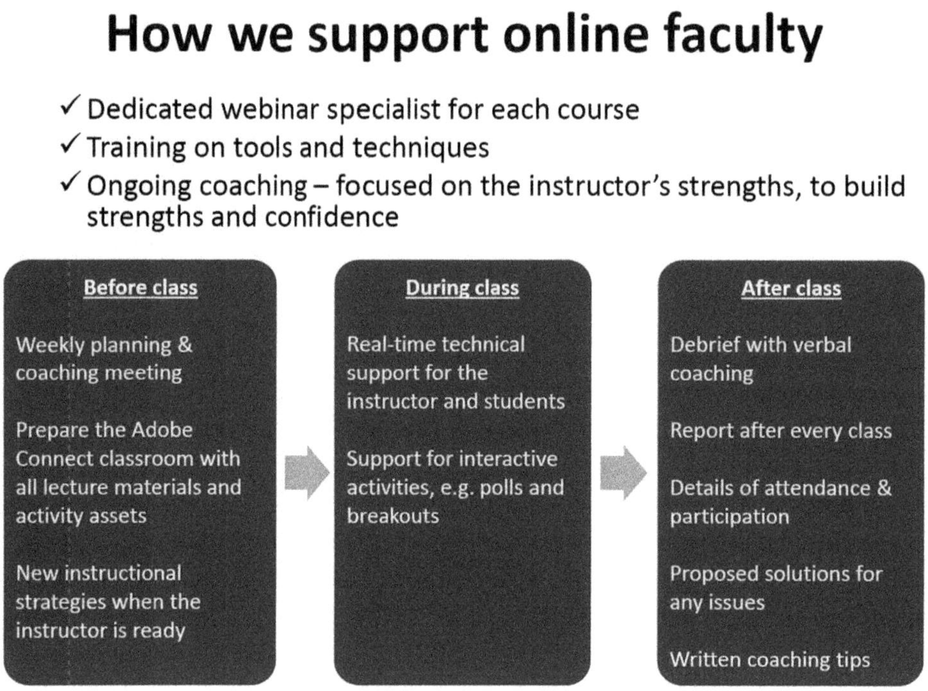

- **Connectivity:** Users will most likely be on different networks, internet connections, and in varying computing environments. Although instructors cannot always control the environment from which users log in, they can encourage users to find a reliable, high-speed Internet connection, preferably Ethernet, or hard-wired, as opposed to Wi-Fi. Failure to secure a reliable connection could result in lag or latency, choppy audio, or in a user dropping out entirely from the web conference platform. Providing a diagnostic URL that includes a speed detection component can help users prepare for the web conference meeting in advance.
- **Audio:** Proper audio configuration for all users is a basic but crucial component to a successful synchronous session. Failure to properly configure audio could result in feedback, inaudible/disruptive volume, or distorted voice. Precautions can be taken by encouraging users to wear recommended headsets with a microphone (to prevent audio feedback and background noise), running an audio configuration diagnostic, double-checking system sound settings on their computer, and muting their microphones when not speaking to reduce disruptions.
- **Visuals:** Ensuring that all users can see the content in a synchronous session can prove more difficult than one might expect. Incompatible or out-of-date web browsers, Adobe Flash Players, or other third-party plug-ins can result in visuals not displaying properly for some users. Users may not be able to properly see the instructor on webcam or might miss important content on PowerPoint slides. Many of these issues can be addressed by having users run a diagnostic URL or double-checking that their computing environment meets the system requirements for your web conference platform.

Table 1. Common challenges to online instruction and recommendations

Challenges	Recommendations
Technology	
The instructor may have technical issues that interrupt class	• Prior to the start of the semester, make sure the instructor's computer and headset are set up properly • Conduct a practice class session with the instructor to identify any needed fixes • Each day of class, restart the instructor's computer and clear browser cache • Stay current on Internet browser updates and updates for needed software • Staff each class session with a support person; if not possible, keep the technical support contact information readily available
Individual students may have technical issues and request help during class	• Require students to set up their technology prior to the start of the course, as part of their course grade for participation • Provide a technology set-up checklist and troubleshooting FAQ • Provide an online test room where students can independently check their technology • Provide a mandatory orientation session to verify that the students' technology is set up and to offer troubleshooting help • Staff each class session with a support person, or provide a chat or phone helpline; if not possible, direct students to the checklist and FAQ rather than stopping instruction, and follow up after class • If students' technology issues prevent them from participating in class, offer a consequence for repeat unresolved issues and possibly a make-up option for reduced participation points
Worst case scenario - the online conferencing platform crashes	• Keep technical support contact information readily available • If class needs to be cancelled and can't be rescheduled, the instructor can record a lecture to send to the students
Instructor Load	
Interactive activities such as polls, videos with debrief discussions, and breakout groups require preparation, which can be time-consuming	Staff the class with a support person or teaching assistant who can do this preparatory setup for the instructor; if not possible, the instructor can use one type of activity until setup has been mastered and takes little time, and then introduce another type of activity
Chat conversations happening during class require constant monitoring	Assign a teaching assistant to monitor the students' chat throughout the class, answer questions, and escalate questions or comments to the instructor as needed; if not possible, assign students to monitor chat on a rotating basis as part of the coursework or on a competitive basis for extra credit
Student attendance and participation require tracking when they impact grades	Staff the class with a support person or teaching assistant who can do this; if not possible, many web conferencing platforms offer time stamped chat tools, which instructors can use to ask students to sign in
Online instructors need to develop online instructional skills over time, and can feel overwhelmed by the many tools and differences from face-to-face classroom instruction	• Provide orientation training to new online faculty, in an online environment so that instructors can get a taste of the student experience • Provide advanced refresher training to returning online faculty • Provide ongoing coaching, peer mentoring, relevant practical literature, classroom observations with feedback
Student Behavior	
Unprofessional behavior, microaggressions, or bullying can happen publicly or behind the scenes	• Establish community agreements or class rules at the start of the semester, reference them periodically, and enforce consequences if broken • Encourage students to speak up if they feel uncomfortable
Students can be tempted by distractions built into their computers or in their environments	• Establish expectations for students to close other computer applications and work in a location with minimal distractions • Plan interactive, whole-class activities periodically throughout class that require students to focus

- **Permissions:** Depending on the level of integration between your LMS and web conference platform you may need to manage certain host permissions to ensure that users have the appropriate access type required for their respective web conference meetings.

- **Software:** Users should ensure that their web browser is current and meets the system requirements and browser compatibility of the web conference platform. Additionally, users may need to download certain plug-ins or extensions to be able to join or host a web conference meeting. It is better to do these things in advance to prevent any delays.
- **Hardware:** Reliable equipment is a must for successful web conferencing. It is recommended that all users have a modern headset with working microphone and webcam, if required for the course. Poor quality equipment will result in poor quality audio and video, and could potentially cause disruptions to the online learning experience.

Assessment Data and Feedback

Once a synchronous session is concluded the online support person creates a live session participation and feedback report to be sent to the instructor and the director of online support and delivery. (A participation report, with identifying information removed, appears below, see figure 3.) This report includes a qualitative summary of what, in the opinion of the online support person, went well and what can be improved, and also includes a description of the technical issues encountered during the session and how these issues were resolved. The participation report also includes quantitative data and analytics downloaded from the backend of the web conference platform. The data compiled generally includes

Figure 3. An example of a participation report, after the SPS model. Student identifying information has been blacked out, but the types of feedback provided are still visible

Live Session Participation Report

Faculty Name: [redacted]

Facilitator: [redacted]

Support: [redacted]

Course Name: [redacted]

Session Week and Date: Week 6 [redacted]

URL of Archive:

What went well?

1. We had another really good class, and very animated discussions. It was great to see students responding really positively to the discussion, and it was clear that this was a topic that was very close to home for most students. As always, it's great that the atmosphere which [redacted] have created makes students feel so confident and disinhibited in discussing work-related issues.
2. I thought the placement of the breakout sessions was really good during this class. It happened a bit earlier in this class and I think students really brought an extra energy to the breakouts. The topic was also a very rich one, and I think that prompting the students to switch in the middle of the breakout time, via broadcast message, was a good way to keep students on task. The debriefs after breakouts were also very rich and covered a wide range of topics, with a lot of student activity in chat as well.
3. Timing was very good again this class. [redacted] was very attentive to the schedule, and did a great job moving class along at a good rate.
4. We had a great discussion about sponsorship after watching the video during class. Students were very animated about the topic. Both of the videos we've seen have had a good impact on class so far, and it might be a good idea to try to use more video media going forward.

What can be improved?

1. I saw a number of students in chat and in the breakouts lamenting that breakouts were only 10 minutes long. I know that extending breakouts would cut into our main room time, but it might be worth considering, especially with topics like these where students seem to have a lot to say.

Technical Issues:

student name, issue, resolution (if unresolved by the end of the session then have student email live@ce.columbia.edu)

Generally speaking, this was a very technically smooth class. There was, however, one very strange moment; when [redacted] came on webcam and began speaking, a number of students, including [redacted] reported that they could not hear her at all. This did not seem to be the case for other students, who were responding to her comments in chat, and was not the case for either myself or [redacted]. This sort of isolated blackout is not too common, and so we should keep an eye on it. None of these students reported issues with being able to see or hear any of the other students who came on webcam or spoke.

****

Attendee List:

Note: [redacted] had previously communicated with [redacted] about a doctor's appointment, which explains the early sign out (bolded below)

[redacted]

6:59 PM → 8:31 PM
6:56 PM → 8:32 PM
6:55 PM → 8:31 PM
6:57 PM → 8:31 PM
6:58 PM → 8:31 PM
7:00 PM → 8:07 PM
6:51 PM → 8:31 PM
7:04 PM → 8:31 PM
6:55 PM → 8:31 PM
7:06 PM → 8:32 PM
6:57 PM → 8:31 PM
6:53 PM → 8:32 PM
6:56 PM → 8:31 PM
6:59 PM → 8:32 PM
6:58 PM → 8:31 PM
6:54 PM → 8:31 PM
6:49 PM → 8:31 PM
6:55 PM → 8:32 PM
6:42 PM → 8:31 PM

Participation Counts from Chat Archive // Main Session (Total Posts)

***Note: this number does not include times students spoke via microphone**

[redacted]

3
12
18
9
18
9
9
12
12

a recording URL, student login/logout times, the chat archive, chat participation counts (indicating the number of times an individual student contributed to the group chat), breakout group notes, poll results, screenshots and anything else that the instructor requests. These report documents, created after each live session, are meant to help our faculty with the learning curve of teaching online. They also provide faculty with a high-level summary of their synchronous sessions which they can use for assessment purposes or as a measure of how the class is progressing over the term.

The ultimate goal of this weekly planning, support, and assessment process is continuous improvement. By providing instructors with real-time support and an opportunity to reflect on their teaching process each week, the aim is to increase the likelihood that instructors will take advantage of interactive features of the web conference platform and engage students in new and innovative ways. In our experience, faculty find this kind of feedback and mentorship, which is particular in character to the online setting, to be very productive.

Promoting Instructor Immediacy Through the Use of Interactive Tools

The technology for web conferencing offers an array of interactive tools that instructors can use to promote immediacy. This array of tools varies depending on which vendor's platform is being used. Table 2, below, provides a reference for uses of these interactive web conferencing tools. As instructors develop their skills with one tool, they can introduce additional tools when they feel ready. Here, we give some descriptions of these various tools, as well as their applications and limitations. We also share comments from experienced online instructors with whom our team has worked; we surveyed them during the fall 2015 semester for the purpose of this chapter. All quotes from instructors are taken from personal communications during November and December 2015. While we have organized this section by tool, our intent is to share the possibilities for interaction that the tool enables, rather than the tool for its own sake. As Palloff and Pratt (2013) write "a well-delivered course provides multiple means by which students and the instructor can interact….it is the interaction and connections made in the course that students will remember as the keys to learning in an online course. Pedagogy, not technology is what is critical to the success of an online course."

Webcam use has a powerful impact on immediacy. Students' ability to see the instructor in real time can help them get to know the instructor and enhance their sense of connection with the instructor. Instructors can foster this by using visuals such as gestures, objects, and facial expressions. Students also enjoy being able to see each other on webcam, as this builds a sense of familiarity and community with their peers. While some instructors may want all of the students on webcam all the time, selective use of student webcam can also have a positive impact, while at the same time conserving Internet bandwidth for a more stable virtual classroom experience. Examples of selective student webcam use include individual students activating their webcams to ask or answer questions, pairs of students coming onto webcam for role-plays or debates, and groups of students using their webcams for panel discussions or group presentations. The use of webcam requires that the instructor and students already own webcams or that they purchase inexpensive webcams. The use of webcam also requires a strong Internet connection.

"I find that the webcam helps students understand lines of reasoning more quickly. Because they can see my facial expressions, they see my encouragement when they are explaining a concept well or my puzzlement if their reasoning seems flawed. Seeing me also seems to enhance their willingness to speak up and ask questions, as it feels more like a seminar," says Barbra Bluestone Rothschild, M.D., who teaches in the Bioethics program at Columbia University's School of Professional Studies. Her online courses use instructor webcam and student mic. "Hearing the intonations in students' voices when they ask questions helps me to more fully understand the inquiry. I find that giving them more time than one might be comfortable with to answer a question that I have posed is essential. Often if I just wait a few seconds longer than seems comfortable, a flood of answers comes through on the mic. This was an adjustment to the medium that I found really helpful."

"Using webcams really builds my connection with the students," says John Robertson, Ph.D., a professor at Columbia University's School of Social Work, who teaches policy courses online. His courses use both instructor and student webcam. "It enriches the teaching, and the connection builds week by week as we share the virtual classroom space using audio, video, and chat. By the end of the semester, I am as connected to my students as I am in a face-to-face classroom setting."

For instructors who need time to adjust to seeing themselves on webcam, or who are concerned about Internet bandwidth, one option is to use webcam only at the start and end of each class session. During class, they can display a headshot photo, so that they still have a visual presence. For courses in which students will use webcams, the instructor must provide advance notice of this expectation, as well as set and reinforce expectations for acceptable on-camera appearance and professionalism. Without guidelines, students may default to wearing pajamas while lying in bed.

"I really enjoy using webcams as a tool for inquiry-centered education," says Amelia Ortega, LMSW, who serves as a Lecturer at Columbia University's School of Social Work. Her courses use both instructor and student webcam. "Incorporating webcams adds depth to the quality of student interaction, as well as helping to create an intentional classroom space to engage new learning processes together. I ask students to use their webcams as a strategy for engaging each other in ways that would not be possible in a campus-based classroom. For example, students can hold paired dialogues in front of their peers – and without the stress of visually seeing their audience, often report feeling more confident in the exchanges. Additionally, using webcams often produces reflections on how students feel they appear, sound, and present themselves. In this way, observing the self through use of webcam during a live session supports critical self-reflection and self-awareness – core components of transformative learning processes."

If student webcams are not an option, inviting students to speak on microphone can also have a powerful impact on immediacy. Hearing each other's voices can create more of a sense of community among students than solely interacting via typed text. Microphone use also enables activities such as role-plays and debates. For a clear audio experience, students should use headsets with microphones and mute their mics when not speaking, to block out background noise.

"While synchronicity is key to enhancing the learning in the online environment, there may not always be an ideal setting for using webcams," says José Pascal da Rocha, J.D., Ph.D., a faculty member and Lecturer with the M.S. program on Negotiation and Conflict Resolution at Columbia University's School of Professional Studies. "The use of audio not only creates a sense of community but can also comfort any students who are in a rather new learning structure. Tonality of voice, modulation of language and, at times, the use of laughter, humor (in appropriate dosage), and speech rhythm are key ingredients for the purposeful delivery of key instructional messages. It encourages synchronous interaction and participation. For audio to work, the setting has to be conducive to learning, with appropriate audio headsets, the previous checking of microphone connectivity and sound, and a calm environment that allows the student to focus solely on listening and interacting, as well as gaining more confidence in the use of online learning environments. Careful preparation is key: match the interaction strategies to the class size, use student names when responding, refer back to the student's words when answering a question to pinpoint your response, establish a crowd-control system (such as raising hands or typing in the chat

Table 2. Uses of interactive tools to promote instructor immediacy

Interactive Tools to Promote Instructor Immediacy	Implementation and Considerations	Modifications for a Variety of Circumstances
Instructor webcam throughout class	• Enables use of visuals and nonverbal communication • Helps students get to know instructor • Requires strong Internet connections • Inexpensive webcams are ok	• Use webcam only at the start and end of the live class session • Display a headshot when not on webcam • Pause the webcam as needed
Student webcam, individually or in groups	• Helps instructor get to know students, builds community • Individual students can ask or respond to questions • Groups of students can role play, present, debate • Requires advance notice to students, and clear expectations	• For large classes, invite students onto webcam only when they speak • For small classes, possible to invite all students onto webcam throughout class
Student microphone	• Conveys student personality • Enables activities such as role plays and debates • To prevent background noise, require that students mute microphones when not speaking • To prevent audio distortion, use headset with microphone	For large classes, withhold whole-class student mic access and enable mics individually
Typed instant chat for two-way interaction and whole-class participation	• Enables whole-class participation, throughout class • Questions for students to answer in chat can lead to inviting particular students onto webcam/mic to elaborate • Potential questions include icebreakers, check-ins, opinions, related experiences, activating prior knowledge • Set expectations for etiquette and encourage use of chat	• Assign a teaching assistant to curate the chat, including escalating questions to the instructor or tracking questions to be answered later • If no teaching assistant, assign students • If class size makes it difficult to keep track of a fast-moving chat, create a second chat area designated for serious questions
Instant polling for whole-class participation	• Learn about students and build community through ice breakers • Assess comprehension, assess learning, gauge opinions to spark discussion, reinforce key points • Differs from instant chat because anonymous and offers whole-class statistics • Gather student feedback on the course	• If no built-in polling tool, can poll by asking questions and using the chat or status icons to gather student responses • Numerous free external polling tools can provide live results, which can be shared verbally or via screenshare
Status icons for whole-class participation	• Students can raise hands with questions • Instructors can ask students to use icons for quick polling	If no status icon functionality, ask students to use chat for these uses
Live on-screen note-taking	• Compile student ideas from brainstorm, discussion, debate • Reinforce key points while lecturing	If no note-taking functionality, share a link to a web-based shared document
Live annotations or drawings	• Highlight key points, focus attention, illustrate answers to questions • Allow students to use drawing tools	If no drawing tool functionality, draw on paper and hold it up to the webcam
Screen share	• Demonstrate specific software • Walk through websites	If no screen share functionality, share the website link with students and clearly narrate a walkthrough
Breakout groups for small group activities	• Enable small group discussions, role plays, collaborative work, interviews, teach-backs • Assign groups different questions for report-backs • Requires strong Internet connection and headset microphones for quality audio	If no breakout functionality, end class early for groups to meet independently via free web conferencing platform, and report back at the start of the next class session
Slides with student work	Incorporate exemplars from public student work into lesson slides, giving students credit by name, e.g. excerpts from discussion forums or blogs	If the instructor doesn't have time or a teaching assistant, assign different students each week to compile exemplar student work to share

pod to indicate you have a question), have a backup plan in case of technical issues, and always use a technical assistant to troubleshoot audio or visual problems."

Typed instant chat is a common feature among web conferencing platforms, and can be used for many purposes. Common uses include requesting that students use the chat area to ask questions, chat socially, or indicate whether they can hear the instructor or support person's audio. The instant chat tool can also enable class-wide participation, rather than participation only by the most engaged students. Instructors can ask questions for all students to answer in chat, and then invite particular students onto webcam or microphone to elaborate. These questions work better when there is more than one correct answer; otherwise, slower typists will have no reason to participate if someone has already answered correctly. Sample questions include icebreakers before the class start time, check-ins to gauge the level of student comfort with the course material, questions about students' opinions or related experiences, and questions that activate prior knowledge. Vu and Fadde (2013) analyzed the on-task questions and comments made via chat and microphone during a course held in Adobe Connect and found that students "made almost twice as many interactions in text (67%) than verbally (33%)." They suggest that chat is a valuable pedagogical tool in synchronous online classes and add that "both the instructor and students interviewed after the course agreed that many of the comments and questions made in the chat box would simply not have been made during typical classroom lecture."

For successful use of typed instant chat, instructors should set expectations or community agreements for respectful conversations, as well as encourage students to use the chat area. Otherwise, some students may consider it disrespectful to chat while the instructor is speaking, and therefore, will be wary of asking questions. In addition, when the web conferencing platform allows, it may be useful to create different chat areas, clearly labeled for different purposes; for example, a general chat area and a specific one used solely to interact with the teaching assistant. If there is no teaching assistant to help monitor the chat area, a particular student (the same one, or different students, newly assigned each week) can be tasked with curating the chat conversation.

"Chat is one of the richest parts of being in a virtual class together, in real time," says Katrina Pugh, M.B.A, the Academic Director of the Information and Knowledge Strategy program at Columbia University's School of Professional Studies, who also teaches in the program. "Before class begins, dozens of hellos, ball scores, and weather reports from students' homes around the world have already flowed up the chat. But that's just the start: when class begins, students start commenting on the lecture ('@Kate: I agree!'), sharing information ('This article from HBR is related to that topic'), and asking questions ('How do you deal with a situation where…?'). As the instructor during class, I appreciate every single syllable of the students' contributions. The chat turns the class sessions into a dialogue, which influences my lecture and the evolution of my own ideas about the material. You see the students' curiosity, generosity, risk-taking, and community."

"The chat is a very useful feature of online education," says Mashura Akilova, Ph.D., a Lecturer at Columbia University's School of Social Work who has taught several subjects online. "It gives all students an equal chance to participate. It is especially important for the involvement of usually shy and non-participating students. This group often involves international students, who may not feel comfortable speaking in class. Furthermore, the use of chat allows a separate space for discussion and integration of the material without interfering with the class agenda and taking time away from planned activities (see Figure 4). Most importantly, the use of chat creates a sense of community, where students can comment, agree, add, or empathize with information being shared in class by the instructor or the students, in a manner that would be impossible in a traditional class setting. After my first online course, I caught

Figure 4. An example of the chat pod functionality in Adobe® Connect™
Note that the instructor, TAs, and support all appear on webcams at the top of the screen, while the public chat is visible beneath. Screenshot of Adobe® Connect™ interface produced by the authors and reprinted with permission from Adobe Systems Incorporated.

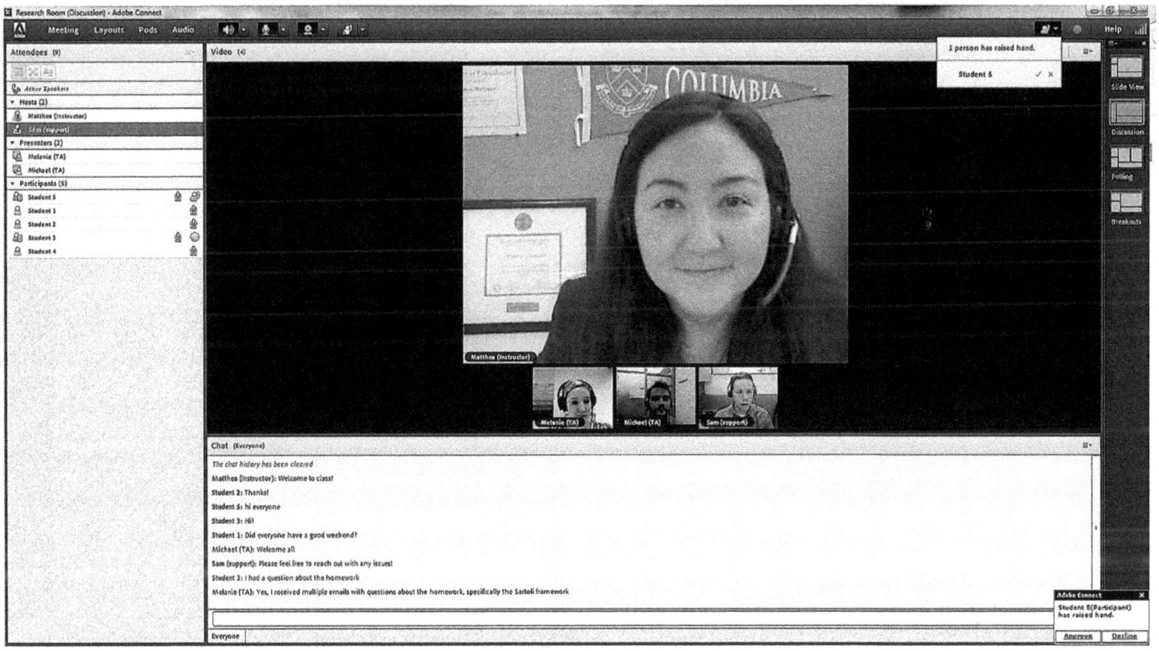

myself thinking that even though I hadn't physically met any of my online students, by the end of the semester, I knew more about them than the students in my residential courses. I think having the opportunity to communicate through chat was one of the contributing factors. Chat is a more comfortable and less scary way for students with different backgrounds to talk about many topics, and especially about sensitive issues."

Another common feature among web conferencing platforms that enables class-wide participation is instant polling. With polling, instructors can quickly learn about students, by using community-building questions such as "where are you from?" or "what personal goals do you have for this course?" Polling tools often offer multiple choice, multiple answer, and short answer options that can be used according to the instructor's goals. Instructors can gauge student opinions on discussion topics, assess comprehension of key concepts, reinforce key points by asking cumulative questions, and assess student learning by asking students to share their key lesson takeaways or summaries of key instructional points. Instructors can also ask for feedback on the course, as students may feel more comfortable responding via an anonymous poll, rather than sharing feedback openly.

"To engage and connect with students, the optimum is to have the students be active themselves," says Basil Rabinowitz, a Lecturer in Discipline in the M.S. in Actuarial Science program at Columbia University's School of Professional Studies. "A great tool for this is polling. An effective poll engages the students, makes students active participants (and keeps them alert), and makes students feel like their opinions count (see figure 5). Polls can also gather helpful anonymous feedback and allow students to gauge their opinions versus those of their peers, which can provide a reality check. Some of the best

Figure 5. This screenshot showcases two types of possible polls; multiple choice and short answer
Screenshot of Adobe® Connect™ interface produced by the authors and reprinted with permission from Adobe Systems Incorporated.

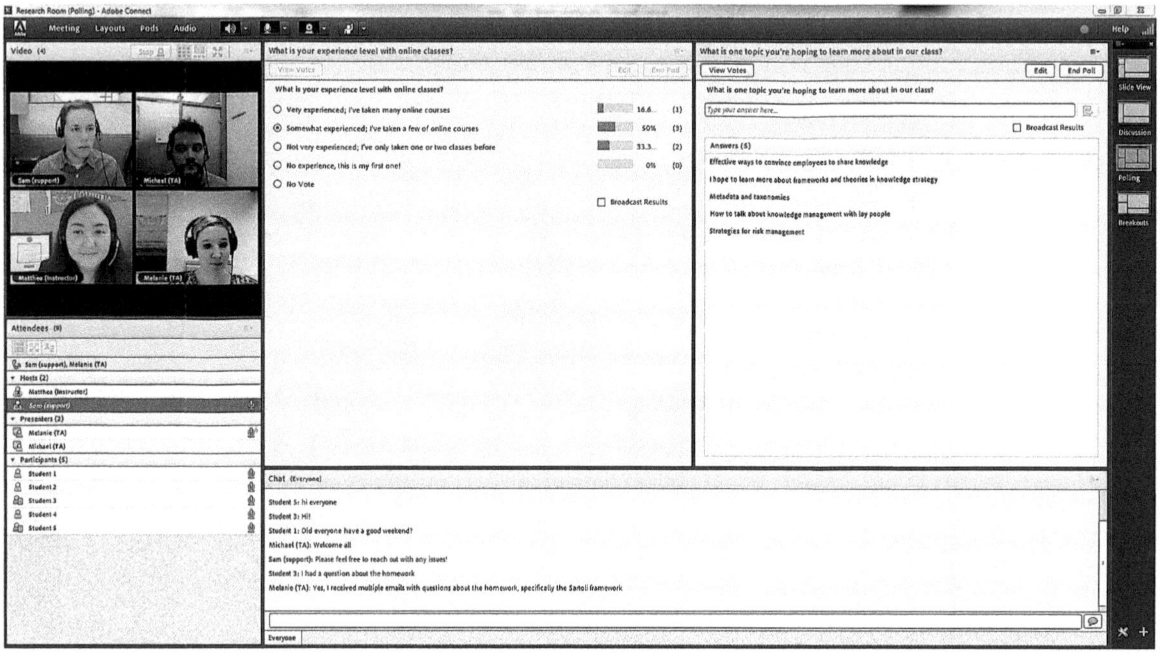

changes that I have made to my course methodology and content have been as a result of feedback from well-structured polls. Best of all, they take seconds to set up and can be multiple choice or open response."

Depending on the web conferencing tool, classes may be able to use status icons such as hand-raising icons, emoticons, and graphics indicating agreement or disagreement. These icons offer another way to encourage class-wide participation. Instructors can quickly gauge whether students feel comfortable with the course material by asking for a particular status icon, such as a green check, if students are ready to move on, or a contrasting status icon, such as a red X, if students have any questions. Then, instructors can follow up and ask students to share their questions on webcam, microphone or via instant chat. Status icons also allow for quick polling on student opinions or course management questions such as whether students need an extension on an assignment.

"I'm a huge fan of official polls as well as the 'informal' polls with hand raising, emoticons, etc. They're easy check-ins to ensure I'm audible or to inquire if students have personally experienced what I am discussing in the moment," says Lauri Harrison, Marketing Adjunct at Columbia University's School of Professional Studies, who teaches Introduction to Marketing/Marketing Management online. "Although I appreciate formal polls for their quantitative aspect, I also favor informal polls for qualitative, in the moment, pulse checks."

Web conferencing tools often offer a whiteboard or note pod tool for live typing, which is visible to the whole class. These can be used to engage with students by compiling student ideas during a brainstorm, discussion, or debate, much as an instructor might do on a flipchart or chalkboard during a face-to-face class. Instructors can also use these to reinforce key points while lecturing.

"I highly encourage online instructors to use the whiteboard or the note pod tool when conducting a live course," says Rebecca Shaffer, CPA, who teaches Financial Accounting at Columbia University's School of Professional Studies. "The switch from lecturing off of a prepared slide to creating an example via a live note pod creates a sense of immediacy in the student. The student turns the focus from 'following along' to engaging in the specific example or explanation being generated. I find it to be an effective tool in teaching a synchronous online course."

Other common tools include drawing or annotating tools, screen share functionality, and breakout groups. Drawing or annotating tools can be used to highlight key points on slides, focus students' attention, or illustrate answers to questions when visuals are helpful for student comprehension. Examples include writing out a formula, drawing a graph, or drawing an illustration. Screen share functionality, in which students see activity on the instructor's computer in real time, can allow instructors to demonstrate specific software or walk through relevant websites.

"For rigorous quantitative courses, which demand a strong connection between theoretical frameworks and their practical applications, the ability to annotate lecture notes in real time can enrich the learning experience in several ways," says Mario A. González-Corzo, Ph.D., a Lecturer in Discipline in the Business Certificate program at Columbia University's School of Professional Studies. "The use of drawing tools or similar functionality, for example, allows online faculty to add an unexpected level of spontaneity and a human touch to their lectures or presentations. I have also found on several occasions that by writing additional examples, and even solving equations and Finance-related word problems on the spot, student engagement and participation tends to increase. Similarly, drawing graphs, illustrations, and diagrams has enabled me, in multiple instances, to reinforce many of the concepts discussed in class and illustrate their practical applications."

Breakout groups allow instructors to divide the class into small groups, so that students can work collaboratively on group projects, have discussions, practice skills via role-plays, interview each other, prepare teach-backs, or do other group activities. During the breakout group activities, instructors should circulate between groups to observe students and provide guidance as needed, as this offers an opportunity for instructors to interact with small groups of students. The increased Internet bandwidth used by breakout groups requires that students have a strong Internet connection. In our experience, students generally want to debrief after group work; this can become monotonous if each group has been doing the same assignment, since they will likely report back the same ideas. Therefore, debriefs can be more interesting wherein each group reports back on only one of a list of questions, or when each group has a different assignment. Bower (2007) analyzed 48 hours of recordings of class sessions held in Adobe Connect with a focus on the course's breakout group activities, concluding that the technical skills of both the instructor and the students were key to effective activities, as the analysis found instances "where an incomplete knowledge of system tools impacted on the quality of the group work activity" and therefore "an incremental approach to difficulty (both technically and collaboratively) is recommended to avoid ineffective activities." Technical coaching and support for both instructors and students can help make breakout activities successful.

"When designing my Marketing Strategy course with our online course development team, I wanted to include student interaction during the live sessions as I would in my face to face courses," says Karl Rutter, MBA, the Associate Dean of Non-Degree and International Programs at Columbia University's School of Professional Studies, who also teaches as an adjunct Lecturer. "Breakout rooms have become my favorite tool because they increase student engagement and team building, contribute to a sense of intimacy within the course, and allow me to monitor student discussion and help guide students towards the goal when necessary. For my breakout activities, prior to class I have students prepare a case study using guided questions, and then during class students work in teams on a given assignment such as constructing a Porter's Five Forces analysis. When we regroup, I call on one team to present their findings. This gives other students the opportunity to comment, and allows for some peer-to-peer exchange as well (see figure 6). The entire experience helps make the online course more engaging and dynamic."

A final, simple interactive tool can be created by incorporating student work into class slides. Most web conferencing tools allow for the sharing of class slides, and instructors can include examples from student coursework in these slides. This works well with student work that has been submitted publicly, such as discussion forum posts; for privately submitted work, instructors should consider asking the student for permission to share.

"I was pleasantly surprised to see that students tend to be quite open and honest when sharing their thoughts, ideas, question and comments about course material in online class discussion forums," says Mary Ann Drury, LCSW, a Lecturer at Columbia University's School of Social Work. "Subsequently sharing excerpts of their work -- original ideas, new insights or thought-provoking questions -- in class provides a natural opportunity to spark lively, interesting, and engaging class discussions."

Developing online instructional skills happens over time. One way to support instructors in developing these skills is by offering feedback from classroom observations. Table 3 offers a checklist of observable instructional behaviors that promote instructor immediacy, which can be useful for conducting classroom

Figure 6. An example of a breakout room in Adobe® Connect™. We can see the class is divided into two different breakout rooms (left side of the screen), and that a student note pod, as well as instructional slide is provided.(Note: student names shown here are created for the purposes of this figure; they do not correspond to actual Columbia University students.)

Screenshot of Adobe® Connect™ interface produced by the authors and reprinted with permission from Adobe Systems Incorporated.

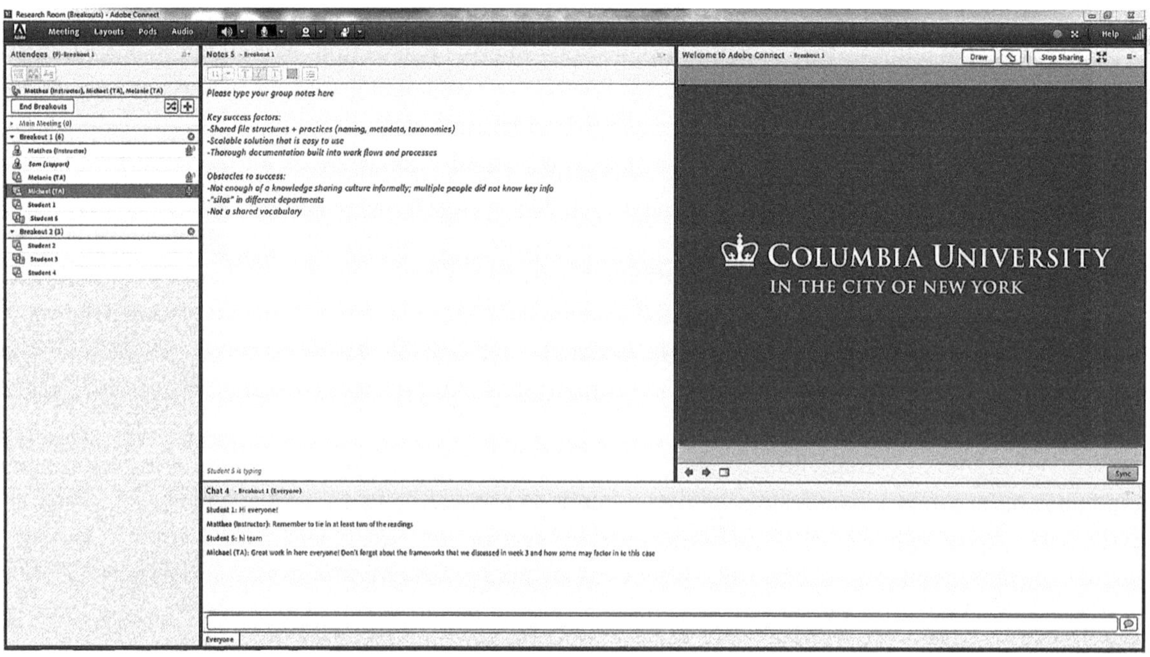

observations, either during a live class session or by viewing a recording. The checklist focuses on three categories of instructional behaviors in online learning environments that are related to instructor immediacy and presence, identified in the literature review: instructor visibility, instructor-student interaction, and interpersonal connection. If the school does not have staff who serve as classroom observers, instructors can partner with fellow instructors to observe each other's classes and debrief using this checklist, or a modified version. The checklist can also be used by independent instructors for self-reflection after a class session or to conduct an observation of their own class by reviewing a recording.

"My experiences in delivering synchronous courses online have profoundly improved my teaching, but my progress has not come easily or quickly," says Steven P. Schinke, Ph.D., the D'Elbert and Selma Keenan Professor of Social Work at Columbia University. He was the winner of the Online Learning Consortium's 2015 Excellence in Online Teaching Award, which honored him "for success in offering a difficult subject online, both with synchronous and asynchronous methods, [and] continuous improvement, while achieving extremely high retention and pass rates with a variable small to large-scale student enrollments" (Online Learning Consortium, 2015). "After teaching in the physical classroom for over 40 years, I thought that I possessed the necessary sensitivities, methods, and tactics to efficaciously transfer new knowledge to my students. However, for my online courses, I needed to learn anew how to engage students, how to communicate effectively, and how to share my course content in ways that students could grasp, master, and apply. Developing high-impact online instructional skills has taken time, and the time investment has not been mine alone. Rather, I have profited immeasurably from a similar investment by outstanding support professionals who have critiqued my online performance, identified areas for me to improve, and passed along ideas gleaned from other online offerings. From what I have learned, I recommend that new online instructors seek out and embrace guidance from experienced online teachers and professionals."

Table 3. Checklist for self-assessment of instructional behaviors promoting instructor immediacy in synchronous class sessions

	Instructional behaviors promoting instructor immediacy
Instructor visibility	• Was the instructor visible on webcam throughout the class session? • If not on webcam, was there an instructor photo? • Was the instructor clearly audible? • If there was a breakout group activity, did the instructor visit each room?

Instructor-student interaction	• Did the instructor arrive early to interact informally with students?
	• Did the instructor create opportunities for instructor-student interaction, using available technology?
	  • Student webcam
	  • Student microphone
	  • Typed instant chat
	  • Instant polling
	  • Status icons
	  • Live on-screen note-taking
	  • Live annotations or drawings
	  • Screen share
	  • Breakout groups and debriefs
	  • Slides with student work
	• Did the instructor acknowledge and respond to students' questions and comments?
	• Did the instructor stay after class to answer student questions, or offer an alternative way to meet?

Interpersonal connection	• Did the instructor use students' names? • Did the instructor share relevant professional experiences to illustrate course concepts? • Did the instructor demonstrate personal passion for the material?

Professor Schinke's comment is supported by Baran, Correia, and Thompson (2013), who found that "programs that prepare faculty to teach online may need to encourage teachers to reflect on their past experiences, assumptions, and beliefs toward learning and teaching and transform their perspectives by engaging in pedagogical inquiry and problem solving." Bower (2011) focused on preparing faculty to teach online by developing their technical skills, as his study of three semesters of a course held in Adobe Connect found that "failure to understand one subtle feature of a tool or its use can have a crippling impact on the learning episode" and noted that "teaching effectively in web conferencing environments is not as simple as directly transferring face-to-face approaches....Given the inherent complexity of teaching using web conferencing systems it would appear that substantial professional development is appropriate." Bower's study identified four different levels of technical competencies, which build on each other:

(1) Operational – the ability to operate the tools and functions of the collaborative technology
(2) Interactional – the ability to effectively interact to perform a task or solve a problem using the technology...
(3) Managerial – the ability to manage a group or class including providing support on how to use the technology and interact effectively
(4) Design – the ability to select and organize tools in a way that optimises interaction and best supports activity management...

These levels of synchronous collaborational competencies were observed to be hierarchical in nature, with technical competencies required for effective interaction, interactional competencies required for management, and management competencies required in order to be able to effectively design....the lower levels of collaborative competencies are more easily mastered than the higher levels.

The SPS support model enables online instructors to begin teaching before they develop expertise in all four levels of technical competencies, as their support specialist can operate the tools for them, guide them on interaction, help manage the group, provide technical support to students, and advise on lesson design. This gives instructors time to develop their skills and frees the School to hire industry leaders and subject matter experts as instructors, regardless of their technical abilities. Institutions that provide less hands-on support may need to place a greater emphasis on technical skills when hiring instructors and then invest in training to develop technical expertise, due to the impact of a lack of such skills. Bower (2011) noted that "deficiencies in synchronous collaboration competencies at best resulted in less efficient collaboration and learning, and at worst could lead to a total communication breakdown." If significant training is not possible, one solution may be to contract teaching assistants who have enough technical expertise to be able to support the instructor and students.

Echoing our introduction to this discussion of tools, Palloff and Pratt (2013) caution that training should not focus on technology itself, but rather what it enables: "training and faculty development should focus on increasing interactivity in online classes, building a learning community among the learners, delivering course content in new and creative ways, incorporating collaboration into the learning process, empowering learners, and evaluating learners and learning outcomes in ways that make sense in the online arena."

FUTURE RESEARCH DIRECTIONS

There are many burgeoning areas of research in the realm of online learning, particularly those related to synchronous webinars. There is an increasing urgency to complete more research in these areas as online and web-based education continues to grow in all arenas (K-12, higher education, corporate training, just-in-time learning modules). Some areas that may prove fruitful include the issue of scale, and how webinar tools can most effectively be leveraged for both small and large groups. Another topic is related to microaggressions in virtual environments, ways in which communication may differ in online environments (rather than face-to-face environments), and how to design for desired behaviors. The affordances of various tools such as webcams also may prove productive for exploration, especially as Internet and video become increasingly high-speed and high-quality.

Regardless of the form this research takes, or of which fronts of investigation prove most fruitful, it is clear that online learning will come to occupy an increasingly central place in all spheres of education.

CONCLUSION

This chapter has attempted to provide some insight into the philosophy and processes of one institution's synchronous online course components. As we have noted throughout, there is no one, correct solution that is broadly applicable, and indeed, many readers may think of this chapter as a point of departure or foundation upon which they can build their own robust synchronous course components, tailored specifically to the needs and strictures of their own institutions or programs. We have highlighted some of the key affordances provided by web conferencing software, discussed the capacities and limitations of conducting an online synchronous session, and identified some of the most frequently encountered issues, while proposing solutions for each. It is our hope that readers can return often to this chapter as they build, or continue expanding, the synchronous program best suited to their institution, faculty, and above all, students.

REFERENCES

Anderson, J., Boyles, J. L., & Rainie, L. (2012). The future impact of the Internet on higher education. *Pew Research Center*. Retrieved from http://www.pewinternet.org/2012/07/27/the-future-of-higher-education/

Babson Survey Research Group. (2014). *Grade change: Tracking online education in the United States* [White paper]. Retrieved from http://www.onlinelearningsurvey.com/reports/gradechange.pdf

Baran, E., Correia, A. P., & Thompson, A. (2013). Tracing successful online teaching in higher education: Voices of exemplary online teachers. *Teachers College Record*, *115*(3), 1–41.

Blignaut, A. S., & Trollip, S. R. (2003). Measuring faculty participation in asynchronous discussion forums. *Journal of Education for Business*, *78*(6), 347–353. doi:10.1080/08832320309598625

Bower, M. (2007, March). Groupwork activities in synchronous online classroom spaces. In *ACM. SIGCSE Bulletin*, *39*(1), 91–95. doi:10.1145/1227504.1227345

Bower, M. (2011). Synchronous collaboration competencies in web-conferencing environments–their impact on the learning process. *Distance Education*, *32*(1), 63–83. doi:10.1080/01587919.2011.565502

Branon, R. F., & Essex, C. (2001). Synchronous and asynchronous communication tools in distance education: A survey of instructors. *TechTrends*, *45*(1), 36–42. doi:10.1007/BF02763377

Cappiccie, A., & Desrosiers, P. (2011). Lessons learned from using Adobe Connect in the social work classroom. *Journal of Technology in Human Services*, *29*(4), 296–302. doi:10.1080/15228835.2011.638239

Ellingson, D. A., & Notbohm, M. (2012). Synchronous distance education: Using web-conferencing in an MBA accounting course. *American Journal of Business Education*, *5*(5), 555–562.

Feenberg, A. (2008). Comments. *Social Epistemology*, *22*(1), 119–124. doi:10.1080/02691720701773585

Gao, T., & Lehman, J. D. (2003). The effects of different levels of interaction on the achievement and motivational perceptions of college students in a web-based learning environment. *Journal of Interactive Learning Research*, *14*(4), 367–386.

Garcia, D. F., Uria, C., Granda, J. C., Suárez, F. J., & Gonzalez, F. (2007, October). A functional evaluation of the commercial platforms and tools for synchronous distance e-learning. *Proceedings of the 3rd WSEAS/IASME International Conference on Educational Technologies*.

Harasim, L. (1996). Computer networking for education. In Decorte & Wienert (Eds.), The International Encyclopedia of Developmental and Instructional Psychology. Pergamon Press.

Jaggars, S. S., Edgecombe, N., & Stacey, G. W. (2013). *What we know about online course outcomes*. New York, NY: Columbia University, Teachers College, Community College Research Center.

Jamrisko, M., & Kolat, I. (2012). Cost of college degree in U.S. soars 12 fold: Chart of the day. *Bloomberg News*. Retrieved from http://www.bloomberg.com/news/2012-08-15/cost-of-college-degree-in-u-s-soars-12-fold-chart-of-the-day.html

Levin, S., Whitsett, D., & Wood, G. (2013). Teaching MSW social work practice in a blended online learning environment. *Journal of Teaching in Social Work*, *33*(4-5), 408–420. doi:10.1080/08841233.2013.829168

Marquart, M., & Fleming, M. (2014, October). *Supporting Successful Live Online Classes: Good Instructional Design is Not Enough*. Workshop presented at the Online Learning Consortium International Conference, Orlando, FL.

Martin, F., & Parker, M. A. (2014). Use of synchronous virtual classrooms: Why, who, and how? *Journal of Online Learning & Teaching*, *10*(2).

McBrien, J. L., Cheng, R., & Jones, P. (2009). Virtual spaces: Employing a synchronous online classroom to facilitate student engagement in online learning. *The International Review of Research in Open and Distributed Learning*, *10*(3).

Meyer, K. A. (2003). Face-to-face versus threaded discussions: The role of time and higher-order thinking. *Journal of Asynchronous Learning Networks*, *7*(3), 55–65.

Noble, D. (1998). Digital diploma mills: The automation of higher education. *First Monday*, *3*(1). doi:10.5210/fm.v3i1.569

Northrup, P. T. (2002). Online learners' preferences for interaction. *The Quarterly Review of Distance Education*, *3*(2), 219–226.

Online Learning Consortium. (2015, September 29). *The Online Learning Consortium Announces Recipients of the 2015 OLC Awards and Effective Practice Awards*. [Press release]. Retrieved from http://onlinelearningconsortium.org/news_item/online-learning-consortium-announces-recipients-2015-olc-awards-effective-practice-awards/

Palloff, R. M., & Pratt, K. (2013). *Lessons from the virtual classroom: The realities of online teaching*. Somerset, NJ: John Wiley & Sons.

Picciano, A. G. (2002). Beyond student perceptions: Issues of interaction, presence, and performance in an online course. *Journal of Asynchronous Learning Networks*, *6*(1), 21–40.

Richardson, J. C., & Swan, K. (2003). Examining social presence in online courses in relation to students' perceived learning and satisfaction. *Journal of Asynchronous Learning Networks*.

Romiszowski, A., & Mason, R. (2004). Computer-mediated communication. In D. H. Jonassen (Ed.), Handbook of Research for Educational Communications and Technology (pp. 397–431). Lawrence Erlbaum.

Schullo, S., Hilbelink, A., Venable, M., & Barron, A. E. (2007). Selecting a Virtual Classroom System: Elluminate Live vs. Macromedia Breeze (Adobe Acrobat Connect Professional). *Journal of Online Learning and Teaching, 3*(4), 331-345.

Stodel, E. J., Thompson, T. L., & MacDonald, C. J. (2006). Learners' perspectives on what is missing from online learning: Interpretations through the community of inquiry framework. *International Review of Research in Open and Distance Learning*, *7*(3).

Vella, J. (1994). *Learning to listen learning to teach: The power of dialogue in educating adults*. San Francisco: JosseyBass.

Vu, P., & Fadde, P. J. (2013). When to talk, when to chat: Student interactions in live virtual classrooms. *Journal of Interactive Online Learning*, *12*(2), 41–52.

Wang, Q., & Woo, H. L. (2007). Comparing asynchronous online discussions and face-to-face discussions in a classroom setting. *British Journal of Educational Technology*, *38*(2), 272–286. doi:10.1111/j.1467-8535.2006.00621.x

Wang, S. K., & Hsu, H. Y. (2008). Use of the webinar tool (Elluminate) to support training: The effects of webinar-learning implementation from student-trainers' perspective. *Journal of Interactive Online Learning*, *7*(3), 175–194.

Woods, R., & Ebersole, S. (2003). Becoming a "Communal Architect" in the Online Classroom-Integrating Cognitive and Affective Learning for Maximum Effect in Web-Based Learning. *Online Journal of Distance Learning Administration*, *6*(1).

Chapter 11
Understanding Strategies of Teacher–Student Interaction:
The Impact on Student Experience and Learning Outcomes in Online Education

Tarryn L. Kille
Griffith University, Australia

ABSTRACT

In this chapter, we discuss the application of teaching strategies as a vehicle for investigating teacher immediacy in the online environment. Through the presentation of a descriptive case study, the chapter explores the theoretical perspective of strategies that intend to reduce psychological distance in the online environment. Specifically, the issue of effective interaction is investigated, including: (1) the application of formative feedback practices; (2) the application of student self-assessment to encourage deeper learning; and (3) the integration of rubric use in assessment activities. The chapter concludes, recommending that practical application of teaching strategies such as: (1) using rubrics; and (2) encouraging student self-assessment, has the effect of enhancing teacher interaction and improving both the student experience and the student learning outcomes in an online environment. The chapter aims to contribute to the literature associated with online university education by validating best practices which assists in developing more effective online courses.

INTRODUCTION

The proliferation of Internet based technologies has had a profound effect on a number of aspects of society, including university education, where the demand for online learning has grown exponentially (Baker, 2010). The growth in online university education offers a fertile ground for empirical based research on how and in what form this relatively firmly established (yet still advancing) medium could be used to improve the student learning experience.

There has been a profusion of studies that offer "no significant difference" regarding the effectiveness of face-to-face compared to online learning (for example, Hiltz, Zhang, & Tuross, 2002; Johnson, Aragon,

DOI: 10.4018/978-1-4666-9995-3.ch011

Shaik, & Palma-Rivas, 2000; McLaren, 2004). As such, researchers are extending inquiry beyond the question of whether online educational delivery is as effective as the traditional forms of learning and are now exploring the area of identifying which strategies of instruction are most effective for the online delivery of a course. Swan (2003) asserts that the main epistemological issue with the "no significant difference" finding is that it disguises the real differences in the online medium that might specifically encourage particular ways of understanding or learning. Thus, researchers need to be less perturbed with the comparison of the value of offering online courses and more intent on understanding specific learner characteristics, models of learning, and the restructuring of curriculum. With that in mind, Grandzol and Grandzol (2006) argued that the extension of the research field beyond "no significant difference" with studies focused on empirically validating best practices are the most useful and influential as they can offer clear guidance for structuring and developing more effective online courses. This transition in research focus towards effective learning in online instruction is the impetus for this study, which sought to explore three specific strategies applied to the online educational environment as a way of further investigating teacher immediacy and its impact on student satisfaction with the quality of online course and teaching and the impact on student learning outcomes.

There is a need to extend the foundational research of instructor immediacy in traditional, face-to-face learning environments to online learning environments (Baker, 2010). Witt, Wheeless, and Allen (2004) conducted a meta-analysis of eighty-one studies that investigated teacher immediacy with respect to learning outcomes in traditional, face-to-face classrooms. Their study found a positive and significant relationship between overall teacher immediacy and overall student learning.

In this chapter we discuss the application of three teaching strategies as a vehicle for investigating teacher immediacy in the online environment. Theoretical perspectives are discussed, which challenge the delivery of online education, and provide a framework for the study. The three challenges discussed include: (1) the application of formative feedback practices; (2) the application of student self-assessment to encourage deeper and more meaningful learning; and (3) the integration of rubric use in assessment activities.

Theoretical perspectives are translated to teaching strategies and tested and discussed in a case study analysis. The descriptive case study research aimed to understand the application of these three practical strategies for improving teacher immediacy in the delivery of university online education, and the impact these strategies have on student overall satisfaction with the quality of the course and teaching in the online environment.

The findings of the case study are discussed within the context of the challenges identified. The case study considers the delivery of the same university course (Contemporary Aviation Management) over a 3 year period. Results of surveys regarding the student experience, and the data regarding the achievement of student learning outcomes are reviewed. Overall, the findings presented in the case study support the application of the three teaching strategies in effective delivery of the university course in the online learning environment.

The chapter offers a synthesis of the earlier discussion and findings, by providing two key solutions. The author recommends that university courses provided in the online environment need to be adjusted to enhance interaction. This may be achieved by: (1) using rubrics to promote transparency, and understanding of the requirements to achieve and demonstrate intended learning outcomes within the course; and (2) encouraging self-evaluation to assist student and teacher interaction that relates to personal student learning requirements.

Finally, the chapter concludes with a discussion of the future research directions that emerged as a result of this study. This discussion highlights the significant gaps in the research relating to teacher immediacy and the need for the construction of suitable teacher resources.

The increased growth of online instruction in university education, combined with the need for empirical research on best practice in online learning environments, provides the base from which this study was conducted. The study aims to contribute to the growing body of knowledge on effective teaching practices in online learning environments.

BACKGROUND

Interaction lies at the core of the learning experience and is a key criteria for successful learning in both traditional and online learning modes (Wanstreet, 2006). Furthermore, interaction has been attributed to the success factors influencing student motivation, active learning and engagement among students, and the attainment of learning outcomes (Tu, 2005). There are two most significant research areas in the field of communications, which offers the theoretical framework for teacher immediacy as a form of interaction. Firstly Moore's transactional distance theory (Moore & Kearsley, 1996) and another concept of communication immediacy defined by Mehrabian (1971).

The transactional distance theory described by Moore and Kearsley (1996) offers an explanation for why the use of electronic communication tools may foster interactions between students and the teacher in an online learning environment. Essentially, the theory acknowledges that the quality of teaching and the interactions between the students and the teacher is less so related to geographical separation and more associated with the structure of the course and the interactions that take place within the course (Lemak, Shin, Reed, & Montgomery, 2005). Distance education was seen as a transaction by Moore (1973) who claimed that the physical distance in online and distance education leads to potential misunderstandings and potential gaps in communication (i.e., transactional distance) between the teacher and the student. Thus, increasing the communication between the teacher and the student translates to reduction in the transactional distance. This theory of transactional distance is important as it considers why the use of electronic communication tools reduces the distance between students and teachers in the online environment. The electronic tools found in many online learning management systems (e.g., discussion boards, email and messaging) enhances the levels of interaction, and allows teachers and students the opportunity to reduce the transactional distance and allows students to achieve levels of interaction similar to those in a face-to-face classroom (Lemak et al., 2005).

While Moore's theory is cogent, it appears that some teachers seem to foster interactions more successfully than others (Baker, 2010). A construct from the field of communications offers teachers a framework for developing the sense of psychological closeness through interactions. Communication immediacy, is a concept suggested by Mehrabian (1971) which uncovers physical and verbal behaviors that effectively reduce the psychological and physical distance between people. The nonverbal immediacy behaviors include physical actions such as leaning forward. However, verbal immediate behaviors include non-physical behaviors (such as using humor, or giving praise). Although the verbal and non-verbal behaviors were often considered as one dimension in early research, the research of Robinson and Richmond (1995) clarified the behaviors in two specific constructs. Verbal immediacy behaviors are particularly relevant to online education as they are more easily controlled and not bound by physical space or proximity as are nonverbal behaviors. Thus, a majority of the immediacy research in the online delivery of education has focused on the teacher's use of verbally immediate behaviors (i.e., teacher immediacy).

As we consider the two key research areas relating to the framework for teacher immediacy as a form of interaction, two questions form the basis of this case study. With regards to Moore's theory of transactional distance, what tools can be used in the online environment that encourage interaction between the student and the learner? Moreover, regarding Mehrabian's concept of communication immediacy, what verbal immediacy strategies further enhance the delivery of online education?

In the main focus of the chapter, the author continues to investigate the framework for teacher immediacy as a form of interaction, discussing three important challenges facing the delivery of online education. It is this discussion that frames the following case study research.

THEORETICAL PERSPECTIVE, ISSUES AND CHALLENGES FOR UNIVERSITY ONLINE EDUCATION

In this section, the discussion relating to teacher immediacy in the online environment is extended to critically examine the challenges of the delivery of university online education and provides the theoretical perspective that frames the case study. The three key issues examined are: (1) the challenge of providing formative feedback on assessment in the online environment; (2) The challenge of encouraging student self-assessment to enhance learner specific student-teacher interaction in the online environment; and (3) the challenge of using rubrics.

The Challenge of Providing Formative Feedback on Assessment in an Online Environment

Feedback plays an essential role in teacher immediacy behaviors and student learning. Importantly, it is the coupling of effective learning goals with feedback that has relevance in instructional settings (Blanchard & Johnson, 1982).

Lin and Lai (2013) emphasize that when consistently integrated into teaching and learning processes of curriculum, formative assessments aim to enhance learning achievements by providing feedback to students while they are developing their abilities. However, the value of feedback is particularly heightened in the learning process when it is thoroughly embedded and clearly articulated with the learning objectives. This ensures that the two adjoining assessment objectives (i.e., 'assessment for learning', and 'assessment as learning') (Clark, 2012) are achieved.

The consistent integration of formative assessment into curriculum provides an opportunity for formative feedback to not only monitor the progress of the student in relation to those specific learning objectives, but it also encourages students to develop skills and strategies that promote life-long learning (Hattie & Timperly, 2007). With this in mind, it is clear that assessment and feedback lie at the heart of pedagogy (Gikandi, Morrow, & Davis, 2011), including the pedagogy applied to university level online education.

According to Cohen (1985):

...feedback is one of the most instructionally powerful and least understood features in instructional design (p. 33).

Over the last fifty years, various studies have provided a similar outcome with respect to learning and performance (Kluger & DeNisi, 1996; Narciss & Huth, 2004). Within this research, we find a number of conflicting findings and relatively little alignment of patterns or guidance. Shute (2008) defines formative feedback as:

...information communicated to the learner that is intended to modify his or her thinking or behavior for the purpose of improving learning (p. 154).

Although a range of inconsistencies and conflicts occur in the literature, the underlying research premise surrounding formative feedback is that high quality feedback can markedly improve learning processes and outcomes. It is essentially, the 'interaction' resulting from the feedback process (i.e., information communicated to the learner) that forms the basis of deeper approaches to learning. The positive learning effect is particularly significant when the feedback is delivered correctly (Shute, 2008). Although teachers understand the importance of formative feedback, the challenge of 'correct delivery' and 'interaction' has been exacerbated within the context of online course delivery.

In online learning, the interaction involved through feedback processes takes on new dimensions (Wolsey, 2008). Traditional forms of face-to-face interaction (i.e., informal discussion after class meeting, questions and answers regarding assignments etc) that underscored some feedback processes become difficult in the online environment. It is not that these interactions are impossible online, only that these interactions require more considered effort on the part of the teacher, or take on a different form.

In the online delivery of university courses, the Internet offers immediacy for some types of communication and interaction. However, feedback scarcely occurs in real time. There may be periods, both long and short, between the question and the reply. With this in mind, Wolsey (2008) suggests that education in online contexts highlights the necessity of effective feedback on student efforts and assessment items. In education of this nature, feedback therefore relates to what the teacher writes on and about student work. However, feedback may also be provided through online tools within learning management software, voice annotations and telephone calls.

P1 (Proposition for Research and Practice): Online education needs to consider the importance of feedback in encouraging deeper approach to student learning. Feedback is a product of interaction. Thus, university level online educators should consider integrating formative assessment into curriculum design, which promotes effective formative feedback opportunities.

The Challenge of Encouraging Student Self-Assessment to Enhance Learner Specific Student-Teacher Interaction in the Online Environment

Formative feedback is useful to the student learning process. Current pedagogical models of effective learning, place the student at the center of the learning experience. In student-centered learning approaches in the online environment, a key component of feedback is the information that students and teachers gain regarding the achievements towards specified learning goals connected to the task or performance (Hattie & Timperly, 2007). However, in the distance and online context, learner specific needs can be difficult to determine. Thus, teacher immediacy behaviors in online course delivery need to take on new forms.

The challenge in online course delivery is identifying specific student learning needs in an effort to help that student achieve the intended learning outcomes. In the online context, teacher immediacy behaviors need to consider how the individual student has progressed towards achieving the intended learning outcomes. Student self-assessment strategies have emerged as a way of assisting teachers and students in discovering a student's personal progress towards learning goal achievement (Huang, 2015).

Previous studies conducted on self-assessment focus predominantly on the correctness of the judgment of the learner (Boud & Falchikov, 1989), while the marks offered by the teacher continue to provide the major measurement of evidence of learning (Huang, 2015). Other research indicates that in the case of self-assessment, more advanced learners are generally found to be more accurate in their judgment (Lew, Alwis, & Schmidt, 2010).

However, a student's self-assessment is not isolated to a matter of accuracy. Recent research has investigated the power relationship that arises in such strategies where transference occurs between the teacher and the student. Specifically, this research considers the potential that self-assessment activities may have in empowering students to take responsibility for learning (Milne, 2009). The studies on student self-assessment however, are not based on assessment alone, nor the appropriateness and correctness of learning power. Rather, the studies on self-assessment focus on the support and development of student learning through participating in self-assessment (Huang, 2015).

Boud (1995) further defines self-assessment as an activity, which asks the students to judge themselves and engage in decisions about minimizing gaps in their knowledge and/or skill. This activity encourages students to ask questions such as:

How am I doing? Is this enough? Is this right? How can I tell? Should I go further? (Huang, 2015) (p. 2).

It is when students ask these questions that they enter into an activity of formative and iterative feedback, inevitably developing a skill in self-regulated learning as they gradually assume ownership of their own learning.

Can student self-assessment strategies enhance interaction and teacher immediacy behaviors?

Student self-assessment has not traditionally included feedback as a critical part of the learning process, from either teachers or peers (Taras, 1999). However, as feedback is inextricably bound to effective learning (Black & William, 1998), it follows that engaging students positively in feedback processes can only further enhance learning (Taras, 2010).

The requirements, however, of integrating self-assessment activities into formative feedback strategies can be challenging for university educators. Taras (2010) highlights two distinctive features of self-assessment, often misunderstood by online educators. Firstly, teacher feedback may be minimal, but ultimately depends on the student's learning needs. Secondly, feedback from the teacher and student self-assessment should occur before students are provided with a grade (Taras, 2010).

Taylor (2014) supports that the feedback students receive through a process of self-assessment supports their development and successful transition into professional careers. Additionally, the feedback gathered through self-assessment strategies encourages the students to engage in more meaningful learning of the course content. While self-assessment in the online delivery mode may offer a student the opportunity to develop life-long learning skills (i.e., inquiry, and development strategies for personal learning improvement), the practice also contains a range of limitations that challenge not only the student, but also the teacher.

Firstly, self-assessments can tend to be biased, unreasonably high, and unreliable when considering a student's ability to assess their own learning, progress and skills (Dunning, 2005). In the aviation industry, Winter, Rice, Reid, and Rian (2015) also revealed that aviation students are more likely to perform poorly on self-assessment activities. The outcome is further exacerbated where a student may not have the knowledge to perform the learning activity, and may lack an understanding of how poorly they are performing (Kruger & Dunning, 1999).

Sedikides (1993) investigated the three principal motivations for self-evaluation. These include: the pursuit of precise self-knowledge (i.e., self-assessment); the pursuit of complimentary self-knowledge (i.e., self-enhancement); and the pursuit of a confirmation of self-knowledge (i.e., self-verification). In the study, the motivating factor associated with self-enhancement was revealed to be the most dominant of the self-evaluation process. This was later confirmed by Baumeister (1999).

While self-assessment provides a sound platform from which to encourage further learning interaction between student and teacher, implementation of self-assessment into teaching and learning strategies must be considered with regards to accuracy and the validity of the information attained from student self-assessment exercises.

P2 (Proposition for Research and Practice): In the student-centered approach to learning, the challenge for university online educators is identifying the individual learning progress of online students. However, in online learning environments, student self-evaluation of work and assessment items potentially presents an opportunity to uncover individual student learning progress. Online educators should consider integrating structured self-assessment opportunities within the curriculum to encourage students to ask questions of their own learning progress, ultimately allowing the teacher to interact and offer feedback that meets the specific needs of the individual student.

The Challenge of Using Rubrics

Kearsley (2000) suggests that designing and conducting learning activities which encourage interaction and engagement is one of the most important roles of the online educator. While self-assessment encourages interaction, the student needs instruction in the practice of self-assessment including appropriate guidance on which to base their assessment of their progress. One approach to self-assessment is the use of rubrics. This includes providing the students with the assessment criteria (Panadero & Romero, 2014). A rubric is a document that clearly communicates the expectations of the assignment or work required by specifying the criteria associated with what is particularly important and detailing the levels of quality on a scale from 'excellent' to 'poor' (Reddy & Andrade, 2010). Three important features characterize rubrics: assessment criteria; a strategy to be applied for grading purposes; and the definition of quality and standards (Popham, 1997).

The use of a marking rubric is one feature of feedback. Publishing the assessment criteria also allows standardization of marking. Norton (2009) agrees that publishing such criteria enacts a process of consensus moderation and assists new staff into the procedures of assessment. This is a process that aims to improve fairness and consistency in marking of student assessment.

Consensus moderation also helps to standardize judgments on assessment across disciplines (Nulty, 2012). Although rubrics help to improve the 'reliability' in marking, it has been argued that they can also have a negative consequence that may drive students to focus on the 'performance' of the task rather than the 'learning' (Norton, 2009). Particularly as the students do not actually engage in the development of the assessment criteria (Race, 1991). Sadler (2008) also questions the validity of marking systems such as this, arguing that rubrics fail to provide sound assessment of complex student works.

More recently, however, Malini Redi and Andrade (2010) suggest that the results of research regarding the relationship between rubrics and learning indicates higher achievement and deeper learning by students who have rubrics to guide their work. The rubric serves to provide fledgling academic writers with an articulation of the expectations for the assignment, listing criteria and the levels of quality. When students use rubrics as part of a formative assessment, rubrics can teach as well as evaluate (Malini Redi & Andrade, 2010).

In successful online learning, it is important for students to realize what is expected of them. As such, the teacher needs to convey the concept of 'quality'. Rubrics go some way to help students understand what is required to meet the necessary standards or criterion, but this is not enough. Issuing exemplars provides the additional clarity students require. With concrete examples of work that is of high quality, students begin to understand what is required of them (Sadler, 2002). Just telling the student about an assessment item (as provided by the course profile), can be abstract to students. As teachers, we try to tell the story through task specifications (written words), followed by more elaborate specifications (spoken words). Sadler (2002) emphasizes that it is important to "show" students what the lecturer's expectations are as well. The rubric, the exemplar and the explanation all assist in improving the 'transparency' of the assessment item (Race, 2010) and reducing cognitive distance between the student and teacher. These are equally important immediacy factors in online learning environments.

P3 (Proposition for Research and Practice): In the online environment, teacher immediacy is enhanced when students clearly understand what is expected of them. As such, online educators should consider the use of rubrics as a way of articulating performance requirements. Yet, immediacy behaviors must not be limited to the simple publication of a rubric. Teachers should encourage interaction with the learning content by offering students: (1) an understanding and appreciation of the value of the self-assessment; (2) access to clear and unambiguous marking criteria on which to support the assessment, (3) a specific task or performance to assess; (4) a model on how to perform the self-assessment; (5) specific instruction in the conduct of self-assessment; and (6) opportunities to revise and improve on the task or performance in which the self-assessment occurred (Andrade and Valtcheva, 2009)

THE CASE STUDY

Methods

The research attempted to translate these challenges by examining the effect of these three theoretical perspectives relating to teacher immediacy behaviors in an effort to enhance student satisfaction of learning in the online learning environment. The three strategies include: (1) the application of formative feedback practices; (2) the application of student self-assessment to encourage deeper and more meaningful learning; and (3) the integration of rubric use in assessment activities. The descriptive case study research aimed to understand the application of these three practical strategies for improving teacher immediacy in the delivery of university online education, and the impact these strategies have on student overall satisfaction with the quality of the course and teaching in the online environment.

The case study research method was selected as the method of inquiry as it offers the researcher the opportunity to capture and describe the complexity of real-life application and events (Yin, 1994). The case study approach presents a disciplined mode of inquiry that can be systematically ordered around issues. The case study researcher is entrusted with the responsibility of managing and implementing a detailed analysis of a case that emphasize "episodes of nuance, the sequentiality of happenings in context, [and] the wholeness of the individual" (Stake, 1995), (p. xii).

This study presents a meaningful analysis and affective attributes of certain strategies to encourage teacher immediacy in the online learning context of university education. The study employed online survey data and analysis of existing student work samples.

Participants

The research was conducted at an Australian University. In this case, the teacher delivered a university course in an online environment over three consecutive years. The course, Contemporary Aviation Management, was a third year level course offered to students in both the Bachelor of Aviation and Bachelor of Aviation Management undergraduate degree programs.

The selected course investigated has been delivered similarly over three subsequent years. In all three semesters of delivery, the researcher has taught the course. In 2013, the Contemporary Aviation Management course (previously named Principles of Management in Aviation) was offered in blended learning mode (providing for both face-to-face delivery and online delivery). In 2013, 75 students enrolled in the course.

In 2014, the course was transitioned to online delivery only. Three strategies were employed in an effort to improve the student overall satisfaction of the quality of course and teaching. These strategies included, (1) the application of formative feedback practices; (2) the application of student self-assessment to encourage deeper and more meaningful learning; and (3) the integration of rubric use in assessment activities. In 2014, 36 students enrolled in the course. In 2015, no changes were made to the course content, learning activities or assessment activities. The same three strategies were employed in this year. In 2015, 77 students enrolled in the course.

Due to the unique nature of the online environment, factors such as ethnicity and race were not considered in the research design. Regarding research in online education, the physical and cultural attributes of participants may dissolve from the researcher's view (Wolsey, 2008). An online identity may also be manufactured or created specifically for the online environment, which may be different from the identities the participant may assume within geographically bound environments (Markham, 2005).

Instruments and Procedures

In week 10 of the thirteen-week semester, students are invited to complete an anonymous and online survey titled 'Student Evaluation of Course' (SEC) and 'Student Evaluation of Teaching' (SET). This invitation is administered through a central university web-based application. The teacher followed up this invitation by posting additional reminders of survey participation in week 11, 12 and 13. The participant responses to each of the surveys (n[SEC] and n[SET]) are listed in the Table 1.

In each of the surveys, participants were asked to respond to statements according to a 5-point Likert scale, where participants could express how much they agree with certain statements. These expressions included 'strongly disagree', 'disagree', 'neutral', 'agree', or 'strongly agree'. Each response is given a value from 1 to 5, where 1 is recorded for 'strongly disagree'. The student evaluation of course survey included the following statements:

Table 1. Number of students enrolled in each course, the number of students that responded to the SEC survey (n[SEC]) and the number of students that responded to the SET survey (n[SET])

Year	Number of Students Enrolled in the Course	Number of Students that Responded to the SEC Survey (n[SEC])	Number of Students that Responded to the SET Survey (n[SET])
2013	75	47	45
2014	36	15	15
2015	77	36	34

1. The course was well organized
2. The assessment was clear and fair
3. I received helpful feedback on my assessment work
4. The course engaged me in learning
5. The teaching (lectures, tutors, online etc) on this course was effective in helping me to learn
6. Overall I am satisfied with the quality of this course.

The student evaluation of teaching survey included the following statements:

1. The staff member presented material in a clearly organized way
2. The staff member presented material in an interesting way
3. The staff member treated students with respect
4. The staff member showed a good knowledge of the subject matter
5. Overall I am satisfied with the teaching of this staff member.

Additionally, surveys offered qualitative data as participants were given the opportunity to express their thoughts and opinions in open-ended questions. The following questions encouraged qualitative responses:

1. What did you find particularly good about this course?
2. How could this course be improved?

Data triangulation is achieved by considering the data provided by the student surveys as well as reviewing results achieved by students for this course between 2013 and 2015.

Limitations of the Research Design

The study relies heavily on student reports, rather than observation of practices. For this reason, the study should not be generalized beyond the conclusions drawn regarding the three strategies specifically applied to online teaching. What we can assume, however, is that the respondents offer useful data that broadly informs the inquiry. Readers may then compare and apply findings to their own teaching situations and environments.

Findings

Student Experience Surveys

As discussed earlier, for the Contemporary Aviation Management course in 2013, 2014 and 2015, the same teacher (i.e., the researcher) delivered the course. However, while the learning content remained the same, from 2014, three strategies were applied in an effort to improve the student responses to the overall quality of course and teaching.

For the 2014 course delivery, firstly the teacher carefully integrated formative assessment into the curriculum design. This was achieved by carefully linking course learning outcomes to the assessment strategy ensuring that students were offered the opportunity to demonstrate the required learning outcomes.

Secondly, the teacher integrated structured self-assessment opportunities within the curriculum to encourage students to ask questions of their own learning progress. This was achieved by requiring students to mark their work on the written assignment against the marking criteria and submit this mark as well as a justification to the teacher. Additionally, to support this activity, the teacher offered an online tutorial on the assignment. This tutorial also offered students instructions in the process of self-assessment. Including self-assessment in the formative assessment allowed the teacher to interact and offer feedback prior to the final submission of the written assignment and also meets the specific needs of the individual student.

This was achieved as the teacher reviewed the student work against the marking criteria, as well as the student's own self-assessment of their work and offered personalized feedback and constructive comments within the student work and via email to encourage students to address learning deficiencies.

Thirdly, the teacher used a rubric as a way of articulating performance requirements for the final written assignment. The teacher encouraged interaction with the learning content by offering students: (1) an online tutorial and weekly online exercises to explain the value of self-assessment; (2) the publication of the marking criteria (rubric) in week 1 of semester, (3) the publication of the written assessment question in week 1 of semester as well as a complete exemplar; (4) the publication of an example of how to perform self-assessment of the written assessment item; (5) specific instruction in the conduct of self-assessment; and (6) the opportunity to submit their work and self-assessment to the teacher for further feedback.

A comparison of both SEC and SET data for the Contemporary Aviation Management course between the 2013 offering (without the three teacher immediacy strategies) and the 2014 and 2015 offerings (with the three teacher immediacy strategies applied), highlights an increase in the mean value of all the questions with "Overall I am satisfied with the quality of this course" increasing from 2.4 out of 5 (2013), to 4.4 out of 5 (2014), and 4.2 out of 5 (2015).

Additionally, the scores for "Overall I am satisfied with the teaching of this staff member" increased from 2.7 out of 5 (2013), to 4.5 out of 5 (2014), and 4.2 out of 5 (2015).

Table 2 highlights significant improvements from the 2013 scores. In the student evaluation of course data, the greatest increases between 2013 and 2014 were the statements relating to "The assessment was clear and fair" (an increase in score of 44%) and "The course engaged me in learning" (an increase in score of 42%).

Table 2. 2013, 2014, and 2015 SEC question [mean] scores

Question	2013	2014 (% Increase Compared to 2013)	2015
The course was well organized	3.2	4.5 (26%)	4.3
The assessment was clear and fair	2.4	4.6 (44%)	4.3
I received helpful feedback on my assessment work	2.9	4.7 (36%)	4.4
The course engaged me in learning	2.3	4.4 (42%)	4.1
The teaching (lecturers, tutors, online etc) on this course was effective in helping me to learn	2.5	4.5 (40%)	4.2
Overall I am satisfied with the quality of this course	2.4	4.4 (40%)	4.2

Table 3 highlights an improvement also in the student evaluation of teaching scores from 2013 to 2014. In the student evaluation of teaching data, the greatest increases between 2013 and 2014 were statements relating to "The staff member presented material in an interesting way" (44% increase) and "Overall I am satisfied with the teaching of this staff member" (36% increase).

In 2013, student responses to the question of "What did you find particularly good about this course?" revolved around one key theme. Students were satisfied with the lecture content and material, with many highlighting a missing link between the content and their assessment and future career. This theme highlights the importance of ensuring that curriculum is designed with learning outcomes clearly linked between all stages of course content, learning activities and assessment strategy (Biggs & Tang, 2007).

In 2013, student responses to "How could this course be improved?" could broadly be categorized into two major themes. Firstly, students expressed dissatisfaction in the assignment guidance material. Many commented that further clarity was required as to the assignment question. Additionally, many commented that they were not aware of how the final assignment allowed them to demonstrate and develop skills that would be useful to their future career. Ultimately, these comments reflect the need for the teacher to carefully and clearly embed formative assessment. Particularly, the research of Lin and Lai (2013) who emphasize that when consistently integrated into teaching and learning processes of curriculum, formative assessments aim to enhance learning achievements by providing feedback to students while they are developing their abilities.

Table 3. 2013, 2014, and 2015 SET question [mean] scores

Question	2013	2014 (% Increase Compared to 2013)	2015
The staff member presented material in a clearly organized way	3.2	4.5 (26%)	4.2
The staff member presented material in an interesting way	2.3	4.5 (44%)	4.0
The staff member treated students with respect	3.5	4.8 (26%)	4.6
The staff member showed a good knowledge of the subject matter	3.4	4.5 (22%)	4.5
Overall I am satisfied with the teaching of this staff member	2.7	4.5 (36%)	4.2

Secondly, in 2013, students commented that more consistency was required across marking. This was extended to the need for additional and more detailed feedback for the final written assignment. The rubric provided in the 2013 offering for the final assignment was limited in detail, offering only single word criteria and a score of 1 to 10 for each. It is clear that students required additional detail as to how they could personally and individually achieve higher marks for their assessment and strategies for how they could individually improve.

After the three immediacy strategies highlighted in this inquiry were implemented in the 2014 offering of the Contemporary Aviation Management course, student qualitative responses were significantly more positive. In both 2014 and 2015, responses to the question "What did you find particularly good about this course?" two key themes emerged.

Firstly, the students commented that the course was very engaging, clearly organized and students could appreciate the need to complete learning activities and the written assessment in developing their abilities as future aviation professionals. This highlighted the success of careful attention to constructive alignment in curriculum design.

Secondly, students were highly satisfied with the material and supporting teacher strategies surrounding the written assignment, including the rubric, and personalized feedback assistance to encourage individual learners to improve their written assignment. While organization in learning is clearly beneficial to online engagement, it was the formative feedback and clarity of assessment that many students enjoyed. One student commented that "[the course] was well organized and as an online student, I feel it was actually set up for online learning…". Another student commented that "[the teacher's] feedback via email was the most detailed I have received…it was a pleasure to have studied this course". Most students however, were highly satisfied with the individual feedback and communication on student progress with comments such as "I felt [the teacher] was clearly committed to providing a good atmosphere for learning" and "[the teacher] always offered feedback and help through emails. [The teacher] was very encouraging, and took time to understand each student from the first day of the course".

In both 2014 and 2015, responses to the question "How could this course be improved?" again, students offered a much more positive response. Many students highlighted sound satisfaction with the online offering with limited need for improvement. Other minor suggestions included the provision of an online quiz at the end of each online lecture to assist in focusing the learning content. Others suggested that the recorded lecture content could be shorter. This further emphasizes the importance of interaction in student learning. While the lecture recordings were only one of the learning activities each week, it is important to note that transmission approaches are limited in their ability to encourage learning in the online environment. What students preferred in the 2014 and 2015 course offering was the instructor-student interaction and the encouragement specific to their learning that the teacher offered.

In general, student qualitative responses were overwhelmingly positive and there was consensus in student satisfaction with the overall quality of course and teachings after the three teacher immediacy strategies were applied. A significant improvement in the qualitative and quantitative data is seen between the 2013 course offering (before the application of the three teacher immediacy strategies) compared to 2014 and 2015 course offerings (after the application of the three teacher immediacy strategies).

Student Learning Outcomes

Enhanced student experiences of learning appear to have been accompanied with the application of the three strategies. This is reflected in improved learning outcomes for the course. In Figure 1, the final

Figure 1. 2013 Histogram of marks for contemporary aviation management course (previously called principles of management in aviation)

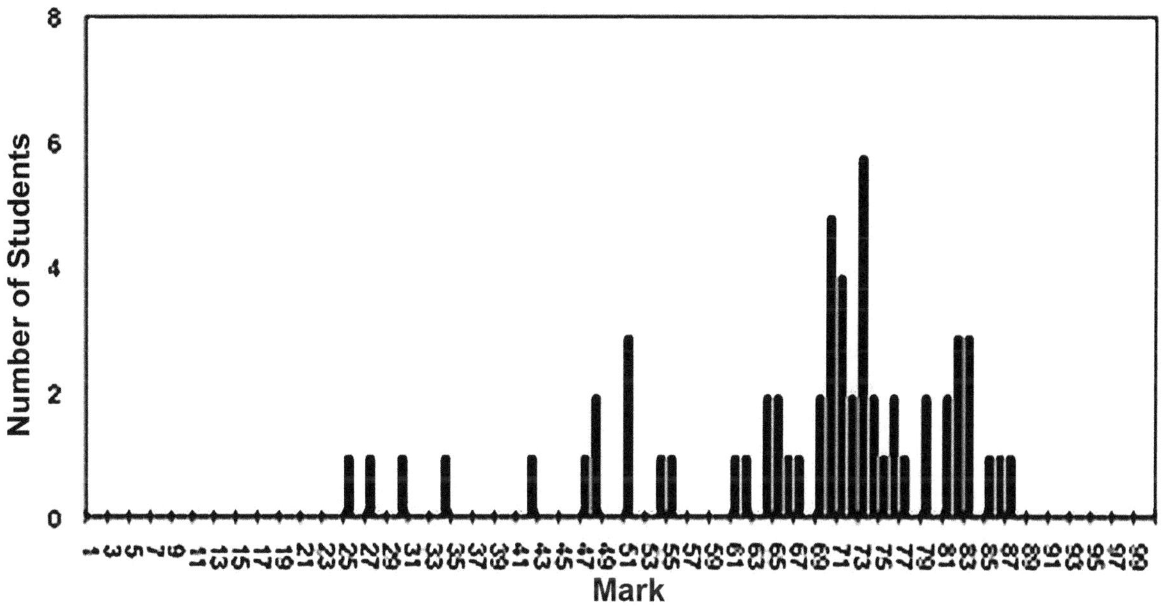

mark distribution for the 2013 cohort (without the application of the three strategies in this inquiry) is seen. Figure 2 indicates the final mark distribution for the 2014 cohort where the three strategies were first applied.

When viewed as variants of normal distribution it is apparent that the ‘tail of failures’ in the 2014 cohort is proportionally much less than that of the 2013 cohort. A minor anomaly in the failure numbers

Figure 2. 2014 Histogram of marks for contemporary aviation management course

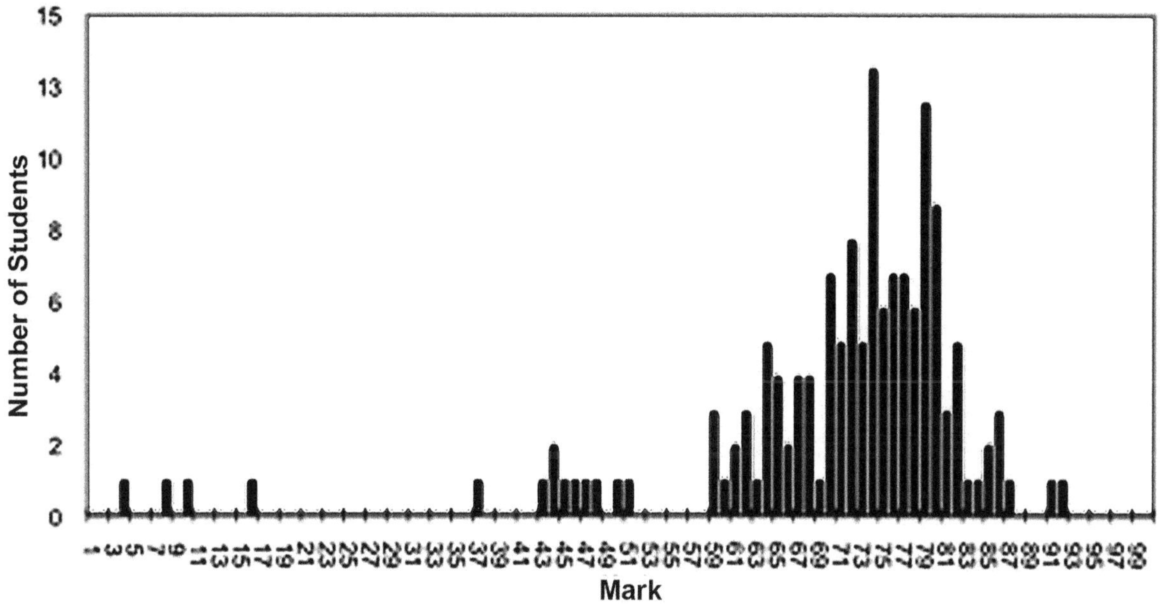

is seen at the lower end of the mark scale for the 2014 cohort and reflects those students that discontinued enrolment in the course during the semester. Never-the-less, the reduced 'tail of failures' indicates improved learning outcomes for the more challenged students in the 2014 cohort. This feature is also accompanied by an increase in the median mark from 70 in 2013 to 74 in 2014, which indicates a rise in the level of engagement and learning (Carini, Kuh, & Klein, 2006).

Table 4 shows the relative distribution of student outcomes in each of the grade ranges from fail to high distinction. It can be seen that there are improvements in the higher grade ranges as well. This may be explained by the teacher's own developing abilities and confidence in the management and provision of personal feedback and learning strategies for students. These results are further supported by the overall positive improvements in learning satisfaction scores and comments identified in the student experience surveys.

The 2014 cohort indicates a lower failure rate and lower pass rate, but higher distinction and high distinction rates. Again, this provides further evidence of improved learning outcomes for students who are exposed to the three investigated strategies that encourage interaction, particularly in the second year of the new methods (as the teacher has had time to practice these).

There are definite indications as detailed in the student experiences of learning and the relative learning outcomes that the three strategies (i.e., (1) the application of formative feedback practices; (2) the application of student self-assessment to encourage deeper and more meaningful learning; and (3) the integration of rubric use in assessment activities have impacted positively on the student learning.

While these strategies have enhanced teacher immediacy, the strategies have also reduced the learning distance between the teacher and the student and supported an improvement in student satisfaction with the quality and teaching of the online delivery of this course.

SOLUTIONS/RECOMMENDATIONS

This case study has confirmed the theoretical perspectives within the literature with regard to improving student satisfaction of the quality and teaching in the online delivery of a university course. The results have highlighted and emphasized the importance of interaction in the student learning process. Moreover, the case study has provided a deeper understanding of effective instructional practices with regards to interaction. In this section, we discuss the solutions and recommendations highlighted by the research and practice of the case study. The author maintains that university courses provided in the online environment need to be adjusted to enhance interaction. This may be achieved by: (1) using rubrics

Table 4. Relative distribution of student outcomes in each of the grade ranges from Fail (F), Pass (P), Credit (C), Distinction (D) to High Distinction (HD) and median marks for the 2013 to 2015 offerings of the Contemporary Aviation Management course

Year (total students enrolled)	%F	%P	%C	%D	%HD	Median Mark %
2013 (75)	18.7	48	28	10.7	0	70
2014 (36)	8.3	8.3	27.8	19.4	36.1	74
2015 (77)	9.1	20.8	18.2	36.4	19.5	73

to promote transparency, and understanding of the requirements to achieve and demonstrate intended learning outcomes within the course; and (2) Encourage student self-evaluation to assist student and teacher interaction that relates to personal student learning requirements.

Effective Uses of Rubrics

Literature suggests that the use of rubrics in university education is widespread, and across a range of disciplines, by a large number of teachers (Malini-Reddy & Andrade, 2010). Published studies regarding rubric use is found in disciplines such as liberal arts, information literacy, medicine, management, nursing, dentistry, food technology, teacher education and film and media technology. As discussed in earlier sections, rubrics have been used to provide feedback and assess a wide range of student work products, including essays, concept maps, literature reviews, reflective writings, oral presentations, portfolios, and projects (Malini-Reddy & Andrade, 2010).

A number of studies (for example, Song (2006)) examine how the diagnostic feedback that is attained by rubric use can be used to identify areas for improvement in teaching, while others have investigated the use of rubrics singularly to assess student work (Campbell, 2005). Never-the-less, the findings of this case study support the work of Andrade (2005) who argues that rubrics can serve purposes to enhance instruction as well as evaluate. Several research reports confirm that rubrics support teaching and learning practices (Andrade & Du, 2005; Schneider, 2006). This case study extends these conclusions, emphasizing that rubrics also provide the opportunity to enhance effective interaction strategies between the student and the teacher.

The research conducted by Petkov and Petkova (2006) asserts that involving students in the development as well as the use of the rubric, or offering an instructor-developed rubric prior to the submission of an assignment showed positive improvements in academic performance. In this case study, the presentation of the instructor-developed rubric prior to submission was widely appreciated by students in the 2014 and 2015 cohorts. However, in the study conducted by (Green & Bowswer, 2006), no difference was found in the quality of the student work with or without the use of a rubric.

The key issue appears that the simple dissemination of a rubric to online students is not enough to enhance learning. Additional teacher immediacy behaviors in the online environment must support the use of rubrics. Ultimately, students must be taught to actively use the rubric for self-assessment and revision in order to garner the benefits of rubric use.

Thus, interaction between teacher and student in the online environment can be enhanced with the use of rubrics providing students are offered: (1) an understanding and appreciation of the value of the self-assessment; (2) access to clear and unambiguous marking criteria on which to support the assessment, (3) a specific task or performance to assess; (4) a model on how to perform the self-assessment; (5) specific instruction in the conduct of self-assessment; and (6) opportunities to revise and improve on the task or performance in which the self-assessment occurred (Andrade & Valtcheva, 2009).

Encourage Self-Assessment to Assist Student-Teacher Interaction that Relates to Personal Student Learning Requirements

There are two elements of inquiry that teachers designing aviation online and distance education programs need to be mindful of. The two elements of inquiry (i.e., reflection and discourse) as described by Garrison and Vaughan (2008) provide the foundation for a meaningful educational experience. Reflection and discourse can be demonstrated in online learning with the use of technology in the application of formative assessment.

With respect to the first element of inquiry, teachers must be mindful that students are engaged in a discourse that is rich and relevant, with careful consideration in the maintenance of a sense of belonging. Yet, the very nature of the online education (i.e., often remote, isolated and distant) means that balancing the social and cognitive presence in an online environment can be complex. However, this challenge can be easily overcome with a strong teaching presence and an understanding of when and how to question and challenge the students (Garrison & Vaughan, 2008).

The second element of inquiry is concerned with self-reflection. One of the essential principles of adult education is deliberate allocation of time for reflective activities (Brookfield, 1989). Karp, McCurry, Turney, and Harms (1999) comment that the technique of self-reflection is slowly being adapted into the teaching and learning activities of some university aviation programs with success. Self-reflective activities may include quizzes, scenario-based questions or philosophical statements associated with the key topics being investigated. These activities assist students in taking responsibility for monitoring and achieving progress through the course, and encourage students to keep up to date with the course content (Walser, 2009).

The elements of inquiry also need to be supported with attention to teaching presence and feedback. University teachers engaged in the provision of online and distance education programs also need to appreciate the value of timely and thorough feedback in the formative assessment process. Ultimately, the formative nature of assessment items relates to the aspect of feedback that promotes the developmental nature of learning. It is the feedback that allows students the opportunity to appreciate the level of their knowledge. Appropriate feedback also gives students the opportunity to improve their abilities towards meeting the intended learning objectives.

This case study has supported the benefits of integrating self-assessment practices into online course delivery. It is argued that when an online student conducts and offers a self-assessment of their achievements against the key learning criteria to the teacher, the teacher has a platform on which to assist the student to developing personalized learning strategies towards attaining those intended learning outcomes. This form of immediacy encourages further learner specific interaction between the teacher and the student.

FUTURE RESEARCH DIRECTIONS

In this chapter, we have established that strategies associated with formative assessment, rubric use and student self-assessment have the potential to enhance interaction in the online learning environment of university courses. However, there is limited discipline specific guidance regarding the application of self-assessment, the integration of formative assessment practices, the use and application of rubrics and its effect on career development skills. Gaps in the research relating to teacher immediacy are emerging and include the need for the construction of suitable teacher resources.

Construction of Suitable Teacher Resources

Gold (2001) investigated the pedagogical function of the teacher in the delivery of online education and established that the transition from face-to-face (in-class) teaching to online teaching is complicated. Teachers adjusting to online delivery modes require special technical training which is centered on delivering high quality education products for students in addition to special training in the practice of engendering effective processes of learning within online environments. Michael Moore and Kearsley (2012) concur, highlighting that teachers using e-learning tools in an online environment also need to be supported by suitable systems with regard to time, resources and guidance.

Regrettably, empirical evidence in the literature specific to the aviation discipline implies that guidance is inadequate. The published literature and research in online education appears to be increasing in support of other disciplines. Of course, much of this research can be garnered to enhance the quality of online higher education. However, considering a future where the student is firmly placed at the center of the learning process, we need a more robust understanding of our specific environment and the students we are intending to nurture. This is particularly relevant to the challenges online education experiences with regards to the integration of self-assessment in formative feedback and assessment strategies.

Thomas (2003) asserts that more empirical research is needed that supports the use of internet-based communication tools, which aim to enhance online learning. Whilst the literature reinforces the application and integration of technology based communication tools, more is required to assure teachers of the validity of these tools with regards to improving self-regulation practices in an online environment.

CONCLUSION

The breadth and intensity of Internet based technologies has had a dramatic effect on a number of aspects of society. University education is not isolated from this effect, where the demand for online learning is experiencing significant growth (Baker, 2010). The rapid increase in online university education offers a fertile ground for empirical based research on how and in what form this well-established (yet still evolving) medium could be used to enhance the student learning experience.

In this chapter we have inquired into the application of teaching strategies as a vehicle for improving our understanding of teacher immediacy in the online environment. Through the presentation of a descriptive case study, the chapter has critically examined the theoretical perspective of strategies that intend to remove psychological and physical distance in the online learning environment. Specifically, we have considered the effective use of interaction in teaching and learning, including: (1) the application of formative feedback practices; (2) the application of student self-assessment to encourage deeper and more meaningful learning; and (3) the integration of rubric use in assessment activities. The chapter concludes by providing recommendations which support the practical application of teaching strategies including: (1) the use of rubrics; and (2) encouraging student self-assessment. These strategies have been shown to have the effect of improving teacher interaction and reducing the physical and psychological distance of online university education. This results in an improvement in both the student experience and the student learning outcomes in the online environment. It is hoped that the chapter provides a contribution to the body of literature relating to online university education by validating best practices and offering clear guidance for structuring and developing more effective online courses.

REFERENCES

Andrade, H., & Du, Y. (2005). Student perspectives on rubric-referenced assessment. *Practical Assessment, Research & Evaluation*, *10*(5), 1–11.

Andrade, H., & Valtcheva, A. (2009). Promoting learning and achievement through self-assessment. *Theory into Practice*, *48*(1), 12–19. doi:10.1080/00405840802577544

Andrade, H. G. (2005). Teaching with rubrics: The good, the bad, and the ugly. *College Teaching*, *53*(1), 27–40. doi:10.3200/CTCH.53.1.27-31

Baker, C. (2010). The Impact of Instructor Immediacy and Presence for Online Student Affective Learning, Cognition, and Motivation. *The Journal of Education Online*, *7*(1), 1–30.

Baumeister, R. F. (1999). The nature of structure of the self: An overview. In R. F. Baumeister (Ed.), *The self in social psychology*. Philadelphia: Psychology Press.

Biggs, J., & Tang, C. (2007). Teaching for quality learning at university. McGraw Hill.

Black, P., & William, D. (1998). Assessment and classroom learning. *Assessment in Education: Principles, Policy & Practice*, *5*(1), 7–74. doi:10.1080/0969595980050102

Blanchard, K., & Johnson, S. (1982). *The one minute manager*. New York: Berkley Books.

Boud, D. (1995). *Enhancing Learning through Self Assessment*. London: Kogan Press.

Boud, D., & Falchikov, N. (1989). Quantitative studies of student self-assessment in Higher Education: A critical analysis of findings. *Higher Education*, *18*(5), 529–549. doi:10.1007/BF00138746

Brookfield, S. (1989). Facilitating adult learning. In S. Merriam & P. Cunningham (Eds.), *Handbook of adult and continuing education*. San Francisco: Jossey-Bass.

Campbell, A. (2005). Application of ICT and rubrics to the assessment process where professional judgement is involved: The features of an e-marking tool. *Assessment & Evaluation in Higher Education*, *30*(5), 529–537. doi:10.1080/02602930500187055

Carini, R. M., Kuh, G. D., & Klein, S. P. (2006). Student engagement and student learning: Testing the linkages. *Research in Higher Education*, *47*(1), 1–32. doi:10.1007/s11162-005-8150-9

Clark, I. (2012). Formative Assessment: Assessment is for self-regulated learning. *Educational Psychology Review*, *2*(2).

Cohen, V. B. (1985). A re-examination of feedback in computer-based instruction: Implications for insturctional design. *Educational Technology*, *25*(1), 33–37.

Dunning, D. (2005). *Self-insight: Roadblocks and detours on the path to knowing thyself*. New York: Psychology Press. doi:10.4324/9780203337998

Garrison, R., & Vaughan, H. (2008). *Designing blended learning to create a community of inquiry. In Blended learning in higher education: Framework principles and guidlines* (pp. 31–48). San Francisco: Jossey-Bass.

Gikandi, J. W., Morrow, D., & Davis, N. E. (2011). Online formative assessment in higher education: A review of the literature. *Computers & Education*, *57*(4), 2333–2351. doi:10.1016/j.compedu.2011.06.004

Gold, S. (2001). A constructivist approach to online training for online teachers. *Journal of Asynchronous Learning Networks*, *5*(1), 36–57.

Grandzol, J., & Grandzol, C. (2006). Best practices for online business education. *International Review of Research in Open and Distance Learning*, *7*(1).

Green, R., & Bowswer, M. (2006). Observations from the field: Sharing a literature review rubric. *Journal of Library Administration*, *45*(1-2), 185–202. doi:10.1300/J111v45n01_10

Hattie, J., & Timperly, H. (2007). The power of feedback. *Review of Educational Research*, *77*(1), 81–112. doi:10.3102/003465430298487

Hiltz, R., Zhang, Y., & Tuross, M. (2002). *Studies of effectiveness of learning networks*. Needham, MA: Academic Press.

Huang, S. (2015). Understanding learners' self-assessment and self-feedback on their foreign language speaking performance. *Assessment & Evaluation in Higher Education*, 1–20. doi:10.1080/02602938.2015.1042426

Johnson, S. D., Aragon, S. R., Shaik, N., & Palma-Rivas, N. (2000). Comparative analysis of learner satisfaction and learning outcomes in online and face-to-face learning environments. *Journal of Interactive Learning Research*, *11*(1), 29–49.

Karp, M. R., McCurry, W. K., Turney, M. A., & Harms, D. (1999). *Aviation education for future airline pilots: An integrated model.* Paper presented at the International Aviation Training Symposium.

Kearsley, G. (2000). *Online education: Learning and teaching in cyberspace*. Toronto: Wadsworth.

Kluger, A. N., & DeNisi, A. (1996). The effects of feedback interventions on performance: A historical review, a meta-analysis, and a preliminary feedback intervention theory. *Psychological Bulletin*, *119*(2), 254–284. doi:10.1037/0033-2909.119.2.254

Kruger, J., & Dunning, D. (1999). Unskilled and unaware of it: How difficulties in recognizing one's own incompetence lead to inflated self-assessments. *Journal of Personality and Social Psychology*, *77*(6), 1121–1134. doi:10.1037/0022-3514.77.6.1121 PMID:10626367

Lemak, D., Shin, S., Reed, R., & Montgomery, J. (2005). Technology, transactional distance, and instructor effectiveness: An empirical investigation. *Academy of Management Learning & Education*, *4*(2), 150–158. doi:10.5465/AMLE.2005.17268562

Lew, M., Alwis, W., & Schmidt, H. (2010). Accuracy of Students' Self-Assessment and their Beliefts about Its Utility. *Assessment & Evaluation in Higher Education*, *35*(2), 135–156. doi:10.1080/02602930802687737

Lin, J.-W., & Lai, Y.-C. (2013). Harnessing Collaborative Annotations on Online Formative Assessments. *Journal of Educational Technology & Society*, *16*(1), 263–274.

Malini-Reddy, Y., & Andrade, H. (2010). A review of rubric use in higher education. *Assessment & Evaluation in Higher Education*, *35*(4), 435–448. doi:10.1080/02602930902862859

Markham, A. N. (2005). The methods, politics, and ethics of representation in online ethnography. In N. K. Denzin & Y. S. Lincoln (Eds.), *The Sage handbook of qualitative research* (3rd ed.). Thousand Oaks, CA: Sage.

McLaren, C. H. (2004). A comparison of student persistence and performance in online and classroom business statistics experiences. *Decision Sciences Journal of Innovative Education*, *2*(1), 1–10. doi:10.1111/j.0011-7315.2004.00015.x

Mehrabian, A. (1971). *Silent messages*. Belmont, CA: Wadsworth.

Milne, C. (2009). Assessing Self-evaluation in a Science Methods Course: Power, Agency, Authority and Learning. *Teaching and Teacher Education*, *25*(5), 758–766. doi:10.1016/j.tate.2008.11.008

Moore, M. (1973). Toward a theory of independent learning and teaching. *The Journal of Higher Education*, *44*(12), 661–679. doi:10.2307/1980599

Moore, M., & Kearsley, G. (2012). *Distance Education: A Systems View of Online Learning*. Belmont, CA: Wadsworth.

Moore, M. G., & Kearsley, G. (1996). *Distance education: A systems view*. Belmont, CA: Wadsworth.

Narciss, S., & Huth, K. (2004). How to design informative tutoring feedback for multi-media learning. In H. Niegemann, D. Leutner, & R. Brunken (Eds.), *Instructional design for multimedia learning* (pp. 181–195). Munster, Germany: Waxmann.

Norton, L. (2009). Assessing student learning. In H. Fry, S. Ketteridge, & S. Marshall (Eds.), *A handbook for teaching and learning in higher education: Enhancing Academic Practice*. London: Taylor and Francis Group.

Nulty, D. (2012). *Griffith University 7014GIH Curriculum Design, Innovation, Assessment and Evaluation: Course Notes*. Griffith University.

Panadero, E., & Romero, M. (2014). To rubric or not to rubric? The effects of self-assessment on self-regulation, performance and self-efficacy. *Assessment in Education: Principles, Policy & Practice*, *21*(2), 133–148. doi:10.1080/0969594X.2013.877872

Petkov, D., & Petkova, O. (2006). Development of Scoring Rubrics for IS Projects as an Assessment Tool. *Issues in Informing Science and Information Technology*, *3*, 499–510.

Popham, J. (1997). What's wrong and what's right with rubrics. *Educational Leadership*, *55*, 72–75.

Race, P. (1991). Practical pointers on peer assessment. In S. Brown (Ed.), Peer assessment in practice (pp. 113-119). Birmingham, UK: Staff and educational Development Association.

Race, P. (2010). *Making Learning Happen*. London, UK: SAGE Publications Ltd.

Reddy, Y., & Andrade, H. (2010). A review of rubric use in higher education. *Assessment & Evaluation in Higher Education*, *35*(4), 435–448. doi:10.1080/02602930902862859

Robinson, R. Y., & Richmond, V. P. (1995). Validity of the verbal immediacy scale. *Communication Research Reports*, *12*(1), 80–84. doi:10.1080/08824099509362042

Sadler, R. (2002). Ah!...so that's 'quality. In P. Schwartz & G. Webb (Eds.), *Assessment: case studies, experience and practice from higher education* (pp. 130–136). Kogan Page Limited and Stylus Publishing Inc.

Sadler, R. (2008). Indeterminacy in the use of preset criteria for assessment and grading. *Assessment & Evaluation in Higher Education.*

Schneider, J. F. (2006). Rubrics for teacher education in community college. *The Community College Enterprise*, *12*(1), 39–55.

Sedikides, C. (1993). Assessment, enhancement, and verification determinants of the self-evaluation process. *Journal of Personality and Social Psychology*, *65*(2), 317–338. doi:10.1037/0022-3514.65.2.317

Shute, V. (2008). Focus on Formative Feedback. *Review of Educational Research*, *78*(1), 153–189. doi:10.3102/0034654307313795

Song, K. H. (2006). A conceptual model of assessing teaching performace and intellectual development of teacher candidates: A pilot study in the US. *Teaching in Higher Education*, *11*(2), 175–190. doi:10.1080/13562510500527701

Stake, R. (1995). *The art of case study research.* Thousand Oaks, CA: Sage.

Swan, K. (2003). Learning effectiveness: What the research tells us. In J. Bourne & J. C. Moore (Eds.), *Elements of quality online education, practice and direction.* Needham, MA: Sloan Center for Online Education.

Taras, M. (1999). Student self-assessment as a means of promoting student autonomy and independence. In M. Taras (Ed.), *Innovations in Learning and Teaching: teaching fellowships at the Univesrity of Sunderland.* Sunderland, UK: University of Sunderland Press.

Taras, M. (2010). To feedback or not to feedback in student self-assessment. *Assessment & Evaluation in Higher Education*, *28*(5), 549–565. doi:10.1080/02602930301678

Taylor, S. (2014). Student self-assessment and multisource feedback assessment: Exploring benefits, limitations, and remedies. *Journal of Management Education*, *38*(3), 359–383. doi:10.1177/1052562913488111

Thomas, M. (2003). Internet-Based Education and Training: Using new Technologies to Facilitate Instruction and Enhance Learning. In A. Henley (Ed.), *Aviation Education and Training: Adult Learning Principles and Teaching Strategies* (pp. 342–362). Ashgate.

Tu, C. H. (2005). From presentation to interaction: New goals for online learning. *Educational Media International*, *42*(3), 189–206. doi:10.1080/09523980500161072

Walser, T. (2009). An action research study of student self-assessment in higher education. *Innovative Higher Education*, *34*(5), 299–306. doi:10.1007/s10755-009-9116-1

Wanstreet, C. E. (2006). Interactions in online learning environments. *The Quarterly Review of Distance Education*, *7*(4), 399–411.

Winter, S., Rice, S., Reid, K., & Rian, M. (2015). Consistency of aviation students when taking the private pilot knowledge exam. *Journal of Aviation/Aerospace Education & Research, 24*(2), 21-38.

Witt, P. L., Wheeless, L. R., & Allen, M. (2004). A meta-analytical review of the relationship between teacher immediacy and student learning. *Communication Monographs, 71*(2), 184–207. doi:10.1080/036452042000228054

Wolsey, T. (2008). Efficacy of instructor feedback on written work in an online program. *International Journal on E-Learning, 7*(2), 311–329.

Yin, R. K. (1994). *Case study research: Design and methods* (2nd ed.). Thousand Oaks, CA: Sage.

Chapter 12
Using Audio and Video Feedback to Increase Instructor Presence in Asynchronous Online Courses

Larisa Olesova
George Mason University, USA

Jered Borup
George Mason University, USA

ABSTRACT

Due to a growing number of online courses and programs, educators' interest in using audio and video feedback in asynchronous online environment has increased. Studies have found evidence that the use of audio and video feedback in asynchronous online courses can increase instructor presence and enhance online community interactions. The purpose of this chapter is to share research findings on audio and video feedback and to overview qualities of effective feedback. The chapter also presents potential benefits and limitations of audio and video feedback in online environments. Researchers and practitioners interested in implementing both types of feedback in online courses will find solutions, recommendations and possible future research directions.

INTRODUCTION

Online courses in U.S. higher education continue to gain popularity. According to the 2014 Babson Survey Research Group report on online education in the United States, the growth in distance enrollments in public institutions is over 160,000 students, at a rate of 4.6% in 2012-2013 (Allen & Seaman, 2015). However, this growth has occurred despite attrition rates that are believed to exceed their face-to-face counterparts. While the cause of this phenomenon is complex, some have pointed to student isolation and poor instructor feedback as contributing factors (Palloff & Pratt, 2007). The majority of online courses have relied predominantly on text-based feedback and communication (Parsad & Lewis, 2009).

DOI: 10.4018/978-1-4666-9995-3.ch012

Although there are several advantages of text-based communication, it lacks communication cues making it difficult to establish instructor presence, resulting in some students feeling isolated and perceiving text communication as restrictive (Palloff & Pratt, 2007). The lack of verbal cues in text-based online communication can also cause misunderstandings and difficulties in interpreting words correctly among students and instructors. Graham (2006) summarized, "Many learners want the convenience offered by a distributed environment yet do not want to sacrifice the social interaction and human touch they are used to in a face-to-face classroom" (p. 9).

Therefore, instructors play a critical role in overcoming the limitations of text-based communication and providing a successful online learning experience for students (Anderson, Rourke, Garrison, & Archer, 2001; Swan, 2003). Indeed, the instructor's role to provide guided instruction, encourage critical reflection, and give constructive feedback may enable students to overcome the limitations of text-based learning environments (Biesenbach-Lucas, 2003) and establish instructor presence (Garrison, Anderson, & Archer, 2000). As a result researchers and practitioners are increasingly looking to new and more effective techniques to promote instructor-student connections while still maintaining the same level of flexibility that has made online learning popular and accessible. One technique, audio and video feedback, has demonstrated that it can strengthen the instructor's ability to affect learning and personalize instructors' communication with students (Borup, West, & Graham, 2012; Ice, Curtis, Phillips, & Wells, 2007).

The purpose of this chapter is to help instructional designers, media specialists, and instructors implement audio and video feedback in ways that increase instructor presence in asynchronous online environments. This chapter overviews what literature suggests about instructional capabilities of both types of feedback and how they support the instructor presence in online courses. This chapter also discusses research findings on the benefits and limitations of both types of feedback for students when they enroll in asynchronous online courses.

BACKGROUND

Anderson (2009) explained that "Distance education has always been to a great degree determined by the technologies of the day...As these technologies have developed, distance education has evolved in parallel to support new forms of interaction, pedagogy and support services" (p. 111). In the early 20th century, distance education courses focused on learner-content interactions and had little personalized human-to-human interactions. Typically learning materials were mailed to students who then completed the work with little to no formative feedback and then mailed the completed work back for it to be assessed by a content expert (Clark, 2007). As communication technology improved, instructors were able to personally communicate with students via the phone. However, phone calls were logistically difficult to coordinate because it required the instructor and student to arrange a common time to talk, often across time zones (Kirschner, van den Brink, & Meester, 1991). As a result, some instructors attempted to simplify the process by mailing students audiotaped feedback on student papers that need more complex response (Harris, 1970; Tanner, 1964).

With the advent of the Internet, distance education enrollments grew at unprecedented rates. These courses were also distinctly different from their predecessors because the Internet enabled a high level of personalized text communication and little cost. The distinction was so stark that Garrison argued

(2009) online learning should not be used synonymously with distance education, as commonly done in the field. Although online courses still rely predominantly on text feedback, faster Internet connections have allowed online instructors to easily provide audio, and even video, feedback to students. One of the first studies on using audio feedback in a distance education course was conducted in the 1980s by Kelly and Ryan (1983). Later, Kirschner et al. (1991) conducted an experiment using audio feedback that was mailed to students regarding their written essays in distance education. The study was conducted at the Open University of the Netherlands for a university level course in photochemistry. Further, the Joint Information Systems Committee, one of the projects in Great Britain, explored the ways of improving human-to-human interactions through the use of digital audio and screen-visual feedback technology. The project aims at the use of emerged technologies in distance education, such as mp3 audio files (Rotheram, 2007), iPod (Nortcliffe & Middleton, 2007), and podcasting (France & Wheeler, 2007; Hill, 2008). The studies are consistent in findings that computerized technologies could speed up the learning process, support a range of learners' styles, increase student engagement through reflection, and give more flexibility for students. For example, students can pause, rewind, and play audio feedback again to make notes while listening.

There are several types of feedback that fit within the larger categories of audio and video feedback. For instance, within audio feedback the following types can be identified:

- **MP3 Audio File:** This is previously recorded feedback on students' assignments, which students can listen to as they read along the instructional comments in the text (Ice, 2008).
- **Embedded Audio Feedback:** Audio comments inserted or embedded in documents such as Microsoft Word or Adobe Acrobat Professional (Ice et al., 2007).
- **Video Feedback:**
    - **Webcam Recording:** Video that only shows the instructor talking to the student about the students' work.
    - **Screencast Recording:** Video that shows the instructors computer screen with audio of the instructor talking to the student. This may also include a smaller window containing a webcam video of the instructor.

Qualities of Effective Feedback

Feedback is one of the core principles of teaching practice (Arbaugh & Hornik, 2006; Chickering & Gamson, 1987) and plays an important role in encouraging and consolidating the learning process (Hyland & Hyland, 2006). Feedback is defined as information provided by an agent (e.g., teacher, peer, book, parent, self, experience) regarding aspects of one's performance or understanding (Hattie & Timperley, 2007) in a way that allows comparison between an actual outcome and a desired outcome (Mory, 2004). Moore (1993) added that feedback should go beyond correction and is an opportunity for instructors to provide important "counsel, support, and engagement" (p. 21).

Gibbs and Simpson (2004-05) reviewed a wide range of studies on feedback to elaborate seven conditions under which feedback may influence students' learning and increase academic success. Gibbs and Simpson's seven conditions are that the feedback: 1) is sufficiently detailed and frequent; 2) focuses on students' performance, on their learning and on actions under students' control, rather than on the students themselves and on their characteristics; 3) timely in that it is received by students while it still matters to them and in time for them to pay attention to further learning or receive further assistance; 4) is appropriate to the purpose of the assignment and to its criteria for success; 5) is appropriate in relation to students' understanding of what they are supposed to be doing; 6) is received and attended to; and 7) acted upon by the students.

Feedback is also viewed as a socially constructed process (Lea & Street, 1998). In a constructivist context, feedback is provided in the form of discussion to help students improve learning, reflection, and academic performance (Mory, 2004; Quinton & Smallbone, 2010). Further, Nicol and Macfarlane-Dick (2006) have emphasized the principles of good feedback in relation to learner self-regulation in learning. Nicol (2006) has suggested that students' self-assessment is at "the heart" of formative feedback; students use the feedback message to modify their own work and improve their own performance. Nicol and Macfarlane-Dick's seven principles of good feedback practice include the following: 1) helps clarify what good performance is (goal, criteria, and standards); 2) facilitates the development of self-assessment and reflection in learning; 3) delivers high quality information to students about their learning; 4) encourages teacher and peer dialogue around learning; 5) encourages positive motivational beliefs and self-esteem; 6) provides opportunities to close the gap between current and desired performance; and 7) provides information to teachers that can be used to help shape teaching (p.3).

To understand students' perception of the effectiveness of feedback, Poulos and Mahony (2008) in their qualitative analysis elaborated the key themes related to the effectiveness of feedback: 1) students' perceptions of feedback were related to the individual meaning attributed to the feedback, the accessibility of lectures to provide feedback, types of feedback, feedback related to criteria, marks and comments; 2) the impact of feedback was related to timeliness, significance and first-year experience. Timeliness related to the need for feedback as early as possible; and 3) credibility of feedback was related to the students' perceptions of the lecturers themselves. The lecturers' ability generally and also their biases influenced the credibility of the feedback they provided (p. 145).

Similarly, Quinton and Smallbone (2010) stated that students need formative feedback that helps them make connections between the characteristics of their work and the way to improve their work in the future. By reviewing applications of feedback in constructivism, Mory (2004) stated that feedback in a constructivist context would provide intellectual tools and serve as an aid to help the learner to construct his or her internal reality. Further, Mory (2004) emphasized the findings of other studies that feedback would enhance intellectual skills (Char, 1978) and might not impact higher-level tasks (Gaynor, 1981; Wager, 1983).

Although feedback is critical in any education context, in online courses the role of feedback becomes one of the most important instructional strategies because students in asynchronous online courses can feel especially stressed, disconnected, or left behind when they do not receive any feedback on their participation (Ertmer, Richardson, Belland, Camin, Connolly, Coulthard, Lei, & Mong, 2007). Schwartz and White (2000) specified the qualities of online feedback, such as multidimensional, nonevaluative, supportive, student controlled, timely, and specific. Mory (2004) outlined the following qualities for online feedback: 1) prompt, timely, and thorough on-line feedback; 2) ongoing formative feedback about on-line group discussions; 3) ongoing summative feedback about grades; 4) constructive, supportive, and substantive on-line feedback; 5) specific, objective, and individual on-line feedback; and 6) consistent on-line feedback (p. 776). In addition, Vasilyeva, Puuronen, Pechenizkiy, and Räsänen (2007) classified the following functions of online feedback: 1) confirming getting the user's response; 2) informing the user about his or her performance (how many tasks were performed, number and ratio of correct answers, time of test processing, etc.); 3) correcting the user (in the case she or he has not given a correct answer); 4) explaining (the feedback could include an explanation about the reasons the user's answer was considered correct or guidance to the correct answers in the case of a wrong answer); 5) evaluating (for example, in the case of an answer until correct feedback); 6) motivating the user; 7) rewarding the user; and 8) attracting his or her attention (p. 11).

In summary, there have been several researchers have attempted to identify to attributes of effective feedback in face-to-face and online learning settings. Although their research addresses a breadth of issues, most of them can be encompassed into three categories:

- **Timing:** Feedback is provided and reviewed in a timely manner that allows students to use the feedback in ways that improve practice.
- **Content and Clarity:** The messages provided to students from the instructor clearly and sufficiently identifies the performance gap and provides necessary information for improving student application of the content.
- **Teacher-Student Relationship Building:** The feedback creates a sense of closeness and care that is motivating and rewarding the student and does not harm students' self-worth and esteem.

The following section will discuss the research that has identified the dimensions of quality feedback and how audio and video feedback may impact the quality of the feedback that is provided.

POTENTIAL BENEFITS OF AUDIO AND VIDEO FEEDBACK

The central component of audio and video feedback provided in online courses is the asynchronous aspect of the instructional comments (Ice, 2008). Audio and video feedback, defined as previously recorded instructional comments, has been viewed as a means to overcome the lack of clarity in text-based communication, to speed up feedback delivery, and to increase student-instructor relationship.

Timing

When students actually receive feedback is especially important in light of research that has found the more time that laps between when the student completes a task and when feedback is provided, the less likely it is that the students will actually use the provided feedback (Wolsey, 2008). Unfortunately, a large study that included 3,135 student survey participants in nearly 150 post-secondary institutions found that 80% of the participants reported commonly waiting three or more weeks for instructor feedback. However, what exactly constitutes effective feedback is difficult to define and appears to be somewhat idiosyncratic. For instance Getzlaf, Perry, Toffner, Lamarche, & Edwards (2009) found that student perceptions of timely feedback ranged from one day to two weeks and was somewhat dependent on the nature of the task that was completed (Getzalf et al., 2009).

Studies in the 1970s and 1980s have examined the time commitment for audio feedback and for written feedback (Clark, 1985; Clark, 1981; Hays, 1978; Hunt, 1989; Hurst, 1975; Kahrs, 1974; Miller, 1973; Petite, 1983; Rubens, 1982; Stratton, 1975). The studies found that audio feedback changed the nature of feedback because it was different in the quantity and quality of instructor's commentary input during the same amount of time. Other studies found that even a cassette tape recorder required no more time than traditional marginal written comments, the process was more enjoyable than writing marginal comments (Sommers, 1989; Vogler, 1971). Moxley (1989) also found taped evaluation of students' papers a powerful and effective way to provide a more efficient use of grading time than marginal comments; instructors could use time more effectively. Similarly, in other experimental research, Carson and McTasney (1973) undertook a pilot cassette-grading program in a technical writing course at the United States Air Force Academy in need of a better grading method. The researchers found that cassette grading allowed the time to explain without exceeding the limits of allotted time in order that students might learn to write. Low cost, privacy with the use of the portable earphone and the ready availability of playback equipment were also advantages in using cassette grading.

More recent research has compared video/audio feedback and text feedback but results have been mixed. Two small case studies found that video (Silva, 2012) and audio (Wood, Moskovitz & Valiga, 2011) feedback was more efficient to create and provide than text. However, a larger study by Borup, West, & Thomas (2015) found that the majority of instructors perceived text feedback to be more efficient because they could easily copy and paste comments for students with similar projects. Instructors also preferred text because they provide it on their mobile devices nearly anywhere whereas they had to be in a quiet location to provide video feedback. Lastly, several instructors encountered technological problems that lessened the efficiency of video feedback, supporting Hew and Cheung (2012) previous warning that technological issues can dramatically increase the amount of time required to provide feedback. However, two instructors actually found text to be more efficient because of "their poor typing and writing skills" (p. 176). Instructors also reported that video feedback was more efficient when they had to provide students with extensive feedback concerning unique aspects of student work. Borup et al. (2015) summarized that the efficiency of providing feedback "is influenced by the communication tool used, instructors' familiarity with that tool, the nature of the assignment, and instructors' communication abilities" (p. 165).

The large majority of the research has only examined the time that it takes teachers to create audio and video feedback and have ignored the amount of time that it takes students to view, listen, or read the feedback. While it's true that instructors can speak faster than they write, students can read and skim text feedback faster than the time it takes to listen to the instructor speaking at a conversational pace (Borup et al., 2015; Rodway-Dyer, Knight, & Dunne, 2011). Furthermore the nature of audio and video feedback can make it more difficult for students to refer back to specific comments within the feedback (Borup et al., 2015). Perhaps it is not surprising that students in Moore and Filling's (2012) case study felt that feedback approaching 20 minutes was excessive.

Content and Clarity

Research has found that in general feedback lacks the level of detail that students desire and require (Price, Handley, Millar, & O'Donovan, 2010; Wolsey, 2008). Mutch (2003) explained that it should not be surprising that "feedback is often terse" (p. 31) considering the time constraints that are placed on instructors. However, providing lengthy feedback in and of itself does not signify quality. Feedback should but correct and confirm students' application in specific and meaningful ways (Price et al., 2010). However, simply identifying the gap between students' current abilities and mastery is not sufficient and instructors should also provide students with resources and supports to help them bridge the gap (Wiliam, 2011). A common obstacle is that students are unable to understand and interpret feedback comments correctly (Higgins, 2000; Quinton & Smallbone, 2010). Indeed, to interpret feedback comments correctly, students need meaningful and clear instructional comments (Biesenbach-Lucas, 2003; Rossman, 1999).

The first research on audio feedback in face-to-face environments has described its effectiveness in providing students with in-depth evaluations of their writing in comparison to traditional marginal written comments (Lumsden, 1962; McGrew, 1969; Tanner, 1964). Studies have found that audio feedback may help students understand instructional feedback better than written comments because the instructor speaks directly to each student on tape, adapting tone, inflection, and explanation to the particular student (Boswood & Dwyer, 1995; Olsen, 1982; Lunt & Curran, 2010; Rodway-Dyer et al., 2011).

While examining the time commitment for audio feedback, other early studies found that the instructor can say much more and can say it more clearly (Klammer, 1973; Logan, Logan, Fuller, & Denehy, 1976). The researchers found that an instructor can speak at least five times faster than he or she can write, which means that audio feedback can convey more information in the same amount of time. This, in turn, may mean that the student no longer feels the need to corner the instructor for so many personal explanations of trivial matters (Klammer, 1973). Hunt (1975) examined how the method could save instructor's time and found that even the method did not save time, it allowed for extensive and more detailed instructional comments. Concerns about misunderstanding between student-writers and teacher-responders led Sommers (1989) to examine whether audio feedback was more understandable to students. The study found that audio feedback allowed instructors to make comments more clearly and in a more detailed fashion. Patrie (1989) found that audio feedback encourages qualitative changes in the content and focus of instructors' comments; it allows putting more feedback because we talk a lot faster than we write.

Research findings about the impact of audio feedback in an online course have reported that students were highly satisfied about effectiveness of using audio feedback and it increased retention of content (Ice, Swan, Kupczynski, & Richardson, 2008). Ice (2008) revealed that students found their ability to detect nuance and inflection in the audio commenting. They believed that verbal feedback gave them increased insight into what the instructor was attempting to convey nuances. Conveying nuance is very important in asynchronous online environment, because as Swan (2003) stated real-time negotiation of meaning is impossible among instructors and students separated by space and time, clarity of meaning is more important in online classes. A lack of nuance can lead to loss of meaning for participants (Ice et al, 2007).

Research examining video feedback is still emerging but the preliminary results indicate that video feedback has the same benefits of audio feedback with the added benefit of visual cues that can add further clarity and context to instructor's comments (Borup, West, Thomas, & Graham, 2014; Griffiths & Graham, 2009; Moore & Filling, 2012; Silva, 2012). For instance, Silva (2012) explained that when giving audio feedback on student writing instructors are required to provide "oral markers to orient students to specific sentences, paragraphs, or pages" (p. 4) and require the student to have their draft in hand to fully understand the feedback comments. A student in Cuthrell, Fogarty, & Anderson's (2009) research added that at times audio feedback was difficult to understand because it lacked the instructor's facial expressions. In contrast, using a screencasting tool instructor can simultaneously provide auditory and visual context that can reduce students' cognitive load and provide a level of clarity that is difficult when visual cues are absent (Borup et al., 2015). Borup et al. (2015) also found that when instructors switched from text to video feedback not only did the word count of the feedback nearly double, on average instructors included more comments that provided students with specific praise and support. However, they also found that text feedback contained slightly more comments that provided students with specific corrections.

Instructor-Student Relationships

In an effort to better understand the effectiveness of audio and video feedback, some studies (Oomen-Early, Bold, Wiginton, Gallien, & Anderson, 2008; Simonsson, Kupczynski, Ice, & Pankake, 2009) have measured the effects of audio and video feedback on course design and teacher-student relationships. A common lens that researchers have used to examine teacher-student relationships is the concept of social presence. Social presence was originally defined as the "degree of salience" of those in mediated communication (Short, Williams, and Christie, 1976). Initially, social presence was considered to be an objective measure of the communication tool—the more communication cues that the tool could transmit the more social presence it contained. However, the concept of social presence has since changed into a product of behavior that can "be cultivated" by those in the mediated communication. This perception was solidified by using the Community of Inquiry (CoI) conceptual framework (Garrison et al., 2000) that defined social presence as "the ability of participants in the Community of Inquiry to project their personal characteristics into the community, thereby presenting themselves to the other participants as 'real people'" (p. 89). Although Garrison et al.'s definition emphasized that social presence was the result of participants' "ability" they acknowledged that it was more difficult to establish social presence in text-based communication as compared to modes of communication with non-verbal communication cues. Research findings have confirmed that audio and video feedback can strengthen the instructor presence and improve student engagement, knowledge of course content, and the instructor-student interaction by making feedback more personal and humanizing (Cuthrell et al., 2009; Ice et al., 2007; Kim, 2004; Wood, Moskovitz, & Valiga, 2011).

Some research has indicated that audio and video feedback can help instructors to more efficiently increase the level of information they provide while simultaneously establishing a strong sense of presence in the course. Similarly, students have reported that they feel a greater connection to their instructors when they the additional communication cues are present (Gould & Day, 2012; Ice et al., 2007; Oomen-Early et al., 2008). Likewise, Cryer and Kaikumba (1987), by looking for a more effective method of giving feedback, found that audio feedback could present feedback in a more informed, helpful and personal manner, i.e., a tone of voice to motivate or to soften criticism and give encouragement.

The visual nature of video feedback also appears to allow instructors to more efficiently establish their presence in the course (Borup et al., 2012; Griffiths, 2010; Silva, 2012). An instructor in Moore and Filling's research (2012) found that she could more easily "express herself" (p. 11) in video through facial expressions. This was confirmed by students in Borup et al.'s (2015) research who reported "more of an emotional connection" with their instructors due—in part—to instructors' facial expressions and their ability to see the instructors' surroundings. Non-verbal cues in video feedback also seemed to add credibility to instructors' positive comments.

DRAWBACKS AND LIMITATIONS

Despite the potential benefits of audio and video feedback, researchers have identified some disadvantages to these modes of communication as compared to text. For instance, while audio and video feedback can be more conversational and elaborate, text is more concise and polished. Some instructors also find creating audio or video comments to be less convenient and more time consuming. The same communication cues that make video feedback more authentic can also convey instructors' frustration and disappointment. For instance, one student explained that she felt like she was being told off when watching video feedback and an instructor acknowledged that it was more difficult to conceal his negative emotions when providing video feedback as compared to text.

The effectiveness of video and audio feedback is also somewhat dependent on the context in which it is given. Students indicated that the fidelity of video feedback is most helpful when receiving complex corrective feedback or at the start of the semester but is not necessary once the instructor-student relationship has been formed or when receiving feedback that is easily communicated in text (Borup et al., 2014). As a result instructors need to be strategic in the use of audio and video feedback and the most effective approach will likely include a combination of multiple modes of communication.

SOLUTIONS AND RECOMMENDATIONS

While providing audio and video feedback can benefit student learning, it is important to note that media alone will not impact student learning. Clark (1983) argued that instructional methods—not media—impacted learning:

[M]edia are mere vehicles that deliver instruction but do not influence student achievement any more than the truck that delivers our groceries causes changes in our nutrition. Basically, the choice of vehicle might influence the cost or extent of distributing instruction, but only the content or the vehicle can influence achievement (p. 445).

The authors of this chapter agree with Clark's assertion and do not argue that the use of audio or video communication tools alone improve student learning. There is no alcamy that changes bad feedback into good feedback just by changing the way it is transmitted. Although it is not guaranteed, research has found that the nature of verbal and visual communication can afford instructors the opportunity to more easily improve the feedback methods that they use. For instance, Graham, Henrie, and Gibbons (2014) condensed the Gibbons and Rodgers' (2009) seven layers of instructional design into two layers—the pedagogical (or method) and the physical (or media) and argued that "the physical layer can impact the availability and effectiveness of the pedagogical layer" (p. 28).

By taking into account that studies investigating audio and video feedback are consistent in their findings that the technique can lead to improved performance and increased students' motivation (Moxley, 1989; Pearce &Ackley, 1995; Yarbro & Angevine, 1982), the following pedagogical implications can be applied.

Audio and video feedback provided online can help instructor deliver meaningful and constructive feedback using the tone of voice, visual and verbal clues. Therefore, instructors are encouraged to provide both types of feedback to increase students' motivation and engagement when they enroll in asynchronous online courses. However, it would be reasonable to start from text-based feedback and give students more time to adapt to audio or video feedback. This can help students internalize feedback better in order to improve learning.

When providing audio or video feedback, instructors can help increase students' perceived feelings of the instructor care. For example, tone of instructor voice can help students overcome challenges in interpreting the comments. However, instructors should remember that there is also an emotional process that students might face while receiving audio or video feedback (Carless, 2006). Sometimes it is difficult for instructors to hide their real, sometimes negative or angry, attitude towards student's work while recording audio or video feedback (Borup et al., 2015). It is highly recommended to record audio or video feedback when the instructor is ready to provide constructive and meaningful feedback.

Furthermore, the length of audio or video files is important. It is recommended to use direct instructional comments on the major points and keep feedback short. For example, the audio file size should be small and whether it is possible to use mono recording. This will allow students download the audio file easily when the Internet connection is slow.

Lastly, instructors need to understand the benefits and drawbacks for providing feedback via text, audio, and video and then select the mode of communication that best fits students' needs. Borup et al. (2015) explained "Therein lies both the challenge and the imperative for the modern online instructor—to understand what media options are available and when to use them" (p. 181).

FUTURE RESEARCH DIRECTIONS

To summarize, taking into consideration that instructional feedback may influence overall student learning and students need constructive feedback to improve their work in the future, further research is needed to examine if audio and video feedback is effective within constructivist learning environments, specifically, in asynchronous online environments. Further research is needed to investigate other types of feedback (e.g., combined written and audio feedback) to determine the value of both types of feedback in online course (Ice, Swan, Diaz, Kupczynski, & Swan-Dagen, 2010). Other types of formats for providing audio feedback are also needed. In addition, more research is needed to examine the effectiveness of the technique across other disciplines and other categories in order to apply findings to larger populations of students. Finally, further research is needed using instructors with diverse backgrounds, i.e. different native languages and ethnicities to examine whether the results may vary.

CONCLUSION

From a constructivist perspective, asynchronous online courses can support students' learning by engaging them in discussions to construct their own knowledge (Romiszowski & Mason, 2004). Asynchronous online courses can enhance rich interactions and flexibility between students and instructors by removing transactional distance when teaching and learning occur in separate locations (Moore, 2007). In addition, asynchronous online courses, by providing time to read and respond to a message, can support the possibility for greater student reflection and critical thinking (Romiszowski & Mason, 2004). However, asynchronous online courses with their flexibility, interaction, and open communication at any time and at any place may present drawbacks or limitations such as the lack of non-verbal cues in text-based communication (Cifuente & Shih, 2001). It is known that text-based online communication can cause difficulties in students' understanding of each other, difficulties in interpreting words correctly, or in understanding specific references (Gunawardena & McIsaac, 2004).

To increase both the verbal and nonverbal cues of asynchronous online interactions, studies have proposed using asynchronous audio or video, specifically, instructional audio or video feedback (Ice et al., 2007; Ice, Swan, Kupczynski, & Richardson, 2008). Audio and video feedback has demonstrated that it can strengthen the instructor's ability to affect learning and to generate more personalized communication with students (Ice et al., 2007).

Research has found video and audio feedback more elaborative and detailed. Video and audio feedback has also been shown to foster a sense of instructor presence by reducing the transactional distance that commonly exists in learning environments where the instructor and student are separated in space and time. However, these benefits are not without their costs and students have reported that text feedback can be more effective in some contexts. As a result, instructors should be strategic in their use of audio and video feedback.

REFERENCES

Allen, I. E., & Seaman, J. (2015). *Grade level: Tracking online education in the United States.* Retrieved from http://www.onlinelearningsurvey.com/reports/gradelevel.pdf

Anderson, T. (2009). A rose by any other name : Still distance education — a response to D. R. Garrison : Implications of online and blended learning for the conceptual development and practice of distance education. *Journal of Distance Education*, *23*(3), 111–116.

Anderson, T., Rourke, L., Garrison, D. R., & Archer, W. (2001). Assessing teaching presence in a computer conferencing context. *Journal of Asynchronous Learning Networks*, *5*(2), 1–17.

Arbaugh, J. B., & Hornik, S. (2006). Do Chickering and Gamson's seven principles also apply to online MBAs? *The Journal of Educators Online*, *3*(2), 1–18.

Biesenbach-Lucas, S. (2003). Asynchronous discussion groups in teacher training classes: Perceptions of native and non-native students. *Journal of Asynchronous Learning Networks*, *7*(3), 24–46.

Borup, J., West, R. E., & Graham, C. R. (2012). Improving online social presence through asynchronous video. *The Internet and Higher Education*, *15*(3), 195–203. doi:10.1016/j.iheduc.2011.11.001

Borup, J., West, R. E., & Thomas, R. (2015). The impact of text versus video communication on instructor feedback in blended courses. *Educational Technology Research and Development*, *63*(2), 161–184. doi:10.1007/s11423-015-9367-8

Borup, J., West, R. E., Thomas, R. A., & Graham, C. R. (2014). Examining the impact of video feedback on instructor social presence in blended courses. *International Review of Research in Open and Distance Learning*, *15*(3), 232–256. Retrieved from http://www.irrodl.org/index.php/irrodl/article/view/1821

Boswood, T., & Dwyer, R. (1995). From marking to feedback: Audio-taped response to student writing. *TESOL Journal*, *5*(2), 20–23.

Carless, D. (2006). Differing perceptions in the feedback process. *Studies in Higher Education*, *31*(2), 219–233. doi:10.1080/03075070600572132

Carson, D.L., & McTasney, J.B. (1973). Grading technical reports with the cassette tape recorder: The results of a test program at the United States Air Force Academy. *Journal of Technical Writing and Communication, 3,* 131-144.

Char, R. O. (1978). *The effect of delay of informative feedback on the retention of verbal information and higher-order learning, for college students*. (Unpublished doctoral dissertation). Florida State University.

Chickering, A. W., & Gamson, Z. (1987). Seven principles for good practice in undergraduate education. *AAHE Bulletin*, *40*(7), 3–7.

Cifuentes, L., & Shih, Y.-C. D. (2001). Teaching and learning online: A collaboration between United States and Taiwanese students. *Journal of Research on Technology in Education*, *33*(4), 456–474.

Clark, I. L. (1985). Audiotapes and the basic writer: A selected survey of useful materials. *Teaching English in the Two-Year College*, *12*, 120–129.

Clark, R. E. (1983). Reconsidering research on learning from media. *Review of Educational Research*, *53*(4), 445–459. doi:10.3102/00346543053004445

Clark, T. (2007). Virtual and distance education in North American schools. In M. G. Moore (Ed.), *Handbook of distance education* (2nd ed.; pp. 473–490). Mahwah, NJ: Lawrence Earlbaum Associates.

Clark, T. D. (1981). Cassette tapes: An answer to the grading dilemma. *The American Business Communication Association Bulletin*, *44*(2), 40–41.

Cryer, P., & Kaikumba, N. (1987). Audio-cassette tape as a means of giving feedback on written work. *Assessment & Evaluation in Higher Education*, *12*(2), 148–153. doi:10.1080/0260293870120207

Cuthrell, K., Fogarty, E., & Anderson, P. (2009). 'Is this thing on?' University Student Preferences Regarding Audio Feedback. In I. Gibson et al. (Eds.), *Proceedings of Society for Information Technology & Teacher Education International Conference 2009* (pp. 32-35). Chesapeake, VA: AACE.

Ertmer, P. A., Richardson, J. C., Belland, B., Camin, D., Connolly, P., & Coulthard, G. et al. (2007). Using peer feedback to enhance the quality of student online postings: An exploratory study. *Journal of Computer-Mediated Communication*, *12*(2), 412–433. doi:10.1111/j.1083-6101.2007.00331.x

France, D., & Wheeler, A. (2007). Reflections on using podcasting for student feedback. *Planet, 18*. Retrieved from http://www.gees.ac.uk/planet/p18/df2.pdf

Garrison, D. R., Anderson, T., & Archer, W. (2000). Critical inquiry in a text-based environment: Computer conferencing in higher education. *The Internet and Higher Education*, *2*(2-3), 87–105. doi:10.1016/S1096-7516(00)00016-6

Garrison, R. (2000). Theoretical challenges for distance education in the 21st Century: A shift from structural to transactional issues. *International Review of Research in Open and Distance Learning*, *1*(1), 1–17.

Garrison, R. (2009). Implications of online learning for the conceptual development and practice of distance education. *Journal of Distance Education*, *23*(2), 93–104.

Gaynor, P. (1981). The effect of feedback delay on retention of computer-based mathematical material. *Journal of Computer-Based Instruction*, *8*(2), 28–34.

Getzlaf, B., Perry, B., Toffner, G., Lamarche, K., & Edwards, M. (2009). Effective instructor feedback: Perceptions of online Graduate students. *The Journal of Educators Online*, *6*(2), 1–22.

Gibbs, G., & Simpson, C. (2004-05). Conditions under which assessment supports students' learning. *Learning and Teaching in Higher Education*, *1*, 3–31.

Gould, J., & Day, P. (2013). Hearing you loud and clear: Student perspectives of audio feedback in higher education. *Assessment & Evaluation in Higher Education*, 38(5), 554-56. http://dx.doi.org/10.1080/02602938.2012.660131.

Graham, C. R. (2006). Blended learning systems: Definition, current trends, and future directions. In C. J. Bonk & C. R. Graham (Eds.), *Handbook of blended learning: Global perspectives, local designs* (pp. 3–21). San Francisco, CA: Pfeiffer Publishing.

Graham, C. R., Henrie, C. R., & Gibbons, A. S. (2014). Developing models and theory for blended learning research. In A. G. Picciano, C. D. Dziuban, & C. R. Graham (Eds.), *Blended learning: Research perspectives* (Vol. 2, pp. 13–33). New York, NY: Taylor & Francis.

Griffiths, M. E. (2010). *Improving the Asynchronous Video Learning Model*. Brigham Young University.

Gunawardena, C. N., & McIsaac, M. S. (2004). Distance education. In D. H. Jonassen (Ed.), *Handbook of research on educational communications and technology* (pp. 355–395). Mahwah, NJ: Lawrence Erlbaum.

Harris, J. S. (1970). The use of the tape recorder in grading. *Brigham Young University Mediated Learning Systems MLS Newsletter*, *2*(3), 1–2.

Hattie, J., & Timperley, H. (2007). The power of feedback. *Review of Educational Research*, *77*(1), 81–112. doi:10.3102/003465430298487

Hays, J. (1978). *Play it again, Sandra: The use of tape cassettes to evaluate student compositions*. Paper presented at the Annual Meeting of the Conference on College Composition and Communication (ERIC Document Reproduction Service No. ED 162332).

Hew, K., & Cheung, W. (2012). Students' use of asynchronous voice discussion in a blended-learning environment: A study of two undergraduate classes. *Electronic Journal of E-Learning*, *10*(4), 360–367.

Higgins, R. (2000, September). *Be more critical': rethinking assessment feedback*. Paper presented at the British Educational Research Association Conference, Cardiff, UK. Retrieved from http://www.leeds.ac.uk/educol/documents/00001548.htm

Hill, D. (2008). *The use of podcasts in the delivery of feedback to dissertation students*. Retrieved from http://www.heacademy.ac.uk/assets/hlst/documents/case_studies/case123_apr08_podcasts_feedback_dissertation_students.pdf

Hunt, A. (1989). Taped comments and student writing. *Teaching English in the Two-Year College*, *16*(4), 269–273.

Hunt, R. A. (1975). Technological gift-horse: Some reflections on the teeth of cassette-marking. *College English*, *36*(5), 581–585. doi:10.2307/374823

Hurst, C. J. (1975). Cassette grading improves student report writing. *English Education*, *65*, 429–430.

Hyland, K., & Hyland, F. (Eds.). (2006). *Feedback in second language writing: Contexts and issues*. New York, NY: Cambridge University Press. doi:10.1017/CBO9781139524742

Ice, P. (2008, April). *The impact of asynchronous audio feedback on teaching, social and cognitive presence.* Paper presented at the First International Conference of the Canadian Network for Innovation in Education, Banff, Canada.

Ice, P., Curtis, R., Phillips, P., & Wells, J. (2007). Using asynchronous audio feedback to enhance teaching presence and students' sense of community. *Journal of Asynchronous Learning Networks*, *11*(2), 3–25.

Ice, P., Swan, K., Diaz, S., Kupczynski, L., & Swan-Dagen, A. (2010). An analysis of students' perceptions of the value and efficacy of instructors' auditory and text-based feedback modalities across multiple conceptual levels. *Journal of Educational Computing Research*, *43*(1), 113–134. doi:10.2190/EC.43.1.g

Ice, P., Swan, K., Kupczynski, L., & Richardson, J. (2008). The impact of asynchronous audio feedback on teaching and social presence: A survey of current research. In *Proceedings of World Conference on Educational Multimedia, Hypermedia and Telecommunications 2008* (pp. 5646-5649). Chesapeake, VA: AACE.

Kahrs, K. A. (1974). Cassette tapes: A medium for personal feedback and learning. *Physical Educator*, *31*, 159–161.

Kelly, P., & Ryan, S. (1983). Using tutor tapes to support the distance learner. *International Council for Distance Education Bulletin*, *3*, 1–18.

Kim, L. (2004). Online technologies for teaching writing: Students react to teacher response in voice and written modalities. *Research in the Teaching of English*, *38*(3), 304–337.

Kirschner, P. A., van den Brink, H., & Meester, M. (1991). Audiotape feedback for essays in distance education. *Innovative Higher Education*, *15*(2), 185–195. doi:10.1007/BF00898030

Klammer, E. (1973). Cassettes in the classroom. *College English*, *35*(2), 179–189. doi:10.2307/375445

Lea, M., & Street, B. (1998). Student writing in higher education: An academic literacies approach. *Studies in Higher Education*, *23*(2), 157–172. doi:10.1080/03075079812331380364

Logan, H. L., Logan, N. S., Fuller, J. L., & Denehy, G. E. (1976). The role of audiotape cassettes in providing student feedback. *Educational Technology*, *16*(12), 38–39.

Lumsden, R. (1962). Evanston, Illinois, Township High School Adds to its Program: The use of dictation machines in grading English themes. *The Bulletin of the National Association of Secondary School Principals*, 223-226.

Lunt, T., & Curran, J. (2010). "Are you listening please?" The advantages of electronic audio feedback compared to written feedback. *Assessment & Evaluation in Higher Education*, *35*(7), 759–769. doi:10.1080/02602930902977772

McGrew, J.B. (1969). *An experiment to assess the effectiveness of the dictation machine as an aid to teachers in the evaluations and improvement of student compositions*. Report to Lincoln Public Schools, Lincoln, NE (ERIC Document Reproductive Service No. ED 034776).

Miller, D. C. (1973). The audio tape cassette in education. *English Education*, *63*(6), 413–440.

Moore, M. G. (1993). Three types of interaction. In K. Harry, M. John, & D. Keegan (Eds.), *Distance education: New perspectives* (pp. 19–24). New York, NY.

Moore, M. G. (2007). The theory of transactional distance. In M. G. Moore (Ed.), *Handbook of distance education* (pp. 89–105). Mahwah, NJ: Lawrence Erlbaum.

Moore, N. S., & Filling, M. L. (2012). iFeedback: Using video technology for improving student writing. *Journal of College Literacy & Learning*, *38*, 3–14.

Mory, E. H. (2004). Feedback research revisited. In D. H. Jonassen (Ed.), *Handbook of research on educational communications and technology* (pp. 745–783). Mahwah, NJ: Lawrence Erlbaum.

Moxley, J.M. (1989). Responding to student writing: Goals, methods, alternatives. *Freshman English News*, 3-11.

Mutch, A. (2003). Exploring the practice of feedback to students. *Active Learning in Higher Education*, *4*(1), 24–38. doi:10.1177/1469787403004001003

Nicol, D. J. (2006). Increasing success in first year courses: Assessment re-design, self-regulation and learning technologies. In *Proceedings of the 23rd Annual Ascilite Conference: Who's learning? Whose technology?* (pp. 589-598). The University of Sydney.

Nicol, D. J., & Macfarlane-Dick, D. (2006). Formative assessment and self-regulated learning: A model and seven principles of good feedback practice. *Studies in Higher Education*, *31*(2), 199–216. doi:10.1080/03075070600572090

Nortcliffe, A. L., & Middleton, A. (2008). A three year case study of using audio to blend the engineers learning environment. *Engineering Education: Journal of the Higher Education Academy Engineering Subject Centre*, *3*(2), 45–57. doi:10.11120/ened.2008.03020045

Olsen, G. (1982). Beyond evaluation: The recorded response to essays. *Teaching English in the Two-Year College*, *8*(2), 121–123.

Oomen-Early, J., Bold, M., Wiginton, K. L., Gallien, T. L., & Anderson, N. (2008). Using asynchronous audio communication (AAC) in the online classroom: A comparative study. *Journal of Online Learning and Teaching*, *4*(3).

Palloff, R. M., & Pratt, K. (2007). *Building Online Learning Communities: Effective Strategies for the Virtual Classroom* (2nd ed.). San Francisco, CA: Jossey-Bass.

Parsad, B., & Lewis, L. (2009). *Distance education at degree-granting postsecondary institutions: 2006–07. World Wide Web Internet And Web Information Systems.* Retrieved from http://nces.ed.gov/pubs2009/2009044.pdf

Patrie, K. (1989). The use of the tape recorder in an ESL composition programme. *TESL Canada Journal*, *6*(2), 87–89.

Pearce, C., & Ackley, R. (1995). Audiotaped feedback in business writing: An exploratory study. *Business Communication Quarterly*, *58*(3), 31–34. doi:10.1177/108056999505800306

Petite, J. (1983). Tape recorders and tutoring. *Teaching English in the Two-Year College*, *9*, 123–125.

Poulos, A., & Mahony, M. J. (2008). Effectiveness of feedback: The students' perspective. *Assessment & Evaluation in Higher Education*, *33*(2), 143–154. doi:10.1080/02602930601127869

Price, M., Handley, K., Millar, J., & O'Donovan, B. (2010). Feedback: All that effort, but what is the effect? *Assessment & Evaluation in Higher Education*, *35*(3), 277–289. doi:10.1080/02602930903541007

Quinton, S., & Smallbone, T. (2010). Feeding forward: Using feedback to promote student reflection and learning – a teaching model. *Innovations in Education and Teaching International*, *47*(1), 125–135. doi:10.1080/14703290903525911

Rodway-Dyer, S., Knight, J., & Dunne, E. (2011). A case study on audio feedback with geography undergraduates. *Journal of Geography in Higher Education*, *35*(2), 217–231. doi:10.1080/03098265.2010.524197

Romiszowski, A., & Mason, R. (2004). Computer-mediated communication. In D. H. Jonassen (Ed.), *Handbook of research on educational communications and technology* (pp. 397–431). Mahwah, NJ: Lawrence Erlbaum.

Rossman, M. H. (1999). Successful online teaching using an asynchronous learner discussion forum. *Journal of Asynchronous Learning Networks*, *3*(2), 91–97.

Rotheram, B. (2007). Using an MP3 recorder to give feedback on student assignments. *Educational Developments*, *8*(2), 7–10.

Rubens, P. M. (1982). Oral grading techniques: An interactive system for the technical writing classroom. *Technical Writing Teacher*, *10*, 41–44.

Schwartz, E., & White, K. (2000). Making sense of it all: Giving and getting online course feedback. In K. W. White & B. H. Weight (Eds.), *The online teaching guide: A handbook of attitudes, strategies, and techniques for the virtual classroom* (pp. 57–72). Boston: Allyn and Bacon.

Short, J., Williams, E., & Christie, B. (1976). *The Social Psychology of Telecommunications*. New York, NY: John Wiley & Sons.

Silva, M. L. (2012). Camtasia in the classroom: Student attitudes and preferences for video commentary or Microsoft Word comments during the revision process. *Computers and Composition*, *29*(1), 1–22. doi:10.1016/j.compcom.2011.12.001

Simonsson, M., Kupczynski, L., Ice, P., & Pankake, A. (2009, April). *The impact of asynchronous audio feedback in the dissertation advising process*. Paper presented at the American Educational Research Association Annual Meeting, San Diego, CA.

Sommers, J. (1989). The effects of tape-recorded commentary on student revision: A case study. *Journal of Teaching Writing*, *8*, 49–75.

Stratton, C. R. (1975). The electric report card: A follow-up on cassette grading. *Journal Tech Writing and Communication*, *5*(1), 17–22. doi:10.2190/PU63-TWLY-QVN2-9JJN

Swan, K. (2003). Learning effectiveness: What the research tells us. In J. Bourne & J. C. Moore (Eds.), *Elements of quality online education: Practice and direction* (pp. 13–45). Needham, MA: Sloan Consortium.

Tanner, B. (1964). Teacher to disc to student. *English Journal, 53*(5), 362–363. doi:10.2307/810191

Vasilyeva, E., Puuronen, S., Pechenizkiy, M., & Räsänen, P. (2007). Feedback adaptation in web-based learning systems. *International Journal of Continuing Engineering Education and Lifelong Learning, 17*(4/5), 337–357. doi:10.1504/IJCEELL.2007.015046

Vogler, S. H. (1971). Grading themes: A new approach, a new dimension. *English Journal, 60*(1), 70–74. doi:10.2307/813344

Wager, S. U. (1983). *The effect of immediacy and type of informative feedback on retention in a computer-assisted task.* (Unpublished doctoral dissertation). Florida State University.

Wiliam, D. (2011). What is assessment for learning? *Studies in Educational Evaluation, 37*(1), 3–14. doi:10.1016/j.stueduc.2011.03.001 PMID:22114905

Wolsey, T. D. (2008). Efficacy of instructor fedback on written work in an online program. *International Journal on E-Learning, 7*(2), 311–329.

Wood, K. A., Moskovitz, C., & Valiga, T. M. (2011). Audio feedback for student writing in online nursing courses: Exploring student and instructor reactions. *The Journal of Nursing Education, 50*(9), 540–543. doi:10.3928/01484834-20110616-04 PMID:21667881

Yarbro, R., & Angerine, B. (1982). A comparison of traditional and cassette tape English composition grading methods. *Research in the Teaching of English, 16*, 394–396.

KEY TERMS AND DEFINITIONS

Audio Feedback: A technique where instructors record their comments on students' assignments, which students can listen to as they read along the instructional comments in the text (Ice, 2008).

Distance Education: Distance education is a concept that covers the learning-teaching activities in the cognitive and/or psycho-motor and affective domains of an individual learner and a supporting organization. It is characterized by non-contiguous communication and can be carried out anywhere and at any time, which makes it attractive to adults with professional and social commitments (Holmberg, 1989, p. 168).

Instructor Presence: Multi-dimensional and consists of three areas of responsibility—design, facilitation and direct instruction. Each of these is associated with the integration of social and cognitive processes in terms of the purposeful nature of the learning experience (Arbaugh, Cleveland-Innes, Diaz, Garrison, Ice, Richardson, & Swan, 2008).

Video Feedback: A technique that combines the instructor's verbal feedback with a video of what is on the instructor's screen and/or a webcam video showing the instructor talking.

Chapter 13
Macromedia Director-MX Lessons Development (MAD-LED) Model:
The Immediacy of Online-Distance Teaching-Learning in Multimedia and Real-Time Environments

Jameson Mbale
Copperbelt University, Zambia

Manish Wadhwa
Salem State University, USA

ABSTRACT

Dissemination of teaching-learning information through online and distance-learning methods can only be effective if the materials are interactively presented among all the stakeholders, that is, the teacher, the learner, and the content itself. The content being used need to dynamically respond according to the prevailing learning circumstances that may demand the interactivity involving text, video, audio, graphics, and animation in a real-time environment. Based on this premise, Macromedia Director-MX Lessons Development system, abbreviated in this work as MAD-LED Model, was envisaged. The MAD-LED Model utilises the combination of nonverbal immediacy and multimedia Macromedia Director-MX technologies. The situational variable of teacher nonverbal immediacy is associated with student's motivation to study and is thus essential for effective classroom instruction. The multimedia Macromedia Director-MX tools such as cast, stage, score, and control panel are used to design and develop animation utilising the text, video, audio, and graphics.

DOI: 10.4018/978-1-4666-9995-3.ch013

INTRODUCTION

Online and distance learning methods are becoming highly popular these day. The growing demand is because of the ease of accessibility and reachability as compared to conventional classroom learning. In order to provide a highly interactive online and distance learning environment, Macromedia Director-MX Lessons Development Model, abbreviated as MAD-LED Model, was envisaged. It must be noted that the latest version of Macromedia Director-MX now goes by the name Adobe Director. We used an older version of the same and hence call it Macromedia Director-MX Lessons Development Model, abbreviated as MAD-LED Model. It can be easily called AD-LED Model based on the newer version name of Adobe Director and hence Adobe Director Lessons Development Model. In truth, it does not matter what this model is called, what matters is how this model is implemented and what is its impact on the online teaching and learning. The model was automated to build highly practical lessons that were demonstrated before the learners. At every lesson, the teacher, lecturer, education administrator, instructional technologists, software designers, or software developers identified the relevant resources to be used to build online lessons.

STATEMENT OF THE PROBLEM

Traditional teaching comprises of teacher and learner interacting in a classroom setting. In a lecture based class, a teacher lectures throughout the class time, and students, for the most part, listen and occasionally interact with the teacher. Also, there are students who are introvert types and don't feel comfortable interacting in front of others. This limits their interaction ability. With the advent of technology and learning tools, education became more reachable to people, including those who live in remote areas as well as those who, for some reason, could not have access to a physical classroom setting. This led to introduction of online and distance education. This was where the lesson was projected to remote site where the teacher was not physically present in the classroom. One important conclusion reported in the paper by Simonson, M. (2006), is the research that found that students have positive attitudes about online learning, and that computer anxiety is not a problem for most students. Well-designed online courses were reported to produce more positive learning outcomes and to be related to overall student satisfaction. Harris, R. A., & Nikitenko, G. O. (2014) compared the online learning with brick-and-mortar stating that, "Overall, students enrolled in the online section (cohort) performed better on the post-test than did students enrolled in traditional ''brick-and-mortar'' classes in quantitative-skill-based-course. An age variable shows that older students performed much better than younger students on the post-test."

The challenge with online mode of teaching is the delivery of practical lessons, as the teacher is not physically present as in conventional classroom setting. For the theory lessons it is acceptable as the learners just sit and listen. The lack of interaction leads to boring lectures and thus leading to short attention span and little learning. Such kind of education thus demands the preparation of online practical lessons of courses using the Information Communication Technology (ICT). That is where another challenge arises regarding the utilisation of ICT technology on the preparation of the lesson. Not only is this a matter of preparing a lesson, it needs to be highly interactive. Harasim (1996) states that "Online education shares certain fundamental characteristics with the face-to-face educational environment: interactive group communication .... [where] people can interact with one another in such formats as dyads, seminars, group projects, or role plays, take part in e-lectures, or contact the instructor, tutors, or subject experts all online" (p. 204).

It was in view of this that the MAD-LED Model was envisaged to utilise the situational variable of teacher nonverbal immediacy, which was essential to effective classroom instruction. Hackman, M. Z., and Walker, K. B. (1990) state that "Results indicate that system design and teacher immediacy behavior strongly impact student learning and satisfaction. System variables such as interactivity and clear audio and video transmission positively influenced perceived learning and satisfaction. Further, instructors who engaged in immediate behaviors such as encouraging involvement, offering individual feedback, maintaining relaxed body posture and using vocal variety were viewed more favorably." The immediacy was integrated with Multimedia Macromedia Director-MX which was used to develop practical lessons utilising the combination of text, video, audio, and graphics to form an animated lesson. The MAD-LED Model was designed and developed such that any TeLI[1] could organise all the relevant teaching resources and group them into the Cast Window (described in the subsection Macromedia Director (MD) of the section System Architecture) and then run the system which would produce a practical lesson in the form of animation. The created lessons on the MAD-LED Model were always highly interactive such that the learners took full control of the lesson.

OBJECTIVES OF THE MAD-LED TOOL

The MAD-LED tool was developed in order to accomplish the following objectives:

- Prepare Online practical lessons by the Teachers, Lecturers, and Instructors (TeLIs).
- Integrate all relevant multimedia tools in order to develop an animation that would be used in an Online practical lesson.
- Build a student learning centred tool.
- Develop a user friendly lesson preparation tool which would easily be operated by any TeLI.
- Organise the relevant teaching materials and be able to place them into the Cast Window.
- Design and write behaviors that would make the animation of the lesson behave according to the desired actions.
- Apply the behavior on the sprites and frames in a movie.
- Attach behaviors to objects in a movie by dragging and dropping them onto sprite or frame script channel.
- Prepare curriculum or syllabus, scheme of work, work sheet and lesson plan.
- Acquire video conferencing facilities.
- Use the video conferencing or Skyping to disseminate the lesson by utilising the MAD-LED tool.
- Connect the Internet to the remote campuses.
- Train the TeLIs and learners on how to use the MAD-LED tool.

ORGANISATION OF THE CHAPTER

The rest of the chapter is organised as follows. The following section is Literature Review that takes into consideration tools similar to MAD-LED tool that were developed and used by other scholars. It is presented in two categories, Immediacy and Multimedia Macromedia Director-MX. The section after the literature review section demonstrates the MAD-LED Model architecture by describing the physical components and functions of the tool. In this section the MAD-LED Model flowchart is illustrated. After this section is presented the System Implementation Section which demonstrates the preparation of online practical lessons by giving specific snapshots of the operation. This is followed by the Discussion and Findings Section, which demonstrates the eligibility and effectiveness of the MAD-LED tool by explaining the results obtained from the diagnostic test given to two groups. The Conclusion Section summarises the functions and benefits of utilizing the MAD-LED tool especially for the remote communities.

RELATED WORK

There are various concerns corresponding to the enhancement and improvement of teaching-learning in the utilization of the situation variable of immediacy and application of Multimedia Director-MX to build interactive animation teaching aids. These are discussed in the following sub-sections as discussed by various scholars.

IMMEDIACY

Frymier, A. A. (1994), Mehrabian (1971) and Weiner and Mehrabian (1968) described a variety of behaviors that communicate immediacy, including closer proximity, eye contact, smiling, verb tense (present vs. past), inclusiveness ("we" vs. "I"), and voluntarism ("want" vs. "should"). Mehrabian (1971) further illustrated and introduced the immediacy metaphor which was described as the universal element of approach and avoidance. For example, people approach things they like and that appeals to them, and avoid things that they dislike, does not appeal to them, or which induces fear. Others such as Christophel (1990) proposed that a teacher's use of immediacy behaviors impacted students' motivation to study, which in turn impacted student learning. He also examined students' level of state and trait motivation to study. He actually found that teacher immediacy (verbal and nonverbal) was positively associated with student motivation to study, with state motivation being more highly related to immediacy than trait motivation and concluded that immediacy had to first modify state motivation to study in order to impact learning. In support of Christophel, Richmond (1990) also found nonverbal immediacy to be positively associated with state motivation to study, affective learning, and perceived cognitive learning.

Titsworth (2004) explained that a students' perceptions of instructors' nonverbal immediacy influence other students' perceptions of the instructor and classroom. Whereas, Witt et al. (2004) cited an example by stating that in their meta-analysis of immediacy in the classroom, that there was ''a low to moderate association between teacher nonverbal immediacy and greater liking for the teacher and course, greater likelihood of engaging in behaviors learned, and greater likelihood of enrolling in another course of the same. Teven and Hanson, 2004; Thweatt and McCroskey, (1998) added that when students perceived their teachers as being immediate, they also perceived them to be more caring, competent, and trustworthy. Also, Rocca (2004) found that college students were more likely to attend classes when they perceived their instructors to be immediate. They further emphasised that overall, prior research has shown teacher nonverbal immediacy and teacher clarity were essential to effective classroom instruction.

MULTIMEDIA MACROMEDIA DIRECTOR-MX

Multimedia Macromedia Director-MX has the capability of building interactive teaching-learning modules utilising the combination of text, video, audio, graphics and animation. Mayer, R. E. (2001) discussed that multimedia teaching integrated verbal material, such as printed and spoken text, and visual material, such as pictures, graphs, photos, and dynamic graphics. It was also supported by various other scholars, such as, Garrison, (2001); Marx & Frost, (1998); Mitchell, (2001); Palmer, (2007); and Shephard, (2003) who emphasised that video as a multimedia application had been viewed as powerful narrative visualization to be of benefit in teaching and learning in various disciplines including engineering, management science, physical, medical and science education.

Ioannis Deliyannis, Christina Simpsiri (2008), and Fluckiger, F. (1995) pointed out that humans remember 20 percent of what they see, 30 percent of what they hear and this increased to 50 percent for audio visual presentation. They further explained that interaction through constructive examples increased the result to 80 percent. They also believed that such observations also stood for students with communication disabilities, where interactive multimedia technology may be utilised to motivate them into learning and enhanced their content-absorbsion and overall understanding.

Manjit Sidhu and Ramesh (2006) described that the Multimedia authoring tools such as Director MX, Flash MX, and Authorware MX had evolved tremendously that today these tools could be successfully integrated and used to aid teaching of undergraduate courses. They further stressed that with the advancement of computer technology, technology-assisted problem solving (TAPS) packages that were used by students to learn had shifted from the model that involved "point and click" with still images and text that lacked interactivity to a dynamic (animation) model that could be used to deliver information in multiple formats such as text, image, animation, audio and video. They also emphasised that the educational benefits offered by multimedia technology included the ability to take users into environments otherwise inaccessible by conventional methods, create a dynamic and interactive environment for learning, the high memory retention of experience, and the ability to reach out to visually oriented learners.

Cairncross and Mannion (2000); Manjit et al., (2002) also emphasised that the Multimedia authoring tools could be used to create high quality TAPS packages, which could engage the user/learner, thereby promoting deep learning and visualization of an area in engineering, medical, science, etc. They also mentioned that under TAPS, the delivery of information, the organization, and timing in which it was delivered could be controlled, the user could engage and interact with the material being presented and it was certainly an added advantage to slow learners.

The Tutorial Guide (2004) described Macromedia Director as a proven multimedia authoring tool for professionals, used to develop high-performance content and could be deployed on CDs, DVDs, intranets, kiosks, or the Internet. The Guide further explained that the Director handles the widest variety of media, letting the user unleash the creativity and build rich, interactive experiences that deliver measurable results. The Guide also emphasised that the Director provided all the tools the user needed to maximize productivity, including a choice of scripting languages such as Lingo, JavaScript syntax, and cross-platform publishing.

SYSTEMS ARCHITECTURE

The Macromedia Director-MX Lesson Development (MAD-LED) architecture is illustrated in Figure 1. The architecture consists of six (6) major components that are, Teaching Resource Repository (TRR), Macromedia Director (MD), Multimedia Tools (MT), Multimedia Interactive-Practical Lesson (MI-PL), the Internet, and a Class at Remote School (CRS).

Teaching Resource Repository (TRR)

The Teaching Resource Repository (TRR) is the reservoir of teaching resources of an institution such as the Curriculum and Syllabus. Other resources, especially those that are prepared in day-to-day's work by

Figure 1. MAD-LED architecture

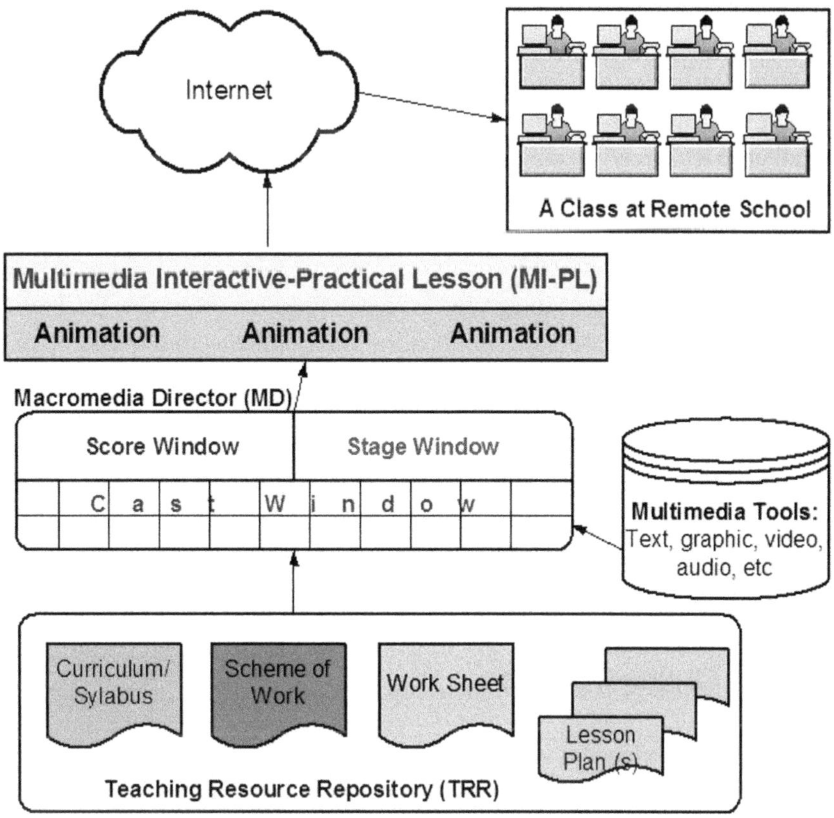

the individual Teachers, Lecturers, and Instructors (TeLI) include the scheme of work, work sheet, and lesson plan. Also note that the terms Curriculum and Syllabus will be used interchangeably. Therefore, in the TRR of a course, the TeLI prepares the teaching / learning materials based on the Curriculum. The TeLI prepares the scheme of work which has a summary of the topic's sections. In a work sheet, he/she organises all the relevant teaching aids. Then the TeLI prepares a lesson plan which has the details of the teaching units. Thereafter, the TeLI organises all the prepared work and load them into the Cast Window of the Macromedia Director as demonstrated in Figure 1.

Macromedia Director (MD)

The MD has a lot of functional windows. However in this work, only the three major ones are discussed such as the Cast, Stage, and Score Windows. The Cast Window is where all the identified and prepared resources from the TRR are imported into. This serves as the Macromedia Director work sheet with all the resources that will be displayed and demonstrated on the Stage Window and relayed online to the recipient screens.

Multimedia Tools (MT)

This component is a reservoir of Multimedia Tools that are the basic functional and building blocks of the targeted practical lessons and these include the text, graphic, video, audio, but to mention a few. The developers of the lessons have to ensure that they make the relevant tools available in this component. As such, the Teachers, Lecturers, and Instructors (TeLI) would prepare the work by ensuring that the named tools are integrated into the lesson. From Figure 1, the tools are integrated into the MD component, where the gathered teaching/learning resources are gathered in the Cast Window.

Multimedia Interactive-Practical Lesson (MI-PL)

Having the teaching/learning resources integrated with Multimedia Tools, the TeLI builds it to form an animation. The TeLI then tests the animated application if it conforms to the desired practical expectation of the learner.

Internet

Having prepared the desired practical work, the TeLI deploys the lesson on the system through the Internet. In this way, the TeLI would administer the lesson either through video conferencing, Skype, or any other online dissemination where the recipients on the remote site or class would interactively participate.

Remote Institution Online Classes

This is actually the targeted component whose majority of beneficiaries are those that may not have any opportunity of face-to-face mode of learning. Also majority of institutions especially in rural areas are not serviced by hydro-electricity. However, many of them are serviced by the solar panels that provide electricity to power-on the computers. For those institutions from the urban areas, a lot of them have adequate electricity, though some have taken initiative of installing backup generators that automatically switched on when the hydro powered electricity went off. These classrooms are also installed with computers that are connected to the network. The students from the remote sites operate the system in an interactive way with the lecturer.

SYSTEM FLOW CHART FOR MAD-LED MODEL

Figure 2 demonstrates the Macromedia Director-MX Lesson Development (MAD-LED) Model Flow Chart, which illustrates step-by-step processes involved in making teaching-learning lessons under the multimedia and real time environment.

When the system is activated, it checks whether the topic exists or not. If the topic does not exist, then the process is terminated. If the topic exists, then the system checks whether the lesson is interactive or not. If the topic is interactive, then the teacher presents it by running the demonstration. If the topic is not interactive, then the process is passed to the next stage to integrate text and graphics. If the system fails to integrate text and graphics, then the process is exited. However, once text and graphics are integrated, the process is passed to the next level to integrate video. Similarly, if it fails to add the video, the process is terminated. If the video is integrated, the process is sent to the next level to integrate audio. When the system fails to integrate audio, the process is exited. Once the audio is integrated, the process

Figure 2. Macromedia director-MX lesson development (MAD-LED) model flow chart

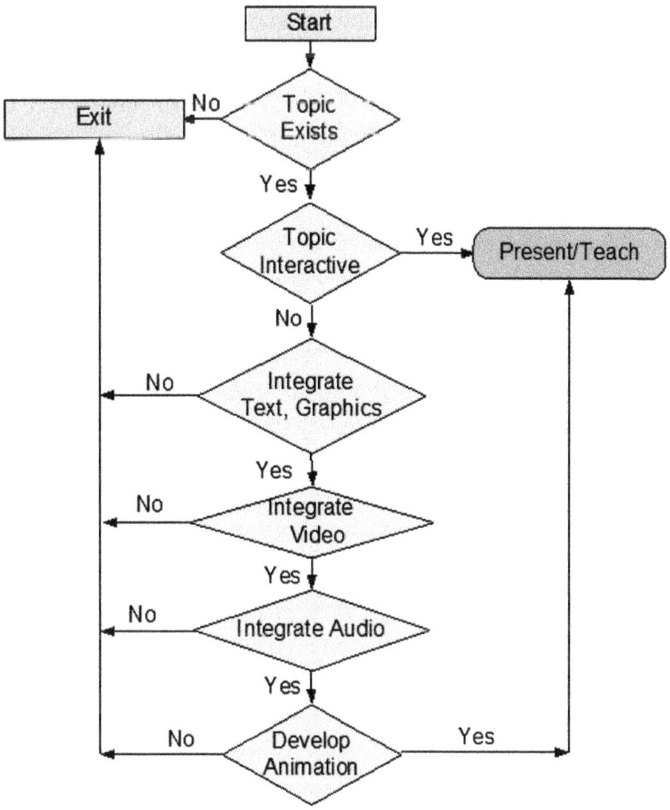

is passed to the next stage. In the next stage if the animation is not built, the system is terminated. If the animation is built, then the teacher runs the demonstration and the students join to actively participate in the demonstration.

SYSTEM IMPLEMENTATION

The system is highly user friendly and any TeLI can use it to build any practical lesson of his/her choice. Three lessons, named Lesson-1, Lesson-2, and Lesson-3 in different fields and levels were developed using the MAD-LED Model. Lesson 1 was a Network course at University level covering the topic of Routing Internet Protocol (RIP). Lesson 2 was prepared for the Secondary School level for a Biology course covering the topic of Blood Circulation. Lesson 3 was Kindergarten level which was prepared for young children of the age between three to four years. All these Lessons were the features of the MAD-LED Model.

Lesson 1: Networking – Routing Internet Protocol (RIP)

The lesson demonstrated how the information in the form of a packet was transmitted from the sender to the recipient on the other network. First and foremost, the Teachers, Lecturers, and Instructors (TeLI) used the Macromedia Fireworks to draw all the relevant teaching materials that included the routers, routing tables, Ethernet cables, serial cables, the network clouds, and arrow and exit buttons.

At the source network, through a network device called router, the packet was sent and transversed on the media such as wire, fibre or air until it was received by the other router at the destination network. This packet passed through different segments of network and was able to locate the destination through the utilisation of the routing tables. These routing tables are analogous to sending a letter through postal mail with details of address composed of - recipient's name, town, location area or area code, street name and number, and house number. These address details always guide the letter to pass through the Post Office system until it is delivered to the targeted or addressed person. Similarly, this was how the information which was transformed into packets was transmitted from one network to another. Each router had a routing table which had the exit interface and the following addresses - source, destination, mac, next hop, and mask. These addresses guided the packet to navigate through the networks until it reached the recipient at the destination network.

Therefore in Lesson 1, the TeLI prepared the practical lesson which demonstrated how the information in the form of packets was transmitted from the router at the source network to the one at the destination network. The lesson also demonstrated how the routing tables using the addresses guided the same information from the source router to the destination one. The TeLI gathered all the relevant resources of the RIP topic and grouped them in the Caste Window as demonstrated in Figure 3.

The TeLI placed the individual resources in the Cast Window boxes numbered 1 to 84 as indicated in Figure 3. In the boxes numbered 1, 5, 6, 7, 8 and 9 he/she put routers. In boxes 2, 3, 4, and 15 were placed the Ethernet cables, whilst in boxes 13 and 14 were serial cables. In the boxes 53, 54, 55, 56, 63, 64, 65, 66, 80, 81, 82, and 83 the TeLI put routing tables. The cloud symbols that present the networks were put in boxes 10 and 11.

In order to develop the lesson that would be more interactive, the TeLI has to construct behaviours that would make the animation behave according to the desired actions. A behavior is a Lingo script that

Figure 3. The cast window with the gathered teaching resources

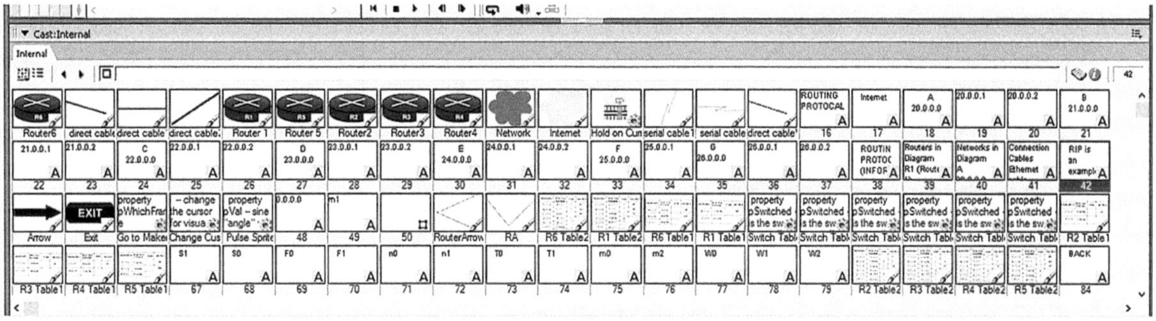

was designed to be easily applied to the sprites and frames in a movie. These behaviors were attached to objects in a movie by dragging and dropping them onto sprite or frame script channel. Note that the Director MX comes with dozens of pre-built behaviors. In this work, the TeLI constructed the following behaviors that were relevant to the lesson of Networking on the topic of RIP:

1. **Speak Word on Click:** The behavior speaks a word or phrase whenever the mouse is clicked on the sprite or frame. The behavior spoke out any word or phrase that was typed in as demonstrated in Figure 4, which shows that when the learner clicked the cursor on router 1, the system spoke the following phrase, "Router 1 is directly connected to network B and network A."
2. **Speak Word on Pointing:** The behavior speaks a word or phrase whenever the mouse is rolled over a sprite or frame on the stage. In that case, whenever the learners rolled the mouse over the router, its converged routing table was displayed showing the addresses of all the connected routers in the network.
3. **Change Cursor:** The behavior changes the appearance of the mouse pointer from the traditional arrow to a finger whenever a mouse pointer is passed over a cast member. That was to make the user know that the element was active and enticed him/her to click on it.
4. **Pulse Sprite:** The behavior made the Cast member or element to pulse. This behavior was embedded to make the lessons more attractive.
5. **Switch Table:** The behavior was responsible for the updating of the routing table. The behavior displayed a fully converged Table. The behavior was written for each Routing Table. Since there are six (6) Routing Tables, there were also six (6) behaviors each specific to each Routing Table. Figure 5 demonstrates the Lingo script written to control the behaviors of Router 1 and its converged Table 1.
6. **Quit:** The behavior was written or constructed to exit the system whenever the learners were through with the lesson

Having gathered all the relevant teaching resources in the Cast Window, the TeLI then organised the channels in the Score Window. These channels controlled the movie's content over time and they were arranged in rows. Also the Score included many sprite channels for the movie's sprites. These Sprite channels were numbered and controlled whenever sprites appeared in the movie. In addition, the Score included the effects channels that controlled the movie's tempo, sound, color palettes, transitions, and scripted behaviors.

Figure 4. Speak word or phrase on click

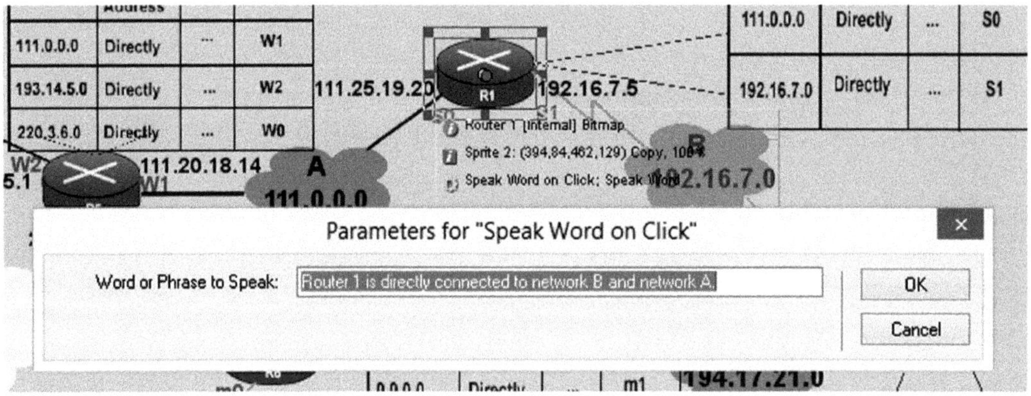

Figure 5. The lingo script controlling behavior of router 1 and its Table 1

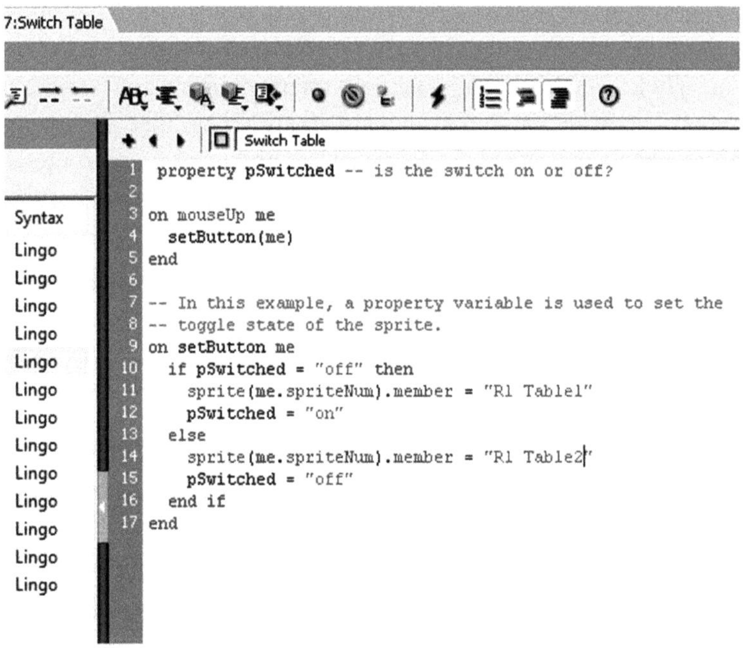

Once the TeLI finished the tasks involved in the Cast and Score Windows, this accomplished the preparatory of the lesson and the programme was ready to run. When the TeLI pressed the run button, the animation of the lesson started playing on the Stage Window. Figure 6 demonstrates a snap shot taken during the animation of the lesson.

Figure 6 demonstrates the full topology exhibiting six (6) networks inter-linked with six (6) routers. From each router a converged table was displayed showing the routing table contents comprised of addresses and exit interface. These were the information that guided the packet to transverse and reach the targeted router at the recipient network.

Figure 6. RIP with Fully converged routing tables

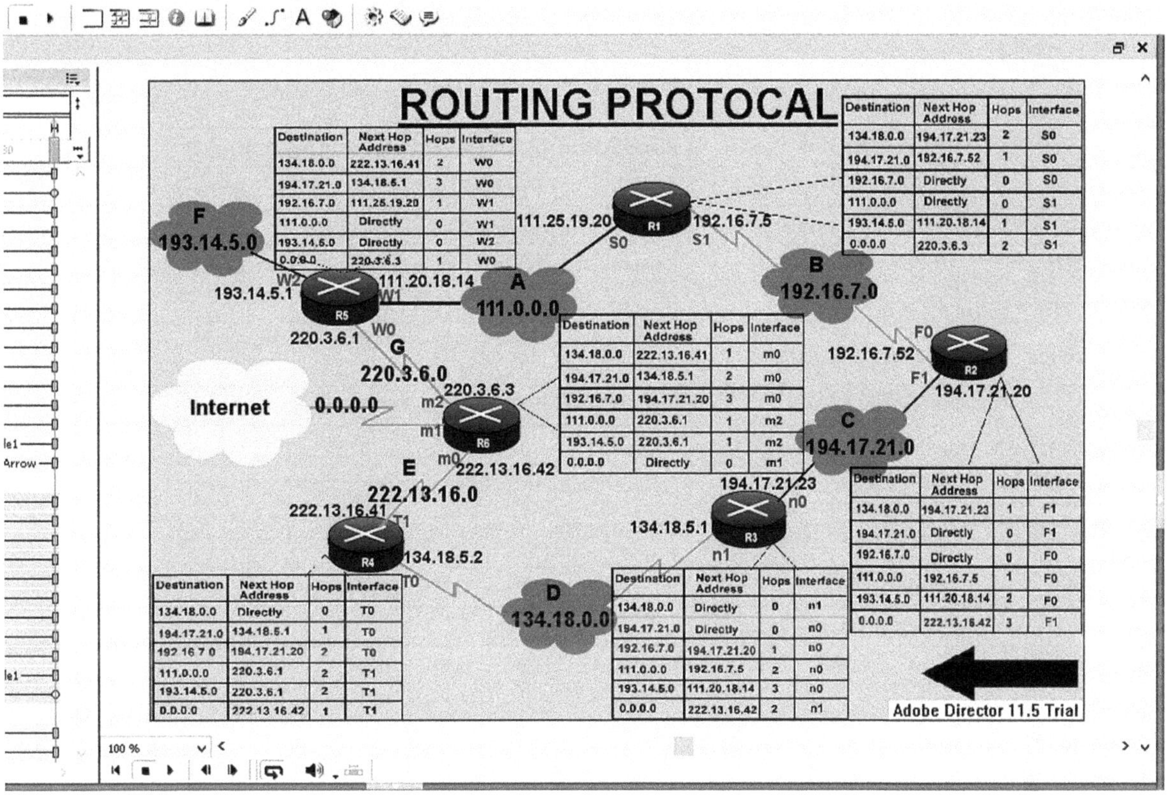

Learner's Class Participation at Remote Site – on RIP Lesson

During the lesson, students at the remote site were able to give real-time response to the lesson. These learners used the mouse to point at any features in Figure 6. A complete class participation was done as demonstrated in Table 1.

Below are some of the examples when the learners clicked the specific rows in the routing tables and the voices were heard describing the scenario involved:

When the learner pointed the cursor at:

Scenario 1: Routing table 4, row 3, the description voice would speak - "the router is connected to a remote network whose address is 21.0.0.0, next hop address is 22.0.0.1, the hop is 2, the exit interface is TO."

Scenario 2: Address 23.0.0.1, the voice would speak - "gateway 23.0.0.1."

Scenario 3: The cable between router 5 and router 6, the voice would speak - "the serial cable."

Scenario 4: The cable between router 5 and network 20.0.0.0, the voice would speak - "the Ethernet cable."

An Example of Sending a Packet from One Network to Another

Scenario 5: Sending a packet from network D through router R3 to network B.

Table 1. Real-time response during class participation

Cursor Pointed-at (p) or Clicked (c)	Feature Response	The System Spoke Louder as
Network A (p)	The network blinked	Network A, with network address 20.0.0.0, it is directly connected to routers R1 and R5
Router R1 (p)	Router was active	Router R1 directly connected to Network A and Network B
Router R1(c)	Routing Table was displayed	Routing Table for router R1
Routing Table 1 (c)	Table was converged	Fully converged routing Table for router R1
Router R5 (p)	Router was active	Router R5 directly connected to Network A, Network F and router R6
Routing Table 5(c)	Table was converged	Fully converged routing Table for router R5
Network B (p)	The network blinked	Network B, with network address 21.0.0.0, it is directly connected to router R1 and R2
Router R2 (p)	Router was active	Router R2 directly connected to Network B and Network C
Router R2 (c)	Routing Table was displayed	Routing Table for router R2
Routing Table 2 (c)	Table was converged	Fully converged routing Table for router R2
Network C (p)	The network blinked	Network C, with network address 22.0.0.0, it is directly connected to router R2 and R3
Router R3 (p)	Router was active	Router R3 directly connected to Network C and Network D
Router R3 (c)	Routing Table was displayed	Routing Table for router R3
Routing Table 3 (c)	Table was converged	Fully converged routing Table for router R3
Network D (p)	The network blinked	Network D, with network address 23.0.0.0, it is directly connected to router R3 and R4
Router R4 (p)	Router was active	Router R4 directly connected to Network D and router R6
Router R4 (c)	Routing Table was displayed	Routing Table for router R4
Routing Table 4 (c)	Table was converged	Fully converged routing Table for router R4
Router R6 (p)	Router was active	Router R6 directly connected to router 4 and router R5
Routing Table 6(c)	Table was converged	Fully converged routing Table for router R6
Internet (p)	The Internet blinked	The Internet, with network address 0.0.0.0, it is directly connected to router R6
Network F (p)	The network blinked	Network F, with network address 25.0.0.0, it is directly connected to router R5

In this case the router checked routing table R3, and identified the record in row three (3) indicated the destination address of the network was 21.0.0.0, the next hop address as 22.0.0.1, the hop was 1, and the exit interface was n0. This information gave the path to the destination and aided packet to reach the targeted network.

Scenario 6: Delivering a packet from network C through router R2 to network F.

As usual, the router checked the routing table and also identified the record in row five (5) showing the network address network F as 25.0.0.0, next hop address as 20.0.0.2, the hop was 2, exit interface as F0. All these records from the routing table established a path of the packet and allowed it to transverse to reach the destination network.

Lesson 2: Biology – Blood Circulatory System in Human Beings

The lesson illustrated on how the blood circulates in the body of human beings. Using the Adobe Photoshop CS6 as photo-editing software, the TeLI created and edited the relevant organs of the body such as the aorta, brain, carotid artery, heart, arteries, superior vena cava, kidneys, lungs, pulmonary veins, renal vein, iliac vein, stomach and intestines, legs and lower body, etc.

The TeLI gathered all the relevant organs and placed them in the Cast Window as demonstrated in Figure 7.

After placing all the relevant teaching resources into the Cast Window, the TeLI organised the channels in the Score Window as discussed in Lesson 1. Thereafter, the TeLI ran the system and all the organs of the body were displayed in the Stage Window as demonstrated in Figure 8.

When the learners clicked on the organs of the body, the system responded by mentioning the parts involved. The learners freely navigated all the body parts as the system identified them with their biological names.

Learner's Class Participation at Remote Site: On Blood Circulatory System Lesson

Table 1 is re-used for the Blood Circulatory System topic which is also projected through online to a remote school. As discussed in the table, the learners pointed the cursor at the organs and the system spoke louder mentioning the parts of the body. Upon clicking the mouse, further, the system gave the description of the blood flow as from the specific organ.

Lesson 3: Kindergarten/Pre-School – Identification of Objects – Fruits

The lesson was prepared to be used by children to identify and spell the names of the fruits. Initially, using the Macromedia Fireworks, the TeLI drew all the relevant fruits that included - apple, avocado, banana, carrot, grape, kiwi, peach, pepaya, guava, pineapple, mango, lemon, raspberry, tomato, and watermelon. Thereafter, the TeLI organised and placed the fruits in the Cast Window, which had a series of windows numbered from 1 to 51 as demonstrated in Figure 9.

Figure 7. Cast window field with human organs

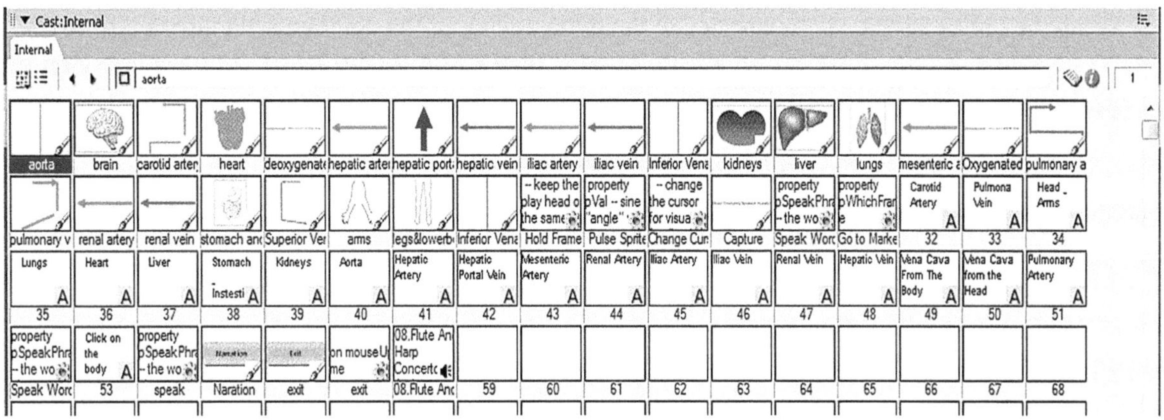

Figure 8. Organs of the body displayed in the stage window

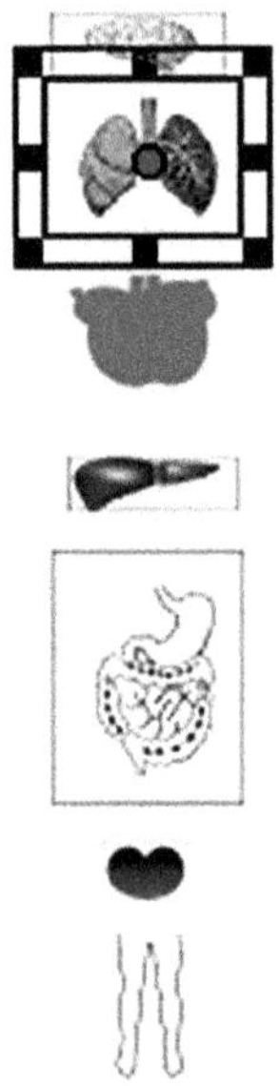

Figure 9. Cast window filled with fruits

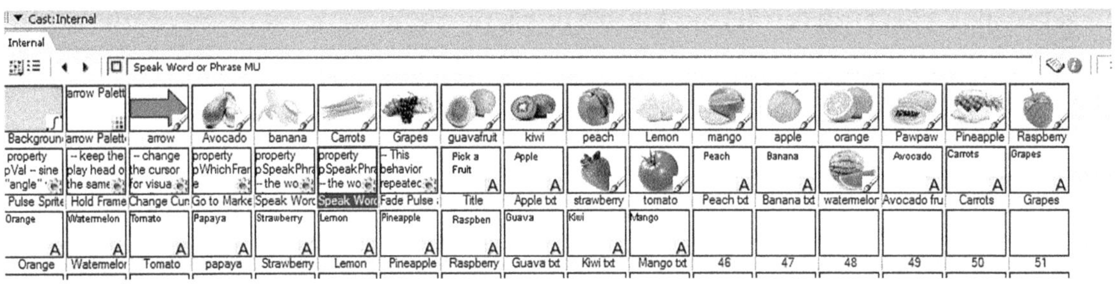

After this, the TeLI organised the channels in the Score Window as already discussed in Lesson 1. After organising the Score Window, the TeLI ran the program and all the fruits were displayed on the Stage Window as demonstrated in Figure 10.

When the online system was connected to the remote schools, the children aged three (3) to four (4) years operated that system. When they ran the system, the fruits were displayed as shown in Figure 10. Using the mouse, the children would point at a fruit, and the voice could aloud mention or read the name of the fruit. For example, when a child pointed at the orange, the system would read louder, "orange", if pointed at mango, it would read "mango," and so on. The children continued pointing at different fruits and the system read and pronounced their names.

Learner's Class Participation at Remote Site: On Identification of Objects Lesson

Again, the re-use of Table 1 is continued on the Identification of Objects topic which is used by the kindergarten children. When the children point the cursor at an individual object, it is highlighted and

Figure 10. Stage window displaying all the fruits

the system mentions louder the name of a fruit. In this way the children are able to identify and know the names of different fruits.

DISCUSSION AND FINDINGS

The MAD-LED Model was designed as a friendly user tool that could be used by any TeLI to prepare a highly interactive and practical online lesson. The tool was designed with six (6) major parts that included - Teaching Resource Repository (TRR), Macromedia Director (MD), Multimedia Tools (MT), and Multimedia Interactive-Practical Lesson (MI-PL), as discussed previously.

During the preparation of the lessons, the MAD-LED Model heavily utilised the integration of multimedia tools such as the text, graphic video, and audio to build an animation practical online lesson. The TeLI needs to gather all the relevant resources to the lesson and place them in the Caste Window. Thereafter, the TeLI creates all the necessary behaviors in the Score Window that would determine specific actions of the animation. Having prepared the behaviors, then the TeLI drags the cast members into the Stage Window. Once the dragging of cast members is completed, the TeLI would connect and run the system to disseminate the online lesson to the remote campuses. The MAD-LED Model has the capability of reaching out many students from the remote campuses through a single TeLI. In addition, the MAD-LED Model has the capability to disseminate interactive lessons whereby the learners would respond to the application involved.

In order to assess the effectiveness of the MAD-LED Model, a test was administered to two groups from one sampled remote campus which offered Networking. A class of eighty (80) students was divided into two - Regular Group (RG) and Control Group (CG). Each group had forty (40) learners.

Regular Group (RG) Lesson

The RG was taught online either through video conferencing or Skype, but without using the MAD-LED Model. In this group, through the video conference the TeLI just explained the concepts of RIP theoretically. The learners at the remote campus just watched and listened to TeLI delivering the lesson. There was no tangible interactive among the TeLI, the lesson, and the learners. The teacher explained the transmission of the information, which was transformed into packet, then the frame was delivered through the media, i.e., cable, fibre or air and received by the recipient at the other network. Further, the TeLI also explained how the addressing in the routing tables was used to guide the message until it reached the targeted destination. All these network devices and other technology involved were only mentioned by the word of mouth and students just grasped through rote learning.

Control Group (CG) Lesson

The CG was also taught through online either video conferencing or Skype, but this time using the MAD-LED Model. In this lesson the MAD-LED Model was connected, the TeLI would practically demonstrate the topology of the network, by displaying routers, cables such as Ethernet and serial. The teacher also illustrated the whole mechanism of how the routing tables were guiding information to reach the recipient. At the remote campus, the learners in the CG would respond on the system by pointing at the tables. The animation would start running, thus operated or controlled by these students. On the routers they were able to see all the mechanism such as the network, destination, next hop addresses, including the interface. In fact, the learners at the remote site were able to play with the animation as much as they could and until they acquired enough hands on skills.

Administering the Test to the Two Groups

The TeLI prepared the test covering the materials of the whole topic. The test was out of 100 marks. The grading category was set as: Very Good = 100 – 80; Good = 79 – 60; Fair = 59 – 50; and Bad = 49 – 0 as demonstrated in Table 2. The online test was administered to the two remote groups at the same time.

The RG had six (6) students who had Very Good results, which was fifteen percent (15%) passing rate, twenty five (25) obtained Good, which was sixty-two point five percent (62.5%) pass rate, about seven (7) got fair results, which was seventeen point five percent (17.5%) pass rate, whereas two (2) failed the test, which was five percent (5%) failure rate as shown in Table 2a and Figure 11. The learners from the RG had opportunity to have hands on interaction on the lesson, as a result they vividly grasped the concepts. They effectively acquired the skills of networking and understood the phenomenon behind

Table 2. Comparison of assessment from two groups

Results	Very Good	Good	Fair	Bad
a: Regular Group – Used the MAD-LED Model				
No. Students	6	25	7	2
b: Control Group – Did Not Use the MAD-LED Model				
No. Students	1	4	9	26

the routing tables. The learners physically saw the composition of the addresses involved in the routing tables. They even operated the movement of the packet from the source router to the destination network in the recipient router. During lesson, the learners played around the system by pressing the cursor on the routers, cables, and Internet, then the systems responded by running an animation at the same time talking, giving the descriptions of the processes involved. In that way, the learners received a practical experience of the lesson and acquired hands on experience. It is easy to remember all the time as the system loudly says the names and thus makes it easier for the learner to remember whatever is learnt. Therefore, the acquisition of hands on skills helped the learners to cement the understanding of the lesson and applied the knowledge gained in the test as a result they all performed very well.

The CG had only one (1) learner who got very good results, which was two point five percent (2.5%) passing rate, four (4) got good results, which translated to ten percent (10%) passing rate, nine (9) obtained fair results, which was twenty-two point five percent (22.5) passing rate, whereby a large number of twenty six (26) students failed the test, and this translated to sixty-five percent (65%) failure rate.

The results demonstrated in Figure 12, gave a true evidence that the CG learners faced a lot of challenges in grasping the concepts that were theoretically disseminated. The sixty-five percent (65%) failure rate signifies that two thirds of the learners from this group never grasped the concepts, hence resulted into higher failure rate. The outcome of the results showed that the learners could not recall what was taught in class as everything was just in abstract. It is easier to forget what was simply mentioned by the word of mouth as nothing was concrete. It was difficult to recall something which you neither saw nor touched. These students never saw the mechanism of the routing tables, especially the composition of the addresses. They never witnessed the mechanism of how the addresses guide the message in the form of a packet to reach the targeted router at the remote network.

CONCLUSION

In this era, the demand of learning has grown to a large extent that people from all walks-of-life have recognised the importance of furthering their education and they have enrolled into some academic programmes. The high demand of education has increased the enrolment in schools. The existing public

Figure 11. Online assessment lesson from regular group

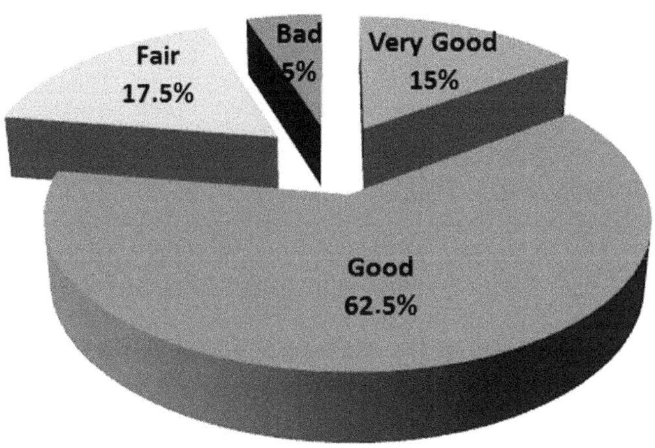

Figure 12. Online assessment lesson from control group

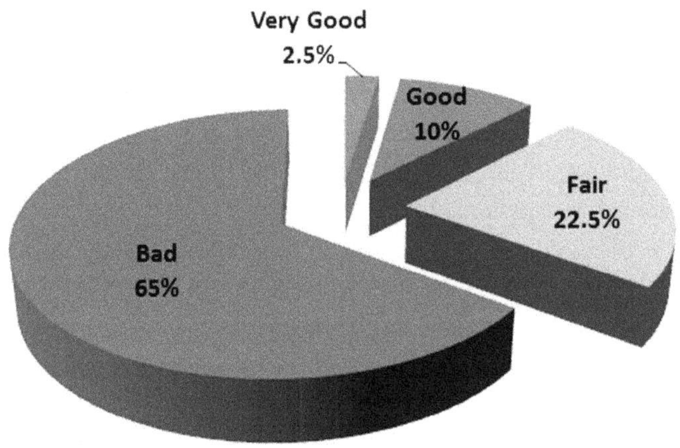

institution infrastructure could not accommodate the student population, especially those from the remote areas. In order to accommodate the large number of learners especially those from disadvantaged community, the introduction of online dissemination of teaching-learning materials to remote centres was inevitable. However, in many cases, the online teaching method is always theoretical which is less effective in information dissemination. Therefore, in order to make an online method effective, the TeLI's had to create highly practical and interactive lessons. It is in view of that the MAD-LED Model was envisaged.

The MAD-LED Model is a user friendly teaching aid where the teacher, lecturer, education administrator, instructional technologists, software designers or software developers can input the relevant resources and a practical lesson is built. The user simply runs the demonstration and the learners actively participate as well. Such a system raises the interest of the learners. In such a learning environment, the student's passing percentage rate is high as demonstrated through the results obtained from two groups where one was a video conferencing lecture based lesson called control group versus a regular group which was administered through MAD-LED Model using video conferencing. The significant improvement in learning performance, as is clear from 72.5% of class getting very good to good results using MAD-LED Model versus only 12.5% of class getting these results under similar scenario in the control group. Having thus understood the importance of the highly interactive MAD-LED Model, it is concluded that it becomes very important to promote such a model for effective teaching and learning.

REFERENCES

Cairncross, S., & Mannion, M. (2000). Multimedia and Learning: Patterns of Interactions. People and Computers XIV-Usability or Else! In *Proceedings of HCI*.

Christophel, D. M. (1990). The relationship among teacher immediacy behaviours motivation, and learning. *Communication Education*, *39*(4), 323–340. doi:10.1080/03634529009378813

Deliyannis, I., & Simpsiri, C. (2008). Interactive Multimedia Learning For Children With Communication Difficulties Using The Makaton Method. *Readings in Education and Technology: Proceedings of ICICTE*.

Fluckiger, F. (1995). *Understanding networked multimedia applications and technology*. Prentice Hall.

Frymier, A. A. (1994, Spring). A model of immediacy in the classroom. *Communication Quarterly*, *42*(2), 133–144. doi:10.1080/01463379409369922

Garrison, W. (2001). Video streaming into the mainstream. *The Journal of Audiovisual Media in Medicine*, *24*(4), 174–178. doi:10.1080/0140110120094949 PMID:11802705

Hackman, M. Z., & Walker, K. B. (1990). Instructional communication in the televised classroom: The effects of system design and teacher immediacy on student learning and satisfaction. *Communication Education*, *39*(3), 196–206. doi:10.1080/03634529009378802

Harasim, L. (1996). Online education. In T. Harrison & T. Stephen (Eds.), *Computer networking and scholarly communication in the twenty-first century university* (pp. 203–214). New York: State University Press.

Harris, R. A., & Nikitenko, G. O. (2014). Comparing online with brick and mortar course learning outcomes An analysis of quantitative methods curriculum in public administration. *Teaching Public Administration*, *32*(1), 95–107. doi:10.1177/0144739414523284

Manjit Sidhu, S. & Ramesh, S. (2006). Multimedia Learning Packages: Design Issues and Implementation Problems. *Malaysian Online Journal of Instructional Technology, 3*(1), 43-56.

Marx, R. D., & Frost, P. J. (1998). Toward optimal use of video in management education: Examing the evidence. *Journal of Management Development*, *17*(4), 243–250. doi:10.1108/02621719810210154

Mayer, R. E. (2001). *Multimedia learning*. New York: Cambridge University Press. doi:10.1017/CBO9781139164603

Mehrabian, A. (1971). Sj7en (messages. Belmont, CA: Wadsworth.

Mitchell, D. (2001). Digitizing video. *Journal of Physical Education, Recreation & Dance*, *72*(4), 11–16. doi:10.1080/07303084.2001.10605730

Palmer, S. (2007). An evaluation of streaming digital video resources in on- and off-campus engineering management education. *Computers & Education*, *49*(2), 297–308. doi:10.1016/j.compedu.2005.07.002

Richmond, V. P. (1990). Communication in the classroom: Power and motivation. *Communication Education*, *39*(3), 181–195. doi:10.1080/03634529009378801

Rocca, K. A. (2004). College student attendance: Impact of instructor immediacy and verbal aggression. *Communication Education*, *53*(2), 185–195. doi:10.1080/03634520410001682447

Shephard, K. (2003). Questioning, promoting and evaluating the use of streaming video to support student learning. *British Journal of Educational Technology*, *34*(3), 295–308. doi:10.1111/1467-8535.00328

Simonson, M. (2006). Teaching courses online. *Quarterly Review of Distance Education*, *7*(4), 7–8.

Study Guide. (2004). Macromedia Director, MX.

Teven, J. J., & Hanson, T. L. (2004). The impact of teacher immediacy and perceived caring on teacher competence and trustworthiness. *Communication Quarterly*, *52*(1), 39–53. doi:10.1080/01463370409370177

Titsworth, B. S. (2004). Students' note taking: The effects of teacher immediacy and clarity. *Communication Education*, *53*(4), 305–320. doi:10.1080/0363452032000305922

Weiner, M., & Mehrabian, A. (1968). *Language within language: Immediacy a channel in verbal communication*. New York: Appleton-Century-Crofts.

Witt, P. L., Wheeless, L. R., & Allen, M. (2004). A meta-analytical review of the relationship between teacher immediacy and student learning. *Communication Monographs*, *71*(2), 184–207. doi:10.1080/036452042000228054

ENDNOTE

1 For convenience sake, in this work, the Teachers, Lecturers, and Instructors will collectively be referred and abbreviated to as "TeLI."

Chapter 14
Students' Perceptions of the Online Instructors' Roles in a Massive Open Online Course

Hengtao Tang
The Pennsylvania State University, USA

Yingxiao Qian
The University of Georgia, USA

Shuyan Wang
University of Southern Mississippi, USA

Kyle L. Peck
The Pennsylvania State University, USA

ABSTRACT

Scholars prefer applying metaphors to interpret the instructor's role in online education, such as facilitators, mentors, e-moderators, and "leading the band", but the rise of Massive Open Online Courses (MOOCs) has reshaped the online teaching and learning practices. Accordingly, the role of instructors in MOOCs is expected to be redefined based on the precedent framework. This research inquiry thus explores students' perceptions of the instructor's role in a MOOC, Technology Applications in Education, regarding four dimensions of Berge's classifications: pedagogical, managerial, social, and technical. An emerging framework of instructor's role in a MOOC is construed to benefit professionals and academics investing in MOOC teaching and learning. Besides, designing a cohesive, structured course is evident in the roles of MOOC instructors, and instructors' timely interaction as a "real person" also influences students' learning experience.

INTRODUCTION

Concerning the role of online instructors, scholars prefer metaphors to elucidate their perceptions, such as mentor (Roger, 2000), e-moderator (Salmoon, 2000), facilitators (Cantor, 2001), and the leader of the band (Heuer & King, 2004). Those metaphors not only reveal the revolution of the instructor's role from traditional classrooms to online instruction, but also interpret the dynamic change of instructor's role encouraged by the technological advancement and students' changing needs. Heuer and King (2004) stress it is online instructor's responsibility of fulfilling flexible roles to meet students' varying needs. Nevertheless, online instructors have confronted unprecedented massive enrollments since online educa-

DOI: 10.4018/978-1-4666-9995-3.ch014

tion morphed into a new landscape featuring the expansion of Massive Open Online Courses (MOOCs). One of MOOCs' core values is to promote top educational resources to a wider scalability of learners (Macdonald & Ahern, 2015). Scalable audiences can thus register for supreme college-level courses in various subjects, for different purposes, and at no costs. For MOOC instructors, it becomes increasingly challenging to satisfy all of the students' needs and foster a desired learning experience for each of them (Robinson, Kerski, Long, & Luo, 2015).

On the other hand, MOOC instructors are "no more or less noticeable and relevant than anyone else who attends the MOOC" (Haavind & Sistek-Chandler, 2015, p.332), as evidenced that students might suffer a sense of isolation, even dropping out of the course because a lack of personalized feedback from the instructor (Macdonald & Ahern, 2015). MOOCs potentially subversively refine the role of online instructors but MOOC instructors are usually not efficiently trained before offering a MOOC. Consequently, an emerging framework of what the MOOC instructors' roles are and how they can fulfill the roles becomes more valuable for a MOOC instructor.

MOOCs embrace the notion of student-centered pedagogy (McAuley, Stewart, Siemens, & Cormier, 2010) and students' voice is an integral segment to delve the teaching practices in MOOC. Therefore, the research inquiry examines students' perceptions of the instructors' roles in a MOOC to generate a new framework envisioning MOOC instructors to fulfill their roles.

LITERATURE REVIEW

Berge's Model of the Online Instructors' Roles

Previously, Berge (1995) classified online instructor's facilitation roles in four perspectives, including pedagogical, managerial, social, and technical. Since then, researchers have attempted to clarify the dynamic roles of instructors in the rapidly evolving online education (Coppola, Hiltz, & Rotter, 2002; Guasch, Alvarez, & Espasa, 2010; Liu, Bonk, Magjuka, Lee, & Su, 2004; Maor, 2003), especially, Liu et al. (2004) further identify subcategories for each perspective in Berge's framework (as Table 1). Berge (2009) argues the framework of online instructors' roles is still valid in spite of the considerable change in the technical environment and pedagogical concepts. Berge's statement resonates with previous attempts before the era of MOOCs as his framework entails dimensions of online instructors commonly revealed in the literature, namely "pedagogical, facilitator, instructional designer, social, managerial, and technical roles" (Baran, Correia, & Thompson, 2011, p. 427).

Pedagogical

Online instructors fulfill the pedagogical roles through facilitating knowledge-based activities to solidify students' mastery of critical concepts and skills (Berge, 1995; Liu et al., 2004). The pedagogical components align with the elements of online teaching practice (Anderson & Dron, 2012), such as addressing designing a course, facilitating interactions, and providing feedback. Accordingly, pedagogical roles denote instructional designer, profession-inspirer, feedback-giver, and interaction-facilitator (Liu et al., 2004). The instructional designer role is salient because the digital-format course enforces the online

Table 1. Summary of the online instructors' roles (Liu et al., 2004)

Dimensions	Roles	Description of Roles
Pedagogical	Course Designer	Design interactive learning experience, structure course materials; refine and update learning materials; share teaching experiences with colleagues
	Profession-Inspirer	Promote professional dialogue among online learners; relate personal experiences and cases to the discipline; point to professional organizations
	Feedback-Giver	Provide timely and high quality feedback; provide formative feedback for continuous learning engagement
	Interaction-Facilitator	Facilitate peer interaction in online discussion through a wide range of facilitation strategies
Managerial	Conference Manager	Ensure equity in online discussion; provide rules and guidelines to augment online discussion; promote knowledge construction
	Organizer and Planner	Provide clear instructions and organization of course structure; achieve a balance between structure and flexibility
Social	Social Rapport Builder	Build social rapport; establish online teams; build online learning community
Technical	Technical Coordinator	Refer students to technical support; communicate technical issues
	Media Designer	Develop multi-media tools; identify and co-design efficient learning tools
	Technology Integrator	Use highly interactive tools to facilitate high quality online interaction

instructors to elaborate in the design to provide online learners high-quality contents and a satisfying learning experience (Anderson et al., 2001; Liu et al., 2004). Further, a majority of online courses cannot compete with traditional classroom teaching in providing face-to-face interaction, thus, it is significant for online instructors to efficiently facilitate the interaction and provide prompt feedback. The discussion is the primary format of interactions in the online environment. Heuer and King (2004) further stress online instructors facilitate the discussion democratically and collaboratively to foster students' equal involvement and ownership. Promoting professional inspiration assists students to approach their ultimate professional aspiration but it is more tailored to professional education. Heuer and King's (2004) "model" role more fits a general educational program. Besides modelling the online presence and behavior, the online instructors model the professional practice for the students.

Managerial

The managerial roles address managing the course logistics and facilitating the communication channel (Baran et al., 2011; Park et al., 2015). Managerial roles contains two perspectives, conference manager and organizer and planner (Liu et al., 2004). The time lag in asynchronous discussion forums results in negative dominancy issues and redundant information (Park & Bonk, 2007). The online instructors thus manage the discussion forum through formulated rules and structures, like agendas, goals, deadlines, and rubrics. In addition, the online instructors have to balance the flexibility and structure in an online course. It is helpful for online instructors to provide a clearly structured timeline to frame students' activities, but timely help and proper flexibility are also rated as two important factors that improve students' learning experience (Heuer & King, 2004).

Social

The social roles endow online instructors the responsibility of weaving a cohesive learning community and developing students' collective identity (Anderson & Dron, 2012). Social dimensions expect online instructors to be a social rapport builder who nurtures an affective bond with students and encourages interaction and participation (Coppola et al., 2002). The key element is to develop group cohesiveness and foster the collective identity to promote students' knowledge sharing and construction (Berge, 2009). However, the online environment restricts the instructor's fulfillment of the social roles because of the asynchronous concerns (Liu et al., 2004).

Technical

The technical roles fundamentally require online instructors to foster a well-developed and comfortable technical environment (Berge, 1995). Liu et al. (2004) interpret the technical roles as a combination of technical coordinator, media designer/developer, and technology integrator. The technical roles of online instructors transform abreast with the technological advancement (Berge, 2009; Guasch et al., 2010). In fact, the technological advancement potentially alters each dimension of online instructors' roles. For example, the cloud computing technology breeds the emergence of MOOCs that is likely to redefine the instructors' roles.

The Rise of MOOCs Challenges Online Instructors

The hype of MOOCs impressively changes the field since George Simons and Stephen Downes facilitated *Connectivism and Connective Knowledge* (CCK08) in 2008. MOOCs are categorized into several formats by distinct purposes as such cMOOC (c means *connectivist*) for connecting students and xMOOC (x means *extended*) for delivering video-based contents, and p-MOOC (p means project-based) for enabling students to work on authentic projects (Haavind & Sistek-Chandler, 2015). One of the core values of MOOC is the accessibility (Macdonald & Ahern, 2015) that otherwise pushes the students-teacher ratio and the diversity of students in a MOOC to a dramatic level. Traditional college-level online courses usually enroll tens of students after they complete several prerequisite courses, if any, and this reduces the difference of previous knowledge levels among students. Unlike the traditional online course, MOOCs enroll worldwide students without prerequisite courses or costs. The large-scale accessibility in part promotes the hype of MOOCs but is also assumed to alter the teaching practices in MOOC. Heuer and King (2004) apply the metaphor of "the leader of a band" to stress online instructors' obligation of satisfying online learners' demands. However, MOOC instructors have been increasingly challenged to satisfy each of the students' objectives.

MOOCs have witnessed the movement of pedagogy from the lecture-based teaching to the distributed learning and teaching (Haavind & Sistek-Chandler, 2015). The interaction of individual and collective learning is a key element in fostering a better understanding of critical contents and concepts (Fournier & Kop, 2015). Online instructors are expected to accordingly adjust the course design and facilitation strategies as a response to the pedagogical shift. For example, the instructor provides more pedagogical supports for novice students with absent pre-required knowledge or user experience. Alternatively, MOOC instructors elaborate in the design perspective to alleviate the misunderstanding by the language barrier and cultural conflicts (Liu et al., 2010).

The social dimension of online instructors' roles is challenged by the dramatic students-teacher ratio and diverse students' demographics. MOOC instructors are not likely to provide individual feedback and personalized instruction for each student (Robinson et al., 2015). Moreover, the geographic boundaries can be a threat for prompt responses from the teacher to solve students' problems. Unfortunately, the aforementioned novice students potentially feel discouraged by the increasing difficulties and then quit without timely assists.

MOOCs instructors confront the challenges from the flexible learning structure in managing the course logistics because students can arbitrarily drop out of the course before the completion for any reason (Macdonald & Ahern, 2015). Further, MOOCs enable students to pursue personal goals with their own desired pedagogy (Cooper & Sahami, 2013). Partial students enroll in the course for personal interests, affective bond, or merely as a "go-to" website for desired contents, but reject completing any assignments.

The integration of automated technology in MOOCs has marginalized the technical dimension but reinforced the pedagogical aspect in online instructors' roles (Haavind & Sistek-Chandler, 2015). On the other hand, students still prefer turning to the instructor for technical support in an online course (Berge, 2009) although it is the primary responsibility of supportive staffs to maintain the technical environment. The role for MOOC instructors as technology coordinators is apparently highlighted.

On top of that, the hype of MOOCs in the field boosts the awareness of the change in MOOC instructors' roles. Haavind and Sistek-Chandler (2015) conclude from the interview with eight MOOC instructors that the pedagogical role of online instructors is emphasized in MOOCs and the course design rather than the real-time interaction influences students' performance. Instead, Macdonald and Ahern (2015) reveal the lack of individual feedback from instructors is one of reasons for students' drop-out. To further investigate the instructors' roles in MOOCs, a dilemma in the current literature is the lack of students' voice in a student-centered environment (McAuley et al., 2010). Therefore, the research question for this inquiry is what it is like for students' perceptions of instructors' roles in a MOOC.

METHODOLOGY

This research inquiry applied grounded theory method to examine learners' perceptions of the online instructor's role in a MOOC, *Technology Applications in Education* (*TAE*). One of the aims for grounded theory method is elaborating additional data to enrich an appropriate, existing theory for the conceptual density in a topic of inquiry (Schram, 2007). Hence, the research used grounded theory method to refine the Berge's (1995) framework of online instructors' roles to fit the MOOC teaching practices. TAE is a pMOOC operated on Canvas for six weeks and intends to empower students to integrate educational technologies in the classroom through working on authentic projects and review peers' assignments (Reeves & Hedberg, 2014). Students were allocated into three groups by the alphabetic sequence of the last names and at least two teaching assistants were assigned to each group. The researchers selected TAE MOOC was based on the consideration of convenience and availability because two of the researchers were co-instructors of the MOOC and had a direct, deep experience with this MOOC.

Data Collection

Crewell (2007) accredits interview and observation as two primary methods of revealing the experience and perceptions of respondents. So the researchers collected data through semi-structured interviews

(Creswell, 2007) with ten respondents from the TAE MOOC and two researchers' participant observations as instructors (Macdonald & Ahern, 2015). The researchers sent out a request for interview participants during the last week of the course and ten respondents approved to voluntarily participate in the research. Those ten respondents were all active "opinion leaders" in the course activities through the completion of the course. They were from various professions, such as college/K-12/EFL teacher, instructional designer, and retired college staff/teacher, in five continents except for Oceania and Antarctica. The semi-structured interview was conducted individually through the video-conferencing software, *Zoom*, which supports video/audio talking and recording. Each of the interviews took approximately 60 to 75 minutes with multiple prepared semi-structured questions inquiring participants' learning experience, their expectation and evaluation of the instructors' performance, as well as suggestions for instructors to facilitate the course. Each of the interviews was recorded upon all of the respondents' approval.

Additionally, two of the researchers co-taught this MOOC so the research applied participant observation as a supplement to the students' perspective. The participant observers kept a journal of highlighted activities for an in-depth interview to generate more patterns in the data analysis.

Data Processing and Analysis

The inquiry applied grounded theory analytic methodology to analyze the transcripts and journals after all the interviews were transcribed. The grounded theory analysis method, intended to enable the theory "earn their way into the analysis" (Charmaz, 2002, p.320) consists of three phases, namely initial coding, focused coding, and theoretical coding (Charmaz, 2006). The initial coding phase required the researchers to remain open, preserve actions, and stay close to the data to generate simple and precise code (Charmaz, 2006; Corbin & Strauss, 2008). Then each of the researchers went through focused coding phase and then collaboratively conducted the constant comparison (Schram, 2007) to produce a set of categories (Charmaz, 2006), such as instructional designer, real person, technical coordinator, role model, and recruiters. Finally, the researchers extracted hypotheses from the categories to build a holistic explanation of the participants' perceptions during the theoretical coding phase (Glaser, 1992; Charmaz, 2006).

RESULTS

The research investigated students' perceptions of instructor's roles in a MOOC based on Berge's (1995) framework. The findings further refined and enriched the framework (Table 2) by adding the perspective of the facilitation practices in MOOCs.

Pedagogical Roles

Course Designer

Participants' responses indicated their primary expectation of MOOC instructors was as a course designer to plan and elaborate the course materials. The respondents admitted the quality of the MOOC course significantly decided whether to complete the course.

Table 2. Students' perceptions of the online instructors' roles in a MOOC

Dimensions	Roles	Description of Roles
Pedagogical	Course Designer	Design an interactive course with a coherent structure; Embed previous teaching experience in the course design; Encourage students to connect with authentic experience; Provide students updated materials and novel challenges; Coordinate personalized and generalized instruction.
	Pre-Instruction Provider	Prepare pre-course instructions and tutorials; Plan and select the contents for the orientation activity.
	Profession Inspirer	Promote professional dialogue among online learners; Motivate students to relate the learning with the disciplines.
	Interaction Facilitator	Facilitate learner-learner interaction; Facilitate learner-instructor interaction; Facilitate learner-content interaction.
Managerial	Consortium Manager	Send weekly announcement and assignment reminders; Ensure equity and fluency in online discussion; Regulate rules, netiquettes, and best practices in the course; Achieve a balance between structure and flexibility.
	Teaching Leader	Recruit qualified teaching assistants to form a team; Diversify the composition of the team roster.
	Organizer and Planner	Provide clear instructions to maintain the course structure; Plan and arrange course activities proactively.
Social	Course Recruiter	Coordinate advertising the course for recruiting students; Establish the personal fame for recruiting students.
	Role Model	Provide a role model for students with professional skills and course facilitation performance.
	Real Person	Enable students to interact with a "real" instructor; Foster an affective bond between the course and the students.
Technical	Technical Coordinator	Refer students to technical support team for solutions; Include FAQ page to address basic technical problems.
	Technology Integrator	Identify the need of integrating tools & multimedia products; Consider the accessibility and flexibility of the official tools.

(Your course was) a great designed course, (with) structured knowledge and great practice! The contents are great and they are (one of the) reasons (why) I finished the course.

In other words, the instructors' capabilities of fulfilling the role of course designers become a key factor influencing the course retention rate. Respondents appreciated a coherent knowledge structure in the course design as an indicator of the course quality. In addition, participant observation journal suggested MOOC instructors applying their previous teaching experience in the course design and arrange the course activities to deliver a productive, interactive learning experience.

I really like your course because your course has a coherent knowledge structure. (The instructor) is an expert and your team brought your expertise (and) your skills in the course. The structure was very clear, (and) very engaging.

MOOC students obtained different levels of expertise in understanding and applying the learning principles in the practice. TAE stressed the importance of working on authentic projects in empowering students to integrate educational technologies into the classroom. The hands-on experience was acknowledged to solidify the knowledge and skills acquired from the course based on the interviews transcripts.

The hands -on practice was very useful because we can work on my own project (that we can) apply the knowledge, the skills (acquired) from the course.

Further, MOOC learners tended to project the pleasure and tortures in their traditional online courses to the selected MOOCs as the interview transcript indicated. For example, one respondent disliked the "same old, same old" assignments (repeated, boring assignments) but adored the updated materials and novel challenges.

The videos, reading materials, and assignments are helpful. I really like the variety of activities you arranged (for the class). They were not 'same old, same old' as some other traditional courses.

What is your impression about this course?

Multiple resources, new resources, and activities to work with resources you gave us. I like the use of Weebly in the course. The hands-on perspective is very useful so that I have common activities to talk with many peers.....and absolutely, the interaction, it is necessary.

Further, the weekly workload was a concern for MOOC instructors in arranging the activity in view that most students might attend to several other responsibilities. Those projected expectations enforced MOOC instructors to be more considerate of their students' multiple personalized demands.

The workload of assignments is good for me because I did not work and got plenty of time to work on them, but (for other classmates,) it will be different.

Pre-Instructions Provider

Both the interviews and the participant observation revealed that the levels of prior expertise vary among the respondents, as commonly in other MOOCs. It is thus essential for online instructors to provide a series of orientation activities for new MOOC learners. The first TAE week featured an orientation activity and the researcher's subsequent participant observation record pinpointed the value of the orientation. Otherwise, students encountered the confusion without an orientation page as the participant observer noted.

Student LS posted the assignment for Module 2 to the discussion forum of Tips & Help. After reviewing her assignment, I left a comment to remind her of referring to course policy in the orientation activity..... Her reply indicated she did not read carefully through that page since it is non-related to the content.

Several participants' responses further confirmed the significance of orientations. They also recommended the instructors clearly outlining the essential contents in the orientation. *Weebly* was the assigned platform for students to develop their website, but students without basic expertise suffered a torture of using *Weebly*. The respondent below predicted the retention rate would be higher if *Weebly* tutorials were available at the very start of the course.

I remember one student said (it was) impossible for her (to work on) Weebly (after the trials), but, if she had (received) pre-instructions about Weebly in the video-conference, she might not drop out of the course.

You (the instructors) can prepare and deliver more instructions on how to design and develop websites on Weebly prior to the course starts (orientation).

The video-conference, the Dr. (Instructor) facilitated during the course, is really great, but (it will be) better if the video-conference was held in the very beginning (of the course) so that students can get clarified of their questions concerning the course.

Professional Inspirer

Respondents agreed connecting the learning with personal experience benefited their professional inspiration. They appreciated the design of embedding course assignments into the classroom teaching. Further, respondents were impressed with the iterative opportunity of continuously refining the assignment based on peers' and instructors' feedback. This profession-based interaction initiated the professional dialogue among students and this design was rated as "a great companion to the hands-on experience" and offered new inspirations for students to refine and improve their projects.

Hands-on experience was helpful for me to learn, to use the technologies in my classroom. I showed the website (the final project) to my boss and he liked it so much. (Currently,) I am still working on the revision so that I can use them in my class of the next semester.

(It was) great (to combine the assignment with the classroom teaching). I worked on the assignment and then shared with my classmates (on the discussion forum). Each time I could get feedback from them, absolutely also from you. Your feedback was a great companion to the hands-on experience and helped revise the assignment and submit a (final) project with a higher quality. I was inspired to design my course (in this way).

Interaction Facilitator

Three common interactions were emerged in TAE MOOC, *learner-content, learner-learner, and learner-instructor interactions,* as Moore (2007) categorized. The instructors' role as an interaction facilitator was further contextualized in the MOOC setting based on the data. First of all, the interview and observation both suggested MOOC instructors increasing the awareness of providing timely and professional feedback to students' posts. The participant observation implied it was labor intensive to facilitate such a massive discussion. The observation further conveyed a potential correlation between the student-teacher interaction and an active community as revealed in the journal that "Group 2 teaching assistants provided timely, detailed responses to students' posts and this group featured the largest number of discussion posts". Besides the time commitment, instructors should be aware of techniques in returning their responses, such as "comment sandwich" (admire, constructive feedback, and encouragement) technique in a student's thread. Another strategy for MOOC instructors was to "pick up interesting topics for the discussion".

The interaction with the instructors was necessary, especially for me, as a new learner (of MOOCs).

I was impressed by your 'comment sandwich'. I really like the way you commented on our project. It is not a put-down but always admiring when giving students feedback.

The second category of interaction is the learner-learner interaction. The interview transcripts supported peer interaction as one of the primary, preferred ways for MOOC students to acquire knowledge. One participant claimed commenting on peers' posts and providing solutions to peers' problems as her "commitment". The transcripts also recommended MOOC instructors to motivate the students' participation in the discussion forum. Geographical boundaries caused untimely responses according to respondents' experience. Further, the disparity in learning styles was another reason for the untimely responses as one respondent complained of not receiving timely responses from peers because she accustomed to the early posting and replies. She added "it was too late for her to read the comments when peers replied to her on the due date".

You have to find the way to encourage people to work collaboratively. More interactions. Yeah. More interactions among peers (should be encouraged) because some of them have answered (the questions) already.

I was disappointed to say no one commented on my posts because I was an early starter...later, I found they were accustomed to commenting near the due day, but it was too late for me to check back because I have already started with the new week.

Moreover, several respondents expected MOOC instructors to take the initiatives of providing more opportunities of collaboration, such as sharing blog posts and learning journals.

It was fun to read other peers' blogs. This format was different from the discussion forum since the post was more from our intuitive. The blog posts were more real.

Another interaction is learner-content interactions. The respondents hoped the instructors to be "learning navigators" while designing the MOOC. It was a great lesson for MOOC instructors to provide clear instructions for the assignment and tutorials for the used techniques/tools. Further, one respondent mentioned she "preferred the course website as a go-to resource even after the course." The tendency advocated the instructors to enable the post-course entry after the course ends.

Managerial Roles

Consortium Manager

Participants insisted MOOC instructors were responsible for managing the online consortium. One respondent assumed instructors informed students of the course rules, netiquettes, and rubrics as the college teacher. Further, respondents generally offered compliments for instructors' endeavors of sending weekly announcement and assignment reminders to alert the incoming tasks and deadlines, but students with strong initiatives might deemphasize the significance of those two endeavors.

Weekly announcement? (it is)Helpful. (It can) Let me know what to expect, yeah, very helpful. Reminder? For most students, yeah, but for me, not so much. I had done my calendar because I am a self-learning person. In fact, I do not need too much support from teacher.

Respondents held mixed feelings towards instructors' efforts in ensuring the equity for global learners. Some favored instructors' attempts for satisfying most students' interests as "a sense of professions". The attempts contained assigning English as the official language and Eastern Standard Time (EST) as the official time. To the contrary, another respondent found the language barrier to using English was a major obstacle for him.

It is a sense of profession to recognize the official language and time zone because it can avoid unpredicted confusions. This is my first MOOC and the management and maintenance (of TAE) was beyond my expectation of an informal course.

When I design a (web) course for soccer, English is even harder for me to find useful information.

The observation also recorded a favorable adjustment in the flexible adoption of tools/software for this course after students argued *Weebly* was not available in certain areas. Another note in the observation journal echoed the favorable adjustment that one student was permitted to use *Wix* as an alternative to *Weebly* because of personal preference and technical concerns.

Teaching Leader

It was almost unlikely for instructors to individually fulfill the teaching responsibility as convinced by the record of the intensive daily workload of dealing with up to hundreds of posts and emails. Thus the role of a teaching leader to coordinate a team of teaching assistants became salient for MOOC instructor. Participants' responses admired the teaching team excelled in solving students' house-keeping questions and providing professional suggestions. One respondent directly expressed the appreciation of the assigned teaching assistant and she "preferred turning to the teaching assistant for help whenever encountering dilemmas because (she) deeply trust the teaching assistant's ability and morals". From another perspective, this posed new challenges for MOOC instructors to select the qualified teaching assistant to organize the team. One of responses suggested diversifying the composition of the teaching assistant team such as including bilingual speakers.

(The teaching assistant) could also speak Spanish. It is really helpful for me since my mother language is Spanish....I am not sure whether it is right, but it is good for me if the teaching assistants can speak multiple languages since MOOC is open to all over the world.

Planner and Organizer

TAE instructors held a video conference to ensure the flow of adaptation to the course at the beginning of the second week. Generally, respondents gave positive remarks to this activity, but suggested moving the conference ahead to the first week of the course. The respondents hoped the instructors organized the course activities in a clear structure but with flexible rules.

Did you find differences between our courses and others?

Completely. I think your course is very well-designed, coherent because the objective of the course is coherent with the content. I really like your course.

Did you encounter any problems while enrolling in the course?

The blog might be helpful, but (it is) tough to do. I have to say that blog did not help keep me engaged. I am a writer but not a blogger. Maybe a little bit more choices of assignments. for se, I do not want a blog. For the video (production assignemnt), could I do with the Garageband?

Social Roles

Course Recruiter

The participant observation recorded online instructors should coordinate the promotion of the course, such as distributing advertisement in online community/forum, portals, or social media accounts to MOOC learners. In an affective perspective, MOOC instructors became a rock star recruited students to enroll in the course as reflected in participants' response:

Yeah, I have heard about (the instructor) when pursuing my master's degree in United States. Coincidentally, I attended her lecture ... right before the course started and she shared about the course information with participants so I intended to register for this course and got an opportunity of working with her.

Role Model

The role model consists of two aspects, the professional role model and the course role model. The MOOC instructors serve as a professional role model to provide inspirations for students as well as reveal the authentic professional attitude. A respondent shared thrilling news that she found a new job of instructional designer right after taking *TAE MOOC* and she stated the instructional design techniques and professional attitudes she acquired from the instructors was an asset. The MOOC instructors serve as a course role model to model students' class performance through their involvement and commitment. The respondents attributed their completion of the course to the role model that MOOC instructors set for the class.

What we want to do is to do our best. Our teachers are trying to do their best to teach us, to do the best thing. I really appreciated that. For other courses, we are gonna see whether we can do this, but here, we have to do this.

Real Person

In particular, a respondent emphasized MOOC instructors' frequent occurrence significantly increased students' learning enthusiasm and attachment to the online community. He sensed the real existence of instructors through a series of individual interactions, timely feedback, and managerial activities (weekly announcement and reminder).

The team is distinct, because each of you help us work on the project and your are all REAL. I know you are all around, like the classroom courses.

Within the course, MOOC instructors constructed an affective bond between students and the course through their active participation and efforts spent in the course design, development, and evaluation.

You know, the reason why we want to work with you because you seem to care about us students. You are very involved, as a member of the big community, so we had the bond to the course.

Technical Roles

Technical Coordinator

It was one of the MOOC instructors' responsibilities to serve as a technical coordinator when students were confused by the use of technologies. Besides referring students to the technical support team, it was wise for instructors to set up a Frequently Asked Questions (FAQ) page equipping solutions to the common technical and policy questions considering the student-to-instructor ratio. The FAQ page was mentioned as "a great resource when the instructor was not available". Further, respondents normally considered the teaching team and discussion forum as "immediate technical support".

Technical Integrator

The participant observation tended to merge the role of "technical incorporator" and "media designer" since the multimedia production phase was completed by an instructional design team. The main role of the instructor was to incorporate the technology and multimedia projects in the course to achieve the best instructional effects. Besides, the themes emerged from respondents' interview reminded instructors of the following issues in technical integration as such the accessibility of tools/software, the alternatives for the official tools, and the length and quality of the multimedia products.

DISCUSSION

The research findings reveal what it is like for online instructor's role in a specific MOOC in terms of students' perceptions. The emerging framework of the MOOC instructors' roles mirrors Berge's (1995) four dimensions, namely pedagogical, social, managerial, and technical, but further enriches the existed framework in the context of a MOOC.. The findings echo Berge's (2009) statement that the traditional framework is still valid, but the subcategories of each dimension are contextualized to fit the MOOC setting. MOOCs are prominent in enabling a large scale of students an open, free access to the high-quality learning resources (McAuley et al., 2012), so the roles of MOOC instructors are also accordingly adjusted to facilitating a course with massive enrollments. This inquiry further confirms the ultimate goal of the instructors' role is to satisfy the learners' needs (Heuer & King, 2004), but the specific roles and mutual relationships transform abreast with the emerging advancement.

The findings in part resonate with Haavind and Sistek-Chandler (2015) that online instructors' roles are highly on the course design in a MOOC. MOOCs enable a flexible learning structure and students can relinquish the course any time before the completion (McDonald & Ahern, 2015). A cohesive course design is thus an integral segment for a MOOC to sustain a high retention rate. Whereas, the course design is not adequate to promote the success of a MOOC and this is where the findings challenge Haavind and Sistek-Chandler (2015). Respondents' preference of working with a real person entails the significance of real-time engagement and interactions in MOOC instructors' roles. The interview transcripts further support the social dimensions motivate students to complete the course because students can recognize the instructors as a role model and develop an affective bond with the learning community. In fact, the emerging framework from this research emphasized three categories of interactions existed in a MOOC as such student-instructor interaction, student-student interaction, and student-content interaction, but how each of the interaction is processed is closely influenced by the instructor's facilitation.

In addition, the findings contextualize Berge's (1995) framework to MOOC settings. For example, the emerging framework adds the significance to the pre-instruction and the orientation activity to address the disparity in students' entry expertise which is common in the current MOOCs. Moreover, the dramatic students-teacher ratio engenders the needs to form a teaching team because the main instructors cannot individually facilitate a course with scalable enrolled students. Another change of instructors' role featuring the MOOC setting is to be the course recruiter. MOOC instructors need assume the responsibility of collaborating with providers and institutions to recruit students. On the other hand, the fame of MOOC instructors can be recruiting advertisement for the course since numerous students register for the course to construct personal relations with the "rock star" in the field (McDonald & Ahern, 2015).

Apart from the emerging framework of MOOC instructors' roles, the research also generated implications for MOOC instructors concerning the teaching and design practices in MOOCs:

1. Provide a cohesive, structured course design as well as ensure freedom for students with flexible options;
2. Encourage students to work on authentic projects and connect the learning with personal experience;
3. Avoid "same-old, same old" and provide new contents, new resources, and new challenges;
4. Empower students the awareness of their own learning path;
5. Emphasize the real-time interaction and timely feedback for students;
6. Recruit qualified teaching assistants and then diversify the composition of the team roster.
7. Establish the orientation and video-conference as basic elements and arrange those activities early at the start of the course;
8. Enable personalized communication as much as possible;
9. Focus on details in the course design and management, such as providing low-technology version of course materials as an alternative, equipping clear screen captures on tutorials, sending weekly announcement and reminders.

The research proposes an emerging framework intended to provide guidance for MOOC instructors, but several shortcomings awaits more revisions and verifications in the future research. For example, the pool of participants in the inquiry was exclusively within the TAE MOOC so the conclusions might lose the validity of generalizing to other MOOCs. In particular, those participants were all active "opinion leaders" who completed the course in the end. The research design can be further improved if more participants with diverse performances, from multiple courses are involved in the inquiry. On top of that, the research project attempted to combine students' and instructors' perspectives to reproduce the real scenario in TAE MOOC. The participant observation experience as instructors is in part supplemental to students' perspective, but tends to mix objective biases in the data collection. The future research may simultaneously collect data from students and instructors in multiple courses to generate a more comprehensive framework of MOOC instructors' roles. Other than those aforementioned, the skepticism towards Berge's (1995) classifications that each of the four dimensions overlaps challenges the researchers to define the boundary among those dimensions.

CONCLUSION

The findings of the research project contribute to an emerging framework of how MOOC instructors fulfill their roles to foster the core value of MOOCs. Berge's (1995) framework is proven to be valid in the context of MOOCs and its four dimensions are integral for the role of MOOC instructors. The role of course designer is increasingly significant for online instructors to facilitate a MOOC, but it is worth noting that the other three dimensions address various aspects for the success of a MOOC. In addition, the research provides suggestions on improving the MOOC teaching and design in the future from students' perspective. The research findings can be a great addition to the existing literature of MOOCs and benefit academics and practitioners investing in MOOC practices of teaching, design, and development.

REFERENCES

Anderson, T., & Dron, J. (2012). Learning Technology through Three Generations of Technology Enhanced Distance Education Pedagogy. *European Journal of Open, Distance and e-Learning, 2012*(2), Retrieved from: http://www.eurodl.org/?p=currentarticle=523

Anderson, T., Liam, R., Garrison, D. R., & Archer, W. (2001). Assessing teacher presence in a computer conferencing context. *The Journal of Asynchronous Learning*, *5*(2).

Bali, M. (2014). MOOC pedagogy: Gleaning good practice from existing MOOCs. *MERLOT. Journal of Online Learning and Teaching*, *10*(1), 44–56.

Baran, E., Correia, A. P., & Thompson, A. (2011). Transforming online teaching practice: Critical analysis of the literature on the roles and competencies of online teachers. *Distance Education*, *32*(3), 421–439. doi:10.1080/01587919.2011.610293

Berge, Z. L. (1995). Facilitating computer conferencing: Recommendations from the field. *Educational Technology-Saddle Brook NJ*, *35*, 22–22.

Braun, V., & Clarke, V. (2006). Using thematic analysis in psychology. *Qualitative Research in Psychology*, *3*(2), 77–101. doi:10.1191/1478088706qp063oa

Charmaz, K. (2002). Qualitative interviewing and grounded theory analysis. In J. F. Gubrium & J. A. Holstein (Eds.), *Inside interviewing: New lenses, new concerns* (pp. 311–330). Thousand Oaks, CA: Sage.

Charmaz, K. (2006). *Constructing grounded theory: a practical guide through qualitative analysis. Thousand* Oaks, CA: Sage.

Collins, A. (2006). Cognitive apprenticeship. In R. K. Sawyer (Ed.), *The Cambridge handbook of the learning sciences*. Cambridge University Press.

Cooper, S., & Sahami, M. (2013). Reflections on stanford's MOOCs. *Communications of the ACM*, *56*(2), 28–30. doi:10.1145/2408776.2408787

Coppola, N., Hiltz, S., & Rotter, N. (2002). Becoming a virtual professor: Pedagogical roles and asynchronous learning networks. *Journal of Management Information Systems*, *18*(4), 169–189.

Corbin, J., & Strauss, A. (2008). *Basics of qualitative research: Techniques and procedures for developing grounded theory* (3rd ed.). Los Angeles, CA: Sage.

Creswell, J. W. (2005). MIxed methods designs. In *Educational research: Planning, conducting, and evaluating quantitative and qualitative research*, (pp. 509-529). Academic Press.

Creswell, J. W. (2007). *Five qualitative approaches to inquiry. In Qualitative inquiry & research design: Choosing among five approaches*. Thousand Oaks, CA: Sage Publications.

Easton, S. S. (2003). Clarifying the instructor's role in online distance learning. *Communication Education*, *52*(2), 87–105. doi:10.1080/03634520302470

Fournier, H., & Kop, R. (2015). MOOC Learning Experience Design: Issues and Challenges. *International Journal on E-Learning*, *14*(3), 289–304.

Glaser, B. (1992). *Basics of grounded theory analysis: Emergence vs. forcing*. Mill Valley, CA: Sociology Press.

Guasch, T., Alvarez, I., & Espasa, A. (2010). University teacher competencies in a virtual teaching/learning environment: Analysis of a teacher training experience. *Teaching and Teacher Education*, *26*(2), 199–206. doi:10.1016/j.tate.2009.02.018

Haavind, S., & Sistek-Chandler, C. (2015). The Emergent Role of the MOOC Instructor: A Qualitative Study of Trends Toward Improving Future Practice. *International Journal on E-Learning*, *14*(3), 331–350.

Heuer, B. P., & King, K. P. (2004). Leading the band: The role of the instructor in online learning for educators. *Journal of Interactive Online Learning*, *3*(1), 1–11.

Jacoby, J. (2014). The disruptive potential of the Massive Open Online Course: A literature review. *Journal of Open. Flexible and Distance Learning*, *18*(1), 73–85.

Liu, X., Bonk, C. J., Magjuka, R. J., Lee, S. H., & Su, B. (2005). Exploring four dimensions of online instructor roles: A program level case study. *Journal of Asynchronous Learning Networks*, *9*(4), 29–48.

MacDonald, P., & Ahern, T. C. (2015). Exploring the Instructional Value and Worth of a MOOC. *Journal of Educational Computing Research*, *52*(4), 496–513. doi:10.1177/0735633115571927

Maor, D. (2003). The teacher's role in developing interaction and reflection in an online learning community. *Educational Media International*, *40*(1-2), 127–138. doi:10.1080/0952398032000092170

McAuley, A., Stewart, B., Siemens, G., & Cormier, D. (2010). The MOOC Model for Digital Practice, Massive Open Online. In *Massive Open Online Courses: Digital Ways of Knowing and Learning*. Academic Press.

Moore, M. G. (2007). The theory of transactional distance. In M. G. Moore (Ed.), *Handbook of distance education* (pp. 89–105). Mahwah, NJ: Lawrence Erlbaum Associates.

Morris, L. V., Xu, H., & Finnegan, C. L. (2005). Roles of faculty in teaching asynchronous undergraduate courses. *Journal of Asynchronous Learning Networks*, *9*(1), 65–82.

Park, J. H., Schallert, D. L., Sanders, A. J., Williams, K. M., Seo, E., Yu, L. T., & Knox, M. C. et al. (2015). Does it matter if the teacher is there? A teacher's contribution to emerging patterns of interactions in online classroom discussions. *Computers & Education*, *82*, 315–328. doi:10.1016/j.compedu.2014.11.019

Park, Y. J., & Bonk, C. J. (2007). Synchronous learning experiences: Distance and residential learners' perspectives in a blended graduate course. *Journal of Interactive Online Learning*, *6*(3), 245–264.

Robinson, A. C., Kerski, J., Long, E. C., Luo, H., DiBiase, D., & Lee, A. (2015). Maps and the geospatial revolution: Teaching a massive open online course (MOOC) in geography. *Journal of Geography in Higher Education*, *39*(1), 65–82. doi:10.1080/03098265.2014.996850

Siemens, G. (2012, July 25). MOOCs are really a platform. *Elearnspace*.

Chapter 15
An Entertaining Game-Like Learning Environment in a Virtual World for Education

Hsiao-Cheng (Sandrine) Han
The University of British Columbia, Canada

Ge Shi
The University of British Columbia, Canada

Junsong Zhang
The University of British Columbia, Canada

Annie Hung
The University of British Columbia, Canada

Nasim Peikazadi
The University of British Columbia, Canada

Colette P. L. Doan
The University of British Columbia, Canada

Sandra Filippelli
The University of British Columbia, Canada

ABSTRACT

This chapter explores the possibilities, benefits, and difficulties of developing game-like virtual environments for education. The goal of this paper is to review the background of game-like environment and impact of game-like environment on learning, discuss the differences on teacher-free and teacher-leading virtual learning environment, and provide examples of game-like environment in the virtual world for education. Finally, this chapter also provides suggestions to readers who would like to create game-like virtual environments for education.

INTRODUCTION

This article explores the possibilities, benefits, and difficulties of developing entertaining game-like virtual environments for education (Han, 2015). The developers are five instructors taking the same class—Visual learning in 3D animated virtual worlds—at the University of British Columbia. The developers are instructors of different subject areas: elementary school level education, leadership education, design education, media education, and museum education. Because of the diversity of these developers,

DOI: 10.4018/978-1-4666-9995-3.ch015

the designs of their virtual learning environments were very different. These developers used their own virtual learning environment design, construction, and teaching demonstration experience to explore the use of game-like environments for education in virtual worlds.

BACKGROUND: LITERATURE REVIEW ON GAME-LIKE ENVIRONMENT

According to Burbules (2006), rethinking the virtual as an educational concept poses a sharp contrast to much current practice by highlighting the centrality of choice, decision, and exploration as important dimensions of learning. Therefore, rather than seeing learning spaces as "delivery systems," it is important to view them as potential sites of collaboration and communities of learners (Rockinson-Szapkiw, 2014; Lounis, Pramatari, & Theotokis, 2014). These perspectives on virtual learning spaces lead us to think about the potentials of education and to ponder how the rising new technologies are being thought about and used in education.

According to Dickey (2005), "educational MOOs (Multiple User Domains Object Oriented) promote an interactive style of learning, collaboration opportunities, and meaningful engagement across time and space" (p. 440). The 3D virtual world is full of educational possibilities (Abbattista, Calefato, De Lucia, Francese, Lanubile, Passero, 2009; Burbules, 2006; Chen, Slau, & Nah, 2008; Dickey, 2005a, 2005b; Han, 2013; Han, 2011); languages, international business, science, math, and art are taught in virtual worlds. Everything students do in the virtual world can be a learning experience. Students in the virtual world are learning through their visual sense; they are seeing and learning from the objects made by other virtual world residents. Moreover, students can travel to different locations and interact with people from other cultures. This kind of learning by doing or learning by seeing fosters self-directed learning (Dewey, 1934; Garris, Ahlers, & Driskell, 2002).

Impact of Game-Like Environment on Learning

We live in a highly technological society that relies on technology from waking up in the morning to succeeding at work to entertaining ourselves in our leisure time. To be a successful member of such a society, students must *be trained* in the use of technology throughout the educational system (Siang & Rao, 2003).

Through playing, we can socialize and observe the world around us, helping us learn to interact with others and understand the world (Han, 2015). Playing provides stronger motivation and experience for learning. From a psychological perspective, a certain amount of excitement is conducive for learning as it potentially pushes what we see and learn into long-term memory (Linehan, Kirman, & Roche, 2014).

Students learn more effectively in an entertaining environment if that environment acquires gaming aspects and educational value simultaneously (Jarvin, 2015; Blumberg, Altschuler, Almonte, & Mileaf, 2013). Savery (2006) believes that students' attention will be focused for a longer period of time if they are trying to solve a problem and/or attain a goal, which are the main objectives of most games. Learning through playing can result in high quality learning. In fact, when a person plays, he or she shows a high level of motivation, observation, and engagement (van der Aalsvoort, Lepola, Overtoom, & Laitinen, 2015). The learning process is very similar to playing. One must have motivation and feel engaged toward what he or she is learning (Vos, van der Meijden, & Denessen, 2011).

When students are exposed to a gamified learning place, the experience of "fun" and "exploration" enhances their motivation and engagement, which, in turn, boosts their level of learning (Han, 2015). However, not every moment of an educational experience needs to be exciting; some things that we have to learn are dull or serious. However, the more we can engage students, the more they will learn. Engaging students within a problem solving or inquiry based learning environment encourages them to discover not only the answers but also formulate the questions they are curious about.

With technological development, play is extended from the physical environment to online (virtual) environments (Han, 2015; Amory, Naicker, Vincent & Adams, 1999). We now have a specific variety of videos or online games that are designed for educational purposes, Serious Games, which aims to enhance learning through games (Michael & Chen, 2006). There are also wider discussions on gamification and gamified pedagogy, which bring game elements into physical and virtual classrooms to enhance teaching and learning by motivating and engaging learners through games and play (Burguillo, 2010; Deterding, 2012; Deterding, Dixon, Khaled, & Nacke, 2011; McGonigal, 2011; Nicholson, 2012).

Using the game-like environment as a part of blended learning is a good way to start, although some schools may face challenges with their technology infrastructure. Because of these challenges with technology, usage will probably depend on school funding and administrative decisions. Planning is also required to incorporate the game-like environment into curriculum and daily teaching activities. For example, use of the game-like environment needs to align with teaching objectives and the values of curriculum (Shelton & Scoresby, 2011). In addition, use of technology or computer-based games can contribute to digital and media literacy for new generations (Prensky, 2001). A review of research shows that curriculum using virtual worlds in K-12 and higher education generally produces enhanced learning outcomes (Hew & Cheung, 2010).

Teacher-Free Environment and Teacher-Leading Environment

The use of technology as part of a blended learning environment is of utmost importance (Graham, 2006; Kirkley & Kirkley, 2005). Students not only use the internet for research/inquiry purposes but also technology, such as Smart Boards, to present their findings. In fact, technology's influence on the traditional classroom could transform the lecture-style teaching that is still pervasive in classrooms around the world.

Traditional forms of education are undergoing significant transformations in their educational environments, which are increasingly founded on the current life-experiences of their learners (Ally, 2008). Specifically, educational environments are being adapted to the contemporary global context (Farrell, 1999), in which we are faced with non-stop development in technology and widespread information through social media (Dabbagh, & Kitsantas, 2011). Freedman (1997) suggests that for education to stay attuned to the fast pacing developments of the contemporary world, the application of technology is required more than ever before. Newer forms of education, rather than providing physical places for transmitting knowledge, provide spaces for the learners to create and share knowledge (Duncum, 1997). According to Efland (2002), there is a shift in theories of knowledge construction from "symbol-processing" views to views more focused on the learners. From this perspective, knowledge is not passively received but "actively constructed by the learner" (p.72). As George Lucas (n.d.) (filmmaker and founder of Edutopia.org) maintains, "New digital multimedia" and "telecommunications" can support the improvement of student learning and also engage them more in the process of learning.

Developing a virtual world for education requires the instructors to have a well-planned curriculum, an interactive pedagogy, and a creative mind to bring their designs to life (Han, Yaro, Gillard, Haugh,

Ihnatovych, & Liu, 2014). Today, educators believe in learning by doing. If students are able to experiment for themselves, the learning will be more profound (Piaget, 1973). Virtual learning environments create opportunities that allow learners to move from one learning environment to the other in order to acquire knowledge. In virtual worlds, educators can incorporate several kinds of software, games and puzzles from different sources into their world and invite students to join and have fun while they learn. Learning can be very relaxing and joyful in the virtual world, and create learners that are more motivated to learn through play as they interact with each other through their avatars. This would broaden the scope of learners on the subject matter and bring about collaborative learning as well.

Generally, virtual learning environments are teacher-lead. Many virtual learning environments that take instructors hours to create become abandoned places after class because these environments cannot be used without the instructors' guidance (Iqbala, Kankaanrantaa, Neittaanmäkia, 2010). Compared with teacher-lead virtual learning environment, teacher-free virtual learning environment does not imply that the teacher is not involved in the learning, but teachers design an environment for students so that, even if the teacher is not present, students are still able to learn. Therefore, in 2014, we decided to create virtual learning environments that can be used by students even when there is no instructor present[1]. And, to increase the positive impact of our work on the current educational environment, we explored how to make this learning space fun as well as educational by incorporate gaming theory into the virtual learning environment (Han, 2015; Barab, Gresalfi, & Ingram-Goble, 2010; Garris, Ahlers, & Driskell, 2002).

EXAMPLES OF GAME-LIKE ENVIRONMENT IN VIRTUAL WORLD FOR EDUCATION

Introducing the Developers

The entertaining game-like learning environment developers are five teachers taking the same class—Visual learning in 3D animated virtual worlds—at the University of British Columbia. Junsong came from China, and his teaching area is in higher education, specifically focussing on leadership. Nasim is an Iranian, and her speciality is design education in higher education. Colette is a Canadian elementary school teacher. Annie came from Taiwan, and she is specialized in museum education; her targeted participants were general museum visitors. Liz, who is from China, specialized in media education in higher education.

Because of the diversity of these developers, the designs of their virtual learning environments were very different. All these developers had little to no virtual world developing experience. They learned about and developed their own entertaining game-like learning environment in about four months. These developers used their own virtual learning environment design, construction, and teaching demonstration experiences to explore the use of game-like environments for education in virtual worlds.

Junsong: Learning Environment for Leadership Development

My purpose was to create a learning environment for higher education leadership development, and I decided to bring game elements into the environment. There are several levels to the game elements. The ground level introduces participants to the rules and goals of the space. Drawing from my experience of playing a variety of role-play games, I designed 3 levels: a gallery (Figure 1), a maze (Figure 2), and a quiz lab for debrief and discussion (Figure 3). Each level is connected by teleportation. The gallery is used to display images related to leadership and to encourage participants to think about what leadership is. The maze is an exploratory environment. Participants must locate materials relevant to leadership and also find the way out. Participants are also exposed again to images first seen in the gallery. The Lab provides a pop quiz on the materials found in the maze and also serves as a place for resources, such as web links, videos, and PowerPoints.

Figure 1. Gallery space made by Junsong

Figure 2. Maze, made by Junsong

Figure 3. Lab, made by Junsong

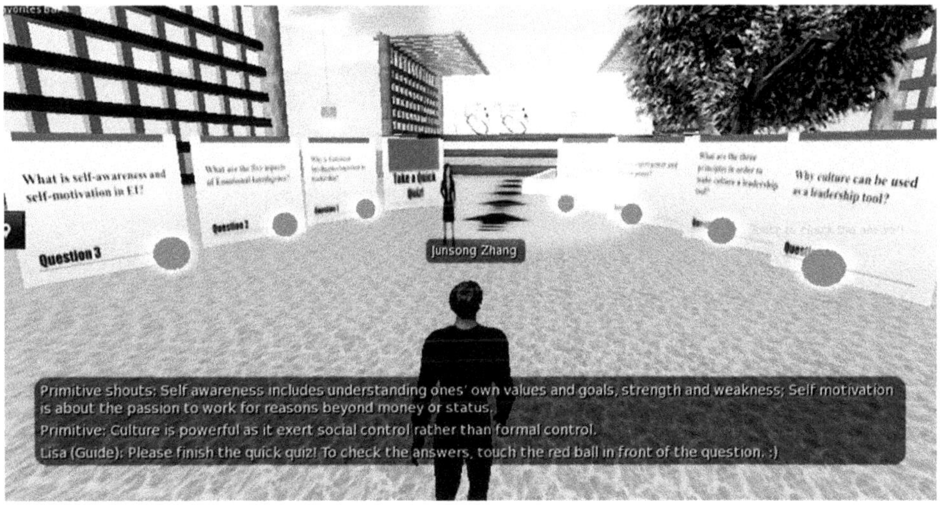

Lessons Learned During the Process of Creating a Virtual Learning Environment

I spent around 30 hours on the project, and I definitely learned how to use different tools to build different things and create special effects. Using those tools creatively is important. It's all about using different tools creatively. I believe conceptualizing the virtual learning environment is also important. You need to have some understanding and theoretical background of games, cognition, and pedagogy. After all, we want the learning environment to support learning effectively.

Lessons Learned after Delivered the Teaching Demonstration

It was impressive to see how others used tools creatively to construct their learning environments, and some of the spaces are really well-designed in terms of texture, color, structure, and landscape. But we all have room for improvement on interactivity and providing immediate feedback. Some environments are well designed but provide limited opportunities regarding what participants can do. And many of the environments do not provide feedback. When we are designing a virtual learning environment, we also need to give more consideration to how the virtual learning environment aligns with or better supports the overall teaching objectives.

Nasim: Elements of Design

For my virtual learning environment, I planned to teach about the elements of design, such as line, colour, and texture, and focus on design of textile. I chose instructions and activities that can be performed and understood in the absence of an instructor. I began by dividing my lessons into three parts. These parts were 1. Getting familiar with the elements of design, 2. Learning hands on design skills, and 3. Establishing a place for design. With these three parts, I created a scaffolding learning process. To do this, I used a path to lead the higher education learners through the environment and help them follow the sequence of spaces and the contents and activities assigned to those spaces (Figure 4). This prevented

Figure 4. Learning about some hands on skills for creating design by Nasim

the learners from getting lost and wondering what they could do or learn in the virtual learning environment. Moreover, I incorporated an activity into each instruction, for instance, writing reflections, playing with patterns, as well as colouring virtual objects, so that the learners could assess their understanding before moving on to the next step (Figure 5).

Lessons Learned During the Process of Creating a Virtual Learning Environment

In the virtual world, one creates a scene within a totally empty area. Because the designer starts from a blank slate, it is crucial to have a story in mind beforehand. While working on my land, I found myself having to think about every single, even tiny, object I was positioning. Keeping a storyline in mind helped

Figure 5. A place for creating some designs by Nasim

me to maintain the unity of my land. I also learned that a creative virtual learning environment is an environment in which knowledge is being transmitted through the participation of the learner interacting with the land, rather than one in which information is given in the form of written text or clear instructions. Therefore, I had to develop activities that would engage the learner in the lessons.

Lessons Learned after Delivered the Teaching Demonstration

Once again, I would like to emphasize activity engagement and its importance in the learning process. After demonstrating my land to my peers, I found that I have to plan for any contingency beforehand, including anything that the users or learners can do and see in my land. I also have to maintain the users' engagement with whatever knowledge or information the land is going to convey.

Colette: Elementary School Level Game-Like Environment

My learning environment was designed to be a teacher- free, game-like environment, where students would be introduced to learning outcomes and would later review those same learning outcomes as part of a blended learning experience. I chose a very small piece of land and created a sparse forest surrounding a vertical "tree-house" like structure with a ramp, which acted like a path, winding around it (Figure 6). On each level of the "tree-house" is an activity related to the "big idea" concept of Patterns and tied into a transdisciplinary scope. The subjects reviewed are Math, Art, and Science, and grade 2 (6-7 year olds) is the age group of my students. I created this simple environment for them to use while getting accustomed to virtual learning environments. I believe the blended learning experience, of individual and group class work along with the virtual learning environment, will keep students interested and facilitate learning to a greater degree than learning through just one or the other.

Lessons Learned During the Process of Creating the Virtual Learning Environment

I found the task of creating a virtual learning environment from scratch to have a huge learning curve. I chose to create most of what was in my environment myself instead of borrowing or copying from

Figure 6. The tree house by Colette

other environments. This may have not been the best strategy as I spent much of my time trying to make elements work the way I wanted them to for my desired learning outcomes. I learned a great deal about scripting and 3D environments. It takes significant spatial awareness to understand how elements look and move in the virtual world. My experience as an artist enabled me to design a space that works on many levels, from the design of the vertical, multileveled "tree-house" structure to the aesthetics of the forest to the activities designed to let students explore the concept of patterns by playing with virtual bricks. Also, as a detail-oriented person, I found that I could spend a great deal of time on very small details, taking away from the time I spent on the overall design. I look at this environment as my sketch for a later more structured and perfected design.

Lessons Learned after Delivered the Teaching Demonstration

My fellow classmates appeared to be able to move through their environments easily enough, but the interactive games that I designed did not seem to be as accessible as I had hoped due to the complicated technological processes. I believe that my instructions were clear enough on each level for my environment to function as a teacher-free environment, but I will need to think about redesigning some of the game elements to make them more user-friendly. Because of my technological inabilities and the limitations of the virtual world, I could not create a smooth and easy-to-follow virtual learning environment that I had imagined.

Annie: Interactive Virtual Museum

I created a teacher-free virtual world to give museum visitors the option of exploring this learning environment themselves. I believe that free choice learning can take the educational experience to another level. Therefore, in my virtual world, learners can choose where to go, what to learn and what to see (Figure 7.). For example, I set up two teleporters to take them to different learning environments, one about identifying the country of the mask, and the other about identifying Tibetan instruments. Instead

Figure 7. The starting point of the interactive virtual museum by Annie

of telling them where they should teleport, I encourage my students to make their own interpretations and choices. This strategy triggers their curiosity about what they will be learning. I also believe it is important to make sure the virtual world I create includes a lot of interactivity. For example, I designed an activity in which students identify the country of a mask (Figure 8.). Students can type in the country in the chat box. If the avatar moves away from the mask, this means they have the right answer!

Lessons Learned During the Process of Creating a Virtual Learning Environment

I found that building my own learning environment and designing my own activity was really enjoyable. Once I began creating my world, I started to reflect on the ways I would like to deliver my lesson: I wanted my students to learn and have fun at the same time. My virtual world is primarily designed for educational museum programs. People often think museums are lifeless and boring, because the interactivity of a museum visit can be very limited. But lessons delivered in a virtual world can be more interactive and fun. I am still seeking the balance of a learning environment that is entertaining while also educational, and I have found that imagination and creativity are very important for the development of this environment. I am also thinking about the many ways to teach as well as to learn. In terms of the overall learning environment, I feel like I have stepped out of my comfort zone and am really trying something new and different.

Lessons Learned after Delivered the Teaching Demonstration

It was a pleasure to see that my classmates were exploring and learning by themselves without needing much of my instruction. I think my goal of creating a free-choice learning environment has succeeded. Although my virtual space is supposed to be a teacher-free environment, I would like to give more attention to the pacing of the lessons and the continuous-engagement of the learners so that they can stay united as a class.

Figure 8. Identifying the country of the mask by Annie

Liz: Expression Training Space

I designed an "expression training space." It is a practice-based and teacher-free learning environment for developing students' "expression" skills. Higher education learners are free to write, draw, narrate, discuss and communicate with classmates. I divided my virtual world into four parts, with each one standing for a season. Spring, winter, and summer were all designed as settings for different teaching materials (Figure 9, 10, and 11). Autumn land holds a Maple Exhibition Center where students can present their learning outcomes (Figure 12).

Figure 9. Spring by Liz

Figure 10. Winter by Liz

Figure 11. Summer by Liz

Figure 12. Maple Exhibition Center

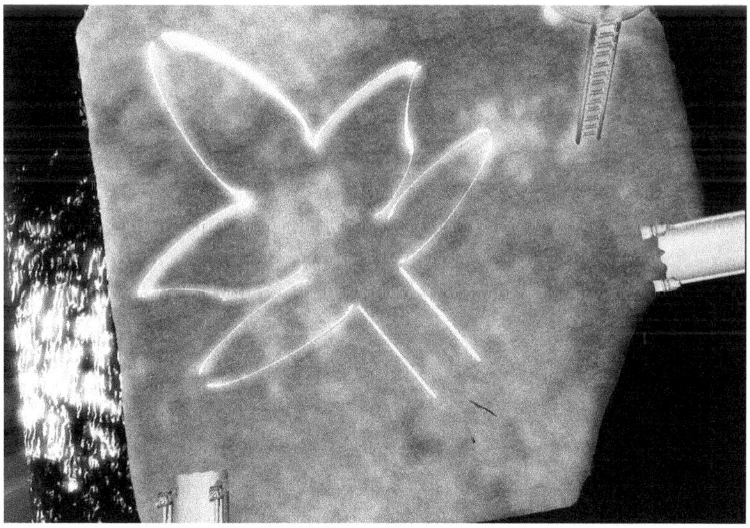

I think my VCER spaces are great environments for students to learn visual symbols, especially students in the Journalism and Mass Communication programs in higher education. Courses like visual communications, visual culture, critical thinking and media literacy could work well in this virtual leaning environment. But I do not want this virtual learning space to replace the traditional classroom. Instead, I hope it could be used as an interactive, multimedia setting to supplement the traditional learning environment. My final goal is to build a blended learning environment for courses in relative expression. For me, the greatest strength of the virtual learning environment is the potential for "practice" of expression, which will complement the theoretical learning of the traditional classroom.

Lessons Learned During the Process of Creating Virtual Learning Environment

I am not proficient at using computers, so I was surprised that it was so easy for me to manipulate elements when constructing the buildings. I found the virtual environment to be an interesting space in which to express my imagination and visualize my thoughts. Honestly, the most challenging part was organization, which was challenging in two ways. One was the spatial organization of my buildings. My blueprint changed several times during construction, many new ideas came to my mind when I observed objects in real life, and creating a visual learning environment required me to improve my observation skills. The other challenge was how to organize the gaming activities, for instance, where, when, and how to provide instructions to visitors. Having spent so much time thinking about how to organize virtual buildings, I now hope everything in the virtual world is meaningful.

Lessons Learned after Delivered the Teaching Demonstration

When giving the demonstration, I found clear visual navigation was necessary for immersing students in the virtual learning environment. I also found that attractive landscape and buildings were necessary for motivating students to learn. But the most important thing was how to guide students to use the settings in the learning environment.

SUGGESTIONS TO THE READERS

It is important to note that teacher immediacy exists in every element in a teacher-free gaming environment. The developers of these teacher-free gaming environments are five instructors in different fields. They found it important to get to know theories on game design, pedagogy, and cognition so the environment you build can better support learning. Also, they recommend that prospective developers ask experts for help and spending a lot of time creating and getting others to try out your creations to test their effectiveness. It is better to do this with a partner who has a different skill set.

Prospective developers should take a look at other virtual educational environments and note down the things they like or dislike to generate ideas for improving their own space. It is always good to keep an open mind and think out of the box. It is also helpful to start with small projects at the beginning for practice. They should start early, work on the overall design first, and then focus on finer details.

It is helpful for the learner to be clearly aware of the learning objectives at the beginning of their journey through the environment. A plan to engage the learner in educational (and entertaining) activities is essential to an effective learning environment. However, this entertaining learning environment cannot merely be a "playground." Time and place, as well as objectives, must be kept in mind when creating the environment. Idle wandering in an environment can quickly bore learners and decrease engagement within the virtual educational setting. The gaming pace, the sequential tasks, and different options for students to choose from engage students in a more focused learning experience.

CONCLUSION

Before we consider whether the game-like environment works in the current educational system, we must address several questions. First, why use games in instruction and what are the benefits of using a game-like environment? Curriculum refers to the organized interactions among students, teachers and instructional facilities, which operate based on learners' life experiences. A game-like learning environment fits the definition of curriculum. Second, what kinds of games are suitable for use in education, and what characteristics should an educational game have? There are many different kinds of games, and the purposes of games can vary. An ideal educational game should include clear gaming purposes, a logical storyline, appropriate challenges, and well planned timing (Han, 2015). Good organization is the basic rule of using games in the classroom.

An entertaining learning environment can relieve the pressures of learning while keeping students interested. However, we must carefully balance the "entertaining" and "educational" when creating an entertaining learning environment, because such an environment is not just about the subjects to be taught, but also about teachers' curriculum, pedagogy, and purpose of using these environments.

REFERENCES

Abbattista, F., Calefato, F., De Lucia, A., Francese, R., Lanubile, F., & Passero, I. (2009). Virtual worlds: Do we really need the third dimension to support collaborative learning? *VIWO 2009 Workshop*, (pp. 1-6). Aachen, Germany.

Ally, M. (2008). Foundations of educational theory for online learning. In T. Anderson (Ed.), *Theory and Practice of Online Learning* (pp. 3–31). Edmonton, Canada: Athabasca University Press.

Amory, A., Naicker, K., Vincent, J., & Adams, C. (1999). The use of computer games as an educational tool: Identification of appropriate game types and game elements. *British Journal of Educational Technology*, *30*(4), 311–321. doi:10.1111/1467-8535.00121

Barab, S. A., Gresalfi, M., & Ingram-Goble, A. (2010). Transformational Play: Using Games to Position Person, Content, and Context. *Educational Researcher*, *39*(7), 525–536. doi:10.3102/0013189X10386593

Blumberg, F. C., Altschuler, E. A., Almonte, D. E., & Mileaf, M. I. (2013). The impact of recreational video game play on children's and adolescent's cognition. In F. C. Blumberg & S. M. Fisch (Eds.), *New Directions for Child and Adolescent Development: No. 139. Digital games: A context for cognitive development* (pp. 59–70). San Francisco, CA: Jossey-Bass.

Burguillo, J. C. (2010). Using game-theory and competition-based learning to stimulate student motivation and performance. Computers & Education. . doi:10.1016/j.compedu.2010.02.018

Chen, X.-F., Slau, K., & Nah, F.-H. (2008). Adoption of 3-D virtual worlds for education. *International Conference on Information Systems*, (pp. 1-12).

Dabbagh, N., & Kitsantas, A. (2011). Personal Learning Environments, social media, and self-regulated learning: A natural formula for connecting formal and informal learning. *The Internet and Higher Education*. doi:10.1016/j.iheduc.2011.06.002

Deterding, S. (2012). Gamification: Designing for motivation. *Social Mediator*, *19*(4), 14–17.

Deterding, S., Dixon, D., Khaled, R., & Nacke, L. (2011). From game design elements to gamefulness: Defining "gamification". In *Proceedings of the 15th International Academic MindTrek Conference: Envisioning Future Media Environments*. doi:10.1145/2181037.2181040

Dewey, J. (1934). *Art as experience*. New York: Penguin.

Dickey, M. (2005b). Three-dimensional virtual worlds and distance learning: Two case studies of Active Worlds as a medium for distance education. *British Journal of Educational Technology*, *36*(3), 439–451. doi:10.1111/j.1467-8535.2005.00477.x

Dickey, M. D. (2005a). Brave new (interactive) worlds: A review of the design affordances and constraints of two 3D virtual worlds as interactive learning environments. *Interactive Learning Environments*, *13*(1-2), 121–137. doi:10.1080/10494820500173714

Duncum, P. (1997). Art education for new times. *Studies in Art Education*, *38*(2), 69–79. doi:10.2307/1320584

Efland, A. (2002). Art and cognition: integrating the visual arts in the curriculum. Reston, VA: National Art Education Association.

Farrell, G. M. (1999). The Development of Virtual Education: A Global Perspective. Vancouver, Canada: The Commonwealth of Learning.

Freedman, K. (1997). Visual art/virtual art: Teaching technology for meaning. *Art Education*, *50*(4), 6–12. doi:10.2307/3193647

Garris, R., Ahlers, R., & Driskell, J. E. (2002). Games, motivation, and learning: A research and practice model. *Simulation & Gaming*, *33*(4), 441–467. doi:10.1177/1046878102238607

Graham, C. R. (2006). Blended learning systems: Definition, current trends, and future directions. In Handbook of blended learning: Global Perspectives, local designs. San Francisco, CA: Pfeiffer Publishing.

Han, H. C. (2011). Second Life, a 3D animated virtual world: An alternative platform for art education. *Art Education*, *64*(4), 41–46.

Han, H. C. (2013). *Teaching visual learning through virtual world viewing, creating, and teaching experiences: Why we need a virtual world for education? IPTEL conference*. UBC.

Han, H. C. (2015). Gamified pedagogy: From gaming theory to create a self-motivated learning environment in studio art. *Studies in Art Education.*

Han, H. C., Yaro, K., Gillard, T., Haugh, D., Ihnatovych, D., & Liu, C. (2014). *From unknown to known: Virtual worlds Interactive Pedagogy*. STEM Conference. UBC.

Hew, K. F., & Cheung, W. S. (2010). Use of three-dimensional (3-D) immersive virtual worlds in K-12 and higher education settings: A review of the research. *British Journal of Educational Technology*, *41*(1), 33–55. doi:10.1111/j.1467-8535.2008.00900.x

Iqbala, A., Kankaanrantaa, M., & Neittaanmäkia, P. (2010). Experiences and motivations of the young for participation in virtual worlds. *Procedia: Social and Behavioral Sciences*, *2*(2), 3190–3197. doi:10.1016/j.sbspro.2010.03.488

Jarvin, L. (2015). Edutainment, games, and the future of education in a digital world. New Directions for Child and Adolescent Development, 147, 33–40. doi:10.1002/cad.20082

Kirkley, S. E., & Kirkley, J. R. (2005). Creating next generation blended learning environments using mixed reality, video games and simulations. *TechTrends*, *49*(3), 42–89. doi:10.1007/BF02763646

Linehan, C., Kirman, B., & Roche, B. (2014). Gamification as behavioral psychology. In Gameful world: Approaches, issues, applications. Cambridge, MA: MIT Press.

Lounis, S., Pramatari, K., & Theotokis, A. (2014). Gamification is all about fun: The role of incentive type and community collaboration. In *Proceedings of ECIS 2014*.

Lucas, G. (n.d.). *A Word from George Lucas: Edutopia's Role in Education*. Retrieved November 27, 2015, from http://www.edutopia.org/word-from-george-lucas-edutopias-role-in-education

McGonigal, J. (2011). *Reality is broken: Why games make us better and how they can change the world*. New York, NY: Penguin Books.

Michael, D., & Chen, S. (2006). *Serious games: games that educate, train and inform*. Boston, MA: Thomson Course Technology.

Nicholson, S. (2012). A user-centered theoretical framework for meaningful gamification. Paper Presented at Games+Learning+Society 8.0, Madison, WI.

Prensky, M. (2001). Digital natives, digital immigrants part 1. *On the horizon*, *9*(5), 1–6. doi:10.1108/10748120110424816

Rockinson-Szapkiw, A. (2014). Technologies that Assist in Online Group Work: A Comparison of Synchronous and Asynchronous Collaboration Technologies on Students' Learning and Community. In *Proceedings of World Conference on Educational Media and Technology 2014* (pp. 672-677). Association for the Advancement of Computing in Education (AACE).

Roussou, M. (2004). Learning by Doing and Learning Through Play: An Exploration of Interactivity in Virtual Environments for Children. *ACM Computers in Entertainment.*, *2*(1), 1–23. doi:10.1145/973801.973818

Savery, J. R. (2006). Overview of Problem-based Learning: Definitions and Distinctions. *Interdisciplinary Journal of Problem-Based Learning*, *1*(1), 9–20. doi:10.7771/1541-5015.1002

Shelton, B. E., & Scoresby, J. (2011). Aligning game activity with educational goals: Following a constrained design approach to instructional computer games. *Educational Technology Research and Development*, *59*(1), 113–138. doi:10.1007/s11423-010-9175-0

Siang, A. C., & Rao, R. K. (2003). Theories of learning: A computer game perspective. *Proceedings of the IEEE Fifth International Symposium on Multimedia Software Engineering*. doi:10.1109/MMSE.2003.1254447

Takatalo, J., Häkkinen, J., Kaistinen, J., & Nyman, G. (2010). Presence, Involvement, and Flow in Digital Games. In J. Karat & J. Vanderdonckt (Eds.), *Evaluating user experience in games: Concepts and methods*. NY: Springer. doi:10.1007/978-1-84882-963-3_3

van der Aalsvoort, G. M., Lepola, J., Overtoom, L., & Laitinen, S. (2015). Motivation of young students: A cross-cultural evaluation of a model for motivational orientations. *Research Papers in Education*, *30*(1), 114–131. doi:10.1080/02671522.2013.787447

Vos, N., van der Meijden, H., & Denessen, E. (2011). Effects of constructing versus playing an educational game on student motivation and deep learning strategy use. *Computers & Education*, *56*(1), 127–137. doi:10.1016/j.compedu.2010.08.013

Whitton, N. (2011). Game Engagement Theory and Adult Learning. *Simulation & Gaming*, *42*(5), 596–609. doi:10.1177/1046878110378587

ENDNOTE

1 The virtual learning environments are taking place in the opensim of VCER (Virtual Commons for Education and Research) at the University of British Columbia. VCER (http://blogs.ubc.ca/educationalvirtualworld/) is Dr. Sandrine Han's research project, funded by the UBC Faculty of Education since 2012. The VCER is a standalone Open Simulator, and the server is located in the UBC IT service. It is a virtual world for educational purposes only and invites educators from around the world, in K-12 and higher education, to participate with their students. The VCER offers the potential of the virtual world for education and avoids the defects that exist in the virtual world of Second Life. Because this is a world for educational purposes only, adult content, violence, and money transfers are not allowed. This is a free virtual world for educators to explore. Educators are encouraged to apply for free land; upload free textures, animations, and sounds; and copy and reuse existing objects. In this world, educators can explore online education in the virtual world, try face-to-face education accompanied by a virtual world environment, and even connect online students with face-to-face students to achieve hybrid education.

Compilation of References

Abbattista, F., Calefato, F., De Lucia, A., Francese, R., Lanubile, F., & Passero, I. (2009). Virtual worlds: Do we really need the third dimension to support collaborative learning? *VIWO 2009 Workshop*, (pp. 1-6). Aachen, Germany.

Abrami, P. C., Bernard, R. M., Borokhovski, E., Waddington, D. I., Wade, C. A., & Persson, T. (2015). Strategies for teaching students to think critically: A meta-analysis. *Review of Educational Research*, *85*(2), 275–314.

Abrami, P. C., Bernard, R. M., Bures, E. M., Borokhovski, E., & Tamim, R. M. (2012). Interaction in distance education and online learning: Using evidence and theory to improve practice. In L. Moller & J. B. Huett (Eds.), *The next generation of distance education: Unconstrained learning*. New York: Springer. doi:10.1007/978-1-4614-1785-9_4

Ahmed, S., Anik, T. A., Tasnim, M., & Ferdous, H. S. (2013). *Statistical analysis and implications of SNS search in underdeveloped countries*. Paper presented at 25th Australian Computer –Human Interaction Conference: Augmentation, application, Innovation, Collaboration, OZCHI 2013, Adelaide, Australia. Retrieved from https://www.academia.edu/4426905/Statistical_Analysis_and_Implications_of_SNS_Search_in_Under-Developed_Countries

Ajjan, H., & Hartshorne, R. (2008). Investigating faculty decisions to adopt Web 2.0 technologies: Theory and empirical tests. *The Internet and Higher Education*, *11*(2), 71–80. doi:10.1016/j.iheduc.2008.05.002

Akyol, Z., & Garrison, D. R. (2010). The development of a Community of Inquiry over time in an online course: Understanding the progression and integration of social, cognitive and teaching presence. *Journal of Asynchronous Learning Networks*, *12*(3–4), 4–22.

Akyol, Z., & Garrison, D. R. (2011). Understanding cognitive presence in an online and blended community of inquiry: Assessing outcomes and processes for deep approaches to learning. *British Journal of Educational Technology*, *42*(2), 233–250. doi:10.1111/j.1467-8535.2009.01029.x

Akyol, Z., & Garrison, D. R. (2011a). Assessing metacognition in an online community of inquiry. *The Internet and Higher Education*, *14*(3), 183–190. doi:10.1016/j.iheduc.2011.01.005

Akyol, Z., & Garrison, D. R. (2014). The development of a community of inquiry over time in an online course: Understanding the progression and integration of social, cognitive and teaching presence. *Journal of Asynchronous Learning Networks*, *12*(3-4), 3–22.

Allen, I. E., & Seaman, J. (2011). Going the distance: Online education in the United States. Sloan Consortium.

Allen, I. E., & Seaman, J. (2015). *Grade level: Tracking online education in the United States*. Retrieved from http://www.onlinelearningsurvey.com/reports/gradelevel.pdf

Allen, I. E., & Seaman, J. (2014). *Grade change: Tracking online education in the United States, 2013*. Babson Survey Research Group and Quahog Research Group, LLC.

Allen, I. E., & Seaman, J. (2015). *Grade level: Tracking online education in the United States*. Wellesley, MA: Babson Survey Research Group and Quahog Research Group, LLC.

Allen, M. W. (2003). *Michael Allen's guide to e-learning: Building interactive, fun, and effective learning programs for any company*. Hoboken, NJ: Wiley.

Allinder, R. M. (1994). The relationship between efficacy and the instructional practices of special education teachers and consultants. *Teacher Education and Special Education*, *17*(2), 86–95. doi:10.1177/088840649401700203

Ally, M. (2008). Foundations of educational theory for online learning. In T. Anderson (Ed.), *Theory and Practice of Online Learning* (pp. 3–31). Edmonton, Canada: Athabasca University Press.

Alutu, A. N. G. (2006). The guidance role of the instructor in the teaching and learning process. *Journal of Instructional Psychology*, *33*(1), 44–49.

Amory, A., Naicker, K., Vincent, J., & Adams, C. (1999). The use of computer games as an educational tool: Identification of appropriate game types and game elements. *British Journal of Educational Technology*, *30*(4), 311–321. doi:10.1111/1467-8535.00121

Andersen, J., & Andersen, P. (n.d.). *Teacher immediacy*. Retrieved November 29, 2015 from http://www.blackwellreference.com/public/uid=3/tocnode?id=g9781405131995_chunk_g978140513199525_ss13-1

Andersen, J. F., Andersen, P. A., & Jensen, A. D. (1979). The measurement of immediacy. *Journal of Applied Communication Research*, *7*(2), 153–180. doi:10.1080/00909887909365204

Anderson, J., Boyles, J. L., & Rainie, L. (2012). The future impact of the Internet on higher education. *Pew Research Center*. Retrieved from http://www.pewinternet.org/2012/07/27/the-future-of-higher-education/

Anderson, L.W., & Krathwohl. (Eds.). (2001). *A taxonomy for learning, teaching, and assessing: A revision of Bloom's Taxonomy of Educational Objectives*. New York: Longman.

Anderson, T. (2004). Towards a theory of online learning. In T. Anderson, & F. Elloumi (Eds.), Theory and practice of online learning (pp. 33-60). Athabasca University Press.

Anderson, T. (2008). *Teaching in an online learning context*. Retrieved December 2, 2015 from http://davidwees.com/content/role-immediacy-feedback-student-learning/

Anderson, T. (2014, December 16). *New report on emotional presence in online education*. [Web log post]. Retrieved from http://terrya.edublogs.org/2014/12/16/new-report-on-emotional-presence-in-online-education/

Anderson, T., & Dron, J. (2012). Learning Technology through Three Generations of Technology Enhanced Distance Education Pedagogy. *European Journal of Open, Distance and e-Learning, 2012*(2), Retrieved from: http://www.eurodl.org/?p=currentarticle=523

Anderson, J. F. (1979). Teacher immediacy as a predictor of teaching effectiveness. In D. Nimmo (Ed.), *Communication Yearbook III* (pp. 543–559). New Brunswick, NJ: Transaction Books.

Anderson, T. (2004). Teaching in an online learning context. In T. Anderson & F. Elloumi (Eds.), *Theory and Practice of Online Learning*. Athabasca University.

Anderson, T. (2008). *The theory and practice of online learning* (2nd ed.). Edmonton, AB: Athabasca University Press.

Anderson, T. (2009). A rose by any other name : Still distance education — a response to D. R. Garrison : Implications of online and blended learning for the conceptual development and practice of distance education. *Journal of Distance Education*, *23*(3), 111–116.

Anderson, T., & Dron, J. (2011). Three generations of distance education pedagogy. *The International Review of Research in Open and Distributed Learning*, *12*(3). Retrieved from http://www.irrodl.org/index.php/irrodl/article/view/890/1826

Anderson, T., Liam, R., Garrison, D. R., & Archer, W. (2001). Assessing teacher presence in a computer conferencing context. *The Journal of Asynchronous Learning*, *5*(2).

Anderson, T., Rourke, L., Archer, W., & Garrison, R. (2001). Assessing teaching presence in computer conferencing transcripts. *Journal of Asynchronous Learning Networks*, *5*(2).

Anderson, T., Rourke, L., Garrison, D. R., & Archer, W. (2001). Assessing teaching presence in a computer conferencing context. *Journal of Asynchronous Learning Networks*, *5*(2), 1–17.

Andrade, H. G. (2005). Teaching with rubrics: The good, the bad, and the ugly. *College Teaching*, *53*(1), 27–40. doi:10.3200/CTCH.53.1.27-31

Andrade, H., & Du, Y. (2005). Student perspectives on rubric-referenced assessment. *Practical Assessment, Research & Evaluation*, *10*(5), 1–11.

Andrade, H., & Valtcheva, A. (2009). Promoting learning and achievement through self-assessment. *Theory into Practice*, *48*(1), 12–19. doi:10.1080/00405840802577544

Anglin, G. J., & Morrison, G. R. (2000). An analysis of distance education research: Implications for the instructional technologist. *Quarterly Review of Distance Education*, *1*(3), 189–194.

Annand, D. (1999). The problem of computer conferencing for distance-based universities. *Open Learning*, *14*(3), 47–52. doi:10.1080/0268051990140307

Annand, D. (2011). Social presence within the community of inquiry framework. *The International Review of Research in Open and Distributed Learning*, *12*(5), 40–56. Retrieved from http://www.irrodl.org/index.php/irrodl/article/view/924/1855

Arbaugh, J. (2001). How instructors immediacy behaviors affect student satisfaction and learning in web-based courses. *Business Communication Quarterly*, *64*(4), 42–54. doi:10.1177/108056990106400405

Arbaugh, J. B. (2010). Sage, guide, both, or even more? An examination of instructor activity in online MBA courses. *Computers & Education*, *55*(3), 1234–1244. doi:10.1016/j.compedu.2010.05.020

Arbaugh, J. B., & Benbunan-Fich, R. (2007). The importance of participant interaction in online environments. *Decision Support Systems*, *43*(3), 853–865. doi:10.1016/j.dss.2006.12.013

Arbaugh, J. B., Cleveland-Innes, M., Diaz, S. R., Garrison, D. R., Ice, P., Richardson, J. C., & Swan, K. P. (2008). Developing a community of inquiry instrument: Testing a measure of the Community of Inquiry framework using a multi-institutional sample. *The Internet and Higher Education*, *11*(3-4), 133–136. doi:10.1016/j.iheduc.2008.06.003

Arbaugh, J. B., & Hornik, S. (2006). Do Chickering and Gamson's seven principles also apply to online MBAs? *The Journal of Educators Online*, *3*(2), 1–18.

Arbaugh, J. B., & Hwang, A. (2006). Does "teaching presence" exist in online MBA courses? *The Internet and Higher Education*, *9*(1), 9–21. doi:10.1016/j.iheduc.2005.12.001

Archibald, D. (2010). Fostering the development of cognitive presence: Initial findings using the community of inquiry survey instrument. *The Internet and Higher Education*, *13*(1-2), 73–74. doi:10.1016/j.iheduc.2009.10.001

Arnett, T. (2013, August 26). Will computers replace teachers? *Clayton Christensen Institute for Disruptive Innovation*. Retrieved from http://www.christenseninstitute.org/will-computers-replace-teachers/

Ash, S. L., Clayton, P. H., & Atkinson, M. P. (2005). Integrating reflection and assessment to capture and improve student learning. *Michigan Journal of Community Service Learning*, *11*(2).

Aslanian, C. B., & Clinefelter, D. L. (2012). *Online college students 2012: Comprehensive data on demands and preferences*. Louisville, KY: The Learning House, Inc.

Austin, A. E. (2002). Preparing the next generation of faculty: Graduate school as socialization to the academic career. *The Journal of Higher Education*, *73*(1), 94–122. doi:10.1353/jhe.2002.0001

Babson Survey Research Group. (2014). *Grade change: Tracking online education in the United States* [White paper]. Retrieved from http://www.onlinelearningsurvey.com/reports/gradechange.pdf

Backs, A. (2012). *Dragging the Y Generation into E-Learning: A study of engaging averse online learners. In 2012 Annual Proceedings* (Vol. 1, pp. 38–40). Bloomington, IN: Association for Educational Communications and Technology.

Bailie, J. L. (2011). *The criticality of verbal immediacy in online education: A modified Delpi study*. Retrieved November 25, 2015 from http://www.thejeo.com/Archives/Volume9Number2/BailiePaper.pdf

Baker, C. (2010). *The impact of instructor immediacy and presence for online student*. Retrieved November 16, 2015 from http://www.thejeo.com/Archives/Volume7Number1/BakerPaper.pdf

Baker, C. (2010). The Impact of Instructor Immediacy and Presence for Online Student Affective Learning, Cognition, and Motivation. *The Journal of Education Online*, *7*(1), 1–30.

Baker, C. (2010). The impact of instructor immediacy and presence for online student affective learning, cognition, and motivation. *The Journal of Educators Online*, *7*(1).

Baker, J. D. (2004). An investigation of relationships among instructor immediacy and affective and cognitive learning in the online classroom. *The Internet and Higher Education*, *7*(1), 1–13. doi:10.1016/j.iheduc.2003.11.006

Baker, J. D. (2010). Perceptions of immediacy, cohesiveness, and learning in online courses. *Christian Perspectives in Education*, *4*(1), 1–14.

Bali, M. (2014). MOOC pedagogy: Gleaning good practice from existing MOOCs. *MERLOT. Journal of Online Learning and Teaching*, *10*(1), 44–56.

Bambara, C. S., Habour, C. P., Davies, T. G., & Athey, S. (2009). *Delicate engagement: The lived experience of community college students enrolled in high-risk online courses*. Retrieved on July 2, 2015 from http://crw.sagepub.com/content/36/3/219.short

Bandura, A. (1997). *Self-efficacy: The exercise of control*. New York: W.H. Freeman.

Bangert, A. (2008). The influence of social presence and teaching presence on the quality of online critical inquiry. *Journal of Computing in Higher Education*, *20*(1), 34–61. doi:10.1007/BF03033431

Bangert, A. W. (2004). The seven principles of good practice: A framework for evaluating on-line teaching. *The Internet and Higher Education*, *7*(3), 217–232. doi:10.1016/j.iheduc.2004.06.003

Barab, S. A., Gresalfi, M., & Ingram-Goble, A. (2010). Transformational Play: Using Games to Position Person, Content, and Context. *Educational Researcher*, *39*(7), 525–536. doi:10.3102/0013189X10386593

Baran, E., Correia, A. P., & Thompson, A. (2011). Transforming online teaching practice: Critical analysis of the literature on the roles and competencies of online teachers. *Distance Education*, *32*(3), 421–439. doi:10.1080/01587919.2011.610293

Baran, E., Correia, A. P., & Thompson, A. (2013). Tracing successful online teaching in higher education: Voices of exemplary online teachers. *Teachers College Record*, *115*(3), 1–41.

Baringer, D. K., & McCroskey, J. C. (2000). Immediacy in the classroom: Student immediacy. *Communication Education*, *49*(2), 178–186. doi:10.1080/03634520009379204

Bauerlein, M. (2009). *The dumbest generation: How the digital age stupefies young Americans and jeopardizes our future (or, don't trust anyway under 30)*. London: Jeremy Tarcher/Penguin.

Baumeister, R. F. (1999). The nature of structure of the self: An overview. In R. F. Baumeister (Ed.), *The self in social psychology*. Philadelphia: Psychology Press.

Bawane, J., & Spector, J. M. (2009, November). Prioritization of online instructor roles: Implications for competency-based teacher education programs. *Distance Education*, *30*(3), 383–397. doi:10.1080/01587910903236536

Beer, V. (2000). *The web learning fieldbook: Using the world wide web to build workplace learning environments*. San Francisco: Jossey-Bass.

Bell, M. (1997). The development of expertise. *Journal of Professional Development*, *68*(2), 34–38.

Bell, R. A., & Daly, J. A. (1984). The affinity-seeking Function of Communication. *Communication Monographs*, *51*(2), 91–115. doi:10.1080/03637758409390188

Bennett, J. (2007). Great actors access vulnerability. *The Jason Bennett Actor's Workshop*. Retrieved from http://www.jbactors.com/actingreading/actorsaccessvulnerability.html

Berge, Z. L. (1995). Facilitating computer conferencing: Recommendations from the field. *Educational Technology-Saddle Brook NJ*, *35*, 22–22.

Berge, Z. L. (2002). Active, interactive, and reflective elearning. *Quarterly Review of Distance Education*, *3*(2), 181–190.

Biesenbach-Lucas, S. (2003). Asynchronous discussion groups in teacher training classes: Perceptions of native and non-native students. *Journal of Asynchronous Learning Networks*, *7*(3), 24–46.

Biggs, J., & Tang, C. (2007). Teaching for quality learning at university. McGraw Hill.

Bischoff, A. (2000). The elements of effective online teaching. In K. W. White & B. H. Weight (Eds.), The Online Teaching Guide: A Handbook of Attitudes, Strategies, and Techniques for the Virtual Classroom, (pp. 57-72). Academic Press.

Blackboard Help. (2011). *Blackboard Collaborate essentials*. Retrieved July 9, 2015, from http://www.open.uwi.edu/sites/default/files/BbC_Essentials_Manual_BbC11_V2_063011.pdf

Blackboard Help. (2015). *Blackboard Collaborate basics for administrators*. Retrieved August 13, 2015, from https://help.blackboard.com/en-us/Learn/Building_Blocks/Blackboard_Collaborate/Administrator/Collaborate_Basics_Administrators

Black, P., & William, D. (1998). Assessment and classroom learning. *Assessment in Education: Principles, Policy & Practice*, *5*(1), 7–74. doi:10.1080/0969595980050102

Blackwell Online Dictionary. (n.d.). *Teacher immediacy*. Retrieved November 29, 2015 from http://www.blackwellreference.com/public/uid=3/tocnode?id=g9781405131995_chunk_g978140513199525_ss13-1

Blanchard, K., & Johnson, S. (1982). *The one minute manager*. New York: Berkley Books.

Blignaut, A. S., & Trollip, S. R. (2003). Measuring faculty participation in asynchronous discussion forums. *Journal of Education for Business*, *78*(6), 347–353. doi:10.1080/08832320309598625

Bloom, B. S. (1984). *Taxomony of educational objectives*. Boston, MA: Allyn and Bacon.

Bloom, B. S., Englhart, M. D., Furst, E. J., Hill, W. H., & Krathwohl, D. R. (Eds.). (1956). *Taxonomy of educational objectives, the classification of educational goals, Handbook I: cognitive domain*. New York: Longmans.

Blumberg, F. C., Altschuler, E. A., Almonte, D. E., & Mileaf, M. I. (2013). The impact of recreational video game play on children's and adolescent's cognition. In F. C. Blumberg & S. M. Fisch (Eds.), *New Directions for Child and Adolescent Development: No. 139. Digital games: A context for cognitive development* (pp. 59–70). San Francisco, CA: Jossey-Bass.

Boettcher, J. (2011). *Ten best practices for teaching online: Quick guide for new online faculty*. Retrieved June 25, 2015, from http://www.designingforlearning.info/services/writing/ecoach/tenbest.html

Bolliger, D., & Waslik, O. (2009). Factors influencing faculty satisfaction with online teaching and learning in higher education. *Distance Education*, *30*(1), 103–116. doi:10.1080/01587910902845949

Bonk, C. J., Wisher, R. A., & Lee, J. Y. (2004). Moderating learner-centered e-learning: Problems and solutions, benefits and implications. In T. S. Roberts (Ed.), Online Collaborative Learning: Theory and Practice, (pp. 54-85). Academic Press.

Bonk, C. J., & Zhang, K. (2008). *Empowering online learning: 100+ activities for reading, reflecting, displaying, and doing*. San Francisco, CA: Jossey-Bass.

Bonwell, C. C., & Eison, J. A. (1991). Active Learning: Creating Excitement in the Classroom. 1991 ASHE-ERIC Higher Education Reports. ERIC Clearinghouse on Higher Education, The George Washington University.

Borup, J., Graham, C. R., & Velasquez, A. (2011). The use of asynchronous video communication to improve instructor immediacy and social presence in a blended learning environment. In *Blended learning across disciplines: Models for implementation*, (pp. 38-57). Academic Press.

Borup, J., West, R. E., & Graham, C. R. (2011). Improving online social presence through asynchronous video. *The Internet and Higher Education*, *15*(3), 195–203. doi:10.1016/j.iheduc.2011.11.001

Borup, J., West, R. E., & Thomas, R. (2015). The impact of text versus video communication on instructor feedback in blended courses. *Educational Technology Research and Development*, *63*(2), 161–184. doi:10.1007/s11423-015-9367-8

Borup, J., West, R. E., Thomas, R. A., & Graham, C. R. (2014). Examining the impact of video feedback on instructor social presence in blended courses. *International Review of Research in Open and Distance Learning*, *15*(3), 232–256. Retrieved from http://www.irrodl.org/index.php/irrodl/article/view/1821

Bosch, T. E. (2009). Using online social networking for teaching and learning: Facebook use at the University of Cape Town. *Communicatio. South African Journal for Communication Theory and Research*, *35*(2), 185–200.

Boswood, T., & Dwyer, R. (1995). From marking to feedback: Audio-taped response to student writing. *TESOL Journal*, *5*(2), 20–23.

Boud, D. (1995). *Enhancing Learning through Self Assessment*. London: Kogan Press.

Boud, D., & Falchikov, N. (1989). Quantitative studies of student self-assessment in Higher Education: A critical analysis of findings. *Higher Education*, *18*(5), 529–549. doi:10.1007/BF00138746

Bower, M. (2007, March). Groupwork activities in synchronous online classroom spaces. In *ACM. SIGCSE Bulletin*, *39*(1), 91–95. doi:10.1145/1227504.1227345

Bower, M. (2011). Synchronous collaboration competencies in web-conferencing environments–their impact on the learning process. *Distance Education*, *32*(1), 63–83. doi:10.1080/01587919.2011.565502

Boyd, D., & Jeffery, H. (2006). *Profiles as Conversation: Networked Identity Performance on Friendster.* Paper presented at the Hawai'i International Conference on Systems Sciences (HICSS-39) Persistent Conversation Track, Kauai, HI. doi:10.1109/HICSS.2006.394

Boyd, D. M., & Ellison, N. B. (2008). Social Network Sites: Definition, History, and Scholarship. *Journal of Computer-Mediated Communication, 13*(1), 210–230. doi:10.1111/j.1083-6101.2007.00393.x

Branon, R. F., & Essex, C. (2001). Synchronous and asynchronous communication tools in distance education: A survey of instructors. *TechTrends, 45*(1), 36–42. doi:10.1007/BF02763377

Bransford, J. D., Brown, A. L., & Cocking, R. D. (Eds.). (1999). *How people learn: Brain, mind, experience, and school.* Washington, DC: National Academy Press.

Brauckmann, S., & Schwarz, A. (2015). No time to manage? The trade-off between relevant tasks and actual priorities of school leaders in Germany. *International Journal of Educational Management, 29*(6), 749–765. doi:10.1108/IJEM-10-2014-0138

Braun, V., & Clarke, V. (2006). Using thematic analysis in psychology. *Qualitative Research in Psychology, 3*(2), 77–101. doi:10.1191/1478088706qp063oa

Brindley, J. E., Walti, C., & Blaschke, L. M. (2009). Creating effective collaborative learning groups in an online environment. *The International Review of Research in Open and Distributed Learning, 10*(3).

Brookfield, S. (1989). Facilitating adult learning. In S. Merriam & P. Cunningham (Eds.), *Handbook of adult and continuing education.* San Francisco: Jossey-Bass.

Brookfield, S. D. (1995). *Becoming a critically reflective teacher.* San Francisco: Jossey-Bass.

Brown, B. (2010, December). The power of vulnerability. *TEDxHouston.* TED Conferences, LCC. Retrieved from http://www.ted.com/talks/brene_brown_on_vulnerability.html

Brown, B. (2011, January). *Brene Brown: The power of vulnerability.* Retrieved from: http://www.youtube.com/watch?v=iCvmsMzlF7o

Brown, J. (2005). *The world café: Shaping our futures through conversations that matter.* San Francisco, CA: Berrett-Koehler Publishers.

Brown, J. S., Collins, A., & Duguid, P. (1989). Situated cognition and the culture of learning. *Educational Researcher, 18*(1), 32–42. doi:10.3102/0013189X018001032

Bruyn, L. L. (2004). Monitoring Online Communication: Can the development of convergence and social presence indicate an interactive learning environment? *Distance Education, 25*(1), 67–81. doi:10.1080/0158791042000212468

Buchanan, T., Sainter, P., & Saunders, G. (2013). Factors affecting faculty use of learning technologies: Implications for models of technology adoption. *Journal of Computing in Higher Education, 25*(1), 1–11. doi:10.1007/s12528-013-9066-6

Buchan, N. R., Croson, R. T., & Dawes, R. M. (2002). Swift Neighbors and Persistent Strangers: A Cross-Cultural Investigation of Trust and Reciprocity in Social Exchange1. *American Journal of Sociology, 108*(1), 168–206. doi:10.1086/344546

Buckingham, D. (1998). *Teaching Popular Culture.* London: UCL Press.

Burguillo, J. C. (2010). Using game-theory and competition-based learning to stimulate student motivation and performance. Computers & Education. . doi:10.1016/j.compedu.2010.02.018

Burnham, B., & Walden, B. (1997). Interactions in distance education: A report from the other side. In *Proceedings of the Adult Education Research Conference*. Oklahoma State University. Available: http://www.edst.educ.ubc.ca/aerc/1997/97burnham.html

Caffarella, R. S., & Zinn, L. F. (1999). Professional development for faculty: A conceptual framework of barriers and supports. *Innovative Higher Education*, *23*(4), 241–254. doi:10.1023/A:1022978806131

Cafferella, R. (2002). *Planning programs for adult learners*. San Francisco, CA: Jossey-Bass.

Cairncross, S., & Mannion, M. (2000). Multimedia and Learning: Patterns of Interactions. People and Computers XIV-Usability or Else! In *Proceedings of HCI*.

Campbell, A. (2005). Application of ICT and rubrics to the assessment process where professional judgement is involved: The features of an e-marking tool. *Assessment & Evaluation in Higher Education*, *30*(5), 529–537. doi:10.1080/02602930500187055

Campbell, D. (2014). The influence of teacher immediacy behaviors on Student Performanc in an online course (and the problem of method variance). *Teaching of Psychology*, *41*(2), 163–166. doi:10.1177/0098628314530351

Cappiccie, A., & Desrosiers, P. (2011). Lessons learned from using Adobe Connect in the social work classroom. *Journal of Technology in Human Services*, *29*(4), 296–302. doi:10.1080/15228835.2011.638239

Caprara, G. V., Barbaranelli, C., Borgogni, L., & Steca, P. (2003). Efficacy beliefs as determinants of teachers' job satisfaction. *Journal of Educational Psychology*, *95*(4), 821–832. doi:10.1037/0022-0663.95.4.821

Carini, R. M., Kuh, G. D., & Klein, S. P. (2006). Student engagement and student learning: Testing the linkages. *Research in Higher Education*, *47*(1), 1–32. doi:10.1007/s11162-005-8150-9

Carless, D. (2006). Differing perceptions in the feedback process. *Studies in Higher Education*, *31*(2), 219–233. doi:10.1080/03075070600572132

Carson, D.L., & McTasney, J.B. (1973). Grading technical reports with the cassette tape recorder: The results of a test program at the United States Air Force Academy. *Journal of Technical Writing and Communication, 3,* 131-144.

Carter, D. (2011). *Successful online learning: Managing the online learning effectively and efficiently*. Sudbury, MA: Jones and Bartlett Publishers.

Carwile, J. (2007). A constructivist approach to online teaching and learning. *Inquiry*, *12*(1), 68–73.

Cavanaugh, C., Gillan, K. J., Kromrey, J., Hess, M., & Blomeyer, R. (2004). *The effects of distance education on K-12 student outcomes: A meta-analysis*. Naperville, IL: Learning Point Associates.

Centre for Teaching Excellence. (2012). *Online discussions: Tips for instructors*. Retrieved July 27, 2015, from https://uwaterloo.ca/centre-for-teaching-excellence/teaching-resources/teaching-tips/developing-assignments/blended-learning/online-discussions-tips-instructors

Chambliss, D., & Takacs, C. (2014). *How College Works*. Boston: Harvard University Press. doi:10.4159/harvard.9780674726093

Chappuis, J. (2014). *Seven Strategies of Assessment for Learning*. New York: Pearson.

Char, R. O. (1978). *The effect of delay of informative feedback on the retention of verbal information and higher-order learning, for college students*. (Unpublished doctoral dissertation). Florida State University.

Charmaz, K. (2002). Qualitative interviewing and grounded theory analysis. In J. F. Gubrium & J. A. Holstein (Eds.), *Inside interviewing: New lenses, new concerns* (pp. 311–330). Thousand Oaks, CA: Sage.

Charmaz, K. (2006). *Constructing grounded theory: a practical guide through qualitative analysis. Thousand* Oaks, CA: Sage.

Cheese, P., Thomas, R. J., & Craig, E. (2008). *The talent powered organization: Strategies for globalization, talent management and high performance*. London, UK: Kogan Page Publishers.

Chen, B., Raible, J., Bauer, & Thompson. (2015). Welcome Message. In K. Thompson & B. Chen (Eds.), *Teaching Online Pedagogical Repository*. Orlando, FL: University of Central Florida Center for Distributed Learning. Retrieved February 27, 2015 from https://topr.online.ucf.edu/index.php?title=Welcome_Message&oldid=3906

Chen, X.-F., Slau, K., & Nah, F.-H. (2008). Adoption of 3-D virtual worlds for education.*International Conference on Information Systems*, (pp. 1-12).

Chickering, A. W., & Ehrmann, S. C. (1996, October). Implementing the seven principles: Technology as lever. *AAHE Bulletin*, *49*(2), 3–6.

Chickering, A. W., & Gamson, Z. F. (1987). Seven principles for good practice in undergraduate education. *AAHE Bulletin*, *3*, 7.

Chickering, A. W., & Gamson, Z. F. (1987, March). Seven principles of good practice in undergraduate education. *AAHE Bulletin*, *39*(7), 3–7. Retrieved from https://scholar.vt.edu/access/content/user/adevans/Public/DVDPortfolio/Samples/samples/training/track_d/Introduction/Best%20Practices/Article%20-%207%20Principles%20of%20Good%20Practice%20in%20Undergrad%20Ed.pdf

Chickering, A. W., & Gamson, Z. F. (1999, Winter). Development and adaptations of the seven principles for good practice in undergraduate education. *New Directions for Teaching and Learning*, *80*(80), 75–81. doi:10.1002/tl.8006

Choi, I., Land, S. M., & Turgeon, A. (2008). Instructor modeling and online question prompts for supporting peer-questioning during online discussion. *Journal of Educational Technology Systems*, *36*(3), 255–275. doi:10.2190/ET.36.3.c

Christophel, D. M. (1990). The relationships among teacher immediacy behaviors, student motivation, and learning. *Communication Education*, *39*(4), 323–340. doi:10.1080/03634529009378813

Churcher, K. M., Downs, E., & Tewksbury, D. (2014). "Friending" Vygotsky: A Social Constructivist Pedagogy of Knowledge Building Through Classroom Social Media Use. *The Journal of Effective Teaching, 33*.

Chute, A., Thompson, M., & Hancock, B. (1999). *The McGraw-Hill handbook of distance learning: An implementation guide for trainers & human resource professionals*. New York: McGraw Hill.

Cifuentes, O. E., & Lents, N. H. (2011). Increasing student-teacher interactions at an urban commuter campus through instant messaging and online office hours. *Electronic Journal of Science Education, 14*(1).

Cifuentes, L., & Shih, Y.-C. D. (2001). Teaching and learning online: A collaboration between United States and Taiwanese students. *Journal of Research on Technology in Education*, *33*(4), 456–474.

Clark, I. (2012). Formative Assessment: Assessment is for self-regulated learning. *Educational Psychology Review*, *2*(2).

Clark, I. L. (1985). Audiotapes and the basic writer: A selected survey of useful materials. *Teaching English in the Two-Year College*, *12*, 120–129.

Clark, R. E. (1983). Reconsidering research on learning from media. *Review of Educational Research*, *53*(4), 445–459. doi:10.3102/00346543053004445

Clark, T. (2007). Virtual and distance education in North American schools. In M. G. Moore (Ed.), *Handbook of distance education* (2nd ed.; pp. 473–490). Mahwah, NJ: Lawrence Earlbaum Associates.

Clark, T. D. (1981). Cassette tapes: An answer to the grading dilemma. *The American Business Communication Association Bulletin*, *44*(2), 40–41.

Cleveland-Innes, M., & Campbell, P. (2012). Emotional presence, learning, and the online learning environment. *International Review of Research in Open and Distance Learning*, *13*(4), 269–292.

Cohen, V. B. (1985). A re-examination of feedback in computer-based instruction: Implications for insturctional design. *Educational Technology*, *25*(1), 33–37.

Coladarci, T. (1992). Teachers' sense of efficacy and commitment to teaching. *Journal of Experimental Education*, *60*(4), 323–337. doi:10.1080/00220973.1992.9943869

Collins, A. (2006). Cognitive apprenticeship. In R. K. Sawyer (Ed.), *The Cambridge handbook of the learning sciences*. Cambridge University Press.

Collins, A., Brown, J. S., & Holum, A. (2011). Cognitive apprenticeship: Making thinking visible. *American Educator*, *6*(11), 38–46.

Cooper, S., & Sahami, M. (2013). Reflections on stanford's MOOCs. *Communications of the ACM*, *56*(2), 28–30. doi:10.1145/2408776.2408787

Coppola, N., Hiltz, S., & Rotter, N. (2002). Becoming a virtual professor: Pedagogical roles and asynchronous learning networks. *Journal of Management Information Systems*, *18*(4), 169–189.

Corbin, J., & Strauss, A. (2008). *Basics of qualitative research: Techniques and procedures for developing grounded theory* (3rd ed.). Los Angeles, CA: Sage.

Cox, M., Preston, C., & Cox, K. (1999). *What Factors Support or Prevent Teachers from Using ICT in their Classrooms?* Paper presented at the British Educational Research Association Annual Conference, Brighton, UK. Retrieved from http://www.leeds.ac.uk/educol/documents/00001304.htm

Crawford, C. (2015). Vulnerability in learning. In J. Spector (Ed.), *The SAGE Encyclopedia of Educational Technology* (pp. 832–835). Thousand Oaks, CA: SAGE Publications, Inc.; doi:10.4135/9781483346397.n338

Crawford, C. M. (2001). Developing webs of significance through communications: Appropriate interactive activities for distributed learning environments. *Campus-Wide Information Systems Journal*, *18*(2), 68–72. doi:10.1108/10650740110386675

Crawford, C. M. (2003). Emerging learning environments: Enhancing the online community. *Academic Exchange Quarterly*, *7*(4), 131–135.

Crawford, C. M., & Smith, M. S. (2015). Rethinking Bloom's Taxonomy: Implicit Cognitive Vulnerability as an impetus towards higher order thinking skills. In Z. Jin (Ed.), *Exploring Implicit Cognition: Learning, Memory, and Social Cognitive Processes* (pp. 86–103). Hershey, PA: Information Science Reference.

Creswell, J. W. (2005). MIxed methods designs. In *Educational research: Planning, conducting, and evaluating quantitative and qualitative research*, (pp. 509-529). Academic Press.

Creswell, J. W. (2007). *Five qualitative approaches to inquiry. In Qualitative inquiry & research design: Choosing among five approaches*. Thousand Oaks, CA: Sage Publications.

Crouch, C. H., & Mazur, E. (2001). Peer instruction: Ten years of experience and results. *American Journal of Physics*, *69*(9), 970–977. doi:10.1119/1.1374249

Cryer, P., & Kaikumba, N. (1987). Audio-cassette tape as a means of giving feedback on written work. *Assessment & Evaluation in Higher Education*, *12*(2), 148–153. doi:10.1080/0260293870120207

Cuban, L. (1986). *Teachers and Machines: the classroom use of technology since 1920*. New York: Teachers College Press.

Curtis, J. (2014, April). *The Employment Status of Instructional Staff Members in Higher Education, Fall 2011*. Washington, DC: American Association of University Professors. Retrieved from http://www.aaup.org/sites/default/files/files/AAUP-InstrStaff2011-April2014.pdf

Cuthrell, K., Fogarty, E., & Anderson, P. (2009). 'Is this thing on?' University Student Preferences Regarding Audio Feedback. In I. Gibson et al. (Eds.), *Proceedings of Society for Information Technology & Teacher Education International Conference 2009* (pp. 32-35). Chesapeake, VA: AACE.

Dabbagh, N. (2007). *The online learner: Characteristics and pedagogical implications*. Retrieved June 30, 2015 from http://www.citejournal.org/vol7/iss3/general/article1.cfm

Dabbagh, N. (2003). Scaffolding: An important teacher competency in online learning. *TechTrends*, *47*(2), 39–44. doi:10.1007/BF02763424

Dabbagh, N., & Kitsantas, A. (2012). Personal Learning Environments, social media, and self- regulated learning: A natural formula for connecting formal and informal learning. *The Internet and Higher Education*, *15*(1), 3–8. doi:10.1016/j.iheduc.2011.06.002

Dabbagh, N., & Reo, R. (2011a). Back to the future: Tracing the roots and learning affordances of social software. In M. J. W. Lee & C. McLoughlin (Eds.), *Web 2.0-based e-learning: Applying social informatics for tertiary teaching* (pp. 1–20). Hershey, PA: IGI Global. doi:10.4018/978-1-60566-294-7.ch001

Dahlstrom, E., & Brooks, D. C. (2014). ECAR Study of Faculty and Information Technology, 2014. Louisville, CO: ECAR.

Dahlstrom, E. (2012). *ECAR study of undergraduate students and information technology*. Louisville, CO: EDUCAUSE Center for Applied Research.

Dass, A. (2015). *The University of the West Indies statistical review, 2009/10 to 2013/14*. The University of the West Indies. Retrieved July 7, 2015 from http://www.mona.uwi.edu/opair/statistics/2013-2014/Survey%20Reports%20-%20UWI%20STATISTICAL%20REVIEW%202009-10%20TO%202013-14.pdf

Dean, P. J., Stahl, M. J., Sylwester, D. L., & Peat, J. A. (2001). Effectiveness of combined delivery modalities for distance learning and resident learning. *Quarterly Review of Distance Education*, *2*(3), 247–254.

Deliyannis, I., & Simpsiri, C. (2008). Interactive Multimedia Learning For Children With Communication Difficulties Using The Makaton Method. *Readings in Education and Technology:Proceedings of ICICTE.*

Dennen, V. P. (2011). Facilitator presence and identity in online discourse: Use of positioning theory as an analytic framework. *Instructional Science*, *39*(4), 527–541. doi:10.1007/s11251-010-9139-0

deNoyelles, A., Cobb, C., & Lowe, D. (2012). Influence of Reduced Seat Time on Satisfaction and Perception of Course Development Goals: A Case Study in Faculty Development. *Journal of Asynchronous Learning Networks*, *16*(2), 85–98.

Designing for Online Learning. (2012). *E-Coaching tip 36: Cognitive presence in online courses — Are you doing it?* Retrieved November 29, 2015 from http://www.designingforlearning.info/services/writing/ecoach/tips/tip36.html

Deterding, S. (2012). Gamification: Designing for motivation. *Social Mediator*, *19*(4), 14–17.

Deterding, S., Dixon, D., Khaled, R., & Nacke, L. (2011). From game design elements to gamefulness: Defining "gamification". In *Proceedings of the 15th International Academic MindTrek Conference: Envisioning Future Media Environments*. doi:10.1145/2181037.2181040

Dewey, J. (1925). Logic: The theory of inquiry (1938). *The Later Works, 1953*, 1-549.

Dewey, J. (1934). *Art as experience*. New York: Penguin.

Dewey, J. (1938). *Experience and education*. New York: The Macmillan Company.

Dewey, J. (1991). *How we think*. New York: Prometheus. (Original work published 1910)

Dickey, M. (2005b). Three-dimensional virtual worlds and distance learning: Two case studies of Active Worlds as a medium for distance education. *British Journal of Educational Technology*, *36*(3), 439–451. doi:10.1111/j.1467-8535.2005.00477.x

Dickey, M. D. (2005a). Brave new (interactive) worlds: A review of the design affordances and constraints of two 3D virtual worlds as interactive learning environments. *Interactive Learning Environments*, *13*(1-2), 121–137. doi:10.1080/10494820500173714

Dick, W., Carey, L., & Carey, J. (2008). *The systematic design of instruction* (7th ed.). New York: Pearson.

Dikkers, A. G., Whiteside, A. L., & Lewis, S. (2013). Virtual high school teacher and student reactions to the social presence model. *Journal of Interactive Online Learning*, *12*(3), 156–170.

Dirkx, J., & Smith, R. O. (2004). Thinking out of a bowl of spaghetti: Learning to learn in online collaborative groups. In T. S. Roberts (Ed.), Online Collaborative Learning: Theory and Practice, (pp. 132-159). Academic Press.

Dixson, M. (2010). *Creating effective student engagement in online courses: What do students find engaging?* Retrieved November 20, 2015 from file:///C:/Users/10018039/Downloads/1744-6523-1-PB%20 (1).pdf

Dixson, M. D. (2012). Creating effective student engagement in online courses: What do students find engaging? *Journal of the Scholarship of Teaching and Learning*, *10*(2), 1–13.

Dobo, N. (2014). *What it's like to have a robot for a teacher*. [Web blog post]. Retrieved from http://www.slate.com/articles/technology/future_tense/2014

Driscoll, M. P. (2004). *Psychology of Learning for Instruction* (3rd ed.). New York: Pearson Education.

Dubuclet, K. S. (2008). *Teaching presence: A focus on the instructor's role in online collaborative learning*. (Unpublished doctoral dissertation). University of Southern Mississippi.

Duncum, P. (1997). Art education for new times. *Studies in Art Education*, *38*(2), 69–79. doi:10.2307/1320584

Dunlap, J. C., & Lowenthal, P. R. (2009). Tweeting the night away: Using Twitter to enhance social presence. *Journal of Information Systems Education*, *20*(2). Retrieved from http://www.patricklowenthal.com/publications/Using_Twitter_to_Enhance_Social_Presence.pdf

Dunlap, J., & Lowenthal, P. (2014). The power of presence: Our quest for the right mix of social presence in online courses. In A. P. Mizell & A. A. Piña (Eds.), *Real life distance education: Case studies in practice*. Charlotte, NC: Information Age Publishing.

Dunlap, J., & Lowenthal, P. (2014). *The power of presence: Our quest for the right mix of social presence in online courses. Real Life Distance Education: Case Studies in Practice*. Charlotte, NC: Information Age Publishing.

Dunning, D. (2005). *Self-insight: Roadblocks and detours on the path to knowing thyself.* New York: Psychology Press. doi:10.4324/9780203337998

Dupin-Bryant, P. A., & DuCharme-Hansen, B. A. (2005). Assessing student needs in web-based distance education. *International Journal of Instructional Technology and Distance Learning, 2*(1), 39-47.

Easton, S. S. (2003). Clarifying the instructor's role in online distance learning. *Communication Education, 52*(2), 87–105. doi:10.1080/03634520302470

Efland, A. (2002). Art and cognition: integrating the visual arts in the curriculum. Reston, VA: National Art Education Association.

El Mansour, B., & Mupinga, D. M. (2007). *Students' positive and negative experiences in hybrid and online classes.* Retrieved on August 9, 2015 from http://www.freepatentsonline.com/article/College-Student-Journal/161282247.html

Ellingson, D. A., & Notbohm, M. (2012). Synchronous distance education: Using web-conferencing in an MBA accounting course. *American Journal of Business Education, 5*(5), 555–562.

Elo, S., & Kynga, H. (2007). *The qualitative content analysis process.* Retrieved November 29, 2015 from http://academic.csuohio.edu/kneuendorf/c63309/ArticlesFromClassMembers/Amy.pdf

Erichsen, E. A., & Bolliger, D. U. (2011). Towards understanding international graduate student isolation in traditional and online environments. *Educational Technology Research and Development, 59*(3), 309–326. doi:10.1007/s11423-010-9161-6

Ertmer, P., Richardson, J., Belland, B., Camin, D., Connolly, P., Coulthard, G., & Mong, C. (2007). Using peer feedback to enhance the quality of student online postings: An exploratory study. *Journal of Computer-Mediated Communication, 12*(2), 412–433. doi:10.1111/j.1083-6101.2007.00331.x

Fahara, M. F., & Castro, A. L. (2015). *Teaching strategies to promote immediacy in online graduate courses.* Retrieved November 20, 2015 from http://www.openpraxis.org/~openprax/index.php/OpenPraxis/article/viewFile/228/181

Farnham, S., Lahav, M., Raskino, D., Cheng, L., & Laird-McConnell, T. (2012). So.cl: An interest network for informal learning. In *Proceedings of the International AAAI Conference on Weblogs and Social Media.*

Farrell, G. M. (1999). The Development of Virtual Education: A Global Perspective. Vancouver, Canada: The Commonwealth of Learning.

Feenberg, A. (2008). Comments. *Social Epistemology, 22*(1), 119–124. doi:10.1080/02691720701773585

Fenwick, T. J. (2000). Expanding conceptions of experiential learning: A review of the five contemporary perspectives on cognition. *Adult Education Quarterly, 50*(4), 243–272. doi:10.1177/07417130022087035

Fink, L. D. (2003). *Creating Significant Learning Experiences: An Integrated Approach to Designing College Courses.* San Francisco, CA: Jossey-Bass.

Fisher, E. A., & Wright, Y. H. (2010). Improving online course design through usability testing. *MERLOT Journal of Online Learning and Teaching, 6*(1), 228–245.

Fluckiger, F. (1995). *Understanding networked multimedia applications and technology.* Prentice Hall.

Fournier, H., & Kop, R. (2015). MOOC Learning Experience Design: Issues and Challenges. *International Journal on E-Learning, 14*(3), 289–304.

France, D., & Wheeler, A. (2007). Reflections on using podcasting for student feedback. *Planet, 18*. Retrieved from http://www.gees.ac.uk/planet/p18/df2.pdf

Fredericksen, E., Pickett, A., Shea, P., Pelz, W., & Swan, K. (2000). Student satisfaction and perceived learning with online courses: Principles and examples from the SUNY learning network. *Journal of Asynchronous Learning Networks*, *4*(2), 7–41.

Freedman, K. (1997). Visual art/virtual art: Teaching technology for meaning. *Art Education*, *50*(4), 6–12. doi:10.2307/3193647

Frymier, A. A. (1994, Spring). A model of immediacy in the classroom. *Communication Quarterly*, *42*(2), 133–144. doi:10.1080/01463379409369922

Fullmer-Umari, M. (2000). Getting ready: The Syllabus and other online indispensables. In K. W. White & B. H. Weight (Eds.), The Online Teaching Guide, (pp. 95-111). Boston: Allyn and Bacon.

Furlich, S. (2013). Enhancing on-line teaching with verbal immediacy through self-theory. In T. Bastiaens & G. Marks (Eds.), *Proceedings of E-Learn: World Conference on E-Learning in Corporate, Government, Healthcare, and Higher Education 2013* (pp. 694-703). Chesapeake, VA: Association for the Advancement of Computing in Education (AACE).

Galant, R. (2013, March 26). What if students learn faster without teachers? *Cable News Network (CNN)*. Retrieved from http://www.cnn.com/2013/02/27/opinion/ted-prize-students-teach-themselves/index.html

Gao, T., & Lehman, J. D. (2003). The effects of different levels of interaction on the achievement and motivational perceptions of college students in a web-based learning environment. *Journal of Interactive Learning Research*, *14*(4), 367–386.

Garay, E. (2011). *Elluminate Live! is now Blackboard Collaborate*. Retrieved July 21, 2015, from https://sites.google.com/a/uic.edu/itlnews/announcements/elluminateliveisnowblackboardcollaborate

Garcia, D. F., Uria, C., Granda, J. C., Suárez, F. J., & Gonzalez, F. (2007, October). A functional evaluation of the commercial platforms and tools for synchronous distance e-learning.*Proceedings of the 3rd WSEAS/IASME International Conference on Educational Technologies.*

Gardner, S. (1995). Inquiry is no mere conversation (or discussion or dialogue): Facilitation is hard work! *Critical and Creative Thinking: The Australasian Journal of Philosophy for Children*, *3*(2), 38–49.

Garrison, D. R. (2003). Cognitive presence for effective asynchronous online learning: The role of reflective inquiry, self-direction and metacognition. In J. Bourne & J. C. Moore (Eds.), Elements of Quality: Practice and Direction (pp. 47-58). Needham, MA: Sloan-C.

Garrison, D. R. (2011). *E-learning in the 21st century: A framework for research and practice*. Taylor & Francis.

Garrison, D. R., & Vaughan, N. D. (2008). *Blended learning in higher education: Framework, principles, and guidelines*. Retrieved November 20, 2015 from http://www.designingforlearning.info/services/writing/ecoach/tips/tip36.html

Garrison, D. R., Anderson, T., & Archer, W. (2000). *Critical inquiry in a text-based environment: Computer conferencing in higher education*. Retrieved November 10, 2015 from http://cde.athabascau.ca/coi_site/documents/Garrison_Anderson_Archer_Critical_Inquiry_model.pdf

Garrison, D., Anderson, T., & Archer, W. (2003). A theory of critical inquiry in online distance education. In M. G. Moore & W. G. Anderson (Eds.), Handbook of Distance Education, (pp. 113-127). Mahwah, NJ: Erlbaum.

Garrison, D. (2011). *E-Learning in the 21st century: A framework for research and practice* (2nd ed.). London: Routledge/Taylor and Francis.

Garrison, D. R. (1989). *Understanding distance education: A framework for the future*. London: Routledge.

Garrison, D. R. (2006). Online collaboration principles. *Journal of Asynchronous Learning Networks*, *10*(1), 25–34.

Garrison, D. R. (2007). Online community of inquiry review: Social, cognitive, and teaching presence issues. *Journal of Asynchronous Learning Networks*, *11*(1), 61–72.

Garrison, D. R. (2007). Online Community of Inquiry Review: Social, Cognitive, and Teaching Presence Issues. *Journal of Asynchronous Learning Networks*, *11*(1), 61–72.

Garrison, D. R., & Anderson, T. (1998). *Learning in a networked world. In Distance learners in higher education: Institutional responses for quality outcomes* (pp. 97–112). Madison, WI: Atwood Publishing.

Garrison, D. R., Anderson, T., & Archer, W. (2000). Critical inquiry in a text-based environment: Computer conferencing in higher education. *The Internet and Higher Education*, *2*(2–3), 87–105.

Garrison, D. R., Anderson, T., & Archer, W. (2010). The first decade of the community of inquiry framework: A retrospective. *The Internet and Higher Education*, *13*(1), 5–9. doi:10.1016/j.iheduc.2009.10.003

Garrison, D. R., & Cleveland-Innes, M. (2005). Facilitating cognitive presence in online learning: Interaction is not enough. *American Journal of Distance Education*, *19*(3), 133–148. doi:10.1207/s15389286ajde1903_2

Garrison, D. R., Cleveland-Innes, M., & Fung, T. S. (2010). Exploring causal relationships among teaching, cognitive and social presence: Student perceptions of the community of inquiry framework. *The Internet and Higher Education*, *13*(1-2), 31–36. doi:10.1016/j.iheduc.2009.10.002

Garrison, D. R., & Shale, D. (1990). *Education at a distance: From issues to practice*. Melbourne, FL: Krieger.

Garrison, D., & Anderson, T. (2003). *E-learning in the 21st century*. London: Routledge Falmer. doi:10.4324/9780203166093

Garrison, D., Anderson, T., & Archer, W. (2000). Critical inquiry in a text-based environment; computer conferencing in higher education. *The Internet and Higher Education*, *2*(2-3), 87–105. doi:10.1016/S1096-7516(00)00016-6

Garrison, R. (2000). Theoretical challenges for distance education in the 21st Century: A shift from structural to transactional issues. *International Review of Research in Open and Distance Learning*, *1*(1), 1–17.

Garrison, R. (2009). Implications of online learning for the conceptual development and practice of distance education. *Journal of Distance Education*, *23*(2), 93–104.

Garrison, R., & Vaughan, H. (2008). *Designing blended learning to create a community of inquiry. In Blended learning in higher education: Framework principles and guidlines* (pp. 31–48). San Francisco: Jossey-Bass.

Garrison, W. (2001). Video streaming into the mainstream. *The Journal of Audiovisual Media in Medicine*, *24*(4), 174–178. doi:10.1080/0140110120094949 PMID:11802705

Garris, R., Ahlers, R., & Driskell, J. E. (2002). Games, motivation, and learning: A research and practice model. *Simulation & Gaming*, *33*(4), 441–467. doi:10.1177/1046878102238607

Gaynor, P. (1981). The effect of feedback delay on retention of computer-based mathematical material. *Journal of Computer-Based Instruction*, *8*(2), 28–34.

Gazi, Z. A., Aksal, F. A., & Öztuğ, O. (2012). *Online Social Networking: A Synergy for Learning*. Retrieved from http://www.iojes.net/userfiles/Article/IOJES_967.pdf_br

Getzlaf, B., Perry, B., Toffner, G., Lamarche, K., & Edwards, M. (2009). Effective instructor feedback: Perceptions of online Graduate students. *The Journal of Educators Online*, *6*(2), 1–22.

Ghamdi, A. A., Samarji, A., & Watt, A. (2016). *Essential considerations in distance education in KSA: Teacher immediacy in a virtual teaching and learning environment.* Retrieved on January 2, 2016 from http://www.ijiet.org/show-62-728-1.html

Gibbs, G., & Coffey, M. (2004). The impact of training of university teachers on their teaching skills, their approach to teaching, and the approach to learning of their students. *Active Learning in Higher Education*, *5*(1), 87–100. doi:10.1177/1469787404040463

Gibbs, G., & Simpson, C. (2004-05). Conditions under which assessment supports students' learning. *Learning and Teaching in Higher Education*, *1*, 3–31.

Giesbers, B., Rienties, B., Tempelaar, D. T., & Gijselaers, W. (2014). Why Increased Social Presence through Web Videoconferencing Does Not Automatically Lead to Improved Learning. *E-Learning and Digital Media*, *11*(1), 31–45. doi:10.2304/elea.2014.11.1.31

Gikandi, J. W., Morrow, D., & Davis, N. E. (2011). Online formative assessment in higher education: A review of the literature. *Computers & Education*, *57*(4), 2333–2351. doi:10.1016/j.compedu.2011.06.004

Gilbert, L., & Moore, D. R. (1998). Building interactivity into web courses: Tools for social and instructional interaction. *Educational Technology*, *38*(3), 29–35.

Glaser, B. (1992). *Basics of grounded theory analysis: Emergence vs. forcing*. Mill Valley, CA: Sociology Press.

Glaser, B. G., & Strauss, A. L. (1967). *The discovery of grounded theory: Strategies for qualitative research.* Chicago: Aldin.

Goa, W. (2006). *Influence of teacher immediacy on student evaluations of teachers in American and Chinese classrooms.* Retrieved December 2, 2015 from http://scholarworks.rit.edu/cgi/viewcontent.cgi?article=8948&context=theses

Gold, S. (2001). A constructivist approach to online training for online teachers. *Journal of Asynchronous Learning Networks*, *5*(1), 36–57.

Gorham, J. (1988). The relationship between verbal teacher immediacy behaviors and student learning. *Communication Education*, *37*(1), 40–53. doi:10.1080/03634528809378702

Gould, J., & Day, P. (2013). Hearing you loud and clear: Student perspectives of audio feedback in higher education. *Assessment & Evaluation in Higher Education*, 38(5), 554-56. http://dx.doi.org/10.1080/02602938.2012.660131.

Graduate Student Instructor Teaching and Resource Center. (n.d.). *Social constructivism.* Retrieved November 8, 2015 from http://gsi.berkeley.edu/gsi-guide-contents/learning-theory-research/social-constructivism/#teaching

Graham, C. R. (2006). Blended learning systems: Definition, current trends, and future directions. In Handbook of blended learning: Global Perspectives, local designs. San Francisco, CA: Pfeiffer Publishing.

Graham, C. R. (2006). Blended learning systems: Definition, current trends, and future directions. In C. J. Bonk & C. R. Graham (Eds.), *Handbook of blended learning: Global perspectives, local designs* (pp. 3–21). San Francisco, CA: Pfeiffer Publishing.

Graham, C. R., Henrie, C. R., & Gibbons, A. S. (2014). Developing models and theory for blended learning research. In A. G. Picciano, C. D. Dziuban, & C. R. Graham (Eds.), *Blended learning: Research perspectives* (Vol. 2, pp. 13–33). New York, NY: Taylor & Francis.

Grandzol, J., & Grandzol, C. (2006). Best practices for online business education. *International Review of Research in Open and Distance Learning*, *7*(1).

Green, B. (1998). Teaching for difference: Learning Theory and Post-critical pedagogy. In D. Buckingham (Ed.), *Teaching Popular Culture* (pp. 177–197). London: UCL Press.

Greenhow, C. (2011). Online social networks and learning. *On the Horizon*, *19*(1), 4–12. doi:10.1108/10748121111107663

Green, R., & Bowswer, M. (2006). Observations from the field: Sharing a literature review rubric. *Journal of Library Administration*, *45*(1-2), 185–202. doi:10.1300/J111v45n01_10

Griffiths, M. E. (2010). *Improving the Asynchronous Video Learning Model*. Brigham Young University.

Grossera, M. M., & Lombard, B. J. J. (2008). The relationship between culture and the development of critical thinking abilities of prospective teachers. *Teaching and Teacher Education*, *24*(5), 1364–1375. doi:10.1016/j.tate.2007.10.001

Guasch, T., Alvarez, I., & Espasa, A. (2010). University teacher competencies in a virtual teaching/learning environment: Analysis of a teacher training experience. *Teaching and Teacher Education*, *26*(2), 199–206. doi:10.1016/j.tate.2009.02.018

Gunawardena, C. N., & McIsaac, M. S. (2004). Distance education. In D. H. Jonassen (Ed.), *Handbook of research on educational communications and technology* (pp. 355–395). Mahwah, NJ: Lawrence Erlbaum.

Gunawardena, C. N., & Zittle, F. J. (1997). Social presence as a predictor of satisfaction within a computer-mediated conferencing environment. *American Journal of Distance Education*, *11*(3), 8–26. doi:10.1080/08923649709526970

Gunderson, B. J., Theiss, M. A., Wood, L. K., & Conti-OHare, M. (2014). Using a telephone call to increase social presence in online classes. *Nursing Education Perspectives*, *35*(5), 338–339. doi:10.5480/11-569 PMID:25291933

Haavind, S., & Sistek-Chandler, C. (2015). The Emergent Role of the MOOC Instructor: A Qualitative Study of Trends Toward Improving Future Practice. *International Journal on E-Learning*, *14*(3), 331–350.

Hackman, M. Z., & Walker, K. B. (1990). Instructional communication in the televised classroom: The effects of system design and teacher immediacy on student learning and satisfaction. *Communication Education*, *39*(3), 196–206. doi:10.1080/03634529009378802

Hadjioannou, X. (2007, June). Bringing the background to the foreground: What do classroom environments that support authentic discussions look like? *American Educational Research Journal*, *44*(2), 370–399. doi:10.3102/0002831207302173

Han, H. C., Yaro, K., Gillard, T., Haugh, D., Ihnatovych, D., & Liu, C. (2014). *From unknown to known: Virtual worlds Interactive Pedagogy*. STEM Conference. UBC.

Han, H. C. (2011). Second Life, a 3D animated virtual world: An alternative platform for art education. *Art Education*, *64*(4), 41–46.

Han, H. C. (2013). *Teaching visual learning through virtual world viewing, creating, and teaching experiences: Why we need a virtual world for education? IPTEL conference*. UBC.

Han, H. C. (2015). Gamified pedagogy: From gaming theory to create a self-motivated learning environment in studio art. *Studies in Art Education*.

Hanover Research Council. (2009). *Best practices in online teaching strategies*. Retrieved from http://www.uwec.edu/AcadAff/resources/edtech/upload/Best-Practices-in-Online-Teaching-Strategies-Membership.pdf

Hanover Research Council. (2009). *Best practices in online teaching strategies*. Retrieved June 19, 2015 from http://www.uwec.edu/AcadAff/resources/edtech/upload/Best-Practices-in-Online-Teaching-Strategies-Membership.pdf

Harasim, L. (1996). Computer networking for education. In Decorte & Wienert (Eds.), The International Encyclopedia of Developmental and Instructional Psychology. Pergamon Press.

Harasim, L. (1996). *Online education. Computer networking and scholarly communication in the twenty-first-century university*. Academic Press.

Harasim, L. (1996). Online education. In T. Harrison & T. Stephen (Eds.), *Computer networking and scholarly communication in the twenty-first century university* (pp. 203–214). New York: State University Press.

Harris, J. S. (1970). The use of the tape recorder in grading. *Brigham Young University Mediated Learning Systems MLS Newsletter*, *2*(3), 1–2.

Harris, K. (2008, October16). Using Social Networking Sites as Student Engagement Tools. *Diverse Issues in Higher Education*, *25*(18). Retrieved from http://diverseeducation.com/article/11837/

Harris, M., Larrier, I., & Castano-Bishop, M. (2011, Winter). Development of the student expectations of online learning survey (SEOLS): A pilot study. *Online Journal of Distance Learning Administration*, *XIV*, V.

Harris, R. A., & Nikitenko, G. O. (2014). Comparing online with brick and mortar course learning outcomes An analysis of quantitative methods curriculum in public administration. *Teaching Public Administration*, *32*(1), 95–107. doi:10.1177/0144739414523284

Hart, C. (2012). Factors associated with student persistence in an online program of study: A review of the literature. *Journal of Interactive Online Learning*, *11*(1), 19–42.

Hativa, N., & Goodyear, P. (Eds.). (2001). *Teacher thinking, beliefs, and knowledge in higher education*. Norwell, MA: Kluwer Academic Publishers.

Hattie, J., & Timperly, H. (2007). The power of feedback. *Review of Educational Research*, *77*(1), 81–112. doi:10.3102/003465430298487

Hays, J. (1978). *Play it again, Sandra: The use of tape cassettes to evaluate student compositions*. Paper presented at the Annual Meeting of the Conference on College Composition and Communication (ERIC Document Reproduction Service No. ED 162332).

Henderson, M., & Phillips, M. (2015). Video-based feedback on student assessment: Scarily personal. *Australasian Journal of Educational Technology*, *61*(1), 51–66.

Herreid, C. F., & Schiller, N. A. (2013). Case studies and the flipped classroom. *Journal of College Science Teaching*, *42*(5), 62–66.

Herrington, J., Reeves, T. C., & Oliver, R. (2010). *A guide to authentic e-learning*. New York: Routledge.

Heuer, B. P., & King, K. P. (2004). Leading the band: The role of the instructor in online learning for educators. *Journal of Interactive Online Learning*, *3*(1), 1–11.

Hewitt, A., & Forte, A. (2006). *Crossing boundaries: Identity management and student/faculty relationships on the Facebook*. Paper presented at the Computer Supported Cooperative Work Conference, Banff, Canada. Retrieved from: http://andreaforte.net/HewittForteCSCWPoster2006.pdf

Hew, K. F., & Cheung, W. S. (2010). Use of three-dimensional (3-D) immersive virtual worlds in K-12 and higher education settings: A review of the research. *British Journal of Educational Technology*, *41*(1), 33–55. doi:10.1111/j.1467-8535.2008.00900.x

Hew, K., & Cheung, W. (2012). Students' use of asynchronous voice discussion in a blended-learning environment: A study of two undergraduate classes. *Electronic Journal of E-Learning*, *10*(4), 360–367.

Higgins, R. (2000, September). *Be more critical': rethinking assessment feedback.* Paper presented at the British Educational Research Association Conference, Cardiff, UK. Retrieved from http://www.leeds.ac.uk/educol/documents/00001548.htm

Higley, M. (2013). *Benefits of synchronous and asynchronous e-Learning in an online learning environment.* Retrieved June 18, 2015 from http://elearningindustry.com/benefits-of-synchronous-and-asynchronous-e-learning

Hill, D. (2008). *The use of podcasts in the delivery of feedback to dissertation students.* Retrieved from http://www.heacademy.ac.uk/assets/hlst/documents/case_studies/case123_apr08_podcasts_feedback_dissertation_students.pdf

Hillman, D., Willis, D. J., & Gunawardena, C. (1994). Learner-interface interaction in distance education: An extension of contemporary models and strategies for practitioners. *American Journal of Distance Education*, *8*(2), 30–42. doi:10.1080/08923649409526853

Hiltz, R., Zhang, Y., & Tuross, M. (2002). *Studies of effectiveness of learning networks.* Needham, MA: Academic Press.

Hodges, C. B., & Forrest Cowan, S. (2012). Preservice teachers' views of instructor presence in online courses. *Journal of Digital Learning in Teacher Education*, *28*(4), 139–145. doi:10.1080/21532974.2012.10784694

Hosler, K. A., & Arend, B. D. (2012). The importance of course design, feedback, and facilitation: Student perceptions of the relationship between teaching presence and cognitive presence. *Educational Media International*, *49*(3), 217–229. doi:10.1080/09523987.2012.738014

Hrastinski, S. (2008). A study of asynchronous and synchronous e-learning methods discovered that each supports different purposes. *EduCause Quarterly,* (1). Retrieved July 5, 2015 from https://net.educause.edu/ir/library/pdf/eqm0848.pdf

Hrastinski, S. (2008). Asynchronous and synchronous e-learning. *EDUCAUSE Quarterly*, *31*(4), 51–55.

Huang, S. (2015). Understanding learners' self-assessment and self-feedback on their foreign language speaking performance. *Assessment & Evaluation in Higher Education*, 1–20. doi:10.1080/02602938.2015.1042426

Hudgins T.L., Orellana, A. & Simonson, M. (2009). *The perfect online course: best practices for designing and teaching*. Academic Press.

Huett, J. (2004). *Email as an educational feedback tool: Relative advantages and implementation guidelines.* Retrieved July 29, 2015 from http://itdl.org/journal/jun_04/article06.htm

Hunt, A. (1989). Taped comments and student writing. *Teaching English in the Two-Year College*, *16*(4), 269–273.

Hunter, C. D. (1998). *Technology in the Classroom: Haven't We Heard This Before?* [Class handout]. Retrieved: www2.le.ac.uk/departments/media/dl/documents.../Reading10.pdf

Hunt, R. A. (1975). Technological gift-horse: Some reflections on the teeth of cassette-marking. *College English*, *36*(5), 581–585. doi:10.2307/374823

Hurst, C. J. (1975). Cassette grading improves student report writing. *English Education*, *65*, 429–430.

Hussain, T. (2015). Influence of Facebook in Pakistani Pedagogy. *Media Watch*, *6*(3), 326–338. doi:10.15655/mw/2015/v6i3/77895

Hyland, K., & Hyland, F. (Eds.). (2006). *Feedback in second language writing: Contexts and issues.* New York, NY: Cambridge University Press. doi:10.1017/CBO9781139524742

Ice, P. (2008, April). *The impact of asynchronous audio feedback on teaching, social and cognitive presence.* Paper presented at the First International Conference of the Canadian Network for Innovation in Education, Banff, Canada.

Ice, P., Swan, K., Kupczynski, L., & Richardson, J. (2008). The impact of asynchronous audio feedback on teaching and social presence: A survey of current research. In *Proceedings of World Conference on Educational Multimedia, Hypermedia and Telecommunications 2008* (pp. 5646-5649). Chesapeake, VA: AACE.

Ice, P., Curtis, R., Phillips, P., & Wells, J. (2007). Using asynchronous audio feedback to enhance teaching presence and students' sense of community. *Journal of Asynchronous Learning Networks*, *11*(2), 3–25.

Ice, P., Swan, K., Diaz, S., Kupczynski, L., & Swan-Dagen, A. (2010). An analysis of students' perceptions of the value and efficacy of instructors' auditory and text-based feedback modalities across multiple conceptual levels. *Journal of Educational Computing Research*, *43*(1), 113–134. doi:10.2190/EC.43.1.g

IGI Global. (2015). *What is social presence?* Retrieved 2015 from http://www.igi-global.com/dictionary/social-presence/27463

Ignatius, E., & Kokkonen, M. (2007). Factors contributing to verbal self-disclosure. *Nordic Psychology*, *59*(4), 362–391. doi:10.1027/1901-2276.59.4.362

Iqbala, A., Kankaanrantaa, M., & Neittaanmäkia, P. (2010). Experiences and motivations of the young for participation in virtual worlds. *Procedia: Social and Behavioral Sciences*, *2*(2), 3190–3197. doi:10.1016/j.sbspro.2010.03.488

Ito, M. (2010). Work. In *Hanging out, messing around and Geeking out* (pp. 295–310). MIT Press.

Jacoby, J. (2014). The disruptive potential of the Massive Open Online Course: A literature review. *Journal of Open. Flexible and Distance Learning*, *18*(1), 73–85.

Jafari, A., McGee, P., & Carmean, C. (2006). Managing Courses, Defining Learning: What Faculty, Students, and Administrators Want. *EDUCAUSE Review*, *41*(4), 50–71. Retrieved from http://www.educause.edu/EDUCAUSE+Review/EDUCAUSEReviewMagazineVolume41/ManagingCoursesDefiningLearnin/158070

Jaggars, S. S., Edgecombe, N., & Stacey, G. W. (2013). *Creating an Effective Online Instructor Presence*. Community College Research Center, Columbia University.

Jaggars, S. S., Edgecombe, N., & Stacey, G. W. (2013). *What we know about online course outcomes*. New York, NY: Columbia University, Teachers College, Community College Research Center.

Jaggars, S. S., Edgecombe, N., & Stacey, G. W. (2014). *Creating an effective online instructor presence*. Community College Research Center, Teachers College, Columbia University.

Jamrisko, M., & Kolat, I. (2012). Cost of college degree in U.S. soars 12 fold: Chart of the day. *Bloomberg News*. Retrieved from http://www.bloomberg.com/news/2012-08-15/cost-of-college-degree-in-u-s-soars-12-fold-chart-of-the-day.html

Jarvin, L. (2015). Edutainment, games, and the future of education in a digital world. New Directions for Child and Adolescent Development, 147, 33–40. doi:10.1002/cad.20082

Jibril, T. A., & Abdullah, M. H. (2013). Relevance of Emoticons in Computer-Mediated Communication Contexts: An Overview. *Asian Social Science*, *9*(4). doi:10.5539/ass.v9n4p201

Johnson, S. D., Aragon, S. R., Shaik, N., & Palma-Rivas, N. (2000). Comparative analysis of learner satisfaction and learning outcomes in online and face-to-face learning environments. *Journal of Interactive Learning Research*, *11*(1), 29–49.

Jones, I. M. (2011). Can you see me now? Defining teaching presence in the online classroom through building a learning community. *Journal of Legal Studies Education*, *28*(1), 67–116. doi:10.1111/j.1744-1722.2010.01085.x

Jones, P., Naugle, K., & Kolloff, M. (2008). *Teacher presence: Using introductory videos in online and hybrid courses*. Learning Solutions Magazine.

Joo, Y. J., Lim, K. Y., & Kim, E. K. (2011). Online university students' satisfaction and persistence: Examining perceived level of presence, usefulness and ease of use as predictors in a structural model. *Computers & Education*, *57*(2), 1654–1664. doi:10.1016/j.compedu.2011.02.008

Joyce, B. R., Weil, M., & Calhoun, E. (2014). *Models of teaching* (9th ed.). Boston, MA: Pearson.

Kahrs, K. A. (1974). Cassette tapes: A medium for personal feedback and learning. *Physical Educator*, *31*, 159–161.

Karp, M. R., McCurry, W. K., Turney, M. A., & Harms, D. (1999). *Aviation education for future airline pilots: An integrated model.* Paper presented at the International Aviation Training Symposium.

Kear, L., Chetwynd, F., & Jefferis, H. (2014). *Social presence in online learning communities: the role of personal profiles*. Retrieved November 22, 2015 from http://www.researchinlearningtechnology.net/index.php/rlt/article/view/19710

Kearsley, G. (2000). *Online education: Learning and teaching in cyberspace*. Toronto: Wadsworth.

Ke, F. (2010). Examining online teaching, cognitive, and social presence for adult students. *Computers & Education*, *55*(2), 808–820. doi:10.1016/j.compedu.2010.03.013

Kelley, D. H., & Gorham, J. (1988). Effects of immediacy on recall of information. *Communication Education*, *37*(3), 198–207. doi:10.1080/03634528809378719

Kelly, R. (2014). *Creating a Sense of Instructor Presense in the Online Classroom.* Retrieved August 4, 2015 from http://www.facultyfocus.com/articles/online-education/creating-a-sense-of-instructor-presence-in-the-online-classroom/

Kelly, P., & Ryan, S. (1983). Using tutor tapes to support the distance learner. *International Council for Distance Education Bulletin*, *3*, 1–18.

Kember, D. (1997). A reconceptualisation of the research into university academics' conceptions of teaching. *Learning and Instruction*, *7*(3), 255–27. doi:10.1016/S0959-4752(96)00028-X

Kennedy, K., & Archambault, L. (2012). Offering Preservice Teachers Field Experiences in K-12 Online Learning A National Survey of Teacher Education Programs. *Journal of Teacher Education*, *63*(3), 185–200. doi:10.1177/0022487111433651

Kerr. (2015). *Behaviourism and adaptive learning*. Retrieved from https://adaptivelearninginelt.wordpress.com/tag/knewton/

Kessler, A. (2013, June 2). Professors are about to get an online education: Georgia Tech's new Internet master's degree in computer science is the future. *The Wall Street Journal*. Retrieved from http://www.wsj.com/articles/SB10001424127887324659404578504761168566272

Kietzmann, J. H., Hermkens, K., McCarthy, I. P., & Silvestre, B. S. (2011). Social media? Get serious! Understanding the functional building blocks of social media. *Business Horizons*, *54*(3), 241–251. doi:10.1016/j.bushor.2011.01.005

Kim, C. (2008). Using email to enable 3 (effective, efficient, and engaging) learning. *Distance Education*, *29*(2), 187–198. doi:10.1080/01587910802154988

Kim, J., Kwon, Y., & Cho, D. (2011). Investigating factors that influence social presense and learning outcomes in distance higher education. *Computers & Education*, *57*(2), 1512–1520. doi:10.1016/j.compedu.2011.02.005

Kim, K.-H., & Yun, H. (2007). Cying for Me, Cying for Us: Relational Dialectics in a Korean Social Network Site. *Journal of Computer-Mediated Communication*, *13*(1), 298–318. doi:10.1111/j.1083-6101.2007.00397.x

Kim, L. (2004). Online technologies for teaching writing: Students react to teacher response in voice and written modalities. *Research in the Teaching of English*, *38*(3), 304–337.

King, K. (2008) *Comparison of social presence in voice-based and text-based asynchronous computer conferencing.* (Doctoral dissertation). Retrieved from Proquest.

Kirkley, S. E., & Kirkley, J. R. (2005). Creating next generation blended learning environments using mixed reality, video games and simulations. *TechTrends*, *49*(3), 42–89. doi:10.1007/BF02763646

Kirschner, P. A., van den Brink, H., & Meester, M. (1991). Audiotape feedback for essays in distance education. *Innovative Higher Education*, *15*(2), 185–195. doi:10.1007/BF00898030

Kirschner, P., Strijbos, J. W., Kreijns, K., & Beers, P. J. (2004). Designing electronic collaborative environments. *Educational Technology Research and Development*, *52*(3), 47–66. doi:10.1007/BF02504675

Klammer, E. (1973). Cassettes in the classroom. *College English*, *35*(2), 179–189. doi:10.2307/375445

Kluger, A. N., & DeNisi, A. (1996). The effects of feedback interventions on performance: A historical review, a meta-analysis, and a preliminary feedback intervention theory. *Psychological Bulletin*, *119*(2), 254–284. doi:10.1037/0033-2909.119.2.254

Knabe, A. P. (2004). Constructivist learning perspectives in online public relations classrooms. *PRism, 2*. Retrieved November 20, 2015 from http://www.prismjournal.org/fileadmin/Praxis/Files/Journal_Files/Issue2/Knabe.pdf

Koestler, A. (1969). *The act of creation* (Danube edition). London: Pan.

Kolb, D. A. (1984). *Experiential learning: Experience as a source of learning and development*. Englewood Cliffs, NJ: Prentice-Hall.

Kopp, W. (2013, April 8). Computers can't replace real teachers. *Cable News Network (CNN)*. Retrieved from http://www.cnn.com/2013/04/08/opinion/kopp-kids-real-teachers/index.html

Kreijns, K., Kirschener, P. A., & Jochems, W. (2003). Identifying the pitfalls for social interaction in computer-supported collaborative learning environments: A review of the research. *Computers in Human Behavior*, *19*(3), 335–353. doi:10.1016/S0747-5632(02)00057-2

Kreijns, K., Van Acker, F., Vermeulen, M., & Van Buuren, H. (2014). Community of inquiry: Social presence revisited. *E-Learning and Digital Media*, *11*(1), 5–18. doi:10.2304/elea.2014.11.1.5

Kruger, J., & Dunning, D. (1999). Unskilled and unaware of it: How difficulties in recognizing one's own incompetence lead to inflated self-assessments. *Journal of Personality and Social Psychology*, *77*(6), 1121–1134. doi:10.1037/0022-3514.77.6.1121 PMID:10626367

Kucuk, M., (2009). Teacher Immediacy Behaviors And Participation In Computer Mediated Communication. *Turkish Online Journal of Distance Education, 10*(2).

Kupczynski, L., Ice, P., Wiesenmayer, R., & McCluskey, F. (2010). Student perceptions of the relationship between indicators of teaching presence and success in online courses. *Journal of Interactive Online Learning*, *9*(1), 23–43.

Kvale, S. (1996). *Interviews*. London: Sage.

Ladyshewsky, R. K. (2013). Instructor presence in online courses and student satisfaction. *International Journal for the Scholarship of Teaching and Learning*, *7*(1), 13. doi:10.20429/ijsotl.2013.070113

Lalor, G., & Marrett, C. (1986). *University of the West Indies distance teaching experiment (UWIDITE) report*. Retrieved July 14, 2015 from http://eric.ed.gov/?id=ED290042

Lalor, G., & Stahmer, A. (1987). *The University of the West Indies distance teaching experiment: A case study*. Retrieved August 13, 2015 from http://pdf.usaid.gov/pdf_docs/pnaax696.pdf

LaRose, R., & Whitten, P. (2000). Re-thinking Instructional Immediacy for Web Courses: A social cognitive exploration. *Communication Education*, *49*(4), 320–338. doi:10.1080/03634520009379221

Laurillard, D. (2002a, January/February). Rethinking teaching for the knowledge society. *Educause Review*. Retrieved from http://net.educause.edu/ir/library/pdf/erm0201.pdf

Laurillard, D. (1993). *Rethinking university teaching: A framework for the effective use of educational technology*. London: Routledge.

Lave, J., & Wenger, E. (1991). *Situated learning: Legitimate peripheral participation*. Cambridge, UK: Cambridge University Press. doi:10.1017/CBO9780511815355

Lavooy, M., & Newlin, M. (2008). Online chats and cyber-office hours: Everything but the office. *International Journal on E-Learning*, *7*(1), 107–116.

Lazonder, A. W., Wilhelm, P., & Ootes, S. A. W. (2003). Using sentence openers to foster student interaction in computer-mediated learning environments. *Computers & Education*, *41*(3), 291–308. doi:10.1016/S0360-1315(03)00050-2

Lea, M., & Street, B. (1998). Student writing in higher education: An academic literacies approach. *Studies in Higher Education*, *23*(2), 157–172. doi:10.1080/03075079812331380364

Lehman, R. M., & Conceição, S. C. (2010). *Creating a Sense of Presence in Online Teaching: How to 'Be There' for Distance Learners*. San Francisco: Jossey-Bass.

Lemak, D., Shin, S., Reed, R., & Montgomery, J. (2005). Technology, transactional distance, and instructor effectiveness: An empirical investigation. *Academy of Management Learning & Education*, *4*(2), 150–158. doi:10.5465/AMLE.2005.17268562

Levine, A., & Dean, D. (2012). Today's students: Same as always, but more so. *Chronicle of Higher Education*. Retrieved from http://chronicle.com/article/Todays-Students-Same-as/134234/ on June 28, 2015.

Levin, S., Whitsett, D., & Wood, G. (2013). Teaching MSW social work practice in a blended online learning environment. *Journal of Teaching in Social Work*, *33*(4-5), 408–420. doi:10.1080/08841233.2013.829168

Levit, A. (2015). Make way for Generation Z. *New York Times*. Accessed April 21, 2015 at http://www.nytimes.com/2015/03/29/jobs/make-way-for-generation-z.html?_r=0

Lew, M., Alwis, W., & Schmidt, H. (2010). Accuracy of Students' Self-Assessment and their Beliefts about Its Utility. *Assessment & Evaluation in Higher Education*, *35*(2), 135–156. doi:10.1080/02602930802687737

Lih-Ching, C. W., & Beasley, W. (2006). Integrating Instant Messenger into Online Office Hours to Enhance Synchronous Online Interaction in Teacher Education. *International Journal of Instructional Media*, *33*(3), 277–287.

Lim, D., & Kim, H. (2002). Motivation and learner characteristics affecting online learning and learning applications. *Journal of Educational Technology Systems*, *31*(4), 423–439. doi:10.2190/0LW0-KE8X-MDYH-X27F

Linehan, C., Kirman, B., & Roche, B. (2014). Gamification as behavioral psychology. In Gameful world: Approaches, issues, applications. Cambridge, MA: MIT Press.

Lin, J.-W., & Lai, Y.-C. (2013). Harnessing Collaborative Annotations on Online Formative Assessments. *Journal of Educational Technology & Society*, *16*(1), 263–274.

Liu, X., Bonk, C. J., Magjuka, R. J., Lee, S. H., & Su, B. (2005). Exploring four dimensions of online instructor roles: A program level case study. *Journal of Asynchronous Learning Networks*, *9*(4), 29–48.

Liu, X., Magjuka, R. J., Bonk, C. J., & Lee, S. H. (2007). Does sense of community matter? An examination of participants' perceptions of building learning communities in online courses. *Quarterly Review of Distance Education*, *8*(1), 9–24.

Livingstone, S. (2002). Changing Media, changing literacies. In *Young people and New Media* (pp. 211–254). London: Sage.

Livingstone, S. (2010). Interactive, engaging but unequal, critical conclusions from Internet studies. In J. Curran (Ed.), *Media and Society* (pp. 122–142). London: Bloomsbury.

Logan, H. L., Logan, N. S., Fuller, J. L., & Denehy, G. E. (1976). The role of audiotape cassettes in providing student feedback. *Educational Technology*, *16*(12), 38–39.

Lortie, D. C. (1975). *School teacher: A sociological inquiry*. Chicago: University of Chicago Press.

Lortie, D. C. (1975). *Schoolteacher: A sociological study*. Chicago, IL: University of Chicago Press.

Lounis, S., Pramatari, K., & Theotokis, A. (2014). Gamification is all about fun: The role of incentive type and community collaboration. In *Proceedings of ECIS 2014*.

Lowenthal, P. R., & Parscal, T. (2008). Teaching presence. *The Learning Curve, 3*(4), 1-2, 4.

Lowenthal, P., & Parscal, T. (2008). *Teaching presence online facilitates meaningful learning*. Retrieved November 22, 2015 from http://www.patricklowenthal.com/publications/TeachingPresenceFacilitatesLearning.pdf

Lowenthal, P., & Parscal, T. (2008). Teaching presence online facilitates meaningful learning. *The Learning Curve*, 3(4), 1-2, 4.

Lowenthal, P. R., & Dunlap, J. C. (2010). From pixel on a screen to real person in your students' lives: Establishing social presence using digital storytelling. *The Internet and Higher Education*, *13*(1-2), 70–72. doi:10.1016/j.iheduc.2009.10.004

Lucas, G. (n.d.). *A Word from George Lucas: Edutopia's Role in Education*. Retrieved November 27, 2015, from http://www.edutopia.org/word-from-george-lucas-edutopias-role-in-education

Lumsden, R. (1962). Evanston, Illinois, Township High School Adds to its Program: The use of dictation machines in grading English themes. *The Bulletin of the National Association of Secondary School Principals*, 223-226.

Lunt, T., & Curran, J. (2010). "Are you listening please?" The advantages of electronic audio feedback compared to written feedback. *Assessment & Evaluation in Higher Education*, *35*(7), 759–769. doi:10.1080/02602930902977772

MacDonald, P., & Ahern, T. C. (2015). Exploring the Instructional Value and Worth of a MOOC. *Journal of Educational Computing Research*, *52*(4), 496–513. doi:10.1177/0735633115571927

Madge, C., Meek, J., Wellens, J., & Hooley, T. (2009). Facebook, social integration and informal learning at university: 'It is more for socialising and talking to friends about work than for actually doing work'. *Learning, Media and Technology*, *34*(2), 141–155. doi:10.1080/17439880902923606

Magee, J., & Smith, P. (2013). The social distance theory of power. *Personality and Social Psychology Review*, *17*(2), 158–186. doi:10.1177/1088868312472732 PMID:23348983

Malini-Reddy, Y., & Andrade, H. (2010). A review of rubric use in higher education. *Assessment & Evaluation in Higher Education*, *35*(4), 435–448. doi:10.1080/02602930902862859

Mandernach, J., Gonzales, R. M., & Garrett, A. L. (2006). *An examination of online instructor presence via threaded discussion participation.* Retrieved November 3, 2015 from http://jolt.merlot.org/vol2no4/mandernach.htm

Manjit Sidhu, S. & Ramesh, S. (2006). Multimedia Learning Packages: Design Issues and Implementation Problems. *Malaysian Online Journal of Instructional Technology, 3*(1), 43-56.

Maor, D. (2003). The teacher's role in developing interaction and reflection in an online learning community. *Educational Media International*, *40*(1-2), 127–138. doi:10.1080/0952398032000092170

Markham, A. N. (2005). The methods, politics, and ethics of representation in online ethnography. In N. K. Denzin & Y. S. Lincoln (Eds.), *The Sage handbook of qualitative research* (3rd ed.). Thousand Oaks, CA: Sage.

Marquart, M., & Fleming, M. (2014, October). *Supporting Successful Live Online Classes: Good Instructional Design is Not Enough.* Workshop presented at the Online Learning Consortium International Conference, Orlando, FL.

Martin, F., & Parker, M. A. (2014). Use of synchronous virtual classrooms: Why, who, and how? *Journal of Online Learning & Teaching*, *10*(2).

Martin, F., Parker, M. A., & Deale, D. F. (2012). Examining interactivity in synchronous virtual classrooms. *The International Review of Research in Open and Distributed Learning*, *13*(3), 228–261.

Marx, R. D., & Frost, P. J. (1998). Toward optimal use of video in management education: Examing the evidence. *Journal of Management Development*, *17*(4), 243–250. doi:10.1108/02621719810210154

Mayer, R. E. (2008). Applying the science of learning: Evidence-based principles for the design of multimedia instruction. *The American Psychologist*, *63*(8), 762–769. doi:10.1037/0003-066X.63.8.760 PMID:19014238

Mayer, R. E. (2009). *Multimedia learning* (2nd ed.). New York: Cambridge University Press. doi:10.1017/CBO9780511811678

McAuley, A., Stewart, B., Siemens, G., & Cormier, D. (2010). The MOOC Model for Digital Practice, Massive Open Online. In *Massive Open Online Courses: Digital Ways of Knowing and Learning*. Academic Press.

McBrien, J. L., Cheng, R., & Jones, P. (2009). Virtual spaces: Employing a synchronous online classroom to facilitate student engagement in online learning. *The International Review of Research in Open and Distributed Learning*, *10*(3).

McGill, J., & Klobas, J. E. (2009). A task-technology fit view of learning management system impact. *Computers & Education*, *52*(2), 496508. doi:10.1016/j.compedu.2008.10.002

McGonigal, J. (2011). *Reality is broken: Why games make us better and how they can change the world.* New York, NY: Penguin Books.

McGrew, J.B. (1969). *An experiment to assess the effectiveness of the dictation machine as an aid to teachers in the evaluations and improvement of student compositions.* Report to Lincoln Public Schools, Lincoln, NE (ERIC Document Reproductive Service No. ED 034776).

McIntosh, P. (2003). White privilege and male privilege. *Privilege. Reading (Sunderland)*, 147–160.

McKerlich, R. (2011). *Student perceptions of teaching presence, social Presence and cognitive presence in a virtual world.* Retrieved December 1, 2015 from http://jolt.merlot.org/vol7no3/mckerlich_0911.htm

McLaren, C. H. (2004). A comparison of student persistence and performance in online and classroom business statistics experiences. *Decision Sciences Journal of Innovative Education*, *2*(1), 1–10. doi:10.1111/j.0011-7315.2004.00015.x

McLoughlin, C., & Luca, J. (2002). A learner–centred approach to developing team skills through web–based learning and assessment. *British Journal of Educational Technology*, *33*(5), 571–582. doi:10.1111/1467-8535.00292

McQuail, D. (2010). *Mass Communication Theory*. London: Sage.

Mehra, B. (2002, March). Bias in qualitative research: Voices from an online classroom. *Qualitative Report*, *7*(1), 1–19. Retrieved from http://nsuworks.nova.edu/cgi/viewcontent.cgi?article=1986&context=tqr

Mehrabian, A. (1971). Sj7en (messages. Belmont, CA: Wadsworth.

Mehrabian, A. (1967). Orientation behaviors and nonverbal attitude communication. *Journal of Communication*, *17*(4), 324–332. doi:10.1111/j.1460-2466.1967.tb01190.x PMID:5588696

Mehrabian, A. (1969). Attitudes inferred from non-immediacy of verbal communication. *Journal of Verbal Learning and Verbal Behavior*, *6*(2), 294–295. doi:10.1016/S0022-5371(67)80113-0

Mehrabian, A. (1969). Some referents and measures of nonverbal behavior. *Behavior Research Methods and Instrumentation*, *1*(6), 205–207.

Mehrabian, A. (1971). *Silent messages*. Belmont, CA: Wadsworth.

Mehrabian, A. (1981). *Silent messages: Implicit communication of emotions and attitudes* (2nd ed.). Belmont, CA: Wadsworth.

Mehradbian, A. (1969). Methods and designs: Some referents and measures of non-verbal behavior. *Behavior Research Methods and Instrumentation*, *1*(6), 203–207. doi:10.3758/BF03208096

Menges, R. (2000). Shortcomings of research on evaluating and improving teaching in higher education. *New Directions for Teaching and Learning*, *83*(83), 5–11. doi:10.1002/tl.8301

Metro-Roland, D. & Farber, P. (2010). Lost causes: Online instruction and the integrity of presence. *Philosophy of Education*.

Meyer, L. (2015). Michigan State telepresence robots for online students. *Campus Technology*.

Meyer, K. A. (2013). Face-to-face versus threaded discussions: The role of time and higher-order thinking. *Journal of Asynchronous Learning Networks*, *7*(3), 55–65.

Michael, D., & Chen, S. (2006). *Serious games: games that educate, train and inform*. Boston, MA: Thomson Course Technology.

Michael, J. (2007). Faculty perceptions about barriers to active learning. *College Teaching*, *55*(2), 42–47. doi:10.3200/CTCH.55.2.42-47

Miller, D. (1973). *George Herbert Mead: Self, language, and the world*. Austin, Texas: University of Texas Press.

Miller, D. C. (1973). The audio tape cassette in education. *English Education*, *63*(6), 413–440.

Milne, C. (2009). Assessing Self-evaluation in a Science Methods Course: Power, Agency, Authority and Learning. *Teaching and Teacher Education*, *25*(5), 758–766. doi:10.1016/j.tate.2008.11.008

Mitchell, D. (2001). Digitizing video. *Journal of Physical Education, Recreation & Dance*, *72*(4), 11–16. doi:10.1080/07303084.2001.10605730

Mollen, A., & Wilson, H. (2009). Engagement, telepresence, and interactivity in online consumer experience: Reconciling scholastic and managerial perspectives. *Journal of Business Research*, *63*(9-10), 919–925. doi:10.1016/j.jbusres.2009.05.014

Mona Information Technology Services. (2015). *Programming and administration of the virtual learning environment (2015)*. Retrieved August 13, 2015 from http://www.mona.uwi.edu/mits/programming-and-administration-virtual-learning-environment

Moore, M. (1973). Toward a theory of independent learning and teaching. *The Journal of Higher Education*, *44*(12), 661–679. doi:10.2307/1980599

Moore, M. (1989). Three types of interaction. *American Journal of Distance Education*, *3*(2), 1–7. doi:10.1080/08923648909526659

Moore, M. G. (1993). Three types of interaction. In K. Harry, M. John, & D. Keegan (Eds.), *Distance education: New perspectives* (pp. 19–24). New York, NY.

Moore, M. G. (2007). The theory of transactional distance. In M. G. Moore (Ed.), *Handbook of distance education* (pp. 89–105). Mahwah, NJ: Lawrence Erlbaum.

Moore, M. G., & Kearsley, G. (1996). *Distance education: A systems view*. Belmont, CA: Wadsworth.

Moore, M., & Kearsley, G. (2012). *Distance Education: A Systems View of Online Learning*. Belmont, CA: Wadsworth.

Moore, N. S., & Filling, M. L. (2012). iFeedback: Using video technology for improving student writing. *Journal of College Literacy & Learning*, *38*, 3–14.

Moreno, R., & Mayer, R. E. (2004). Personalized messages that promote science learning in virtual environments. *Journal of Educational Psychology*, *96*(1), 165–173. doi:10.1037/0022-0663.96.1.165

Morgan, T. (2011). Online classroom or community-in-the-making? Instructor conceptualizations and teaching presence in international online contexts. *Journal of Distance Education*, *25*(1).

Morris, L. V., Xu, H., & Finnegan, C. L. (2005). Roles of faculty in teaching asynchronous undergraduate courses. *Journal of Asynchronous Learning Networks*, *9*(1), 65–82.

Morrison, D. (2012). *Critical thinking in the online classroom*. Retrieved on August 7, 2015 from https://onlinelearninginsights.wordpress.com/2012/05/24/critical-thinking-in-the-online-learning-classroom/

Morrison, G. R., Ross, S. M., Kalman, H. K., & Kemp, J. E. (2012). *Designing effective instruction* (7th ed.). Hoboken, NJ: Wiley.

Mory, E. H. (2004). Feedback research revisited. In D. H. Jonassen (Ed.), *Handbook of research on educational communications and technology* (pp. 745–783). Mahwah, NJ: Lawrence Erlbaum.

Moxley, J.M. (1989). Responding to student writing: Goals, methods, alternatives. *Freshman English News*, 3-11.

Mullane, R. R. (2014). *Students' perception of teacher immediacy behaviors on student success and retention*. Retrieved November 13, 2015 from http://dc.uwm.edu/cgi/viewcontent.cgi?article=1480&context=etd

Mullen, G. E., & Tallent-Runnels, M. K. (2006). Student outcomes and perceptions of instructors' demands and support in online and traditional classrooms. *The Internet and Higher Education*, *9*(4), 257–266. doi:10.1016/j.iheduc.2006.08.005

Mumtaz, S. (2000). Factors affecting teachers' use of information and communications technology: A review of the literature. *Journal of Information Technology for Teacher Education*, *9*(3), 319–342. doi:10.1080/14759390000200096

Murphy, E. (2004). Recognising and promoting collaboration in an online asynchronous discussion. *British Journal of Educational Technology*, *35*(4), 421–431. doi:10.1111/j.0007-1013.2004.00401.x

Mutch, A. (2003). Exploring the practice of feedback to students. *Active Learning in Higher Education*, *4*(1), 24–38. doi:10.1177/1469787403004001003

Myers, S., Zhong, M., & Guan, S. (1998). (1998) Instructor immediacy in the Chinese college classroom. *Communication Studies*, *49*(3), 240–254. doi:10.1080/10510979809368534

Nagel, L., Blignaut, S., & Cronjé, J. (2007). Methical Jane: Perspectives on an Undisclosed Virtual Student. *Journal of Computer-Mediated Communication, 12*(4), 1346–1368. doi:10.1111/j.1083-6101.2007.00376.x

Nagel, L., & Lotze, T. (2010). Supersizing e-learning: What a CoI survey reveals about teaching presence in a large online class. *The Internet and Higher Education, 13*(2), 45–51. doi:10.1016/j.iheduc.2009.12.001

Naisbitt, J. (1999). *High tech/ high touch: Technology and our search for meaning*. New York: Broadway Books.

Narciss, S., & Huth, K. (2004). How to design informative tutoring feedback for multi-media learning. In H. Niegemann, D. Leutner, & R. Brunken (Eds.), *Instructional design for multimedia learning* (pp. 181–195). Munster, Germany: Waxmann.

National Standards for Quality Online Courses. (n.d.). Retrieved from http://www.inacol.org/cms/wp- content/uploads/2013/02/iNACOL_CourseStandards_2011.pdf_br

Nespor, J. (1987). The role of beliefs in the practice of teaching. *Journal of Curriculum Studies, 19*(4), 317–328. doi:10.1080/0022027870190403

Neuhauser, P., Bender, R., & Stromberg, K. (2000). *Culture.com*. Toronto: John Wiley & Sons.

Nicholson, S. (2012). A user-centered theoretical framework for meaningful gamification. Paper Presented at Games+Learning+Society 8.0, Madison, WI.

Nicol, D. J. (2006). Increasing success in first year courses: Assessment re-design, self-regulation and learning technologies. In *Proceedings of the 23rd Annual Ascilite Conference: Who's learning? Whose technology?* (pp. 589-598). The University of Sydney.

Nicol, D. J., & Macfarlane-Dick, D. (2006). Formative assessment and self-regulated learning: A model and seven principles of good feedback practice. *Studies in Higher Education, 31*(2), 199–216. doi:10.1080/03075070600572090

Nielsen, J. (2000). *Designing web usability: The practice of simplicity*. Indianapolis, IN: New Riders.

Nisbett, R., & Ross, L. (1980). *Human inference: Strategies and shortcomings of social judgment*. Englewood Cliffs, NJ: Prentice-Hall, Inc.

Noble, D. (1998). Digital diploma mills: The automation of higher education. *First Monday, 3*(1). doi:10.5210/fm.v3i1.569

Nortcliffe, A. L., & Middleton, A. (2008). A three year case study of using audio to blend the engineers learning environment. *Engineering Education: Journal of the Higher Education Academy Engineering Subject Centre, 3*(2), 45–57. doi:10.11120/ened.2008.03020045

Northrup, P. T. (2002). Online learners' preferences for interaction. *The Quarterly Review of Distance Education, 3*(2), 219–226.

Norton, L. (2009). Assessing student learning. In H. Fry, S. Ketteridge, & S. Marshall (Eds.), *A handbook for teaching and learning in higher education: Enhancing Academic Practice*. London: Taylor and Francis Group.

Nulty, D. (2012). *Griffith University 7014GIH Curriculum Design, Innovation, Assessment and Evaluation: Course Notes*. Griffith University.

Nussbaum, M., Alvarez, C., McFarlane, A., Gomez, F., Claro, S., & Radovic, D. (2009). Technology as small group face-to-face Collaborative Scaffolding. *Computers & Education, 52*(1), 147–153. doi:10.1016/j.compedu.2008.07.005

O'Sullivan, P. B., Hunt, S. K., & Lippert, L. R. (2004). Mediated immediacy: A language of affiliation in a technological age. *Journal of Language and Social Psychology, 23*(4), 464–490. doi:10.1177/0261927X04269588

Obasa, A., Eludire, A., & Ajao, T. (2013). A comparative study of synchronous and asynchronous e-learning resources. *International Journal of Innovative Research in Science, Engineering and Technology, 2*(11). Retrieved from http://www.ijirset.com/upload/2013/november/3_A-COMPARATIVE.pdf

Ogden, L., Pyzdrowski, L., & Shambaugh, N. (2014). A teaching model for the college algebra flipped classroom. In J. Keengwe, G. Onchwari, & J. Oigara (Eds.), *Promoting active learning through the flipped classroom model* (pp. 47–70). Hershey, PA: IGI Global. doi:10.4018/978-1-4666-4987-3.ch003

Oleson, A., & Hora, M. T. (2012, September). *Teaching the way they were taught? Revisiting the sources of teaching knowledge and the role of prior experience in shaping faculty teaching practices.* Wisconsin Center for Education Research, School of Education, University of Wisconsin-Madison. Retrieved from http://www.wcer.wisc.edu/publications/workingpapers/Working_Paper_No_2012_09.pdf

Olsen, G. (1982). Beyond evaluation: The recorded response to essays. *Teaching English in the Two-Year College, 8*(2), 121–123.

Online Learning Consortium. (2015, September 29). *The Online Learning Consortium Announces Recipients of the 2015 OLC Awards and Effective Practice Awards.* [Press release]. Retrieved from http://onlinelearningconsortium.org/news_item/online-learning-consortium-announces-recipients-2015-olc-awards-effective-practice-awards/

Oomen-Early, J., Bold, M., Wiginton, K. L., Gallien, T. L., & Anderson, N. (2008). Using asynchronous audio communication (AAC) in the online classroom: A comparative study. *Journal of Online Learning and Teaching, 4*(3).

Oztok, M., & Brett, C. (2011). Social presence and online learning: A review of the research. *Journal of Distance Education, 25*(3), 1–10.

Pajares, M. F. (1992). Teachers' beliefs and educational research: Cleaning up a messy construct. *Review of Educational Research, 62*(3), 307–332. doi:10.3102/00346543062003307

Palloff, R. M., & Pratt, K. (2003). *The virtual student: A profile and guide to working with online learners.* John Wiley & Sons.

Palloff, R. M., & Pratt, K. (2007). *Building Online Learning Communities: Effective Strategies for the Virtual Classroom* (2nd ed.). San Francisco, CA: Jossey-Bass.

Palloff, R. M., & Pratt, K. (2013). *Lessons from the virtual classroom: The realities of online teaching.* Somerset, NJ: John Wiley & Sons.

Palmer, S. (2007). An evaluation of streaming digital video resources in on- and off-campus engineering management education. *Computers & Education, 49*(2), 297–308. doi:10.1016/j.compedu.2005.07.002

Panadero, E., & Romero, M. (2014). To rubric or not to rubric? The effects of self-assessment on self-regulation, performance and self-efficacy. *Assessment in Education: Principles, Policy & Practice, 21*(2), 133–148. doi:10.1080/0969594X.2013.877872

Panko, M. (2005). Teaching beliefs and the practice of e-moderators: Presage, process, and product. *Education in a Changing World.*

Pappas, C. (2014). *9 tips to apply adult learning theory to eLearning - eLearning industry.* Retrieved July 20, 2015 from http://elearningindustry.com/9-tips-apply-adult-learning-theory-to-elearning

Pappas, C. (2015). *Ten Invaluable tips to develop asynchronous learning.* Retrieved July 2, 2015 from https://www.docebo.com/2015/06/22/10-invaluable-tips-to-develop-asynchronous-learning/

Park, Y. J., & Bonk, C. J. (2007, September). Is online life a breeze? A case study for promoting synchronous learning in a blended graduate course. *MERLOT Journal of Online Learning and Teaching, 3*(3), 307-323. Retrieved from http://www.anitacrawley.net/Articles/Park2007%20pedagogical%20strategies%20for%20integ%20of%20syn.pdf

Park, J. H., Schallert, D. L., Sanders, A. J., Williams, K. M., Seo, E., Yu, L. T., & Knox, M. C. et al. (2015). Does it matter if the teacher is there? A teacher's contribution to emerging patterns of interactions in online classroom discussions. *Computers & Education*, *82*, 315–328. doi:10.1016/j.compedu.2014.11.019

Park, J. Y. (2013). Student interactivity and teacher participation: An application of legitimate peripheral participation in higher education online learning environments. *Technology, Pedagogy and Education*, *24*(3), 389–406. doi:10.1080/1475939X.2014.935743

Park, Y. J., & Bonk, C. J. (2007). Synchronous learning experiences: Distance and residential learners' perspectives in a blended graduate course. *Journal of Interactive Online Learning*, *6*(3), 245–264.

Parsad, B., & Lewis, L. (2009). *Distance education at degree-granting postsecondary institutions: 2006–07. World Wide Web Internet And Web Information Systems*. Retrieved from http://nces.ed.gov/pubs2009/2009044.pdf

Patrie, K. (1989). The use of the tape recorder in an ESL composition programme. *TESL Canada Journal*, *6*(2), 87–89.

Pearce, C., & Ackley, R. (1995). Audiotaped feedback in business writing: An exploratory study. *Business Communication Quarterly*, *58*(3), 31–34. doi:10.1177/108056999505800306

Perkel, D. (2006). *Copy and Paste Literacy: Literacy practices in the production of a MySpace profile.* Retrieved April 28, 2014, from http://people.ischool.berkeley.edu/~dperkel/media/dperkel_literacymyspace.pdf

Petite, J. (1983). Tape recorders and tutoring. *Teaching English in the Two-Year College*, *9*, 123–125.

Petkov, D., & Petkova, O. (2006). Development of Scoring Rubrics for IS Projects as an Assessment Tool. *Issues in Informing Science and Information Technology*, *3*, 499–510.

Picciano, A. G. (2002). Beyond student perceptions: Issues of interaction, presence, and performance in an online course. *Journal of Asynchronous Learning Networks*, *6*(1), 21–40.

Plante, K., & Asselin, M. E. (2014). Best practices for creating social presence and caring behaviors online. *Nursing Education Perspectives*, *35*(4), 219–223. doi:10.5480/13-1094.1 PMID:25158415

Popham, J. (1997). What's wrong and what's right with rubrics. *Educational Leadership*, *55*, 72–75.

Poulos, A., & Mahony, M. J. (2008). Effectiveness of feedback: The students' perspective. *Assessment & Evaluation in Higher Education*, *33*(2), 143–154. doi:10.1080/02602930601127869

Preisman, K. A. (2014). Teaching Presence in Online Education: From the Instructor's Point of View. *Online Learning, 18*(3). Retrieved from http://files.eric.ed.gov/fulltext/ EJ1043166.pdf

Preisman, K. A. (2014). Teaching Presence in Online Education: From the Instructor's Point of View. *Online Learning*, *10*(3), 1–16.

Prensky, M. (2001). Digital natives, digital immigrants part 1. *On the horizon*, *9*(5), 1–6. doi:10.1108/10748120110424816

Price, M., Handley, K., Millar, J., & O'Donovan, B. (2010). Feedback: All that effort, but what is the effect? *Assessment & Evaluation in Higher Education*, *35*(3), 277–289. doi:10.1080/02602930903541007

Putnam, R. T., & Borko, H. (2000). What do new views of knowledge and thinking have to say about research on teacher learning? *Educational Researcher*, *29*(1), 4–15. doi:10.3102/0013189X029001004

Quinton, S., & Smallbone, T. (2010). Feeding forward: Using feedback to promote student reflection and learning – a teaching model. *Innovations in Education and Teaching International*, *47*(1), 125–135. doi:10.1080/14703290903525911

Race, P. (1991). Practical pointers on peer assessment. In S. Brown (Ed.), Peer assessment in practice (pp. 113-119). Birmingham, UK: Staff and educational Development Association.

Race, P. (2010). *Making Learning Happen*. London, UK: SAGE Publications Ltd.

Ragan, L. (2008). *Best practices in online teaching*. Retrieved July 19, 2015 from http://florida.theorangegrove.org/og/file/489805c0-7346-6cb7-320a-5610cb10f9da/1/onlineedu.pdf

Ragan, L. C., Bigatel, P. M., Kennan, S. S., & Dillon, J. M. (2012). From Research to Practice: Towards the Development of an Integrated and Comprehensive Faculty Development Program. *Journal of Asynchronous Learning Networks*, *16*(5), 71–86.

Rallis, H. (1994). *Creating teaching and learning partnerships with students: Helping faculty listen to student voices*. Academic Press.

Ravitch, D. (2013, July17). Diane Ravitch: 3 dubious uses of technology in schools: Technology can inspire creativity or dehumanize learning. *Scientific American*, *309*(2). Retrieved from http://www.scientificamerican.com/article/diane-ravitch-3-dubious-uses-technology-in-schools/

Ray, J., & Kafka, S. (2014). Life in college matters for life after college. *Gallup Latest News, Economy*. Retrieved from http://www. gallup.com/poll/168848/life-college-matters-life-college.aspx

Redmond, P. (2014). Reflection as an indicator of cognitive presence. *E-Learning and Digital Media*, *11*(1), 46-46. Retrieved July 19, 2015 from http://ldm.sagepub.com/content/11/1/46.full.pdf html.

Reilly, C. (2014). Online teaching as the art of hosting: Designing social interactions to promote engagement. In *Proceedings of World Conference on E-Learning in Corporate, Government, Healthcare, and Higher Education 2014* (pp. 1635-1641). Chesapeake, VA: Association for the Advancement of Computing in Education (AACE).

Reilly, J. R., Gallagher-Lepak, S., & Killion, C. (2012). "Me and My Computer": Emotional Factors in Online Learning. *Nursing Education Perspectives*, *33*(2), 100–105. doi:10.5480/1536-5026-33.2.100 PMID:22616408

Remesal, A., & Colomina, R. (2013). Social presence and online collaborative small group work: A socioconstructivist account. *Computers & Education*, *60*(1), 357–367. doi:10.1016/j.compedu.2012.07.009

Richards, C. (2004). From old to new learning: Global imperatives, exemplary Asian dilemmas as a key to cultural change in education. *Globalisation, Societies and Education*, *2*(3), 337–352. doi:10.1080/1476772042000252470

Richardson, J. C., Koehler, A. A., Besser, E. D., Caskurlu, S., Lim, J. E., & Mueller, C. M. (2015). Conceptualizing and investigating instructor presence in online learning environments. *International Review of Research in Open and Distributed Learning*, *16*(3), 256–297.

Richardson, J. C., & Swan, K. (2003). Examing social presence in online courses in relation to students' perceived learning and satisfaction. *Journal of Asynchronous Learning Networks*, *7*(1), 69–83.

Richardson, J. C., & Swan, K. (2003). Examining social presence in online courses in relation to students' perceived learning and satisfaction. *Journal of Asynchronous Learning Networks*, *7*, 68–82.

Richmond, V. P. (1990). Communication in the classroom: Power and motivation. *Communication Education*, *39*(3), 181–195. doi:10.1080/03634529009378801

Rienties, B., & Alden Rivers, B. (2014). *Measuring and Understanding Learner Emotions: Evidence and Prospects.* Learning Analytics Review 1, Learning Analytics Community Exchange (LACE). Retrieved from http://www.laceproject.eu/learning-analyticsreview/meas

Ritchhart, R., Church, M., & Morrison, K. (2011). *Making thinking visible: How to promote engagement, understanding, and independence for all learners.* San Francisco, CA: Jossey-Bass.

Robinson, A. C., Kerski, J., Long, E. C., Luo, H., DiBiase, D., & Lee, A. (2015). Maps and the geospatial revolution: Teaching a massive open online course (MOOC) in geography. *Journal of Geography in Higher Education, 39*(1), 65–82. doi:10.1080/03098265.2014.996850

Robinson, R. Y., & Richmond, V. P. (1995). Validity of the verbal immediacy scale. *Communication Research Reports, 12*(1), 80–84. doi:10.1080/08824099509362042

Roblyer, M., & Ekhaml, L. (2000). How interactive are YOUR distance courses? A rubric for assessing interaction in distance learning. *Online Journal of Distance Learning Administration.* Retrieved on November 8, 2015 from http://www.westga.edu/distance/roblyer32.html

Roblyer, M. D., & Ekhaml, L. (2000, Spring). How interactive are YOUR distance courses? A rubric for assessing interaction in distance learning. *Online Journal of Distance Learning Administration, 3*(2). Retrieved from http://www.westga.edu/~distance/roblyer32.html

Rocca, K. A. (2004). College student attendance: Impact of instructor immediacy and verbal aggression. *Communication Education, 53*(2), 185–195. doi:10.1080/0363452041000l682447

Rockinson-Szapkiw, A. (2014). Technologies that Assist in Online Group Work: A Comparison of Synchronous and Asynchronous Collaboration Technologies on Students' Learning and Community. In *Proceedings of World Conference on Educational Media and Technology 2014* (pp. 672-677). Association for the Advancement of Computing in Education (AACE).

Rodriguez, A. L., & Fahara, M. F. (2010). Online teaching styles: A study in distance education. *International Journal of University Teaching and Faculty, 1*(2), 1–14.

Rodway-Dyer, S., Knight, J., & Dunne, E. (2011). A case study on audio feedback with geography undergraduates. *Journal of Geography in Higher Education, 35*(2), 217–231. doi:10.1080/03098265.2010.524197

Romiszowski, A., & Mason, R. (2004). Computer-mediated communication. In D. H. Jonassen (Ed.), Handbook of Research for Educational Communications and Technology (pp. 397–431). Lawrence Erlbaum.

Romiszowski, A., & Mason, R. (2004). Computer-mediated communication. In D. H. Jonassen (Ed.), *Handbook of research on educational communications and technology* (pp. 397–431). Mahwah, NJ: Lawrence Erlbaum.

Root, M. V., Molgaard, L. K., & Malone, E. (2015). Creation of a metric for faculty effort in teaching in the veterinary curriculum. *Journal of Veterinary Medical Education, 42*(3), 66-68. 10.3138/jvme.0414-046R

Roscoria, T. (2015, May). *Telepresence helps universities connect virtual students with campus life.* [Web Blog Post]. Retrieved fromhttp://www.govtech.com/education/Telepresence-Helps-Universities-Connect-Virtual-Students-With-Campus-Life.html

Rose, D. H., & Meyer, A. (2002). *Teaching every student in the digital age: Universal design for learning.* Alexandria, VA: Association for Supervision and Curriculum Development.

Rosenberg, M. J. (2001). *Building successful online learning in your organization: E-learning strategies for delivering knowledge in the digital age.* New York: McGraw Hill.

Ross, J. A. (1992). Teacher efficacy and the effects of coaching on student achievement. *Canadian Journal of Education, 17*(1), 51–65. doi:10.2307/1495395

Rossman, M. H. (1999). Successful online teaching using an asynchronous learner discussion forum. *Journal of Asynchronous Learning Networks, 3*(2), 91–97.

Rotheram, B. (2007). Using an MP3 recorder to give feedback on student assignments. *Educational Developments, 8*(2), 7–10.

Rourke, L., Anderson, T., Garrison, D. R., & Archer, W. (2007). Assessing social presence in asynchronous text-based computer conferencing. *International Journal of E-Learning & Distance Education, 14*(2), 50–71.

Roussou, M. (2004). Learning by Doing and Learning Through Play: An Exploration of Interactivity in Virtual Environments for Children. *ACM Computers in Entertainment., 2*(1), 1–23. doi:10.1145/973801.973818

Rovai, A. P. (2002). Building sense of community at a distance. *International Review of Research in Open and Distance Education, 5*(2). Retrieved from http://www.irrodl.org/index.php/irrodl/article/view/79/152

Rovai, A. P., Ponton, M. K., & Baker, J. D. (2008). *Distance learning in higher education: Programmatic approach to planning, design, instruction, evaluation, and accreditation.* New York: Teachers College Press.

Rubens, P. M. (1982). Oral grading techniques: An interactive system for the technical writing classroom. *Technical Writing Teacher, 10*, 41–44.

Rubin, B., Fernandes, R., & Avgerinous, M. D. (2013). The effects of technology on the Community of Inquiry and satisfaction with online courses. *The Internet and Higher Education, 17*, 48–57. doi:10.1016/j.iheduc.2012.09.006

Ruffalo Noel Levitz. (2015). 2015 *Adult learner marketing and recruitment practices benchmark report.* Retrieved November 8, 2015 from www.noellevitz.com/BenchmarkReports

Russo, T., & Benson, S. (2005). Learning with invisible others: Perceptions of online presence and their relationship to cognitive and affective learning. *Journal of Educational Technology & Society, 8*(1), 54–62.

Ryan, R. M., & Deci, E. I. (2000). Intrinsic and extrinsic motivation: Classic definitions and new directions. *Contemporary Educational Psychology, 25*(1), 54–67. doi:10.1006/ceps.1999.1020 PMID:10620381

Sadat, A., & Rahman, K. (n.d.). *Prospect of email communication as an educational tool for distance education in Bangladesh.* Retrieved August 5, 2015 from http://wikieducator.org/images/7/73/PID_266.pdf

Sadler, D. R. (1989). Formative assessment and the design of instructional systems. *Instructional Science, 18*(2), 119–144. doi:10.1007/BF00117714

Sadler, R. (2002). Ah!...so that's 'quality. In P. Schwartz & G. Webb (Eds.), *Assessment: case studies, experience and practice from higher education* (pp. 130–136). Kogan Page Limited and Stylus Publishing Inc.

Sadler, R. (2008). Indeterminacy in the use of preset criteria for assessment and grading. *Assessment & Evaluation in Higher Education.*

Said, A. (2006) Accessing Electronic Information: A study of Pakistan's Digital Library. *INASPR Research and Education Case studies 1.* Oxford, UK: Antony Rowe Ltd. Retrieved from: http://www.hec.gov.pk/PublishingImages/454_diglibpak/454_diglibpak.html

Saroyan, A., & Amundsen, C. (2004). *Rethinking teaching in higher education: From a course design workshop to a faculty development framework.* Sterling, VA: Stylus Publishing.

Sathik, M., & Jonathan, S. G. (2013). *Effect of facial expressions on student's comprehension recognition in virtual educational environments*. Retrieved June 28, 2015 from http://www.ncbi.nlm.nih.gov/pmc/articles/PMC3795200/

Savery, J. (2005). BE VOCAL: Characteristics of successful online instructors. *Journal of Interactive Online Learning*, *4*(2), 141–153.

Savery, J. R. (2006). Overview of Problem-based Learning: Definitions and Distinctions. *Interdisciplinary Journal of Problem-Based Learning*, *1*(1), 9–20. doi:10.7771/1541-5015.1002

Schank, R. (1997). *Virtual learning, A revolutionary approach to building a highly skilled workforce*. New York: McGraw-Hill.

Schneider, J. F. (2006). Rubrics for teacher education in community college. *The Community College Enterprise*, *12*(1), 39–55.

Schullo, S., Hilbelink, A., Venable, M., & Barron, A. E. (2007). Selecting a Virtual Classroom System: Elluminate Live vs. Macromedia Breeze (Adobe Acrobat Connect Professional). *Journal of Online Learning and Teaching, 3*(4), 331-345.

Schwartz, E., & White, K. (2000). Making sense of it all: Giving and getting online course feedback. In K. W. White & B. H. Weight (Eds.), *The online teaching guide: A handbook of attitudes, strategies, and techniques for the virtual classroom* (pp. 57–72). Boston: Allyn and Bacon.

Seaman, J., & Tinti-Kane, H. (2013). *Social media for teaching and learning*. Pearson Learning Systems.

Seaton, J. X., & Schwier, R. (2014). An exploratory case study of online instructors: Factors associated with instructor engagement. *International Journal of E-learning &. Distance Education*, *29*(1), 1–16.

Sedikides, C. (1993). Assessment, enhancement, and verification determinants of the self-evaluation process. *Journal of Personality and Social Psychology*, *65*(2), 317–338. doi:10.1037/0022-3514.65.2.317

Seidman, I. (2012). *Interviewing as qualitative research: A guide for researchers in education and the social sciences*. New York: Teachers College Press.

Selinger, J. (2015). The view from the top: What presidents think about financial sustainability, student outcomes, and the future of higher education. *The Chronicle of Higher Education*.

Selwyn, N. (2007). Technology and Education: Learning in the Information Age. In F. Option (Ed.), *Unit 83, MA in Mass Communications (By Distance Learning)*. Department of Media and Communication, University of Leicester.

Selwyn, N. (2009). Faceworking: Exploring students' education-related use of Facebook. *Learning, Media and Technology*, *34*(2), 157–174. doi:10.1080/17439880902923622

Sener, J. (2006). Quality Matters: Inter-institutional quality improvement for online courses. *Journal of Asynchronous Learning Networks*, *10*(1), 69–80.

Shambaugh, R. N., & Magliaro, S. G. (2005). *Instructional design: A systematic approach to reflective practice*. Boston, MA: Allyn & Bacon.

Shavelson, R. J., & Stern, P. (1981). Research on teachers' pedagogical thoughts, judgments, decisions, and behavior. *Review of Educational Research*, *51*(4), 455–498. doi:10.3102/00346543051004455

Shea, P. J., Fredericksen, E. E., Pickett, A. M., & Pelz, W. E. (2003). A preliminary investigation of "teaching presence" in the SUNY learning network. *Elements of Quality Online Education: Practice and Direction, 4*, 279-312.

Shea, P., Li, C. S., & Pickett, A. (2006). *A study of teaching presence and student sense of learning community in fully online and web-enhanced college courses*. Retrieved November 22, 2015 from http://www.sunyresearch.net/hplo/wp-content/uploads/2012/08/Shea-Li-Pickett.pdf

Shea, P., Swan, K., Fredericksen, E., & Pickett, A. (2002). Student satisfaction and reported learning in the SUNY learning network. *Elements of Quality Online Education*, *3*, 145-156.

Shea, P. (2006). A study of students' sense of learning community in online environments. *Journal of Asynchronous Learning Networks*, *10*(1), 35–44.

Shea, P., & Bidjerano, T. (2012). Learning presence as a moderator in the community of inquiry mode. *Computers & Education*, *59*(2), 316–326. doi:10.1016/j.compedu.2012.01.011

Shea, P., Hayes, S., Vickers, J., Gozza-Cohen, M., Uzuner, S., Mehta, R., & Rangan, P. et al. (2010). A re-examination of the community of inquiry framework: Social network and content analysis. *The Internet and Higher Education*, *13*(1), 10–21. doi:10.1016/j.iheduc.2009.11.002

Shea, P., Li, C. S., & Pickett, A. (2006). A study of teaching presence and student sense of learning community in fully online and web-enhanced college courses. *The Internet and Higher Education*, *9*(3), 175–190. doi:10.1016/j.iheduc.2006.06.005

Shea, P., Li, C. S., Swan, K., & Pickett, A. (2005). Developing learning community in online asynchronous college courses: The role of teaching presence. *Journal of Asynchronous Learning Networks*, *9*(4), 59–82.

Shea, P., Vickers, J., & Hayes, S. (2010). Online instructional effort measured through the lens of teaching presence in the community of inquiry framework: A re-examination of measures and approach. *The International Review of Research in Open and Distributed Learning*, *11*(3). Retrieved from http://www.irrodl.org/index.php/irrodl/article/view/915

Shelton, B. E., & Scoresby, J. (2011). Aligning game activity with educational goals: Following a constrained design approach to instructional computer games. *Educational Technology Research and Development*, *59*(1), 113–138. doi:10.1007/s11423-010-9175-0

Shephard, K. (2003). Questioning, promoting and evaluating the use of streaming video to support student learning. *British Journal of Educational Technology*, *34*(3), 295–308. doi:10.1111/1467-8535.00328

Sheridan, K., & Kelly, M. A. (2010). The indicators of instructor presence that are important to students in online courses. *Journal of Online Learning and Teaching*, *6*(4).

Sheridan, K., & Kelly, M. A. (2010). The indicators of instructor presence that are important to students in online learning. *Journal of Online Learning and Teaching*, *6*(4).

Short, J., Williams, E., & Christie, B. (1976). *The social psychology of telecommunications*. London: John Wiley and Sons.

Short, J., Williams, E., & Christie, B. (1976). *The Social Psychology of Telecommunications*. New York, NY: John Wiley & Sons.

Shulman, L. (1987). Knowledge and teaching: Foundations of the new reform. *Harvard Educational Review*, *57*(1), 1–21. doi:10.17763/haer.57.1.j463w79r56455411

Shute, V. (2008). Focus on Formative Feedback. *Review of Educational Research*, *78*(1), 153–189. doi:10.3102/0034654307313795

Siang, A. C., & Rao, R. K. (2003). Theories of learning: A computer game perspective.*Proceedings of the IEEE Fifth International Symposium on Multimedia Software Engineering*. doi:10.1109/MMSE.2003.1254447

Siddiqui, S. Z. (2006). Study approaches of students in Pakistan: The revised two-factor study process questionnaire experience. *2006 Occasional Report 1*. Retrieved from: http://www.hec.gov.pk/PublishingImages/684_Study-Approaches-of-Students-in-Pakistan/684_Study-Approaches-of-Students-in-Pakistan.html

Siemens, G. (2002, September 30). *Instructional design in elearning*. Retrieved from http://www.elearnspace.org/Articles/InstructionalDesign.htm

Siemens, G. (2012, July 25). MOOCs are really a platform. *Elearnspace*.

Silva, M. L. (2012). Camtasia in the classroom: Student attitudes and preferences for video commentary or Microsoft Word comments during the revision process. *Computers and Composition*, *29*(1), 1–22. doi:10.1016/j.compcom.2011.12.001

Simonson, M. (2006). Teaching courses online. *Quarterly Review of Distance Education*, *7*(4), 7–8.

Simonson, M., Smaldino, S., Albright, M., & Zvacek, S. (2003). *Teaching and learning at a distance: Foundations of distance education* (2nd ed.). Upper Saddle River, NJ: Merrill.

Simonsson, M., Kupczynski, L., Ice, P., & Pankake, A. (2009, April). *The impact of asynchronous audio feedback in the dissertation advising process*. Paper presented at the American Educational Research Association Annual Meeting, San Diego, CA.

Sims, R. (1999). Interactivity on stage: Strategies for learner-designer communication. *Australasian Journal of Educational Technology*, *15*(3), 257–272. Retrieved from http://www.ascilite.org.au/ajet/ajet15/sims.html

Smith, G. G., & Taveras, M. (2005, January). The missing instructor: Does e-learning promote absenteeism? *eLearn Magazine*, 1.

Smith, P., & Ragan, T. (2005). *Instructional design* (3rd ed.). Hoboken, NJ: Wiley.

Smylie, M. A. (1989). Teachers' views of the effectiveness of sources of learning to teach. *The Elementary School Journal*, *89*(5), 543–558. doi:10.1086/461591

Sobel, D. M., Sands, D. I., & Dunlap, J. C. (2009). Teaching intricate content online: It can be done and done well. *Action in Teacher Education*, *30*(4), 28–44. doi:10.1080/01626620.2009.10734450

So, H. J., & Brush, T. A. (2008). Student perceptions of collaborative learning, social presence and satisfaction in a blended learning environment: Relationships and critical factors. *Computers & Education*, *51*(1), 318–336. doi:10.1016/j.compedu.2007.05.009

Sommers, J. (1989). The effects of tape-recorded commentary on student revision: A case study. *Journal of Teaching Writing*, *8*, 49–75.

Song, K. H. (2006). A conceptual model of assessing teaching performace and intellectual development of teacher candidates: A pilot study in the US. *Teaching in Higher Education*, *11*(2), 175–190. doi:10.1080/13562510500527701

Sorensen, C. K., & Baylen, D. M. (2009). *Learning online. The perfect online course: Best practices for designing and teaching*. Academic Press.

Sorensen, E. K. (2004). Reflection and intellectual amplification in online communities of collaborative learning. In T. S. Roberts (Ed.), Online Collaborative Learning: Theory and Practice, (pp. 242-261). doi:10.4018/978-1-59140-174-2.ch011

Spear, L. R. (2012). *Social presence, social interaction, collaborative learning, and satisfaction in online and face-to-face courses*. Retrieved November 29, 2015 from http://lib.dr.iastate.edu/cgi/viewcontent.cgi?article=3983&context=etd

St. Phard, J., Jr. (2015). Distance education through the lens of USDLA members: A white paper. *Distance Learning 12*(2), 15-21. Retrieved from http://search.proquest.com/openview/fdbfe622e1eb011eafa1cafe097c3c6e/1?pq-origsite=gscholar

Stake, R. (1995). *The art of case study research*. Thousand Oaks, CA: Sage.

Stenbom, S., Cleveland-Innes, M., & Hrastinski, S. (2014). Online Coaching as a Relationship of Inquiry: Mathematics, online help, and emotional presence. In *Eden 2014*. Oxford, UK: Eden.

Stewart, M. (2014, August 21,) *Designing for emergence: The role of the instructor in student- centered learning*. [Web Blog Post]. Retrieved from http://www.hybridpedagogy.com/ Journal/designing-emergence-role-instructor-student-centered-learning

Stewart, C., Bachman, C., & Johnson, R. (2010). Students' characteristics and motivation orientations for online and traditional degree programs. *Journal of Online Learning and Teaching*, *6*(2). Retrieved from http://jolt.merlot.org/vol6no2/stewart_0610.htm

Stodel, E. J., Thompson, T. L., & MacDonald, C. J. (2006). Learners' perspectives on what is missing from online learning: Interpretations through the community of inquiry framework. *International Review of Research in Open and Distance Learning*, *7*(3).

Stratton, C. R. (1975). The electric report card: A follow-up on cassette grading. *Journal Tech Writing and Communication*, *5*(1), 17–22. doi:10.2190/PU63-TWLY-QVN2-9JJN

Study Guide. (2004). Macromedia Director, MX.

Sung, E., & Mayer, R. (2012). Five Facets of social presence in online distance education. *Computers in Human Behavior*, *28*(5), 1738–1747. doi:10.1016/j.chb.2012.04.014

Swan, K. (2003). Developing social presence in online course discussions. In *Learning and teaching with technology: Principles and practices*, (pp. 147-164). Academic Press.

Swan, K., Garrison, D. R., & Richardson, J. (2009). *A constructivist approach to online learning: The Community of Inquiry framework*. Retrieved November 15, 2015 from http://www.academia.edu/398997/A_Constructivist_Approach_to_Online_Learning_The_Community_of_Inquiry_Framework

Swan, K. (2002). Building learning communities in online courses: The importance of interaction. *Education Communication and Information*, *2*(1), 23–49. doi:10.1080/1463631022000005016

Swan, K. (2003). Learning effectiveness: What the research tells us. In J. Bourne & J. C. Moore (Eds.), *Elements of quality online education, practice and direction*. Needham, MA: Sloan Center for Online Education.

Swan, K. (2003). Learning effectiveness: What the research tells us. In J. Bourne & J. C. Moore (Eds.), *Elements of quality online education: Practice and direction* (pp. 13–45). Needham, MA: Sloan Consortium.

Swan, K., Garrison, D. R., & Richardson, J. (2009). *A constructivist approach to online learning: the Community of Inquiry framework. In Information technology and constructivism in higher education: Progressive learning frameworks*. Hershey, PA: IGI Global.

Swan, K., & Ice, P. (2010). The Community of Inquiry framework ten years later: Introduction to the special issue. *The Internet and Higher Education*, *13*(1), 1–4. doi:10.1016/j.iheduc.2009.11.003

Swan, K., & Shea, P. (2005). The development of virtual learning communities. In S. R. Hiltz & R. Goldman (Eds.), *Learning together online: Research on asynchronous learning networks* (pp. 239–260). Mahwah, NJ: Erlbaum.

Swan, K., & Shih, L. F. (2005). On the nature and development of social presence in online course discussions. *Journal of Asynchronous Learning Networks*, *9*(3), 115–136.

Tag Archives. (2004). *Synchronous tools for online learning the next big thing in online education… learning in real time*. Retrieved June 30, 2015 from https://onlinelearninginsights.wordpress.com/tag/synchronous-tools-for-online-learning/

Takatalo, J., Häkkinen, J., Kaistinen, J., & Nyman, G. (2010). Presence, Involvement, and Flow in Digital Games. In J. Karat & J. Vanderdonckt (Eds.), *Evaluating user experience in games: Concepts and methods*. NY: Springer. doi:10.1007/978-1-84882-963-3_3

Tanner, B. (1964). Teacher to disc to student. *English Journal*, *53*(5), 362–363. doi:10.2307/810191

Taras, M. (1999). Student self-assessment as a means of promoting student autonomy and independence. In M. Taras (Ed.), *Innovations in Learning and Teaching: teaching fellowships at the Univesrity of Sunderland*. Sunderland, UK: University of Sunderland Press.

Taras, M. (2010). To feedback or not to feedback in student self-assessment. *Assessment & Evaluation in Higher Education*, *28*(5), 549–565. doi:10.1080/02602930301678

Taylor, S. (2014). Student self-assessment and multisource feedback assessment: Exploring benefits, limitations, and remedies. *Journal of Management Education*, *38*(3), 359–383. doi:10.1177/1052562913488111

Tekian, A., McGuire, C. H., McGaghie, W. C., & Associates. C (1999). Innovative simulations for assessing professional competence. Chicago, IL: Department of Medical Education, University of Illinois, Chicago.

Teven, J. J., & Hanson, T. L. (2004). The impact of teacher immediacy and perceived caring on teacher competence and trustworthiness. *Communication Quarterly*, *52*(1), 39–53. doi:10.1080/01463370409370177

The Online Learning Definitions Project. (n.d.). Retrieved from http://www.inacol.org/cms/wp-content/uploads/2013/04/iNACOL_DefinitionsProject.pdf_br

Thomas, M. (2003). Internet-Based Education and Training: Using new Technologies to Facilitate Instruction and Enhance Learning. In A. Henley (Ed.), *Aviation Education and Training: Adult Learning Principles and Teaching Strategies* (pp. 342–362). Ashgate.

Thomson, S. (2014). 6 online collaboration tools and strategies for boosting learning - eLearning industry. *E-Learning industry*. Retrieved May 31, 2015 from http://elearningindustry.com/6-online-collaboration-tools-and-strategies-boosting-learning

Thweatt, K. S., & McCroskey, J. C. (1996). Teacher Non-immediacy and Misbehavior: Unintentional negative communication. *Communication Research Reports*, *13*(2), 198–204. doi:10.1080/08824099609362087

Titsworth, B. S. (2004). Students' note taking: The effects of teacher immediacy and clarity. *Communication Education*, *53*(4), 305–320. doi:10.1080/0363452032000305922

Traver, A. E., Volchok, E., Bidjerano, T., & Shea, P. (2014). Correlating community college students' perceptions of community of inquiry presences with their completion of blended courses. *The Internet and Higher Education*, *20*, 1–9. doi:10.1016/j.iheduc.2013.09.001

Trigwell, K., Prosser, M., & Waterhouse, F. (1999). Relations between teachers' approaches to teaching and students' approaches to learning. *Higher Education*, *37*(1), 57–70. doi:10.1023/A:1003548313194

Trucano, M. (2015, February 24). Will technology replace teachers? No, but … *EduTech*. Retrieved from http://blogs.worldbank.org/edutech/tech-and-teachers

Tu, C. (2002). The relationship of social presence in an online learning environment. *The Internet and Higher Education*, *5*, 293–318. doi:10.1016/S1096-7516(02)00134-3

Tu, C. H. (2005). From presentation to interaction: New goals for online learning. *Educational Media International*, *42*(3), 189–206. doi:10.1080/09523980500161072

Tu, C., & McIsaac, M. (2002). The relationship of social presence and interaction in online classes. *American Journal of Distance Education*, *16*(3), 131–150. doi:10.1207/S15389286AJDE1603_2

Umbach, P. (2007). Faculty cultures and college teaching. In R. P. Perry & J. C. Smart (Eds.), *The Scholarship of Teaching and Learning in Higher Education: An Evidence-Based Perspective* (pp. 263–317). Netherlands: Springer. doi:10.1007/1-4020-5742-3_8

University of Victoria. (2013). *The continuing studies instructor's welcome message*. Retrieved August 13, 2015 from http://distance.uvic.ca/pdfs/instructors/CS-Instructor-Welcome-Message.pdf

UWI Open Campus. (2014). *The learning exchange*. Retrieved from http://2014.tle.courses.open.uwi.edu/course/view.php?id=272

UWI Open Campus. (2015). *About the open campus, UWI*. Retrieved June 15, 2015 from http://www.open.uwi.edu/about/welcome-uwi-open-campus

Vai, M., & Sosulski, K. (2011). *Essentials of online course design: A standards-based guide*. New York: Routledge.

Valez, J. L., & Cano, J. (2008). The relationship between teacher immediacy and student motivation. *Journal of Agriculture*, *49*(3).

van der Aalsvoort, G. M., Lepola, J., Overtoom, L., & Laitinen, S. (2015). Motivation of young students: A cross-cultural evaluation of a model for motivational orientations. *Research Papers in Education*, *30*(1), 114–131. doi:10.1080/02671522.2013.787447

Vasilyeva, E., Puuronen, S., Pechenizkiy, M., & Räsänen, P. (2007). Feedback adaptation in web-based learning systems. *International Journal of Continuing Engineering Education and Lifelong Learning*, *17*(4/5), 337–357. doi:10.1504/IJCEELL.2007.015046

Veletsianos, G., & Navarrete, C. (2012). Online social networks as formal learning environments: Learner experiences and activities. *The International Review of Research in Open and Distributed Learning*, *13*(1), 144–166.

Vella, J. (1994). *Learning to listen learning to teach: The power of dialogue in educating adults*. San Francisco: JosseyBass.

Vesely, P., Bloom, L., & Sherlock, J. (2007). Key elements of building online community: Comparing faculty and student perceptions. *MERLOT Journal of Online Learning and Teaching*, *3*(3), 234–246.

Vogler, S. H. (1971). Grading themes: A new approach, a new dimension. *English Journal*, *60*(1), 70–74. doi:10.2307/813344

Vos, N., van der Meijden, H., & Denessen, E. (2011). Effects of constructing versus playing an educational game on student motivation and deep learning strategy use. *Computers & Education*, *56*(1), 127–137. doi:10.1016/j.compedu.2010.08.013

Vu, P., & Fadde, P. J. (2013). When to talk, when to chat: Student interactions in live virtual classrooms. *Journal of Interactive Online Learning*, *12*(2), 41–52.

Vygotsky, L. (1934). Thinking and speaking. Cambridge, MA: The MIT Press.

Vygotsky, L. S. (1933/1966). Play and its role in the mental development of the child. *Social Psychology*, *12*(6), 62–76.

Vygotsky, L. S. (1935). *Mental development of children during education*. Moscow: Uchpedzig.

Vygotsky, L. S. (1962). *Thought and Language*. Cambridge, MA: MIT Press. doi:10.1037/11193-000

Vygotsky, L. S. (1978a). *Mind in society*. Cambridge, MA: Harvard University Press.

Vygotsky, L. S. (1978b). *Mind in society: The development of higher psychological processes* (M. Cole, V. John-Steiner, S. Scribner, & E. Souberman, Trans. & Eds.). Cambridge, MA: Harvard University.

Vygotsky, L. S. (1981). The genesis of higher mental functions. In J. V. Wertsch (Ed.), *The Concept of Activity in Soviet Psychology*. Armonk, NY: Sharpe.

Vygotsky, L. S. (1987). *The collected works of L. S. Vygotsky* (R. W. Rieber & A. Carton, Eds.). New York: Plenum Press. (Original work published 1934)

Wager, S. U. (1983). *The effect of immediacy and type of informative feedback on retention in a computer-assisted task.* (Unpublished doctoral dissertation). Florida State University.

Wagner, E. D. (1994). In support of a functional definition of interaction. *American Journal of Distance Education*, *8*(2), 6–26. doi:10.1080/08923649409526852

Wagner, E. D. (1997). In support of a functional definition of interaction. *New Directions for Teaching and Learning*, *71*, 19–26. doi:10.1002/tl.7103

Walkem, K. (2014). Instructional immediacy in elearning. *Collegian (Royal College of Nursing, Australia)*, *21*(3), 179–184. doi:10.1016/j.colegn.2013.02.004 PMID:25632711

Walser, T. (2009). An action research study of student self-assessment in higher education. *Innovative Higher Education*, *34*(5), 299–306. doi:10.1007/s10755-009-9116-1

Walther, J. B., & Boyd, S. (2002). Attraction to computer-mediated social support. In C. A. Lin & D. Atkin (Eds.), *Communications technology and society: Audience adoption and uses of the new media* (pp. 153–188). Cresskill, NJ: Hampton Press.

Wang, Q., & Woo, H. L. (2007). Comparing asynchronous online discussions and face-to-face discussions in a classroom setting. *British Journal of Educational Technology*, *38*(2), 272–286. doi:10.1111/j.1467-8535.2006.00621.x

Wang, Q., Woo, H. L., Quek, L. C., Yang, Y., & Liu, M. (2011). Using the Facebook group as a learning management system: An exploratory study. *British Journal of Educational Technology*, *43*(3), 423–438.

Wang, S. K., & Hsu, H. Y. (2008). Use of the webinar tool (Elluminate) to support training: The effects of webinar-learning implementation from student-trainers' perspective. *Journal of Interactive Online Learning*, *7*(3), 175–194.

Wang, Y. M., & Chen, D. V. (2011). Instructors as Architects—Designing Learning Spaces for Discussion-Based Online Courses. *Journal of Educational Technology Systems*, *39*(3), 281–294. doi:10.2190/ET.39.3.e

Wanstreet, C. E. (2006). Interactions in online learning environments. *The Quarterly Review of Distance Education*, *7*(4), 399–411.

Wasko, M., Teigland, R., Leidner, D., & Jarvenpaa, S. (2011). Stepping into the Internet: New ventures in virtual worlds. *MIS Quarterly: Management Information Systems*, *35*(3), 645–652.

Waters. (2015). *Education technology and skinners box.* Retrieved from https://educationfuturism.com/education-technology-and-skinners-box-76a669c48461#.63cts8qee

Watkins, C. (2009). What schools are learning about themselves and young technology users. In *The Young and the Digital: What the Migration to Social Network Sites, Games, and Anytime, Anywhere Media Means for Our Future* (pp. 19–46). Beacon Press.

Wei, A. C. Y. (2012). *Emoticons and the non-verbal communication: With reference to Facebook.* (Unpublished master's thesis). Department of Media Studies, Christ University, Bangalore, India.

Weiner, M., & Mehrabian, A. (1968). *Language within language: Immediacy a channel in verbal communication*. New York: Appleton-Century-Crofts.

Wenger, E. (2009). *Digital habitats*. Portland: CPsquare.

Wenger, E. (1998). *Communities of practice: Learning, meaning, and identity*. Cambridge: Cambridge University Press. doi:10.1017/CBO9780511803932

Wenger, E. (2010). Communities of practice and social learning systems: the career of a concept. In C. Blackmore (Ed.), *Social Learning Systems and Communities of Practice*. Springer Verlag and the Open University. doi:10.1007/978-1-84996-133-2_11

Wenger, E., McDermott, R., & Snyder, W. M. (2002). *Cultivating communities of practice*. Harvard Business Press.

Wenger, E., White, N., & Smith, J. (2009). *Digital habitats: Stewarding technology for communities*. CP Square Press.

Whipp, J., & Lorentz, R. A. (2008). *Cognitive and social help Giving in online teaching: An exploratory study*. Retrieved November 30, 2015 from http://epublications.marquette.edu/cgi/viewcontent.cgi?article=1038&context=edu_fac

Whitton, N. (2011). Game Engagement Theory and Adult Learning. *Simulation & Gaming*, *42*(5), 596–609. doi:10.1177/1046878110378587

Wicks, D. J., & Cano, J. (2009). *Educational technology: Emerging theories and online learning environments for adults*. Retrieved November 8, 2015 from https://sites.google.com/a/boisestate.edu/edtechtheories/emerging-theories-and-online-learning-environments-for-adults-1

Wiggins, G., & McTighe, J. (2006). Understanding by design (2nd ed.). Upper Saddle River, NJ: Merrill/Prentice-Hall.

Wiggins, E. B., & Bowers, G. B. (2014). Memes as genre: A structurational analysis of the memescape. *New Media & Society*, 1–21.

Wiggins, G. (2012). Seven keys to effective feedback. *Educational Leadership*, *70*(1), 10–18.

Wiley, D. A. (2002). *Instructional use of learning objects*. Bloomington, IN: AECT. Retrieved June 26, 2015 from http://www.reusability.org/read/

Wiliam, D. (2011). What is assessment for learning? *Studies in Educational Evaluation*, *37*(1), 3–14. doi:10.1016/j.stueduc.2011.03.001 PMID:22114905

Wilson, B. M., Pollock, P. H., & Hamann, K. (2007). Does active learning enhance learner outcomes? Evidence from discussion participation in online classes. *Journal of Political Science Education*, *3*(2), 131–142. doi:10.1080/15512160701338304

Wilson, C. (1998, Fall). Concerns of instructors delivering distance learning via the WWW. *Online Journal of Distance Learning Administration*, *1*(3). Retrieved from http://www.westga.edu/~distance/ojdla/fall13/wilson13.html

Winograd, D. (2002). Guidelines for moderating online educational computer conferences. *TechTrends*, *46*(5), 53–57. doi:10.1007/BF02818310

Winter, S., Rice, S., Reid, K., & Rian, M. (2015). Consistency of aviation students when taking the private pilot knowledge exam. *Journal of Aviation/Aerospace Education & Research, 24*(2), 21-38.

Witt, P. L., Wheeless, L. R., & Allen, M. (2004). A meta-analytical review of the relationship between teacher immediacy and student learning. *Communication Monographs, 71*(2), 184–207. doi:10.1080/036452042000228054

Wojciechowski, A., & Palmer, L. B. (2005). Individual student characteristics: Can any be predictors of success in online classes? *Online Journal of Distance Learning Administration, 8*(2).

Wolf, M. A. (2010). Innovate to educate: System [Re]design for personalized learning: A report from the 2010 symposium. Washington, DC: Software & Information Industry Association (SIAA).

Wolfe, C. (2000). Learning and teaching on the World Wide Web. In C. R. Wolfe (Ed.), *Learning and teaching on the World Wide Web* (pp. 1–22). San Diego, CA: Academic Press.

Wolsey, T. (2008). Efficacy of instructor feedback on written work in an online program. *International Journal on E-Learning, 7*(2), 311–329.

Wolsey, T. D. (2008). Efficacy of instructor fedback on written work in an online program. *International Journal on E-Learning, 7*(2), 311–329.

Wood, K. A., Moskovitz, C., & Valiga, T. M. (2011). Audio feedback for student writing in online nursing courses: Exploring student and instructor reactions. *The Journal of Nursing Education, 50*(9), 540–543. doi:10.3928/01484834-20110616-04 PMID:21667881

Woods, R. H., & Baker, J. D. (2004). *Interaction and immediacy in online learning*. Retrieved November 29, 2015 from http://www.irrodl.org/index.php/irrodl/article/view/186/268

Woods, R. H., & Baker, J. D. (2004, August). Interaction and immediacy in online learning. *The International Review of Research in Open and Distributed Learning, 5*(2). Retrieved from http://www.irrodl.org/index.php/irrodl/article/view/186/268

Woods, R., & Baker, J. (2004). Interaction and Immediacy in Online Learning. *International Review of Research in Open and Distance Learning, 5*(2), 1–13.

Woods, R., & Ebersole, S. (2003). Becoming a "Communal Architect" in the Online Classroom-Integrating Cognitive and Affective Learning for Maximum Effect in Web-Based Learning. *Online Journal of Distance Learning Administration, 6*(1).

Wright, R. (2009). Effective kickoff meetings. *Internal Aditor*.

Xu, D., & Jaggars, S. S. (2013). *Adaptability to Online Learning: Differences across Types of Students and Academic Subject Areas*. CCRC Working Paper No. 54. Community College Research Center, Columbia University.

Yarbro, R., & Angerine, B. (1982). A comparison of traditional and cassette tape English composition grading methods. *Research in the Teaching of English, 16*, 394–396.

Yin, R. K. (1994). *Case study research: Design and methods* (2nd ed.). Thousand Oaks, CA: Sage.

Young, S., & Bruce, M. A. (2011). Classroom community and student engagement in online courses. *MERLOT Journal of Online Learning and Teaching, 7*(2), 219–230.

About the Contributors

Steven D'Agustino holds a doctorate from Fordham University's Graduate School of Education and is the Director of Online Learning for the Office of the Provost where his responsibilities include supporting the development of distance learning programs across Fordham University. He has published research in the area of instructional enhancement through the integration of technology and has been awarded a number of grants while at Fordham, the largest of which was a 2.5 million dollar grant to provide access to technology through online learning. Dr. D'Agustino is the editor of two books: Adaptation, Resistance and Access to Instructional Technologies and Immersive Environments, Augmented Realities, and Virtual Worlds: Assessing Future Trends in Education published in 2010 and 2012, respectively. His most recent publications, both in 2013, include "Toward a course conversion model for distance learning: a review of best practices" in Frontiers of Distance Learning in Business Education and "Providing innovative opportunities and options through online credit recovery and afterschool programs" in Expanding Minds and Opportunities.

* * *

Rachael Olubukola Afolabi is an experienced Instructional Designer and Adjunct Faculty. Her areas of expertise include developing creative eLearning experiences for different learning audiences, game based learning and open education. She teaches in the areas of Humanities, Information Technology, Global Studies and Education.

Jered Borup is an assistant professor of learning technologies at George Mason University. His research currently focuses on online and blended learning communities and interactions in K-12 and higher education settings. His current research publications can be found online at: https://sites.google.com/site/jeredborup/.

Caroline M. Crawford, Ed.D., is an Associate Professor of Instructional Technology at the University of Houston-Clear Lake in Houston, Texas, United States of America. She earned her doctoral degree from the University of Houston in Houston, Texas, United States of America, in 1998, with specialization areas in Instructional Technology and Curriculum Theory, and began her tenure at the University of Houston-Clear Lake (UHCL) the same year. At this point in Dr. Crawford's professional career, her main areas of interest focus upon communities of learning and the appropriate and successful integration of technologies into the learning environment; the learning environment may be envisioned as face-to-face, blended and online (virtual or text-driven) environments.

Colette P. L. Doan is currently teaching Grade 2 PYP at a public IB school, having recently completed a Master of Education in Art Education at UBC. She enjoys integrating technology and Art into her everyday lessons.

Oliver Dreon is an associate professor and director for the Center for Academic Excellence at Millersville University of Pennsylvania. He teaches a wide variety of education and instructional technology courses both in face-to-face and online formats, and also coordinates the university's Digital Learning Studio. He is the co-author of the book Authentic Instruction with Technology: A Student-Centered Approach and has published in various journals, including the Middle Level Journal, TechTrends, Teachers and Teaching, Science Education, Online Classroom and Teacher Education & Practice. Dr. Dreon also contributes to Faculty Focus, an online newsletter providing pedagogical and technological strategies for higher education. Dr. Dreon has spent over twenty years teaching in various educational environments. His research examines how technology can be used to support student learning through online, blended and hybrid environments. Dr. Dreon also examines the role that technology plays in supporting communities of practice for educators across the educational landscape.

Ashley Dugan has a B.S. in Business Administration from Chapman University, and recently completed an M.S. in Instructional Technology at Mississippi State University. She is working professionally as an instructional designer.

Kelly Elander has a B.S. in Communication from Ohio University, a Master's in adult instruction and performance technology from the University of Michigan, and a Ph.D. in instructional design for online learning from Capella University. He currently coordinates the web design and interactive media program at Harding University in Searcy, Arkansas.

Sandra Filippelli is currently a PhD student in the Faculty of Education specializing in Arts Based Research.

Michael Fleming is the Director of Online Support and Delivery at the School of Professional Studies, Columbia University.

Adrienne A. Garber is a Senior Instructional Designer for the School of Professional Studies, Columbia University. Prior to joining SPS, Adrienne worked on innovative technology projects for the Columbia Center for New Media Teaching and Learning, the EdLab at Teachers College, Carnegie Mellon's Language Technologies Institute, and Carnegie Mellon's Field Robotics Center. Adrienne is currently a doctoral candidate at Teachers College, Columbia University; her academic areas of interest include multimedia annotation, cognitive development, and human computer interaction. She earned her B.S. from Lehigh University, an M.S. from Carnegie Mellon University, a J.D./M.B.A from Duquesne University, and most recently her Ed.M. from Teachers College, Columbia University.

Hsiao-Cheng (Sandrine) Han, PhD., is an assistant professor at the University of Columbia, Faculty of Education, Department of Curriculum and Pedagogy. Her research focuses on the visual culture and cultural studies, and on the integration of art education and educational technology specifically in virtual worlds. She also looks at the ways in which media have influenced cultures.

Melanie Hibbert is the Associate Director of Instructional Media at Barnard College, Columbia University. She holds a Doctor of Education in Instructional Media from Teachers College, Columbia University. Her professional interests include producing media and videos; researching learning from videos and online spaces; and other forms of digital production and scholarship.

Kun Huang is Assistant Professor in the Department of Instructional Systems and Workforce Development at the Mississippi State University. She is an experienced instructional designer who has designed and developed numerous interactive learning materials to scaffold students' critical thinking, metacognition, and problem solving. Her research focuses on the development of technology-supported learning environments and their effects on students' metacognition, knowledge transfer, and epistemic beliefs. Dr. Huang has published several empirical studies in refereed journals, and presented her research and instructional design works at various national and international conferences.

Tazeen Hussain is Assistant Professor at Indus Valley School of Art and Architecture and visiting faculty at the department of Visual Studies, University of Karachi and Szabist. She has a diverse teaching experience including teaching 2D and 3D design studios, supervising dissertation and design thesis research. Apart from academia Tazeen is also a visual artist with multi faceted portfolio, covering visual arts, television, theatre, journalism, and social work. Currently she is serving as a trustee for Indus Earth Trust an NGO working in the field of sustainable development. This allows her the liberty to 'walk the talk' and practice design and social responsibility. Tazeen Hussain received a Bachelors degree in Communication Design from Indus Valley School of Art and Architecture, and completed her MA in New Media and Society from the University of Leicester, UK.

Kristine Rodriguez Kerr is interested in multimodal composing practices, new literacy studies, and cosmopolitan-minded education. She is currently an Instructional Designer for Columbia University School of Professional Studies and an Assistant Adjunct Professor at Teachers College Columbia University. She holds a Doctor of Education in Communication and Education from Teachers College Columbia University and a Masters of Professional Writing from Carnegie Mellon University.

Tarryn Kille is a Senior Lecturer at Griffith University lecturing in aviation leadership and management. Tarryn commenced her aviation career as a professional pilot and flight instructor. Whilst working in the industry, she completed an undergraduate degree in aviation at Curtin University and a Masters of Business Administration, majoring in Aviation Management. Prior to joining Griffith, Tarryn served as Manager, Policy and Business Development with the Australian Civil Aviation Safety Authority and held membership on the Operations Panel with the International Civil Aviation Organization. In 2009, Tarryn commenced her doctoral studies focusing on economic and environmental sustainability in the aviation industry.

Sang Joon Lee is an assistant professor in the Department of Instructional Systems and Workforce Development at Mississippi State University where he teaches multimedia and web design courses. His research focuses on the use of emerging technologies for teaching and learning in online and blended courses.

Matthea Marquart is the Associate Director of the Online Program at Columbia University's School of Social Work. She is also a Lecturer at the School of Social Work; she teaches in the Social Enterprise Administration method area, preparing the next wave of nonprofit and human services leaders. Her writing, speaking, and research interests focus on online education.

Jameson Mbale is a Professor in the Department of Computer Science at the Copperbelt University, in Zambia. He is a Director of Research and Innovations. He teaches the following courses: Multimedia Computing and Web Service, Advanced Mobile Computing and Networking, and Telecommunications,

Larisa Olesova, Ph.D., is an instructional designer and adjunct professor specializing in distance education at George Mason University. Her research focuses on the effectiveness of instructional strategies in online learning environments.

Kyle L. Peck is Co-Director of the Center for Online Innovation in Learning and Professor of Education and Research Fellow in the Learning, Design, and Technology program at Penn State University. He studies and applies innovations in education, and his current interests include Massive Open Online Courses (MOOCs) and digital badges in education.

Nasim Peikazadi is a PhD student at the University of British Columbia at the faculty of Educational Studies. She got her Masters of Education in Art Education from UBC in 2015.

Yingxiao Qian is a Ph.D student in the Learning, Design, and Technology program at The University of Georgia. Her research focuses on the case-based learning, STEM education, and cognition and instruction.

Sam A. Rosenthal is a webinar specialist in the School of Professional Studies at Columbia University. In addition to his work at the SPS, he has written and done research in the areas of education, technology, sociology and music.

Neal Shambaugh is a Professor of Learning Sciences and Human Development. He is a former Associate Dean of Academic Affairs and a Graduate Programs Coordinator of Instructional Design and Technology (IDT) in the College of Education and Human Services at West Virginia University. The master's IDT program has been 100% online delivered since 2010, and he teaches courses in IDT and Educational Psychology. He has been a university liaison to an elementary/middle public school for a dual-degree, five-year teacher education program. Prior to academia, his work experiences included radio station ownership, engineering, announcing, and sales; training program consultant, and an audio and video producer.

Ge Shi is a graduate student in the Department of Curriculum and Pedagogy. Research interests include Visual Communication, Media Education and Media Literacy Education.

Paulette Stewart is the Head of the Department of Library and Information Studies at The University of the West Indies, (UWI) Mona. She teaches both graduate and undergraduate students at The UWI, Mona and is a Course Coordinator and Instructor at The UWI Open Campus. Dr. Stewart was elected

Librarian of the Year in 2009 by the Library and Information Association of Jamaica and served as the President of this Association in 2010. She received the Ken Haycock International Association of School Librarianship (IASL) Leadership Award in 2006 for her outstanding contribution to librarianship in Jamaica. Presently, she is the IASL Director for Latin American and the Caribbean. Her research interests include information literacy and school libraries, library education and online learning.

Hengtao Tang is a Ph.D student in the Learning, Design, and Technology program at The Pennsylvania State University. His research focuses on the educational innovation, learning environment, and knowledge structure.

Manish Wadhwa, Ph.D., is working as Assistant Professor in the Department of Computer Science at Salem State University (Salem, MA) since September 2013. He is also coordinating the Information Technology Program and chairing IT related committees. Previously, he worked as Program Director of Information Technology at South University in Virginia Beach, Virginia. Dr. Wadhwa joined South University in July 2011 and was responsible for managing the department of Information Technology within the College of Business and overseeing the Associates, Bachelors, and Masters in Information Technology. Dr. Wadhwa has published in various elite Journals and Conferences. His research work spans Cognitive Radio Networks, Dynamic Spectrum Sharing, Sensor Networks, and Biofield Sciences. Dr. Wadhwa is also the editor of an interdisciplinary book in the field of Technology and Business entitled, "Technology, Innovation, and Enterprise Transformation."

Shuyan Wang is a professor of Instructional Technology at The University of Southern Mississippi. Her research interests include the integration of technology through curriculum development, professional development in the use of technology for teaching and learning, distance education, m-learning, e-learning, and online course development, and assessment, evaluation, and issues related to electronic portfolios.

Junsong Zhang completed his masters program at UBC in Technology Studies Education. Prior to that he worked as a school teacher and later on moved to business organizations in learning and development. He is interested in gamified pedagogy, e-learning, instructional design, technology-enhanced teaching, and faculty development in terms of using appropriate learning technology and pedagogical practices.

Index

I

L

M

N

O

P

R

S

T

U

V

W

www.ingramcontent.com/pod-product-compliance
Ingram Content Group UK Ltd.
Pitfield, Milton Keynes, MK11 3LW, UK
UKHW050951290926
15470UKWH00005B/1769

9 781466 699953